1000 GREAT WINES

THAT WON'T COST A FORTUNE FROM THE WORLD'S BEST WINERIES

EDITOR-IN-CHIEF JIM GORDON

London, New York, Melbourne, Munich, and Delhi

Editor David Williams
Photography Peter Anderson

DK LONDON
Project Editor Andrew Roff
Project Art Editor Katherine Raj
Editorial Assistant David Fentiman
Design Assistant Danaya Bunnag
Managing Editor Dawn Henderson
Managing Art Editor Christine Keilty
Senior Jackets Creative Nicola Powling
Senior Presentations Creative Caroline de Souza
Production Editor Ben Marcus
Senior Production Controller Alice Sykes
Creative Technical Support Sonia Charbonnier

DK INDIA
Editorial Assistants Aditi Batra, Priyanka Chatterjee
Project Designer Era Chawla
Managing Editor Glenda Fernandes
Managing Art Editor Navidita Thapa
Creative Technical Support Sunil Sharma
DTP Designers Rajdeep Singh, Anurag Trivedi

First published in Great Britain in 2011
by Dorling Kindersley Limited
80 Strand, London WC2R 0RL
Penguin Group (UK)

This paperback edition published
in Great Britain in 2014

2 4 6 8 10 9 7 5 3 1
001–253670–Jun/2014

A CIP catalogue record for this book
is available from the British Library

ISBN 978 1 4093 5632 5

Colour reproduction by Colourscan, Singapore

Printed and bound in China

Discover more at **www.dk.com**

Contents

Foreword 6
Reading Old World wine labels 8
Reading New World wine labels 10

FRANCE 12
Bordeaux 14
Burgundy 46
Champagne 68
The rest of France 74

ITALY 104

SPAIN 142

PORTUGAL 170

GERMANY 180

AUSTRIA 206

NORTH AMERICA 214
California 216
Washington 248
Oregon 252
The rest of the US 254
Canada 256

SOUTH AMERICA 260
Chile 262
Argentina 272
Brazil 278

SOUTH AFRICA 280

AUSTRALIA 290

NEW ZEALAND 314

EMERGING REGIONS 326

Glossary 338
Index 344
Acknowledgments 351
About the authors 352

Foreword

Why do most wine books, magazines, and blogs concentrate on the rarest and most expensive wines in the world – wines made for once-in-a-lifetime events – when what most of us want is simply a really good bottle to open tonight?

1000 Great Wines that Won't Cost a Fortune isn't most wine books. Wine drinkers from newcomers to aficionados will find more than 1000 excellent wines from trusted wineries around the world that cost no more than the price of an entrée at a good restaurant. Our team of expert authors used a simple rule to select the wines: find the best wineries around the world, those that actually do make the once-in-a-lifetime wines, and then taste their less expensive wines. They found fantastic second wines from famous Bordeaux châteaux, compelling house reds from California vineyards, undervalued white varietals from Germany, and hundreds of other great buys.

This book is first and foremost a guide to buying wonderful affordable wines. We include red wines, white wines, sparkling wines, rosés, dessert wines, and fortified wines. While lending the most space to the classic regions of France, Italy, Spain, and North America, this guide also covers every other major winemaking country in the world as well as emerging stars, such as South Africa and Argentina.

The task of each contributor was not to find the cheapest, most generic mass-market wines, but to recommend wines with sophistication, authenticity, and regional character. They were not to select specific outstanding vintages that may be sold out or fluctuate in price, but to endorse brands, varietals, and types that are consistently high quality and affordable.

That's all good. But what is wine without food, glassware, or a party at which to pour it? With questions like these in mind we added food and wine pairings, profiles of the most popular grape varieties, and a wealth of other practical advice on how to select and enjoy great-value wines.

While this guide brims over with information, it's important to remember that wine is not a difficult subject to appreciate. Dig as deep as you like into details of grape varieties and wine appreciation. Come back to the book when you have questions about wine. Most of all, we hope you will use our wine recommendations to take the stress out of wine buying.

With this new guide you never need to overspend on a bottle again.

Jim Gordon

READING OLD WORLD WINE LABELS

European wine labels tend to emphasize the vineyard location, sometimes down to the individual plot of land in which the grapes were grown, and the vast majority do not state the main grape variety. To get the most from the label, therefore, it is useful to have some background knowledge about the wine-growing region: only certain types of grape will be grown there, wines will be produced in particular styles and to legally defined standards, and the "terroirs" of each region will have varying reputations and produce wines with specific characteristics. The alcohol content and volume are legal requirements in most countries where the wine is sold and will be printed on the front, neck, or back label.

FRANCE – BORDEAUX

Bordeaux labels give prominence to the château (winery) name and the vine-growing district in which the grapes were grown. The term *mise en bouteille au château*, often printed on the back label, means that the wine was bottled on the same property where the grapes were grown.

Wine name Often in Bordeaux the name of the wine is also the name of the estate, as here. This means the wine is the superior "first wine" or "grand vin" produced by the estate. Second wines and blends tend to have their own names to distinguish them from the grand vin.

Classification of quality "Cru" means literally "growth" and, in practical terms, "vineyard site" in a superior area. "Grand cru classé en 1855" is an historical designation specific to the Médoc and Haut-Médoc and identifies this as a wine from one of the highly ranked chateaux ("premier cru" being the top designation).

Region of origin This indicates the wine has been produced from grapes grown in a specific region and according to the legally defined requirements of that region. Labels often, but not always, include the origin certification, in France "Appellation (d'Origine) Contrôlée" or AOC.

Vintage The year the grapes were harvested is particularly important for wines grown in continental climates as in most of Europe, where weather can be extreme and affect wine quality significantly from year to year.

Ownership A "vignoble" (vineyard) owns this château and vineyard. Often individual persons are listed as owners, and sometimes legal terms for the business entities of the owners are indicated.

FRANCE – BURGUNDY

The system of AOC certifies French wines' origins, as well as regulating labels, grape-growing, and winemaking. On Burgundy labels, the region is usually most prominent and the vintage is often printed on the neck label.

Bourgogne The French word for Burgundy is the name of the region, and the generic name of any wine from the region.

Winery name Family-owned domaines often say "pére et fils" (father and son) or "pére et fille" (father and daughter).

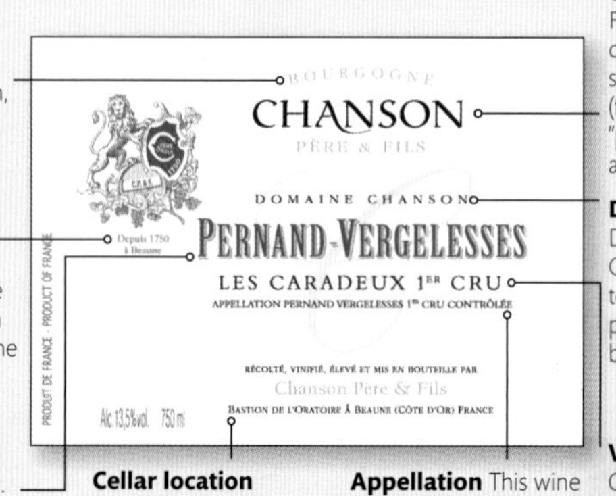

Domaine Domaine Chanson refers to the vineyard property owned by the winery.

Château details "Depuis 1750 à Beaune" means the company has been in the city of Beaune since 1750.

Village This is the village where the grapes were grown. Wines that use grapes from many villages give a less specific area on the label, such as Côte de Beaune.

Cellar location This fine print says the winery's cellars are located in the city of Beaune, home to many Burgundy wine firms.

Appellation This wine comes from an official vineyard appellation. "1er cru" is a quality vineyard, second in Burgundy to "grand cru".

Vineyard "Les Caradeux" is the section of vines in the village of Pernand-Vergelesses where the grapes grew.

FRANCE – CHAMPAGNE

This informative Champagne label goes into detail about the wine's origin and style. Its main identification is the winery name and the place it comes from, which is, of course, the region of northeastern France called Champagne. All wines in the Champagne appellation are sparkling wines whose "fizz" is produced via a second fermentation in the bottle.

Champagne This wine was grown and made in the Champagne region of France, an officially recognized Appellation d'Origine Contrôlée.

Winery name Pierre Gimonnet & Fils (son) is the winery's name.

Wine style "Blanc de Blancs" means "white of whites", a white sparkling wine made from white wine grapes. Blanc de Noirs is a white bubbly made from dark, red wine grapes where the wine gains little or no colour from the skins.

Vineyard location "Cuis 1er Cru" means the grapes come from a vineyard that is rated as a first growth (high quality location, second only to "grand cru") in the village or commune of Cuis.

Sweet or dry? "Brut" is the most popular style of champagne, a dry style with no detectable sweetness, that may contain up to 1.2 per cent sugar. Brut zero or brut natural are completely dry. Extra dry is sweeter than brut; demi-sec is sweeter still.

Volume This is a magnum-size bottle, with double the volume of a standard 750ml bottle. Larger bottles such as Jeroboam (3 litres) and Rehoboam (4.5 litres) are also available.

Type of winery "RM" indicates a "recoltant-manipulant" – a grower who makes its own champagne. "NM" means the firm is a "négociant-manipulant" – it buys grapes rather than growing its own. CM, RC, and SR identify champagnes from cooperatives.

Winery details The full legal name of the winery and its location.

Grape variety Chardonnay is the sole grape variety used in this wine. Most champagnes are blends of two or three varieties, which are not stated on labels.

GERMANY

Grape varieties appear prominently on many German labels, and this tells you most about the style of wine. The vineyard name or producer name may appear in large type, too.

Village and vineyard Vineyard locations for German wines usually state the village; in this case Wolf in the Mosel River valley, followed by the particular plot of land, Goldgrube.

Vintage Indicates that at least 85 per cent of the grapes for this wine were grown in 2007. Higher priced, higher classifications can be expected to be closer to 95 per cent.

Quality "Prädikatswein" indicates that no extra sugar has been added, so the wine is better quality than QbA, Landwein, and Tafelwein (see glossary).

Sulphites Indicates that a form of sulphur dioxide was added to the wine, which is a standard way to preserve freshness.

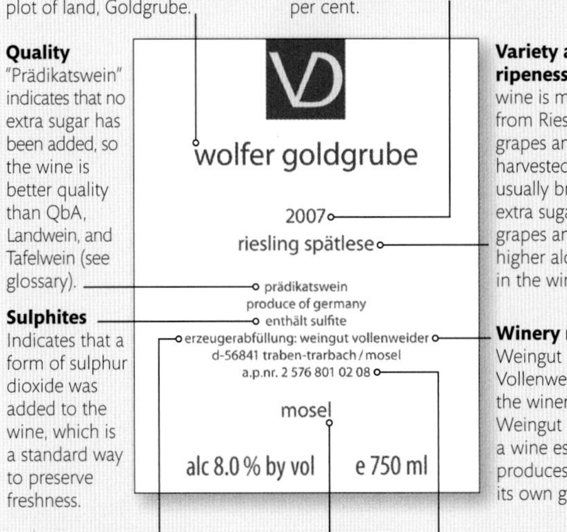

Variety and ripeness The wine is made from Riesling grapes and late harvested. This usually brings extra sugar in the grapes and thus higher alcohol in the wine.

Winery name Weingut Vollenweider is the winery name. Weingut means a wine estate that produces all of its own grapes.

Producer versus bottler "Erzeugerabfüllung" means bottled by the same firm that fermented the wine. Estates that produce and bottle their own wine may use the term "Gutsabfüllung". "Abfüllung" indicates a bottler or shipper.

Region of origin The Mosel River valley is part of the larger Mosel-Saar-Ruwer wine-growing region in which the Wolfer Goldgrube vineyard lies.

A.P.Nr. The AP number is the wine's identification number confirming who made the wine and when it was bottled. This helps track a wine back to its source if any complaints arise.

ITALY

Like many Old World labels, this Italian label emphasizes the legally defined region of origin. Many Italian labels also emboss the vintage on the bottle or declare it on the neck label.

Region of origin Barbaresco is the classified village and vineyard district, in the Piedmont region of Italy, where the grapes were grown.

Classification "Denominazione d'Origine Controllata e Garantita" (DOCG) is the highest quality designation in Italy. Next is DOC, then Indicazione Geografica Tipica (IGT), and Vino da Tavola (VDT).

Winery name Produttori del Barbaresco is the winery name. The small print says it is a cooperative. On other labels, "fattoria" and "tenuta" mean farm or estate. "Azienda agraria" and "azienda agricola" are estates producing wine from their own grapes; an "azienda vinicola" buys in grapes.

Bottling "Imbottigliato all'origine dai produttori riuniti" means the wine was bottled at the source (not transported elsewhere), and jointly by the producers. "Imbottigliato da" means simply bottled by the named winery and the wine could have been grown and fermented elsewhere.

READING NEW WORLD WINE LABELS

Unlike Old World wines that often give top billing to the place where the grapes were grown, on New World labels it is the winery name and grape variety that tend to stand out most, though the vine-growing region must be shown and the individual vineyard may be identified, too. It is much more common for New World producers to give their wines fanciful names to catch the imagination, but these usually have no legal meaning. Beware of New World labels that use traditional Old World terms such as "Almond Champagne" and "Mountain Chablis" – these are not an indication of the quality of the wine in the bottle. Alcohol content and volume are legal requirements in most countries where the wine is sold and will be printed on the front, neck, or back label.

SOUTH AFRICA

Although wine has been made in South Africa for more than 300 years, wine labels nevertheless follow the New World pattern, emphasizing the winery name and grape variety name in most cases. This straightforward label is typical of many from South Africa.

Winery name The name of the winery is the largest feature on many South African labels.

Region The Wine of Origin (WO) system covers about 60 growing areas in four categories. The biggest are Geographical Units such as the Western Cape, then regions, districts such as Walker Bay, and wards such as Elgin, shown here.

Grape variety As in many New World countries, the overwhelming majority of the grape content of a wine must come from the grape variety named on the label. The rule is 85 per cent in South Africa.

Vintage year In South Africa, 85 per cent of grapes must come from the specified year, but wine saved from earlier vintages may be blended in.

CHILE

Chile adopted labelling regulations regarding vintage, grape variety, and region in the 1990s. The winery name is usually most prominent; the grape variety often second.

Winery name The winery name tells you which wine company bottled the wine. By itself it doesn't necessarily mean this winery grew the grapes or even fermented the wine.

Wine name "Antiguas Reservas" literally means "old reserves", implying that this bottle is the winery's best stuff, kept in cask until it was mature. It is a marketing rather than a legal term.

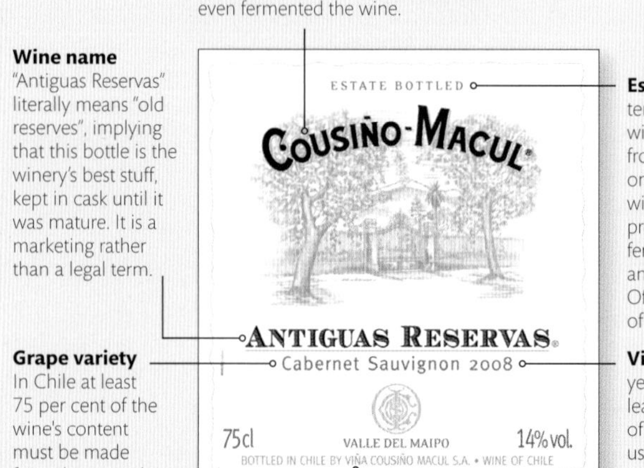

Estate bottled This term indicates the wine was made from grapes grown on the named winery's own property, and fermented, aged, and bottled there. Often a good sign of quality.

Grape variety In Chile at least 75 per cent of the wine's content must be made from the named grape variety.

Vintage The year in which at least 75 per cent of the grapes used to make this wine were grown.

Region of origin In Chile an official wine region is a "Denominación de Origen" (DO). At least 75 per cent of the grapes were grown there.

CALIFORNIA

Californian wine labels are typical of New World regions. They usually emphasize the name of the winery foremost, and the grape variety second. The officially recognized region in which the grapes were grown is often prominent, too. Unlike in Europe, however, the regional designation indicates nothing legally about the wine style, or methods of grape-growing and winemaking.

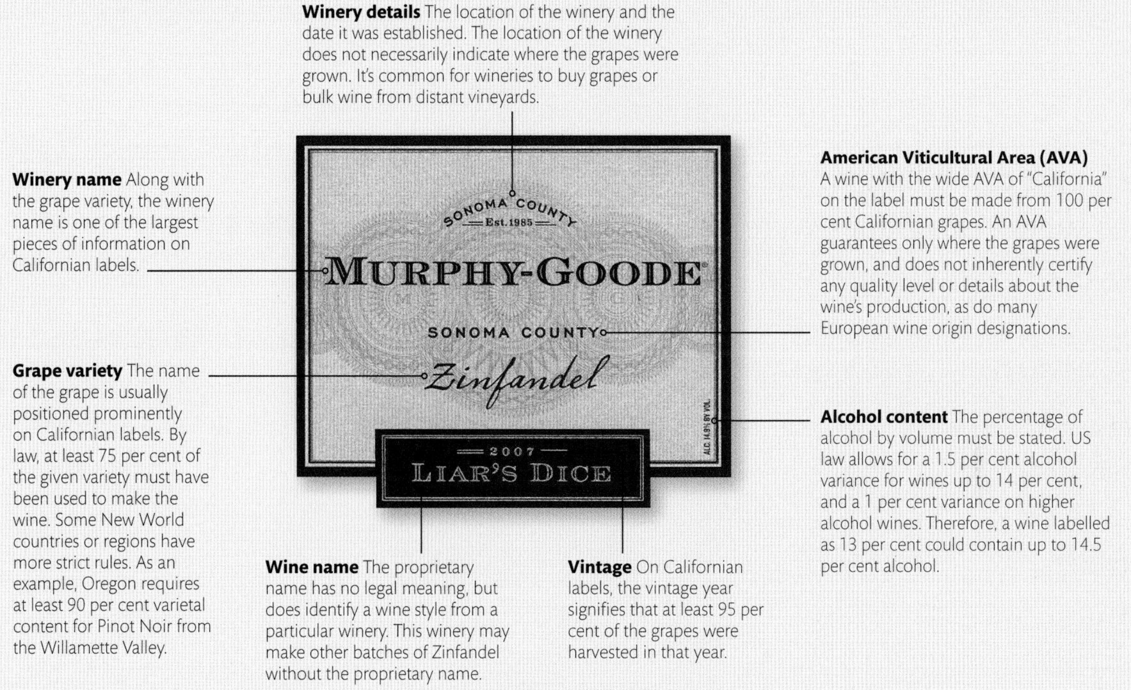

Winery details The location of the winery and the date it was established. The location of the winery does not necessarily indicate where the grapes were grown. It's common for wineries to buy grapes or bulk wine from distant vineyards.

Winery name Along with the grape variety, the winery name is one of the largest pieces of information on Californian labels.

American Viticultural Area (AVA) A wine with the wide AVA of "California" on the label must be made from 100 per cent Californian grapes. An AVA guarantees only where the grapes were grown, and does not inherently certify any quality level or details about the wine's production, as do many European wine origin designations.

Grape variety The name of the grape is usually positioned prominently on Californian labels. By law, at least 75 per cent of the given variety must have been used to make the wine. Some New World countries or regions have more strict rules. As an example, Oregon requires at least 90 per cent varietal content for Pinot Noir from the Willamette Valley.

Alcohol content The percentage of alcohol by volume must be stated. US law allows for a 1.5 per cent alcohol variance for wines up to 14 per cent, and a 1 per cent variance on higher alcohol wines. Therefore, a wine labelled as 13 per cent could contain up to 14.5 per cent alcohol.

Wine name The proprietary name has no legal meaning, but does identify a wine style from a particular winery. This winery may make other batches of Zinfandel without the proprietary name.

Vintage On Californian labels, the vintage year signifies that at least 95 per cent of the grapes were harvested in that year.

AUSTRALIA AND NEW ZEALAND

Labels from Australia and New Zealand follow the New World pattern of emphasizing the winery name and the grape variety, while also showing the region of origin. Use of a proprietary name such as "The Custodian" is fairly common in the New World and fairly rare in the Old World. It's best to look at the grape variety first, so you know what kind of wine to expect, and then consider the winery and region of origin for their quality attributes.

Winemaking method On New World labels, notations like this usually are not verified by legal authorities, but are generally truthful. "Foot trod, basket pressed" indicates a traditionally made wine. Other common terms are "barrel-fermented", "sur lie" (which translates literally as "on lees" and means the wine was aged while still containing a portion of the lees from fermentation), "unfined", "unfiltered", and "unoaked".

Winery name The winery name or brand name is usually prominent on an Australian or New Zealand label, but in cases like this one it plays third or fourth fiddle in the label design. You can tell d'Arenberg is the winery because of the "established" date. Many winery names include the words "winery", "cellar", "vineyard", or "estate" to indicate winery or brand name.

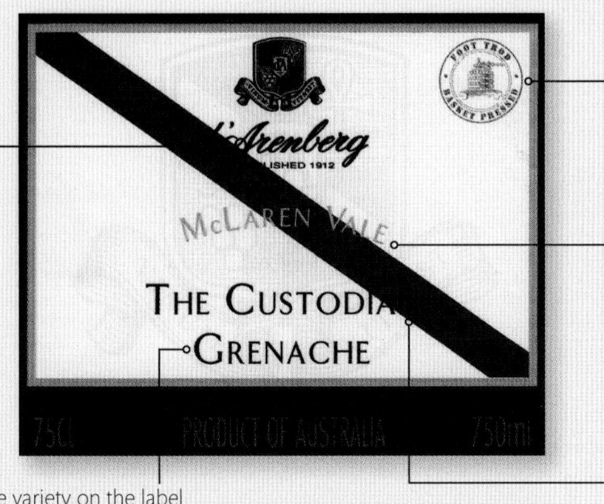

Geographical Indications (GI) The official certification of where the grapes were grown, in this case McLaren Vale.

Wine name The name, "The Custodian", has no legal meaning but describes a certain style of wine made from Grenache grapes by the d'Arenberg winery. Australian producers are particularly fond of pet names for their wines.

Grape variety The name of the grape variety on the label means you have a varietal wine. In Australia and New Zealand a wine must contain at least 85 per cent of the named variety.

France

The great joy of French wine is its unmatched diversity. No other country produces such a range of different styles (many of them imitated all over the world) – at all prices. A tour of France's wine regions could start with the grassy Sauvignons and rich Chenin Blancs of the Loire. Next stop would be Champagne, home of many of the world's greatest sparkling wines, before moving on to the ethereal Pinot Noirs and complex Chardonnays of Burgundy and the aromatic whites of Alsace. Heading south, you find the spicy Syrahs and Grenache-led blends of the Rhône, the delicate rosés of Provence, the powerful red blends of the Languedoc-Roussillon, and the structured reds, zesty whites, and unctuous dessert wines of Bordeaux. Even this tour would only scratch the surface of a country that most wine lovers still regard as the wine world's spiritual home.

Bordeaux

When seeking value in Bordeaux, remember that vintage matters. Less celebrated vintages, such as 2007 and 2008, can offer good value. In the best vintages, although wine from the top estates is expensive, there is plenty of chance to try smaller, less expensive appellations. For these, consider 2005, 2009, and 2010. Also look for Bordeaux's unsung heroes – the second wines of the big estates.

Château d'Agassac Cru Bourgeois, Médoc

L'Agassant d'Agassac, Haut-Médoc (red)

Château d'Agassac is one of the Médoc's smaller properties. But what it lacks in size it more than makes up for in charm. It is a fairytale château, built in the 13th century, and it is one of the few wineries in the area where children are genuinely welcomed – the little ones can take advantage of an iPod-guided tour of the grounds in search of a princess. There is charm, too, when it comes to the wines at this 39ha (96 acre) estate. The second wine, L'Agassant d'Agassac, has a full 90% Merlot in the blend, and offers silky tannins and ripe red fruits. It represents quite a departure from many Médoc wines, but it works.

15 rue d'Agassac, 33290 Ludon-Médoc
www.agassac.com

Château Beauregard Pomerol

Benjamin de Beauregard, Pomerol (red)

A good proportion of Cabernet Franc gives a floral edge to the cranberry and redcurrant fruits in Benjamin de Beauregard, the second wine from this excellent Pomerol estate. From young vines grown on sandy plots, it is gentle and appealing, with subtle white pepper notes on the finish. It comes from the property's 17.5ha (43 acre) estate, which is planted 70% to Merlot and 30% to Cabernet Franc, and on which you'll find one of Pomerol's few genuine châteaux. It is a beautiful building, and it is easy to see why the Guggenheim family chose to build a replica at home in Long Island. It is also a very modern winery, thanks to the major renovations undertaken since the 1990s by the owners, Vignobles Foncier.

1 Beauregard, 33500 Pomerol
www.chateau-beauregard.com

Château Beauséjour Premier Grand Cru Classé B, St-Emilion

Croix de Beauséjour, St-Emilion Grand Cru (red)

Both the 2008 and 2009 vintages of Croix de Beauséjour, the second wine of Château Beauséjour, offer sweet red fruit flavours, and some nutty edges of hazelnut and crushed almonds. The latter vintage is the first under a new winemaking team, headed by Nicolas Thienpont (who is also the winemaking director of Pavie Macquin) and assisted by two of Bordeaux's most famous wine consultants, Michel Rolland and Stéphane Derenoncourt. The team has 5ha (12 acres) of vineyards on which to draw, with 70% Merlot, 20% Cabernet Franc, and 10% Cabernet Sauvignon, and they have introduced such Burgundian winemaking techniques as open-vat fermentation and manual punching down in order to extract flavours more gently from the grapes, and to obtain richer fruit. The château is owned by the Duffau-Lagarrosse family, although they have long since removed the family name from the château's labels.

No visitor facilities
05 57 24 71 61

Château Beau-Séjour Bécot Premier Grand Cru Classé B, St-Emilion

Tournelle de Beau-Séjour Bécot, St-Emilion Grand Cru (red)

Château Beau-Séjour Bécot has seen its fortunes fall and rise over the past few decades. The château (not to be confused with Château Beauséjour) was demoted by the local wine board in 1986 (for using non-classified vines), but rose back up again in 1996, and was recently granted "B" status. The wines certainly deserve their current ranking. They are produced from 17ha (42 acres) of vineyards planted to 70% Merlot, 24% Cabernet Franc, and 6% Cabernet Sauvignon, and located on the western plateau of the village. Those grapes are transformed by gentle, hands-on winemaking, including manual punch-downs during maceration (fermentation on the skins) and the passing of the wine into barrels without using pumps. In Tournelle de Beau-Séjour Bécot, the high-quality second wine, a hefty 20%-plus of Cabernet Franc makes its presence felt with gently warming spices and, if you are lucky (look for the 2009 vintage), touches of violets.

33330 St-Emilion
www.beausejour-becot.com

Château La Bécasse Pauillac
Château La Bécasse, Pauillac (red)

The tiny Château La Bécasse is the kind of estate that lovers of Bordeaux on a budget would like to see more of: a producer dedicated to making good quality, non-classified Pauillac at prices that everyone can afford. Black cherry and damson flavours dominate the wine produced here; these are well-knitted wines that are carefully made, and sold unfiltered to emphasize the natural tannic structure. A great deal of credit for the La Bécasse style has to go to the owner, Roland Fonteneau, who took over the 4.2ha (10.4 acre) estate from his father. Fonteneau inherited a vineyard that is highly fragmented, spread over 20 miniscule plots that had been slowly acquired by his father over a period of several years. To age his wines, Fonteneau uses very high-quality secondhand oak barrels, cannily snapped up from the five first growth châteaux. All the work at La Bécasse is carried out by hand, and the sense that a dedicated artisan is at work here is inescapable.

21 rue Edouard de Pontet, 33250 Pauillac
05 56 59 07 14

Château Belgrave Fifth Growth, Médoc
Château Belgrave, Haut-Médoc (red)

A classified Bordeaux that you can still get for a reasonable price is increasingly rare these days. But Château Belgrave manages to deliver on price *and* taste. That the price is not higher is largely down to the fact that Belgrave has only recently begun to come up with the goods. Reputation counts for a great deal in Bordeaux, and before current owners Dourthe, a négociant house, took over, the château was underperforming. Over the past few years, however, Dourthe has worked hard to remodel the 61ha (150 acre) estate. The company has also invested in a new winery, complete with stainless steel vats, and the winemaking is now much more sensitive, eschewing the use of pumps for moving the grapes around. Today the wine has stylish, precise red fruits, and plenty of swagger. A bargain now, but probably not for much longer.

No visitor facilities
www.dourthe.com

Château Belle-Vue Cru Bourgeois, Médoc
Château Belle-Vue, Haut-Médoc (red)

The late Vincent Mulliez, who died suddenly in 2010, was the driving force behind Château Belle-Vue, which is now owned by his family. Mulliez was once a high-flying banker. But in 2004, this former director of the JP Morgan bank in London felt the urge to return to his native Bordeaux, snapping up three estates in the Haut-Médoc, Belle-Vue, de Gironville, and Château Bolaire. The vineyards were well chosen, with vines right next to the Margaux classified growth Château Giscours. In the case of Belle-Vue, they yield big chewy tannins in a wine that veers towards opulence, but which also has dense plums and damsons to pad things out nicely in the mid-palate, and rich tannins for it all to slide along on – a wine with good development ahead, and one that is always sensibly priced.

103 route de Pauillac, 33460 Macau-en-Médoc
www.chateau-belle-vue.fr

Château Bellevue de Tayac Margaux
Château Bellevue de Tayac, Margaux (red)

There is a decidedly modern feel to Château Bellevue de Tayac's Margaux, with dense brambly blackcurrant fruits from the blend of Merlot, Cabernet Sauvignon, and Petit Verdot, and a hint of charred smoke on the finish. The estate is one of several owned by Jean-Luc Thunevin, who is perhaps more commonly associated with Bordeaux's Right Bank, and with estates such as Château de Valandraud. Thunevin, and his winemaker Christophe Lardière, have reworked the 3ha (7.5 acre) estate, ripping it up and then replanting around a third of the vines in 2005. Those vines, plus a small parcel that Thunevin leases, account for an annual production of 16,000 bottles at this fast-improving estate.

No visitor facilities
www.thunevin.com

Château Bertinerie Côtes de Bordeaux
Château Bertinerie, Blaye Côtes de Bordeaux (red)

Château Bertinerie in Blaye in the Côtes de Bordeaux is one of those estates that shows just how much influence the vintage continues to have on the quality of the wines produced in Bordeaux. In smaller vintages, the fruit in the wine here can be subdued, but if you stick to the sure-fire hits (such as 2005, 2008, 2009, and, judging by early tastings of the unfinished wines, 2010), Château Bertinerie has an elegance, combined with sweet red fruits and a touch of softness, that is very appealing. The vineyard here is organic, and like everything here it is cleverly managed by Daniel Bantegnies, one of the most respected winemakers in Blaye. Bantegnies's tricks in the vineyard include growing the vines using double-curtain trellising, which improves photosynthesis and creates less shade on the grapes, boosting maturity. He is similarly attentive in the winery, whether working at Bertinerie or at his family's other Blaye estate, Château Manon La Lagune.

33620 Cubnezais
www.chateaubertinerie.com

Château Beychevelle Fourth Growth, St-Julien
Les Brulières de Beychevelle, St-Julien (red)

The prices of the estate wines of the classified growths of the Médoc are heading in just one direction: upwards. Everyday drinking is increasingly found, therefore, in these estates' second wines, or other ventures. Château Beychevelle's Les Brulières de Beychevelle – an AOC Haut Médoc from vines owned by Beychevelle but not located in St-Julien – is a good example. It has plenty of Médoc structure and elegance at a fraction of the estate wine's price. Now in the joint ownership of French beer and wine company Castel and their Japanese counterpart Suntory, Château Beychevelle is a fine estate on Bordeaux's famous Route des Châteaux as it enters St-Julien.

33250 St-Julien-Beychevelle
www.beychevelle.com

Château Brane-Cantenac Second Growth, Margaux
Baron de Brane, Margaux (red)

Baron de Brane is a delightful, easy-drinking claret. It is softer than its big brother at this second-growth Margaux estate, spending less time in oak, with just 30% new barrels. In terms of flavour, it is deliciously plummy, with a touch of violets from the 5% Cabernet Franc included in the blend. Henri Lurton, the owner at Château Brane-Cantenac, is a humble character, who would rather spend his time tending his 85ha (210 acres) of vines than pursuing the glitzier side of a top Bordeaux estate-owner's life. Lurton's team are in the same mould, quietly getting on with their jobs, and, in the case of estate manager, Christophe Capdeville, leading research into the effects of different types of barrels on the estate's wines.

33460 Cantenac
www.brane-cantenac.com

Château Calon-Ségur Third Growth, St-Estèphe
Marquis de Calon, St-Estèphe (red)

Château Calon-Ségur is the furthest north of all the classified estates of the Médoc. It has some 74ha (183 acres) of vines planted to 65% Cabernet Sauvignon, 20% Merlot, and 15% Cabernet Franc, producing powerful wines of great texture and depth. Those wines have many fans around the world, including the actor Johnny Depp – clearly a man of taste. The estate, which is owned today by the Casqueton family, puts a great deal of effort into its second wine, the Marquis de Calon, and in doing so it has certainly managed to recreate some of the excitement of the first wine. Produced from the estate's younger vines, the Marquis nevertheless has real finesse, with subtle oak on the nose, and good depth of black cherry fruits on the palate.

2 Château Calon-Ségur, 33180 St-Estèphe
05 56 59 30 08

Château Cambon la Pelouse
Cru Bourgeois, Médoc
Château Cambon la Pelouse, Haut-Médoc (red)

There is a touch of the New York hipster about Nicolas Marie, the son of owner Jean-Pierre, who now runs this estate. But while he may not look the part of a vigneron, he is clearly a very talented winemaker. The Château Cambon la Pelouse is a high quality, unshowy wine, with pleasing freshness, good balance, and lots of ageing potential if you can hold onto it long enough. It is worth seeking out cooler vintages, such as 2006, 2007, and 2008, as the alcohol can be a touch high in some years.

5 chemin de Canteloup, Macau, 33460 Margaux
www.cambon-la-pelouse.com

Château Camensac Fifth Growth, Médoc
La Closerie de Camensac, Haut-Médoc (red)

Notes of spice and tobacco lend a touch of complexity to La Closerie de Camensac, but the overall feel is of easy drinking – summer rather than autumn fruits, and soft tannins. It is the second wine of an estate that lies between two of the area's other classified châteaux, Belgrave and La Tour Carnet. There used to be a Spanish connection here: until 2005 Camensac was one of the properties owned by the Forner Brothers behind the famous Rioja estate, Marqués de Cacères. It is now in the hands of Jean Merlaut, who works with his niece, Celine Villars, and uses the popular Eric Boissenot as consultant. The vineyards, planted at a high density of 10,000 vines per hectare (4,000 per acre), are evenly divided between Merlot and Cabernet Sauvignon.

Route de St-Julien, 33112 St-Laurent-Médoc
www.chateaucamensac.com

Château Canon

Premier Grand Cru Classé B, St-Emilion

Clos Canon, St-Emilion Grand Cru (red)

The Wertheimer brothers have an enviable collection of assets to their name. Among them are the fashion house, Chanel, and two top Bordeaux châteaux, Rauzan-Ségla and Château Canon. The last of these has been completely renovated in recent years. Its 22ha (54 acre) estate produces some polished and smooth wines. The second wine, Clos Canon, has plenty of rich summer fruits and ripe tannins – and lots of Cabernet Franc making its subtly spicy presence felt. Some vintages may be a special occasion price, but they're worth it.

4 Saint Martin, 33330 St-Emilion www.chateau-canon.com

FOOD & WINE POMEROL

Pomerol is a tiny appellation in Bordeaux's Right Bank area. It predominantly produces Merlot – and it is the best in the world. Cabernet Franc is sometimes blended with the Merlot, but in very small proportions. Ultra-elegant, fruity, refined, and with a full body, Pomerols pair well with myriad ingredients.

The best, most expensive Pomerols are richly layered with fruit and fine tannins. They offer a Burgundian intensity of raspberry and cherry fruit and complement classics such as *Tournedos Rossini* (pan-fried *filet mignon* served on a crouton with foie gras).

Softer, more affordable Pomerols are typically ethereal, soft, rich, and earthy, with plum and berry fruit, and tobacco notes. They are supple, full of flavour, elegant, and balanced. These wines pair well with straightforward, earthy, soft-textured meat dishes including braised oxtails or cheek, chateaubriand of beef with *demi-glace*, rack of lamb with mustard and herbs, or even a modern dish such as potato-wrapped lamb chop with Merlot and vanilla bean sauce.

Wines from less reputable regions that neighbour Pomerol, such as Lalande-de-Pomerol, are lighter and delicious with a simple roast chicken served with sautéed mushrooms, a vegetarian burger with mushrooms and a mild cow's milk cheese such as Cheddar, or a picnic of duck confit and pâté.

Enjoy light Merlots from Lalande-de-Pomerol with roast chicken.

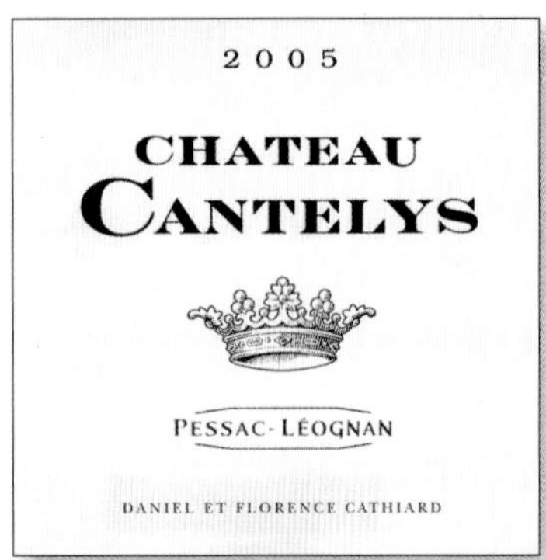

Château Cantelys Pessac-Léognan

Château Cantelys, Pessac-Léognan (red and white)

Owned by the Cathiard family of Château Smith Haut Lafitte, Château Cantelys has a reputation for making wines that are distinctly modern in character. Certainly, the estate's Cabernet Sauvignon-led red wine is plushly international and pleasantly flashy in feel, with toasty oak notes and rich red berry fruits coming through on the palate. The well-made white, which blends Sauvignon Blanc, Sauvignon Gris, and just a little Sémillon, is full of toasty oak flavours and exotic fruit.

No visitor facilities
www.smith-haut-lafitte.com

Château Cantenac Brown Third Growth, Margaux

Brio de Cantenac Brown, Margaux (red)

There is a distinctly English ambience at Château Cantenac Brown. That is not surprising – the estate's first owner, one John Lewis Brown, modelled the château on an English country mansion, and the owner today is the Syrian-born British businessman, Simon Halabi. The second wine, Brio de Cantenac Brown, is a contemporary take on traditional claret. New oak is kept to a minimum during the ageing process, meaning that the style emphasizes exuberant fruit.

33460 Margaux
www.cantenacbrown.com

Château Cap de Faugères Côtes de Bordeaux

Château Cap de Faugères, Castillon Côtes de Bordeaux (red)

A spicy mix of Merlot (60%) and Cabernet Franc (40%), Château Cap de Faugères offers great concentration of rich berry fruits, and a gently toasted note, like roasted chestnuts. It is a wine that many believe outshines some of the bigger names in the more glamorous neighbouring appellation, St-Emilion. The estate has been owned by Silvio Denz since 2005.

33330 St-Etienne-de-Lisse
www.chateau-faugeres.com

Château Caronne-Ste-Gemme

Cru Bourgeois, Médoc

Château Caronne-Ste-Gemme, Haut-Médoc (red)

Expect dense black fruits from Château Caronne-Ste-Gemme. Produced from grapes sourced from 45ha (111 acres) of vines, averaging 25 years in age, around the sleepy village of St-Laurent, it is a wine that lasts, and you will want to decant young vintages. It is a classic Médoc mostly made from Cabernet Sauvignon and aged for a year in oak. The château's ownership is also very traditional Bordeaux: François Nony is a cousin of the Borie family at Château Ducru-Beaucaillou. Modernity is not entirely absent here, however. Oenologist Olivier Dauga has introduced the concept of green harvesting, which helps to concentrate flavours.

33112 St-Laurent-Médoc
www.chateau-caronne-ste-gemme.com

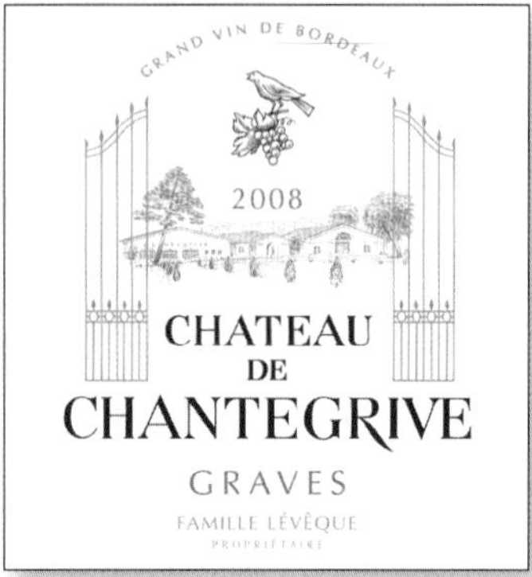

Château de Chantegrive

Pessac-Léognan

Château de Chantegrive, Graves (red)

Château de Chantegrive is one of the largest estates in Graves, with vineyards extending over 97ha (240 acres) of land. Hélène Lévêque is in charge of operations, although the winemaking benefits greatly from the consultant oenologist, Hubert de Boüard. The wines are aged in an impressive barrel cellar, and the grapes from each plot of vineyard are vinified separately. Savoury rosemary and touches of earthy warmth give a sense of uncomplicated charm to the estate's red, a 50/50 blend of Cabernet Sauvignon and Merlot. It is one of Bordeaux's best value wines from one of the region's most dynamic producers.

33720 Podensac
www.chantegrive.com

Château Chasse-Spleen Cru Bourgeois, Médoc

L'Ermitage de Chasse-Spleen, Moulis-en-Médoc (red)

A blend of grapes from young Cabernet Sauvignon, Merlot, and Petit Verdot vines, L'Ermitage de Chasse-Spleen is the very classy second wine of Château Chasse-Spleen. In the best years, it has silky tannins and manages to pack some of the power of its big brother, which is itself a cru bourgeois that regularly out-punches some of the classified growths. Both wines live up to the promise suggested by the château's name: Chasse Spleen roughly translates as "chase the blues away". Owned by the Villars-Merlaut family, the estate has 80ha (198 acres) of vines, with Cabernet Sauvignon the major component.

32 chemin de la Raze, 33480 Moulis-en-Médoc
www.chasse-spleen.com

Château Citran Cru Bourgeois, Médoc
Moulin de Citran, Haut-Médoc (red)

With its supple and soft tannins, Château Citran's second wine, Moulin de Citran, manages to be both elegant and subtle. In some vintages the wine can in fact seem a little too light, at least in its early stages, with the fruit coming across as unexpressive. When the wine gets into its stride after a few years in bottle, however, it shows a firm blackberry core. The estate is managed by Céline Villars-Merlaut (whose sister, Claire, has the same role at Chasse-Spleen), and it has ballooned in size so that it now stands at 90ha (222 acres) after once having been as small as 4ha (10 acres).

Chemin de Citran, 33480 Avensan
www.citran.com

Château Clarke Cru Bourgeois, Médoc
Rosé de Clarke, Listrac-Médoc (Bordeaux Rosé)

There are increasing numbers of rosé wines coming out of the Médoc, and Château Clarke's version is a good example of why they are worth exploring. It has much more structure than many rosés, with a healthy strawberry colour, and plenty of raspberry fruit. Château Clarke has been around since the 12th century, but in winemaking terms, it is a relatively recent concern: it was not until 1978 that the first wine was bottled here, five years after the estate was acquired by Baron Edmund de Rothschild. Today, it is run by Edmund's son, Baron Benjamin, a cousin of Baron Eric at Château Lafite. Benjamin also has estates in South Africa and Argentina.

No visitor facilities
www.cver.fr

Château Clément-Pichon Cru Bourgeois, Médoc
Château Clément-Pichon, Haut-Médoc (red)

Some serious investment in recent years has begun to pay off at Château Clémont-Pichon. Owner Clément Fayat has completely overhauled the 25ha (62 acre) vineyard since he bought the château in 1976, and it shows. Made from 50% Merlot, 40% Cabernet Sauvignon, and 10% Cabernet Franc, the estate wine has coffee and chocolate hints on the nose and the palate (thanks to ageing in softly charred oak barrels), and smooth, confident fruit.

30 avenue du Château Pichon, 33290 Parempuyre
www.vignobles.fayat.com

Château Climens
First Growth, Sauternes
Cyprès de Climens, Barsac (dessert)

As befits its first-growth status, Château Climens is one of the greatest names of the world-famous dessert wine appellation of Sauternes. Owned by Bérénice Lurton and located in Barsac, the estate covers 30ha (74 acres) of 100% Sémillon vines. It is a charming estate, and it makes this excellent second wine, too, at a considerably more accessible price. As you might expect, Cyprès de Climens is lighter and fresher than its big sister, but it still has the luscious sweetness of a Barsac. There is plenty of honeyed fruit, and a delicate flourish on the finish – in sum, this is a seriously enjoyable dessert wine.

2 Climens, 33720 Barsac
www.chateau-climens.fr

CABERNET SAUVIGNON

Vineyards in Bordeaux grow five different red grape varieties, but only one of them, Cabernet Sauvignon, is the primary ingredient in all of the five famous first-growth wines recognized in the 1855 classification of the top Bordeaux estates.

The qualities that Cabernet Sauvignon grapes bring to those rare wines (celebrated names such as Château Mouton-Rothschild and Château Lafite Rothschild), they also bring to many less expensive wines from Bordeaux and other places around the world – deep colour, full body, vivid blackcurrant aromas, and a famously astringent texture that helps the wines to age gracefully.

FAMILY RESEMBLANCE

The shape of Cabernet Sauvignon leaves is very similar to that of Sauvignon Blanc, a white wine variety native to Bordeaux. Scientists have confirmed that Sauvignon Blanc and the red variety Cabernet Franc are the genetic parents of Cabernet Sauvignon.

SMALL BERRIES

Cabernet Sauvignon grapes are known for their small size, which gives big flavours to the wine. Since most wine flavour comes from the grape skins, small berries increase the proportion of flavour compounds to juice when the wine ferments, and can result in extra concentration in the finished wines.

LATE BLOOMER

Cabernet Sauvignon vines send out shoots later in the spring, and ripen later in the autumn than Merlot, the most widely grown variety in Bordeaux. This helps Cabernet Sauvignon avoid damage from spring frosts, and since it has good resistance to vine diseases in the autumn it can still ripen fully.

THICK-SKINNED

One reason grape growers like Cabernet Sauvignon is that this variety has grapes with thick skins. These skins help the grapes to resist damage from sunburn and mildew during the growing season, and various moulds that can attack and damage grapes in the autumn harvest season.

WHERE IN THE WORLD?

Bordeaux is the birthplace of Cabernet Sauvignon, and grows the most famous and expensive examples, but wine drinkers have other options for affordable Cabernet Sauvignon.

In Bordeaux, lower priced wines often carry the place name of simply Bordeaux on the label, or of appellations such as Bordeaux Supérieur, Médoc, Haut-Médoc, Entre-deux-Mers, Côtes de Bourg, and Côtes de Blaye. Most of these will be lighter and smoother than wines from the top estates. The US, Chile, and Australia are all great sources of Cabernet Sauvignon. Napa Valley is best known for its high-priced Cabernet Sauvignons, but other parts of California and Washington State make more affordable versions.

The following regions are among the best for Cabernet Sauvignon. Try bottles from these recommended vintages for the best examples:

Médoc/Haut-Médoc: 2010, 2009, 2005
Pauillac: 2009, 2008, 2006, 2005
Napa Valley: 2009, 2007, 2006
Australia: 2009, 2006, 2005

Washington's Columbia Crest makes fine, affordable Cabernet Sauvignon.

Château Clos Chaumont
Côtes de Bordeaux

Château Clos Chaumont, Cadillac Côtes de Bordeaux (red)

Dutch timber merchant Pieter Verbeek has worked wonders at Château Clos Chaumont, a rising star in Côtes de Bordeaux, one of Bordeaux's less-established appellations. With the help of his friend Kees van Leeuven, a winemaker at Cheval Blanc and d'Yquem, he has built up this fine estate in the tiny village of Haux from scratch. His red (60% Merlot, 22% Cabernet Franc, 18% Cabernet Sauvignon) has firm redcurrant fruits, with a tingle of freshness. There is no need to think too hard about this wine. Just enjoy it.

8 Chomon, 33550 Haux
05 56 23 37 23

Château La Conseillante Pomerol

Duo de Conseillante, Pomerol (red)

Château La Conseillante is undoubtedly one of Pomerol's finest and most exciting estates. It is owned by the Nicolas-Artefeuille family, although it is the director, Jean-Michel Laporte, who is in charge of the day-to-day running of the 12ha (30 acre) estate. The vineyard is mostly planted to Merlot with a little (14%) Cabernet Franc, and Laporte is not afraid to try modern ideas such as cold soaking, micro-oxygenation, and co-innoculation (initiating both alcoholic and malolactic fermentation at the same time). But whatever technique is employed, it is always applied sensitively. With the price of the estate wine rising all the time, wine lovers were delighted when La Conseillante introduced a second wine, Duo de Conseillante, in 2008. Fleshy, joyful, and packed with fruit, it is an exquisite slice of Pomerol. And while it is not the easiest wine to track down and its price tag requires a slight splurge, it is well worth trying.

130 rue Catusseau, 33500 Pomerol
www.laconseillante.fr

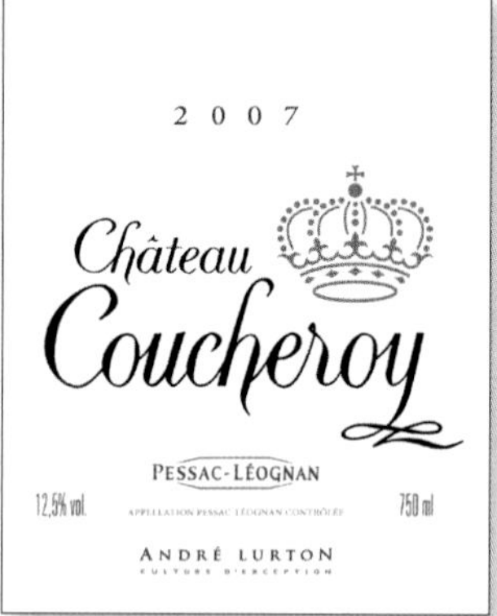

Château Coucheroy Pessac-Léognan

Château Coucheroy, Pessac-Léognan (red and white)

Both the red and white wines from André Lurton's Château Coucheroy offer great drinking. The estate is split between 25ha (60 acres) or red vines and 6ha (15 acres) of white. Whatever the colour of the wine, the estate makes extensive use of modern winemaking techniques to capture bright fruit flavours at their most exuberant. The estate's red wine is an equal-parts blend of Cabernet Sauvignon and Merlot that spends some 12 months ageing in barrel. It has soft tannins and ripe red fruits that only need a few years in bottle before becoming expressive. The white, meanwhile, is perhaps even better. It is a crisp 100% Sauvignon Blanc taken from vines planted at high density (8,000 vines per hectare/3,400 per acre). But there is more to it than just freshness and vitality. There is complexity, too, thanks to a winemaking regime that begins with fermentation taking place at low temperatures in stainless steel tanks before transferring the wine to age gracefully in barrel.

c/o La Louvière, 33850 Villenave d'Ornon
05 57 25 58 58

Château Couhins
Grand Cru Classé de Graves, Pessac-Léognan

Château Couhins, Pessac-Léognan (red)

Château Couhins is no ordinary winery. Owned by the INRA (a national body for the science of plants), it doubles up as a research and development centre. When it comes to the wines that are made here, however, it is worth looking for bottles that date from 2005 onwards, the point at which the investment from the new winemaking team really started to pay off. Post-2006, the red wines have well-padded density in the mid-palate, and great crunchy fruit. Clearly fruit selection has been improved here, allowing for the creation of a second and third wine.

No visitor facilities
www.chateau-couhins.fr

Château La Croix Mouton Bordeaux Supérieur

Château La Croix Mouton, Bordeaux Supérieur (red)

Château La Croix Mouton consistently makes wine that over-delivers for the price. In fact, the estate red here is a brilliant wine irrespective of how much it costs, reminding you of what Bordeaux can achieve with smart winemaking, even in the small appellations. Full of cleverly teased-out brambly fruits, with a fresh finish, it is joyously drinkable. The man to thank for this is Jean-Philippe Janoueix, one of the Right Bank's most dynamic characters. Working with 50ha (124 acres) of vines just across the border from St-Emilion he lets the wine ferment in stainless steel, with malolactic fermentation in barrel, before finishing it off with eight months of barrel age.

33240 Lugon-et-l'Ile-du-Carnay
www.josephjanoueix.com

Château de la Dauphine Fronsac

Delphis de la Dauphine, Fronsac (red)

Château de la Dauphine in Fronsac is an increasingly acclaimed estate, and deservedly so. It has been owned by Jean Halley since he acquired it from the Moueix group in 2001, and the winemaking is carried out by Halley's son, Guillaume, who works in tandem with consultant winemaker, Denis Dubourdieu. Having incorporated a second estate in the neighbouring Canon-Fronsac area (although all the wines produced here are labelled as Fronsac), there are now 32ha (79 acres) of vines at Dauphine, averaging 33 years in age, and divided 80/20 between Merlot and Cabernet Sauvignon. Large-scale investment has brought about a new winery, complete with vats and a circular underground barrel cellar. The second wine, Delphis de la Dauphine, is a gentle introduction to the charms of Fronsac. Majoring on blackberry and vanilla cream, it has soft tannins that make it an early-drinking favourite.

33126 Fronsac
www.chateau-dauphine.com

Château Duhart-Milon Fourth Growth, Pauillac

Baron de Milon, Pauillac (red)

Château Duhart-Milon is affectionately known to many as "Lafite's little brother". It earned the soubriquet both because of its location – right next door to Château Lafite Rothschild – and because it has been owned since 1962 by the Rothschild family (the same as, you guessed it, Lafite). Though somewhat overshadowed by its all-conquering big brother, Duhart-Milon nevertheless has charms of its own, and is a sizeable producer in its own right. The estate covers some 73ha (180 acres), roughly divided into 70% Cabernet Sauvignon and 30% Merlot, and produces 240,000 bottles annually. The third wine, Baron de Milon, is the most affordable. It is a very different experience from the estate wine, of course – far more approachable when young, with red Merlot fruit dominating the whole experience.

17 rue Castéja, 33250 Pauillac
05 56 59 15 33

Château de Fieuzal

Grand Cru Classé de Graves, Pessac-Léognan

L'Abeille de Fieuzal, Pessac-Léognan (white)

Businessman Lochlann Quinn became the latest in a long line of Irishmen to take an active interest in the Bordeaux wine industry when he purchased Château de Fieuzal in 2001. He installed Stephen Carrier as director and Hubert de Boüard as consultant shortly afterwards, and he has made considerable investments ever since. Recent vintages have seen higher proportions of Sauvignon Blanc in L'Abeille de Fieuzal, the reliable second wine, which offers enticing aromas of sweet wet grass, with hints of gooseberry on the palate.

124 avenue de Mont de Marsan, 33850 Léognan
www.fieuzal.com

Château Figeac Premier Grand Cru Classé B, St-Emilion

Le Grand Neuve de Figeac, St-Emilion Grand Cru (red)

As the first wine of Château Figeac pulls ever further away in price, the second wine starts to look like serious value. Like the estate wine, Le Grand Neuve de Figeac has an unusually high proportion of Cabernet Sauvignon for the Right Bank. It also shares some of its brooding dark fruits, although it does not need the same 10-year ageing period to get into its stride. The estate is run today by Eric d'Aramon, the son-in-law of the man who put Figeac on the map, Thierry Manoncourt, who died in 2010.

33330 St-Emilion
www.chateau-figeac.com

Château La Fleur de Boüard

Lalande-de-Pomerol

Fleur de Boüard, Lalande-de-Pomerol (red)

Fleur de Boüard is open and easy-going in style, with a rich mouthfeel and soft tannic structure that packs a punch with summery red fruits. It is a blend of 85% Merlot, 10% Cabernet Franc, and 5% Cabernet Sauvignon made by Coralie de Boüard, the daughter of celebrated winemaker Hubert de Boüard, the driving force of Château Angélus. Coralie is very much at the centre of operations here: the property was even renamed after her by her father when he bought it in 1998. The vineyards extend to 19.5ha (48 acres), and are worked by hand.

33500 Pomerol
www.lafleurdebouard.com

Château La Fleur Morange St-Emilion

Mathilde, St-Emilion (red)

Jean-François and Veronique Julien are the perfectionist couple behind the high-achieving, small-scale Château La Fleur Morange. A (famous) cabinet maker by trade, Jean-François has brought a number of ingenious innovations to his new field of endeavour. Malolactic fermentation, for example, takes place on a specially constructed balcony to take advantage of the rising heat. The couple farm biodynamically, and they are able to draw on very old vines, including some that are more than a century old. Those vineyards are divided between 70% Merlot, 15% Cabernet Franc, and 15% Cabernet Sauvignon, but the delicious Mathilde is a 100% Merlot. One of the most exciting second wines on the Right Bank, it is full of fleshy, insistent red berry fruits.

Ferrachat, 33330 St-Pey-d'Armens
www.lafleurmorange.com

Château Fonbadet Cru Bourgeois, Pauillac
Château Fonbadet, Pauillac (red)

Though she is a law graduate, it was perhaps inevitable that Pascale Peyronie would one day get involved in the wine business. Both sides of her family tree have been associated with some of Bordeaux's finest wines, whether at Château Mouton Rothschild on her mother's side, or Château Lafite Rothschild on her father's. Peyronie got her chance when her family bought Château Fonbadet, and she now runs the 20ha (49 acre) estate, where the vines average 50 years in age. The unfiltered wine is led by Cabernet Sauvignon, with a touch of Malbec that gives a dark, spicy edge. A brooder when young, make sure you decant it for a few hours to let the black fruits out.

45 route des châteaux, St-Lambert, 33250 Pauillac
www.chateaufonbadet.com

Château Fonplégade Grand Cru Classé, St-Emilion
Fleur de Fonplégade, St-Emilion Grand Cru (red)

Château Fonplégade is one of St-Emilion's most improved estates. Renovations here have been literally bankrolled by the château's owner, US banker Stephen Adams, and the winemaking has been overseen by consultant Michel Rolland. The estate extends to some 18ha (44 acres), of which the overwhelming majority (91%) are planted to Merlot. The house style is one of slick, poised, and polished luxury; hedonistic wines that have been given plenty of time in new French oak. La Fleur de Fonplégade, the second wine, is a delicious entry-point. With its uncomplicated, flirtatious red berry fruits, it is a seriously enjoyable wine, and excellent value.

1 Fonplégade, 33330 St-Emilion
w[illegible]adamsfrenchvineyards.fr

RATINGS ON THE 100-POINT SCALE

Why do wine critics and retailers rate wines on the 100-point scale? The practice emerged in the 1980s when the US wine newsletter *Wine Advocate* adopted a popular method used by US schoolteachers to grade students' papers, and applied it to wine, to indicate the quality level of wines it reviewed.

The world's largest circulation wine magazine, *Wine Spectator*, adopted the scale soon after and it seems to be everywhere today. It is a quick way to express how much a critic likes or dislikes a wine, and it has proved to be an equally quick way to sell wines, especially when they get scores of 90 points or above. The scale gives some people the impression of objective precision, as if it were a laboratory test of wine quality. It's more like the grade for an essay test: an informed but subjective judgment.

As used by most critics, wines scoring 90-plus are outstanding or classic in quality, those from 80 to 89 are good to very good, wines in the 70s are merely drinkable, while most at 60 and under are considered very poor.

Wine consumers, particularly in the US but increasingly elsewhere, too, have embraced and followed the 100-point scale, finding that they can't go too far wrong with an 85-point wine and they might have a great and rare experience with a 95-point wine. Wine writers who don't use the scale, however, never seem to tire of criticizing it as too simplistic, too inconsistent, and too powerful.

Many winemakers in regions including Bordeaux, California, and Tuscany have changed their grape-growing and winemaking practices to gain higher scores from critics. The danger of this, claim the 100-point opponents, is that only wines with big flavours and obvious personalities earn the highest scores, and thus the system doesn't reward the equally positive attributes of elegance and subtlety.

Château Fonréaud Cru Bourgeois, Médoc

Château Fonréaud, Listrac-Médoc (red)

This estate sits at the highest point in the Médoc. Although, at 43m (141ft) above sea level, that is perhaps not quite as impressive as it first sounds. Whether or not the altitude affects the style of wine made by owner Henri de Mauvezin, is somewhat moot, however. The wine takes on balance, complexity, and plenty of fruit with age, developing subtle but convincing cedar and vanilla oak on the nose, and a fresh finish on the palate, but can be rather tough and tannic in its infancy. It improves with five years or more in the cellar.

138 Fonréaud, 33480 Listrac-Médoc
www.chateau-fonreaud.com

Château Fourcas Dupré Cru Bourgeois, Médoc

Château Fourcas Dupré, Listrac-Médoc (red)

Château Fourcas Dupré is a very reliable Listrac name, which, like a number of producers here, has been greatly improved by recent investments. This is not an exuberant wine by any means, but it has well-controlled black fruit, and its restrained style suits lovers of classic Bordeaux. It is a blend of 50% Cabernet Sauvignon, 38% Merlot, 10% Cabernet Franc, and a smidgen of Petit Verdot. The vines grow on gravel soils, which explains why the wine has the structure of some of the more prestigious Médoc wines.

Le Fourcas, 33480 Listrac-Médoc
www.fourcasdupre.com

Château Fourcas Hosten Cru Bourgeois, Médoc

Château Fourcas Hosten, Listrac-Médoc (red)

As with the neighbours at Fourcas Dupré, recent investment has begun to pay off in the wine at Château Fourcas Hosten, and it is finally fulfilling its true potential. There has certainly been a noticeable step-up in quality since the 2008 vintage, and the wine is now characterized by smooth, rich fruits and a well-buttoned tannic waistcoat – appropriate given that the estate has been owned, since 2006, by Renaud and Laurent Mommeja, the brothers behind the Hermès fashion house.

2 rue d'Eglise, 33480 Listrac-Médoc
www.fourcas-hosten.fr

Château Franc Mayne Grand Cru Classé, St-Emilion

Les Cèdres de Franc Mayne, St-Emilion Grand Cru (red)

Château Franc Mayne is at the forefront of what might be called the modernist side of St-Emilion. Owned by a Belgian couple, Griet and Hervé Laviale, the modern stylings are immediately apparent to the visitor in the top-notch boutique hotel and wine tourism centre that the couple have added to the property. Modernity is also discernible in the estate's wines, which are produced from 7ha (17 acres) of vineyard planted to Merlot (90%) and Cabernet Franc (10%), and which are made with the emphasis on fruit. This is particularly true of the second wine, Les Cèdres de Franc Mayne, which has soft toasted tannins from the oak, wrapped up with red cherry flavours and vanilla cream. Not everything here is new, however; the limestone cellars date back several centuries.

La Gomerie, 33330 St-Emilion
www.chateau-francmayne.com

Château La Garde Pessac-Léognan

Château La Garde, Pessac-Léognan (red)

Château La Garde is one of several well-managed properties owned by the Dourthe wine merchant business. It was acquired by the company in 1990, and it stretches across 54ha (133 acres) of top-quality vineyard. There has been a great deal of research into the vineyard and its soils carried out here, enabling the team to plant and harvest with precision. Made under the guidance of consultant Michel Rolland, the red wine is a blend of around 60% Merlot with the balance made up by the Cabernets and Petit Verdot. It is vinified in small stainless steel tanks and aged in barrel for 18 months. Excellent value for the quality, it has rich, powerful fruits and yet is balanced by smooth and supple tannins.

No visitor facilities
05 56 35 53 00

Château Giscours Third Growth, Margaux

La Sirène de Giscours, Margaux (red)

Château Giscours is a grand estate that makes an immediate impression on the visitor with its long driveway snaking off behind the imposing gates. Now in the hands of Dutch owner Eric Albada

Jelgersma (who also owns Château du Tertre), Château Giscours has made great improvements in recent vintages thanks to a series of major investments. Much of that money has been focused on restructuring the 83ha (205 acre) of vines, which cover four hillocks composed of white gravel, with vines averaging 40 years in age. The red wines made here are a blend of 55% Cabernet-Sauvignon, 35% Merlot, and a smattering of Petit Verdot and Cabernet Franc, and are known for their appealing richness and tight-knit tannic structure. La Sirène de Giscours is an excellent value second wine from this well-known Médoc estate, with some of the slick, plump blackcurrant fruits of its big brother. The 2008 and 2009 vintages are particularly good.

10 route de Giscours, Labarde, 33460 Margaux
www.chateau-giscours.com

Château Grand Corbin-Despagne
Grand Cru Classé, St-Emilion
Petit Corbin-Despagne, St-Emilion Grand Cru (red)

There is tradition to spare at the 27ha (67 acre) Château Grand Corbin-Despagne, which has been in the hands of the Despagne family for seven generations. But there is innovation, too, under current owner François Despagne. Despagne is committed to organic vineyard practices, and he is well on the way to converting the vineyards to biodynamic farming. He is also committed to experimenting with technology in the vineyard and winery (including a laser-optic sorting table) to ensure he ends up with the best grapes. Whether inspired by tradition or the latest ideas, attention to detail is clearly the guiding principle here, and all work is carried out by hand. The second wine, Petit Corbin-Despagne offers truly excellent value. Gently roasted black cherries are balanced out by seams of freshness that reflect the personality and precision of the estate's first wine. A blend of 75% Merlot and 25% Cabernet Franc from young vines, it is aged in a mixture of stainless steel and oak.

33330 St-Emilion
www.grand-corbin-despagne.com

Château Greysac Cru Bourgeois, Médoc
Château Greysac, Médoc (red and white)

Smart winemaking and a refreshingly modern approach make Château Greysac's Cru Bourgeois a good value, reliable Bordeaux red wine, with well-placed black fruits and a hint of liquorice on the palate. The estate, which has a fairly sizeable 95ha (235 acres) of vineyard, can be found some distance to the north of St-Estèphe, in the small town of By. Around 70% of its 540,000-bottle annual production goes into the first wine, with the remaining 30% going to the second wine, Château de By. The estate is managed by the charming Philippe Dambrine (of Cantemerle), who also makes a complex 100% Sauvignon Blanc dry white from 2ha (5 acres). Fermented and aged for six months in oak barrels of which 30% are new, it is well worth looking out for.

18 route de By, 33340 Bégadan
www.greysac.com

Château Haut-Bailly Grand Cru Classé de Graves, Pessac-Léognan
La Parde de Haut-Bailly, Pessac-Léognan (red)

Château Haut-Bailly was one of the first estates in Bordeaux to create a second wine. First produced in 1967, La Parde de Haut-Bailly has all the elegance that you would expect from an estate of this quality, with soft tannins, firm plum fruits, and savoury herbs. Today, however, the wines of the Haut-Bailly estate, with its 30ha (74 acres) of vines sitting high on a ridge in Léognan, have become some of the most sought-after in the region so the second wine becomes ever more important as a better-priced entry point.

Avenue de Cadaujac, 33850 Léognan
www.chateau-haut-bailly.com

Château Haut-Bergey Pessac-Léognan

Château Haut-Bergey, Pessac-Léognan (red and white)

Sylviane Garcin-Cathiard, who also owns Clos l'Eglise in Pomerol, has added a certain dynamism to the improving Château Haut-Bergey. With Alain Reynaud acting as consultant, the estate produces excellent quality red and white wine, although grape varieties for the former take up considerably more space (38ha/94 acres of Cabernet Sauvignon and Merlot, 2ha/5acres of Sauvignon Blanc and Sémillon). Notes of blackcurrant leaf and clean graphite make the red a highly enjoyable, contemporary-styled wine. Aged in new oak, the white is also modern in style, with attractive tropical-fruit notes.

69 cours Gambetta, 33850 Léognan
www.chateau-haut-bergey.com

Château Haut Peyrous Graves

Château Haut Peyrous, Graves (red)

Marc Darroze took the global route to becoming a Bordeaux château owner. He worked in Armagnac, California, and Hungary before snapping up Château Haut Peyrous in 2008. A lot of his work since then has focused on converting this promising 12ha (30 acre) estate to organic production (the first organic vintage will be 2012). The red wine shows the benefit of Darroze's belief in low yields, ripe grapes, and a gentle approach to vinification. Produced from Merlot, Cabernet Franc, Cabernet Sauvignon, and a little Malbec, it offers gourmet flavours with toasty red fruits and soft, supple tannins.

No visitor facilities
www.darroze-armagnacs.com

Château d'Issan Third Growth, Margaux

Blason d'Issan, Margaux (red)

Regularly cited as one of the best value, most reliable second wines in the Médoc, Blason d'Issan offers soft black fruits and blackberry crumble, with the oak providing a smoky edge. It comes from an attractive estate, Château d'Issan, that is also one of the oldest in the Médoc. D'Issan has grown enormously in the post-war years, both in reputation and size. Run by Emmanuel Cruse, a key figure in the politics of Bordeaux wine, Château d'Issan had a mere 2ha (5 acres) when it was bought by the Cruse family in 1945. Today there are 53ha (131 acres) of vineyard, with plantings mostly devoted to Cabernet Sauvignon, which dominates the estate's blends.

33460 Cantenac
www.chateau-issan.com

Château Joanin Bécot Côtes de Bordeaux

Château Joanin Bécot, Castillon Côtes de Bordeaux (red)

Though the alcohol can seem a little high in warmer vintages, Château Joanin Bécot is an outstanding example of a Côtes de Bordeaux red. Ripe damsons and roasted vanilla pods give the wine some of the seductive power of the best Right Bank wines. Like many of the new breed of wines produced in this part of Bordeaux, it is the work of a young member of a famous winemaking family from a more celebrated neighbouring appellation. In this case it is Juliette Bécot from Château Beau-Séjour Bécot in St-Emilion who has made the short journey to Castillon to make her name. In tandem with oenologists Sophie Porquet and Jean-Philippe Fort, Bécot works 7ha (17 acres) of 75% Merlot and 25% Cabernet Franc vines.

33330 St-Emilion
www.beausejour-becot.com

Château Kirwan Third Growth, Margaux

Les Charmes de Kirwan, Margaux (red); Rosé de Kirwan, (Bordeaux Rosé)

There are Irish roots at Château Kirwan, but the roots of the prize-winning rosés are French. They were planted by Camille Godard, a former owner of the estate who was also a botanist. It all adds to the appeal of this most romantic of Margaux estates, which is today in the hands of the eighth generation of the Schyler family. It is run by general manager, Philippe Delfault, who believes Bordeaux should be about elegance and balance rather than power, and the estate's wines certainly live up to those beliefs. Vinified to favour fresh fruit over extracted tannins, the second wine, Les Charmes de Kirwan, is soft and gentle, very much a little sister wine of the Margaux appellation. The rosé is also delightful.

Cantenac, 33460 Margaux
www.chateau-kirwan.com

Château Lafon-Rochet Fourth Growth, St-Estèphe

Les Pelerins de Lafon-Rochet, St-Estèphe (red)

Château Lafon-Rochet's excellent second wine, Les Pelerins de Lafon-Rochet, provides terrific value when you consider the level of winemaking know-how you are getting. As is the case in a number of the second wines produced in St-Estèphe, Les Pelerins has a relatively high proportion of Merlot in the blend, which means you can be confident in cracking it open young. Lafon-Rochet has been run by Michel Tesseron, ably assisted by his son, Basile, since 2007. The pair manage an estate that extends to 45ha (111 acres), planted at high density to 55% Cabernet Sauvignon, 40% Merlot, 3% Cabernet Franc, and 2% Petit Verdot.

Blanquet, 33180 St-Estèphe
05 56 59 32 06

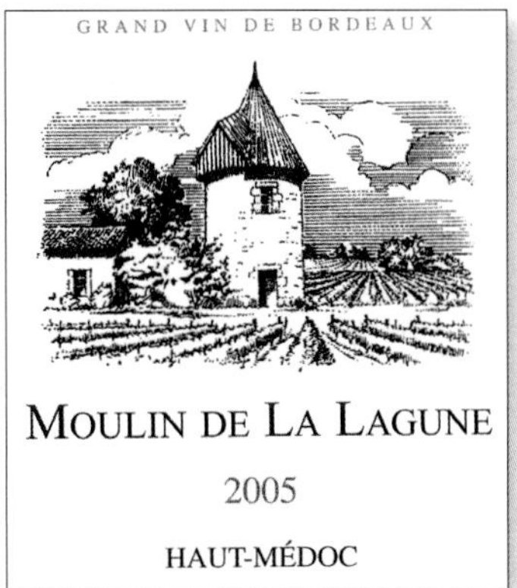

Château La Lagune Third Growth, Médoc

Moulin de La Lagune, Haut-Médoc (red); Mademoiselle L, Haut-Médoc (red)

Château La Lagune's second wine, Moulin de La Lagune, owes much of its character to the high proportion of Cabernet Franc in its blend. There is as much as 15% of the variety used in Moulin in most years, which is high for the Médoc. It gives the wine a gently perfumed nose, although the taste still manages to pack plenty of punch. Mademoiselle L is a lighter and fresher wine made from vines grown on a different plot, located higher up in the Médoc. The château has a proud history of employing female winemakers, and today's incumbent is Caroline Frey. Frey works in an impressive winery that features some 72 gravity-fed tanks, enabling her to vinify many plots separately.

83 avenue de l'Europe, 33290 Ludon-Médoc
www.chateau-lalagune.com

Château Léoville-Las-Cases Second Growth, St-Julien

Le Petit Lion, St-Julien (red)

The high-performing second-growth estate Château Léoville-Las-Cases uses vines from other estates to produce its first wine, Clos du Marquis. The 2007 vintage saw the arrival of a second wine, Le Petit Lion, made from vines grown on the main estate. Le Petit Lion is full of charm, with autumn fruits, and some summery touches of redcurrant and even elderflower from its high degree of Merlot. Las-Cases is run today by Jean-Hubert Delon, the fifth generation to take charge of an estate whose vineyards are next to Château Latour on the border of St-Julien and Pauillac.

Route Pauillac, 33250 St-Julien-Beychevelle
05 56 73 25 26

Château Léoville Poyferré Second Growth, St-Julien

Pavillon de Poyferré, St-Julien (red)

Pavillon de Poyferré is an early-drinking wine created from the young vines of the increasingly acclaimed Léoville Poyferré. For a relatively inexpensive Médoc, this manages to capture some of the slick delivery of the first wine, with a silky mouthfeel and fresh coffee aromas from the oak. The estate has been owned by the Cuvelier family of wine traders from northern France since the 1920s. The team today is led by Didier Cuvelier, with Isabelle Davin as full-time oenologist, and Michel Rolland as consultant. Recent work here has been influenced by extensive research into the estate's soils.

Le Bourg, 33250
St-Julien-Beychevelle
www.leoville-poyferre.fr

Château Lucas Lussac St-Emilion
Château Lucas, Lussac St-Emilion (red)

A little insider knowledge can pay dividends when bargain-hunting in Bordeaux. Château Lucas is a case in point. A little-known estate in Lussac St-Emilion, Lucas is owned and worked by the Vauthier family, who have polished their winemaking skills as owner of the rather more celebrated St-Emilion estate, Château Ausone. Here Frédéric Vauthier works his magic on a little more than 52ha (128 acres) of vines with 50% Merlot and 50% Cabernet Franc, in sustainable (soon-to-be organic) fashion. He produces three cuvées in total, all of which offer a measure of Ausone charm for a fraction of the price. The basic Château Lucas is arguably the best in terms of value. It has a delightful floral nose from its high proportion of Cabernet Franc, with touches of redcurrants on the palate.

33570 Lussac
www.chateau-lucas.fr

Château de Lussac Lussac St-Emilion
Le Libertin de Lussac, Lussac St-Emilion (red)

The notion of a wine being flirtatious might seem slightly preposterous, but if there is a wine that justifies the adjective it would be Château de Lussac's second wine, Le Libertin de Lussac. A blend of 80% Merlot and 20% Cabernet Franc, it is full of seductive damson and ripe berry flavours, with hints of mocha and liquorice from the oak. It is produced in appropriately kitschy surroundings, by Belgian couple, Griet and Hervé Laviale, who have converted the 19th-century Château de Lussac into a country manor, complete with gilt-edged chandeliers. The winemaking facilities are thankfully less frivolous, however, and the circular layout is kitted out with all the necessary modern winemaking gadgets, including a Tribaie machine to assess sugar levels.

15 rue de Lincent, 33570 Lussac
www.chateaudelussac.fr

Château Lynch-Bages Fifth Growth, Pauillac
Echo de Lynch-Bages, Pauillac (red)

Price rises have seen Echo de Lynch-Bages, Château Lynch-Bages's excellent quality second wine, reach more serious levels in recent years. However, the wine, which had its name changed in 2008, still provides a great example of the bold, seductive pleasure offered by this estate. Considerably less Cabernet Sauvignon goes into the blend in Echo de Lynch-Bages than the main wine, usually around 50%, meaning the softer Merlot and Cabernet Franc can make their influence felt, giving high aromatics on the nose, and hints of violets in the mouth. Owned by Jean-Michel Cazes, Château Lynch-Bages is currently run by his son, Jean-Charles. The family has been active (and successful) in promoting wine tourism in Pauillac, and are well respected for the sincerity, consistency, and sophistication of everything they turn their hand to at their 96ha (237 acre) estate.

33250 Pauillac
www.lynchbages.com

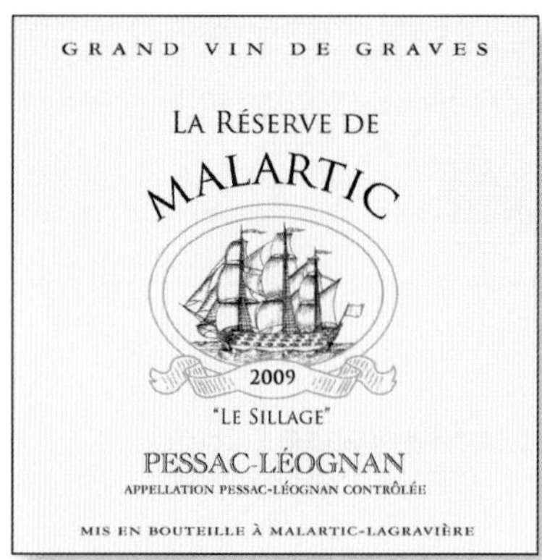

Château Malartic Lagravière
Grand Cru Classé de Graves, Pessac-Léognan
La Réserve de Malartic, Pessac Léognan (white); Rosé de Malartic (Bordeaux Rosé)

Owned by the Bonnie family since 1997, the 53ha (131 acre) Château Malartic Lagravière has rapidly become one of the most exciting estates in the Pessac-Léognan appellation. Over the past decade, fastidious work in the vineyard (which is now farmed sustainably) and the winery (which is one of the most technically advanced in the appellation) have brought enormous improvements to the wines. The vineyards are divided between 46ha (114 acres) of red varieties and 7ha (17 acres) of white. Bargains at this estate include the classic cut-grass aromas of the deft, enjoyable white La Réserve de Malartic, which has tart gooseberry, and a well-controlled lift, on the finish. There is also an excellent value, and deliciously juicy, bright rosé.

No visitor facilities
www.malartic-lagraviere.com

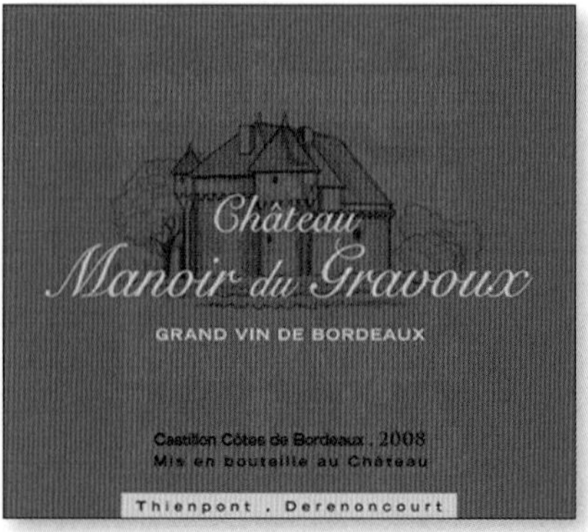

Château Manoir du Gravoux
Côtes de Bordeaux
Château Manoir du Gravoux, Castillon Côtes de Bordeaux (red)

Situated directly opposite Stéphane Derenoncourt's celebrated Domaine de l'A in Castillon, Philippe Emile's 19ha (47 acre) rising star estate, Château Manoir du Gravoux, is beginning to make a name of its own. Derenoncourt has offered plenty of expert advice to Emile, who tends his Merlot (88%) and Cabernet Franc (12%) vines with the same gentle and intelligent touch for which Derenoncourt is famed. At Manoir du Gravoux this results in a wine that is packed with fruit from beginning to end, with plenty of blackberries and damsons, and a touch of aromatic Cabernet Franc lightness on the finish.

33350 St-Genes-de-Castillon
www.terraburdigala.com

Château Marjosse Bordeaux
Château Marjosse, Bordeaux (red)

Buying a bottle of Château Marjosse is a very affordable way to get your hands on a slice of the red winemaking know-how of Château Cheval Blanc, since the estate is owned by Pierre Lurton, director of the legendary St-Emilion estate. The wine is made in a different style to Cheval Blanc, and is not designed to offer the same complexity, but it is exquisitely well made all the same. Its soft, smooth tannins and firm fruits are simply full of charm. The estate is found in Entre-deux-Mers, where Lurton has recently begun using a spanking new 2,400 sq m (25,824 sq ft) modernist winery designed by architect Guy Tropes. Lurton has 80ha (198 acres) of vines to work with, and Merlot is the dominant grape variety, making up 75% of the red blend, which also includes 3% Malbec to add a touch of spice.

33420 Tizac-de-Curton
05 57 74 94 66

Château Mondésir-Gazin Côtes de Bordeaux
Château Mondésir-Gazin, Blaye Côtes de Bordeaux (red)

Marc Pasquet has brought all of the flair, creativity, and attention-to-detail that made him a successful photographer to his second career as a winemaker. The owner of Château Mondésir-Gazin since 1990, he also owns Château Haut-Mondésir (Bourg) and Château Gontey (St-Emilion). At Mondésir-Gazin, Pasquet has 14ha (35 acres) of vines up to 60 years old, from which he makes 24,000 bottles of a red that is widely regarded as one of the best in Blaye. Unfined and unfiltered to emphasize the chunky, upfront structure, the wine shows off fruit that combines wild strawberries with spicy liquorice from 20% Malbec, the balance being 60% Merlot and 20% Cabernet Sauvignon.

10 le Sablon, 33390 Plassac
www.mondesirgazin.com

Château Le Moulin Pomerol
Le Petit Moulin, Pomerol (red)

Château Le Moulin may be small at just 2.5ha (6 acres) but it is run with considerable élan by Michel Querre, and produces some fine modern wines. The soil here is a mix of clay and gravel, and Querre works it intensively but sensitively, keeping yields very low. For the winemaking, Querre favours a Burgundian-inspired approach, with the wooden vats kept open during punching down, and with malolactic fermentation and ageing taking place in 100% new oak. The successful second wine, Le Petit Moulin, is a touch flashy, and certainly on the modern side in style, but it is undeniably enjoyable. Cassis and fig flavours keep things full of punch. It is worth decanting for an hour or so to open it up.

Moulin de Lavaud, La Patache, 33500 Pomerol
www.moulin-pomerol.com

Château Moulin St-Georges St-Emilion
Château Moulin St-Georges, St-Emilion Grand Cru (red)

Because it shares the same winemaking team as the famous St-Emilion estate, Château Moulin St-Georges is sometimes dubbed the "mini Ausone". It does not suffer too badly from the implied comparison. The 7ha (17 acres) of vines are dominated by Merlot (80%) with 20% Cabernet Franc. Low yields are one of the goals in the vineyard, where all work is carried out by hand. The wine is fermented in stainless steel, and given 18 months in 100% new oak. It takes a while to come round, but the wait is worth it. Well structured, with deep fruit flavours, it is also extremely well priced.

33330 St-Emilion
05 57 24 70 26

Château Nenin Pomerol
Fugue de Nenin, Pomerol (red)

Now in the hands of the Delon family of Léoville-Las-Cases (who took over in 1997), Château Nenin has been on an upward curve in the past decade. The Delons have invested heavily in restoration and renovation, including adding an extra 4ha (10 acres) of vineyards from the now-defunct Château Certan-Giraud, making a total of 33ha (81 acres). Other moves undertaken by director Jacques Depoizier, his son, Jérome, and consultant Jacques Boissenot include raising the proportion of Cabernet Franc to 40%, increasing the canopy cover, and introducing picking dates based on the age of the vines. The improvements are clear in Fugue de Nenin, the well-respected second wine. Full of dark chocolate and black cherry flavours, it is seductive and good value, particularly in recent years.

66 route de Montagne, 33500 Libourne
www.chateau-nenin.com

HOW TO TASTE WINE

The real objective with wine is to drink and enjoy it, not to make a pretentious show of twirling the glass and thrusting your nose in the bowl for a sniff. But if you are interested in enjoying wine to its limit, that requires a measure of connoisseurship. Being a connoisseur doesn't mean being a snob, but in its original form means being someone who knows. The best way to know wine and to understand your own likes and dislikes about it is to, at least sometimes, taste wine thoughtfully rather than simply swallowing it. Here are the six basic steps in tasting wine. When you have practiced them a bit you can even use them unobtrusively when you are at a party or dinner.

1 Hold the glass at an angle in front of a piece of white paper. Study the wine. Is it light in colour, suggesting a light taste too? As they age, reds go from bright purple or ruby to a brick-like colour; whites take on a deeper, more golden hue.

4 Taste a good-sized sip of wine and concentrate on its flavours. Does it taste like it smells? Maybe even better? Or do unpleasant flavours intrude? Great wines tend to have complex flavours that hang together in balance.

2 Swirl the wine carefully to coat the sides of the glass. This allows more wine to evaporate into the air, making it easier to smell. Heavy drip lines or "legs" indicate viscosity.

3 Smell deeply by putting your nose into the glass and slowly inhaling. Think about what you smell, to help you remember similar wines later. Are there fruit or spicy oak aromas, for instance?

5 Feel the wine's texture. Sense its viscosity in your mouth. The drying sensation of tannin is common in reds. Dessert wines tend to feel especially rich. Fresh whites are crisp with mouth-cleaning acidity.

6 Take the time to savour the finish. A good quality wine's flavour lingers in your mouth after swallowing (or after spitting, if you are tasting many wines in the same sitting). Great wines tend to have long finishes.

Château Ormes de Pez
St-Estèphe

Château Ormes de Pez, St-Estèphe (red)

The very stylish new label at Château Ormes de Pez depicts the elm (orme) trees that used to grow around the estate, and from which this château takes its name. The wine – a blend of 51% Cabernet Sauvignon, 39% Merlot, 8% Cabernet Franc, and 2% Petit Verdot – is stylish too, which is not surprising when you learn that it is owned by the Cazes family of the classified growth, Château Lynch-Bages. With its exuberant black fruits, its emphasis on purity of fruit and its lightness of touch, this is a wine that will make you smile.

Route des Ormes,
33180 St-Estèphe
www.ormesdepez.com

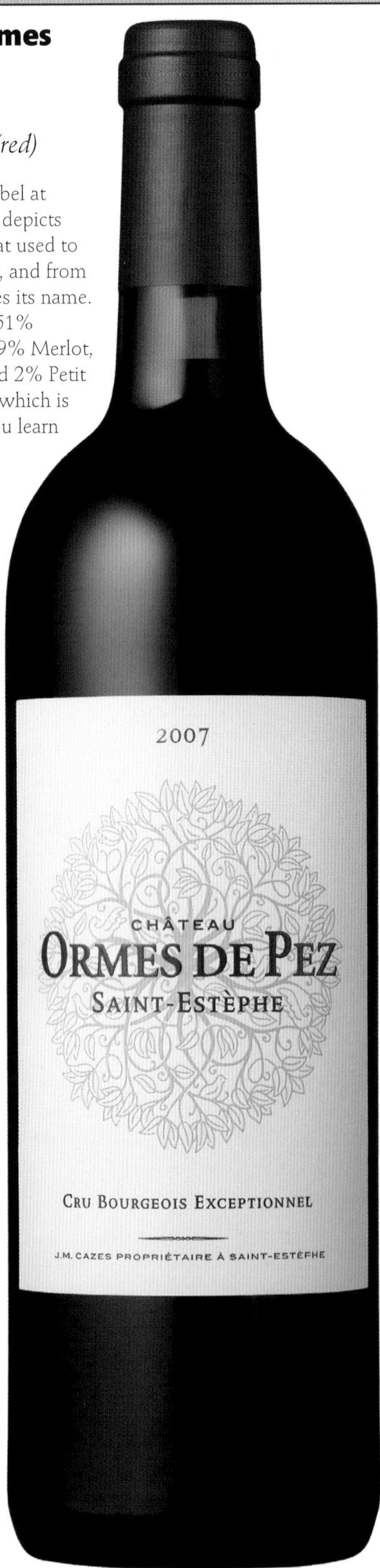

Château Penin Bordeaux Supérieur
Château Penin, Bordeaux Supérieur (red)

Château Penin's owner, Patrick Carteyron, makes his wine with 100% Merlot grapes, all of them taken from vines that are more than 30 years old. It is a delightful wine, very easy to drink and full of fresh red fruits, with little evident tannin, despite having spent one year ageing in barrel. Carteyron has been at the helm of this 40ha (99 acre) estate since 1982, and his approach is to have as little intervention in the cellar as possible (including making some wines with no added sulphur dioxide). He produces more than 270,000 bottles each year of a range of wines that are consistently of a higher quality than the humble Bordeaux Supérieur appellation might suggest. With attractive pricing the norm, this is most certainly an estate to look out for.

33420 Port Génissac
www.chateau-penin.com

Château Petit-Village Pomerol
Le Jardin de Petit Village, Pomerol (red)

Château Petit-Village is owned by the AXA Millésimes group, which has interests in a handful of top estates around the world, including fellow Bordeaux estate Château Pichon-Baron, and the celebrated port producer, Quinta do Noval. Run by the Englishman Christian Seely, who uses Stéphane Derenoncourt as a winemaking consultant, Château Petit-Village is atypical for Pomerol in that it has a high proportion of Cabernet Sauvignon in its blend (as much as 18%), something that reflects the gravelly soil here. There is also a little Cabernet Franc planted, although Merlot is still king, with around 80% of the blend. The château's second wine, Le Jardin de Petit Village, features classic Pomerol flavours coming through strongly – notably violets and redcurrant fruits. There is oak, but it is restrained and wraps the fruit rather than smothering it. The estate itself is well-worth a visit to see the new cellars and a visitor centre designed by architect Alain Triaud.

33500 Pomerol
www.petit-village.com

Château Peyrabon Cru Bourgeois, Haut-Médoc
Château Peyrabon, Haut-Médoc (red)

Château Peyrabon is a wine made from vines grown in the Haut-Médoc appellation by an estate that also has a small patch of vines in Pauillac that are bottled as a cru bourgeois under the label, Château La Fleur Peyrabon. Owned by Patrick Bernard of the Millésima wine merchants (and a cousin of Olivier Bernard at the famous Pessac-Léognan estate, Domaine de Chevalier), both Peyrabon and La Fleur Peyrabon have been the subject of a good deal of investment since they were acquired in 1998. And that investment can certainly be felt in the wines. The Château Peyrabon is a really good value, well-made claret, with pleasingly soft coffee aromas, and some charming summery fruits.

Vignes des Peyrabon, 33250 Pauillac
www.chateaupeyrabon.com

Château Phélan Ségur St-Estèphe
Frank Phélan, St-Estèphe (red)

Redcurrant and black cherry flavours, and a subtle wash of cedary oak are the key characteristics of Frank Phélan, the second wine at Château Phélan. It is light in style for a St-Estèphe, but it has real spirit and elegance. The property is owned by Thierry Gardinier, a well-known figure in Bordeaux as owner of Hotel les Crayères in Champagne and the Taillevent Group in Paris. The estate covers 68ha (168 acres), with 47% Merlot, 22% Cabernet Sauvignon, and the remainder Cabernet Franc. Michel Rolland is the consultant winemaker.

33480 St-Estèphe
www.phelansegur.com

FOOD & WINE SAUTERNES

The Sémillon grape variety originated in Bordeaux in the 18th century, and is still widely planted today. When over-ripe and allowed to become affected by the fungus *Botrytis cinerea* (noble rot), Sémillon is the major component of the unique wines of Sauternes, where it produces the world's most famous dessert wine, Château d'Yquem.

Thin skin and a tendency to rot give Sémillon grown in the cool, misty climate of Sauternes the ability to easily host *Botrytis cinerea*. The fungus concentrates and shrivels the grapes so that the wine they produce is exquisitely honeyed and complex with notes of pineapple, peach, lanolin, toasted pecans, white mushroom, candlewax, and orange blossom.

These unctuous, nuanced sweet whites are most often paired with desserts. Ideal choices include crème brûlée, sabayon with peaches, peach tart, lemon angel food cake, almond cookies, jasmine wafers with brown sugar, or banana and ginger ice cream. Avoid chocolate, however.

Savoury dishes such as seared foie gras with poached apple or pineapple is a classic pairing even with well-priced satellite wines such as Monbazillac. Salty, crispy, fried chicken is also worth a try. For cheese lovers, Roquefort and other blues work, with the salt of the cheese contrasting nicely with the richness and sweetness of the wine.

Sauternes contrasts deliciously with salty Roquefort cheese.

Château Pibran Cru Bourgeois, Pauillac
La Tour Pibran, Pauillac (red)

La Tour Pibran is one of the more accessible Pauillacs on the market, with a high degree of Merlot that means it does not need long ageing to reveal its leather-and-blackberry flavours. It is made by an estate, Château Pibran, that has been improving in quality, and shaking off its somewhat dowdy reputation, since its acquisition by insurance company, AXA Millésimes. Under the guidance of the debonair Englishman, Christian Seely, a new winery has been built, enabling all the winemaking to now take place on site (grapes were previously sent to Château Pichon-Longueville Baron). The château's vineyards, which have been extensively replanted in recent years, cover 17ha (42 acres), divided 50/50 between Cabernet Sauvignon and Merlot.

c/o Château Pichon-Longueville Baron, Route des Châteaux, 33250 Pauillac; 05 56 73 17 28

Château Plince Pomerol
Pavilion Plince, Pomerol (red)

A series of big improvements in recent years have made the Pomerol property Château Plince an estate to watch. It is owned by the Moureau family, but more pertinently it is run by the Moueix family – producers of some of the Right Bank's top wines (and owners of the legendary Château Pétrus). The estate covers 8.6ha (21 acres), planted largely to Merlot (72%), with a fair amount of Cabernet Franc (23%), and a little Cabernet Sauvignon (5%). Among the key changes made by the Moueix family at what used to be very much a workhorse estate (and one of the very few to use mechanical harvesting in Bordeaux) has been the introduction of green harvesting. In the second wine, Pavilion Plince, all that Moueix winemaking expertise translates into a well-structured wine with sweet black fruits.

Chemin de Plince, 33500 Libourne
http://chateauplince.chez-alice.fr

Château La Pointe Pomerol
Château La Pointe, Pomerol (red)

Although the price has been creeping up (quite justifiably) in recent vintages, Château La Pointe is still one of the best value Pomerols you can find. Brimming with clearly defined red fruits and subtle hints of vanilla oak, it is a wine that is utterly delicious, a real delight to drink, with its silky-soft tannins caressing the palate. The estate was bought by Generali France in 2007, since when a number of changes have been made. There is a new director (Eric Monneret), and a new consultant winemaker (Hubert de Boüard). The team has undertaken a major study of its vineyards which has shown that there is considerably greater complexity in the soils than was previously thought. Plantings have been adjusted, and the vineyards are now solely composed of Merlot (85%) and Cabernet Franc (15%). The winery has also been renovated with smaller vats.

33501 Pomerol
www.chateaulapointe.com

Château Poujeaux
Cru Bourgeois, Médoc
Château Poujeaux, Moulin-en-Médoc (red)

The last few years have been kind to Château Poujeaux, with new owner (Philippe Cuvelier of Clos Foutet in St-Emilion) and new investment reaping rewards. The young team, which is led by Cuvelier's son, Mathieu, with winemaking consultant Stéphane Derenoncourt offering sage advice, have managed to turn this 52ha (128 acre) estate into a very serious proposition. They work hard at ensuring soft, silky tannins. A good 40% of Merlot in most years plumps out and softens the power, rich intensity, and spice of Cabernet Sauvignon and Petit Verdot. Expect stacks of fruit and plenty of attitude.

No visitor facilities
www.chateaupoujeaux.com

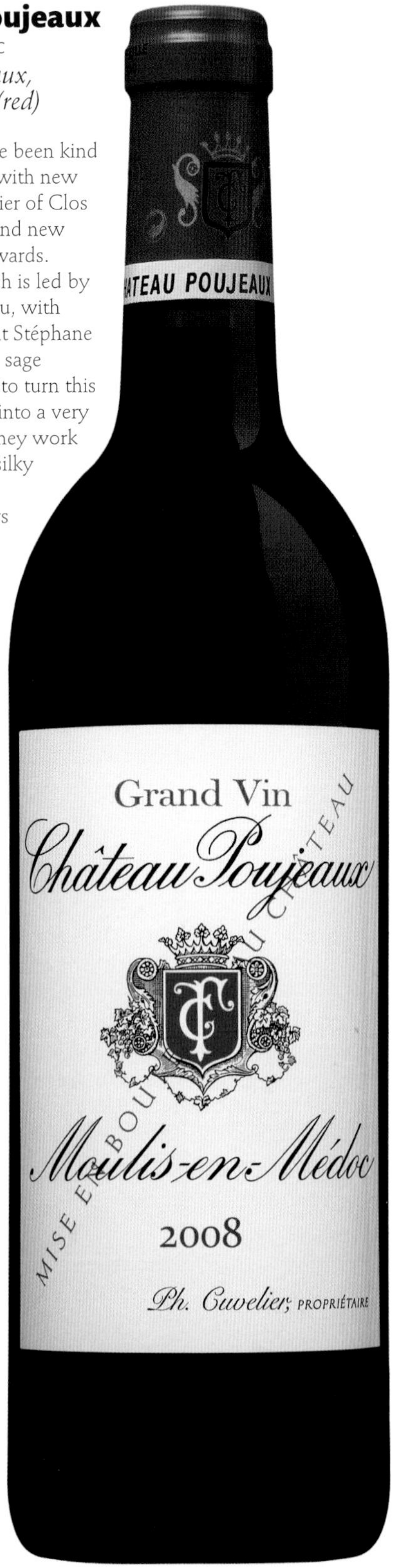

Château Preuillac Cru Bourgeois, Médoc

Château Preuillac, Médoc (red)

Château Preuillac is an underrated estate. After more than ten years under the dynamic and enlightened ownership of Jean-Christophe Mau, however, it really should not be. Mau took over as proprietor of Preuillac in 1998, backed by investment from the Dutch drinks company, Dirkzwager. Since then he has introduced a raft of improvements, including new drainage channels, increased planting density, and a new, fully equipped, modern winery. Stéphane Derenoncourt is the consultant winemaker here, and the wine is improving every vintage, with smooth, plumped-out black fruits, silky tannins, and touches of redcurrant.

33340 Lesparre-Médoc
www.chateau-preuillac.com

Château Rahoul Graves

L'Orangerie de Rahoul, Graves (red)

The influence of the Champagne region can be felt at Château Rahoul. The estate has been owned for 25 years by Alain Thiénot, the founder and proprietor of Champagne Thiénot, and, since 2007, a majority shareholder of the Bordeaux wine merchant business, CVBG Dourthe Kressman. This latter investment has helped give a new impetus to Rahoul, since Thiénot has been able to call on Dourthe's considerable winemaking, and wine-selling, expertise. The wines are made sustainably from grapes grown on the 42ha (104 acres) of vines. The red, L'Orangerie de Rahoul, offers smoky overtones and black cherry flavours.

No visitor facilities
www.chateau-rahoul.com

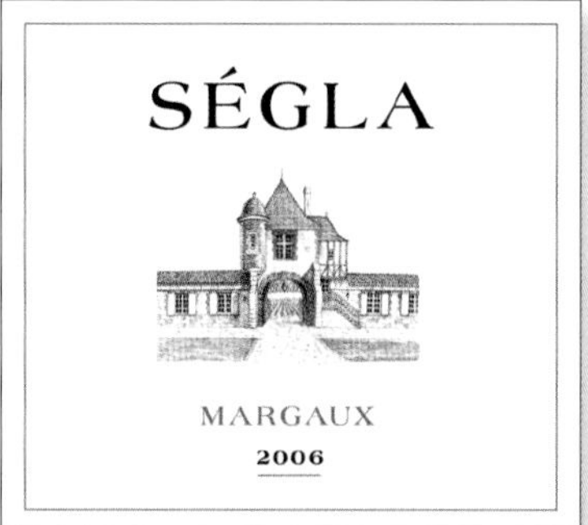

Château Rauzan-Ségla Second Growth, Margaux

Ségla, Margaux (red)

From the very first taste of Ségla, it is apparent that it is the work of the same winemaking team behind the celebrated first wine at Château Rauzan-Ségla. You may pay a special occasion price for this magnificent second wine, but you are rewarded with cassis and tobacco and a lovely structure that holds on tight. Seek out older vintages for a keener price. It seems incredible to think now that this estate was in the doldrums when the Wertheimer brothers (who also own the fashion house and luxury goods business, Chanel) snapped it up in 1993. Today, the château, with its 60ha (148 acres) of land, is one of the top names in the region once again, thanks to the improvements made by director John Kolasa, who developed his approach to wine at Château Latour.

rue Alexis Millardet, 33460 Margaux
www.rauzan-segla.com

Château Raymond-Lafon Sauternes

Les Jeunes Pousses de Raymond-Lafon, Sauternes (dessert)

If you are looking for a high quality but affordable Sauternes, try the second wine from the excellent Raymond-Lafon estate. This is a lighter, fresher version of its big brother, but still with a balance of sweetness and acidity. Expect lime, apricot, and white flowers. The estate has been in the Meslier family since it was bought by Pierre Meslier, a longtime employee of Château d'Yquem, in 1972. Managed today by Charles-Henri and Jean-Pierre Meslier, it has 16ha (40 acres) of Sémillon and Sauvignon Blanc.

4 aux Puits, 33210 Sauternes
www.chateau-raymond-lafon.fr

Château Réal Médoc

Château Réal, Médoc (red)

Château Réal is not one of the Médoc's best-known estates, but should be considered a real rising star. Owned by Didier Marcellis of Château Sérilhan, it is located right next to Château Tronquoy in St-Seruin-de-Cadourne. The vineyard is relatively small at 5ha (12 acres), planted to Cabernet Sauvignon (55%), Cabernet Franc (10%), and Merlot (35%). The vineyard is now worked using organic practices, with everything done by hand. The winemaking, meanwhile, is highly intelligent, bringing out intense blackcurrant flavours from the Cabernet Sauvignon fruit, while the 10% dose of Cabernet Franc adds a floral touch to the nose that is very seductive. The wine is bottled unfiltered.

No visitor facilities
www.chateau-serilhan.fr

Château Reine Blanche St-Emilion

Château Reine Blanche, St-Emilion Grand Cru (red)

Château Reine Blanche produces a polished and accomplished wine that is little known outside the region but is certainly one to watch out for. It is an understated, grown-up kind of wine, characterized by silky red fruits with a touch of mocha on the finish. The talented François Despagne of Château Grand Corbin-Despagne, is the man responsible for this estate. He works 6ha (15 acres) of mainly sandy and stony soil, to come up with the 65% Merlot and 35% Cabernet Franc blend.

No visitor facilities
www.grand-corbin-despagne.com

MERLOT

One could say that the Merlot and Cabernet Sauvignon grape varieties grew up together in Bordeaux. They became great friends, mixing readily and easily in many of the red wines produced there, yet providing different benefits, both to winemakers and to the people who drink their wines.

If Cabernet Sauvignon wine has the stiffer, more angular personality, then Merlot is more feminine, with a softer texture and more mellow and friendly fruit flavours. Merlot is, in fact, the most widely grown grape in the large region of Bordeaux, and is particularly important in the smaller districts of Pomerol and St-Emilion.

WHY "MERLOT"?

The word "Merlot" means young "merle" or blackbird in French. The term may have stemmed from the blue-black colour of the ripe grapes, or from the way that blackbirds like to eat the grapes before they are harvested.

THIN-SKINNED

Merlot is a thin-skinned grape variety. This means various insects, fungi, and even rain can damage it rather easily. It's difficult to grow successfully, but makes delicious, elegant wines when all turns out right.

EARLY BLOOMER

One reason vineyard owners in Bordeaux have grown Merlot for centuries is that its buds burst in early spring and the fruit ripens for harvest in the late summer or early autumn, beating Cabernet Sauvignon by a few weeks. This means the Merlot grapes are less likely to remain hanging on the vine when damaging autumn rains arrive.

BLENDS WELL

Winemakers in Bordeaux like Merlot because they can blend their barrels of Merlot wine with barrels of other wine they make from Cabernet Sauvignon, Cabernet Franc, Petit Verdot, and Malbec. Merlot's softer, sweeter characteristics help balance out tougher traits in the others.

WHERE IN THE WORLD?

While few Pomerol and St-Emilion wines are priced for everyday drinking, Bordeaux makes great value wines using Merlot and other grape varieties in bottles labelled as Bordeaux Supérieur, Médoc, Haut-Médoc, Entre-deux-Mers, Côtes de Bourg, Côtes de Blaye, and others.

Merlot is grown in almost every wine region in the world to at least some extent, so value-priced Merlot of good quality come from such places as Chile, South Africa, northern Italy, Australia, California, New York State, Washington State, the Languedoc-Roussillon area of France, and eastern Europe. Merlot wine may not be easy to make, but it is easy to find, to afford, and to drink, which is why it is so popular.

The following regions are among the best for Merlot. Try bottles from these recommended vintages for the best examples:

St-Emilion: 2009, 2008, 2006, 2005
Chile: 2009, 2008, 2007
Washington: 2008, 2007, 2006
South Africa: 2009, 2007

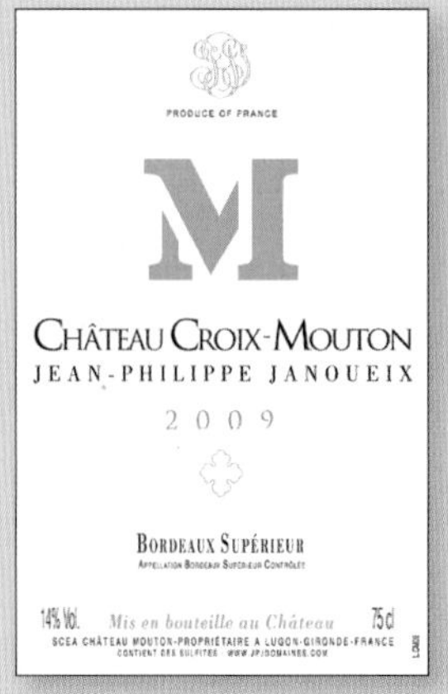

Merlot is often the main grape variety in affordable Bordeaux Supérieur blends.

Château Reynon
Bordeaux Blanc

Château Reynon, Bordeaux Blanc (white)

Denis Dubourdieu is arguably Bordeaux's most celebrated white winemaker, and it is the great value white that shines at his family estate, Château Reynon. Made from 89% Sauvignon Blanc and 11% old-vine Sémillon from 17ha (42 acres) of vines, this is a classic Bordelais interpretation of white wine. In character, therefore, it veers towards the cut grass, rather than grapefruit, end of the Sauvignon Blanc flavour spectrum. Crisp, clean, juicy, and highly (dangerously) drinkable, it is a wine that is made for summer-garden sipping and shellfish or fish dishes.

33410 Beguey
www.denisdubourdieu.fr

Château de la Rivière Fronsac

Château de la Rivière, Fronsac (red)

Château de la Rivière is quite a large estate by the standards of the Fronsac appellation. The vineyards extend across some 59ha (148 acres), divided between 82% Merlot, 13% Cabernet Sauvignon, 4% Cabernet Franc, and 1% Malbec. There is also a beautiful stretch of parkland. This is underrated terroir, that shares the same limestone found in many St-Emilion classified growths, and yields wines with silky, well-worked red fruits. With good length and no harsh edges, this is an accomplished example of Fronsac's potential.

33126 La Rivière, Fronsac
www.vignobles-gregoire.com

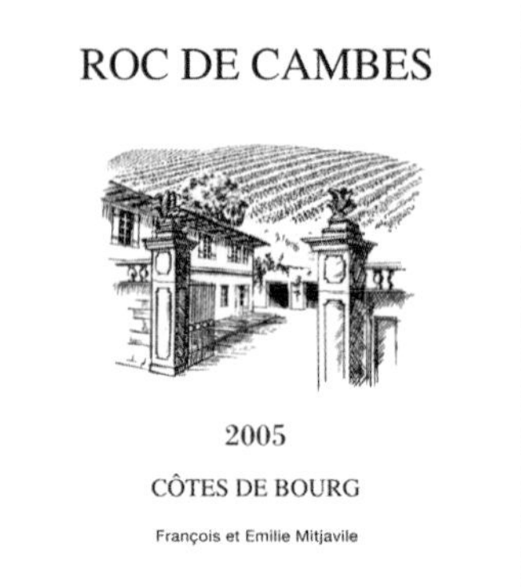

Château Roc de Cambes Côtes de Bourg

Roc de Cambes, Côtes de Bourg (red)

The Côtes de Bourg is one of Bordeaux's lesser-known appellations. But if there is one estate in the region to transcend its origins and gain an international image, that estate would be Château Roc de Cambes. It helps that François Mitjavile, of Château Le Tertre-Roteboeuf (St-Emilion) fame, has been the owner here since 1988. But the wines are consistently excellent, too. Produced from 65% Merlot, 25% Cabernet Sauvignon, and 10% Cabernet Franc, grown in a natural 10ha (25 acre) amphitheatre, the flavour profile here is often similar to the better wines of the Left Bank – savoury, refined black fruits, with good backbone and dense tannins.

33330 St-Laurent-des-Combes
www.roc-de-cambes.com

Château Rollan de By Cru Bourgeois, Médoc

Château Rollan de By, Médoc (red)

It has been a long journey for Jean Guyon at Château Rollan de By. When Guyon bought what was then a tiny (2ha/5 acre) estate in an unfashionable corner of the Médoc in 1989, it was scarcely known at all. But Guyon has transformed the estate, both increasing its size (it now stands at 83ha/205 acres) and introducing quality-conscious vineyard and winemaking practices. He has been helped by Alain Reynaud, his consultant winemaker, who made his reputation working on the Right Bank. The wine uses a majority of Merlot grapes and plenty of new French oak during the ageing process which combine to make this an exuberant, gourmet experience.

3 route du haut Condissas, 33340 Begadan
www.rollondeby.com

Château Rouget Pomerol
Carillon de Rouget, Pomerol (red)

There is a Burgundian sense of restraint and purity to the rich red fruits in Château Rouget's Carillon de Rouget that is highly appealing. It is a slow-burner rather than a crowd pleaser, with real elegance and a weighty mid-palate that makes you smile as the fruit unfolds. That Burgundian character is perhaps to be expected given the ownership of this estate. Eduard Labruyère's family, who bought the 18ha (44 acre) Château Rouget in 1992, do in fact originate from Burgundy, and are the owners of Domaines Jacques Prieur in France's other iconic red wine region. And they have imported some Burgunidan touches to the winemaking at Rouget, such as open vats and naturally started malolactic.

6 route de St-Jacques de Compostelle, 33500 Pomerol
www.chateau-rouget.com

Château Seguin Graves
Château Seguin Cuvée Prestige, Graves (red)

Château Seguin Cuvée Prestige is an enjoyable wine that reliably offers good value. It has ambitious notes of coffee and mocha, which in the best years are well integrated and play with the blackberry fruits. The owner here, in partnership with property group, Foncière Loticis, is Jean Darriet, and it was under Darriet's instructions that the vineyards at Seguin were completely reconfigured in 1988. The policy is for low impact winemaking, using 60% Cabernet Sauvignon and 40% Merlot grapes that are frequently among the last to be picked in the region.

33360 Lignan-de-Bordeaux
www.chateau-seguin.fr

Château Sérilhan Cru Bourgeois, St-Estèphe
Château Sérilhan, St-Estèphe (red)

An emigré from the computer business, Didier Marcellis swapped a high-flying career at Cisco Systems in Paris for a more uncertain, rural existence at Château Sérilhan in St-Estèphe in 2003. But he has lost none of the dynamism that made his business career such a success. He has invested heavily in both expertise – his technical director is Bernard Franc from Château Pontet-Canet, the wine consultant is Hubert de Boüard of Château Angélus in St-Emilion – and in the vineyard and cellar. He now has 23ha (57 acres) of vineyards, from which he produces a confident, modern-feeling wine with plentiful silky blackcurrant fruits.

No visitor facilities
www.chateau-serilhan.fr

Château Siaurac Lalande-de-Pomerol
Le Plaisir de Siaurac, Lalande-de-Pomerol (red)

Slick, pleasingly fruity flavours abound in Le Plaisir de Siaurac, the charming second wine of Château Siaurac. Consistently good from vintage to vintage, it is a reliable, easy-drinking wine that uses fruit sourced from the estate's younger vines. It comes from an estate whose owners have a fine pedigree: Domaines Baronne Guichard also own Le Prieuré in St-Emilion and Vray Croix de Gay in Pomerol. Siaurac's vineyards extend over 39ha (96 acres) just across the border from Pomerol in Lalande.

33500 Néac
05 57 51 64 58

Château Smith Haut Lafitte
Grand Cru Classé de Graves, Pessac-Léognan
Les Hauts de Smith, Pessac-Léognan (red)

Château Smith Haut Lafitte is one of the key estates in the quality revolution that has transformed Pessac-Léognan in recent decades. Owned since 1990 by the Cathiard family, it features 67ha (166 acres) of organically tended vines, a modern winery, and even its own on-site barrel-maker. The red Les Hauts de Smith has muscular tannins that open up (try decanting for an hour) to allow through the sweet, damson plums on the palate, and the cherry-toasted nose.

4 chemin de Bourran, 33650 Martillac
www.smith-haut-lafitte.com

Château Sociando-Mallet Médoc
La Demoiselle de Sociando Mallet, Médoc (red)

Something of a cult estate, Château Sociando-Mallet has a devoted worldwide following among winelovers. Owned by the detail-obsessed Belgian Jean Gautreau, it lies some 3km (1.9 miles) north of St-Estèphe, and La Demoiselle is an excellent introduction to what it is about. Only 20% of the wine sees new oak during the ageing process, with the rest kept in stainless steel tanks, which ensures it is the fruit that takes centre stage, rather than the smokier, more intense flavours developed by a long oak ageing.

33180 St-Seurin-de-Cadourne
05 56 73 38 80

Château Talbot Fourth Growth, St-Julien

Caillou Blanc du Château Talbot, St-Julien (white)

The Caillou Blanc du Château Talbot is one of the rare white wines produced by Médoc estates. But there is much more to this 80/20 blend of Sauvignon Blanc and Sémillon than curiosity value. It is a delightfully unpretentious, crisp, and fresh white wine, with an abundantly aromatic nose from the oak ageing. Château Talbot is located in the very centre of St-Julien, atop one of the highest gravel hills. It is owned by two Cordier sisters, Lorraine and Nancy. Oenologist Stéphane Derenoncourt has consulted since 2008.

33250 St-Julien-Beychevelle
www.chateau-talbot.com

Château du Tertre Fifth Growth, Margaux

Haut du Tertre, Margaux (red)

Inconsistency is now thoroughly in the past at the top Margaux estate, Château du Tertre. After more than a decade of ownership, which has seen considerable investment in the vineyards, Eric Albada Jelgersma and his director, Alexander Van Beek, now produce some of the most elegant wines in Margaux. The second wine, Haut du Tertre, is no exception. Better vineyard selection has refined the supple fruit flavours, and the wine is alive with blackcurrant, wet stones, and some earthy undertones.

33460 Arsac
www.chateaudutertre.fr

Château Teyssier St-Emilion

Château Teyssier, St-Emilion Grand Cru (red)

The red wine of Château Teyssier is rich, deeply fruited, and well-structured – especially for the price. Owner Jonathan Maltus now has some 52ha (128 acres) of vineyards on the Right Bank, and he has improved the grapes for Château Teyssier, a blend of 85% Merlot and 15% Cabernet Sauvignon, by including some good plots from near Château Monbusquet, higher up on the St-Emilion slopes. It is still made for immediate pleasure, however, and it is perfectly suited to early drinking.

33330 Vignonet
www.teyssier.fr

Château Thieuley

Entre-deux-Mers

Château Thieuley, Entre-deux-Mers (white)

Marie and Sylvie Courselle, the two sisters who run Château Thieuley, are making one of the most acclaimed white wines from the AC Entre-deux-Mers region. The acclaim is deserved. They have 30ha (74 acres) of white varieties, divided between Sémillon (50%), Sauvignon Blanc (35%), and Sauvignon Gris (15%). And they use a variety of techniques to emphasize the fruity freshness of their blend, including cold soaking and ageing in only stainless steel. The result is a pin-sharp, and refreshingly drinkable, crisp white wine.

33670 La Sauve
www.thieuley.com

Château La Tour de Bessan Cru Bourgeois, Margaux

Château La Tour de Bessan, Margaux (red)

Marie-Laure Lurton assumed control of Château La Tour de Bessan from her father, Lucien, in 1992. She has been impressing everyone with her determination and energy ever since. Lurton likes to approach her work on the 19ha (47 acre) estate with a mixture of modern and more traditional attitudes. The modern includes such innovations as growing the vines with larger canopies and using stainless steel in the winery. The traditional side of her personality can be found in her use of manual picking and extended oak-ageing. She has worked hard on replanting the vineyards, too, and the balance is now 40% Cabernet Sauvignon, 24% Cabernet Franc, and 36% Merlot. It results in a wine where spiced plum fruit abounds, with touches of liquorice and truffles in the best years.

Route d'Arsac, 33460 Margaux
www.marielaurelurton.com

Château La Tour de Mons Cru Bourgeois, Margaux

Terre du Mons, Margaux (red)

You can expect an elegant, classically styled Margaux red wine from Terre du Mons, the second wine made by Château La Tour de Mons. The touch of smoky cedar on the nose, and the restrained soft fruits, add further lustre to this delicious 60% Merlot, 40% Cabernet Sauvignon blend. It is just one of the wines responsible for giving Château La Tour de Mons its deserved reputation for being one of the most reliable estates in Margaux. Currently owned by a French bank (which is an increasingly common occurence in Bordeaux), the estate is run by the talented director Patrice Bandiera. Manual picking is used throughout the 35ha (86 acre) vineyard, and the vinification is traditional.

No visitor facilities
05 57 88 33 03

Château de Valandraud St-Emilion

3 de Valandraud, St-Emilion (red)

Some refreshingly simple, straight-to-the-point thinking has gone into the naming of 3 de Valandraud, since this is in fact the third wine of Château Valandraud. The tannins have been stripped right

BIODYNAMIC WINE

A biodynamic wine is like an organic wine that also meditates. The vineyard owner will have adopted an especially philosophical approach to its care, making wines from carefully nurtured grapes, grown as free from industrial enhancements as possible.

Biodynamic farming was inspired by the lectures of Austrian philosopher Rudolf Steiner in the 1930s. He's the same man who conceived and lent his name to the Steiner and Waldorf schools that offer an alternative education to children around the world today. Steiner's followers interpreted his teachings for grape growing and winemaking.

Biodynamic wines don't have a particular flavour or style, but their makers maintain that a biodynamic wine shows its terroir – or the flavour of the place where it was grown – more readily than a normal wine. Beyond composting and other proven organic measures, biodynamic farmers must pay especially close attention to their land, their plants, the seasons, and many other elements of the vineyard environment. One of the most important goals is to close the farming loop and use only materials from the property to sustain the property. Animal manure is essential as a fertilizer, for example. Sometimes adherents use preparations that can sound more ritualistic than scientific. One is made by stuffing cow horns with manure and burying them over the winter, then extracting the composted manure from the horns, mixing it to make a solution, and spraying it in the vineyard.

Not surprisingly many agricultural scientists are sceptical of such measures. Some sceptics, however, do allow that a method that encourages farmers to pay special attention to the health of their soil and strive to maintain harmony with nature has much to commend it.

back here, leaving a soft structure that allows the 70% Merlot to show off its summery fruits. It is made by a fabled estate that was at one point synonymous with the garage wine movement of tiny start-up boutique producers that shook the Right Bank's winemaking establishment during the 1990s. Back then, owners Jean-Luc Thunevin and his wife Murielle Andraud had a mere 0.6ha (1.5 acres) of vineyard to play with. They have since grown the estate to 10ha (25 acres), and their wines are now cherished for their quality, rather than as symbols of the anti-establishment.

33330 Vignonet
05 57 55 09 13

Château Vieux Pourret St-Emilion

Château Vieux Pourret, St-Emilion Grand Cru (red)

Attention was focused on Château Vieux Pourret long before any of its wines had been put on the market. In part that is because it is involved in the growing biodynamic movement in Bordeaux, but also because the estate is a joint-venture between two winemaking celebrities: the Rhône's Michel Tardieu, and Bordeaux's Olivier Dauga. The pair have brought a fastidious approach to the project: all the grapes are hand-picked, and the various plots are vinified separately. The result is an 80% Merlot, 20% Cabernet Franc wine that is full of ripe red fruits with wild berry aromas.

Miaille, 33330 St-Emilion
www.chateau-vieux-pourret.fr

Clos Floridène Graves

Clos Floridène, Graves (white)

Clos Floridène is relatively expensive for a Bordeaux white wine. But the style itself is still undervalued, meaning that in a global, and certainly a French, context, it still represents fine value for money. Top Bordeaux white winemaker, Denis Dubourdieu, manages to get fresh mouth-watering flavours from this blend of 55% Sauvignon Blanc, 44% Sémillon, and 1% Muscadelle, which is grown in Dubourdieu's own 31ha (77 acre) vineyard. Even in warmer years, the wine is fresh and packed with crisply defined citrus elements.

33210 Pujols-sur-Cirons
www.denisdubourdieu.fr

Clos Fourtet

Premier Grand Cru Classé B, St-Emilion

La Closerie de Fourtet, St-Emilion Grand Cru (red)

One of St-Emilion's most fetching estates, located just a short walk from the town's most important church, Clos Fourtet has been owned, since 2001, by the Cuvelier family. The family employs Stéphane Derenoncourt as winemaking consultant, and his influence is apparent in the elegant wines made on the 19ha (47 acre) estate, where Merlot (85%), dominates over Cabernet Sauvignon and Cabernet Franc. La Closerie de Fourtet is dominated by delightful brambly autumn fruits, but retains some structure and tannic backbone.

1 Le Châtelet Sud,
33330 St-Emilion
www.closfourtet.com

Clos Puy Arnaud Côtes de Bordeaux
Clos Puy Arnaud, Castillon Côtes de Bordeaux (red)

Rich in colour and structure, the best vintages of Clos Puy Arnaud are truly excellent. Produced from 65% Merlot, 30% Cabernet Franc, 3% Cabernet Sauvignon, and 2% Carmenère, there is a purity to the damson and redcurrant fruits that simply steals over you. The estate lies in the Castillon area, and has been owned since 2000 by Thierry Valette. Stéphane Derenoncourt was initially employed as a consultant winemaker, and he instructed Valette in the basics of biodynamic viticulture. The estate's 7ha (17 acres) are now worked entirely according to biodynamic principles, and Valette's winemaking avoids over-extraction in favour of elegance.

33350 Belvès de Castillon
05 57 47 90 33

Domaine de Chevalier
Grand Cru Classé de Graves, Pessac-Léognan
L'Esprit de Chevalier, Pessac-Léognan (red)

L'Esprit de Chevalier is the second red wine from an estate that is justly celebrated for both its red and white wines. It has firm fruit, with an inviting nose that opens up almost immediately upon opening. Produced from young vines, it nonetheless needs a little ageing, so stash it in the cellar for a couple of years before drinking. When it is ready, however, the good-value red has enough spice to stand up to even the richest meat dishes. It is a good introduction to the talents of Olivier Bernard, who, with the help of consultant winemaker, Stéphane Derenoncourt, heads up this 43ha (106 acre) estate with plantings largely taken up by Cabernet Sauvignon (60%), Merlot (30%), and a little of both Petit Verdot and Cabernet Franc.

102 chemin Mignoy, 33850 Léognan
www.domainedechevalier.com

La Goulée Médoc
La Goulée, Médoc (red)

La Goulée is a new player in Bordeaux, but it has quickly made a name for itself. That is not perhaps surprising given that it shares the same owners (the Reybier family) and winemaking team as the celebrated Cos d'Estournel. The estate, which was conceived as a smart, modern, word-of-mouth brand to rival the likes of New Zealand's Cloudy Bay, takes its name from the Port du Goulée at the mouth of the Gironde Estuary, where its vineyards are located. The estate red hovers on a special occasion price, but it is a silky smooth wine, clearly made by people who know what they are doing. It is deliberately modern in style, with velvety, well-knitted tannins and heaps of crushed blackberries.

c/o Château Cos d'Estournel, 33180 Saint-Estèphe
www.estournel.com

Vieux Château Certan Pomerol
La Gravette de Certan, Pomerol (red)

La Gravette de Certan, the second wine of Vieux Château Certan, is a real find. It manages to balance both opulence and restraint – opulence on the nose and in the rich fruits, restraint with the tannins and the sweet oak barrels. Both those adjectives are also regularly applied to the building at Vieux Château Certan, which is the oldest château in Pomerol, with some parts built as far back as the 12th century. It is owned by the very respected Alexandre Thienpont, whose grandfather Georges bought the estate in 1924. As with Pétrus right next door, the soil here is rich in iron ore, although there is more gravel at VCC than clay. It is planted with 60% Merlot, 30% Cabernet Franc, and 10% Cabernet Sauvignon, and extends to some 14ha (35 acres).

1 route du Lussac, 33500 Pomerol
www.vieux-chateau-certan.com

Vieux Château Gaubert Graves
Vieux Château Gaubert, Graves (red and white)

Owned by Dominique Haverlan, Vieux Château Gaubert is a highly reliable estate, and, even though it is not officially classified as such, it is one of the finest in the region. It deals in both red and white, with 20ha (49 acres) devoted to the former, and 6ha (15 acres) the latter. Whether it is making red or white wines, however, it offers a superb value taste of this exciting appellation. The white has rounded stone fruit flavours of peach and apricot; the red is elegant yet rich.

33640 Portets
05 56 67 52 76

Burgundy

Burgundy may not be the obvious choice when looking for value, but there are plenty of well-priced wines to be found. Look for bottles from top producers in the less celebrated, more generic appellations such as Bourgogne, Côte de Beaune, or Côte de Nuits, or for Village wines rather than those from top (Grand or Premier Cru) vineyards. The white grape Aligoté also provides good value, as do the underrated reds from the Gamay grape in Beaujolais.

Domaine Daniel Barraud Mâconnais

Mâcon-Vergisson (white)

Mâcon Chardonnays tend to be on the light, crisp side, but Domaine Daniel Barraud's are considerably more than that. This Mâcon-Vergisson is lemony and dry and has Barraud's trademark silky texture. Like all of Barraud's wines, it is worthy of comparison to bottles from starrier appellations in the Côte d'Or such as Meursault or Chassagne-Montrachet. Also like the rest of the portfolio, it is produced from organically grown grapes. Now working with his son, Julien, Daniel Barraud has some fine vineyards in the Mâconnais, including very old vines in Vergisson.

71960 Fuissé
www.domainebarraud.com

Château de Beauregard Mâconnais

Pouilly-Fuissé (white)

Another Mâconnais family who are producing wines to challenge the supremacy of the much pricier Côte d'Or, Château de Beauregard is run by Frédéric Marc Burrier, the fifth generation of his family to work in the wine business. Like his counterparts to the north, Burrier puts the emphasis on terroir, and his wines bring out the chalky minerality and individuality of the different sub-regions of the Mâconnais, with a range of *lieu-dit* (or single-vineyard) releases. He farms some 20ha (49 acres) in Pouilly-Fuissé, and 7ha (17 acres) in St-Véran. His straight Pouilly-Fuissé is exceptionally well-balanced and has a distinct chalky flavour.

71960 Fuissé
www.joseph-burrier.com

Domaine Roger Belland Santenay, Côte de Beaune

Santenay Rouge (red); Maranges Rouge (red)

Increasingly under the supervision of Julie Belland, the daughter of owner Roger Belland, this excellent family domaine is a great source of well-priced red burgundy. The Santenay Rouge is a nicely plump Pinot Noir from this erstwhile backwater behind Meursault. Ripe, juicy, and smoothly spicy, it shows off the domaine's modern but authentic style. The red from neighbouring Maranges is similarly luscious, with a seductive texture. This lesser-known village is fertile hunting ground for (relatively) inexpensive red burgundy.

3 rue de la Chapelle, 21590 Santenay
www.domaine-belland-roger.com

Danjean Berthoux Côte Chalonnaise

Givry (red)

Pascal Danjean's vineyards at Danjean Berthoux lie at a relatively high elevation in the hilly hamlet of Jambles. Does this give him an advantage when it comes to producing quality? Perhaps, but the way he has steadily gone about making some of the best wines in contemporary Givry is highly impressive. The wines are made in very small quantities, and have attracted a vocal following among sommeliers and critics. Danjean has slowly added to the vines he inherited from his grower parents in the early 1990s, and the estate now has more than 12ha (30 acres). His lovely Givry is medium-bodied and has inviting aromas of red berries and baking spice – a nice way to experience red burgundy without spending a fortune.

Le Moulin Neuf, 45 route de St-Désert, 71640 Jambles
03 85 44 54 74

Domaine Louis Boillot et Fils Chambolle-Musigny, Côte de Nuits

Gevrey-Chambertin (red)

Domaine Louis Boillot et Fils Gevrey-Chambertin is selected from six parcels of 50- to 60-year-old vines dotted around Gevrey-Chambertin. The harmonious marriage of raspberries and blackberries, roses, red cherries, and brown spices with a long, silky mouthfeel results in a really joyful wine. Louis Boillot is married to Ghislaine Barthod and the couple share their winery on the edge of the village of Chambolle, which has views across the vines. Louis's wines are very much a complement to Ghislaine's range of Chambolles, and they offer a broad overview of styles.

21220 Chambolle-Musigny
03 80 62 80 16

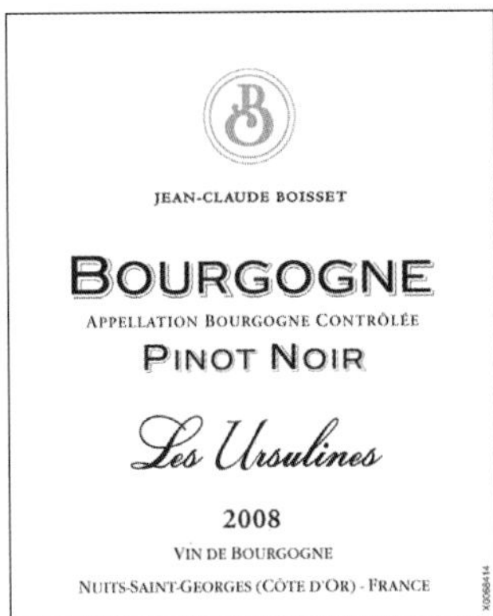

Maison Jean-Claude Boisset Côte de Nuits

Bourgogne Pinot Noir Les Ursulines (red)

One of Burgundy's largest wine operations, Maison Jean-Claude Boisset is a family-run merchant that until recently had been struggling to stay relevant. Under the leadership of the dynamic, creative Jean-Charles Boisset, however, things have improved dramatically, and swiftly. Boisset brought in the well-regarded Grégory Patriat (who used to work at Domaine Leroy) to oversee not just the winemaking, but also major improvements in the vineyards. Rather than simply buy in finished wines to be marketed, Patriat and his team now give strict instructions on how they want their grapes to be grown, and the wines are made at the Boisset winery. Today the business works more as a partnership between grape-grower and merchant than as a traditional négociant, and the quality is improving all the time. The Boisset Bourgogne Pinot Noir Les Ursulines is now one of the most reliable produced in the region. A refreshing, bright red, it is an example of Pinot Noir's lighter side that is zesty and zippy. It can be drunk on its own or served lightly chilled with fish.

Les Ursulines, 5, quai Dumorey, 21700 Nuits-St-Georges
www.jcboisset.com

Bouchard Père et Fils Beaune, Côte de Beaune

Meursault (white)

Another of Burgundy's historic, larger négociant-éleveurs (merchant-producers) to undergo major change for the better in recent years, Bouchard Père et Fils has improved enormously since it was taken over by champagne producer Joseph Henriot in 1995. Much of the credit for this must go to Bernard Hervet, who led the company astutely until he departed to rival firm Faiveley at the end of the 2000s. Hervet was backed by major funds from Henriot, and he invested in an impressive winery near Savigny that has everything a modern winemaker could need. The company has also overhauled its work in the vineyards. It has some 130ha (320 acres) of its own holdings, many in top Grand Cru sites, and it employs a team of 250 pickers so that they have sufficient flexibility to pick the different parcels at the right time. As an example of the quality on offer here now, the Meursault is an impressive place to begin. Meursault is never cheap, but this well-priced example gives you a feel for the toasty, savoury, nutty character of Chardonnay grown in this famous village.

Château de Beaune, 21200 Beaune
www.bouchard-pereetfils.com

Domaine Jean-Marc et Thomas Bouley Volnay, Côte de Beaune

Bourgogne Rouge (red); Bourgogne Hautes-Côtes de Beaune Rouge (red)

Domaine Jean-Marc et Thomas Bouley's Bourgogne Rouge is a succulent, pure, and raspberry-scented Pinot. Very Burgundian in its freshness and purity, it also has a delicious, friendly plumpness. Their Bourgogne Hautes-Côtes de Beaune Rouge is fragrant and intense, a fresh but substantial Pinot that has a core of ripe fruit and is great with game. The wines are made by Thomas Bouley, who worked in Oregon and New Zealand before taking the helm here in 2002.

12 chemin de la Cave, 21190 Volnay
www.jean-marc-bouley.com

Domaine Michel Bouzereau et Fils
Meursault, Côte de Beaune
Bourgogne Aligoté (white); Bourgogne Blanc (white)

More sinned against than sinner, Aligoté produces beautifully zesty, fresh wines when treated with respect, as it is by Jean-Baptiste Bouzereau, the 10th generation of his family to run this estate in Meursault, with its cool cave built into the cliff. Bouzereau's Bourgogne Aligoté is nuanced and juicy, as is his Bourgogne Blanc. A beautifully pure, appealing Chardonnay with a kiss of vanilla-scented oak and a sleek, sophisticated texture, it is satisfyingly ripe yet fresh.

3 rue de la Planche Meunière, 21190 Meursault
03 80 21 20 74

Jean-Paul Brun Côte de Brouilly, Beaujolais
Brouilly Terres Dorées (red)

In Jean-Paul Brun's Brouilly Terres Dorées, you can expect dense, rich flavours of blackberry, coffee, and raspberries that fill out the mid-palate and give a long, satisfying finish. Quality winemaking and consistently good quality makes these wines hard to get hold of at times, but their popularity is deserved, and it's worth making the effort. The iconoclastic Jean-Paul Brun is a natural winemaker, who uses only indigenous yeasts, and works his 16ha (40 acre) family vineyard in the town of Charnay organically.

69380 Charnay
www.louisdressner.com/Brun

Jean-Marc Burgaud Morgon, Beaujolais
Cuvée Les Charmes, Morgon (red)

Seductively easy to drink, and showing all the pleasure offered by the fresh, firm, and succulently red-fruited Gamay grape, Jean-Marc Burgaud's Morgon Cuvée Les Charmes is a star of Beaujolais. The vines here grow almost directly on granite rock, and the whole bunches are macerated for just 10 days, then fermented, briefly aged, and bottled six months after harvest. From a family that has been growing vines for generations, Burgaud founded his estate in 1989, after finishing his winemaking studies, and he now has some 19ha (47 acres) of vineyards in several appellations.

La Côte du Py, 69910 Villié-Morgon
www.jean-marc-burgaud.com

Château de Cary-Potet Côte Chalonnaise
Bourgogne Aligoté (white)

The latest generation of the du Besset family is carrying on a fine tradition of making white burgundies of great finesse at Château de Cary-Potet, in Buxy. One of the oldest domaines in the Côte Chalonnaise, wine has been made at Cary-Potet for more than 200 years, and the cellars beneath the château date back to the 17th and 18th century. The estate has 13ha (32 acres) of vineyards, and makes wines in the Montagny and Côte Chalonnaise appellations, as well as very striking Bourgogne Aligoté. This fragrant, minerally dry white comes from vines that were planted in the Great Depression. While it is regarded as one of the best Aligotés of Burgundy, it is extremely well-priced.

Route de Chenevelles, 71390 Buxy
www.cary-potet.fr

Champy Père et Fils Beaune, Côte de Beaune
Bourgogne Blanc (white)

Champy Père et Fils is the oldest négociant house in Burgundy, founded back in 1720. Its continued relevance today is thanks to the wine broker Henri Merguey and his son, Pierre, who bought the business in the early 1990s, and have worked hard to improve quality. Champy now has 17ha (42 acres) of vineyards, owned and rented, in the Côte de Beaune. Much of it is farmed biodynamically and the family believe the biodynamically managed plots show much greater ripeness and considerably less rot. They recruited Dimitri Bazas as winemaker in 1999, and Bazas makes wines that have the ability to keep for several years, but are always accessible in their youth. The Champy Bourgogne Blanc is clear, crisp Chardonnay in a smooth but restrained style. If you find New-World Chardonnay a little too much, you should give this a try.

5 rue Grenier à Sel, 21200 Beaune
www.champy.com

Domaine et Maison Chanson Beaune, Côte de Beaune
Pernand-Vergelesses Premier Cru Les Caradeaux Blanc (white)

Domaine et Maison Chanson's impressive modern reputation is thanks in no small part to one man, Gilles de Courcel, who took over as president here in 2002. The company's revival dates back slightly earlier than that, to its acquisition by the champagne house Bollinger in 1999, but it was the radical changes instituted by de Courcel that really ushered in the most significant improvements at a business that began its life in 1750. De Courcel moved the company out of buying wines, preferring instead to buy grapes from growers on long-term contracts, where quality, rather than quantity, is rewarded. He oversaw the renovation of the original winery, in the medieval centre of Beaune, and the impressive cellars in the Bastion de l'Oratoire in Beaune's fortified medieval walls, and the construction of a new winery near Savigny. He also recruited the other significant figure in Chanson's revival, winemaker Jean-Pierre Confuron, of the Vosne Confuron-Cotétidot family. Nuanced, racy, rich yet taut, the Pernand-Vergelesses Premier Cru Les Caradeaux Blanc is a fine example of Burgundy Chardonnay.

Au Bastion de l'Oratoire, rue Paul Chanson, 21200 Beaune
www.vins-chanson.com

Domaine David Clark Morey-St-Denis, Côte de Nuits

Côte de Nuits-Villages (red)

The Scotsman, David Clark, left the bright lights and excitement of Formula 1 racing – where he was a trackside engineer – behind to make wines in Burgundy. While he was studying at the Lycée Viticole in Beaune, he found a tiny plot of vines in Morey-St-Denis, thinking this would give him a little hands-on experience. The project took off, and Clark is now starting a modest expansion. His Côte de Nuits-Villages is a carefully hand-crafted wine that has a concentrated and generous charm, with succulent black fruit and a subtle peppery quality to the lingering finish.

17 grande rue, 21220 Morey-St-Denis
www.domainedavidclark.com

Domaine Laurent Cognard Côte Chalonnaise

Montagny Premier Cru Les Bassets (white)

In a story that is common in Burgundy and, indeed, much of Europe, Laurent Cognard changed the emphasis of his family's wine business from growing grapes for selling on to négociants, to bottling and marketing the wine themselves. That was not his only brave decision, however. Cognard has also changed the way the family's vineyards are managed, introducing organic and biodynamic methods, and implementing more natural winemaking. The new direction has paid off in wines such as the Montagny Premier Cru Les Bassets. This Chardonnay is rich, round, and creamy with soft apple, pear, and butter notes, while also offering the house's trademark honeyed character.

9 rue des Fossés, 71390 Buxy
06 15 52 74 44

FOOD & WINE
RED BURGUNDY

The Pinot Noir grape variety takes on many forms in the red wines of Burgundy, from the feminine Chambolle-Musigny to the exotic Richebourg.

Wines here are on the lighter, more delicate side, with fairly high but not aggressive natural acidity, giving them a wide range of pairing ability especially with softer, earthier dishes. They can be powerful when coming from the best vineyards in the best vintages, but it is a discreet, stealthy power.

When pairing food with red burgundy, it is good to have an idea of the wine's structure. Flavours of berry, mushroom, and earth are easy to compare or contrast, but many young burgundies will offer quite a tart, chewy mouthfeel that is easily softened by adding fat. Duck confit served on a bed of potatoes, for example, is ideal. Anything heavier would make the dish too rich.

Delicate beef dishes work well, especially when accompanied by duck-fat French fries, but quail and coq au vin are sure-fire winners. Snails cooked in garlic and parsley butter are delicious with the younger, simpler wines. The richer wines of the region, when mature, are ideal for game dishes, and in general the range of pairable cheese selections is wide, with the very gamey, distinct-tasting Époisses being a local favourite.

The richness and fat of duck confit softens Pinot Noir's acidity.

Domaine Jack Confuron-Cotétidot

Vosne-Romanée, Côte de Nuits

Bourgogne Rouge (red)

Yves Confuron, son of Jacky, is a man of great humour and charm. His family has been involved in wine in Vosne as far back as Louis XIV, and today he and his brother, Jean-Pierre make high-quality, ageworthy wines. Domaine Jack Confuron-Cotétidot's sophisticated Bourgogne Rouge, like most wine made from grapes with their stems attached, has principally floral aromas and flavours. The silky raspberry and blackberry bud fruit displays great precision and clarity, reflecting the masterful work of Yves and Jean-Pierre. Treat yourself.

10 rue de la Fontaine, 21700 Vosne Romanée
03 80 61 03 39

Domaine Cordier Père et Fils Mâconnais

St-Véran (white)

Though Domaine Cordier is based in St-Véran in the Mâconnais, the wines here are on a par with many a top bottle of Puligny-Montrachet or Chassagne-Montrachet. Christophe Cordier uses biodynamic methods, crops at very low yields, and gives his wine a long, slow fermentation in oak barrels, many of which he buys from the legendary Côte d'Or producer, Ramonet. His St-Véran is much richer, concentrated, and toastier than most St-Véran's; it is a wine of scintillating high quality.

Les Molards, 71960 Fuissé
03 85 35 62 89

Domaine Daniel Dampt Chablis

Chablis Premier Cru Lys (white)

Domaine Daniel Dampt is a family affair, where the different personalities of Daniel and his two sons combine to make a range of Chablis Premiers Crus of great transparency and purity. The family have a well-equipped winery in Milly, and one son, Vincent, has made wine in New Zealand. On the fresh, minerally side of the Chablis spectrum, the Premier Cru Lys is a supremely controlled, elegant wine. It offers great concentration of citrus and grapefruit flavours, and real persistence on the finish.

1 rue des Violettes, 89800 Milly-Chablis
www.chablis-dampt.com

Domaine Bernard Defaix

Chablis

Chablis (white)

You can expect a full-on expression of citrus fruit with Domaine Bernard Defaix's Chablis. The effect is a wine that is juicy and taut at the same time, but with plenty of characteristic Chablis flint and minerality, too, and always excellent value for money. It is one of several fine bottlings produced by Sylvain and Didier Defaix, who source fruit from their 25ha (62 acres) of vineyards – including a sizeable holding in the Côte de Lechet – supplemented by fruit from growers. Sylvain likes to retain the typical character of Chablis, and uses old oak barrels sparingly.

17 rue du Château, Milly, 89800 Chablis
www.bernard-defaix.com

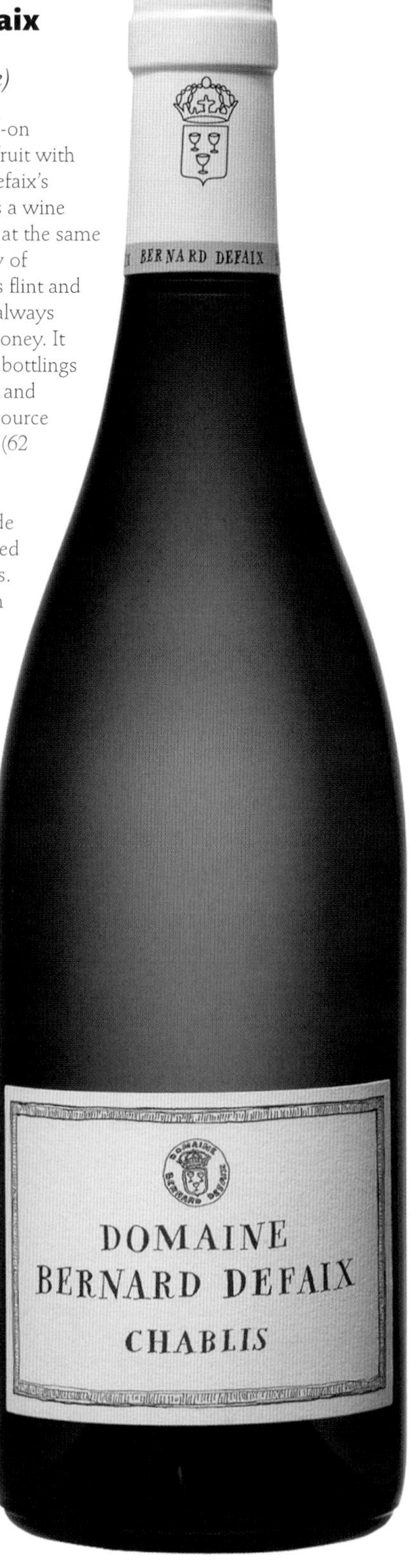

Domaine des Deux Roches Mâconnais

Mâcon-Villages (white)

Like the wines of Meursault in the Cote d'Or, Domaine des Deux Roches Mâcon-Villages offers a nutty component to round out the citrus and apple notes. It is a very elegant, dry, medium-bodied Chardonnay that is made by two childhood friends, Christian Collovray and Jean-Luc Terrier, who own this winery in Davayé. The domaine takes its name from the "two rocks" of Vergisson and Solutré, although the duo's wines are now almost as famous as these celebrated landmarks.

Route de Fuissé, 71960 Davayé
03 85 35 86 51

Jean-Yves Devevey Demigny, Côte de Beaune

Bourgogne Hautes-Côtes de Beaune Blanc (white)

Jean-Yves Devevey returned to his family domaine in 1992, and began to make a name for himself with his fine basic Bourgogne Blanc. Since then he has consolidated the reputation of this producer in the little-known village of Demigny, and his business is now thriving thanks to his conscientious approach to the less famous appellations in which he works (although he has since acquired holdings in more illustrious sites). Devevey's Bourgogne Hautes-Côtes de Beaune Blanc is always lively and vibrant, with that fine tension between toasty richness and stimulating freshness. As with all of his wines, this refined Chardonnay punches well above its official ranking.

Rue de Breuil, 71150 Demigny
www.devevey.com

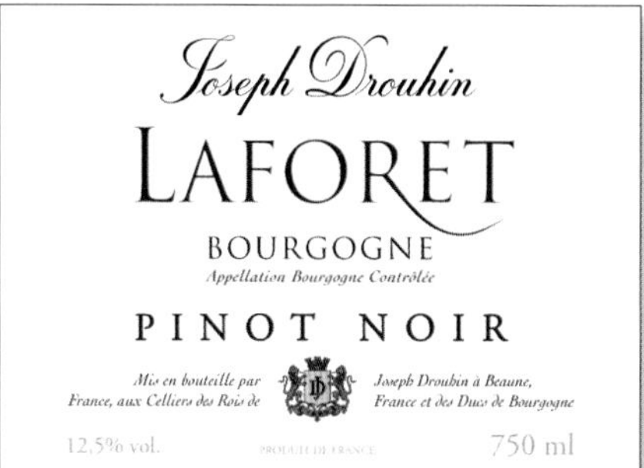

Joseph Drouhin Chablis and Beaune, Côte de Beaune

Laforêt Pinot Noir Bourgogne (red); Chorey-lès-Beaune Rouge (red); Domaine de Vaudon, Réserve de Vaudon (white)

Maison Joseph Drouhin is one of the most impressive of Burgundy's larger négociant houses. It is a business that has shown it is possible to produce consistent quality at larger volumes in Burgundy, both with its négociant wines and those from the Drouhin family's fine collection of vineyards. Drouhin's fortunes are currently the ultimate responsibility of Philippe Drouhin, who manages the vineyards and keeps an eye on the contract land. Drouhin is joined by winemaker Jérôme Faure-Brac, who has made a name for his sensitive approach in the winery since his first vintage in sole charge in 2006. Faure-Brac is the guardian of the house style, which is all about purity of fruit, with well-integrated tannins in the red wines such as the Laforêt Pinot Noir Bourgogne Rouge. This is a light and delicate style of red, with sweet-smelling floral fruit and very pure Pinot character that is best in ripe vintages. Also highly attractive in terms of both price and flavour is the Chorey-lès-Beaune Rouge, which is softly grippy, with lashings of ripe red berry fruit. The Drouhin family also own a fine domaine in Chablis, Domaine de Vaudon, whose name comes from a watermill that stands near the vines. The Réserve de Vaudon is a simply delicious wine, with soft pink grapefruit aromas and an excellent concentration of pure citrus on the palate.

7 rue d'Enfer, 21200 Beaune
www.drouhin.com

Domaine Faiveley Nuits-St-Georges, Côte de Nuits

Bourgogne Rouge Hautes-Côtes de Nuits Dames Huguettes (red)

In recent years there has been a renaissance at Domaine Faiveley, an important estate in Nuits-St-Georges. Erwan Faiveley, who took over the business while still in his 20s, is the driving force behind the renaissance, although he is helped in no small part by the wisdom of general manager, Bernard Hervet, and their very talented winemaker, Jerome Flous. The trio have shaken up the business, which was founded in 1825 by Pierre Faiveley, and which has some 120ha (297 acres) of high quality vineyards supplying 80% of the company's grape requirements. The reds have shown a marked improvement, with the hard tannins and smoky notes of yore replaced by succulence and supple tannins, in wines such as the seductive entry level Bourgogne Rouge Hautes-Côtes de Nuits Dames Huguettes. Exuding supple red and black fruits, a round and juicily plump body, and a refreshing finish, it has that "something extra" quality.

21700 Nuits-St-Georges
www.domaine-faiveley.com

Domaine J A Ferret Mâconnais

Pouilly-Fuissé (white)

With a history dating back to 1760, Domaine J A Ferret was recently sold to the consistently good local merchant, Louis Jadot. It is easy to see why Jadot would have been interested. This widely respected 15ha (37 acre) domaine sits in the heart of Fuissé, and was among the first in the village to bottle its own-label wines (in 1942), blazing a trail for others to follow. It produces several lieu-dit (single-vineyard) wines, such as Les Sceles, Les Vernays, Le Clos, and the old-vine plots of Les Ménétrières, Le Tournant de Pouilly, and Les Perrières, as well as a fine Pouilly-Fuissé. Made with fruit from the amphitheatre of Fuissé, and aged 50% in French oak, this elegant Chardonnay is rich and dry with a hint of tropical fruit.

71960 Fuissé
03 85 35 61 56

Domaine William Fèvre Chablis

Chablis (white)

Another part of the collection of fine Burgundy properties owned by Henriot Champagne, Domaine William Fèvre is a major land owner in Chablis, including some 12ha (30 acres) of Premier Cru vineyard. Indeed, it is the largest producer of Premier and Grand Cru wines in Chablis, but quality is never behind quantity. The sites, many of them planted by the eponymous founder in 1950, are all good quality and the winemaking, by Didier Séguier, is meticulously skilful. The domaine's straight Chablis is a flinty-edged, classically dry wine that is excellent value. With its elegant profile it just begs for a pairing with shellfish.

21 avenue d'Oberwesel, 89800 Chablis
www.williamfevre.fr

Domaine Jean-Philippe Fichet Meursault, Côte de Beaune

Bourgogne Aligoté (white)

Jean-Philippe Fichet is an atypical Meursault producer. Rather than the richer, fuller, fatter style that tends to be associated with the village, he prefers to make wines with precise acidity and a pronounced mineral streak. His portfolio – which includes a number of different Meursault cuvées and a Puligny-Montrachet Premier Cru – recalls Chablis rather than Côte de Beaune, and that is certainly the case with his fantastic Bourgogne Aligoté. A brilliant expression of the variety from a still under-hyped winemaker, it has Chablis-like precision, purity, savoury fruit, and lovely intensity. It is an officially "modest" wine that consistently over-performs.

2 rue de la Gare, 21190 Meursault
09 63 20 79 04

Domaine Germain, Château de Chorey

Chorey-lès-Beaune, Côte de Beaune

Chorey-lès-Beaune (red); Pernand-Vergelesses Blanc (white)

Domaine Germain, Château de Chorey has a long history, and its parcels of fine Beaune vineyards have been passed through the generations. It is only in recent years, however, under the leadership of Benoît Germain that it has really begun to hit the heights. The Chorey-lès-Beaune, while not the cheapest wine in the appellation, is always one of the best, with a succulent texture and good depth of lightly spicy fruit. The Pernand-Vergelesses Blanc is an intriguing Chardonnay that combines zesty freshness with stony, intense fruit.

Rue Jacques Germain, 21200 Chorey-lès-Beaune
www.chateau-de-chorey-les-beaune.fr

Vincent Girardin Meursault, Côte de Beaune

Santenay Blanc (white)

Though Vincent Girardin is now based in Meursault, it was in Santenay-le-Haut that his winemaking adventure started, when he inherited a small plot of vineyard land. He now has a négociant business as well as his own estate wines, but everything he makes is biodynamic. His beguilingly scented Santenay Blanc has all the trademark Girardin intensity of fruit, and supple, slinky texture. It is expansive and generous, but not too obvious.

Les Champs Lins, 21190 Meursault
www.vincentgirardin.com

Maison Camille Giroud Côte de Beaune

Santenay Rouge (red); Maranges Premier Cru Croix aux Moines Rouge (red)

Maison Camille Giroud is another example of that modern Burgundian theme – the ailing négociant that has been brought back from the brink by new investment and enlightened management. In this case, the revival starts with the maison's acquisition in 2001 by a consortium of Americans. They recruited David Croix, a talented young winemaker, to lead the winemaking just 11 days after he left winemaking school. Croix has imposed a new style of winemaking with little new oak, in wines such as the fine Santenay Rouge. A bright, refreshing wine with very pure Pinot fruit and a nicely dry little whiplash on the finish, it is great with poultry. The Maranges Premier Cru Croix aux Moines Rouge, meanwhile, is scented and fragrant, but absolutely no pushover. Intense, very fresh, and finely dry, it cries out for *boeuf bourgignon*.

3 rue Pierre Joigneaux, 21200 Beaune
www.camillegiroud.com

Pascal Granger Juliénas, Beaujolais

Juliénas (red)

Pascal Granger's fine Beaujolais domaine has been in his family for more than 200 years. It is based in a disused (since the 14th century) church, where Granger uses large and small oak barrels alongside stainless steel casks. Light-weight in structure, the straight Juliénas recalls delicate redcurrants in colour, and displays supreme elegance, with gentle redcurrant and soft cherry fruit flavours and aromas. Aged entirely in stainless steel, the best years capture hints of violets on the nose and palate.

Les Poupets, 69840 Juliénas
www.cavespascalgranger.fr

Domaine Jean Grivot Vosne-Romanée, Côte de Nuits

Bourgogne Rouge (red)

Few winemakers in Burgundy command greater respect than Étienne Grivot, of Domaine Jean Grivot, who is unquestionably one of the finest in the region. The man himself is famed for his sensitive winemaking approach and his engagingly serene personality, his wines for their ability to express terroir and a delicate purity of fruit, always with an alluring freshness. His much sought after Bourgogne Rouge is no exception. Elegant, silky, and very desirable, with notes of fresh violets and black cherries, it has a caressing quality that makes you want to linger over each glass. In a word: classy.

6 rue de la Croix Rameau, 21700 Vosne-Romanée
www.domainegrivot.fr

Domaine Anne Gros Vosne-Romanée, Côte de Nuits

Haut-Côtes de Nuits, Cuvée Marine (white)

When she was a young woman in the 1980s, the admirable Anne Gros knew she wanted a career that involved hands-on work. But it took the death of her father later on in the decade to persuade her that wine would be her calling. Today her name is recognized by wine lovers the world over as one of the best producers in Vosne. Grown in the Concouer in the hills above Vosne-Romanée, this exotic white wine displays lemon citrus and exotic tropical fruits on the nose, with a light-bodied, green plum, white flower, and preserved lemon palate, which is both refreshing and enjoyable.

11 rue des Communes, 21700 Vosne-Romanée
www.anne-gros.com

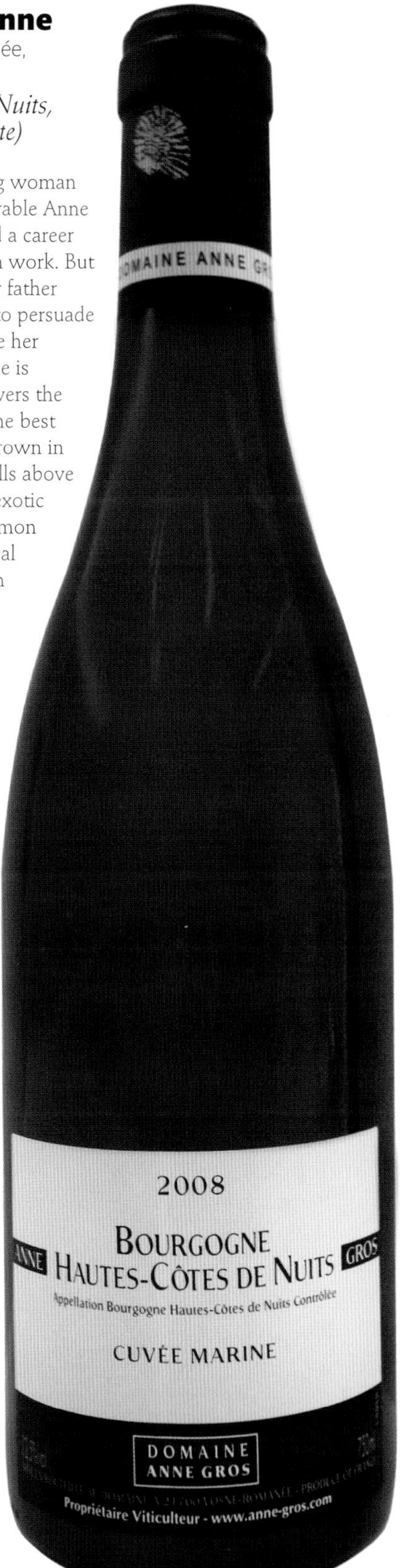

HOW GRAPES BECOME WINE

The basic process by which grapes become wine is so simple that a winemaker is hardly necessary. Pile ripe grapes into a vat of any kind and wild yeast will take over in a few days and turn them into wine a couple of weeks later. Grapes and yeast are the only essential ingredients, and nature can provide the yeast, ever-present in the air. The winemaker's job is to guide the grapes through the process in such a way that nothing goes wrong. That's why winemakers say their job is essentially about finding excellent grapes and not making a mess of them.

1 Once the grapes are ripe they are harvested. Farm workers – and in some wineries, machines – will sort the fruit, discarding rotten grapes, leaves, and even spiders.

4 Pressing separates the juice or new wine from the grape skins and seeds. Winemakers press most whites before fermentation; for reds this takes place afterwards.

2 The grapes are placed in a hopper from where they are sent to be gently crushed, just breaking the grape skins enough to release some juice ready for fermentation.

3 Fermenting is the crucial step for all wines. The winemaker adds yeast or may let the natural yeast take over; its billions of tiny cells convert the grape sugar into alcohol.

5 Ageing takes place largely in tanks for many white wines and in barrels for traditional reds. After as little as a few months, or up to three years, the new wines are ready.

6 Bottling ends the winemaker's job. The wine usually undergoes filtration to remove sediment and any remaining micro-organisms, then it flows into bottles.

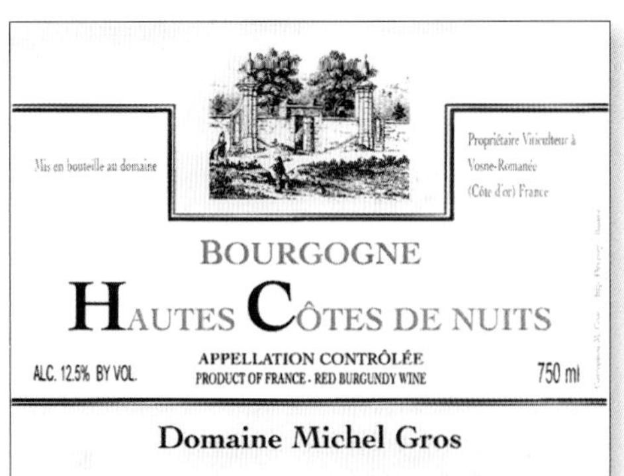

Domaine Michel Gros Vosne-Romanée, Côte de Nuits

Hautes Côtes de Nuits (red)

A consistently reliable performer, Michel Gros's Hautes Côtes de Nuits comes from the hills behind the Côte de Nuits. Dark, mellow, and round, the cool black fruit and subtly earthy body make for a pleasing result, both in the mouth and in your wallet. Domaine Michel Gros is perhaps best known for its monopole vineyard, Clos des Reas, which can be found at the southern edge of the village of Vosne-Romanée, and which Michel (the brother of Bernard) received when the holdings of the Gros family were divided some years ago. In general, Michel's style is for very pure, lucid, flowing wine, where the fruit is allowed to sing.

7 rue des Communes, 21700 Vosne-Romanée
www.domaine-michel-gros.com

Domaine Guffens Heynen Mâconnais

Mâcon-Pierreclos Le Chavigne (white)

The charismatic Jean-Marie Guffens has done an enormous amount to raise the profile of the Mâconnais, pushing the boundaries of what the region was capable of, and making some of its very best wines. He works from a 3.6ha (9 acre) family estate in Pouilly-Fuissé, and also acts as négociant through his Verget label. Clarity of flavour and pronounced minerality are the hallmarks of the house style, whatever the wine, and both are certainly on show in the Mâcon-Pierreclos Le Chavigne. This superb Mâcon Chardonnay is edgy in style, with an almost bracing tartness and complex minerality. The wine is lean and expressive, needing a white meat or rich fish dish to coax out its depth of character.

71960 Vergisson
www.verget-sa.com

Domaine Hudelot-Noellat Vougeot, Côte de Nuits

Vosne-Romanée (red)

The friendly Domaine Hudelot-Noellat is always a welcoming place to visit. The wines, too, share in the conviviality – they are made with great restraint and sensitivity, with careful use of new oak leading to a range of bottlings that clearly articulate their origins, rather than being showy, flashy blockbusters. As well as its range of three Grands Crus, Hudelot-Noellat also make a very authentic village Vosne-Romanée, where delicious violet, plum, and redcurrant aromas are integrated into a black and red-fruited core that is harmonious, rewarding, and very enjoyable.

21640 Chambolle-Musigny
03 80 62 85 17

Maison Louis Jadot Beaune, Côte de Beaune

Bourgogne Pinot Noir (red)

Maison Louis Jadot is one of the best-known names in Burgundy, famed the world over for its vast range of estate and négociant wines. It is a very good thing, then, that the company is such a consistently reliable producer of all of the many quality levels in which it operates. The house was founded in 1859, and it still owns an elegant town house in rue Eugène Spuller in Beaune, where a labyrinth of cellars runs beneath the offices above. Winemaking in fact takes place in the rather more prosaic surroundings of a modern winery on the outskirts of Beaune. Here, Jadot's highly skilled and individualistic winemaker, Jacques Lardière, a believer in the biodynamic approach, oversees a complex wine operation that makes use of a collection of open-topped wooden vats complete with an automated system for punching down the cap of fruit that rises to the top of the vat during fermentation. Lardière also uses a traditional implement known as a *pichou* to perform the same task – a tough job when the vats are as large as they are here – and he likes to destem the grapes and ferment at high temperatures. Today the company, which was sold to the Korbrand Corporation by the Jadot family in 1985, owns and runs a total of five domaines (Louis Jadot; des Héritiers Louis Jadot; Gagey; Duc de Magenta; and Clos de la Commaraine) which between them amount to around 154ha (380 acres), as well as the négociant business. The portfolio stretches from the Côte d'Or to the Mâconnais, including a number of Grands Crus, but for everyday wine it is tough to beat the reliable Bourgogne Pinot Noir. A restrained, traditional style of Pinot (this is no fruit bomb), with a finely drying finish, it is best consumed with a dish of classic *boeuf bourguignon*.

2 rue du Mont Batois, 21200 Beaune
www.louisjadot.com

Domaine Patrick Javillier Meursault, Côte de Beaune

Bourgogne Blanc Cuvée Oligocène (white)

Domaine Patrick Javillier's Bourgogne Blanc Cuvée Oligocène is a gorgeously exuberant, floral yet refined Chardonnay with excellent intensity, interest, and sophisticated richness. An impressively consistent wine, it always over-delivers for the price. It is made by the ebulliently enthusiastic Patrick Javillier, a blizzard of energy whose cellar is full of chalk diagrams written directly on the walls showing how he intends to mature his wines.

19 place de l'Europe, 21190 Meursault
www.patrickjavillier.com

Domaine Alain Jeanniard Morey-St-Denis, Côte de Nuits

Côte de Nuits-Villages, Vieilles Vignes (red)

The sheer concentration of flavours in the summery red fruits of Domaine Alain Jeanniard's Côte de Nuits-Villages Vieilles Vignes gives complexity and interest. The mid-palate is full and round, and there is real staying power on the finish, making it a great-value wine that offers a taste of good red burgundy for a reasonable price. Alain Jeanniard worked as an electrician for more than a decade before studying winemaking and then founding this relatively young domaine in 2000.

4 rue aux Loups, 21220 Morey-St-Denis
www.domainealainjeanniard.fr

Domaine Emile Juillot Côte Chalonnais

Mercurey Blanc (white)

The quality of Chardonnay produced in southern Burgundy can be somewhat variable, but there is no doubt that Domaine Emile Juillot's Mercurey Blanc is a stunning expression. It is medium-bodied, dry, and flavoursome with notes of apple, pineapple, lemon zest, and chalk. The estate is run today by Jean-Claude and Natalie Theulot, who bought it from Natalie's grandfather, Emile Juillot, in the 1980s. The couple have plots in the Mercurey Premier Cru vineyards of Les Champs Martin, Les Combins, Les Croichots, and Les Saumonts, and they own La Cailloute. Most of the vineyards are in the prime hillside zones of the region.

4 rue de Mercurey, 71640 Mercurey
03 85 45 13 87

Domaine Michel Lafarge Volnay, Côte de Beaune

Bourgogne Passetoutgrains L'Exception (red); Bourgogne Aligoté (white)

A family domaine, run by Michel Lafarge and his son, Frédéric, Domaine Michel Lafarge is unquestionably one of Burgundy's best producers. The duo make some seriously fine wines at the top end, which are characterized by the elusive, haunting quality that attracts so many people to the region, but their talent extends to everything they put their hands to. The Bourgogne Passetoutgrains L'Exception is a light-bodied and delicious blend of Gamay and Pinot Noir that is perfumed and gossamer-textured. The Bourgogne Aligoté, which is sourced from old-vine Aligoté, has notable depth of aroma and citrussy intensity. And because the family are known for red wines, this fine white is very well priced.

15 rue de la Combe, 21190 Volnay
www.domainelafarge.fr

Domaine François Lamarche Vosne-Romanée, Côte de Nuits

Bourgogne Rouge (red)

Blended from nine vineyards around Vosne-Romanée, Domaine François Lamarche Bourgogne Rouge is an attractive wine that has good depth to its spicy, fresh violet, and black cherry core. It has a smooth, creamy mouthfeel that rewards and refreshes. Though the name may suggest otherwise, this is an estate with a decidedly feminine influence, run by a trio of women. Madame Marie-Blanche Lamarche is the matriarch in charge, while her daughter, Nicole, has been in sole charge of the winemaking since 2007, and Nicole's cousin, Natalie, runs the commercial side of the business. The trio have transformed the fortunes of this estate by breathing new life into their many fine vineyard sites, including Vosne-Romanée Premier Cru Croix-Rameau, which adjoins Romanée-St-Vivant, and their monopole La Grande Rue, which sits next to La Tache and looks across a small dividing road to Romanée-Conti.

9 rue des Communes, 21700 Vosne-Romanée
www.domaine-lamarche.com

PINOT NOIR

The Côte de Nuits of the Burgundy region has over many centuries bred legendary wines from such famous parcels as Clos de Vougeot, Romanée-Conti, La Tache, Chambertin, and Le Musigny. Here, as in most of France, the wines are named for their vineyard districts rather than the grape variety from which they were made, but behind all the great names is one red grape variety – Pinot Noir.

The Côte de Nuits, and its sibling the Côte de Beaune just to the south, long ago set the standard for Pinot Noir wines: medium to full-bodied, smooth-textured red wines that are not as "noir" as their name suggests.

MORNING SUN

The Pinot Noir variety is uncommonly sensitive to growing conditions. On the Côte de Nuits, the vineyards face east to catch the warming morning sun while the 400m (1,310ft) peaks behind them cast early shadows in the late summer afternoons, protecting vines from the oppressive late-day heat.

EARLY BLOOMER

The vines' buds burst early in the spring, making them susceptible to damage from spring frost.

LESS IS MORE

Pinot Noir wines can taste boring, bland, and watery if the grower doesn't prune the vines severely to reduce the number of grape bunches per vine. Low yields often produce better wines, but they also reduce the amount of wine that can be sold.

THIN-SKINNED

Pinot Noir berries have notoriously thin skins, which contributes to the wine's lighter red colour and rather delicate flavours, but also leaves them vulnerable to mildew and bunch rot from wet weather during the growing season.

WHERE IN THE WORLD?

The legend has spread far and wide from Burgundy's Côte de Nuits. In modern times, the Pinot Noir grape is grown in Italy, Germany, California, Oregon, New Zealand, Chile, southern France, and elsewhere. The variety always manages to express the taste of the place it was grown.

Talented winemakers in all these regions are capable of making excellent Pinots, but it can be difficult to find good-value bottles. Because low yields are required, many Pinot Noir makers charge more per bottle than other wine growers to make up the difference, so value-priced versions are especially vexing to find. Shopping for Pinot Noir can be a challenge, but the reward awaits for wine drinkers willing to educate themselves about Pinot Noir or find a good wine merchant who can direct them.

The following regions are among the best for Pinot Noir. Try bottles from these recommended vintages for the best examples:

Côte de Nuits: 2009, 2008, 2005
Côte de Beaune: 2009, 2008, 2005
Oregon: 2008, 2005
New Zealand: 2010, 2007, 2006

Seresin Estate's bright-fruited wine shows what New Zealand Pinot Noir is all about.

Domaine Leflaive Puligny-Montrachet, Côte de Beaune

Bourgogne Blanc (white)

For a little taste of the thrilling vitality of top burgundy, try Domaine Leflaive's Bourgogne Blanc, an entry-level Chardonnay from a genuine superstar producer. Vibrant, smoky, intense, and utterly singular, it is partly made from declassified fruit grown in Puligny, but comes at a fraction of the price of a wine bearing that name on its label. Domaine Leflaive is run by the legendary Anne-Claude Leflaive, and is unquestionably among Burgundy's elite. Her domaine is the most famous in Puligny, and was one of the first big name estate's anywhere in the world to make the transistion to biodynamics. In doing so, Domaine Leflaive has played an important role in convincing winemakers the world over that this form of agriculture is not necessarily eccentric, but is something to be taken seriously for fine wine production. Leflaive's winemaking style is all about unforced intensity and a fine balance between full flavours and finesse, and she has parcels in a range of fine vineyard sites, with 10ha (25 acres) of Premier Cru, and an unusually large 5ha (12 acres) of Grand Cru, comprising plots in such legendary, historic names as Bâtard, Chevalier, and Bienvenues-Bâtard-Montrachet.

Place des Marronniers, 21190 Puligny-Montrachet
www.leflaive.fr

Maison Olivier Leflaive Puligny-Montrachet, Côte de Beaune

Bourgogne Blanc Les Setilles (white); Auxey-Duresses La Macabrée Blanc (white)

Founded by Olivier Leflaive, cousin of the celebrated Anne-Claude of Domaine Leflaive, in 1984, Maison Olivier Leflaive has become an important négociant that has established itself as a highly consistent producer of drinker-friendly white wines. Frank Grux (who has been with the company for more than two decades, having previously made wine for his godfather, Guy Roulot) heads up a team of two winemakers and an oenologist, who between them make wines from a range of sources that includes 14ha (35 acres) of domaine land. As part of the drive to improve quality, the house no longer buys in wine for its blends, preferring to buy in grapes (60%) and juice (40%). The Bourgogne Blanc Les Setilles is a smooth and creamy Chardonnay in a juicy but refreshing style that is nicely balanced between a little toasty oak and floral fruit, and is rich, full, and full of impact. The Auxey-Duresses La Macabrée Blanc is quite a serious white, with intensity and persistence. Not a delicate flower – but plenty of character and good length.

Place du Monument, 21190 Puligny-Montrachet
www.olivier-leflaive.com

Benjamin Leroux Beaune, Côte de Beaune

Auxey-Duresses Blanc (white); Savigny-lès-Beaune Rouge (red)

Top winemaker Benjamin Leroux (formerly of Domaine du Comte Armand) is the man behind this rising-star négociant. With its headquarters in a large warehouse near the ring road in Beaune, it sources grapes from a wide array of appellations, drawing on specific, high-quality vineyards, a third of which are organic. Highlights include a very fine Auxey-Duresses Blanc, which Leroux has been buying for many years. It is a lovely – and classically Côte de Beaune – combination of ripe, citrussy fruit with tingling freshness and a kiss of savoury oak. The red wines are a more recent concern, and include Pinot Noirs drawn from "lighter" appellations than the tannic terroir that Leroux was used to working with at Comte Armand. The Savigny-lès-Beaunes Rouge is a wonderfully fruity, juicy, and rounded Pinot Noir, where Leroux emphasizes fruit but keeps vitality.

5 rue Colbert, 21200 Beaune
03 80 22 71 06

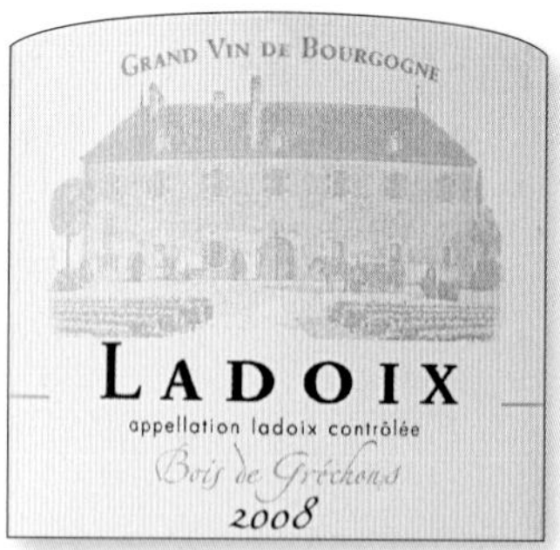

Domaine Sylvain Loichet Chorey-lès-Beaune, Côte de Beaune

Ladoix Blanc (white)

Ladoix is a little-known appellation not far from the Grand Cru of Corton-Charlemagne. In Domaine Sylvain Loichet's white example, the wine is full-bodied with a classic balance of savoury oak and zesty fruit. Loichet is a young (20-something) winemaker who, unlike many of his contemporaries in the region, is already hitting the heights. He comes from a family of stonemasons in Comblanchien, and his domaine is based on vineyards that once belonged to the family that Loichet has reclaimed in Côte de Nuits-Village, Ladoix, and Clos du Vougeot. His wines are characterized by their vibrancy, clarity, and purity.

2 rue d'Aloxe Corton, 21200 Chorey-lès-Beaune
06 80 75 50 67

Domaine Long-Depaquit Chablis

Chablis Premier Cru Les Vaucopins (white)

With its headquarters in a grand stately château surrounded by a small park, Domaine Long-Depaquit is steeped in history. Its origins in fact go back to 1791, although its current owners, the Beaune négociant, Albert Bichot, only took over in the 1970s. The wines are made by Jean-Didier Basch, and include the Chablis Premier Cru Les Vaucopins, which is is a wonderful, flinty but full Chablis, which can stand up well to white meat just as it can to delicate fish dishes. Aromatically, it has a gentle white-flower perfume which is set off against a rich, mouth-filling lemon zest palate.

89800 Chablis
03 86 42 11 13

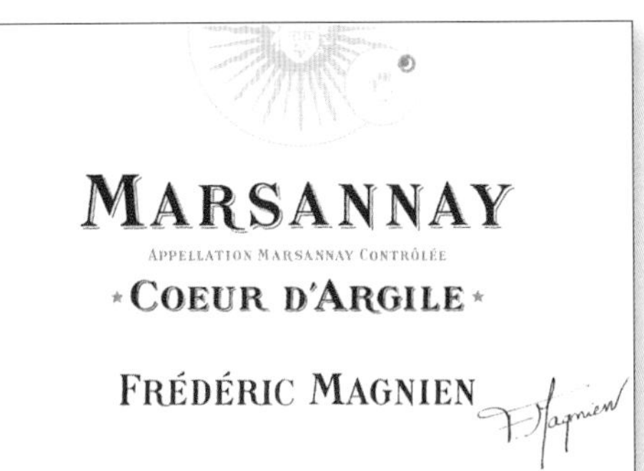

Maison Frédéric Magnien Morey-St-Denis, Côte de Nuits

Marsannay Coeur d'Argile (red)

Though it has only been going for a little more than a decade, Maison Frédéric Magnien is already among the most successful small-scale négociants in the Côte d'Or. It is run by Frédéric, son of Michel Magnien, vineyard manager for Maison Louis Latour and owner of his own eponymous domaine. The Marsannay Coeur d'Argile ("Heart of Clay") delivers warm, spicy aromas and flavours of plum, ginger, and mulberry, with a subtle smokiness lingering on the supple and generous finish.

26 route nationale, 21220 Morey-St-Denis
www.frederic-magnien.com

Domaine des Malandes Chablis

Chablis Premier Cru Côte de Lechet (white)

Domaine des Malandes was established in the 1980s by the charming Jean-Bernard and Lyne Marchive. Lyne is now in charge, along with the couple's daughter Marion and son-in-law Josh, while Guénolé Breteaudeau is the winemaker. There is fairly obvious oak in the Chablis Premier Cru Côte de Lechet, but Chardonnay can handle oak pretty much better than any other white grape variety, so this is still an enjoyable, good-value Chablis. With its rich mouth-feel, it is a good choice for seafood and light meat.

63 rue Auxerroise, 89800 Chablis
www.domainedesmalandes.com

Domaine Jean Marechal Côte Chalonnaise

Mercurey Les Nuages (white)

Known for its power, Domaine Jean Marechal Mercurey Les Nuages is a richer Pinot Noir than most in the area. Old vines help give complexity and there are also hints of toasty oak. It is typical of the 10ha (25 acre) Domaine Jean Marechal which consistently offers elegance and power at much better prices than more famous northern neighbours. The estate has been in the Marechal family since 1570.

20 grande rue, 71640 Mercurey
www.jeanmarechal.fr

Domaine Alain Michaud Côte de Brouilly, Beaujolais

Brouilly (red)

Founded by Jean Marie Michaud in 1910, this domaine has been in the hands of the Michaud family ever since. Alain Michaud took up the reins in 1973, and he works 9ha (22 acres) of vineyards in Brouilly, plus some smaller parcels in Morgon and the wider Beaujolais appellation. Way too easy to sink into, the domaine's mouth-watering Brouilly tastes of ripe cherries and summer afternoons. The structure is light enough for easy drinking, but also sufficiently firm and rich to make it memorable.

Beauvoir, 69220 St-Lager
www.alain-michaud.fr

Domaine Denis Mortet Gevrey-Chambertin, Côte de Nuits

Marsannay Les Longeroies (red)

Denis Mortet made his eponymous domaine a huge success with his modern take on Pinot Noir before his untimely death in 2006. Mortet made polished wines with a considerable new oak influence that appealed to the modern drinker, and his top wines developed a cultish reputation. Mortet's son, Arnaud, took over after his father's death when he was just 25 years old, and the style has changed slightly under his direction; Arnaud prefers to see more elegance and restraint in the wines, and so uses less new oak and seeks out finer tannins. The house style remains forward and rich, however, and the superb Marsannay Les Longeroies is an explosive mouthful of mulberry, black cherries, sweet raspberries, and violets from one of the best vineyards in Marsannay, brought to vibrant life by Arnaud.

22 rue de l'Eglise, 21220 Gevrey-Chambertin
www.domaine-denis-mortet.com

Domaine Georges Mugneret-Gibourg Vosne-Romanée, Côte de Nuits

Bourgogne Rouge (red)

Velvety, deep, and succulent, the sumptuous blackberry, fresh violet, and black cherry infusion of Domaine Georges Mugneret-Gibourg is beautifully balanced, svelte, and classy. It comes from a domaine that embodies the spirit of St-Vincent, the patron saint of vignerons who is depicted on the Chagall-style labels. The domaine is managed today by Jacqueline Mugneret and her daughters Marie-Christine and Marie-Andrée, with the emphasis always on wines with grace, vibrancy, and definition.

5 rue des communes, 21700 Vosne-Romanée
www.mugneret-gibourg.com

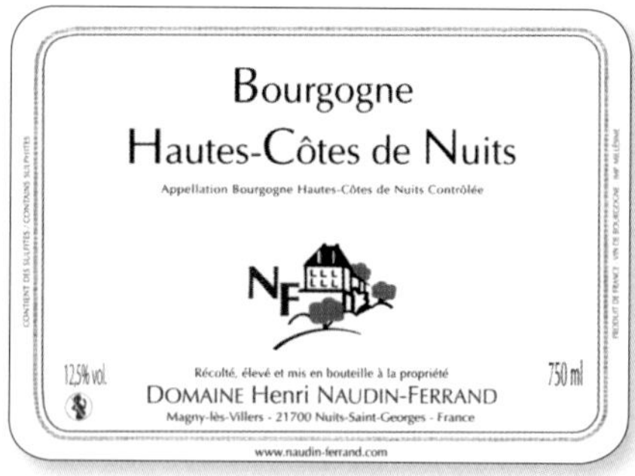

Domaine Henri Naudin-Ferrand Côte de Nuits

Bourgogne Hautes-Côtes de Nuits Rouge (red)

While some winemakers earn their spurs working on the greatest terroirs, others do a fine job finding magic in lesser appellations. Claire Naudin has been one of the latter, crafting wines of great depth of flavour and personality in appellations such as Hautes-Côtes de Nuits. An exceptionally talented winemaker, her red wine from that appellation has a pleasant sweetness to the redcurrant fruits, coupled with a light structure, and there is a softness to the fruit that is very appealing.

Rue du Meix Grenot, 21700 Magny les Villers
www.naudin-ferrand.com

Domaine François Parent Pommard, Côte de Beaune

Bourgogne Pinot Noir (red)

There are many examples of basic Bourgogne Rouge that are unpleasantly tart and lacking in generosity. But not Domaine François Parent's example, which is a warm, gluggable incarnation that is softly spicy, with easy-going fruit and velvety texture. It is made by François Parent, who is the 13th generation of his venerable family to make wine. Though he never loses sight of his heritage, he is nonetheless one of Burgundy's more approachable vignerons. He inherited his share of the family's Pommard vineyards in 1990, and he makes wines both under his own label "François Parent", as well as those from the Côte de Nuits vineyards belonging to his wife, Anne-François Gros.

5 grande rue, 21630 Pommard
www.parent-pommard.com

Domaine Jean-Marc et Hugues Pavelot

Savigny-lès-Beaune, Côte de Beaune

Savigny-lès-Beaune Blanc (white); Savigny-lès-Beaune Rouge (red)

The management of Domaine Jean-Marc et Hugues Pavelot is currently in the transition from father (Jean-Marc) to son (Hugues) but the wines have not suffered in the slightest. From an appellation best known for its whites, the Savigny-lès-Beaune Blanc is an intriguing, fern- and nut-scented Chardonnay that is full of character and is delicious with food such as roasted Bresse chicken. The Pavelot's Savigny-lès-Beaune Rouge, meanwhile, is a very smart buy from a region whose days as a source of burgundy bargains are over: it is a lushly textured, sweet-fruited Pinot Noir of delicious drinkability.

1 chemin des Guettottes, 21420 Savigny-lès-Beaune
www.domainepavelot.com

Domaine Henri Perrusset Mâconnais

Mâcon-Villages (white)

A chance encounter with the celebrated US wine importer Kermit Lynch in the mid-1980s was the catalyst for Henri Perrusset's rise to fame. The two happened to be sharing the same bench at a French truckstop when the 21-year-old Henri mentioned he had just made his first wines. Kermit tasted them, and he bought as much as he could. The rest, as they say, is history. Today, the wines are as good as ever, including the Mâcon-Villages. With notes of candied lemon, chalk, and pear tart, this light, friendly Chardonnay is easy to enjoy every day, especially at its incredible price.

71700 Farges lès Mâcon
03 85 40 51 88

GAMAY

Most popular French grape varieties have been imitated in other countries. But the fresh, vibrant red wines of the Beaujolais countryside in the south of Burgundy, which are made with Gamay grapes, have yet to be successfully copied. Only in Beaujolais, and to a lesser extent in the Loire Valley, is Gamay important for winemaking.

Beaujolais wines are the second red wines of Burgundy in prestige, behind Pinot Noir, yet they are ideal for many occasions thanks to their relative low cost and versatility. Simple Beaujolais is a light to medium red wine that once dominated Parisian cafés. Its famous, fresh, raspberry-like flavours and bright acidity make Beaujolais a good match for many different foods.

Nouveau or "new" Beaujolais may be a marketing phenomenon but gulping the nouveau when it's first released each year on the third Thursday of November is a suitably hedonistic way to celebrate the brand-new vintage. Nouveau wine is light, jammy, and banana-like in aroma, and seemingly sweet in the mouth.

The highest quality Gamay wines of the world are called Beaujolais-Villages and cru Beaujolais, and come from villages such as Morgon, Juliénas, and Moulin-à-Vent. The best cru Beaujolais are excellent and sometimes age-worthy estate-bottled wines that rival fine burgundies for complexity and finesse.

Early-ripener Gamay adapts well to cooler climates.

Domaine Jean-Marc Pillot Chassagne-Montrachet, Côte de Beaune

Chassagne-Montrachet Rouge (red); Santenay Rouge (red)

After studying oenology at Beaune's renowned Lycée, Jean-Marc Pillot assumed control of his family domaine from his father, Jean, in 1991. He has since taken the well-regarded domaine to another level of quality, and it is in the upper echelon of Chassagne producers. His Chassagne-Montrachet Rouge is pure, intense, dense but supple – a benchmark Côte de Beaune Pinot Noir. In his fresh, vibrant Santenay Rouge, delicacy with intensity – that very Burgundian paradox – are nicely combined in a beautifully made Pinot Noir.

21190 Meursault
03 80 21 33 35

Villa Ponciago Fleurie, Beaujolais

Fleurie (red)

Villa Ponciago is a producer with a centuries-long tradition that is enjoying a new lease of life under new owners, the Henriot family of Champagne and Burgundy. Coming from a selection of the estate's most valued plots of vines, this Fleurie easily proves just how out-dated it is to dismiss Beaujolais today as a centre for exciting, terroir-led wines. This wine has a finely woven structure, with tannins that are present but restrained, and add weight to the rich cherry flavours, and soft white pepper spice.

69820 Fleurie
04 37 55 34 75

Potel-Aviron Morgon, Beaujolais

Morgon Côte du Py (red)

Two young winemakers, Nicolas Potel from Burgundy and Stephane Aviron (whose family have roots in Beaujolais), are behind this new project, founded in 2000, and working on a négociant model. The Morgon Côte du Py can be very tannic when young, so don't expect a classic light and fresh Beaujolais, but within a year or two it evolves into an elegant, well-structured delight. Aged in Burgundian oak barrels, this holds tight to the palate with gripping dark brambly fruits.

2093 route des Deschamps, 71570 La-Chapelle-de-Guinchay
03 85 36 76 18

Domaine Michèle et Patrice Rion Nuits-St-Georges, Côte de Nuits

Bourgogne Rouge Les Bon Bâtons (red)

Patrice and his wife Michèle left the Rion family business in 2000 to form a new domaine and négociant business in Prémeaux-Prissey. The domaine's high quality Bourgogne Rouge comes from the top Bon Bâtons vineyard near Chambolle-Musigny. A consistently delicious wine that performs well from vintage to vintage, it speaks powerfully of this special vineyard. It is fragrant and floral, with the Griotte cherries, raspberries, and redcurrants really singing a sweet song. Delicious and affordable.

1 rue de la Maladière, 21700 Prémeaux-Prissey
www.patricerion.com

Domaine de Roally Mâconnais

Mâcon-Villages (white)

Domaine de Roally is situated on a limestone ridge that overlooks the River Saône. It was originally founded by Henri Goyard and is part of what is now the Viré-Clessé AC. Gautier Thévenet, son of the celebrated Jean Thévenet (Domaine de la Bongran), now owns the domaine with its 5.6ha (14 acres) of old vines – a mix of several old Chardonnay clones that Thévenet manages sustainably. Made in a somewhat controversial style (it has a little residual sugar, which is forbidden in the Viré-Clessé appellation), the Mâcon-Villages Chardonnay is tank-fermented only, is distinctly petrolly and yeasty, and has a slight sweetness.

Quintaine Cidex 654, 71260 Clessé
03 85 36 94 03

Maison Roche de Bellene Beaune, Côte de Beaune

Côte de Nuits-Villages, Vieilles Vignes (red)

In Maison Roche de Bellene's Côte de Nuits-Villages Vieilles Vignes, the skills of Nicolas Potel are on full display. The wine is an elegantly concentrated mélange of blackberries, raspberries, and creamy espresso flavours, with a lingering, refreshingly juicy finish, and it is highly enjoyable. Nicolas (also of Potel-Aviron) is the son of the famed Gérard Potel and grew up at Domaine de la Pousse d'Or in Volnay. He worked for a time at top Australian wineries Mount Mary, Mosswood, and Leeuwin Estate, before establishing his eponymous négociant house in 1997. He left that business in 2008 before starting out again with Roche de Bellene the same year.

41 rue Faubourg Saint Nicolas, 21200 Beaune
www.maisonrochedebellene.com

Antonin Rodet Côte Chalonnais

Château de Chamirey Mercurey Blanc Premier Cru La Mission Monopole (white)

An historic négociant house that makes and distributes wines from across the Burgundy region, Antonin Rodet was first established in 1875. It has been through a series of ownership changes since then, and today it is a part of the much larger Boisset group. It still has its headquarters in Mercurey, however, and as well as making wine under its own label, it sells wines from estates such as the ancient fortress Château de Rully, Givry's Domaine de la Ferte, and Château de Chamirey. The last is round and creamy with apple, pear, floral, and mineral notes – a lovely award-winning French Chardonnay that offers tremendous value.

Grande rue, 71640 Mercurey
www.rodet.com

Clos de la Roilette Fleurie, Beaujolais

Fleurie, Cuvée Tardive (red)

At his family estate, Clos de la Roilette, Alain Coudert makes a heartier, more brooding take on Fleurie than many in this appellation. The Cuvée Tardive, for example, uses vines aged between 50 and 80 years old, aged in wooden vats, and bottled unfiltered. In taste, you can expect rich strong flavours and plenty of brambly berry fruit; blackberry crumble with a gentle touch of vanilla and cinnamon spice.

La Roilette, 69820 Fleurie
www.louisdressner.com

Domaine Nicolas Rossignol-Jeanniard Volnay, Côte de Beaune

Bourgogne Pinot Noir (red); Volnay (red)

The likeable, talkative Nicolas Rossignol is a passionate advocate of all things Burgundian. He makes a huge array of wines in Volnay and Pommard, with low yields, sustainable viticulture, and always paying close attention to the health of the soil. His Bourgogne Pinot Noir is substantial and vigorous, with Rossignol's trademark exuberant perfume and firm, dry grip. Quite serious, it deserves and demands a good dinner of lamb cutlets or light game. His Volnay is one of the most consistent and characterful "basic" Volnays that is scented and juicy, with a slinky texture and proper intensity.

Rue de Mont, 21190 Volnay
www.nicolas-rossignol.com

Domaine Michel Sarrazin et Fils Côte Chalonnaise

Givry Champs Lalot (red)

Michel Sarrazin began bottling wines on his family domaine in 1964, after taking over from his parents. Today, Michel has passed control of the family business, which is situated in the relatively high-altitude Jambles, to his sons, Guy and Jean-Yves Sarrazin. The brothers have proved themselves worthy incumbents at an estate whose history dates back to the 17th century, making a range of wines as naturally as possible, without fining or filtration. With notes of wild strawberry, spice, and earth, this medium-bodied dry red of Givry Champs Lalot is a lovely, understated expression of Pinot Noir with the ability to age well.

Charnailles, 71640 Jambles
www.sarrazin-michel-et-fils.fr

Domaine Servin

Chablis

Chablis Premier Cru Montée de Tonnerre (white)

François Servin's family have been established as vignerons in Chablis for more than 300 years, and François himself continues the fine tradition today. He is helped in the cellar by his American assistant, the well-liked and highly respected Marc Cameron, and between them the duo have a thoughtful approach to winemaking that pays off in wines such as the Chablis Premier Cru Montée de Tonnerre. White flowers and juicy pears abound in this finely wrought wine, which is vinified in 100% stainless steel. There is plenty of tongue-tingling acidity that suggests it could age well.

89800 Chablis
www.domaine-servin.fr

CHABLIS
PREMIER CRU
VAILLONS
SIMONNET-FEBVRE
À CHABLIS

Domaine/Maison Simonnet-Febvre

Chablis

Chablis Premier Cru Vaillons (white)

Though Domaine Simonnet-Febvre was bought by Maison Louis Latour in 2003, its house style remains the same, and is far removed from Louis Latour's Côte d'Or-style take on Chablis. The house in fact dates back to 1840, when it was established by Jean Febvre, a cooper, as a specialist in traditional-method sparkling wines. It still makes sparkling wines, the only producer in Chablis to make the Burgundy fizz, Crémant de Bourgogne. The winemaking today is in the hands of Jean-Philippe Archambaud, who has the run of a modern winemaking facility outside Chablis. Because freshness is the guiding principle of all the wines here, Archambaud uses Stelvin screwcaps for some wines, including the village-level bottlings, and he eschews oak in all but the Grands Crus. The Chablis Premier Cru Vaillons is a richer, rounder Chablis than some you will come across in the Simonnet-Febvre portfolio. It is a wine that goes long on stone fruits, with touches of peach blossom to soften out the zing of lemon.

9 avenue d'Oberwesel, 89800 Chablis
www.simonnet-febvre.com

Michel Tête (Domaine du Clos du Fief)

Juliénas, Beaujolais

Domaine du Clos du Fief Juliénas (red)

Several things mark out Michel Tête's operation Domaine du Clos du Fief as a place for high quality wine production. First, there is the location, on sloping sites in the Juliénas, where Tête has some old, untrellised Gamay vines. Second, there is the winemaking, which is as natural and traditional as possible, with open-vat fermentations and manual punching down of the grape skins. Then there is the viticulture, which is organic, although not in fact certified as such. Finally there is Tête himself, a highly talented winemaker whose attention to detail goes as far as having his own bottling line despite his relatively small scale. His Domaine du Clos du Fief Juliénas is a wine that is built to age, or decant for a few hours if you are drinking it young (in other words, for its first four years after vintage), with good structure and some firm tannins. The old vines lend some swirling dark spices to the blackberry fruits.

69840 Juliénas
www.louisdressner.com/Tete

Domaine Trapet Père et Fils

Gevrey-Chambertin, Côte de Nuits

Marsannay Rouge (red)

Jean-Louis Trapet is a warm-hearted and dedicated biodynamic producer who makes some of the finest wines in the Côte de Nuits. His Marsannay Rouge displays a luminous beauty and sensuality. With fresh mulberry fruit, warm brown spices, and a radiant quality throughout, it really shines, and is typical of the Trapet approach. That approach is marked by a genuine (and not in the least bit marketing-driven) feel for the land and the wines that spring from it. Trapet has been working with organics and then biodynamics for 15 years, and it has brought about a philosophical transformation of his views on wine and life in general. He is committed to the idea that wines are best if they are left in peace during their creation, and he believes producers should work as respectfully and gently as possible, whether that is in the vineyard or the winery. He is also inspired by the history of Burgundy, and its strong winemaking traditions, which date back to monastic times, informing everything he does.

53 route de Beaune, 21220 Gevrey-Chambertin
www.domaine-trapet.com

Domaine A et P de Villaine Côte Chalonnais

Bourgogne Aligoté (white)

Aubert de Villaine, the urbane guiding force of Burgundy's most famous estate, Domaine de la Romanée-Conti, established Domaine A et P de Villaine in 1970, four years before assuming control at DRC. Today the domaine in Bouzeron is run by Aubert's nephew, Pierre de Benoît, and it is producing wines from organically produced grapes that are marked by their elegance and ability to age, but which fortunately do not touch the astronomic prices commanded by the bottlings from DRC. Among the stars at this estate is the Bourgogne Aligoté. This is more than simply a benchmark example of this sometimes maligned grape variety; it is one of the best wines produced from Aligoté in the world. Like Chardonnay, it has characteristic apple and pear notes, but it also has soft grassy flavours and a slightly heavier mouthfeel. With its precise, singing acidity it is the perfect wine for springtime.

2 rue de la Fontaine, 71150 Bouzeron
www.de-villaine.com

FOOD & WINE
WHITE BURGUNDY

Chardonnay reaches its ultimate expression in Burgundy – although you won't find the grape's name on many of the region's labels.

In Burgundy you can find the steely wines of Chablis; the nutty, creamy style of Meursault; the decadent, mineral-laced Corton-Charlemagne; and the rich, layered, and complex Montrachet.

From light, crisp, and tart to full-bodied, opulent, and ripe, one common flavour denominator is butter, coming from malolactic fermentation, the conversion of tart malic acid to the soft lactic acid. White burgundies also have notes of pear, apple, citrus, and varying levels of both minerality and oakiness. When pairing the wine with food, consider its weight as well as its beautiful earthiness, an element that is showcased nicely with mushrooms.

Chablis, the lightest and most mineral of the classic burgundies, often has a salinity that works with oysters. It is also perfect for the local escargot cooked in Chablis with garlic and butter. Medium-bodied white burgundies pair nicely with richer dishes such as Bresse chicken, morel, and asparagus ragout in puff pastry, or those incorporating the local mustard into a sauce of wine and cream. Even the richest of these wines offer refreshing citrus and apple notes, and are easy to pair with rich dishes such as *ris de veau* (sweetbreads) or the creamy white Chaource, a fine and tasty local cheese.

Oysters are a classic match with crisp minerally Chablis.

Champagne

The world's greatest sparkling wine is a model for producers around the globe, and remains the choice for any celebratory occasion. Produced in the Champagne region in northeast France, champagne is principally made from one or all of three grape varieties, Chardonnay, Pinot Noir, and Pinot Meunier. It can be made in a variety of styles, but the best examples marry complex flavours with thrilling acidity.

Agrapart & Fils Côte des Blancs

Brut Blanc de Blancs Les 7 Crus

A blend of two different years, Agrapart & Fils' Brut Blanc de Blancs Les 7 Crus is a classic Chardonnay champagne. Lively and crisp, it shows fragrant, floral aromas of pear and citrus. It is made by the Agrapart brothers, Pascal and Fabrice, who believe work in the vineyard is every bit as important as the winemaking, a belief that is not as common in Champagne as you might think. The emphasis is on environmentally sensitive viticulture in the family's estate in Avize, and the wines exhibit great terroir character, with a distinctive mineral edge offset by a depth of flavour that comes from the judicious use of oak in the winery.

57 avenue Jean Jaures, 51190 Avize
www.champagne-agrapart.com

L Aubry Fils Montagne de Reims

Brut NV

The Aubry twins, Philippe and Pierre, are known for sticking up for Champagne's lesser-spotted grape varieties, producing wines from such neglected varieties as Arbanne, Petit Meslier, and Fromenteau. They are also believers in the potential of the least regarded of Champagne's "big three" grape varieties, Pinot Meunier, and their Brut NV is based primarily on that grape, giving it a round, spicy succulence. The wine is also full-bodied and generous in feel, finishing with vibrant aromas of strawberry and citrus. L Aubry would be an interesting and innovative estate even without this varietal experimentation. Located in the village of Jouy-lès-Reims, they have become known for making highly individual wines.

4 et 6 Grande Rue, 51390 Jouy-lès-Reims
www.champagne-aubry.com

Bérèche et Fils Montagne de Reims

Brut Réserve

Bérèche et Fils was founded in 1847, and today it is a rising star among Champagne's grower-estates. A small estate in the village of Ludes, it is run by the Bérèche family, with Raphaël and Vincent Bérèche working with their father, Jean-Pierre. In recent years the family have taken an increasingly natural direction in the vineyards, and they have also started using more cork while the wines age on their lees. The results of their approach can be seen to full effect in the family's excellent Brut Réserve. A blend of Chardonnay, Pinot Noir, and Pinot Meunier, this champagne feels unusually sophisticated for a non-vintage brut, combining a rich depth of flavour with crystalline purity and grace.

Le Craon de Ludes, 51500 Ludes
www.champagne-bereche-et-fils.com

Charles Heidsieck Reims

Brut Réserve

Charles-Camille Heidsieck, who founded Charles Heidsieck in 1851, was a colourful character. He became well known in the US during his frequent (successful) sales trips to the country, and even earned a nickname, "Champagne Charlie". Today the wines are made by the highly respected *chef de cave* (cellarmaster), Régis Camus, who continues to look for the rich and complex style developed by his successor, Daniel Thibault. The Brut Réserve is a non-vintage brut of uncommon complexity and character which contains a high percentage of older wines, giving it a rich fragrance and firm, confident depth.

4 boulevard Henry Vasnier, 51100 Reims
www.charlesheidsieck.com

Chartogne-Taillet Montagne de Reims

Brut Cuvée Ste-Anne

Brut Cuvée Ste-Anne takes its name from the patron saint of Merfy, the village where Chartogne-Taillet is based. It is harmonious and sleekly sculpted, its dark flavours of cherry and plum feeling energetic and pure. Like all of the wines produced at this 12ha (29.5 acre) estate, the Cuvée Ste-Anne has been climbing to new heights in recent years under the direction of Alexandre Chartogne, who makes champagnes that express the sandy and chalky–clay soils of Merfy, which lies in the far north of the Champagne appellation. The current owners have a long tradition in the area, having made wines as far back as the early 1800s.

37 Grande Rue, 51220 Merfy
03 26 03 10 17

Diebolt-Vallois Côte des Blancs
Brut Blanc de Blancs

Diebolt-Vallois is indisputably in the front-rank of Champagne's grower-estates. It is the product of two families: the Diebolt family, who have been making wine in Cramant since the late 19th century, and the Vallois family, who have been growing vines in Cuis since the 1400s. The modern-day business really began to get going in the late 1970s, however, when the vineyards were extended, and a winery and cellars constructed. Run today by Jacques Diebolt and Nadia Vallois, in conjunction with their two children, Arnaud and Isabelle, Diebolt-Vallois now has some 11ha (27 acres) of vineyards in Cramant, and it produces a range of fine Blanc de Blancs that are marked out by their purity and vibrancy. Elegant and lithe, the Brut Blanc de Blancs is a pure Chardonnay champagne that is the very model of refinement, its flowery fruitiness feeling delicate and summery against a textural backdrop of chalky minerality.

84 rue Neuve, 51530 Cramant
www.diebolt-vallois.com

Doyard Côte des Blancs
Brut Blanc de Blancs Cuvée Vendémiaire

Doyard Brut Blanc de Blancs Cuvée Vendémiaire is aged on its lees for at least four years, an unusually long time for a non-vintage champagne. Its lemony, smoky flavours show a detailed complexity and fine balance that demand the drinker returns for another glass. It is made by Yannick Doyard, who uses the best fruit from his 10ha (25 acres) of vines in the Côte des Blancs (the other half is sold on to local négociants). Doyard has a justified reputation for making highly sophisticated champagnes that see some time in oak barrel during the winemaking process. Doyard works his six vineyards – five of them in grand cru sites, the other in the top premier cru village of Vertus – biodynamically. The estate was founded in the 1920s by Doyard's grandfather, Maurice Doyard.

39 avenue Général Leclerc, 51130 Vertus
03 26 52 14 74

Drappier Aube
Brut Nature Zéro Dosage

Made entirely of Pinot Noir, Drappier Brut Nature Zéro Dosage is deliciously ripe and fruity, with a luscious, succulent charm. There is also a non-sulphured version of this champagne (it will say "sans souffre" on the label) that is even more vibrant and complex and well worth looking out for. The family-owned and run Drappier is a top producer in the Aube. It is managed by Michel Drappier who works the 55ha (136 acres) of vineyards (the family also buys in some grapes) with sustainable practices, vinifying individual parcels separately.

Rue des Vignes, 10200 Urville
www.champagne-drappier.com

SERVING CHAMPAGNE

Champagne and other sparkling wines are such treats that one can hardly complain about the complicated process of opening a bottle. It involves a series of tasks: peeling the foil wrap, loosening the wire cage, removing the cork, cleaning the messy overflow, and finally pouring the wine. Still, it's a chore that can be simpler and less messy if you follow a few easy steps used by sommeliers. Remember to have the bubbly well chilled first, not to shake it about as you open it, and don't waste it by letting the cork fly and the bubbles overflow. Remember, too, that the cork is under pressure and capable of harming people and property.

1 The little tab designed to remove the foil casing rarely works as intended. Rip or cut and unwrap the foil casing however you can. The point is to get at the wire cage underneath.

4 Hold the cork firmly with one hand and twist the whole bottle at the base with the other to loosen the cork. Pressure will push it out. Go for a "poof" rather than a pop. Then return the bottle to an upright position, covered with a cloth.

2 Position one thumb over the cork, and twist the loop to loosen the cage. Quickly, lift your thumb long enough to remove the cage, and return your thumb, to prevent the cork ejecting.

3 Here is the first thing you need to know to pour champagne like a professional. If you tilt the bottle 45 degrees down from vertical before removing the cork and keep it angled, the bubbles will rarely overflow.

5 Ah, the payoff. Slowly pour a thin stream into a flute glass (the best shape for retaining the bubbles) until the foam approaches the top, without spilling over. Wait for it to slump, and then pour a second time to fill the glass.

Gosset Épernay
Brut Excellence

A champagne house with a long history, Gosset has had a home in Aÿ since it was founded in the village in 1584. It recently moved production to larger cellars in Épernay, but it has retained its distinctive style. Made without malolactic fermentation, Gosset's champagnes balance power with complexity and finesse. This is certainly true of the aptly named Brut Excellence. Pinot Noir accounts for nearly half the blend in this entry-level cuvée. This gives the wine a mouthfilling richness and dark, sappy fruit flavours. The fresh, apple-like acidity keeps it feeling silky and focused, however.

69 rue Jules Blondeau, 51160 Aÿ
www.champagne-gosset.com

Henriot Reims
Brut Souverain

Made of equal parts Chardonnay and Pinot Noir, the Brut Souverain shows off the rich, opulent Henriot style, allying its velvety depth with an elegantly fine texture. It is a fitting introduction to a house that was established in Reims in 1808 by Apolline Henriot. With a fine and longstanding reputation for making rich, mouthfilling cuvées, Henriot's champagnes develop a great deal of their renowned complexity and finesse from a long period of ageing on the lees.

81 rue Coquebert, 51100 Reims
www.champagne-henriot.com

Louis Roederer Reims
Brut Premier

Even people who have never drunk it have heard of Louis Roederer's most famous champagne, the remarkable prestige cuvée, Cristal. The wine was originally made for Russia's Tsar Alexander II, and today it is a favourite of the rich and famous, and the connoisseur, all over the world. But Louis Roederer has much more to offer than this very expensive wine. With a history dating back to 1776, the house is one of the finest in champagne, producing a range of consistently high quality wines. A great introduction to Roederer's hallmark complexity, the suave, creamy non-vintage Brut Premier demonstrates all the elegance and class of the house style.

21 boulevard Lundy, 51053 Reims
www.champagne-roederer.com

Mailly Grand Cru Montagne de Reims
Grand Cru Brut Réserve

Is Mailly Grand Cru the finest co-operative in Champagne? It is certainly hard to think of another that manages to maintain such high standards as this association of 80 growers in the north-facing village of Mailly. Established in 1929, the members own some 70ha (173 acres) of vines, all in Mailly, which is renowned for producing fine Pinot Noir with good structure. The quality of that Pinot Noir shines through in the Grand Cru Brut Réserve. A blend of three-quarters Pinot Noir and one-quarter Chardonnay, it shows impressive finesse, its notes of redcurrant and grapefruit feeling vivid and taut.

28 rue de la Libération, 51500 Mailly
www.champagne-mailly.com

Michel Loriot Vallée de la Marne
Brut Réserve Blanc de Noirs

The independent grower Michel Loriot tends an estate of some 7ha (17 acres) of vines on clay soils in and around the Flagot Valley, on the southern banks of the river Marne. His vineyards mainly (but not exclusively) comprise Pinot Meunier and, unusually for the region, he produces some cuvées that are solely based on that grape variety. The Brut Réserve Blanc de Noirs is one of those wines, and it is a fine example of what Pinot Meunier, the least regarded of the champagne varieties, is capable of in the right hands. A serious wine, it shows lively, assertive flavours of apple, red berry, and freshly baked bread.

13 rue de Bel Air, 51700 Festigny
www.champagne-michelloriot.com

Pierre Gimonnet & Fils Côte des Blancs

Brut Blanc de Blancs

A well-regarded house in the Côte des Blancs, Pierre Gimonnet was established by its eponymous founder in 1935. Today Pierre's grandsons, Didier and Olivier Gimonnet, look after the operation, which is devoted to Chardonnay. All but one of Gimonnet's champagnes are Blanc de Blancs, drawing on Chardonnay grapes sourced in the villages of Cuis, Cramant, and Chouilly (the exception is the special cuvée, Paradoxe, which has some Pinot Noir from Aÿ and Mareuil). Gimonnet's Brut Blanc de Blancs is a benchmark example of the house's style of pure Chardonnay champagne. Racy and brisk, it is driven by a saline, knife-like zestiness that keeps the citrus and apple flavours bright and fresh.

1 rue de la République, 51530 Cuis
www.champagne-gimonnet.com

Raymond Boulard/Francis Boulard & Fille Montagne de Reims

Brut Nature Les Murgiers

Made of 70% Pinot Meunier and 30% Pinot Noir, the Brut Nature Les Murgiers is bone-dry without feeling aggressive, thanks to its ripe fruit flavours. It is one of several excellent wines made by Francis Boulard under his new label, which he founded with his daughter, Delphine, in 2010. Francis used to make the wines for his father, Raymond Boulard's, eponymous estate. The new label arose when the 10ha (25 acre) Raymond Boulard estate, which was spread across Marne and Aisne, was divided between Raymond's three children. Francis Boulard's winery is now in Cauroy-lès-Hermonville, north of Reims, from where he sources the grapes for his best cuvées. The estate aims to have all of its production certified organic in the near future.

Route Nationale 44, 51220 Cauroy-lès-Hermonville
www.champagne-boulard.fr

René Geoffroy

Grande Vallée

Brut Expression

Though the Geoffroys are perhaps usually associated with wines from Cumières, the cellars today are in fact located in Aÿ, where the company moved in 2008. The wines, made by Jean-Baptiste Geoffroy, have lost none of their trademark character in their move, however, as is amply shown by the Brut Expression. With its bold red-fruit flavours, this Pinot-dominated blend feels extroverted and inviting, combining its full-bodied depth with lively, citrussy finesse. It is made from parcels of grapes that are grown sustainably and that are vinified separately.

4 rue Jeanson
51160 Aÿ
www.champagne-geoffroy.com

The rest of France

Outside the famous classic regions, there are sources of some of the finest affordable wines in the world. The Rhône is home to elegant Syrah and spicy Syrah-Grenache blends. Alsace is all about aromatic whites such as Riesling and Gewurztraminer. In the Loire, try crisp Sauvignon Blanc and complex Chenin Blanc whites, and leafy, fragrant Cabernet Franc reds. In Languedoc-Roussillon and the Southwest, you'll find intriguing grape varieties of both colours.

Antech Limoux, Languedoc

Blanquette de Limoux Cuvée Françoise (sparkling)

Françoise Antech runs this family business in Limoux, where the speciality is sparkling wines from appellations such as AC Crémant de Limoux, AC Blanquette de Limoux, and AC Blanquette Méthode Ancestrale. This area has a very long history of making sparkling wine, and some experts believe that the traditional method – where the sparkling wine takes on its fizz with a second fermentation in the bottle – was actually developed around here, in the Abbey of Saint Hilaire in 1531, some time before the method reached Champagne. Today, producers in Limoux still use the traditional method, although the blend is different from champagne – Mauzac, Chenin Blanc, and Chardonnay. With its 60ha (150 acre) lots of vines, Antech is one of the best producers in the region. Its Blanquette de Limoux Cuvée Françoise is a dry, crisp, minerally, and vivacious sparkling wine that is a fraction of the price of champagne and nearly as good.

Domaine de Flassian, 1150 Limoux
www.antech-limoux.fr

Cave de Mont Tauch Fitou, Languedoc

Muscat de Rivesaltes Tradition (dessert)

Though it has a history dating back to 1913 that makes it one of the oldest co-operatives in the Languedoc, Cave de Mont Tauch is also one of France's most forward-looking wine producers. Its home is in the village of Tuchan, although its 250 members have vines in the villages of Paziols, Tuchan, Durban, and Villeneuve. Mont Tauch is usually associated with the Fitou appellation, on the Languedoc-Roussillon border, which was first established in 1948 (it is the oldest AC in the Languedoc), and where Mont Tauch dominates production to the tune of around 50% of all wines made each vintage. But typically excellent, good-value red wines are also made in the Corbières AC, and winemaker Michel Marty produces some excellent dessert wines, too. The Muscat de Rivesaltes Tradition is a fine example of the latter. At once showy and subtle with exotic orange blossom and spice notes intermingling with honey, this is a very elegant French dessert wine.

Les Vignerons Du Mont Tauch, 11350 Tuchan
www.mont-tauch.com

Caves des Vignerons de Saumur

Saumur, Saumur-Champigny, Loire

La Réserve des Vignerons, Saumur Champigny (red); Les Poyeux, Saumur Champigny (red)

The Caves des Vignerons de Saumur is a vast operation. Its 200 member-growers tend some 1,800ha (4,450 acres), and their grapes go into a wide variety of wines of all styles. The Réserve des Vignerons Saumur Champigny is a smooth, slightly creamy red with bright damson and red cherry fruit, a hint of graphite, and fine powdery tannins. Les Poyeux Saumur Champigny is a seductive single-vineyard red with peony, violet, and cinnamon spice notes to its silky cassis and black and red cherry fruit.

Route de Saumoussay, 49260 St-Cyr-en-Bourg
www.cavedesaumur.com

M Chapoutier Northern Rhône

Deschants, St-Joseph (red)

There are few bigger names in the contemporary French wine scene than Chapoutier. That this is the case is largely down to one man, the charismatic Michel Chapoutier, who has led the family firm, which began its life more than 200 years ago, with great foresight and skill since he took the helm in 1990. Chapoutier is one of the foremost exponents of biodynamic viticulture, something he has applied not just to his estates in the Rhône Valley, but to projects in the Ardèche, Roussillon, Portugal, and Australia. Michel is, in fact, the seventh generation of his family to lead the business, a line that goes back to 1808 when Polydor Chapoutier began making wine. Today the Chapoutier have interests throughout the Rhône, but the house's spiritual home remains the north of the valley, with wines such as the excellent St-Joseph, Deschants, which has fresh aromas and flavours of red and black fruits with accents of smoked meat, fresh herbs, and cured olives.

18 ave Dr Paul Durand, 26600 Tain l'Hermitage
www.chapoutier.com

Château d'Aussières Corbières, Languedoc
A d'Aussières, Corbières (red)

Château d'Aussières has been completely transformed since it was acquired by Domaines Barons de Rothschild (Lafite) from Bordeaux in 1999. It now has a spanking new winery, and some 170ha (420 acres) have been replanted to the traditional local grape varieties, Syrah, Grenache, Mourvèdre, and Carignan. The Lafite influence can be literally tasted in the wines, which are aged using barrels that have been made at the famous château in Pauillac. And there is certainly an extra level of class and quality in wines such as the A d'Aussières, which is a juicy and vibrantly fruity red from the Corbières AC. This is a wine with a slightly wild side, but its spicy drinkability makes it the perfect dry red for a weeknight dinner of pizza or roast chicken.

Départementale 613, Route de l'Abbaye de Fontfroide, 11100 Narbonne
www.lafite.com

Château La Canorgue Luberon, Southern Rhône
Château La Canorgue, Luberon (red)

There is a touch of Hollywood glamour about the exquisitely faded, 300-year-old Château La Canorgue: it was used as the setting for the 2006 film, *A Good Year*, made by Ridley Scott and starring Russell Crowe. Scott became a fan of the wines during filming, and many more visitors of the estate, inspired to make the journey having seen the film, have had the same experience. The wines are made by the château's owners, Jean-Pierre Margan and his daughter Nathalie. The estate's red offers stylish evidence of Syrah's natural ability to play the lead part in Luberon reds. Delicacy and purity mark this fine-boned, strawberry-and-herb-scented organic beauty.

Route du Pont Julien, 84480 Bonnieux
04 90 75 81 01

Château de Caraguilhes Corbières, Languedoc
Solus Corbières Blanc (white)

Made with 100% organically farmed Grenache Blanc, Château de Caraguilhes' lovely full-bodied and creamy dry Corbières white, Solus, has notes of limoncello, white rose, pink grapefruit, and toasted nuts. It is emblematic of an estate, based near St-Laurent de la Cabrerisse in the Corbières-Boutenac region, that was among the first in the region to use organic methods in the 1950s, thanks to the visionary thinking of the owner at the time, Lionel Faivre. The estate, which dates back to the 12th century, is now owned by Pierre Gabison.

11220 St-Laurent de la Cabrerisse
www.caraguilhes.fr

Château Cazal Viel St-Chinian, Languedoc

St-Chinian, Vieilles Vignes (red)

Château Cazal Viel St-Chinian Vieilles Vignes is a blend of Syrah, Grenache, Mourvèdre, and other southern grapes that has been oak-aged for 12 months. It offers notes of blackberry, bay leaf, and extra dark chocolate, is medium-bodied with firm structure, and is well suited for rich dishes such as duck. The estate itself is located by Cessenon-sur-Orb at the foot of the Caroux Mountains, and has been in the hands of the Miquel family since the French Revolution in 1789. Now run by the talented Laurent Miquel, it has more than 135ha (335 acres) of vines, and is the biggest private producer in St-Chinian.

Hameau Cazal Viel, 34460 Cessenon-sur-Orb
www.laurent-miquel.com

Château de Cazeneuve Pic St-Loup, Languedoc

Les Calcaires, Pic St-Loup (red)

Medium-bodied with just a hint of oak, Château de Cazeneuve Pic St-Loup Les Calcaires is a Syrah-based blend that has inviting notes of berries, *herbes de Provence*, and vanilla. It is one of several high quality wines being produced by André Leenhardt at this estate, which he bought two decades ago, rebuilding the winery soon after in 1991. The estate extends to some 35ha (90 acres), largely planted to red varieties (Syrah, Grenache, Cinsault, and Carignan) with a fifth of the area given over to white grapes (Roussanne, Viognier, Marsanne, with a little Rolle, Muscat, and Petit Manseng). The vines are divided into 30 parcels at altitudes of between 150 and 400m (490 and 1,300ft). Leenhardt manages the vineyards using organic methods, and keeps yields low.

34270 Lauret
www.cazeneuve.net

Château de Chambert Cahors, Southwest France

Chambert Gourmand Fruité Intense, Cahors (red)

Château de Chambert was not a particularly well-known estate until it was snapped up by Philippe Lejeune in 2007. It is now, however, thanks to the major series of investments that Lejeune has introduced since taking over. Among other things, he has bought new barrels and other new equipment for the cellar, and he has replanted and repaired the vineyards (taking out all the Tannat grapes and bringing the total area down to some 60ha/148 acres in the process). Most eye-catching of all, perhaps, has been Lejeune's recruitment of the top Bordeaux-based wine consultant, Stéphane Derenoncourt, who has helped Lejeune transfer the whole property to biodynamic practices. The range of wines here is now much more focused, in terms of both the winemaking and the size of the portfolio. The Chambert Gourmand Fruité Intense shows all the work is paying off. An earthy, black pepper spice dominates in this 80% Malbec, 20% Merlot wine, with rich black cherries underpinning the whole thing – a successful modern take on Cahors.

Les Hauts Coteaux, 46700 Floressas
www.chambert.com

Château Clément Termes Gaillac, Southwest France

Cuvée Tradition Rouge, Gaillac (red)

An even blend of the traditional Gaillac grape varieties Braucol, Syrah, and Duras form the basis of Cuvée Tradition Rouge, the main wine at Château Clément Termes. Brambly autumn fruits are the dominant note, with plenty of blackberries and redcurrants. Firm fruit tannins give a natural structure to the wine, which is made without the use of oak. The estate itself, situated atop a ridge, looking down on the picturesque town of Lisle-sur-Tarn, started its life in 1860. Today it is still run by descendants of the founder: Olivier David directs operations and makes the wines, while his sister, Caroline, looks after sales and marketing. The 80ha (198 acres) of vineyards are planted to Braucol, Duras, Sauvignon Blanc, Syrah, and Loin de l'Oeil, along with Cabernet Sauvignon and Merlot.

Les Fortis Rd 18, 81310 Lisle-sur-Tarn
www.clement-termes.com

Château des Erles Fitou, Languedoc

Cuvée des Ardoises, Fitou (red)

The Lurton brothers, Jacques and François, have wine in the blood, having grown up in a winemaking family in Bordeaux. Looking to establish their own personality in wine, they went into business themselves at the end of the 1980s, and were soon making wines in far-flung places such as Chile and Argentina, and closer to home in Spain and, with the acquisition of Château des Erles in Fitou in 2001, the Languedoc. François is now in sole charge here, and he has 90ha (220 acres) to play with. With notes of jam, herbs, and toast, Château des Erles Cuvée des Ardoises Fitou is a silky, lush Languedoc blend of 30% Syrah, 40% Grenache, and 30% Carignan that is well-made and well-priced.

Villeneuve-les-Corbières 11360
www.francoislurton.com

Château d'Esclans Côtes de Provence, Provence

Whispering Angel, Côtes de Provence (rosé)

Any sceptics about how good rosé wine can be owe themselves the favour of buying a bottle of Château d'Esclans' Whispering Angel. There is a delicate structure that majors on fresh wild strawberries with a creamy swirl. And if you like it, you can head upwards in both price and quality of rosé at the same estate. This is certainly a most impressive operation: a 267ha (660 acre) property in La Motte, southeast of the town of Draguignan. It was acquired in 2006 by Sacha Lichine, the son of Alexis Lichine, former owner of Château Prieuré-Lichine in Margaux, and includes some 44ha (109 acres) of vines, averaging 80 years in age. Heavyweight consultants Patrick Léon (once of Château Mouton Rothschild) and the globetrotting Bordelais, Michel Rolland, are both employed in this venture that has always set about proving that rosé can be seriously fine wine.

4005 route de Callas, 83920 La Motte en Provence
www.châteaudesclans.com

Château des Eyssards Bergerac, Southwest France

Château des Eyssards, Bergerac Blanc (white)

A light touch is exercised with Château des Eyssards Bergerac Blanc, which is largely made from Sauvignon Blanc (the remainder is Muscadelle). It is a wine that emphasizes fresh white flowers against the refreshing citrus zing. Eyssards is run by Pascal Cuisset, a well-liked figure who exports much of his production, proving that this is a man who understands what drinkers around the world – rather than simply in the local area – really enjoy. The jovial Cuisset is very much a man of the local area, however, playing the French horn in a band he started up with a group of his friends in the local winemaking community. Today, Cuisset's estate extends to some 44.5ha (110 acres) of vines, with slightly more white grapes than red. The family also makes some intriguing sweet Saussignac and a Vin de Pays Chardonnay.

24240 Monestier
05 53 24 36 36

Château de Haute Serre Cahors, Southwest France

Château de Haute Serre, Cahors (red)

There is a seductively romantic story behind Château de Haute Serte. It begins with Georges Vigouroux who, in the early 1970s, was looking for somewhere to plant Malbec vines. He noted that the rundown Château de Haute Serre, with its overgrown, derelict vineyards, had been ranked among the best producers in France before phylloxera struck in the late 19th century, and so he decided to revive the estate. It took him two years to plant what is the highest vineyard in the Cahors AC, with the overwhelming majority being Malbec plus a little Merlot and Tannat. The first vintage arrived in 1976, and the estate began to attract wide acclaim. In 1989, Vigouroux passed the business onto his son, Bertrand, who has kept up the good work in wines such as the estate red. Expect plenty of gourmet flavours here – raspberry coulis over blackberry crumble, together with gently toasted oak, but the natural tannins and acidity stop it from being too much.

46230 Cieurac
www.hauteserre.fr

Château de Jau
Roussillon

Le Jaja de Jau Syrah (red)

The name of Château de Jau's Le Jaja de Jau Syrah – "Jaja" translates as "everyday" – aptly summarizes the style of the wine in the jaunty, simple bottle: it is a fruit-forward, ebullient dry red with expressive blackberry, cherry, and plum notes, and is delicious served slightly chilled. Originally founded by Cistercian monks in the 12th century, the Château de Jau at Cases de Pène has views of the Agly Valley. It has been owned since 1974 by the Dauré family, and is managed today by brother and sister Simon and Estelle.

66000 Cases de Pène
www.chateau-de-jau.com

Château Lagrézette Cahors, Southwest France
La Rosé de Grézette

Under the ownership of Alain Dominique Perrin, Château Lagrézette has shot to the top of the list of the best producers in Cahors. Perrin, owner of the Richemont Group (known for luxury brands like Cartier and Chloé), acquired the property originally as a country retreat in 1980, and he has since invested a great deal of money into the restoration of the 15th-century château and Malbec-dominated vineyards. The main wine at this estate sells for consistently high prices, but it is worth trying the rosé for some everyday drinking. This is made entirely in stainless steel, at low temperatures, from grapes (80% Malbec and 20% Merlot) that are hand harvested. Rich raspberry in colour, it carries through red summer fruits onto the palate, with good structure, making it a perfect barbecue wine.

46140 Caillac
www.chateau-lagrezette.tm.fr

Château La Liquière Faugères, Languedoc
Sous l'Amandier Faugères Rouge (red)

Château La Liquière's Sous l'Amandier Faugères Rouge shows that packaging a wine in the bag-in-box format can work for premium wines. It is a lovely, bright, and fruity red wine, that is just the thing for warm weather entertaining. A family-run estate, Château La Liquière extends to some 60ha (150 acres) of vineyards, planted to Grenache, Syrah, Carignan, Mourvèdre, and Cinsault.

34480 Cabrerolles
www.chateaulaliquiere.com

Château Mourgues du Grès
Costières de Nîmes, Southern Rhône

Les Galets Dorés, Costières de Nîmes (white); Les Galets Rosés, Costières de Nîmes

Few wines at a similarly reasonable price conjure up the essence of summer in southern France with quite as much panache as these two fresh, lively numbers from Château Mourgues du Grès. Both the white (Les Galets Dorés), and rosé (Les Galets Rosés), provide a touch of tangy mineral intrigue alongside their exuberant fruit. Made by François and Anne Collard, the wines are ample proof that the motto that was carved into the front of the estate centuries ago – *sine sole nihil*, "without the sun, nothing" – is as true at this fine Costières de Nîmes estate today as it has ever been.

Route de Bellegarde, 30300 Beaucaire
www.mourguesdugres.com

Château de la Negly La Clape, Languedoc
La Falaise, Coteaux du Languedoc (red)

La Falaise Coteaux du Languedoc by Château de la Negly is a concentrated and deep red wine – one of the more serious efforts from this area. Full-flavoured and dry, it has the dark berry fruit and garrigue flavour typical of the area, and is able to cross over from fish to meat at the table. The château itself has been improving rapidly over the past decade, taking advantage of its excellent position on the chalky terrain of La Clape. That is largely thanks to Jean-Paul Rosset, who made the decision to start bottling the fruit of the family vineyard, which had previously disappeared into the anonymous fare of the local co-op. Today yields are kept low, and Rosset works with winemaker Cyril Chamontin and the consultant Claude Gros.

11560 Fleury d'Aude
04 68 32 36 28

Château Pesquié Ventoux, Southern Rhône
Les Terrasses, Ventoux (rosé and red)

If the top wines of polished Pesquié lie outside your budget, raise three cheers for the temptingly priced Terrasses. The terrifically vibrant rosé is genuinely refreshing while the red is an attractive all-rounder with a peppery, herbal edge. The estate has been at the forefront of rising quality in Ventoux since the 1980s. The Chaudière family farm their 83ha (205 acres) organically.

Route de Flassan, 84570 Mormoiron
www.chateaupesquie.com

Château de Pibarnon Bandol, Provence
Rosé de Pibarnon, Bandol

For an affordable entry to this excellent quality estate, try Château de Pibarnon's Rosé de Pibarnon – a 50/50 blend of Cinsault (pressed direct from the grapes) and Mourvèdre (free-run juice from the first maceration of grapes intended for their red wine). There is a real complexity to the summer fruit flavours, which offer depth and a silky mouthfeel as well as a streak of freshness. Pibarnon has been owned by Henri and Catherine de Saint Victor since 1978, since when it has expanded tenfold in terms of size and, in many people's view, quality.

Comte de Saint Victor, 83740 La Cadière d'Azur
www.pibarnon.fr

Château Pierre-Bise Anjou, Loire
Clos Le Grand Beaupreau Savennières (white); Gamay Sur Spilite, Anjou (red)

Claude Papin makes a bewildering range of different wines at Château Pierre-Bise. That they are all eminently drinkable is all the more remarkable when you consider that Papin only took over at his wife's family estate in 1990. Clos Le Grand Beaupreau Savennières is a bone-dry, fresh, vibrant, and focused white with a dash of ginger spice to its crisp apple and steely grapefruit. The Gamay Sur Spilite Anjou shows how the Loire's cooler climate and rocky spilite soils produce a leaner Gamay style than Beaujolais. It is mineral-driven, with jewel-bright tightly coiled briar fruit.

49750 Beaulieu-sur-Layon
02 41 78 31 44

FOOD & WINE RHÔNE VALLEY REDS

When considering what to pair with Rhône reds, first determine whether you will select a rich, pure Syrah from the north of the Rhône Valley, or a bold and robust blend with Grenache and Mourvèdre from the south. Both have a good affinity with a variety of dishes.

Côte Rotie and Hermitage, the world's best Syrahs, are deeply coloured and powerful with notes of dark berry fruit, earth, smoke, bacon, lilacs, white and pink peppercorns, and *herbes de Provence*. These wines are medium-bodied and dry, as are the less expensive Syrahs from Cornas, St-Joseph, and Crozes-Hermitage. Aim to partner their pronounced flavours with rich dishes such as *Tournedos Rossini* or squab pigeon with offal sauce.

Blended in the south with Syrah, Grenache brings body and a pleasant strawberry note, while Mourvèdre brings a gamey chewiness. The light and fruity Côtes du Rhône wines are easy to enjoy with weeknight meals. Try a glass with roast chicken; flank steak with mustard sauce; ham and gruyère paninis; pumpkin and sausage soup; French onion soup; baked brie with garlic; or lentils with (or without) salted pork. The more robust Châteauneuf-du-Pape (a blend of Syrah, Grenache, Mourvèdre as well as some others) pairs nicely with daube of beef (French beef stew), beef en croute with figs and mushrooms, roast suckling pig, or roasted lamb.

Enjoy flank steak with a light, fruity, Côtes du Rhône.

Château Plaisance

Fronton, Southwest France

Le Grain de Folie, Côtes du Frontonnais (red)

Soft tannins and warming red fruits are the order of the day for this 70% Négrette, 30% Gamay wine. Only natural yeasts are used to start fermentation, and everything takes place in stainless steel, with no oak. There is still plenty of body and mid-palate to hang on to here, but nothing too intense. The wine's vibrant flavours are typical of the results obtained from the careful, natural approach favoured by Louis Penavayre and his son Marc at their 30ha (74 acre) estate. They farm the land organically, and produce some 150,000 bottles a year of consistently excellent wine that are a benchmark of today's Fronton scene.

Place de la Mairie, 31340 Vacquiers
www.chateau-plaisance.fr

Château La Roque Pic Saint-Loup, Languedoc

Coteaux du Languedoc Blanc (white)

With a recent conversion to biodynamic farming, the fruit from Château La Roque's estate is pristine. The light, dry white Coteaux du Languedoc is a blend of local grapes (Marsanne, Rolle, Grenache Blanc, Viognier, and Roussanne), and is zesty and fresh with lime, apricot, and jasmine notes. The estate's origins date back to the 8th century, when it was a posting house, and vines made their first appearance here in the 13th century. Today it has some 32ha (79 acres) and is owned by Jacques Fiquette who employs Claude Gros as his winemaking consultant.

84210 La Roque Sur Pernes Vaucluse
www.chateau-laroque.fr

Château de St-Cosme Gigondas, Southern Rhône

St-Cosme, Côtes du Rhône (red)

Sidestep that ocean of light, fruity, forgettable Côtes du Rhône, in favour of this excellent choice from Louis Barruol. A multi-layered, firm red, the St-Cosme Côtes du Rhône echoes Barroul's impressive estate Gigondas. Barruol is one of the key figures in the Gigondas appellation, the 14th generation of his family to look after St-Cosme, which the family have owned since 1570, although wine was made here long before that. Barruol brings a mixture of charm, intelligence, and energy to his work, and his wines are always rich but refined, whether they are made on the 15ha (37 acre) estate, or in the high-quality négociant business started by Barruol in 1997.

La Fouille et les Florets, 84190 Gigondas
www.saintcosme.com

Château St-Jacques d'Albas Minervois, Languedoc

Domaine St-Jacques d'Albas, Minervois (red)

Grapes have been grown for many years at Château St-Jacques d'Albas, which lies towards the west of the Minervois region. Initially, those grapes were sold on to the local co-operative, but that all changed in 2001, when the estate was bought by Graham Nutter, an Englishman, and his wife, Beatrice. The couple renovated the vineyards and recruited consultant Jean-Pierre Cousine to help them adapt a more holistic way of working. The Domaine St-Jacques d'Albas is a sultry red that has notes of wild strawberry, plum, thyme, and tarragon. It is medium-bodied and one of the best deals in the area.

11800 Laure Minervois
www.chateaustjacques.com

Château St-Martin de la Garrigue
Picpoul de Pinet, Languedoc

Château St-Martin de la Garrigue, Picpoul de Pinet (white)

A long and chequered history lies behind Château St-Martin de la Garrigue. Documents from 847 AD refer to the existence of the Roman chapel here, and Iron Age relics were discovered on the site in the 1970s. By the time of that discovery, the château had been abandoned, and it was not until 1992, when the current owners took over, that it was restored to its former glory, building a winery and replanting the vineyards. They now make a range of interesting wines, including their Picpoul de Pinet. This delicate dry white is brisk and lemony with complex notes of pine needle and the sea.

34530 Montagnac
04 67 24 00 40

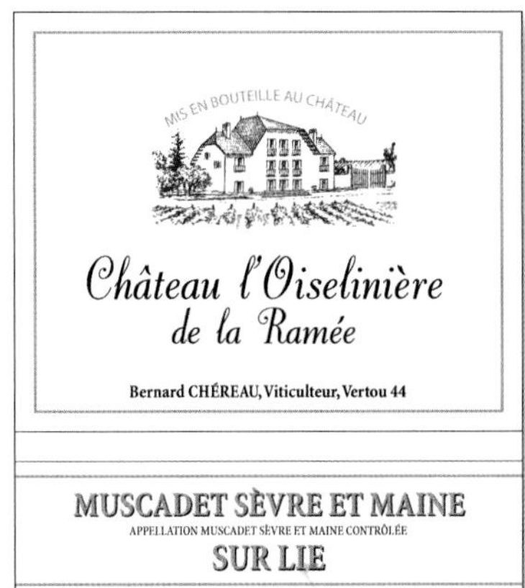

Chéreau Carré Muscadet Sèvre et Maine, Loire

Château l'Oiselinière de la Ramée Muscadet Sèvre-et-Maine sur Lie (white); Château l'Oiselinière Le Clos du Château Muscadet Sèvre-et-Maine sur Lie (white)

Chéreau Carré makes great Muscadet Sèvre et Maine at four top estates, and two stand out for inclusion here. Aged on the lees, the Château l'Oiselinière de la Ramée offering is a classic Muscadet with a salty tang to its fresh pear and pear skin fruit. The flagship Château l'Oiselinière Le Clos du Château, from a south-facing site with schist and orto-gneiss soils, is weighty, with poached pear and melon fruit. It reminds you that Muscadet's grape variety, Melon de Bourgogne, hails from Burgundy.

44690 Saint Fiacre sur Maine
www.chereau-carre.fr

Clos de l'Anhel Corbières, Languedoc

Le Lolo de l'Anhel, Corbières Rouge (red)

Sophie Guiraudon and Philippe Matthias have worked hard to establish their estate since buying a plot of old vines in the Orbieu valley in 2000. A young couple, they work their organic vineyard, which stands at 220m (720ft) near Lagrasse, with great care, eschewing chemicals and calling on family and friends to help them out. They have added some new plantings of Syrah and Mourvèdre to the original old-vine Carignan, Grenache, Cinsault, and Syrah, and their Le Lolo de l'Anhel red blend is wild, savoury, and fragrant, marking them out as producers to watch.

11220 Lagrasse
www.anhel.fr

Clos Mireille Côtes de Provence, Provence

Clos Mireille Rosé Coeur de Grain, Côtes de Provence

Clos Mireille is part of the fabled Domaines Ott stable. Bought by Marcel Ott, from Alsace, in 1936, the estate covers some 170ha (420 acres) near to the sea in La Londe, close to Hyères. Here there is a beautiful house and palm tree-lined grounds of which 47ha (116 acres) are covered by vineyards planted to Sémillon, Ugni Blanc, Grenache, Syrah, and Cinsault. The Rosé Coeur de Grain, one of two wines made here, has the lovely orange-blush flavours and floral heather aromas of a classic Provence rosé.

2 bis bd des Hortensias, 83120 Ste-Maxime
04 94 49 39 86

Clos Nicrosi Cap Corse, Corsica

Clos Nicrosi Blanc, Coteaux du Cap Corse (white)

You have to head to the white wines at Clos Nicrosi, the most northerly vineyard in Corsica, which lies in Rogliano, right at the top of the ruggedly beautiful Cap Corse. The standout is the crisp, elegant 100% Vermentino (some years with a touch of the Codiverta grape) Clos Nicrosi Blanc. Taut and sinewy, this has a lovely white flower perfume, with a touch of savoury herbs, and is almost always light in alcohol (12.5% in most vintages). The estate was founded in 1959 by Toussaint Luigi and his brother, Paul, who began making and bottling their own wines in the late 1960s. Today it is run by Jean-Noël Luigi and his son, Sebastien.

Pian Delle Borre, 20247 Rogliano
04 95 35 41 17

Clos Ste-Magdeleine Cassis, Provence

Rosé Cassis

A blend of Grenache, Cinsault, and Mourvèdre, Clos Ste-Magdeleine Rosé Cassis is a little more of a pink blush colour than many Provence rosés, and correspondingly the flavours have a touch more red summer fruits than savoury herbs. The added structure (while still fresh and delicate) gives you good food-and-wine matching choices. This beautiful estate on the Cap de Canaille has been much improved over the past four decades by Georgina and François Sack and their children, Grégoire and Jonathan. It has some 20ha (50 acres) of terraced vineyards running right down to the sea.

Avenue du Revestel,
13260 Cassis
wwwclossainte magdeleine.fr

Clos du Tue-Boeuf Cheverny, Loire

Rouillon Cheverny (red)

Jean-Marie and Thierry Puzelat are stars of the natural wine movement, a growing group of winemakers who look to make their wines as naturally as possible. That means organic viticulture, but it also means using as few interventions in the winery as possible, with little or no sulphur dioxide and wild rather than cultivated strains of yeast for fermentation. The couple took up the reins at their father's estate in the 1990s, and they have retained the huge variety of rare, heirloom grape varieties planted in its 16ha (40 acres) of vineyards. The deliciously vibrant wines they produce are testament to the wisdom of the brave choices they have made in both the vineyards and the winery. The Rouillon Cheverny, for example, is a floral, summery blend of Gamay and Pinot Noir that combines red cherry, berry, and currant fruit with savoury white pepper and smoky bacon.

6 route de Seur, 41120 Les Montils
02 54 44 05 06

Delas Frères Northern Rhône

Domaine des Grands Chemins, Crozes-Hermitage (red)

Until relatively recently, Delas Frères was in danger of slipping into mediocre obscurity. A famous négociant house, it was originally founded in 1835, but by the 1980s and early 1990s, its wines had not kept up with the quality being produced by its peers. Then, in 1996, things began to change, thanks largely to the visionary leadership of managing director, Fabrice Rosset. It was Rosset who instituted wide-ranging and radical changes, overhauling both the infrastructure and the personnel. He employed the oenologist Jacques Grange and winemaker Jean-François Farinet to head up the winemaking team, and recruited Vincent Girardini to improve the vineyards. The winemaking facilities were redeveloped, and the vineyards restructured. The work soon bore fruit, and now Delas has established itself as a fine producer of wines once more, in both the Southern and Northern Rhône, producing a broad range of négociant and estate wines. Delas has some notable vineyards (amounting to some 14ha/35 acres in total) in such top Northern Rhône appellations as Hermitage, St-Joseph, and Crozes-Hermitage, and it is in the last appellation that one of its top value wines can be found. The Crozes-Hermitage Domaine des Grands Chemins is sourced from an estate owned by Delas, and is a surpassingly interesting Crozes-Hermitage that combines some intricate aromas with deep, satisfying flavours.

07300 St-Jean de Muzols
www.delas.com

Denis et Didier Berthollier Savoie

Chignin Vieilles Vignes, Savoie (white); Chignin Bergeron, Savoie (white)

The Berthollier brothers, Denis and Didier, are rising stars of the Savoie region, thanks to their unremitting insistence on quality. They have become particularly identified with white wines of great freshness, verve, and character. The Chignin Vieilles Vignes is a surprisingly supple dry white from the Jacquère variety, with lovely flowery scents and an Alpine freshness. The brothers also make a much richer, full-bodied white, the Chignin Bergeron, from Roussanne, which has lightly spiced scents and flavours of apricot, with a mineral edge.

Le Viviers, 73800 Chignin
www.chignin.com

Domaine Alain Graillot Northern Rhône

Domaine Alain Graillot, Crozes-Hermitage (red)

Dark in colour and intense in all respects, Domaine Alain Graillot Crozes-Hermitage offers a wild ride from the first whiff of cured meat and spices to the bright, focused finish. It is a benchmark example of Crozes-Hermitage's spicy reds, as well as a great introduction to an estate that has contributed enormously to the appellation's rise in prestige in the past couple of decades. The energetic, committed former chemical engineer, Alain Graillot, is still at the helm at his domaine, and he now works his 21ha (52 acres) of vineyards with his son, Maxime.

Les Chênes Verts, 26600 Pont-de-l'Isère
04 75 84 67 52

Domaine Alary Cairanne, Southern Rhône

La Chèvre d'Or Côtes du Rhône Blanc (white); Tradition Cairanne, Côtes du Rhône Villages (red)

Organic producer Denis Alary makes his wines from three sites in Cairanne in the Southern Rhône, and whether red or white, they always show the same deft touch. Among the most enticing Southern Rhône whites at its price, La Chèvre d'Or Côtes du Rhône spins pear, peach, citrus, and honey notes together in perfect harmony. And, with its raspberry and blackberry succulence, Alary's Tradition Cairanne, which includes his trademark dash of Carignan, is a super introduction to Cairanne's elegant reds. The intelligent, open-minded Alary comes from a talented winemaking family: he is a cousin of the brothers behind Oratoire St-Martin.

Route de Rasteau, 84290 Cairanne
04 90 30 82 32

Domaine André et Michel Quenard

Savoie

Abymes, Savoie (white); Chignin Mondeuse, Savoie (red)

The village of Chignin is home to several producers with the surname Quenard, but this estate has, over several generations, been the most consistent. Today, it is run by Michel, who is now helped by his son, Guillaume, fresh from his winemaking studies. From a fine portfolio produced in steep vineyard sites, the simple, fresh dry white Abymes is a really versatile, inexpensive Savoie white that works brilliantly with fondue and other cheese dishes. On the red side, the spicy, deep Mondeuse is aged in large oak vats, and this fleshes out the rustic, blackberry flavours.

Torméry, 73800 Chignin
04 79 28 12 75

Domaine André et Mireille Tissot Jura

Crémant du Jura (sparkling); Arbois Poulsard Vieilles Vignes (red)

Made from a blend of the Chardonnay and Savagnin grape varieties, Domaine André et Mireille Tissot Crémant du Jura is an elegant, dry, bubbly wine with lemony flavours, available at a bargain price. It is made by Stéphane Tissot, son of André and Mireille, who has raised the quality bar at this 40ha (99 acre) Arbois estate to increasingly impressive levels. He works the vineyards biodynamically, and is not afraid to bring in new winemaking ideas that may go against the grain of tradition in this area. As well as the Crémant, look out for the elegant Arbois Poulsard Vielles Vignes. The difficult red Poulsard grape needs careful handling and Stéphane coaxes out lovely redcurrant fruits melding with a touch of oak for this deftly made, deliciously light red.

Place de la Liberté, 39600 Arbois
www.stephane-tissot.com

Domaine Arretxea Irouléguy, Southwest France

Rouge Tradition, Irouléguy (red)

The Pyrenees Mountains loom over Irouléguy in Southwest France, and they play a major role in defining the wines produced in the appellation. At Domaine Arretxea, for example, at least half of the the 8.5ha (21 acre) vineyard is carved into terraces in very steep slopes, while the balance is largely planted at a gradient of 40°. The domaine is owned and run by Thérèse and Michel Riouspeyrous, who are long-time believers in organic and biodynamic methods, having been certified organic since 1996. They make a small amount of white wine, but it is red wine that dominates production here. For their fine Rouge Tradition, the Riouspeyrous blend Tannat, Cabernet Franc, and Cabernet Sauvignon, ageing it in cement vats rather than oak. It is an excellent example of the little known but truly pleasurable wines of Irouléguy, which offer the punch and smoothness of well-worked red fruits without a high price tag, making them fantastic everyday drinking choices.

64220 Irouléguy
05 59 37 33 67

Domaine Belle Northern Rhône

Les Pierrelles, Crozes-Hermitage (red); Blanc Les Terres Blanches, Crozes-Hermitage (white)

Domaine Belle has quite substantial holdings in Crozes-Hermitage: the majority of its 20ha (50 acres) of vineyards are in the appellation, with a small percentage in Hermitage. In terms of its winemaking, the domaine approaches its red and white wines very differently. The reds are made in traditional fashion, with long maceration times and whole clusters, which, in the case of Les Pierrelles, yields a satisfying Syrah that is dark in colour and deep in flavour, with pure fruit showing notes of both red and black berries. For whites, such as Les Terres Blanches, more modern techniques are used, such as carrying out fermentation in temperature-controlled stainless steel tanks, and this leads to a fresh but still complex wine, with some citrus-edged fruit recalling quince and wild honey.

Les Marsuriaux, 26600 Larnage
04 75 08 24 58

Domaine de Bellivière Jasnières, Coteaux du Loir, Loire

Prémices, Jasnières (white)

It's not an exaggeration to say that Eric and Christine Nicolas have done more than anybody else to revive the fortunes of Jasnières and Coteaux du Loir. These two obscure appellations, which are located some 50km (30 miles) north of Tours, along the banks of the Loir River (a tributary of the Loire), were all but forgotten until the couple discovered some old vineyards in the appellations and set about restructuring them. They took quite radical steps: yields were cut back dramatically, and in one vineyard they planted the vines to an astonishingly high density of 40,000 vines/ha (16,200/acre). They have made their name with their fabulous range of whites made from Chenin Blanc, including the fine Prémices, which was introduced as an affordable alternative to top wines such as Calligrame. The Prémices fufils its brief perfectly: vibrant, mouthwatering citrus, and tart yellow plum fruit is deftly balanced with a dash of residual sugar; just off-dry.

72340 Lhomme
www.belliviere.com

Domaine Bernard Baudry Chinon, Loire

Les Granges, Chinon (red)

Burgundy-trained winemaker, Bernard Baudry, is one of the Loire's best red wine producers. Now working with his son, Matthieu – who travelled in Tasmania and California after studying winemaking in France – Baudry has vineyards in some top sites, amounting to 30ha (75 acres). From Les Granges, a vineyard next to the Vienne River, where Baudry has his youngest vines, Chinon Les Granges, is an elegant, medium-bodied perfumed Cabernet Franc that has a bright and beautiful core of cinnamon-edged ripe but juicy red cherry.

9 Coteau de Sonnay, 37500 Cravant-les-Côteaux
www.chinon.com/vignoble/Bernard-Baudry

Domaine Bott-Geyl Alsace

Les Pinots d'Alsace Métiss (white)

Domaine Bott-Geyl is a critical favourite, which has attracted attention with its extensive range of stunning small-production wines. Les Pinots d'Alsace Métiss is a blend of four different members of the Pinot family of grape varieties, combining a mix of Auxerrois, Pinot Blanc, Pinot Gris, and Pinot Noir. Together, the quartet form a distinctively delicious wine with a beautiful deep palate and an intense mineral finish. Flavours of orange and lemon with a touch of honey and some herbal elements abound. It is superb drinking on its own but equally versatile with food.

Rue du Petit-Chateau, 68980 Beblenheim
www.bott-geyl.com

Domaine Brana Irouléguy, Southwest France

Domaine Brana Rouge, Irouléguy (red); Domaine Brana Blanc, Irouléguy (white)

Jean Brana has been a pioneer in the Irouléguy area of Southwest France. Among other things, he was the first to revive white wine production in the appellation, and he was the first producer to cut loose from the important local co-operative, which dominates production here, making wine for more than 90% of the area's growers. Brana, who used to contribute to the co-operative himself, began bottling his own wines in 1988, and he has carved out a fine reputation ever since. The Domaine Brana Rouge is a lovely wine; delicate despite using some fairly meaty red grapes, and overall full of confidence and pleasure. The blend is 60% Cabernet Franc, 30% Tannat, and 10% Cabernet Sauvignon, worked together to offset the dense black fruits with a fresh aromatic structure. Brana's white is also excellent. Making use of classic southwestern grape varieties, with 50% Gros Manseng, 25% Petit Courbu, and 25% Petit Manseng, this is floral and summery, majoring on a crisp rendition of exotic fruits.

64220 St-Jean-Pied-de-Port
www.brana.fr

Domaine Le Briseau

Jasnières, Coteaux du Loir, Loire

Patapon, Coteaux du Loir (red)

Innovative, stubbornly individualist – often of the bloody-minded variety – winemakers seem to be attracted to Jasnières and Coteaux du Loir, turning this once-sleepy backwater into a hotbed of vinous experimentation. Christian and Nathalie Chaussard of Domaine Le Briseau, who came to the area in 2002, are two prime examples of this phenomenon. The couple work their estate biodynamically, and they have been certified as organic since 2006. The winemaking is minimalist and natural, leading to a distinctive house style which puts the accent on vibrancy, life, and energy. All of which apply to the Coteaux du Loir Patapon, which blends Pineau d'Aunis and Côt into a joyous, perfumed, silky unoaked red with lifted white pepper and smoky clove edging its bright red cherry fruit.

Les Nérons, Marçon carte, Sarthe
02 43 44 58 53

Domaine de Cazes Roussillon

Muscat de Rivesaltes (dessert)

The Cazes family's Roussillon wine empire began its life in 1895, when Michel Cazes tended a few hectares of vines producing grapes to sell on to other producers in the region. Today it covers some 200ha (490 acres) of terraced vineyards in the Agly Valley, it produces 1 million bottles spread across 15 different wines each year, and it is France's largest organic and biodynamic wine estate. One of the highlights of this extensive range is the delicious, honeyed, medium-sweet white Muscat de Rivesaltes. With notes of orange blossom, candied orange, vanilla bean, and fruitcake, its richness is balanced with fresh underlying acidity.

4 rue Francisco Ferrer BP 61, 66602 Rivesaltes
www.cazes-rivesaltes.com

Domaine Chaume-Arnaud

Vinsobres, Southern Rhône

Domaine Chaume-Arnaud, Vinsobres (red)

Certified biodynamic in 2007, having already achieved organic status in 1997, Domaine Chaume-Arnaud is one of the best estates in Vinsobres. Its rise has been masterminded by the dynamic and driven Valerie Arnaud, who took over the family estate from her parents in 1987. At the time, it was rare to see a woman head up a wine estate in the Southern Rhône, but Arnaud, helped by her husband, Philippe Chaume, developed a wine style that put the emphasis on terroir and authenticity. Brambly in flavour and finely textured, the domaine's Vinsobres is a textbook example.

Les Paluds, 26110 Vinsobres
04 75 27 66 85

Domaine Combier Northern Rhône

Domaine Combier, Crozes-Hermitage (red)

Luxuriously ripe, soft, and fleshy, in many vintages Domaine Combier Crozes-Hermitage is more generous and expressive than big-ticket Northern Rhônes costing twice as much. It is made by Laurent Combier, who produces wines that are driven by the same principles as his father, Maurice: organic practices abide in the family vineyards, with Maurice converting to this form of agriculture way back in 1970. The estate today has some 22ha (54 acres) of Syrah in Crozes-Hermitage and a further 2ha (5 acres) in Marsanne and Roussanne, plus a small plot of Syrah, in St-Joseph.

2 route de Chantemerle, 26600 Tain l'Hermitage
www.domaine-combier.com

Domaine Cosse Maisonneuve

Cahors, Southwest France

Cuvée La Fage, Cahors (red)

The wines of Domaine Cosse Maisonneuve have provided a new direction for the Cahors appellation, offering great style, polish, and poise. They are the work of Matthieu Cosse, a retired rugby player, and his partner, Catherine Maisonneuve, who have earned rave reviews for their approach. The couple farm 17.5ha (43 acres) in the appellation biodynamically, and make three cuvées from the local Malbec grape variety, of which the Cuvée La Fage is the best priced. A touch of smoky oak envelops you instantly here, followed by the spicy black fruits of Malbec. An intense, concentrated, and highly controlled wine.

46800 Fargues
05 65 24 22 37

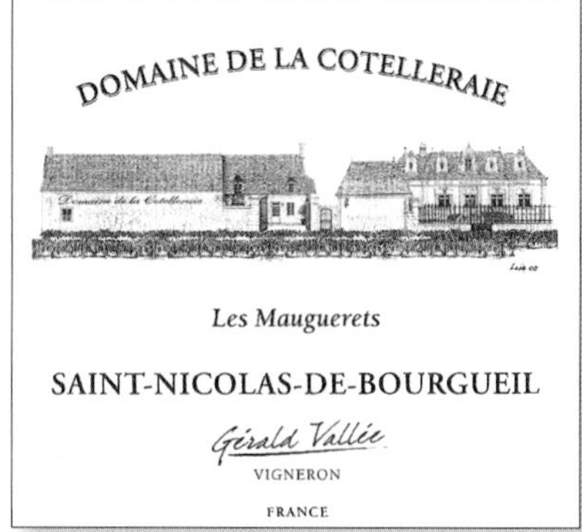

Domaine de la Cotellaraie

St-Nicolas-de-Bourgueil, Loire

Les Mauguerets, St-Nicolas-de-Bourgueil (red)

Elegant, silky, and perfumed with fresh-picked peonies, red and black cherry fruit, and a subtle hint of lead pencil, St-Nicolas-de-Bourgueil Les Mauguerets is a beautiful example of Loire Cabernet Franc from Domaine de la Cotellaraie, one of the region's finest exponents of the variety. The domaine owes its reputation to the skill and dedication of Gérald Vallée, who has brought a sensitive and terroir-driven approach to the 25ha (62 acre) property. Vallée works his vineyards, where a small (10%) amount of Cabernet Sauvignon is planted alongside the Cabernet Franc.

2, La Cotellaraie, 37140 St-Nicolas-de-Bourgueil
02 47 97 75 53

Domaine du Cros Marcillac, Southwest France

Cuvée Lo Sang del Païs, Marcillac (red)

Domaine du Cros Cuvée Lo Sang del Païs is a wine that is desperate to be drunk. Joyfully bright purple in colour, it is aged without oak to ensure that the raspberry flavours, with a touch of gooseberry, are given full expression. A 100% Fer Servadou (known in Marcillac as Mansois), this wine should be consumed within five years of the vintage. It is made from grapes grown by Philippe Teulier in his 26ha (64 acres) of vineyards (some owned, some rented), which are hidden away in steep hills where the ruby-red soil (known locally as rougier) betrays the high iron content.

12390 Goutrens
www.domaine-du-cros.com

Domaine Dupasquier Savoie

Roussette de Savoie (white); Mondeuse, Savoie (red)

The vineyards of Noël Dupasquier and his son David are extremely steep, and they produce some wonderful wines whose quality is not reflected in their prices. Made from the Altesse grape, their Roussette de Savoie can be enjoyed young or with a few years age. A dry, minerally, mid-weight white, it reveals delicate white peach and pear flavours. Dupasquier's Mondeuse is a light-bodied, soft red with a blackberry fruit character.

Aimavigne, 73170 Jongieux
04 79 44 02 23

Domaine Duseigneur Lirac, Southern Rhône

Antarès, Lirac (red)

An ultra-suave, concentrated, modern red made in collaboration with prominent sommelier Philippe Faure-Brac, Domaine Duseigneur Antarès Lirac is slightly more expensive than the other wines in this book – but it is lusciously rewarding, packing layers of flavour inside a velvet cloak. All of the wines produced by brothers Bernard and Frédéric Duseigneur on this biodynamic estate underscore the exciting potential of Lirac. Across the river from Châteauneuf-du-Pape, its vineyards are similarly carpeted with stones.

Rue Nostradamus, 30126 St-Laurent-des-Arbres
www.domaineduseigneur.com

Domaine de la Ferme Blanche

Cassis, Provence

Cuvée Cassis Blanc, Provence (white)

Showing why Cassis is so well regarded for its white wine, Domaine de la Ferme Blanche's Cuvée Cassis Blanc has a freshness and delicacy that makes it a perfect summer wine. It is not merely simple, however, since it is rounded out with honeysuckle aromas and a candied citrus note that adds complexity. Founded in 1714, and owned by the Imbert family for generations, Domaine de La Ferme Blanche has 30ha (74 acres) of vines, managed today by François Paret.

Route de Marseille, 13260 Cassis
04 42 01 00 74

GEWÜRZTRAMINER

This grape variety makes dry and sweet white wines with easily recognizable aromas and excellent fruit flavours, but it divides opinion.

The fans love Gewürztraminer for its sheer exuberance, the exotic floral aroma, like roses, and the fruit flavours that resemble sliced pears drizzled with honey. Others find the aroma overpowering, or associate its floral character with sweetness, thinking (erroneously) that it cannot be enjoyed with a meal. Yet the dry versions drink beautifully with many dishes, including sausages with Dijon mustard, and off-dry examples pair with spicy Asian dishes and smoked salmon.

Alsace in France is home to most of the world's best Gewurztraminer (there is no umlaut on the word here), though it is made in Germany, Australia, New Zealand, California, and elsewhere, sometimes under synonyms. The best examples tend to come from cool climates, and are often made by the same winemakers who bottle Riesling.

The name incorporates gewürz ("spicy" in German) with Tramin (a town in Northern Italy). A grape variety known simply as Traminer can be traced back hundreds of years. Grapevine scientists believe that variety, which is green-skinned, mutated to create the pink-skinned Gewürztraminer as recently as 150 years ago.

Today, Gewürztraminer's relative unpopularity is an advantage. It keeps the demand down, so prices for excellent bottles can be quite reasonable.

Pink-skinned Gewürztraminer fares best in cool climates.

Domaine Frantz Saumon Montlouis, Loire

Minérale+ Sec Montlouis-sur-Loire (white); Un Saumon dans la Loire Romorantin Vin de France (white)

Frantz Saumon made his living as a forester before turning his attention to wine with the acquisition of 5ha (12 acres) of vineyards in Montlouisi-sur-Loire in 2001. A newcomer he may be, but he has already proved himself a fine exponent of pure Chenin Blanc. Perhaps his background has helped in at least one respect: Saumon seems to have an inbuilt understanding for how to use oak in his winemaking: it is always employed judiciously here. In the Minérale+ Sec, a streak of citrus acidity balances subtly sweet honeyed apple fruit. The wine is clear as a bell with, as might be guessed from the wine's name, a mineral undertow. The punningly named, Un Saumon dans la Loire Romorantin, is taut, long, and lingering with a savoury, nutty edge; this bone-dry wine from the local Romorantin grape variety has lipsmacking lemon zest and crunchy green apple fruit.

15 B Che des Cours, 37270 Montlouis-sur-Loire
06 16 83 47 90

Domaine Frédéric Mabileau

St-Nicolas-de-Bourgueil, Bourgueil, Anjou, Saumur, Loire

Les Rouillères, St-Nicolas-de-Bourgueil (red); Racines, Bourgueil (red)

Frédéric Mabileau could have joined the family estate to pursue his winemaking career. But he was impatient to do his own thing, and back in 1991 he decided to start his own domaine instead. Over the years, he has progressively added to his vineyard holdings, which means he now has some 27ha (67 acres) of vines to play with, all of them certified organic in 2009. Though he makes some white wines from Chenin Blanc in Anjou, it is his reds, from Cabernet Franc (he has a little Cabernet Sauvignon, too), that have earned him his global following. Of these, two stand out for inclusion in this book: Les Rouillères St-Nicolas-de-Bourgueil is a sophisticated yet approachable expression of Cabernet Franc that delivers delicious juicy red and black berry fruit tinged with warm earth and gravel. The Racines Bourgueil is more structured and sturdy with a rich veneer of spicy vanilla oak to its deep seam of pure, ripe, perfumed cassis fruit.

6 rue du Pressoir, 37140 St-Nicolas-de-Bourgueil
www.fredericmabileau.com

Domaine Gauby Roussillon

Les Calcinaires Blanc, Côtes du Roussillon Villages (white)

When you consider that Gérard Gauby's top-level wines sell for the price of Grand Cru Burgundy, the Côtes du Roussillon Villages Les Calcinaires Blanc begins to seem like even more of a bargain. A blend of 50% Muscat, 30% Chardonnay, and 20% Macabeu, it is produced, like all of Gauby's wines, biodynamically. An elegant, focused, rich dry white, it has notes of pineapple, white peach, and honey. It is the kind of wine that has made Gauby a superstar of the Roussillon, someone who has provided inspiration for the younger generation of winemakers that is making the region such an exciting place. The estate, located 20km (12 miles) to the northwest of Perpignan in the village of Calce, has been in the Gauby family for many years, but it was Gérard, who took the helm in 1985, who proved it could make great wine. Over the years he has added a number of parcels to the 11ha (27 acres) he inherited. The estate now extends to 45ha (110 acres) of vines up to 120 years old, all of it biodynamic since 2001, and mostly planted on the chalky soils that dominate around Calce (which derives from "calcaire", or chalky).

La Muntada, 66600 Calce
www.domainegauby.fr

Domaine Gayda Languedoc

Gayda Cépages Syrah, IGP Pays d'Oc (red)

Domaine Gayda's Cépages Syrah is a rich and meaty wine, with some fragrant redcurrant and violet notes, and gentle black pepper spices. It is smooth and easy to drink, although watch out for high alcohol in warmer years. This estate has a cosmopolitan background. It is owned by an Englishman (Tim Ford) and a South African (Anthony Record) who recruited their French winemaker (Vincent Chansault) while he was working in Franschoek, South Africa, at top producer, Boekenhoutskloof, whose winemaker (Marc Kent), is also a non-executive director at Gayda. The cosmopolitan approach also carries over to the way the company sources its raw materials. With some 11ha (27 acres) of their own vineyards in Brugairolles, to the southeast of Carcassonne, plus another 8ha (20 acres) at La Livinière in Minervois, the team also has partnerships with a number of growers dotted around the Languedoc and Roussillon.

11300 Brugairolles
www.gaydavineyards.com

Domaine Georges Vernay Condrieu, Northern Rhône

Le Pied de Samson, Vin de Pays des Collines Rhodaniennes Viognier (white)

Viognier is the speciality of Domaine Georges Vernay. The grape variety is used for the estate's top wine, the flagship Condrieu that is one of the finest produced in this highly prized, small (just 8ha/20 acres) and, consequently, somewhat expensive appellation. But the domaine also makes a more affordable version of Viognier as a Vin de Pays des Collines Rhodaniennes. This has lovely floral aromas leading the way to plush fruit with flavours recalling peaches and ripe melon, and a fresh edge of citrus providing a balanced finish. Today the influential Georges Vernay has passed control of the estate to his daughter, Christine, who works alongside her husband, Paul, and her brother Luc.

1 route nationale, 69420 Condrieu
www.georges-vernay.fr

Domaine La Grange aux Belles Anjou, Loire

Fragile, Anjou (white); Princé, Anjou (red)

Marc Houtin was a geologist, before bringing his talents to wine. He worked as an intern at the legendary Sauternes producer, Château d'Yquem, where he learned all about making fine sweet wines. So it was not surprising that his first forays into production at his own estate, Domaine La Grange aux Belles, founded in Anjou in 2004, were with sweet wines. He was soon experimenting with dry styles, however, and today these are the primary focus at the domaine. Houtin recruited the viticulturist Julien Bresteau, formerly of Mongilet, in 2006, and the vineyards are now managed sustainably. The two Anjou wines, the white Fragile and the red Princé, are both excellent demonstrations of the house style. Fragile is well endowed with mouthwatering, tangy apple fruit and is a beautifully balanced wine with a flinty, long finish. Princé is an extremely refined, elegant Cabernet Franc from the domaine's best vines which has a lovely purity to its fresh-picked, silky black fruits.

Quartier artisanal de l'églantier, 49610 Murs-Erigne
02 41 80 05 72

Domaine du Grapillon d'Or Gigondas, Southern Rhône

Cuvée Classique, Gigondas (red)

Domaine du Grapillon d'Or sits beneath the Dentelles de Montmirail, with most of the vineyards on clay-limestone soils around Gigondas. The estate is run today with considerable élan by Céline Chauvet, who succeeded her father, Bernard, a decade ago. Bernard still helps Céline in the tradition, however, as she goes about crafting her ripe, rich wines from Grenache (80%) and Syrah (20%). Her supple Cuvée Classique Gigondas marries supreme drinkability with relative affordability. Whereas Gigondas can often be meaty, almost chewy, this one stands out for its silky elegance.

84190 Gigondas
www.domainedugrapillondor.com

Domaine Jacques Puffeney Jura

Chardonnay, Arbois (white); Poulsard M, Arbois (red)

From his vineyards in Montigny-les-Arsures, one of the largest of the Arbois wine villages, Jacques Puffeney is crafting some of the finest wines in the region. He has an entirely uncompromising attitude to winemaking, according to what nature provides, comparing weather conditions in each vintage with those from decades past. His style is traditional, and he grows all five of the Jura grape varieties (Trousseau, Poulsard, Savagnin, Chardonnay, and Pinot Noir) in his 7.5ha (19 acres) of vineyards. Puffeney's Arbois Chardonnay is an intriguing Jura version of the grape that shows the minerality characteristic of the region, combined with ripe appley fruit and a dry, fresh, elegant palate. Puffeney's Poulsard M, aged in large foudres, is outstanding. Surprisingly powerful and lively, there is an earthy red-fruit character behind its very pale ruby colour.

Quartier Saint Laurent, 39600 Montigny-les-Arsures
03 84 66 10 89

Domaine de la Janasse

Châteauneuf-du-Pape, Southern Rhône

Domaine de la Janasse, Côtes du Rhône (red)

Domaine de la Janasse Côtes du Rhône is a consistent standout in the range of humbler wines produced by this Châteauneuf-du-Pape superstar. Perfumed, lavishly fruity, and sleek, it is typical of the Janasse style. Incredibly, Christophe Sabon was only 19 when his father passed him ownerhsip of the estate he had founded and developed. Sabon, now joined by his winemaking sister, Isabelle, has expanded the estate considerably since then, adding land in Côtes du Rhône and Côtes du Rhône-Villages, to 15ha (37 acres) across the Châteauneuf-du-Pape appellation.

27 chemin du Moulin, 84350 Courthézon
www.lajanasse.com

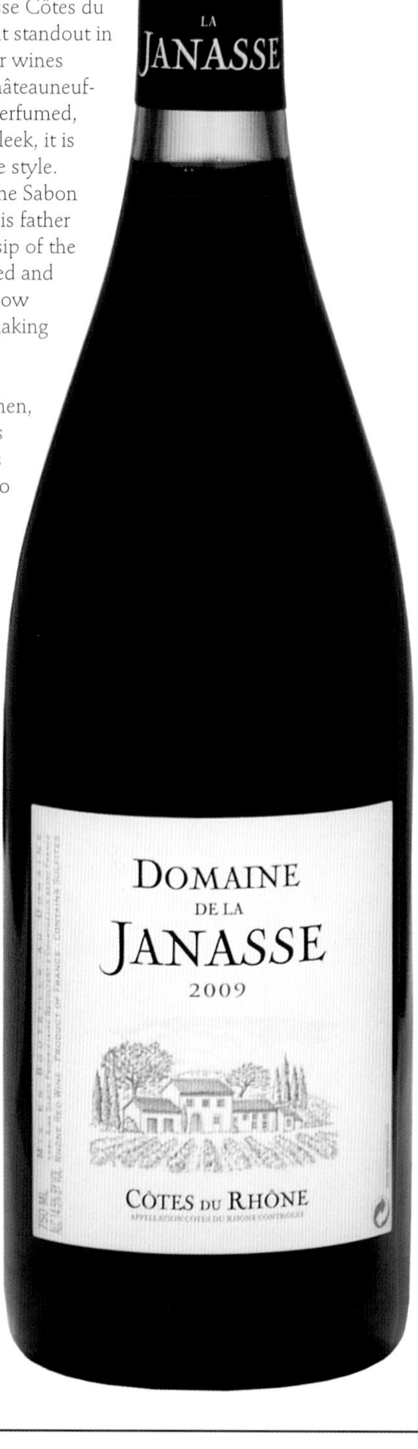

Domaine Jean-Luc Matha

Marcillac, Southwest France

Cuvée Pèirafi, Marcillac (red)

The older vines of the estate provide the Fer Servadou grapes for Domaine Jean-Luc Matha Cuvée Pèirafi, that really is excellent value for such a personality-driven bottle. No mistaking this for a branded wine, with its soft red fruits and touch of cinnamon spice. It has 20 months of gentle ageing in large casks made from old oak, a move designed to lend the wine texture, depth, and a softening effect, rather than overt oak flavours. The eponymous owner here trained to be a priest before ending up as a wine producer. Today, his thoughtful approach is applied to some 16ha (38 acres) of organically farmed vineyards, all of them planted to Fer Servadou, the local speciality. This estate is sometimes referred to as Domaine du Vieux Porche.

12330 Bruéjouls
www.matha-vigneron.fr

Domaine Jean-Luc Colombo Northern Rhône

Les Fées Brunes, Crozes-Hermitage (red)

Jean-Luc Colombo was regarded as a bit of an *enfant terrible* when he first came to the Northern Rhône as a young man in the 1980s. As a consultant, he was instrumental in bringing modern winemaking and viticultural techniques to this part of the Rhône, pioneering practices such as green harvesting, de-stemming of grape clusters, and the use of new oak barriques. He is still seen as the public face of modernist winemaking in the Rhône, and he still consults widely. However, he is no longer regarded as a divisive figure, and he makes a broad portfolio of négociant and domaine wines under his own label across the Rhône, including Châteauneuf-du-Pape and Tavel in the south, plus Cotes du Rhône, St-Joseph, St-Péray, Crozes-Hermitage, Hermitage, Condrieu, and four highly-esteemed cuvées from Cornas. In many vintages his Les Fées Brunes tastes more like an expensive Cornas than a relatively affordable Crozes-Hermitage, with impressive concentration and complex aromas and flavours.

La Croix des Marais, 26v600 La Roche-de-Glun
04 75 84 17 10

Domaine de Joÿ

Côtes de Gascogne, Southwest France
L'Etoile, Côtes de Gascogne (white)

The family roots of the owners of this delightfully named estate go back to Switzerland. Véronique and André Gessler and their sons, Olivier and Roland, are descended from Swiss families who moved to this part of Southwest France in the early 20th century. Their production is dominated by white grape varieties, with much of the 110ha (272 acres) being devoted to Bas-Armagnac and Floc de Gascogne aperitifs. The white wines they make use modern techniques, with low temperature fermentations in stainless steel aimed at retaining the aromatic fresh fruit. Underlining the effortlessly light and fresh flavours of Côtes de Gascogne white wines is Domaine de Joÿ's charming L'Étoile, where a blend of 50% Colombard and 25% Ugni Blanc is given a little fattening out with 25% of Gros Manseng.

32110 Panjas
www.domaine-joy.com

Domaine Laffont

Madiran, Southwest France
Cuvée Erigone, Madiran (red)

With its pleasantly complex nose, brooding dark fruits, and some lovely coffee and chocolate notes, Domaine Laffont's Cuvée Erigone uses fruit from old Tannat vines, where the yields are kept low, and the grapes are given a cold soaking to gently extract the fruit flavours. It is a wine that pretty much begs to be served alongside a hefty, rich meat stew or a vast slab of steak. Domaine Laffont was bought by the Belgian businessman Pierre Speyer in 1993. Speyer, who also owns and runs a business supplying equipment to the film industry, currently has 4ha (10 acres) of vineyards in Maumusson in the heart of the Madiran appellation, which he supplements with grapes bought in from another 3ha (7 acres) of vineyards. Speyer converted to organic production in 2005, and he is now well on the way towards converting to biodynamics at the estate.

32400 Maumusson
05 62 69 75 23

WHAT'S THAT GUNK IN THE BOTTLE?

Most beverages are so thoroughly pasteurized, homogenized, and filtered that nothing but liquid ever appears in the bottle. Wine is an exception, however. Small crystals sometimes form in white and red wines, and muddy sediment can agglomerate in some reds.

These do not look attractive, but neither one presents a health concern. In fact, both indicate that the wine has been made more naturally than most, and processed minimally.

The crystals are about the size of dry sea salt and you might see an amount the size of a teaspoon in the bottom of the bottle. These crystals are potassium tartrate, an innocent by-product of the natural tartaric acid in wine grapes. They are harmless and do not alter the taste of the wine. Try not to pour them into your glass, and avoid swallowing them. They will not harm you but their texture is quite unpleasant.

A finer-grained gunk known as sediment or lees affects red wines almost exclusively. It is most common in minimally filtered wines that have been saved for several years before opening. This sediment forms over time, making stripes down the sides of bottles if stored properly on their sides, or stains in the bottoms of bottles if stored standing up. A little sediment is a good sign; it indicates the wine is probably in good condition. Lots of sediment and cloudy wine indicates it may have spoiled.

Decanting is the solution to getting the clear wine off the sediment before drinking. It is a good idea to stand up an old bottle of red wine two days before you plan to drink it, to let the sediment fall to the bottom. (See page 148 for decanting advice).

Domaine Leon Barral Faugères, Languedoc

Domaine Leon Barral, Faugères Rouge (red)

Few people are more committed to the land and environmentally friendly practices than Didier Barral, grandson of the eponymous founder of this fine Languedoc estate. This is a man who is, frankly, obsessed with soil and manure – as is immediately apparent to any visitor to his 25ha (60 acres) of old vines at the estate in the hamlet of Lenthéric, close to Cabrerolles. Barral farms biodynamically, which means there are no chemicals or weed-killers. Cows are used to fertilize the soil, which is thoroughly ploughed, and biodiversity is encouraged: the vineyards are full of spiders, insects, birds, and plant life. The winemaking is equally natural with a minimal approach to intervention and the use of traditional methods such as an antique-style basket press. The fruit of this approach can be seen in the broad spectrum of flavours in the dry red wine of the estate's Faugères Rouge. With delicious notes of bramble, wild herbs, and mushroom, it is easy-going and easy to enjoy.

Lenthéric Faugères, 34480 Cabrerolles
www.domaineleonbarral.com

Domaine Marcel Deiss Alsace

Vendanges Tardives Pinot Blanc, Alsace (white)

Generally speaking, Domaine Marcel Deiss is not one of the cheapest producers you will find in Alsace or, for that matter, France. But the estate's Vendanges Tardives Pinot Blanc is a highly affordable introduction to their distinctive winemaking style. Marcel Deiss, grandson of the eponymous founder of the estate (and part of a family of winegrowers that have roots in Bergheim dating back to 1744), is at the forefront of biodynamic viticulture, insisting this is the only way their vineyards can fully express themselves in the wines. With some bottle age, this wine can develop a deep golden hue, the aroma becomes more subdued but the flavours – backed up by some sweetness – are forthright and intense. Honeyed and richer than many (the sweetness emphasizing this), this is a magnificent, affordable, Pinot Blanc. You can see why many wine merchants keep the wines of Deiss all for themselves.

68750 Bergheim
www.marceldeiss.com

Domaine du Mas Blanc Roussillon

Cosprons Levants, Collioure Rouge (red)

One of the very best – and most innovative – producers in Banyuls, Domaine du Mas Blanc has been owned by the same family since 1639. Its current lofty reputation is thanks in no small part to the work of Dr André Parcé, who did much to shape Banyuls' contemporary identity, reintroducing noble varieties, lobbying hard for the introduction of the Collioure appellation, and developing the term "rimage" (equivalent to vintage port) in the Banyuls appellation. Today it is run by Jean-Michel Parcé, who took over in 1976 and now works some 21ha (52 acres) of old vines on steep terraces to make his range of top Banyuls and Collioure wines. The Collioure Rouge Cosprons Levants is an intriguing dry red that offers immediately appealing notes of wild berry jam, dried herbs, and earth. Using fruit from the domaine's oldest vines, it is a blend of 60% Syrah, 30% Mourvèdre, and 10% Counoise.

66650 Banyuls-sur-Mer
www.domainedumasblanc.com

Domaine Michel & Stéphane Ogier

Northern Rhône

La Rosine Syrah, Vin de Pays des Collines Rhodaniennes (red); Viognier de Rosine, Vin de Pays des Collines Rhodaniennes (red)

Domaine Michel & Stéphane Ogier is a Rhône producer on the rise. It took on its current form relatively recently, when Michel Ogier decided to start bottling his Côte-Rôtie rather than selling it to négociants as had been the tradition at the family estate for many years. Today, the estate is run by Stéphane, the son of Michel and Hélène, who has added his own imprimatur to the operation, including a variety of winemaking innovations and expansion into other parts of the Rhône. Of particular relevance to this book are Ogier's forays into the production of Vins de Pays des Collines Rhodaniennes. The flavorsome but structured La Rosine Syrah from Ogier is a consistent over-achiever when it comes to value, all the more so given that this is a region where price is always an issue. The Viognier de Rosine, meanwhile, likewise offers great value, as well as being unusually fresh and focused, with subtle floral aromas and pleasantly persistent flavours.

3 chemin du Bac, 69420 Ampuis
04 74 56 10 75

Domaine de Montvac

Vacqueyras, Southern Rhône

Domaine de Montvac, Vacqueyras (red)

A distinctly feminine influence prevails at the 24ha (60acre) Domaine de Montvac. It has been passed down the female line, from mother to daughter, for four generations. The latest to take on the estate is Cécile Dusserre, who initially wanted to be a ballet dancer rather than a winemaker. Still, the wines she makes here have a certain elegant charm which calls to mind Dusserre's original ambition: they are remarkable in their poise and grace, positively dancing across the tongue, while retaining the trademark power of the Vacqueyras and Gigondas appellations where she works. Dusserre's gift for making hedonistic wines means that her entry-level red represents Vacqueyras at its most pleasurable, oozing the direct appeal of a summer berry compote.

84190 Vacqueyras
www.domaine-de-montvac.com

Domaine Oratoire St-Martin

Cairanne, Southern Rhône

Réserve des Seigneurs, Cairanne (red)

The Alary family is an established presence in Cairanne, having been involved in making wine here for more than 300 years. Run today by François and Frédéric Alary, Domaine Oratoire St-Martin, is one of the most consistently impressive estates in the Southern Rhône. There is an air of tradition about everything they do – as you would expect from a family with 10 generations of experience – but they have never rested on their laurels, introducing biodynamic practices on their 26ha (64 acre) estate (organic since 1993), as well as taking away heat-absorbing stones from the vineyards in a bid to slow down ripening and lend greater freshness to their wines. Like all the wines produced at the estate, the unoaked red Réserve des Seigneurs carries the savoury stamp of mineral-rich terroir within a poised, elegant frame.

Route de St-Roman, 84290 Cairanne
www.oratoiresaintmartin.fr

Domaine Paul Blanck Alsace

Pinot Noir, Alsace (red); Gewurztraminer, Alsace (white)

Sometimes you do have to wonder why they bother making red wines in Alsace; after all, the white wines are just so excellent and the generally lacklustre reds can be a little uninspiring. And then you discover a Pinot Noir with such an appealing streak of red berried fruit and pure drinkability that you see what they are striving for. Paul Blanck Pinot Noir is one such wine. Made by a top Alsace estate, it offers a little strawberry freshness, and a smoky edge adds to the whole. This is a light wine, well suited to a little chilling in the fridge before serving. The intriguing Gewurztraminer is an equally beguiling mix of nutmeg, cinnamon, and ginger, with a kick of black pepper, a dash of Turkish Delight, and a hint of sweetness.

32 grand-rue, 68240 Kientzheim
www.blanck-alsace.com

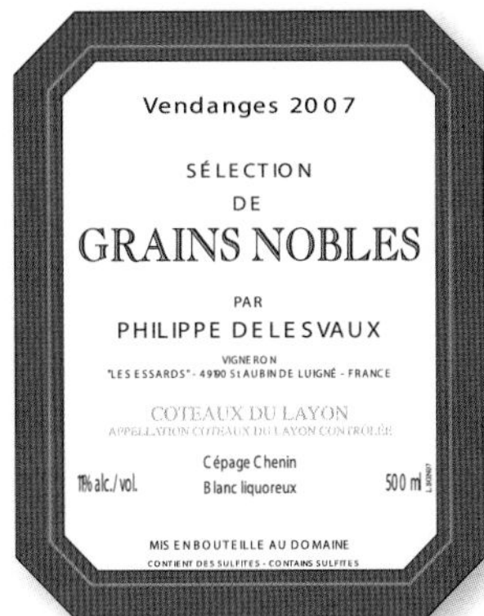

Domaine Philippe Delesvaux

Coteaux du Layon, Loire

Domaine Philippe Delesvaux, Coteaux du Layon (dessert)

Since 1983, when he founded his eponymous 10ha (25 acre) estate, the Paris-born Philippe Delesvaux has been a major force in rebuilding the reputation of the once-beleaguered Coteaux du Layon appellation in the Loire. The estate, which is now worked biodynamically, has enjoyed high praise almost from the beginning for its highly concentrated, rich, dessert wines that are nonetheless never lacking in balance or a certain lightness of touch. All the work here – including the rigorous pruning, debudding, bunch thinning, and leaf thinning that Delesvaux carries out to keep his yields low – is done by hand. Delesvaux's sweet Coteaux du Layon shows the benefits of all the attention to detail that comes with his hand-crafted approach. Delicately sweet with complex flavours and aromas of stone fruits and crème caramel, it has a wonderfully fresh, clean finish. It is also a very versatile food match, being the perfect partner for such choices as foie gras and a range of desserts and cheeses.

Les Essarts, La Haie Longue, 49190, St-Aubin-de-Luigné
02 41 78 18 71

Domaine Philippe Faury Condrieu, Northern Rhône

Domaine Philippe Faury, St-Joseph (red)

Graceful and elegant, Domaine Philippe Faury St-Joseph combines a core of red fruit with accent notes of smoked bacon and cracked pepper leading to a silky, soft finish. Made entirely from Syrah, and aged in a variety of different-sized oak barrels for 12 months, this wine is typical of this fine, family-owned and managed Northern Rhône estate. The domaine was developed significantly by Philippe Faury during his several years in charge, a period which saw the family's holdings swell from 2.5ha (6 acres) to its current 7ha (17 acres) of vines in St-Joseph, Condrieu, Côte-Rôtie, and the IGP Collines Rhodaniennes. Run since 2006 by Philippe's son, Lionel, the estate is based in the charming little hamlet of La Ribaudy, which sits on the slopes in the Condrieu appellation.

La Ribaudy, 42410 Chavanay
www.domaine-faury.fr

Domaine Philippe Gilbert

Menetou-Salon, Loire

Domaine Philippe Gilbert, Menetou-Salon (red and white)

Philippe Gilbert was a playwright before he returned to his family's wine estate in the Loire in 1998. In doing so he was following a family tradition of grape growing that dates back to 1768. Both Gilbert and his father studied in Burgundy, the home of Pinot Noir, and unusually for this appellation there is more Pinot Noir planted in the domaine than Sauvignon Blanc. Gilbert uses biodynamic practices in the vineyards, and his winemaker, Jean-Philippe Louis, is renowned for his gentle approach, always looking for the clearest terroir expression. The estate white is a flavoursome Sauvignon Blanc with blackcurrant bud and dried herb notes as well as riper white peach fruit. The estate red is a pretty Pinot Noir with crunchy red cherry and redcurrant flavours and classic Pinot savoury, earthy notes to the finish.

Les Faucards, 18510 Menetou-Salon
www.domainephilippegilbert.fr

Domaine Pieretti Cap Corse, Corsica

Vieilles Vignes, Coteaux du Cap Corse (red)

Domaine Pieretti is one of the best-known estates in Corsica and a reliable bet for quality drinking at a good price. The Coteaux du Cap Corse Vieilles Vignes is their top red blend (the entry level is also excellent), produced from a blend of old vine Grenache and Nielucciu. Good acidity gives the wine tension and there are just the right amount of tannins to help concentrate the intense black fruits. It is a wine with a real sense of place. Lina Venturi-Pieretti took up the reins from her father, Jean, in 1989 and the estate has since swelled from 3ha (7 acres) to 10ha (25 acres) of vineyards. These are planted at 100m (330ft) altitude in Santa Severa, right by the coast near the port of Luri in Cap Corse, with the winery, which was built in 1994, even closer to the sea.

Santa Severa, 20228 Luri
www.vinpieretti.com

Domaine de la Pigeade Beaumes-de-Venise, Southern Rhône

Domaine de la Pigeade, Muscat de Beaumes-de-Venise (dessert)

If you are looking for a treat to enhance a fruit dessert or blue cheese, consider this finely tuned, zesty Muscat de Beaumes-de-Venise made by Marina and Thierry Voute at Domaine de la Pigeade. Enticingly light-footed in its youth, it has exotic lychee and tangerine notes which intensify with age – so, will-power permitting, it may be worth cellaring some bottles for a few years. (The Voutes claim it ages well for up to two decades.) Tireless promoters of the Muscat de Beaumes-de-Venise appellation, they have devoted around three-quarters of their 42ha (104 acre) estate to the Muscat à Petits Grains variety used for production in one of France's most famous dessert wines.

Route de Caromb, 84190 Beaumes-de-Venise
www.lapigeade.fr

Domaine de la Rectorie Roussillon

L'Argile Vin de Pays de la Côte Vermeille Blanc (white)

The brothers Marc and Thierry Parcé inherited the old family vineyard – managed until 1969 by their grandmother, Theresa Parcé, and in the family for several generations before that – of Domaine de la Rectorie at the beginning of the 1980s. They produced their first wine in 1984, and they have gone on to build an enviable reputation for quality ever since. The brothers work some 27ha (67 acres) of vines, which are spread across more than 30 small plots, each planted at a different altitude, ranging from sea level right up to 400m (1300ft), and with different sun exposures. The brothers are careful to harvest and then vinify these plots separately, since each one has its own character. L'Argile Vin de Pays de la Côte Vermeille Blanc is a rich, dry white made from Grenache Gris (90%) with a little Grenache Blanc. Fermented and aged in oak barrels, it has chalky minerality, peach and honey notes, a tangy character, and just a hint of oak smoke for complexity.

65 rue de Puig del Mas, 66650 Banyuls-sur-Mer
www.la-rectorie.com

Domaine La Réméjeanne

Côtes du Rhône and Côtes du Rhône-Villages, Southern Rhône

Les Arbousiers, Côtes du Rhône (red and white)

While all the wines produced at Domaine La Réméjeanne showcase the Côtes du Rhône at its most accomplished, the Arbousiers duo reliably combines depth with charm. The white is mouthfilling without feeling heavy; the spicily complex red keeps well for five years or more. The highly regarded Rémy Klein has been pushing up the quality of his ambitious range of wines for the past 20 years, when he took over the family estate founded by his father, François, in the early 1960s on the family's return from Morocco. Klein now has 38ha (94 acres) of vineyards in the Northern Gard, and his wines rank alongside any being made in the Côtes du Rhône-Villages. The scenery here is somewhat wilder, with stronger winds, than down in the more sun-baked heartland of the Southern Rhône, resulting in wines with pronounced freshness and vibrancy. Klein himself is a lover of nature in the wild, and he has named his wines after different wild plants – arbutus (arbousiers), honeysuckle, juniper, and dog-rose.

Cadignac, 30200 Sabran
www.laremejeanne.com

Domaine des Remizières Northern Rhône

Domaine des Remizières, Crozes-Hermitage (red)

Domaine des Remizières Crozes-Hermitage is an exceptionally complex wine for the money. It features lovely floral scents that lead into soft, sweetly fruity flavours of red and black raspberries with a spicy edge. But then, exceptional wines are now par for the course at Domaine des Remizières. The estate has been in the hands of the same family for three generations, with Alphonse Desmeures, the original proprietor, passing it on to his son Philippe in 1977, and with Philippe now working with his daughter, Emilie. Philippe and Emilie have added more than 25ha (62 acres) to its vineyard holdings in the past few years so that it now stands at 30ha (74 acres). Today, the domaine's holdings are largely focused on Crozes-Hermitage (24ha/60 acres), with a little in St-Joseph and Hermitage. More importantly, quality has certainly kept pace with the rise in quantity. The wines are made in a modern style with plenty of new oak and ripe, rich flavours.

Route de Romans, 26600 Mercurol
www.domaineremizieres.com

Domaine Ricard Touraine, Loire

Le Petiot Sauvignon Blanc, Touraine (white)

Many of the main players of contemporary French wine were once grape growers who sold all their fruit to the local co-operative or négociants, but who now bottle their own wines. Domaine Ricard is one such case. Until Vincent Ricard founded his 17ha (42 acre) domaine in 1998, his family sold all the production to third parties. But, after working in Chinon (with Philippe Alliet) and Vouvray/Montlouis (with François Chidaine), Ricard became more ambitious and wanted to get hands-on. Situated near Saint Aignan sur Cher in Touraine, on the other side of the river Cher, he now makes a highly regarded range of wines, including reds from Cabernet Franc and Malbec (known in the Loire as Côt), as well as the occasional Chardonnay. But it is the estate's excellent Sauvignon Blanc that really dominates both his vineyards and his production, much of which is exported. The unoaked Le Petiot Sauvignon Blanc Touraine, produced from younger (20- to 30-year-old) vines, is as bright, cheeky, and fun as its label, with a hint of spicy bay leaf to its pert gooseberry and crunchy green apple fruit.

19 rue de la Bougonnetière, 41140 Thesee La Romaine
www.domainericard.com

CHENIN BLANC

In several parts of the world, Chenin Blanc is considered cheap and cheerful. But this is a great disservice to this wonderful white grape variety. In the relatively cool region of the Loire Valley, Chenin Blanc produces some great dry and sweet wines, with floral, fruity aromas reminiscent of Anjou pears or crisp apples, and floral accents.

Loire wines don't carry the name Chenin Blanc on their labels, but can be identified as such by the wine-growing districts they come from, including: Anjou (usually dry wines), Bonnezeaux, Coteaux du Layon, Montlouis, Quarts de Chaume, Saumur, Savennières, and Vouvray (often slightly sweet wines, or even very sweet dessert wines). Crémant de Loire is a sparkling version.

Think of dry Chenin Blanc as an interesting substitute for Sauvignon Blanc or Pinot Grigio/Gris, when you want to stretch your tastes into new, but not really foreign, territory. The Loire versions are rather light in alcohol, and since they have lively acidity, they make good pairings with light or creamy fish dishes, salads, chicken, and even pâté.

Chenin Blanc is a major grape variety in South Africa, also, where it has been grown since early colonial times and accounts for approximately 20% of vineyards. Sometimes referred to by the local name, Steen, it has enjoyed a revival among quality-oriented winemakers in the past couple of decades.

Chenin Blanc grapes have high levels of acidity.

Domaine Le Roc

Fronton, Southwest France

Le Classique, Fronton (red)

Redcurrant and white pepper notes are classic markers of the Négrette grape variety, which finds a home in the Fronton appellation near Toulouse in Southwest France. In Domaine Le Roc's Le Classique Fronton, those classic flavours are mixed with the darker, more structured flavours of Syrah and Cabernet Sauvignon. The wine is spicy, distinctive, and aromatic: no wonder some refer to it as the Pinot Noir of the Southwest. Domaine Le Roc is run by Frédéric Ribes, a practical, conventionally trained winemaker, who nonetheless likes to take a creative, artistic approach to his job – the labels and tanks feature floral motifs.

31620 Fronton
www.leroc-fronton.com

Domaine Le Roc des Anges Roussillon

Vieilles Vignes, Cotes du Roussillon Rouge (red)

Domaine Le Roc des Anges started its life in 2001, the project of Marjorie Gallet, whose first vintages drew on 10ha (25 acres) of vines (including a parcel of 100-year-old Carignan) near the village of Montner. Gallet was soon snapping up more parcels, until the vineyard reached its current dimensions, 25ha (62 acres), planted to, among others, low-yielding Carignan Noir, Grenache Noir, Grenache Gris, Maccabeu, and Carignan Blanc. Gallet makes her wines in an old cellar she has restored in the village, using concrete tanks to get as much fruit and terroir character as possible. The style comes through in the Vieilles Vignes, where old-vine Carignan, Grenache, and Syrah give complexity and length to this flavoursome, discreetly powerful wine with its fleshy, supple texture.

2 place de l'Aire, 66720 Montner
www.rocdesanges.com

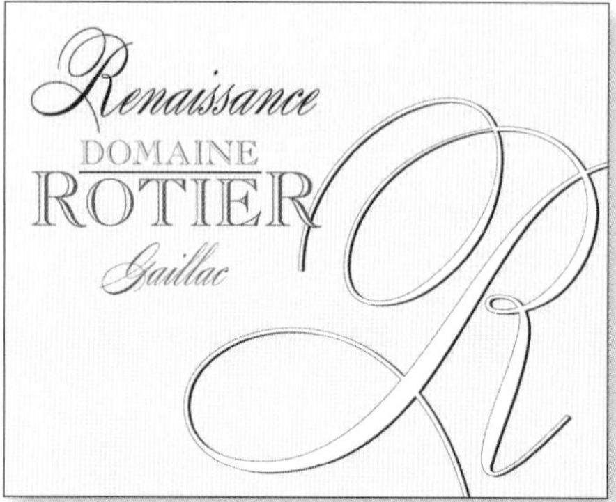

Domaine Rotier Gaillac, Southwest France

Renaissance Rouge, Gaillac (red)

Domaine Rotier Renaissance Rouge is a classic Gaillac blend of 30% Duras, 30% Braucol, and 40% Syrah, that spends one year in oak (just 15% of which is new). It usually needs a few years to open up, by which time you should be rewarded with a touch of liquorice that gives depth to the tight black fruits. This is just the kind of traditional but quality-conscious winemaking that the brothers-in-law Alain Rotier and Francis Marre have become known for. Long-term believers in sustainable viticulture, they have not used chemical fertilizers for more than 25 years, growing oats and barley between the rows of vines to encourage microbiological activity instead.

Petit Nareye, 81600 Cadalen
www.domaine-rotier.com

Domaine des Savarines Cahors, Southwest France

Domaine des Savarines, Cahors Rouge (red)

Domaine des Savarines Cahors Rouge is great value, supremely enjoyable, green (the wine is certified both organic and biodynamic), and very food-friendly. A good 20% of Merlot softens the Malbec grapes, and the tannins are soft and silky, but still earthy enough to feel French. The 4ha (10 acre) estate is owned by Eric Treuille, who also owns the Books for Cooks bookshop in London's Notting Hill. In a welcome change from many estates, Treuille likes to hold onto his wines until they are ready to drink – about five years after bottling.

Trespoux, 46090 Cahors
www.domainedessavarines.com

Domaine La Soumade Rasteau, Southern Rhône
Cuvée Tradition, Rasteau (red); Vin Doux Naturel Rasteau, Rouge (dessert)

La Soumade's Cuvée Tradition Rasteau is an elegant wine that is sumptuous but never jammy. There is elegance and subtlety, too, in the Vin Doux Naturel Rasteau Rouge. A luxuriously textured sweet red, wafting notes of loganberries and coffee, it is divine when served alongside some dark chocolate or desserts made from it. These wines are produced by a family that have strong ties to Rasteau, having grown peaches and grapes there for generations. Today, André Romero and his son Frédéric tend to some 28ha (69 acres), and while they make a little Châteauneuf-du-Pape and Gigondas too, it is with Rasteau that they are most commonly associated.

84110 Rasteau
04 90 46 11 26

Domaine Tariquet Côtes de Gascogne, Southwest France
Tariquet Classic, Vin de Pays de Côtes de Gascogne (white)

There is a wide range of wines from Domaine Tariquet, many of them excellent value for money, but for true easy-drinking, everyday wine that matches with a wide range of foods, the slightly floral, unoaked blend of Ugni Blanc-Colombard, Tariquet Classic takes some beating. It is unpretentious, light, and citrussy. Tariquet's Yves Grassa put the domaine on the map when he became the first to grow Chardonnay, Sauvignon Blanc, and Chenin Blanc in Armagnac country a quarter of a century ago, and his crisp, modern whites have since set the standard for this part of Southwest France.

32800 Eauze
www.tariquet.com

Domaine La Tour Vieille Banyuls, Collioure, Roussillon
Banyuls Vendanges (fortified)

Christine and Vincent Cantié's Domaine La Tour Vieille is a beautiful estate that sits on terraced hillsides reaching down towards the Mediterranean. The estate extends to 12ha (30 acres), which is divided into 12 different plots dotted around the Banyuls and Collioure appellations. These different plots, with their varied altitudes and variations in sun and wind exposure, contribute complexity to the finished wines, which include both table wines and fortified styles. A fine example of the latter is the Banyuls Vendanges. Very port-like, this decadent sweet wine has notes of dark cherry, red rose, mocha, caramel, and sea salt. It is well-textured with some bite and grip for balance.

12 route de Madeloc, 66190 Collioure
04 68 82 44 82

Domaine du Tunnel Northern Rhône
Roussanne, St-Péray (white); St-Joseph (red)

Domaine du Tunnel began its life in 1994, when the winemaking prodigy, Stéphane Robert, then aged just 24, started making wines from grapes sourced from leased vineyards. He was soon adding vineyards of his own, and in the intervening years he has added nearly 3.5ha (9 acres) in Cornas, 2.5ha (6 acres) in St-Joseph, and 2ha (5 acres) in St-Péray, most of which he owns. The domaine itself is found in St-Péray, and Robert is responsible for some of that appellation's best wines, such as his St-Péray Roussanne, which shows alluring scents recalling fresh flowers, toasted nuts, bread crust, and wild honey, followed by luscious flavours of white peach and quince. Robert's St-Joseph, by contrast, is generously flavoursome but still fresh and focused.

20 rue de la République, 07130 St-Péray
04 75 80 04 66

Domaine Yann Chave Northern Rhône
Domaine Yann Chave, Crozes-Hermitage (red)

It is hard to believe that Yann Chave is only just into his 40s, so great has his impact been since he began making wines in the 1990s. It seems equally incredible that this star of the Northern Rhône had once planned to go into banking and economics, before realizing he was not really cut out for the corporate world. Chave joined his father Bernard, who still works the vines, at the family estate instead, and he has since made it into one of the Rhône's most impressive rising stars. Chave now has some 15ha (37 acres) of vineyards in Crozes-Hermitage (mostly Syrah) and a little more than 1ha (2.4 acres) in Hermitage to play with, and his wines are always convincing, complex, and delicious. Pure, fresh aromas and flavours of red raspberries and black cherries are the driving forces in his exceptionally fine Crozes-Hermitage, for example. The wine also has some engagingly light peppery accents and very subtle oak.

26600 Mercurol
04 75 07 42 11

Domaines Paul Mas Languedoc

La Forge Varietal Wines (Syrah and Viognier) (white); Arrogant Frog (white)

The restless, dynamic Jean-Claude Mas has turned his family firm in the Hérault department into a strikingly consistent, large-scale producer. Mas has an avowedly New World approach, both in his winemaking and marketing, to the range of wines from across southern France. Head to his La Forge estate where he makes some excellent value Vins de Pays d'Oc. The soft leather whiff to the Syrah is particularly appealing, as is the apricot and lemon zest of the Viognier Forge Estate and Arrogant Frog.

Route de Villeveyrac, 34530 Montagnac
www.paulmas.com

Domaines Schlumberger Alsace

Riesling Grand Cru Saering, Alsace (white)

Domaines Schlumberger is the largest estate in Alsace, run today by two generations of the family – Alain Beydon-Schlumberger (sixth generation) and Séverine Schlumberger (seventh generation). It has some 148ha (366 acres) of vineyards, many of them planted on vertiginously steep slopes. The real delights in the Schlumberger range can be found in the wines that sit above its entry-point portfolio, and the Riesling Grand Cru Saering, from a prime Grand Cru vineyard, is one superb example. You would anticipate a little class and refinement from this vineyard, and this wine offers both. A wonderful palate, fresh, lively, clean, and crisp, silky with a little weight and a burst of intense, lime-drenched flavour on the finish.

100 rue Theodore Deck, 68501 Guebwiller
www.domaines-schlumberger.com

Ferraton Père & Fils Northern Rhône

La Malinière, Crozes-Hermitage (red)

Ferraton is a producer that is very much on the rise since the celebrated Rhône producer, Michel Chapoutier, a family friend of the founders, took charge. As is the Chapoutier way wherever he is involved, the vineyards are farmed biodynamically (and have been certified as such for more than 10 years), and the quality is rising across Ferraton's range of négociant and estate wines. The Crozes-Hermitage La Malinière is prime evidence of the Ferraton revival. Aged in oak barrels for 12 months, it is pure, pretty, and pleasing at every turn; a Syrah built for freshness and elegance, where red berry notes lead into a soft finish.

13 rue de la Sizeranne, 26600 Tain l'Hermitage
www.ferraton.fr

François Crochet Sancerre, Loire

François Crochet, Sancerre (white)

François Crochet's Sancerre is a fresh, precise example of modern Loire Valley Sauvignon Blanc. It is characterized by its vivid nettle and gooseberry aromas and flavours and a long, mouthwatering finish. François Crochet assumed control of his father's 10.5ha (26 acre) estate in 1998. He added a new cellar full of all the equipment required for modern winemaking, and his portfolio now covers a range of single-vineyard Sauvignon Blancs from his variety of different terroirs – silex, stony limestone, and chalky clay – plus some well-made, fruity, but elegant Pinot Noirs.

Marcigoué, 18300 Bué
02 48 54 21 77

François Lurton Languedoc

Fumées Blanches Sauvignon (white); Terra Sana Syrah, Vin de Pays d'Oc (red)

Although he has now separated from his brother, Jacques, François Lurton continues to make fresh, modern wines including a number in France. Crisp, zingy gooseberry abounds in the classic Sauvignon Blanc of Fumées Blanches: it is practically bursting with varietal flavours that come from a cool vinification to encourage the fruit. It is worth looking for the most recent vintage for freshness. The Terra Sana Syrah is a well-priced organic wine, full of clean fruit that delivers black spicy fruit flavours balanced by a fresh seam of acidity. It has reasonable alcohol levels too, at 13.5%.

Domaine de Poumeyrade, 33870 Vayres
www.francoislurton.com

Gérard Bertrand Languedoc

Gris-Blanc, Vins de Pays d'Oc (rosé)

Rugby player-turned-winemaker, Gérard Bertrand's well-priced Gris-Blanc rosé is light as a feather, but with candy-sweet undertones that make it easy to drink. You don't need to think too hard about it, which is exactly as it should be with a picnic-perfect summer wine. Bertrand is an important presence in today's Languedoc scene. He owns five properties himself, and collaborates with 40 growers and 10 co-operatives on other projects. He now sells upwards of 12 million bottles around the world each year, but he is never less than 100% commited to quality. Visitors to the area should make a beeline for his estate in La Clape, Château Hospitalet, where there is a hotel, restaurant, and wine shop.

Route de Narbonne plage, 11104 Narbonne
www.gerard-bertrand.com

E Guigal

Northern Rhône

E Guigal, Crozes-Hermitage (red)

Headed by the driven Marcel Guigal, E Guigal is among the most familiar names in French wine. It is one of the most important producers and négociants in the Northern Rhône (producing more than 40% of all the wine made in Côte-Rôtie and Condrieu), as well as being a significant player in the southern part of the region. The Crozes-Hermitage offers a delicious, relatively affordable introduction to the smoky, sexy, exotically-perfumed world of Northern Rhône Syrah. It is soft in texture but packed with complexity and character.

Château d'Ampuis,
69420 Ampuis
www.guigal.com

Hugel et Fils Alsace

Hugel Muscat Tradition, Alsace (white); Hugel Riesling Tradition, Alsace (white)

Hugel et Fils is a family-run business that has been flying the flag for the aromatic wines produced in this region with verve and panache for generations. It specializes in varietally true wines of clarity and precision, made from an estate that covers some 65ha (160 acres), making Hugel one of the largest landholders in Alsace. These are planted exclusively to the noble varieties Gewurztraminer, Riesling, Pinot Gris, and Pinot Noir, with some vines up to 70 years old. From the Tradition range try the Hugel Muscat Tradition or the Hugel Riesling Tradition. The Riesling offers an edge of maturity revealing that classic, distinctive, petrol-esque edge to the aroma and one that overlays a fresh palate with lashings of orange peel and lime juice backed up with a little weight and a stony edge. In contrast the Muscat offers grapey vibrancy of a mish-mash of white grapes, ginger, and all-spice with added lime and tropical fruit juice.

68340 Riquewihr
www.hugel.com

Jean-Louis Chave Selection Northern Rhône

Silène, Crozes-Hermitage (red)

Chave is not simply one of the Rhône's best producers, this estate is widely regarded as one of the handful of top estates in France. Certainly, it has long been synonymous with great Hermitage, and it produces some of the top wines from that appellation. Jean-Louis Chave recently took charge at this family estate, but his father, the highly regarded but unfailingly modest Gérard, is still very much involved in the business, even though he claims to have retired. As well as maintaining the quality of Chave's top wines, Jean-Louis has also expanded his eponymous négociant business – Jean-Louis Chave Selection – and it is here, rather than the famed estate wines from the family's 14ha (36 acre) vineyard holdings in Hermitage, that fans of the Chave signature can find wines that are priced more for everyday drinking. The Crozes-Hermitage Silène, for example, is a highly expressive, gutsy Syrah that shows smoky, spicy, and meaty accents on a core of rich, dark fruit. A serious wine in classic Northern Rhône style, it is built for pairing with serious food, such as rich red meat dishes.

37 ave St-Joseph, 07300 Mauves
04 75 08 24 63

Josmeyer Alsace

Pinot Gris Le Fromenteau, Alsace (white)

The Josmeyer estate has built its modern reputation on two core principles. The first of those is biodynamics, to which the estate is passionately committed. The second is a focus on making wines that can work well with food, which means much of the production here is of dry styles. As a way into this fine producer's house style, one bottle that is well worth sampling is the Josmeyer Pinot Gris Le Fromenteau, which is as smooth and as pure a take on Pinot Gris as you would wish for. A hands-on approach to winemaking reflects itself in the quality of all the Josmeyer range across the board, this Pinot Gris being no exception. Apples, quinces, and pears abound with an edge of minerality and something equating to a Riesling's distinctiveness on the finish.

68920 Wintzenheim
www.josmeyer.com

Kuentz-Bas Alsace
Pinot Gris Tradition, Alsace (white)

After resolving the financial troubles and family infighting that beset this venerable estate in recent years, Kuentz-Bas is finally producing wines worthy of its name once more, such as the delicious Kuentz-Bas Pinot Gris Tradition. The Pinot Gris grape is so food-friendly and yet it is frequently overlooked and under-appreciated. This Kuentz-Bas rendition offers a mouth-filling wine full of apple and pear flavours, as you would expect, but also with a tantalizing edge of coffee bean and a touch of spice.

14 route des Vins, 68420 Husseren-Les-Chateaux
www.kuentz-bas.fr

Le Clos de Caveau Vacqueyras, Southern Rhône
Fruits Sauvages, Vacqueyras (red)

Le Clos de Caveau is a distinctive estate: the vineyard is a single plot encircled by trees, high up in the Dentelles de Montmirail, and the owner is a clinical psychologist and psychoanalyst (Henri Bungener), who took over from his father Gérard, a Swiss parfumier, in 2005. The wines, organic for almost 30 years, are fresher than many others in Vacqueyras because the grapes are harvested earlier. Fruits Sauvages offers notes of kirsch, juicy allure, and a silky texture in an attractively light body.

Route de Montmirail, 84190 Vacqueyras
www.closdecaveau.com

Leon Beyer Alsace
Gewurztraminer, Alsace (white); Pinot Gris, Alsace (white)

Having made wine in Eguisheim since the late 16th century, the Beyer family is today applying all of its know-how to a range of fine clean, varietally true, well-balanced wines. The Leon Beyer Gewurztraminer is a case in point. Offering a little restraint on the exotic aromas, this bottle reveals a touch of Middle-Eastern mysticism with rose petals, tangerine, pineapple, and lychees in a dry style. Equally delicious is the rounded, highly drinkable Leon Beyer Pinot Gris, with its soft apple core.

Rue de la 1ère Armée, 68420 Eguisheim
www.leonbeyer.fr

Les Vins de Vienne Northern Rhône
Heluicum, Vins de Pays des Collines (red)

Three modern legends of the Northern Rhône – Pierre Gaillard, Yves Cuilleron, and François Villard – are the men behind the fascinating and original project, Les Vins de Vienne. The trio got together when they discovered some texts that suggested there had been vineyards in Seyssuel above Vienne in the 17th century. Inspired by this discovery, the trio decided that it would be worth reviving this lost tradition, and they planted some vineyards in the area in 1996, on schist slopes facing south in a secluded spot on the east of the Rhône River. The venture now produces a range of

FOOD & WINE ALSACE PINOT GRIS

It is hard to believe that a rich, honeyed, tangy, minerally Alsace Pinot Gris is related to often neutral, rather quaffable Italian Pinot Grigio. As it ripens under the plentiful Alsace sun, the grape acids soften and the resultant wines are rounder, softer, and creamier than those from Italy.

Alsace Pinot Gris has notes of lemon, toasted almonds, minerals, honey, and that unique Alsace yeasty tang. The wines are rich and range in style from bone-dry to decadently sweet. Late-harvest versions include the intense and often (but not always) dry Vendange Tardive, and the concentrated, botrytis-imbued Sélection de Grains Nobles. These wines pair beautifully with the local charcuterie, German-influenced pastries, stews, and desserts. Elegant, understated and not too fruity, the wines go well, too, with spicy Asian dishes.

Dry Pinot Gris is perfect for savoury tarts including onion, or cheese and bacon (quiche Lorraine), or a ham-and-mushroom crêpe. Lobster with lime butter or halibut with lemon confit would work nicely too. The slight amount of sugar in the off-dry and medium-sweet versions gives them versatility with spicy dishes – sugar cools the fire – and they are commonly paired with seared foie gras. A dry Vendange Tardive is lovely with Munster cheese, or pâté. With the sweetest wines, chefs love to serve luxurious and delicate desserts including apricot tart or passion fruit crêpes.

Quiche Lorraine is a great regional match for Alsace Pinot Gris.

wines, with three Syrahs – Sotanum, Heluicum (from more recent plantings), and Taburnum (a parcel selection) – at the core of their activities. Of these, the Heluicum is the best value. The young vines give the wine the dusky black cherry flavours and gently rich spices of Syrah, but it doesn't need the same ageing or decanting of Sotanum. Soft, gentle tannins make this a pleasurable choice.

42410 Chavanay
www.vinsdevienne.com

Mas Amiel Roussillon
Maury (dessert)

Have you ever wondered which wine you can serve with chocolate? Well, look no further: Mas Amiel Maury is just that wine. This well-priced sweet red has notes of dark chocolate, ginger cake, molasses, and dried banana, flavours that are only enhanced by a nibble of cocoa bean. It comes from an estate that has always had a high reputation, but which had been through some tough times until it was bought, in 1999, by Olivier Decelle, who was at the time the managing director of the Picard frozen food chain. Decelle has since quit his job to give his full attention to Mas Amiel, overseeing a revival of the 155ha (385 acre) estate, replanting many of the vines and employing a new winemaking team, including top consultant Stéphane Derenoncourt.

66460 Maury
www.masamiel.fr

Mas Champart St-Chinian, Languedoc
St-Chinian Rosé

Mas Champart St-Chinian Rosé is the perfect wine for those who love a great French rosé at an amazing price. It is fresh and gentle with notes of raspberry coulis, cream, savoury, thyme, and chalk. It is the work of Matthieu and Isabelle Champart, who arrived in the Languedoc in 1976. Since buying the estate, they have completely transformed it, growing the vineyard from 8ha (20 acres) to 16ha (40 acres), renovating the rundown house, and constructing a winery. The first vintage was 1988.

34360 St-Chinian
04 67 38 20 09

Mas de Libian Côtes du Rhône-Villages, Southern Rhône
Khayyam, Côtes du Rhône-Villages (red)

Glamorous Hélène Thibon has made a huge impression since taking over Mas de Libian, an old hunting estate in the Ardèche. Working biodynamically on vineyards which are covered with large stones as in Châteauneuf-du-Pape, Thibon has some 17ha (42 acres), from which she makes charming and highly drinkable wines. So seductive is the Libian flagship, Khayyam, that the bottle is half-empty before you reflect on its heady aromas, gorgeous berry flavours, and velvety length. Could there be a better signal of a wine's quality than that?

Quart Libian,
07700 St-Marcel d'Ardèche
06 61 41 45 32

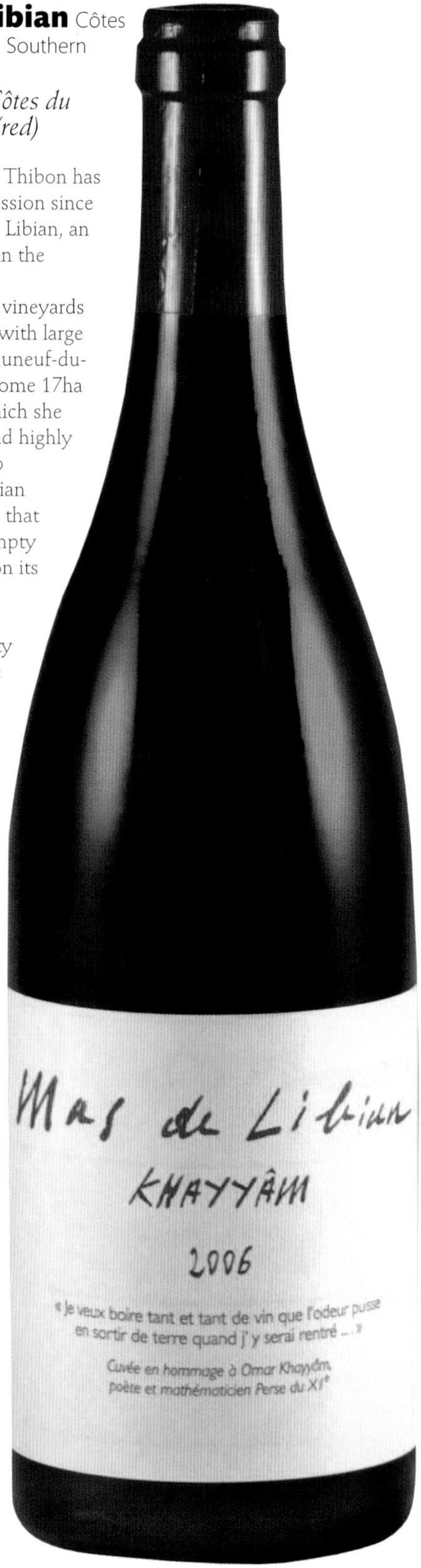

Paul Jaboulet Aîné Northern Rhône

Domaine de Thalabert, Crozes-Hermitage (red)

During the 20th century, Paul Jaboulet Aîné, which came into being in 1834, developed a fine reputation for its Rhône wines, doing much to establish the region on the global wine-drinking map. It held its pre-eminent position until the death of Gérard Jaboulet in 1997, after which quality seemed to take a pronounced dip for a time. Things have been moving rapidly in the right direction since the company was acquired by the Frey family (owners of La Lagune in Bordeaux and Champagne Billecart-Salmon), however. The Crozes-Hermitage Domaine de Thalabert is a delicious wine that has set off countless love affairs with Rhône Syrah around the world with its accents of smoked meat and saddle leather.

Les Jalets RN7, 26600 La Roche-de-Glun
www.jaboulet.com

Pierre-Jacques Druet Bourgueil, Chinon, Loire

Bourgueil Rosé, Les Cent Boisselées Bourgueil

Having studied with the celebrated winemaker and teacher Emile Peynaud at Bordeaux University, Pierre-Jacques Druet set out on his winemaking adventure in Bourgueil in 1980. The Peynaud influence was certainly apparent in Druet's work, with careful selection in the vineyard and with wines vinified separately by parcel. His house style mixes spice, deep fruit, and minerality. His food-friendly, dry Bourgueil Rosé has an attractive leafy edge to its delicate red cherry and crisp redcurrant fruit. Les Cent Boisselées Bourgueil, meanwhile, is a spicy, supple red from Cabernet Franc with succulent blackberry and blackcurrant fruit, which develops an attractive gamey quality with age.

Le Pied Fourrier, 37140 Benais
02 47 97 37 34

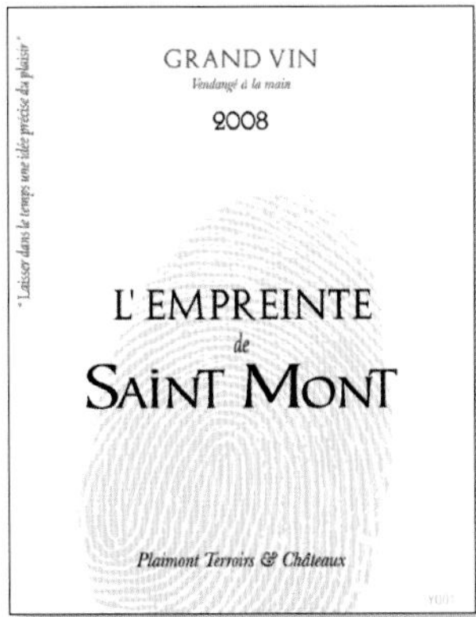

Producteurs Plaimont Côtes de St-Mont

L'Empreinte de Saint Mont Rouge (red)

One of France's most dynamic and quality-driven co-operatives, Producteurs Plaimont dominate the winemaking scene in Armagnac country. As one might expect from their location, the grower members of the co-op used to earn their crust supplying Armagnac producers, but as sales of the dark spirit fell away, they began making attractive white and red wines instead. L'Empreinte de Saint Mont Rouge is full of uncomplicated satisfaction. With toasty yet earthy raspberries, there is a real concentration to the Tannat, Pinenc, and Cabernet Sauvignon fruit, and plenty of liquorice on the finish.

32400 St-Mont
www.plaimont.com

Rimauresq Côtes de Provence, Provence

R de Rimauresq Rosé

Now under Scottish ownership (it was bought by the Wemyss family in 1988) Rimauresq is a fine old estate. The family have done much to reinvigorate its fortunes, adding a winery and renovating the vineyards (they now have 36ha/89 acres at Pignans on the north side of the Massif des Maures). In a consistent line-up, the top rosé cuvée, R de Rimauresq Rosé, just pips the rest, with its fragrant stone fruit notes of apricot and peach, and its honeysuckle aromas.

Route Notre Dame des Agnes, 83790 Pignans
www.rimauresq.fr

Skalli Languedoc

Chardonnay, Vins de Pays d'Oc (white)

Robert Skalli led the way when it came to improving the quality of wines in the south of France. He was one of the first to see the potential for varietal wines in the south, and, having established his cellar in Sète, he persuaded growers of the merits of so-called "improving" varieties such as Chardonnay, Sauvignon Blanc, Syrah, Merlot, and Cabernet Sauvignon. The company's influence is still strong in the region today, and they make a wide range of wines that manage the rare feat of quality and quantity. The Chardonnay Vins de Pays d'Oc is a good example of the Skalli style. It has some gourmet, toasty notes from a touch of oak, but there is still enough fresh citrus bite to keep a sense of lightness.

No visitor facilities
www.robertskalli.com

Yannick Pelletier St-Chinian, Languedoc

Yannick Pelletier, St-Chinian (red)

Yannick Pelletier's St-Chinian is unique in style. A dry, rich red, it offers flavours of blackberry, barnyard, lavender, and smoke. It is rather chewy on its own, but softens beautifully with rich meat dishes. Pelletier did not even get started at his estate in the north of the St-Chinian appellation until 2004, but his wines are already highly regarded. He farms some 10ha (24 acres) of vines divided into several parcels and soil types, with the main grape varieties being Syrah, Grenache, Carignan, Cinsault, and Mourvèdre.

52400 Coiffy le Haut
03 25 90 21 12

Italy

As you would expect from a country that ranges from the cool, Alpine climate of the Alto-Adige near Austria to the sun-baked warmth of Sicily, and all climatic points in between, Italy's wine scene is hugely diverse. It has a vast source of indigenous grape varieties to draw upon, and hundreds of different appellations. For reds, Italy is world-famous for two great grape varieties: haunting Nebbiolo from Piedmont in the Northwest, and cherry-and-leather-flavoured Sangiovese from Tuscany. Northeast Italy offers distinctive reds from part-dried grapes in Valpolicella, while the south has a range of rich reds such as Nero d'Avola and Aglianico. For whites, varieties such as Cortese, Arneis, and Verdicchio are all fine alternatives to the ubiquitous, crisp quaffable Pinot Grigio, while Prosecco makes for a fine, light fizz: perfect for an aperitif.

Abbazia di Novacella Südtirol/Alto Adige/Eisacktaler, Northeast Italy
Müller-Thurgau (white)

With a history that can be traced back to 1142, the Abbazia di Novacella is a strikingly beautiful winery and working monastery in the foothills of the Alps. Along with the monks, the mix of medieval and renaissance buildings houses an operation whose specialities include aromatic white grape varieties such as Gewürztraminer, Sylvaner, Kerner – and a delicious Müller-Thurgau. A lean, mineral-driven wine, the Müller-Thurgau exemplifies the Austro-Germanic wine culture in upper Alto Adige, the northern limit of Italian wine production. Made from grapes grown on steeply terraced vineyards, it melds appealing citrus flavour to a graphite frame.

Via Abbazia 1, 39100 Varna
www.kloster-neustift.it

Accademia dei Racemi Puglia, Southern Italy
Puglia Rosso IGT Anarkos (red)

Accademia dei Racemi is one of Southern Italy's most dynamic wineries, producing a huge variety of wines and styles. It is the project of Gregory Perrucci, a businessman with a passionate interest in indigenous Puglian varieties, and with holdings of almost 200ha (500 acres) of vineyards. Not everything Perrucci grows is native: the estate has some Chardonnay planted alongside the sizeable area devoted to Sussumaniello and Ottavianello. The authentic Puglia Rosso Anarkos is a lusty, generously proportioned red centred by a juicy core of dark fruit that finishes on a bright note with lasting flavours of blackberry.

Via Santo Stasi I – ZI, 74024 Manduria
www.accademiadeiracemi.it

Adriano Adami Valdobbiadene, Northeast Italy
Prosecco di Valdobbiadene Bosco di Gica (sparkling)

Franco Adami is a producer aiming to prove that Prosecco can be made with artisan-levels of care and attention. He does so with considerable panache, producing wines of grace and style that belie this sparkling wine's mass-market reputation. A consistent theme runs throughout the wines produced here: vivid fruit with incisive but fresh acidity. That style is very much on show in the Bosco di Gica. An elegant, serious take on Prosecco, with fresh apple flavours and floral notes, this easily qualifies as a go-to bottle.

Via Rovede 27, 31020 Colbertaldo di Vidor
www.adamispumanti.it

Alois Lageder Alto Adige, Northeast Italy
Pinot Bianco Dolomiti (white)

Alois Lageder's Pinot Bianco packs a lot of tangy, bright citrus flavour onto its chalky frame; the minerality grows more pronounced with air. It is well balanced, too, with good length. But then, these are all characteristic of Lageder's winery, which is located in a sunny spot towards the south of the Adige Valley. Lageder cares deeply about the local environment and uses organic and biodynamic practices.

Vicolo dei Conti 9, 39040 Magrè
www.aloislageder.eu

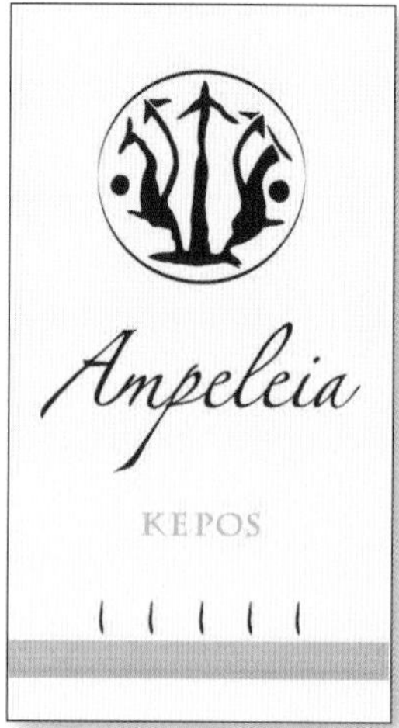

Ampeleia Maremma, Tuscany
Kepos IGT Maremma (red)

The thinking behind the ambitious Ampeleia estate is rather different to that of many of its neighbours in the burgeoning Maremma wine scene. Founded by Elisabetta Foradori, Giovanni Podini, and Thomas Widmann in southern Tuscany near Grosseto in 2002, this relatively young operation has chosen not to look to Bordeaux, but to the Mediterranean basin for inspiration.The deliciously different and affordable Kepos is a fragrant, vibrant example of what Mediterranean grape varieties can do in the region. A blend of Grenache, Mourvèdre, Carignan, Alicante, and Marselan, it is a spicy, rich, and unconventional departure from the norms of coastal Tuscany.

Località Meleta, 58036 Roccastrada
www.ampeleia.it

Anna Maria Abbona Dogliani, Northwest Italy
Dolcetto di Dogliani Sori dij But (red)

From a hillside parcel of Dolcetto vines in Dogliani, Anna Maria Abbona's Dolcetto di Dogliani Sori dij But shows that Dolcetto can be more than easy-drinking. Balancing its dark concentration and rich fruit flavours with a lively, focused acidity, it is one of the best of the new breed of more serious Dolcettos emerging from Dogliani. The story behind the wine is rather typical for the area. Anna Maria Abbona and her husband, the current proprietors, left their careers in the city behind to assume control of the family business started by her grandfather, Giuseppe, as a grape-growing concern in the 1930s. Their hand was forced in 1989, when Anna's father, who had been running the vineyards as a side-project from his full-time job in industry, decided to tear out the vines. The couple came back to rescue the family winery, and, using the old vines planted by her grandfather, have helped to raise the reputation of Dolcetto, with a range of powerful, concentrated wines.

Frazione Moncucco 21, 12060 Farigliano
www.amabbona.com

Antonelli San Marco Umbria, Central Italy
Montefalco Rosso (red); Grechetto dei Colli Martani (white)

Filippo Antonelli's Montefalco Rosso is a plush, refined expression of Sangiovese and Sagrantino, that balances dark, chewy tannins with a lasting high-toned cherry flavour. It is the kind of wine that is perfect for decanting in readiness for a grilled steak, and the kind of wine that Antonelli delivers with seeming ease. But then, wine is in Antonelli's blood. His family has been growing vines in the hills of Montefalco since 1881, when Francesco Antonelli bought the 160ha (395 acre) estate in the centre of the current DOCG. As well as the excellent Sagrantino that dominates production here, there is also a great white from the Grechetto grape variety.

Località San Marco 60, 06036 Montefalco
www.antonellisanmarco.it

Apollonio Puglia, Southern Italy
Rocca dei Mori Salice Salentino (red)

The Apollonio brothers, Massimiliano and Marcello, make a wide range of intriguing wines from a variety of DOCs. With a long history of grape growing, the family firm began bottling its wines in 1975, since when they have earned a deserved reputation for value as well as quality. Nowhere is that more true than in their Rocca dei Mori range of wines, of which the Salice Salentino is a particular highlight. Using grapes sourced from growers under strict instructions from the Apollonio brothers, this is a heady and stylish take on Salice Salentino, combining the dark fruit character of Negroamaro with notes of liquorice and spice.

Via San Pietro in Lama 7, 730470 Monteroni di Lecce
www.apolloniovini.it

Argiolas Sardinia
Cannonau di Sardegna Costera (red)

Like a ripe strawberry covered in damp earth, the hearty red Cannonau di Sardegna Costera is for many their introduction to Sardinian wine. Bright acidity gives it focus, and it is just the ticket for sausage pizza. The wine is one of the flagships of an operation begun by Antonio Argiolas, and since taken on by his children and grandchildren, who have between them turned it into one of Sardinia's most important, and biggest, wineries. The family now has more than 250ha (618 acres) of vineyards, all planted exclusively to local varieties, with most at altitudes above 350m (1,150ft).

Via Roma 56, 09040 Serdiana
www.argiolas.it

FOOD & WINE TUSCAN REDS

The red wines of Tuscany are the quintessential expressions of Sangiovese. They are slightly earthy, often bitter, and always zesty. Their high natural acidity brings balance and gives the wines the ability to pair easily with both traditional Tuscan and contemporary international dishes.

For Chianti, the lightest of Tuscan reds, the classic pairing is chicken liver pâté piled on unsalted crostini, the gamey component of the dish mirroring the earth in the wine, and the lemony acidity of the wine cleansing the palate. Playing on the tomato notes, Chianti is easily paired with such dishes as *pappa al pomodoro* (tomato-bread soup with basil and olive oil) or lighter pasta dishes such as *pici pomodoro* (Tuscan-style noodles with cherry tomatoes and ricotta cheese).

Light- or medium-bodied Chianti Classico or slightly richer Chianti Classico Riserva is traditionally paired with fish dishes such as *pesce al ragù Toscano* (pan-roasted white fish with butter beans, asparagus, and smoked bacon), *galleto alla brace* (baby chicken with bitter greens and truffle vinaigrette), or rich pasta dishes such as pappardelle with wild boar ragù. The powerful, oaky Brunello di Montalcino and the Cabernet-based Super Tuscans fit well with steak and with rich dishes such as *osso bucco* (slow-braised veal shank) or *carre d'agnello* (grilled rack of lamb).

Brunello's tannins work well with the fat in grilled rack of lamb.

Avide Sicily
Cerasuolo di Vittoria (red)

Avide's wonderfully lithe and gentle Cerasuolo di Vittoria combines floral and red-fruit aromas with a juicy palate of rich strawberry flavour. The brightness and supple nature of the wine makes it a great alternative to the similarly styled cru Beaujolais from France. It seems hard to believe that the winery behind such a well-executed wine started out as little more than a hobby. But that is exactly how the Demonstene family, a Sicilian legal dynasty, got involved in producing wine in the 19th century. Starting with no more than a handful of vines, they made a little wine for themselves each year. Quality steadily improved, and production rose, until Avide had become one of the most significant producers in the Cerasuolo di Vittoria DOCG. Today they produce some of the finest wines on the island, with many being great value.

Corso Italia 131, 97100 Ragusa
www.avide.it

Badia a Coltibuono Chianti Classico, Tuscany
Coltibuono Cetamura Chianti (red)

The architecture of the High Renaissance meets the medieval at this beautiful estate. It has been owned since 1987 by Tuscan grandees, the Antinori family, who own several estates in Tuscany and other regions of Italy, and have interests in such far-flung places as Washington State and New Zealand. The complex was once a monastery, but is now home to one of Chianti Classico's top estates. There are around 50ha (123 acres) of vineyards here, all given over to the local Sangiovese. The grapes for the Coltibuono Cetamura Chianti, however, are sourced from contracted growers in the surrounding area. But the wine is very much in keeping with the house style. Fermented in stainless steel, it is a blend of Sangiovese and Canaiolo. It is a bright and fresh Chianti, with juicy cherry and lasting mint scents.

No visitor facilities
www.coltibuono.com

Bellavista Franciacorta, Northwest Italy
NV: Franciacorta Brut (sparkling)

Situated between Brescia and Bergamo in the very heart of Franciacorta, Italy's best region for champagne-method (known here as "*metodo classico*") sparkling wine, Bellavista is the work of the driven Vittorio Moretti. The estate was built from scratch starting in 1977, when Moretti snapped up the first parcels of land. Today it has reached an impressive 190ha (470 acres), and makes a range of fine sparkling wines. The Franciacorta Brut is the company's entry point, and it offers a great introduction to the complexity, depth of flavour, and refinement of the best Franciacorta wines. A refreshing, light-bodied wine made with the second, fizz-giving fermentation taking place in bottle, this well-priced wine is a consistently good expression of the Bellavista house style.

Via Bellavista 5, 25030 Erbusco
www.bellavistawine.com

Benanti Sicily
Rosso di Verzella (red)

Benanti's lively Rosso di Verzella red is based on the local Nerello Mascalese grape, which has become one of the trendiest names to drop in wine circles in recent years. In this example, it is framed by elegant tannins with lasting red apple and cherry fruit. Its freshness is very much a function of the intriguing micro-climate on the slopes of Mount Etna, where the vineyards for the wine are found. The climate here has more in common with the Alps than the Mediterranean, and Benanti's three centuries of experience have clearly taught them how to take advantage of it.

Via Garibaldi 475,
95029 Viagrande
www.vinicolabenanti.it

Bisson Liguria, Northwest Italy
Vermentino Vignaerta (white)

For a project that started its life as a wine shop, Bisson has come a long way. Pierluigi Lugano, the man behind Bisson, opened his shop in Chivari on the Ligurian coast in 1978. He started dabbling in bulk wine, followed by grapes soon after, before setting up a full-blown winery. Lugano is a believer in such traditional white varieties as Pigato, Bianchetta Genovese, and Vermentino. The Vignaerta shows what the last is capable of in the right hands. A hint of bitter almond adds complexity to the citrus flavours in a refreshing coastal white that shows still more mineral character once it is opened and has come into contact with air.

Corso Gianelli 28, 16043 Chiavari
www.bissonvini.com

Boroli Barolo, Northwest Italy
Dolcetto d'Alba Madonna di Como (red)

Dense with ripe blueberry and blackberry flavours, Boroli's Dolcetto d'Alba Madonna di Como is an aromatic and fresh red wine, with lasting violet scents and gentle, gripping tannin. It is a wine that has won many friends for a winery that only arrived on the scene in the 1990s, but which has consistently provided wines that offer more flavour than their prices might suggest. Initially run by Silavano and Elena Boroli, Boroli is now headed up by the couple's son, Achille, who has carried on his parents' excellent work with his own stylish approach.

Frazione Madonna di Como 34, 12051 Alba
www.boroli.it

Broglia Gavi, Northwest Italy
Gavi di Gavi La Meirana (white)

One of the Gavi DOCG's most consistent producers, Broglia came into being in 1972, when Piero Broglia rented his father's 73ha (180 acre) farm and vineyard, La Meirana. The aim (successfully achieved) at Broglia is to make modern wines that marry the freshness of clean, bright fruit with some texture and weight in the mouth, and the consultant winemaker, Donato Lanati, has clearly helped in that regard. The basic Gavi di Gavi La Meirana is clean and focused, with refreshing lime and floral notes. It is a textbook modern Gavi with enough mouthfeel and weight to match most seafood, including the many local specialities.

Località Lomellina 22, 15066 Gavi
www.broglia.eu

Candido Puglia, Southern Italy
Salice Salentino Riserva (red)

Candido's savoury, earthy Salice Salentino Riserva has been a flagship not just for this winery, but for the entire DOC for many years now. It is easy to understand why: it is a wine that is brimful of authentic Puglian flavours. Combining dried cherry and plum with umami-edged tannin, it feels focused and lean, a good match for braised duck legs. Production of the Riserva accounts for a great deal of Alessandro and Giacomo Candido's 2 million-bottle annual output, which is sourced from their 140ha (346 acres) of vineyards. But this is a winery with a reputation for excelling at producing large quantities of wine of consistently good quality across its range. In terms of grape varieties, the local Negroamaro is by far the most significant at the estate, although the Candidos also use small amounts of Cabernet Sauvignon.

Via Armando Diaz 46, 72025 San Donaci
www.candidowines.it

Cantina Gallura Sardinia
Vermentino di Gallura (white)

Inviting and warm, with subtle notes of bitter almond and anise to add complexity to the citrus flavours, Cantina Gallura's Vermentino di Gallura is an exceptional white wine that was just made to be served with grilled fish. It is one of a number of highly impressive bottlings produced from the Vermentino grape variety by this important co-operative, located in the island of Sardinia's only DOCG, Vermentino di Gallura. The co-op began its life in 1956, and now has a total of 160 members who between them cover 325ha (800 acres) of vineyards high above the sea on Sardinia's northern coast. It has helped to lead the island's vinous culture away from high yealds and high volumes towards quality winemaking.

Via Val di Cossu 9, 07029 Tempio Pausania
www.cantinagallura.com

Cantina del Locorotondo Puglia, Southern Italy
Primitivo di Manduria Terre di Don Peppe (red)

With a history stretching back to 1930, Cantina del Locorotondo is one of Italy's most prosperous co-operative wineries. Its power has proved so great, in fact, that it has even managed to lobby successfully for its own DOC, Locorotondo, for wines produced from the local white grape variety, Verdeca. The Cantina's members now have more than 1,000ha (2,500 acres) of vineyards between them, which provide fruit for a whopping 3.5 million bottles a year and a similarly hefty 30 different labels. Among the many of its bottles worth looking out for is the powerful Primitivo di Manduria

Terre di Don Peppe. This is a very well-structured Primitivo, which has plenty of powerful, savoury tannic muscle to support the ripe plum fruit flavours. It is the kind of big, bold wine that marries well with full-flavoured foods such as meaty stews and grilled or barbecued meats.

Via Madonna della Catena 99, 70010 Locorotondo
www.locorotondodoc.com

Cantina del Pino Barbaresco, Northwest Italy
Barbera d'Alba (red)

Renato Vacca's family have lived in Barbaresco for several generations. But Cantina del Pino, Vacca's small-scale winery, is, in fact, a relatively new arrival on the area's winemaking scene. Vacca has the considerable headstart of owning several vineyards clustered in and around the top cru of Ovello, which makes for some consistently excellent Barbaresco. But for a more affordable idea of what Cantina del Pino is all about, Vacca's Barbera d'Alba is an excellent alternative. There's a higher-toned edge to the earthy red cherry fruit in this vibrant, fleshy red. It feels refreshing and lean, a great match for braised pork.

Via Ovello 31, 12050 Barbaresco
www.cantinadelpino.com

Cantina Terlan Alto Adige, Northeast Italy
Pinot Bianco Classico (white)

There is considerable depth and focus to the seemingly humble white wine of Cantina Terlano's Pinot Bianco Classico. Well-structured and energetic, it balances green melon notes with a savoury minerality. It is emphatic, attractively priced proof, that Cantina Terlano is one of the classiest co-operative wineries around. Formed in 1893 in the foothills of the Alps, Cantina Terlano is a formidably well-organized operation. It has more than 100 growers on its books, and they provide fruit for a wide range of the region's white and red styles, including some life-affirmingly vivid expressions of grape varieties such as Gewürztraminer, Sauvignon Blanc, and, of course, Pinot Bianco.

Via Silberleiten 7, 39018 Terlano
www.kellerei-terlan.com

Cantina Tramin
Südtirol/Alto Adige, Northeast Italy
Gewürztraminer Classic (white)

Along with Cantina Terlan, Cantina Tramin is arguably the best co-operative winery in the far northeastern region of Alto Adige. It was founded in 1898, and the vineyards of its 290 member-growers now stretch across the villages of Tramin, Neumarkt, Montan, and Auer. Gewürztraminer is the winery's calling card, a grape variety that has taken on a whole new pitch of complexity in the hands of Cantina's winemaker (since 1992), Willi Stürz. The Classic is a touchstone for Gewürztraminer in Alto Adige, a golden wine that combines heady aromas of ginger and pear and bright acidity, resulting in a rich yet brisk mouthful.

Strada del Vino 144, 39040 Termeno
www.tramin-wine.it

Cantine de Falco Puglia, Southern Italy
Salice Salentino Salore (red)

With its headquarters and winery located just outside the beautiful baroque city of Lecce, this well-respected, very consistent producer has been a great source of good-value, typically Puglian wines since 1960. Currently under the leadership of Salvatore de Falco, it has 25ha (62 acres) of vineyards, with production averaging 200,000 bottles each year. The range is wide, with Primitivo a speciality, and it includes well-made wines from the Squinzano DOC. The best-value selection, however, is the Salice Salentino Salore. This is very much a modern take on Salice Salentino. It has been aged in small oak barrels, and this both emphasizes the wine's inherently rich fruit and lends it a plush texture. All told, it is a bargain red for simple meat dishes such as grilled steak, barbecued lamb chops, or meaty, herby sausages.

Via Milano 25, 73051 Novoli
www.cantinedefalco.it

Cantine Giorgio Lungarotti Umbria, Central Italy
Rosso di Torgiano Rubesco (red)

Cantine Giorgio Lungarotti is one of Italy's largest producers, with a huge production of nearly 3 million bottles a year, and vineyard holdings of some 300ha (750 acres). It completely dominates the Torgiano Rosso Riserva DOCG with which it is intimately associated – indeed there is only one other, much smaller, producer making wines in the appellation. Though it produces many other well-regarded wines, Lungarotti's most consistently good-value bottling is the wine that first put it on the map: the Rosso di Torgiano Rubesco blend of Sangiovese and Canaiolo. Today this iconic wine is a juicy, brightly flavoured Central Italian red that goes well with a variety of meaty pasta sauces.

Via Mario Angeloni 16, 06089 Torgiano
www.lungarotti.it

Cantine Gran Furor Divina Costiera di Marisa Cuomo Campania, Southern Italy
Ravello Bianco (white)

Marisa Cuomo's Ravello Bianco is a captivating blend of the Falanghina and Biancolella grape varieties that shows what is possible in the volcanic soils of the Amalfi Coast: vibrant aromas, lasting fruit, and great minerality. It is produced by Cuomo and her husband Andrea Ferraioli in a quite breathtaking vineyard perched some 500 metres above the beach, and planted over a series of narrow terraces that cling to the rocks on what at first glance looks to be an inaccessible cliff face. Given that the vines grown here produce vanishingly small yields, and that the grape varieties used are unfamiliar to many, it is in many ways a wonder that the wine is produced at all. The couple's difficulties have not gone unnoticed, however. Their hard work was rewarded a few years ago when the Italian government acknowledged the region's increasing quality, and granted DOC status to the Costa d'Amalfi.

Via GB Lama 16/18, 84010 Furore
www.granfuror.it

Casa Emma Chianti Classico, Tuscany
Chianti Classico (red)

Casa Emma takes its intriguing name from Emma Bizzarri, the Florentine aristocrat who sold this 20ha (50 acre) estate near Castellina to the Bucalossi family in the early 1970s. Today, Casa Emma, under the guiding hand of winemaker Carlo Ferrini, does a good job of balancing the old and the new, using traditional grape varieties, but ageing them in French barriques. Among the many highlights here is the firm and earthy Chianti Classico, which combines ripe strawberry and cherry notes with gentle, savoury tannin resulting in a wine that feels polished and refined.

SP di Castellina in Chianti 3, San Donato in Poggio, 50021 Barberino Val d'Elsa
www.casaemma.com

Casale del Giglio Lazio, Central Italy
Lazio Bianco Satrico (white)

Casale del Giglio's Lazio Bianco Satrico is typical of this forward-looking winery's approach. It takes some familiar international grape varieties – in this case Chardonnay and Sauvignon Blanc –

and blends them, in equal parts, with the more traditional Trebbiano. It makes for a zesty white that combines citrus flavours and floral aromas. It is an ideal partner for shellfish, but it is not the kind of wine that appeals to purists. Not that Antonio Santarelli, the man behind Casale del Giglio, will be too concerned by that. Santarelli – who took over from his father, Dr Bernadino Santarelli, who founded the estate in 1969 – has been researching the potential of international varieties in Lazio for more than 25 years. And he is happy to remind his detractors that, far from being a place with a long viticultural history, the land was formerly nothing more than a swamp.

Strada Cisterna-Nettuno Km 13, 04100 Le Ferriere
www.casaledelgiglio.it

Cascina Morassino Barbaresco, Northwest Italy
Dolcetto d'Alba (red)

Violet scents lift the fresh blackberry flavours in Cascina Morassino's fruit-forward, full-bodied Dolcetto. It is substantial and rich but not at all heavy, a perfect wine for lasagne, in fact. It comes from a talented young winemaker, Robert Bianco, who is responsible for some of the finest Dolcettos currently on the market. The heart of the Cascina Morassino operation is in Barbaresco, however, where Bianco has some 3.5ha (9 acres) of vineyards in the top cru of Ovello. The operation is the definition of small-scale, and the work is kept in the family, with Bianco sharing the work with his father, Mauro, and all tasks being carried out by hand.

Strada Da Bernino 10, 12050 Barbaresco
0173 635149

Castel de Paolis Lazio, Central Italy
Frascati Superiore (white)

Frascati does not have the best of reputations outside its home region. The staple of many an indifferent trattoria wine list, it has been devalued over the years by the insipid, mass-produced wines that tend to make it overseas. Castel de Paolis is very much not to be counted in this company, however. Owner Giulio Santarelli, whose family took over the estate in the 1960s, has overseen a complete renovation of every aspect of the estate, which now has 13ha (32 acres) of vineyards, and is now among the upper tier of Italian producers. The Frascati Superiore is unusually deep for Frascati, combining ripe melon and pear flavours with a saline mineral aspect. It is lovely with grilled fish and lemon.

Via Val De Paolis, 00046 Grottaferrata
www.casteldepaolis.it

Castello di Ama Chianti Classico, Tuscany
Chianti Classico (red)

The relatively high altitude in the hills around Gaiole gives wines made here a distinctive freshness and excellent, natural acidity. Castello di Ama is no exception. With vineyards at 490m (1,600ft), the wines are deliciously well balanced. The estate has been in the hands of a group of Roman families since 1977, and it is now managed by one of the owners' daughters, Lorenza Sebasti, who works alongside the winemaker, Marco Pallanti. The fine straight Chianti Classico produced here relies on some pleasingly brisk acidity to bring freshness to the savoury, dark tannins, and ripe, juicy berry flavours.

Località Ama, 53013 Gaiole in Chianti
www.castellodiama.com

Castello Banfi Montalcino, Tuscany
Rosso di Montalcino (red)

An American-owned estate that has done much to promote Montalcino's status overseas, Castello Banfi is also one of the area's biggest producers. It was founded, in 1978, by John and Harry Mariani, and it has since grown to include some 2,800ha (7,000 acres), on which you'll find a restaurant and an extensive visitor centre, including a museum, alongside the winery. Banfi has been at the forefront of research into the local Sangiovese grape variety, and it makes a consistently high quality range of wines, too. As an entry-point to its extensive portfolio – and, indeed, the region itself – the Rosso di Montalcino takes some beating. There is an attractively cool mintiness to the ripe cherry and vanilla flavours in this fruit-forward gem. Bright, juicy, and extremely approachable, it is a good match for pasta.

Castello di Poggio alle Mura, Località Sant' Angelo Scalo 53024
www.castellobanfi.com

Castello di Brolio Chianti Classico, Tuscany
Ricasoli Brolio Chianti Classico (red)

A Tuscan winery with an aristocratic heritage, Castello di Brolio is the family seat of the Ricasoli family, who retain control of the winery to this day. One of the larger estates in Chianti, it is widely credited with helping to shape the region's modern form thanks to Bettino Ricasoli, who developed the blend of Sangiovese and Canaiolo, along with white grapes, that was the blueprint for the Chianti DOC. Now in the hands of Francesco Ricasoli, the winery makes use of the international varieties, such as Cabernet

wine, with a polished edge to its structure. For all the ripe flavours, there is an appealing savoury element that provides length to what has to be one of the best-value wines in Tuscany.

Cantine del Castello di Brolio, 53013 Gaiole in Chianti
www.ricasoli.it

Castello di Montepò Maremma, Tuscany

Sassoalloro Toscana IGT (red)

The legendary Franco Biondi Santi of the eponymous Montalcino estate, is one of the key figures in the development of Italian wine. He was one of a handful of producers who, from the 1960s onwards, proved that Italian wines could compete with the world's finest. A tough act to follow, then, for his son, Jacopo Biondi Santi, who set out on his own in the mid-1990s. Initially, Jacopo worked with contracted vineyards, but he soon bought the Montepò estate in Scansano. He has since added to the vineyards, so that he now has some 50ha (123 acres), and he makes wines that mix modernity and traditional Tuscan character. The Sassoalloro Toscana IGT layers ripe plum and cherry notes with tobacco and cooling notes of mint. It feels polished and full, with lasting red-fruit sweetness.

Castello di Montepò, 58050 Scansano
www.biondisantimontepo.com

Castello di Verduno Barolo, Northwest Italy

Verduno Pelaverga (red)

While Castello di Verduno has belonged to the Burlotto family for more than a century, it has only recently joined the front rank of Barolo producers. Its rise is largely down to the work put in by Gabriella Burlotto and Franco Bianco, the current owners, aided and abetted by their oenologist, Mario Andrion. They are best known for their slick but traditional Barolos, produced from two crus, Massara and Monvigliero, and their Barbaresco from Faset and Rabajà. But just as interesting is their Verduno Pelaverga. This feisty grape is native to the commune of Verduno, and here it makes for a light, spicy, refreshing red with lasting flavours of cherry and rose.

Via Umberto 9, 12060 Verduno
www.castellodiverduno.com

Castello di Volpaia

Chianti Classico, Tuscany

Chianti Classico (red)

Behind the walls of the delightful hilltop village of Volpaia, is the home of one of Chianti's most respected producers. Castello di Volpaia looks down on slopes of carefully, organically tended vineyards,that range in altitude from 450 to 640m (1,470 to 2,100ft). Now owned by the Mascheroni Stianti family, Volpaia makes consistently fine Chianti. The Chianti Classico is elegant and fresh, with cool savoury earth notes marked by the brisk red-fruit flavours of a wine twice its price.

Di Giovanna Stianti,
Località Volpaia, 5317
Radda in Chianti
www.volpaia.it

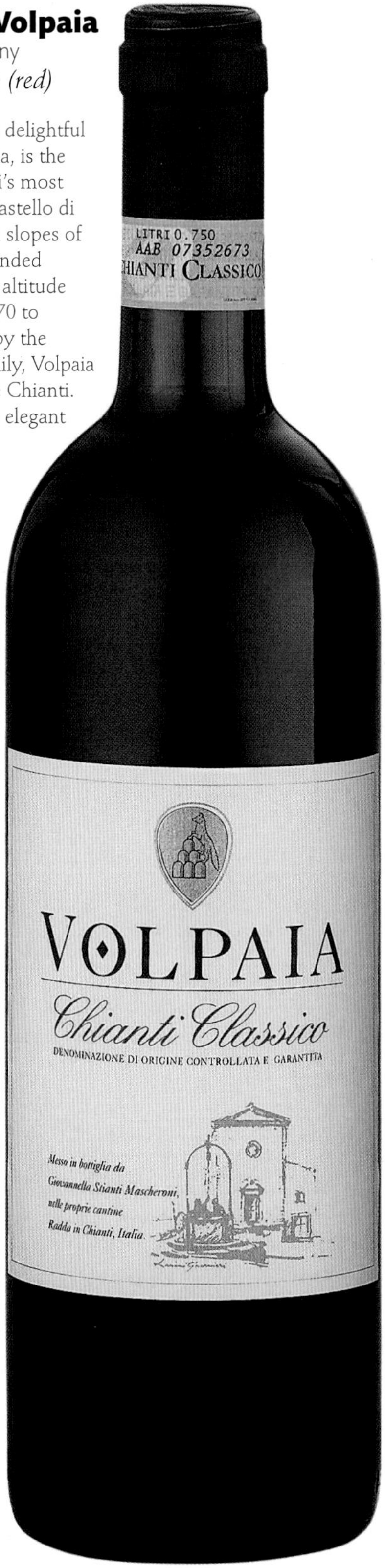

WHAT FOOD? WHAT WINE?

Choosing an appropriate wine for a dish is no more technical than selecting two dishes to serve at the same meal. Apply equal parts tradition and taste experience. In Texas, tradition dictates that coleslaw goes well with barbecued beef brisket. In France, red Bordeaux is a traditional match for roast lamb. Most good pairings are based on the wine having enough "grip" in your mouth to wash the food down easily and leave your mouth fresh for the next bite. So, choose wines that match the relative lightness or richness of the dish. There are no rights or wrongs, only accumulated opinion. Experiment to find what pleases you.

SEAFOOD

Seafood with white wine is a given but different white wines are best with different seafoods.

- Lighter, crisper whites, such as Pinot Grigio/Gris, Riesling, Muscadet, and Chablis pair with simply prepared seafood, from raw oysters to crab salad to sole meunière and sea bass in black bean sauce.
- Richer whites such as white burgundy and other Chardonnays, and ripe Riesling styles make good partners for denser, fattier seafood such as lobster, halibut, and salmon.

VEGETABLES AND SALAD

Vegetables and salads contain little or no fat, unless it's in the dressing, so avoid full-bodied, tannic wines which would overwhelm the fresh, light flavours.

- Choose crisp white wines such as Sauvignon Blanc, dry rosés, and lighter-style, simply fruity reds such as Beaujolais Villages.

MEAT

When serving meat, match the red wine to the richness of the meat, and also consider the flavour and texture of the sauce.

- Cabernet Sauvignon, Merlot, and Syrah/Shiraz love heavy, rich meats, such as beef, lamb, and venison, and duck and game birds.
- Lighter reds, such as Beaujolais, Pinot Noir, or red burgundy, and richer dry white wines such as Chardonnay and ripe Riesling work better with leaner meats, such as pork and chicken.

CHEESE

Don't limit yourself to just reds when pairing with cheese.

- Crisp, light whites go with fresh cheeses such as ricotta.
- Richer whites including Viognier and Chardonnay can take on Brie and Taleggio.
- Sweet whites go with salty cheeses such as Parmesan.
- Rich, late-harvest whites tame blue cheeses.
- Port with Stilton and toasted walnuts is a fine, traditional match.

DESSERT

It's best to serve a wine that is sweeter than the dessert.

- An apple or pear tart works with a late-harvest Riesling or Sauternes.
- Sponge cake is much better with a slightly sweet bubbly than a brut.
- Super-sweet ingredients – chocolate, butter icing, and so on – overpower almost everything but port, and are best with coffee.

GOES WITH EVERYTHING

Some wines transcend these rules and pair well with everything.

- Lighter-style reds including red burgundy/Pinot Noir, Beaujolais, Chianti/Sangiovese, and Cabernet Franc from the Loire go well with slow-braised beef, rich fish dishes such as grilled or sautéed salmon, and with mushrooms and many vegetarian dishes that have protein elements including beans, cheese, and lentils.

Cataldi Madonna Abruzzo, Central Italy
Montepulciano d'Abruzzo (red)

There is a rustic, earthy edge to the violet-scented fruit in the dark, concentrated red that is Cataldi Madonna's Montepulciano d'Abruzzo. It is a gutsy wine, but it also comes with sufficient levels of refreshing acidity to cope with the full-flavoured delights of a meaty ragù, or other rich dishes. The wine gets its full-bodied character from the searing heat of this part of the region, which is known locally as the "oven of Abruzzo". Situated on either side of the River Tirino, Cataldi Madonna has some 25ha (62 acres) of vineyards planted to traditional varieties.

Località Piano, 67025 Ofena
0862 954252

Ceretto Barolo, Northwest Italy
Arneis Blangé (white)

It is a truth universally acknowledged that the most widely admired Barolo is the work of small-scale, artisan producers. But there is also a handful of larger companies whose wines are well worth looking out for, and which provide great value, too. Ceretto certainly falls into that latter camp. After being established in the early 20th century, Ceretto now has more than 120ha (300 acres) of vineyards. But quality is excellent too, as in the refreshing, light-bodied white, Arneis Blangé, which combines ripe pear flavours with a slightly chalky texture. The perfect apéritif wine for summer drinking.

Località San Cassiano 34, 12051 Alba
www.ceretto.com

Cima Colli Apuani, Tuscany
Massaretta Toscana IGT (red)

In the hands of the Cima family estate, the quirky indigenous grape variety Massaretta yields a charming, rustic red, with notes of cola and red plum. It is savoury and bright, and a good partner for roast pork. The Cima family has had a presence on the steep foothills of western Tuscany for the best part of two centuries. With Aurelio Cima now heading up operations, and with consultant winemaker Donato Lanati working wonders in the cellar, the estate has expanded and updated in the past few years, making it one of the best estates in this area of Tuscany.

Via del Fagiano 1, Frazione Romagnano, 54100 Massa
www.aziendagricolacima.it

Collemattoni Montalcino, Tuscany
Rosso di Montalcino (red)

Impressively structured for a humble Rosso di Montalcino, Collemattoni's gripping Sangiovese is one of Montalcino's biggest bargains. Combining firm tannin, savoury earth, and high-toned cherry notes, this should be stashed in the cellar for a few years before it comes round. Marcello Bucci, who took up the reins at this boutique estate near Sant'Angelo in Colle from his father Aldo in 1995, has transformed its reputation.The vineyard is now managed organically, and the winemaking is traditional, employing long maceration times and large Slavonian oak casks.

Località Podere Collemattoni 100, 53020 Sant'Angelo in Colle
www.collemattoni.it

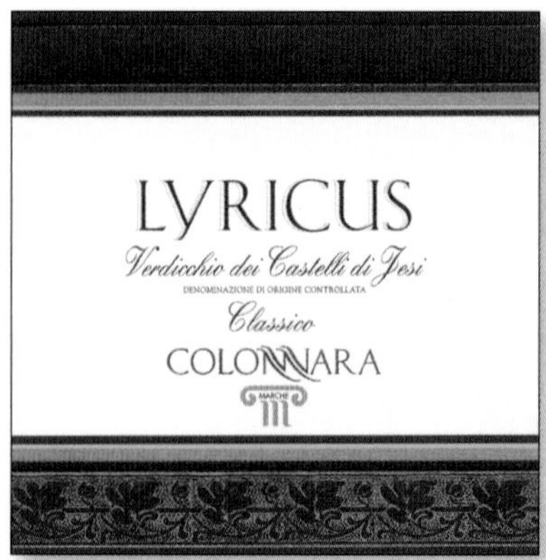

Colonnara Marche, Central Italy
Verdicchio Lyricus (white)

The refreshing and crisp white Verdicchio Lyricus has a lime-like acidity that gives it real cut and focus. It would make an ideal aperitif wine, but it works equally well with fish. It is produced from the unique Marche grape variety Verdicchio, the origins of which can be traced to the hills around Cupramontana, where Colonnara is based. The maritime-meets-alpine climate of this area of the Marche seems ideally suited to the variety, and Colonnara's is certainly among the best, and best-value, examples around. One of Italy's finest co-operative wineries, Colonnara was established in 1959, and includes 200 members who cultivate 250ha (618 acres) of vineyards between them.

Via Mandriole 6, 60034 Cupramontana
www.colonnara.it

Conti Costanti Montalcino, Tuscany
Rosso di Montalcino (red)

There is a remarkable purity to the wines of Conti Costanti, and this excellent Rosso di Montalcino is no different. Poised and elegant, with nervy acidity, it will be at its best about five years from the vintage. The Costanti family have been important players in Montalcino's wine scene since the mid-1600s. Their reputation as pioneers, however, dates back to 1865, when Tito Costanti made his first vintage of Brunello.The current director of the family firm is Andrea Costanti, who was fresh out of university when he took over in 1983. He has since taken a path between the traditional and the modern, using both large casks and small barriques for ageing, leading to wines that are about elegance rather than power.

Località Colle al Matrichese, 53024 Montalcino
www.costanti.it

Contucci Montepulciano, Central Italy
Rosso di Montepulciano (red)

With its cellars based beneath the family palazzo within the walls of the medieval town of Montepulciano, Contucci is a producer of great heritage that has been making wine in the area for hundreds of years. As you might expect from a family estate with such a long and distinguished history, the approach here has no truck with modernity. Winemaking methods are instead highly traditional which means that only indigenous grapes such as Prugnolo (Sangiovese), Canaiolo, and Colorino are used, and that the wines are left to age in large oak casks, rather than smaller barriques. This leads to wines that are marked out by their distinctively gentle, elegant structure, and the Rosso di Montepulciano amply demonstrates those charms: a delightfully traditional wine with soft tannins and focused flavours, it has the freshness and balance to match meat that has been left to marinate for some time in a wintry casserole.

Via del Teatro 1, 53045 Montepulciano
www.contucci.it

COS Sicily
Cerasuolo di Vittoria (red)

A lively, fine, juicily fruity blend of Nero d'Avola and Frappato, the COS Cerasuolo di Vittoria is a benchmark for this Sicilian DOCG. Strikingly reminiscent of a top cru Beaujolais, it deftly balances fresh fruit with a dark earthiness and really bright acidity. The producer behind it was formed back in 1980, when three school friends decided to go into business together, buying a farm and naming it COS after the first letter of each of their surnames. Of the original trio, only Giusto Occhipinti and Titta Cilía are still involved in the business, but the remaining duo has earned considerable respect and worldwide attention for its wines, which are produced using biodynamic practices in the vineyard and a distinctly natural, minimal-intervention approach in the cellar. They now have a not-inconsiderable 25ha (62 acres) of vineyards to work with, and they have become synonymous with Cerasuolo di Vittoria, Sicily's first DOCG.

SP 3 Acate-Chiaramonte, 97019 Vittoria
www.cosvittoria.it

Cusumano Sicily
Nero d'Avola (red)

Diego Cusumano is a fervent believer in the local varieties and traditions of his native Sicily. And, since 2001, he has certainly been prepared to back his beliefs with investment. He now runs an operation that produces some 2.5 million bottles a year, and he has earned effusive praise and numerous awards for his efforts. Cusumano's beloved local grape varieties are at the heart of that production. And the consistently brilliant Nero d'Avola shows just how good those varieties can be. A juicy core of dark, plummy fruit forms the heart of this ripe red. It is forward and appealing, perfect for a weeknight pizza.

Contrada San Carlo
SS113, 90047
Partinico
www.cusumano.it

DeForville di Anfosso Barbaresco, Northwest Italy
Langhe Nebbiolo (red)

DeForville di Anfosso's Langhe Nebbiolo is a pure expression of the quintessential Piedmont variety, with scents of red cherries, rose, and dried porcini. It drinks easily, the gentle tannins a subtle contrast to the fresh fruit. It is the work of a Belgian-Italian family, whose roots in the Barbaresco region date back to 1860, when the DeForville family arrived in the region from Belgium. Brothers Paolo and Valter Anfosso now run the estate in traditional fashion using long maceration periods and ageing in large oak casks.

Via Torino 44, 12050 Barbaresco
0173 635140

Di Majo Norante Molise, Central Italy
Terre degli Osci Sangiovese (red)

Di Majo Norante's Terri degli Osci Sangiovese is a wine that shows how good the Molise region can be. A juicy, full-bodied red that is the ideal foil for spaghetti with meatballs or other meaty pasta dishes, it balances sweet spice with notes of ripe cherry and plum, and is quite delicious. Di Majo is one of the longest-established producers in Molise, which is Italy's smallest and youngest wine region. Somewhat off-the-beaten-track in terms of the contemporary Italian wine scene, Molise is located some distance away from the better-known, and more fashionable, likes of Piedmont, Tuscany, or even Campania. But the estate's 200 years of experience in the region shine through in the wines, and the di Majo family has earned respect for the way it has stuck to its guns, making an impressive range from indigenous grape varieties, both on their own and as components of some clever and tasty blends.

Contrada Ramitelli 4, 86042 Campomarino
www.dimajonorante.com

Donnafugata Sicily
Passito di Pantelleria Ben Ryé (dessert)

The fortified wine of Marsala is Sicily's most famous wine style. Back in 1983, however, it had fallen from favour. Concerned for the future of his family business, Giacomo Rallo decided to end his family's 150-year-old association with the style, and switched instead to making wines without adding alcohol. It was a gamble that paid off. The estate now has 300ha (750 acres) of vineyards, and makes delicious wines like the elegant, beautifully aromatic, complex dessert wine, Passito di Pantelleria Ben Ryé, which has a golden amber colour and scents of flowers, peach, and honey.

Via San Lipari 18,
81015 Marsala
www.donnafugata.it

Elio Grasso Barolo, Northwest Italy
Nebbiolo d'Alba Gavarini (red)

Elio Grasso is one of Italy's most celebrated winemakers, a widely respected figure who has done much to elevate the red wines of Piedmont in general, and Barolo in particular, to their current lofty status in the wine world. He comes from a family of growers in Barolo who have long had holdings in the Monforte zone's top two vineyards, Gavarini and Ginestra. Today, Elio Grasso himself continues to produce magnificent wines, helped by his son, Gianluca. The winemaking style is a blend of the traditional and the modern, a halfway house in a region where adherents of the two methods are often vociferously opposed to each other. Nebbiolo here is treated to long, slow fermentations, and both large Slavonian oak casks and smaller barriques are used. There is a pristine, elegant quality to the fruit at the base of the Nebbiolo d'Alba Gavarini. Released young for early consumption, it is fresh and inviting.

Località Ginestra 40, 12065 Monforte d'Alba
www.eliograsso.it

Falesco Umbria, Central Italy
Vitiano Rosso (red)

Falesco is the estate that first put the now world-famous Italian winemaker, Riccardo Cotarella on the map. It was here that Cotarella developed his modern style of winemaking, which favours ripe fruit and soft tannins, and he is not afraid to use international varieties to get there. Today, Cotarella acts as a consultant to numerous wineries across Italy, but the Falesco estate continues to show off his style at its best in wines such as the affordable Vitiano Rosso. A blend of Cabernet Sauvignon, Sangiovese, and Merlot, this rich red combines dark notes of plum and ripe cherry with soft, gentle tannins and vanilla spice.

Località San Pietro, 05020 Montecchio
www.falesco.it

Fantinel Collio, Northeast Italy
Vigneti Sant' Helena Ribolla Gialla (white)

Lively notes of citrus and spices (such as coriander) help the richly textured white Vigneti Sant' Helena Ribolla Gialla to feel distinctly light on its feet. The finish combines appetizingly savoury minerality and drinkably brisk acidity. It is the kind of concentrated but fresh modern wine that has been the stock in trade of this wide-ranging winery with holdings in a number of areas of Northeast Italy since 1969. That was the year that Mario Fantinel, a businessman with interests in a number of hotels and restaurants in the region, decided to try his hand at the vinous branch of the hospitality industry. Now run by Mario's three sons, Loris, Gianfranco, and Luciano Fantinel, the Fantinel operation has expanded considerably since its inception, and it has become a consistently high quality, and good-value, producer across its large and varied range of wines.

Via Tesis 8, 33097 Tauriano di Spilimbergo
www.fantinel.com

NEBBIOLO

Winemakers in Northwest Italy's Piedmont region count the Nebbiolo grape variety as their most valuable although Barbera is much more widely grown. The great red wines known as Barolo and Barbaresco come from Nebbiolo grown in vineyards around the two villages by those names.

Connoisseurs consider these expensive, concentrated and robust wines the aristocracy of Piedmont because of their unique flavours, their ability to improve with age for decades, and the interesting way their flavour personalities vary from one small vineyard to the next.

Not all Nebbiolo wine is expensive. Grapes grown in Piedmont outside the Barolo and Barbaresco boundaries can make excellent wines labelled as Gattinara and Ghemme, and simply Nebbiolo d'Alba, which all tend to be the most affordably priced. Nebbiolo wines are occasionally produced in other parts of the world, but few, if any of these attempts have captured the mysterious rose-petal aromas and tart raspberry flavours of an Italian Nebbiolo.

The best Nebbiolo wines are grand, but not "big" in the sense of a Châteauneuf-du-Pape or California Cabernet Sauvignon. A Nebbiolo is relatively light in colour for a red, but has lots of tannin to give it a chewy feel. They are crisp and appetizing because of their acidity, and as they age they develop mushroom, herb, and dark cherry nuances.

Nebbiolo is a late-ripening grape, harvested from mid-October.

Fattoria di Fèlsina Chianti Classico, Tuscany

Chianti Classico Berardenga (red)

Run by the Sangiovese-obsessed Giuseppe Mazzoclin, Fattoria di Fèlsina is justly renowned for its collection of impressively structured, long-lived wines. The estate's vineyards in the southern end of the Chianti Classico zone were considerably replanted and remodelled in the 1980s and 1990s, improving the quality of wines such as the Chianti Classico Berardenga. Combining savoury, cool tannins and high-toned cherry notes within an elegant frame, this delicious Tuscan red is a seriously good wine for the price.

Via del Chianti 101, 53019 Castelnuovo Berardenga
www.felsina.it

Fattoria Nicodemi Abruzzo, Central Italy

Montepulciano d'Abruzzo (red)

A perfect wine for serving with roast meats and game, Fattoria Nicodemi's Montepulciano d'Abruzzo is a dark, inky-coloured red that balances rich dark fruit flavours with notes of anise and black pepper. With its beefy structure, it is a heady, potent wine that is also a good candidate for short-term ageing. It is made by Elena Nicodemi, who, in 1998, took over the family estate originally founded by her grandfather, Carlo, in the early 20th century. Going into the wine business had never been Nicodemi's plan. But when her father, Bruno, who had been running the estate since the early 1960s, died suddenly, she abandoned her career as an architect and, with great determination, transformed its reputation. She is assisted in her work by the winemakers Federico Curtaz and Paolo Caciorgna, and her wines have become excellent representatives of the unmatched value found in the Abruzzo.

Contrada Ventriglio, 64024 Notaresco
www.nicodemi.com

Fattoria Le Pupille Scansano, Tuscany

Morellino di Scansano (red)

Elisabetta Geppetti has been a formidable figure in Scansano. Having assumed control of the family estate near to Scansano in 1985, she has done much to develop this region's identity, and was the prime mover behind the formation of the growers' consortium for Morellino di Scansano. Of course, she has been just as active on behalf of her own estate, and the wines are uniformly excellent, fashioned with an eye on appealing to the tastes of drinkers throughout the world, not just in Italy. Fattoria Le Pupille's straight Morellino di Scansano is a great introduction to the region. Juicy and bright, with sweet raspberry flavours, it is an easy-going, hearty red to pair with a weeknight dinner of spaghetti and meatballs.

Piagge del Maiano 92/A, Località Istia d'Ombrone, 58100 Grosseto
www.elisabettageppetti.com

Fattoria di Selvapiana Chianti Rùfina, Tuscany

Chianti Rùfina (red)

If you are looking for classically Tuscan Sangiovese produced in a traditional style, then Fattoria di Selvapiana is a great place to start. Originally bought by Michele Giuntini Selvapiana in 1827, Selvapiana was run by his descendant Francesco Giuntini Antinori for several years. Now under the control of Federico Giuntini Masetti and his sister Silva, the wines have been made under the guidance of consultant winemaker, Franco Bernabei, since 1979, and they are without doubt among the best in the Rùfina subzone. From the Rùfina highlands northeast of Florence, the straight Chianti Rùfina is textbook mountain-grown Sangiovese. Featuring brisk cherry and mint flavours, it is elegant, rather than rich, and very food friendly. Try it with a Tuscan classic dish such as roast pork loin with rosemary and garlic.

Località Selvapiana, 50068 Rùfina
www.selvapiana.it

Feudi di San Gregorio Campania, Southern Italy

Falanghina Campania Sannio IGT (white)

Feudi di San Gregorio's Falanghina is a rich, full-bodied white from the volcanic vineyards of inland Campania. Combining ripe melon and citrus with smoky minerality, it is a perfect introduction to the talents of Riccardo Cotarella, who has been consulting at Feudi di San Gregorio for more than 20 years. The approach mixes traditional and modern, with an indigenous grape variety given the latest winemaking technology, but with Cotarella's deft touch always apparent.

Località Cerza Grossa, 83050 Sorbo Serpico
www.feudi.it

FALANGHINA DEI FEUDI DI SAN GREGORIO

Francesco Rinaldi e Figli Barolo, Northwest Italy

Grignolino d'Asti (red)

The Francesco Rinaldi e Figli estate began its life in 1870, when the eponymous founder inherited some vineyard land in Barolo. It is still owned by the family, and its fortunes are currently in the capable hands of Luciano Rinaldi and his niece, Paola. The guiding principle here is to maintain local traditions, both in the winemaking and the grape varieties used. That is very much the case with Francesco Rinaldi's Grignolino d'Asti, which uses the little-known local grape variety, Grignolino. Here it is fashioned into a wine that, while light in colour and body, is nonetheless packed with flavour. In character it is lively, vibrant, with an inviting combination of fresh strawberry, cherry, and a cooling mintiness. A real original, this is a wine that is not to be missed.

Via U Sacco 4, 12051 Alba
www.rinaldifrancesco.it

Fratelli Alessandria Barolo, Northwest Italy

Verduno Pelaverga (red)

Another fine producer in the Barolo zone with a history dating back to the 1800s, Fratelli Alessandria is based in Verduno, one of the region's lesser-known communes. Judging by the quality of the aromatic, elegant wines produced by Gian Battista Alessandria and his son Vittorio, however, it deserves to be much better known. One of the stars of the Fratelli Alessandria range is produced from a grape that is perhaps even more obscure than the Verduno commune: Pelaverga. Their Verduno Pelaverga is well worth hunting down, however. It is the kind of zesty, cherry-scented red that is so appealing and drinkable you need to remind yourself that it is actually wine – an alcoholic drink – before you consume too much of it! The perfect accompaniment to pretty much any food you care to serve it with, it is a good idea to stock up on plenty of bottles of this wonderfully quaffable classic if you can.

Via Beato Valfre 59, 12060 Verduno
www.fratellialessandria.it

Fuligni Montalcino, Tuscany

Rosso di Montalcino Ginestreto (red)

A wine that does not reach its delicious peak until around five years after the vintage in which it was produced, Fuligni Ginestreto is quite a substantial example of Rosso di Montalcino. Firm and powerfully structured, it has savoury tannins that grip and ground the ripe berry flavours. With much more structure and concentration than the average Rosso, it is the kind of wine upon which the Fuligni family have built their reputation for almost 100 years – they have been tending their estate towards the east of Montalcino (which many argue is the best, most classical part of the region) since 1923. Today operations are managed by Maria Flora Fuligni and her nephew, Robert Guerrini, and the estate is among Montalcino's most traditional in approach and style.

Via S Saloni 32, 53024 Montalcino
www.fuligni.it

Gulfi Sicily
Nero d'Avola Rossojbleo (red)

Vito Catania made his name, and his fortune, as a major player in the automotive industry. But he returned to his native Sicily to head up this impressive operation on the island's southeastern tip. Catania is a great believer in Nero d'Avola, and he tends some 70ha (173 acres) of this classic southern grape variety, using organic practices, near Chiaramonte Gulfi. The Nero d'Avola Rossojbleo is a fine example of his approach to the variety. Juicy and ripe without feeling heavy, it finds its focus thanks to bright acidity and brisk flavours of raspberry and plum – a delicious wine for any occasion.

Contrada Partia, 97010 Chiaramonte Gulfi
www.gulfi.it

Hilberg-Pasquero Roero, Northwest Italy
Barbera d'Alba (red)

The estate at Hilberg-Pasquero may have a long history of vine-growing – it can trace its roots back to 1915 – but, under the current owners, who lend the estate its name, this is every inch a modern producer. Michele Pasquero and Annette Hilberg take charge of every aspect of production here, always retaining the ecologically aware methods they believe in, and with equally sensitive work in the winery. Stylistically speaking, they tend to look for a more extracted version of Barbera, and their straight Barbera d'Alba is certainly darkly coloured and rich, although it also feels light and nervy on the palate.

Via Bricco Gatti 16, 12040 Priocca
www.hilberg-pasquero.com

J Hofstätter Alto Adige, Northeast Italy
Lagrein (red)

Do not be deceived by the dark, brooding colour of J Hofstätter Lagrein. This vibrant, dangerously drinkable red wine is fresh and light on the palate, with lasting notes of plum and savoury spice. That is a style that drinkers have come to love about Hofstätter, which has cellars just off the main square of the Alpine village of Tramin, thought by many to be the birthplace of the Gewürztraminer grape variety.

Piazza Municipio 7, 39040 Tramin-Termeno
www.hofstatter.com

I Clivi di Ferdinando Zanusso Collio/Colli, Northeast Italy
Galea Bianco (white)

Blended from a host of local varieties including Friulano and Verduzzo, Galea is a powerfully structured, complex white wine. Though delicious now, it is worth holding on to: it will benefit from being held for a few years in the cellar before it reaches its optimum flavour and complexity. It has been produced organically, and with a minimum of intervention in the cellar, by Ferdinando Zanusso, who acquired and rennovated the estate in the 1990s.

Località Gramogliano 20, 33040 Corno di Rosazzo
www.clivi.it

I Poderi di San Gallo Montepulciano, Central Italy
Rosso di Montepulciano (red)

I Poderi di San Gallo, Olimpia Roberti's top quality, traditional Montepulciano estate, is built around two fine vineyards – Le Bertille and Casella – which together cover some 7.5ha (19 acres) of prime land. Roberti's winemaking style is one that favours giving the grapes a long maceration during the fermentation, leading to deep ruby-coloured wines that have a real grip and firm texture. A great example of Roberti's style can be found in the I Poderi di San Gallo Rosso di Montepulciano. This is a meaty, hearty blend of the Sangiovese grape variety with other traditional varieties that feels quite sturdy and full for a second wine. It balances dark fruit flavour with mineral tannin in a captivatingly stylish and savoury way that places it among the very best wines of the region. A fine food wine, you could try drinking it with a Florentine T-bone steak, served on the bone.

Via delle Colombelle 7, 53045 Montepulciano
www.ipoderidisangallo.com

Il Molino di Grace Chianti Classico, Tuscany
Chianti Classico (red)

Top Chianti Classico estate, Il Molino di Grace, has risen to its current exalted status in the region with remarkable speed. This is all the more remarkable when you consider that it is the work of an expatriate, the American Frank Grace, who only bought the property in 1995. Over the past couple of decades, and with the help of his winemaker, German-born Gerhard Hirmer, and the consultant Franco Bernabei, Grace has fashioned one of the top estates in Panzano. The house style here – polished and suave – leans towards international tastes, but it retains some distinctive Tuscan grit and charm in the tannin department. The Chianti Classico is savoury and firm, with potent mineral expression – a highly impressive Chianti that drinks more like a riserva-level wine than a basic *normale*.

Località Il Volano Lucarelli, 50022 Panzano in Chianti
www.ilmolinodigrace.com

Il Poggione Montalcino, Tuscany
Rosso di Montalcino (red)

One of Montalcino's more sizeable producers, Il Poggione is nonetheless generally regarded as something of a standard-bearer for the region's wines. Owned by Leopoldo Franceschi, the winemaking is in the hands of Fabrizio and Alessandro Bindocci, a father-and-son team who have developed their own take on Montalcino. It is an approach that looks to create balanced wines that show the typicity of Sangiovese in the region, rather than cloaking the wines in oak and going for heavy extraction during the winemaking process. And it leads to wines that prove Sangiovese can be capable of displaying great subtlety and aromatic lift when it is handled carefully. That is certainly the case with Il Poggione Rosso di Montalcino. The entry-level wine from this firmly traditional house, this Rosso shows off the foresty, earthy side of Sangiovese grown in Montalcino. It is a stylish, characterful wine of real finesse that would marry wonderfully with a truffly pasta or risotto.

Frazione Sant'Angelo in Colle, Località Monteano, 53020 Montalcino
www.tenutailpoggione.it

Inama Soave, Northeast Italy
Soave Classico (white)

The innovative Inama estate is one of the finest in Northeast Italy, and it has done much to challenge stereotypical assumptions about the producing zone at the core of its operation – Soave. Inama's roots go back to the 1950s, when it was founded by Giuseppe Inama. But it is under Giuseppe's son, Stefano, that this 30ha (74 acre) estate has begun to really spread its wings. Stefano makes Soaves that are a far cry from the cheap bottles that dominate pizza and pasta restaurants the world over. Produced with artisanal levels of attention, they marry great concentration and texture with freshness and drinkability, and they are wildly popular. The range is extensive, but the Soave Classico is the wine with which this producer is most commonly associated in the minds of most wine lovers. Richly textured for a Soave, with lasting notes of lemon curd and kaffir lime, it shows depth with air, the fruit stretching long through the finish; a great match for seafood and simple fish dishes.

Località Biacche, 50, 37047 San Bonifacio
www.inamaaziendaagricola.it

SANGIOVESE

Sangiovese is one of those grape varieties that prefers to stay at home. While it has made delicious, tangy red wines in Tuscany for hundreds of years, and has adapted well to different locations within Italy, few of the attempts to grow it elsewhere have resulted in memorable wines. This has not been the case with French varieties such as Merlot, Syrah, and Cabernet Sauvignon.

Tuscany is home base for Sangiovese. Some winemakers there craft it as a light, simple, fruity wine for gulping rather than savouring, while others turn it into medium- and full-bodied fine wines that earn high marks from critics and age well.

VARIETY OF SIZES

Sangiovese has evolved into various clonal selections or sub-varieties over time. The Sangiovese vines in the Chianti area of Tuscany have mostly small berries, while the Sangiovese Grosso vines in Montalcino have larger berries with thicker skins. The latter make richer wines.

TEXTURE AND TANNIN

Compounds in the juice and skins of Sangiovese grapes have an unusual abundance of tannin, the same substance that gives tea its bite, and a healthy portion of fruit acidity. Together these components create an appetizingly dry texture that complements food and helps Sangiovese wines stand apart from softer red wines.

MULTIPLE PERSONALITIES

Sangiovese is like Pinot Noir in that the variety expresses the taste of the place where it is grown. A Sangiovese vineyard in Chianti Classico on the north side of a hill might make a peppery smelling wine, while the same grape variety on the sunny, south-facing side might create more strawberry aromas.

SMALL YIELDS

One of the reasons that Sangiovese hasn't made many top-quality wines outside of Italy is that it is especially sensitive to crop yields. Growers can encourage grape types such as Syrah/Shiraz to grow a large number of bunches per vine, yet Sangiovese vines must be pruned severely.

WHERE IN THE WORLD?

A few regions in the New World, such as Argentina and California, make Sangiovese wines, but their performance is spotty and when there is so much good and good-value Italian Sangiovese it doesn't make much sense to stray.

Much of central Italy is planted to Sangiovese, which is used to make everything from sparkling wine to light- and full-bodied reds and dessert wines. For dry red table wines, the best wines are labelled Chianti Classico, Chianti Classico Riserva, and Brunello di Montalcino, with the last requiring long-ageing to reach its full potential.

Extraordinary wines known as Super Tuscans are sometimes labelled as Toscana. For value, look for Vino Nobile de Montepulciano and Sangiovese di Romagna.

The following regions are among the best for Sangiovese. Try bottles from these recommended vintages for the best examples:

Tuscany: 2009, 2008, 2007, 2006
Emilia-Romagna: 2009, 2008, 2007, 2006

Brunello di Montalcino can be tough in its youth, but matures beautifully in the bottle.

Isole e Olena Chianti Classico, Tuscany
Chianti Classico (red)

Situated towards the north of the official Chianti Classico region, Isole e Olena is a family-run operation that has been making wines of great authenticity and style since the mid-1950s. It was then that the family of today's owner, Paolo de Marchi, assumed control of the estate, and they have been passionate advocates of the local Sangiovese grape variety ever since, believing it works best on its own. Classically proportioned, with earthy tannins and dark cherry fruit, the estate's straight Chianti Classico feels graceful and poised, as much a reflection of the warm Tuscan hills as anything.

Località Isole 1, 50021 Barberino, Val d'Elsa
0558 072763

La Mozza Scansano, Tuscany
Morellino di Scansano I Perazzi (red)

This 35ha (90 acre) estate belongs to an American restaurateur, Joseph Bastianich, and his mother Lidia Bastianich. They do not make the wine, however. That responsibility is in the hands of the Italian Maurizio Castelli, who makes powerful wines from the Sangiovese, Syrah, and Alicante grape varieties. The Morellino di Scansano I Perazzi is a hearty, juicy blend of Sangiovese with other Mediterranean varieties, that balances ripe plum and berry flavours with a cooling liquorice note. It is very food friendly.

Monte Civali, Magliano in Toscana, 68061 Grosseto
www.bastianich.com

Le Presi Montalcino, Tuscany
Rosso di Montalcino (red)

When it comes to Sangiovese, Bruno Fabbri is a true believer. He even goes so far as to design T-shirts proclaiming his love for the grape variety. Fabbri's devotion to the variety dates back to 1970, when he founded the small Le Presi estate. His son Gianni has been in charge since 1998, and he has taken on his father's traditional winemaking approach and organic methods. Le Presi Rosso di Montalcino is an energetic, engaging Sangiovese, combining dried rose and cherry aromas with darker fruit tones on the palate. Firm and well structured, it is a great introduction to Montalcino.

Via Costa della Porta, Frazione Castelnuovo Abate, 53020 Montalcino
0577 835541

Leone de Castris Puglia, Southern Italy
Salice Salentino Riserva Donna Lisa (red)

Leone de Castris is a large producer that makes more than 2.5 million bottles of wine each year. It is also historic: founded by the Duke Oronzo, the estate has been around for almost 350 years on the same site. The Donna Lisa Salice Salentino Riserva makes a great introduction to the many wines produced here. A deliciously earthy, old-style southern Italian red, it combines rich fruit, savoury tannin, and high-toned acidity. It is an agreeably food-friendly wine, ready for rich meat dishes.

Via Senatore De Castris 50, 73015 Salice Salentino
www.leonedecastris.com

Librandi Calabria, Southern Italy
Cirò Riserva (red)

There's a warm sun-kissed quality to the bright cherry and plum flavours in the hearty Cirò Riserva. It feels classically Italian, a versatile red choice for the dinner table. It is one of many excellent wines produced by Librandi, a large, family-owned winery that is a significant presence in the Calabrian wine scene with more than 250ha (625 acres) of vineyards, producing a dozen labels. Very much rooted in the local community, Librandi has led the way in reviving ancient local varieties that were in danger of falling into obscurity. Today, the estate grows eight different grape varieties, with international varieties such as Sauvignon Blanc and Chardonnay rubbing shoulders with the local Gaglioppo.

SS 106, Contrada San Gennaro, 88811 Cirò Marina
www.librandi.it

Livio Felluga Colli Orientali, Northeast Italy

Pinot Grigio (white)

A sense of minerality adds complexity to this generously textured white from Friuli winemaking star, Livio Felluga. The ripe apple and pear flavours on the finish suggest pairing it with richer seafood dishes. The estate, which is now run by Felluga's children, is one of the pioneers of modern winemaking in this northeastern region, helping to pave the way for the vivid, fresh whites that are now common in the area. With an active presence in markets all over the world, Livio Felluga remains a great ambassador for Friuli's wines.

Via Risorgimento 1, 34071 Brazzano-Cormons
www.liviofelluga.it

Majolini Franciacorta, Northwest Italy

NV: Franciacorta Brut (sparkling)

Franciacorta, part of the Brescia region in Lombardy, has developed a reputation for being Italy's finest area for sparkling wine made in the champagne-method (where the secondary fermentation that brings the fizz takes place in the bottle). As one of the region's top producers, Majolini has played an important role in establishing Franciacorta's reputation. The producer's story goes back to the 1960s, when Valentino Majolini founded the family winery. But it was not until the early 1980s, when brothers Gianfranco, Piergiorgio, Stefano, and Ezio Majolini took over, that it really began to make progress. Located towards the east of the Franciacorta zone, in the village of Ome, Majolini produces elegant, age-worthy sparkling wines. Richly textured with heady notes of brioche and apple, the non-vintage Franciacorta is nevertheless an energetic wine.

Via Manzoni 3, 25050 Ome
www.majolini.it

Marchesi di Grésy Barbaresco, Northwest Italy

Nebbiolo d'Alba Martinenga (red)

Marchesi di Grésy has long been an important presence in the Barbaresco region, with its holdings of vineyard land dating back generations. As a modern wine producer, however, the estate's year zero is as recent as 1973, when Alberto di Grésy made the decision to start producing and bottling his own wine, rather than selling the grapes from the family vineyards for others to use. The estate stretches across the Langhe and Monferrato regions, although its heart can be found in the Martinenga cru, which is widely regarded as one of the Barbaresco region's best sites. The estate makes three Barbarescos from this precious slice of land in Martinenga, including two from the sub-sections, Gaiun and Camp Gros. These two are very serious wines made with plenty of oak. But arguably the best window on the site's character is the Nebbiolo d'Alba Martinenga. Made in an unoaked style (unusual for Nebbiolo), it's nevertheless still a serious wine with attractively grippy tannins and some high-toned cherry fruit followed by the lasting scents of rose characteristic of this grape variety.

Via Rabaja Barbaresco 43, 12050 Barbaresco
www.marchesidigresy.com

Marco Porello Roero, Northwest Italy
Roero Arneis Camestrì (white)

Marco Porello's Roero Arneis boasts two things that the Arneis grape variety often lacks: nervy acidity and a gently gripping palate. It is also refreshing and long, with lasting notes of lime and melon. A delicious wine, in fact, but then, since he took over the family wine business in 1994, this charming young winemaker has seemed incapable of making anything less than delicious. Porello has entirely changed the working practices since assuming control: lowering yields in the vineyard and modernizing the wine cellar in Canale, the principal town in the Roero. Porello's Arneis comes from his own Camestrì vineyard near to the winery, where the vines are planted on steep slopes composed of sandy soils.

Via Roero 3, 12050 Guarene
www.porellovini.it

Masciarelli Abruzzo, Central Italy
Montepulciano d'Abruzzo (red)

Few figures in Italian wine have had more influence, and earned more respect, in their native regions than the late, great Gianni Masciarelli in Abruzzo. Masciarelli, who passed away in 2008 at the age of just 53, bestrode the region like a colossus. In part that was due to the sheer scale of his operation, which extended to some 275ha (680 acres) of vineyards, and production of 3 million bottles a year. But it is also due to his tireless work in promoting the region, and in his endlessly innovative and open-minded approach to winemaking. Masciarelli was always willing to experiment with new grape varieties or winemaking ideas. Whatever he did, however, he never lost sight of the need to protect the Abruzzo wine region's distinctive identity and traditions. The result is one of Italy's most dynamic producers, one that is still working well without its guiding light and inspiration. You can taste that for yourself in the hearty, earthy red Montepulciano d'Abruzzo, which balances sun-kissed flavours of strawberry and plum with savoury tannins. It finishes on a high note: perfect for a rustic pasta.

Via Gamberale 1, 66010 San Martino sulla Marrucina
www.masciarelli.it

Melini Chianti Classico, Tuscany
Chianti Classico Granaio (red)

If you are looking for a well-made, tasty red that will work just fine with pizza or pasta, then Melini's widely available Chianti Classico Granaio is hard to beat. This is not a wine built for complexity and contemplation. It is, however, good, honest, unpretentious Sangiovese, showing cherry and rose notes, along with gentle, savoury tannin. Now in the hands of the Gruppo Italiano Vini, Melini is one of Chianti's largest producers. And though it has modernized in recent years, it is one of the region's more traditionally minded, as befits a place founded in 1705.

Località Gaggiano, 53036 Poggibonsi
www.gruppoitalianovini.com/melini

Michele Chiarlo Barolo, Northwest Italy
Barbera d'Asti Le Orme (red)

Reliably direct and easy to drink, Barbera d'Asti Le Orme is a juicy, forward red that is perfect for spaghetti or pizza. It is a great introduction to the elegant, racy house style of a producer that has a fine reputation for making eminently drinkable Barbera. Founded in 1956 by Michele Chiarlo, initially as a grape grower specializing in Barbera (Nebbiolo from Barolo and Barbaresco came soon after), the company has gone on to become one of the largest producers in Piedmont, with interests all over the region.

Strada Nizza, Canelli, 14042 Calamandrana
www.chiarlo.it

Montesecondo Chianti Classico, Tuscany
Toscana Rosso IGT (red)

From vineyards farmed biodynamically, Montesecondo's Toscana Rosso is a blend of Sangiovese and Canaiolo that is all about purity: there's vivid fruit expression and firm, minerally tannins. It is the kind of unarguably lovely wine that justifies the decision made by Silvio and Catalina Messana in the 1990s to move their family from New York to a farm near Florence owned by Silvio's parents. The farm contained a vineyard, planted by Silvio's father in the 1970s, which the Messanas started to work on, applying the organic and biodynamic methods they believed in. These methods extend to the winery, where naturally present yeasts are used for fermentation.

Via per Cerbaia 18, Località Cerbaia, 53017 San Casciano Val di Pesa
www.montesecondo.com

Montevertine Chianti Classico, Tuscany
Pian del Ciampolo IGT (red)

Like the other, more expensive bottlings produced at this estate, the gorgeous Pian del Ciampolo favours finesse and elegance over raw power; here Sangiovese is shown with vivid purity and depth. That has been the case ever since Montevertine was founded in 1967, when the late Sergio Manetti bought an old farm in Radda, and planted the Le Pergole Torte vineyard. Now in the hands of Sergio's son, Martino, the estate's philosophy follows the same principles as it always has, with the accent forever on elegance.

Località Montevertine, 53017 Radda in Chianti
www.montevertine.it

FOOD & WINE
PIEDMONT REDS

Piedmont is the most celebrated of Italian wine regions, not only for rich red Barolo and Barbaresco, both made from the Nebbiolo grape, but for the far more commonly consumed and easy-going Barbera and Dolcetto.

Nebbiolo gives wines that are both incredibly acidic and incredibly tannic when young – serious reds that need serious dishes. The sultry but polished Barolo and Barbaresco wines from the best sites offer delicate notes of orange rind, black liquorice, cherry, violet, white rose, white truffle, and earth. Piedmont is home to the world famous *tartufo bianco*, or white truffle, whose heady perfume is ideally suited to these wines as are *Cinghiale* (wild boar), beef short ribs with a bone marrow crust, and beef braised in the wine. Roast duck also has an affinity for these wines, especially when paired with mushrooms.

Barbera and Dolcetto, both named after the grapes they're made from, are high in acid but give softer, typically unoaked, and more fruit-forward wines with notes of plum and dark berry. They are ready to drink upon release and are a good choice to enjoy with dishes from a range of international cuisines. The local meat- and spinach-filled ravioli, *agnolotti*, is a great starter with a glass of fruity, easy-going Barbera or Dolcetto, but these wines really shine with flavoursome Italian ingredients, such as olives, anchovies, garlic, artichokes, and tomato.

Dolcetto and Barbera work well with intense, salty anchovies.

Morgante Sicily
Nero d'Avola (red)

Since starting out in 1998, Carmelo Morgante has become a specialist in the local red grape variety, Nero d'Avola. Morgante, who has followed several generations of his family by growing grapes on Sicily's southern highlands, has some 30ha (75 acres) of vineyards to play with. From these he makes three versions of Nero d'Avola, including this straight version. As with all the wines he makes using the variety, it is full and rich, combining ripe notes of plum with substantial weight and structure. It is well worth trying with grilled lamb.

Contrada Racalmare, 92020 Grotte
www.morgantevini.it

Moris Farms Maremma, Tuscany
Morellino di Scansano (red)

Although they have been farmers in the southern Maremma for several generations, it is only relatively recently that the Moris family have got into the local wine business. That they have taken that involvement very seriously indeed, however, is immediately apparent once you've tasted their wines. The family now have two estates, one in the Scansano region, another in Massa Marittima, both of which have been established with the express purpose of producing the highest quality wine possible. It is from the Scansano property that Moris Farms' most consistently tasty everyday wine is drawn, however. The Morellino di Scansano combines ripe blackberry and plum notes with liquorice and spice. Dry and firm, with medium structure, this is a food-friendly red (pasta, all kinds of meat dishes) from the Tuscan coast.

Fattoria Poggetti, Località Cura Nuova, 58024 Massa Marittima
www.morisfarms.it

Muri-Gries Alto Adige, Northeast Italy
Lagrein (red)

In Muri-Gries' delicious interpretation of Lagrein, the dark and savoury side of the variety is out in force. This is a potent red from the Alps, with lasting flavours of ripe plum and spice marking the finish. Its origins are just as intriguing as its taste. Muri-Gries is a Benedictine monastery, which began its life as a fortress in the 11th century, with ownership reverting to the church in 1407. Wine has been produced here ever since, and the monastery is today the proud owner of some of the most sought-after Lagrein vineyards around Bolzano. The estate still draws its workforce from the monks who live there, although a winemaker oversees their work in the cellar and vineyard. Among the varieties produced here are Müller-Thurgau and Pinot Grigio, but it is the Lagrein which has attracted the most attention.

Grieser Platz 21, 39100 Bolzano
www.muri-gries.com

Nino Franco
Valdobbiadene/Conegliano, Northeast Italy
Prosecco Rustico (sparkling)

Nino Franco's Prosecco Rustico is a sparkling wine that is far more than just an easy-drinking aperitif. Bright and refreshing, it is marked by brisk apple and pear flavours, and there is enough acidity to enjoy it well beyond cocktail hour and into dinner. It is made by one of Valdobbiadene's longest-running wineries. Founded in 1919 by Antonio Franco, Nino Franco is now in the capable hands of Antonio's grandson, Primo. The epitome of the well-travelled modern winemaker, Primo Franco has incorporated a lot of the ideas learned from his frequent overseas trips into his intelligent winemaking.

Via Garibaldi 147, 31049 Valdobbiadene
www.ninofranco.it

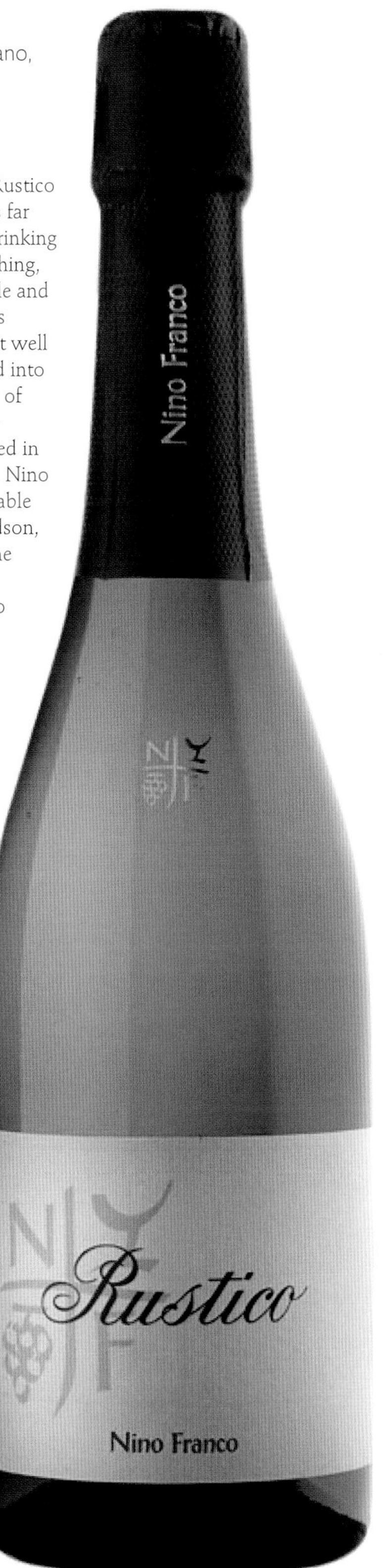

Orsolani Caluso, Northwest Italy
Erbaluce di Caluso La Rustia (white)

Erbaluce is a versatile white grape variety from northern Piedmont that is used to make a range of different wine styles. You can find Erbaluce made as a sparkling wine, as a passito (from dried grapes), or as a dry white, as is the case with this thirst-quenching example, La Rustia. A chalky, refreshing white, this Erbaluce di Caluso is the perfect partner for everything from cheese to seafood. It comes from Orsolani, a specialist in the variety, based in the Canavese area of Piedmont, to the north of Turin among the mountain passes that lead into the Valle d'Aosta. The business began its life in the late 19th century as an inn and farm, but it is now very much associated with winemaking in general, and Erbaluce in particular, from which it makes a variety of different wines that are never less than deliciously interesting.

Via Michele Chiesa 12, 10090 San Giorgio Canavese
www.orsolani.it

Pieropan Soave, Northeast Italy
Soave Classico (white)

With its notes of lime zest and brisk, focused acidity, Pieropan's celebrated Soave Classico sets a benchmark for a region whose name is not always the guarantee of quality that it should be. Classically proportioned and graceful, refreshing, and balanced, the wine is perfect with simply grilled fish and other seafood dishes. Leonildo "Nino" Pieropan, the guiding force at the family winery, is one of a handful of producers that has helped to improve the image of Soave, which is often associated with cheap, characterless supermarket own-labels. Together with his wife Teresita and their sons, Nino runs the winery, located in the medieval city of Soave, along unashamedly traditional lines. His wines have a cultish following worldwide, and, in La Rocca and Calvarino (both of which produce splendid single-vineyard wines), Pieropan has access to some of the finest vineyards in the region.

Via Camuzzoni 3, 37038 Soave
www.pieropan.it

Pietracupa Campania, Southern Italy
Fiano di Avellino (white)

With just 3.5ha (8.5 acres) of vineyard, Sabino Loffredo's Pietracupa operation in the hamlet of Montefredane in Campania is small by anybody's standards. But to his great credit (and to his customers' surprised delight), Loffredo has always managed to keep the prices of his wines at everyday, rather than boutique, levels – all the more impressive when you consider his increasingly lofty reputation. Loffredo produces some arresting wines from Greco and Aglianico, but it is the white Fiano which stands out for its simply incredible quality-to-price ratio. It has stony minerality and brisk acidity that bring focus to the ripe melon and apple notes. The finish is firm, marked by notes of flint and gun smoke.

Via Vadiaperti 17, 83030 Montefredane
0825 607418

TEMPERATURE MATTERS

Cocoa tastes best when piping hot. Soft drinks taste best when icy cold. Wine isn't quite that simple. The temperature at which wine is served can have a great effect on its taste, just as warm soft drinks and tepid cocoa veer wildly from the ideal. It is another wine issue that appears complex, but doesn't have to be. Rich white wines, rosés, and many dessert wines should be served cold, but not too cold. Light red wines should be served cool. You can accomplish this with the 20-minute rule: take rich whites out of the refrigerator, and put light reds into the refrigerator, about 20 minutes before serving.

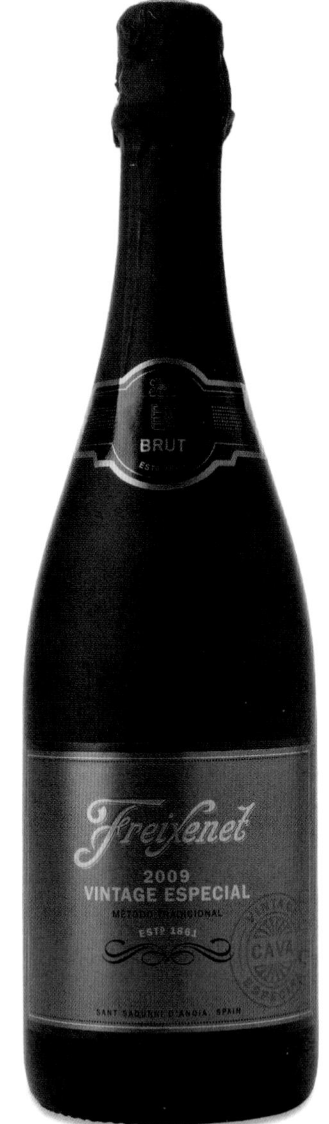

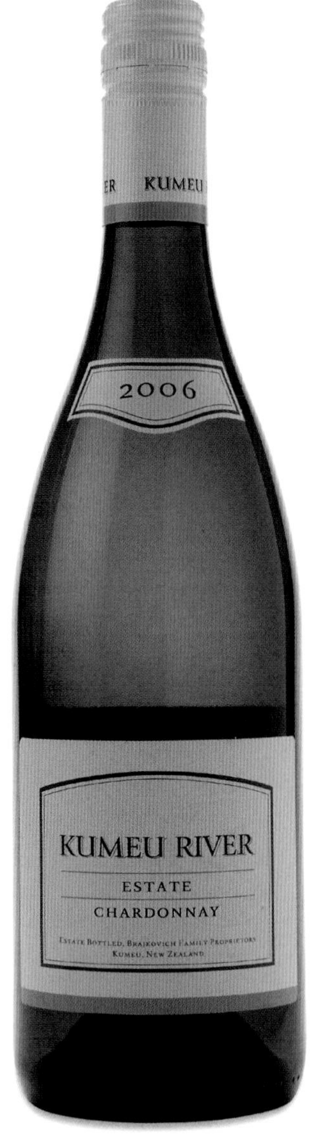

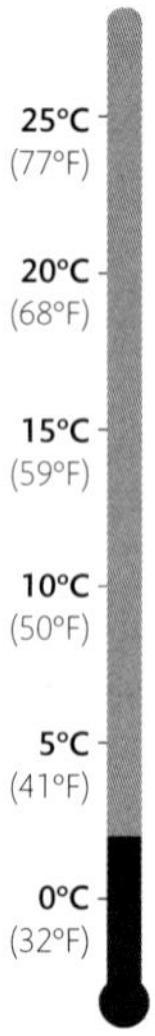

BRUT
Freixenet
2009
VINTAGE ESPECIAL
CAVA

KUMEU
2006
KUMEU RIVER
ESTATE
CHARDONNAY

25°C
(77°F)
20°C
(68°F)
15°C
(59°F)
10°C
(50°F)
5°C
(41°F)
0°C
(32°F)

CRISP WHITES AND BUBBLY

SERVE AT: 2°C (35°F)

Tart, refreshing white wines including Pinot Grigio, Sauvignon Blanc, Albariño, lighter Riesling, Muscadet, and most sparkling wines taste refreshing and crisp served straight from the refrigerator at a temperature of around 2°C (35°F).

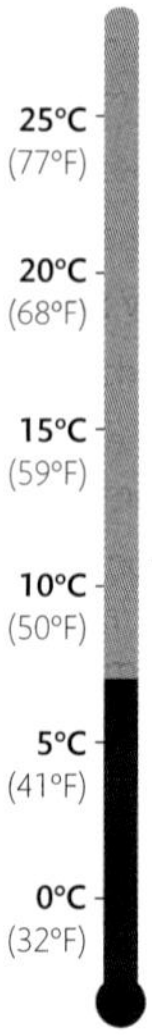

25°C
(77°F)
20°C
(68°F)
15°C
(59°F)
10°C
(50°F)
5°C
(41°F)
0°C
(32°F)

RICH WHITES, ROSÉS, AND DESSERT AND FORTIFIED WINES

SERVE AT: 7°C (45°F)

All these styles have plenty of body and flavour which mean that cooling them too much will inhibit your enjoyment. They taste best chilled but not ice-cold so remove them from the refrigerator 20 minutes early.

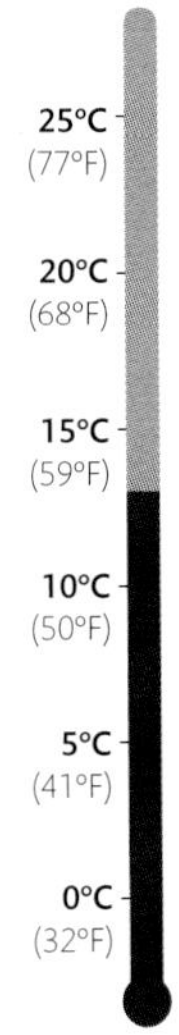

25°C (77°F)
20°C (68°F)
15°C (59°F)
10°C (50°F)
5°C (41°F)
0°C (32°F)

LIGHT REDS

SERVE AT: 13°C (55°F)

Contrary to the received wisdom for red wines, light reds including Beaujolais, inexpensive Pinot Noir, Chianti, and lighter Syrah/Shiraz taste better and are more refreshing when they are chilled for 20 minutes in the refrigerator or given five minutes in an ice bucket.

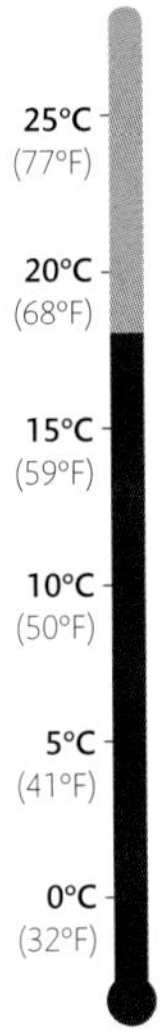

25°C (77°F)
20°C (68°F)
15°C (59°F)
10°C (50°F)
5°C (41°F)
0°C (32°F)

RICH REDS AND VINTAGE PORT

SERVE AT: 18°C (65°F)

Full-bodied reds such as Bordeaux, burgundy, Malbec, Cabernet Sauvignon, and serious Syrah/Shiraz should be served at 18°C (65°F). This may mean briefly chilling a wine or leaving it in a warm room for an hour, depending on where the wine has been stored.

TEMPERATURE TIPS

Everyone has different tastes: there is nothing wrong with drinking your white wines warm or your reds ice-cold, or even putting ice cubes in your rosé. Generally speaking, however, you'll find optimum enjoyment from wine if you follow these tips.

Draughty castle
The conventional wisdom that red wine should be served at room temperature dates to a time before central heating, when a draughty Scottish castle's great room might have measured 16°C (60°F).

Too cold?
It's better to serve wine a bit too cold than too warm, because it always warms up as it's poured and enjoyed.

Ice bucket
Add water to the ice bucket to maximize its cooling power. The ice-cold water touches the bottle all around and cools more quickly than simply ice with fewer contact points.

Freezer
Use the freezer cautiously. An overnight stay can push out the cork and make a mess. And an ice bucket works more quickly.

Adding water to ice cools wine faster.

Pietratorcia Campania, Southern Italy

Ischia Bianco (white)

At the turn of the millennium, three young entrepreneurs came together to form Pietratorcia, a new wine venture on the island of Ischia. The trio were driven by a desire to help conserve the island's farming traditions, and with that in mind they planted 6ha (15 acres) with unusual local grape varieties. Ischia Bianco is a great example of the kind of new-meets-old thinking that has come to characterize this estate: blended from indigenous white varieties such as Biancolella and Forastera, it's a refreshing, citrus-tinged wine that would go well with seafood pasta.

Via Provinciale Panza 267, 80075 Forio d'Ischia
www.pietratorcia.it

Planeta Sicily

Cerasuolo di Vittoria (red)

Planeta is one of Sicily's largest producers, making in excess of 2 million bottles each year. It is also one of the island's (and Italy's) best, attracting global attention for wines produced from both international and native grape varieties. It is the latter that give the three cousins Alessio, Francesca, and Santi Planeta the most pride, however. None more so than the Cerasuolo di Vittoria, a forward, easy-drinking red that balances ripe cherry and sweet raspberry notes with gentle acidity, making it a great choice for pizza.

Contrada Dispensa, 92013 Menfi
www.planeta.it

Poderi e Cantine Oddero Barolo, Northwest Italy

Barolo (red)

In the hands of the Oddero family for more than 100 years, this venerable estate near La Morra has an estimable collection of vineyards in some of Barolo's finest areas. Crus such as Vigna Rionda, Villero, Rocche di Castiglione, and Bussia Soprana provide the fruit for wines of great character. The estate's straight Barolo is delightfully traditional with notes of damp earth, sour cherry, and rose. Unlike many Barolos, it is often approachable when young.

Frazione S Maria 28, 12064 La Morra
www.oddero.it

Produttori del Barbaresco Barbaresco, Northwest Italy

Barbaresco (red)

High quality is sadly not always the first thing that people associate with co-operative wineries in Italy. But the long-running Produttori del Barbaresco is most certainly an exception. First established in 1894, and then brought back to life in the late-1950s, it is today one of Barbaresco's best producers, with a collection of fine vineyards, such as Rio Sordo, Ovello, Asili, and Rabajà. The winemaking team is headed by the well-regarded Aldo Vacca, whose approach is entirely focused on ensuring that the wines in his care are as faithful an expression of their origins as possible. Each of the wines is also good value, not always the case in a region that tends to be one of Italy's most expensive. That includes the straight Barbaresco, which is a benchmark of its kind. Combining grace and structure in a sinewy frame, it is an age-worthy bargain for your cellar.

Via Torino 54, 12050 Barbaresco
www.produttoridelbarbaresco.com

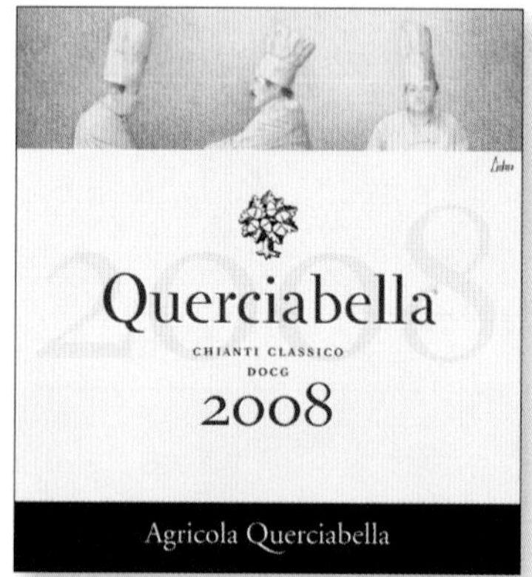

Querciabella Chianti Classico, Tuscany

Chianti Classico (red)

The late Giuseppe Castiglioni was the original driving force behind Querciabella. It was Castiglioni who, in the 1970s, began the process of buying up land around Greve and Radda that would form the basis of this top Chianti Classico producer. The estate then passed into the hands of Castiglioni's son, Sebastiano, in the late 1980s, and it was under Sebastiano's direction that Querciabella really began to attract worldwide attention. Sebastiano is committed to environmentally aware agriculture, and he has been responsible for transferring production to biodynamic practices. The success of the approach can be seen throughout the Querciabella portfolio, which includes reds and whites made from both international and indigenous grape varieties. The estate-labelled Chianti Classico included here is predominantly Sangiovese, with a tiny proportion of Cabernet Sauvignon. An elegant, stylish take on Chianti, with ripe cherry and mocha scents balanced by medium tannins, it is a sophisticated wine to enjoy in its youth.

Via di Barbiano 17, 50022 Greve in Chianti
www.querciabella.com

Rocca di Montegrossi Chianti Classico, Tuscany
Chianti Classico (red)

Marco Ricasoli-Firidolfi, the founder and driving force of Rocca di Montegrossi, is a member of one of Chianti's most influential families. His ancestor, Bettino Ricasoli, was widely credited with being the father of Chianti in the 19th century, and the Ricasoli name is still intimately associated with the region today. Ricasoli-Firidolfi's own project, Rocca di Montegrossi, is a fitting continuation of the family tradition. It began in the late 1990s, when Ricasoli-Firidolfi assumed control of his family's Vigneto San Marcellino estate. By 2000 he had completed construction of a winery, and he has slowly added new plantings to the vineyard, expanding it to some 18ha (45 acres), with classic Chianti grapes such as Sangiovese and Canaiolo. Ricasoli-Firidolfi consistently releases an elegant, mineral-laden, and refined Chianti Classico – a serious wine for the money.

Località Monti in Chianti, San Marcellino, 53010 Gaiole in Chianti
www.roccadimontegrossi.it

Salcheto Montepulciano, Central Italy
Rosso di Montepulciano (red)

The Salcheto estate began its life as a farm, before moving into wine production with the planting of its first vineyards in the late 1980s. Consultant winemaker Paolo Vagaggini was brought on board to make the wines, alongside the estate's manager Michele Manelli, and Salcheto began to make waves in the region, earning a reputation for producing wines that were both classically structured, and ripe and fruity. The house style, with its lipsmackingly fresh acidity, is well demonstrated by Salcheto's excellent Rosso di Montepulciano. Made without any oak influence (the wine is aged in steel tanks), the Rosso di Montepulciano is a mouthwatering blend of Sangiovese, Canaiolo, and Merlot. Highly refreshing, it is a versatile red for the dinner table.

Via di Villa Bianca 15, 53045 Montepulciano
www.salcheto.it

Sartarelli Marche, Central Italy
Verdicchio dei Castelli di Jesi (white)

That Sartarelli is one of the leading producers in the Marche region of Italy today, is thanks to Donatella Sartarelli and Patrizio Chiacchiarini. The pair have completely reinvigorated this family estate since taking it over in 1972, when they decided to start producing wines from grapes that they had previously sold to other producers. They focus on pure varietal Verdicchio, made using grapes from their 60ha (150 acres) of vineyards, spread over various sites. The estate produces a number of different bottlings, all of which are concentrated, beautifully crafted modern white wines. The Verdicchio dei Castelli di Jesi is clean and crisp, with bright lime-scented flavours and floral notes and it is wonderfully focused and pure thanks to its zesty acidity.

Via Coste del Molino 24, 60030 Poggio San Marcello
www.sartarelli.it

Sassotondo Maremma, Tuscany
Ciliegiolo Toscana Rosso IGT (red)

Founded in the southern Maremma in 1990, Sassotondo is one of a group of brave producers that has attempted to prove that Sangiovese isn't the only native Tuscan grape variety worth looking out for. Since their debut vintage in 1997, Edoardo Ventimiglia and Carla Benini, the couple behind Sassotondo, have instead focused their attentions on Ciliegiolo, a red variety that is capable of producing some highly distinctive, not to mention delicious, wines. This unoaked expression is feisty and bright on the palate – a juicy, charming red to pair with many foods.

Pian di Conati 52,
58010 Sovana
www.sassotondo.it

PINOT GRIGIO / PINOT GRIS

Although the grape variety known as Pinot Grigio in Italy originated in France's Burgundy region, it spread around the world a long time ago. It is called Pinot Gris in Alsace today, but used to be known there as Tokay d'Alsace. Germans call it Ruländer. Ukrainians call it something that can't be spelled in our alphabet. In California, wines can be called either Pinot Grigio or Pinot Gris.

Pinot Grigio is especially important to Northern Italian winemakers, who set the style that goes with the name internationally: a very light colour, crisp, and fresh, with delicate fruit flavours.

GREY OR PINK?

Gris and Grigio mean grey in French and Italian. These not-quite-dark grapes traditionally made a pink- or orange-coloured wine when fermented in the same way as red wines.

LATE HARVEST

In the northern French region of Alsace, Pinot Gris makes delicious, dessert wines. Winemakers let the grapes hang on the vines until late in the autumn so they develop a high sugar concentration and rich honey flavours.

A MUTANT

Grapevine researchers say the Pinot Grigio/Gris grape variety was born in Burgundy, through an accidental mutation of Pinot Noir, the dark-coloured grape that makes Burgundy's great red wines. The mutant vines grew semi-dark grapes, neither blanc nor noir, but gris.

PRESSING MATTERS

Modern Pinot Grigio became popular after Italian winemakers in the 1960s began treating it like a white wine. They pressed the grapes immediately after harvest, and fermented the juice without the skins, which provide colour. It has been primarily a white wine ever since.

WHERE IN THE WORLD?

Italians make Pinot Grigio mostly in the northern part of the country, particularly in Trentino-Alto Adige and in Friuli-Venezia Giulia. The variety does well in the cool and mountainous terrain of Italy near the Alps.

Spurred largely by the sales success of Italian Pinot Grigio, growers around the world have planted lots of it in the past two decades. It is New Zealand's third most planted white variety. In California, plantings have more than quadrupled since 2000, and many Oregon Pinot Noir producers have adopted Pinot Gris.

Italian versions can be merely fresh and light. Those from Alsace, Oregon, and New Zealand have more citrus-like flavours and some still have a pink tinge to the colour.

The following regions are among the best for Pinot Grigio/Gris. Try bottles from these recommended vintages for the best examples:

Northeast Italy: 2009, 2008, 2007
Alsace: 2009, 2008, 2007
Oregon: 2009, 2008, 2007

Alsace Pinot Gris tends to have a fuller flavour because of the long, hot summers.

Scarbolo

Pavia di Udine, Northeast Italy

Friulano (white)

Valter Scarbolo is a man of many talents. A celebrated restaurateur, his restaurant, La Frasca, is one of Italy's best. But he is also a winemaker, with a tiny estate that shares his family name, and which is no less well regarded throughout Italy. Scarbolo's winemaking, like his cooking, is modern in style, but he's not afraid to look to traditional methods, too. His Friulano is a balanced, juicy white with snappy acidity that lifts the broad flavours of tangerine and lemon. To match its richness and cut, it is best served with gently seared scallops.

Viale Grado 4, 33050 Pavia di Udine
www.scarbolo.com

Sergio Mottura Lazio, Central Italy

Orvieto Classico (white)

Porcupines are a feature of this picturesque estate in the Lazio portion of the Orvieto DOC. The animals are regarded with great affection by the owners – so much so they play a starring role on each of the estate's instantly recognizable labels. It is all part of Sergio Mottura's holistic view of viticulture, a philosophy that also extends to organic production in the estate's 37ha (91 acres) of vineyards. Regularly winning awards for its multi-faceted whites, the estate is one of Orvieto's finest, but its Orvieto Classico is also delightfully inexpensive. A crisp white, it feels refreshing and bright thanks to its mouthwatering acidity. It would be comfortable being paired with a range of fish and seafood dishes.

Località Poggio della Costa, 01020 Civitella d'Agliano
www.motturasergio.it

Sorelle Bronca Valdobbiadene/Conegliano, Northeast Italy

Prosecco di Valdobbiadene Extra Dry (sparkling)

Generally speaking, Prosecco sparkling wines are made by adding yeast and sugar to a base wine that has already finished its first fermentation, in a pressurized tank. But the team behind Sorelle Bronca – Antonella and Ersiliana Bronca, and winemaker Federico Giotto – are one of a handful of producers to do things differently, with just a single fermentation. The process works by chilling the just-pressed grapes (produced organically at Sorelle Bronca), and then putting them into a tank where the sugars present in the grapes lead to fermentation *and* carbonation. This results in wines that have great natural vibrance and purity. Certainly, the substantial mid-palate weight of the refreshing extra dry sparkling wine lends it more depth and complexity than other Prosecco. It finishes bright, ideal for prosciutto.

Via Martiri 20, 31020 Colbertaldo di Vidor
www.sorellebronca.it

Talenti Montalcino, Tuscany

Rosso di Montalcino (red)

The Talenti name has been synonymous with well-made, traditional Brunello and Rosso di Montalcino since 1980. That was the year when the winemaker Pierluigi Talenti established his eponymous family estate in Montalcino. Though the estate is now run by Pierluigi's grandson, Riccardo, the wines have continued to impress and to retain their distinctive, classic personality. The wines are made to accompany the local cuisine, and the Rosso di Montalcino, which is considerably cheaper than the estate's Brunello, is a great match for a variety of authentic Tuscan dishes. Produced from Sangiovese, this vivid, evocative red wine is centred with flavours of dried porcini, rose petal, and light cherry fruit, and is a wine that, stylistically speaking, is firmly rooted on the traditional side of Montalcino Sangiovese.

Pian di Conte, S Angelo in Colle, 53020 Montalcino
www.talentimontalcino.it

Tasca d'Almerita
Sicily

Regaleali Rosso (red)

With a history that dates back almost 200 years, few estates in Italy can rival Tasca d'Almerita's long record of quality wine production. Still under the control of the original family, it has sustained its position at the top of Sicilian wine thanks to its willingness to add innovation to its years of experience. The family controls five estates, including the 400ha (1,000 acre) Tenuta Regaleali, in the central highlands, the source of the Regaleali Rosso. Bright acidity lends elegance to notes of high-toned cherry and plum in this juicy red. Rich in flavour yet light in body, it's a great choice for a summer barbecue.

Contrada Regaleali, 90020 Sciafani Bagni
www.tascadalmerita.it

Tenimenti Fontanafredda Barolo, Northwest Italy

Serralunga Barolo (red)

There's a regal history to this fine Piedmontese estate. Its founder, back in 1878, was the Count Emanuele Alberto Cuerrieri di Mirafiori, the illegitimate son of King Vittorio Emmanuel II of Italy. The Count established the vineyards on land that had been used by the king as a hunting estate, and they became some of the best in the region. The estate is now in the capable hands of Oscar Farinetti (who also owns another Barolo estate, the Borgogno winery) and, since 1999, when winemaker Danilo Drocco assumed control of the winemaking, the wines have begun to live up to their pedigree once again. The very well priced Serralunga Barolo combines a core of generous fruit – a soft, juicy pillow of cherry and plum – with classically structured Serralunga tannins. The finish is savoury and long.

Via Alba 15, 12050 Serralunga d'Alba
www.tenimentifontanafredda.it

Tenuta Belguardo Maremma, Tuscany

Serrata Maremma Toscana IGT (red)

The Maremma has become a hotbed of investment in Tuscany, as producers flock to the region to make powerful reds inspired by the wines of Bordeaux. One such producer is the Mazzei family of the Fonterutoli estate in Chianti Classico, who bought Tenuta Belguardo in the 1990s to boost their presence in the Maremma. The family was eager to do more than produce just another Cabernet Sauvignon-led blend, however (although the Tenuta Belguardo wine is exactly that). Indeed, arguably the more interesting wine in the Mazzei's Maremma portfolio is Serrata, a wine that is not at all Bordelais in character, being much more traditionally Italianate. A graceful blend of Sangiovese and Alicante, Serrata is firm and rich, yet has bright mouthwatering acidity that gives the wine an appealing freshness.

Località Montebottigli, VIII° Zona, 58100 Grosseto
www.mazzei.it

Tenuta Pèppoli Chianti Classico, Tuscany
Chianti Classico (red)

One of the many properties owned by the Antinori family from Tuscany, Tenuta Pèppoli is just a short distance from the vineyard for Tignanello, the family's celebrated Super Tuscan red blend. The property is a source of very drinkable, unpretentious Chianti, such as the accessible Pèppoli Chianti Classico. A blend of 90% Sangiovese, topped up with a little Merlot and Syrah (the proportion varies from vintage to vintage), this sleek, modern-styled Chianti combines ripe strawberry and plum flavours with sweet vanilla spice. It is an attractive, plush red to serve with steak.

No visitor facilities
www.antinori.it

Terredora Campania, Southern Italy
Campania IGT Aglianico (red)

There is a firm, savoury grip to the tannins in Terredora's Campania IGT Aglianico. It is the kind of red wine that needs a little time in a decanter to soften, the rich plum fruit and bright acidity making it a really good match for braised pork. The wine is the work of Lucio Mastroberardino, whose branch of the famous Campanian wine family controls more than 125ha (308 acres) of vineyards at the meeting point of the top southern DOCGs of Fiano d'Avellino, Greco di Tufo, and Taurasi.

Via Serra, 83030 Montefusco
www.terredora.com

Thurnhof Alto Adige, Northeast Italy
Lagrein Riserva (red)

Thurnhof Lagrein Riserva is a great introduction to the intriguing winemaking philosophy of Andreas Berger, the dynamic young winemaker at the helm of this family estate in Alto Adige. It is very much on the refreshing and nervy side for a wine made from the Lagrein variety, with snappy acidity and bright red apple and plum flavours. Like all the Thurnhof wines, it shows off Berger's third way: using traditional methods (including ageing wines in large oak casks) to make bright, modern wines.

Küepachweg 7, 39100 Bozen
www.thurnhof.com

Trappolini Lazio, Central Italy
Orvieto Classico (white)

Roberto Trappolini heads up this family estate, founded by his grandfather in the 1960s. It is located in the Lazio half of the Orvieto DOC, and, under Roberto's leadership, it has established a fine reputation for producing Orvieto wines that appeal to the modern palate without sacrificing traditional virtues. True to that reputation, the vineyards are largely given over to white varieties for the production of Orvieto (although a reasonable amount of red wine from Sangiovese is also made). The Orvieto Classico is a fragrant, vibrant white, with subtle notes of chalk that add a layer of complexity to the wine's bright citrus and green apple flavours.

Via del Rivellino 65, 01024 Castiglione in Teverina
www.trappolini.com

Triacca Valtellina, Northwest Italy
Valtellina Sassella (red)

There's a distinctly Swiss flavour to Triacca. The operation, which has interests in Valtellina and Tuscany, is run by a Swiss family originating from Poschiavo, just over the border from Valtellina. The family crossed over into Italy in 1897, when Domenico and Pietro Triacca bought a vineyard in Valgella. The La Gatta estate in the same region was added to the portfolio in 1969. The Valtellina Sassella is an energetic, nervy expression of Nebbiolo from near the Swiss border. It feels gentle yet firm, with focused acidity and bright flavour; a fascinating wine.

Via Nazionale 121, 23030 Villa di Tirano
www.triacca.com

Umani Ronchi Marche, Central Italy
Verdicchio dei Castelli di Jesi (white)

One of the Marche's largest producers, Umani Ronchi has vineyard holdings of some 200ha (500 acres), reaching from Cónero DOCG in the north to Colline Teramane DOCG in the Abruzzo. In an average year, it produces 4 million bottles, but fortunately winemaker Michele Bernetti does an admirable job of ensuring that quality is not sacrificed for quantity. The company's Verdicchio dei Castelli di Jesi, for example, is a richer style of Verdicchio, with savoury notes of honey and fresh herbs mixed with ripe apple flavours. Try it with a rich, creamy cheese.

Via Adriatica 12, 60027 Osimo
www.umanironchi.com

Valle dell'Acate Sicily
Sicilia IGT Il Frappato (red)

The Jacono family have a long tradition of growing grapes on the alluvial terraces that line the Acate River as it works its way across Sicily. But it took Gaetana Jacono, a pharmacist by training who left her career behind to join the family business in the 1990s, to finally help those grapes reach their full potential. Today, Gaetana Jacono's wines are consistently among the best in Sicily, including the excellent-value Il Frappato. A delightfully refreshing red, with notes of rose and fresh strawberries, this is the perfect wine for a late-afternoon picnic.

Contrada Bidini, 97011 Acate
www.valledellacate.it

Velenosi Marche, Central Italy
Rosso Piceno Superiore Il Brecciarolo (red)

Over the past few years, Velenosi, a relatively recent arrival on the Marche's wine scene, has become one of the region's most significant producers. From its home in the centre of the Rosso Piceno DOC, the company now produces around a million bottles each year, and it controls some 105ha (359 acres) of vineyards. The operation is led by the impressive and forward-thinking Angela Velenosi, and she presides over a range that is both consistently good, and consistently well-priced. Production covers a variety of styles, but of all Velenosi's output it is perhaps the Rosso Piceno Superiore Il Brecciarolo that best displays these qualities. In terms of flavour, this excellent red at first seems to be rich, dark, and brooding, but it gains lift and lightness thanks to brisk acidity. As for the food you should drink it with, this great value red is pretty much the ideal steak wine.

Via dei Biancospini 11, 63100 Ascoli Piceno
www.velenosivini.com

Vietti Barolo, Northwest Italy
Nebbiolo d'Alba Perbacco (red)

Vietti is one of the greatest names in Barolo, one of Italy's greatest wine regions. Like many in the region, the family's beginnings in Piedmont's wine industry were relatively humble: they began in the 19th century as growers who sold their grapes to other wine producers. The family moved into bottling their own wines just after WWII, and from that point on their reputation continued to grow. They are renowned for their white Arneis and for Barbera reds from the Scarrone vineyard, but it is Nebbiolo with which most people associate them. They produce numerous examples of the great Piedmontese grape in both Barolo and Barbaresco, many of which command prices to match their reputations. But it is the Nebbiolo d'Alba Perbacco that is a wonderful example at a very reasonable price. Using grapes from the same vineyards as Vietti's Castiglione Barolo, Perbacco is a classically structured, savoury wine that is best enjoyed about six years after the vintage.

Piazza Vittorio Veneto 5, 12060 Castiglione Falletto
www.vietti.com

Villa Bucci Marche, Central Italy
Verdicchio dei Castelli di Jesi (white)

Wine is but one of the concerns at the enormous Villa Bucci estate in the Marche. Its 400ha (1,000 acres), which are located in the very centre of the Verdicchio dei Castelli di Jesi DOC, include significant areas devoted to agricultural crops such as wheat, sugar beet, and sunflowers. More importantly for the purposes of this book, however, the estate contains a 21ha (52 acre) patch of carefully maintained, organically cultivated vineyards. It is here that the Bucci family produces some of the finest, most intense white wines in the region, from seriously low-yielding vines. The straight Verdicchio dei Castelli di Jesi has a distinctive savoury herbal note that lends this coastal white complexity and depth. The texture grows broad when it comes into contact with air, making this a great match for fish stew.

Via Cona 30, 60010 Ostra Vetere
www.villabucci.com

Vittorio Bera e Figli Asti, Northwest Italy
Moscato d'Asti (sparkling)

Moscato d'Asti is a wine style that is not usually taken particularly seriously. That's not surprising – this gently sparkling, gently sweet, light-alcohol white is just made for easy-sipping on summer afternoons. But Vittorio Bera e Figli has made a point of challenging Moscato's lightweight reputation, and its straight Moscato d'Asti makes a mockery of the idea that the style can't do complexity. Matching apple and pear flavours with a minerally texture that finishes on a savoury note, it's a serious wine by any stretch of the imagination. The wine is the work of Gianluigi and Alessandra Bera, who between them own an estate with roots that go as far back as the 18th century. A brother-and-sister team, the Beras are major players in the Italian natural wine scene, a group of winemakers who believe wine should be made from grapes grown organically or biodynamically. They also use as few additions as possible in the winery, relying on naturally present yeasts to do the work of fermentation.

Regione Serra Masio 21, 14053 Canelli
0141 831157

Spain

For many years, international interest in Spanish wine centred on three wine styles: the soft but full-flavoured oak-aged reds of Rioja, the sparkling wines of Cava, and the multi-faceted fortified wines of Jerez, or sherry. These classic styles remain benchmarks, but the past couple of decades have brought an explosion of interest in the rest of the country's varied wine styles. Many of these wines hail from regions with a long history of wine production that have been reinvigorated by new investment, new ideas, and a younger generation of winemakers. Places such as Priorat and Montsant in Catalonia, home to complex, mineral, powerful reds; or Rías Baixas in Galicia, with its fresh, aromatic whites. Look out, too, for the plush reds of Ribera del Duero, the violet-scented reds of Bierzo, and the crisp, aromatic whites of Rueda. Indeed, you are spoilt for choice in the "new" Spain.

Abadía Retuerta
Sardon de Duero,
Castilla y León
Rívola Sardon de Duero (red)

Though the Abadía Retuerta estate lies just outside the Ribera del Duero DO boundaries, the quality of its wines are such that it really deserves to be considered as a Duero wine. The estate was established in 1996, and the wines are made by Angel Anocibar, the first Spaniard to receive a doctorate in oenology from the University of Bordeaux. Ripe and rounded with fleshy plum damson fruit, the Rívola is a big, bold Tempranillo-Cabernet Sauvignon blend with spicy, vanilla notes that will keep for up to five years.

47340 Sardón de Duero, Valladolid
www.abadía-retuerta.es

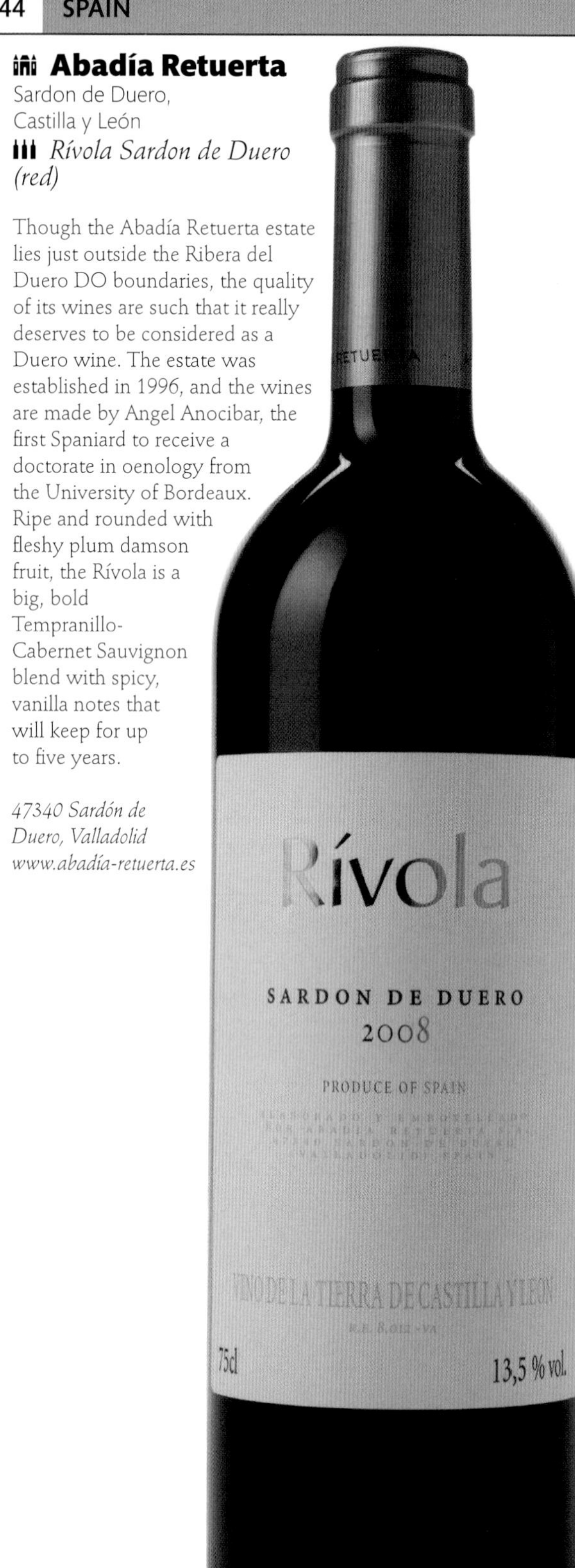

Abel Mendoza Rioja
Abel Mendoza Joven (red)

There is a long tradition of winegrowing in cult Rioja producer Abel Mendoza's family: both his father and his grandfather were wine-growers. All the same, Mendoza is far from cowed by history. Closer in spirit to the modernist wing of Rioja's wine scene, he has developed his own distinct winemaking style since starting his own estate in 1988. It is a style that looks to make the most of his collection of more than 30 different, tiny vineyard plots, some of which include vines of up to 80 years in age. From traditional local grape varieties – all grown in his own vineyards – he produces a number of wines in many styles including a fine example of Rioja Joven (literally "young Rioja"). Made using the same techniques employed in France's Beaujolais region, it results in a very juicy, medium-bodied red that is ready for drinking on release.

Carretera de Peñacerrada 7, 26338 San Vicente de la Sonsierra, La Rioja
941 308 010

Acústic Montsant, Catalonia
Acústic Blanc (white)

The name of this winery gives a clue to the kind of wines you can expect here: they are acoustic, in the sense that the flavours come to the fore, without the amplification of too much oak or over-ripeness. This is all part of the plan for owner Albert Jané Ubeda, who tries to avoid what he sees as modern, globalized winemaking. All of this is immediately apparent in the Acústic Blanc. A blend of Garnacha Blanca, Macabeo, and Pansàl, it is a fine example of the potential of Montsant's whites. Much like a white from the Rhône Valley, up-front fruit is not the point here. Instead, the wine is all about its intriguing texture and complexity.

St Lluis 12, 43777 Els Guiamets, Tarragona
629 472 988

Agrícola Castellana Rueda, Castilla y León
Cuatro Rayas Verdejo (white); Cuatro Rayas Sauvignon Blanc (white)

Agrícola Castellana started its life in difficult circumstances: it was founded in 1935 shortly before the outbreak of the Spanish Civil War. A co-operative winery, it was formed by a group of 30 wine-growers, and the concrete vats they installed are still used to this day. There are plenty of modern touches here, too, however, including a great many temperature-controlled stainless steel tanks, which are used in the production of the clean cut, crunchy wines that are the latter-day Agrícola Castellana's speciality. Many of those wines are bottled as the Cuatro Rayas brand, which with 11 million bottles produced each year is one of Spain's most successful brands, accounting for some 20% of all the wine made in the Rueda appellation. Fortunately for Rueda, those wines are extremely tasty. The Cuatro Rayas Verdejo is all lime and cream; the Sauvignon Blanc from the same label has a grapefruit zest.

Carretera Rodilana, 47491 La Seca, Valladolid
www.cuatrorayas.org

Agustí Torelló Mata Cava

Brut Reserva (sparkling)

Agustí Torelló's infectious enthusiasm for Cava and the Cava grape varieties comes through clearly in the Brut Reserva. Made in the traditional method, this sparkling white is deliciously drinkable with creamy, floral, herbal notes. Torelló Mata founded his eponymous winery at a very young age in 1950. Now moving onto the second generation, his estate remains devoted to Cava, and its wines have an immediately recognizable style, based on purity and precision. Unlike many other Cava producers, the family avoids Pinot Noir and Chardonnay, in favour of the classic Cava grape varieties, Macabeo, Xarel-lo, and Parellada.

La Serra (Camino de Ribalata), Apartado de Correos 35, 08770 Sant Sadurní d'Anoia
www.agustitorellomata.com

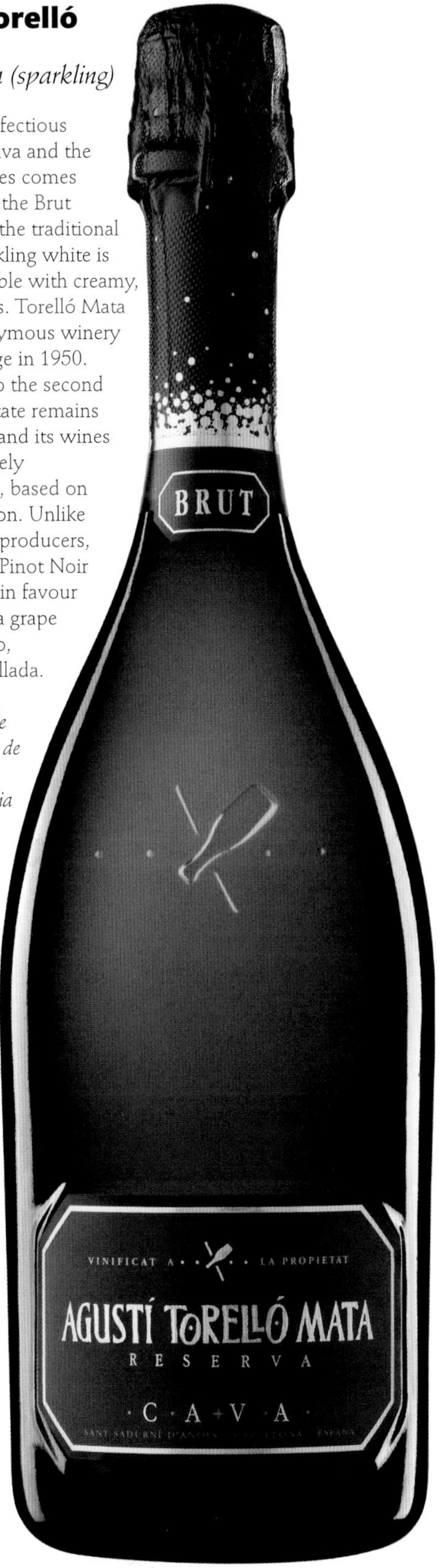

Albet i Noya Penedès, Catalonia

Petit Albet (sparkling)

Albet i Noya is renowned the world over for its green credentials. An organic pioneer, the company's production is now entirely based on organically grown grapes. It also uses a minimum of sulphur dioxide in the winemaking process, a boon for asthmatics as well as for drinkers who favour wines that taste as natural as possible. The company makes a wide range of consistently good wines, using both native Spanish and international grape varieties, of which the Petit Albet Cava is a highlight. A traditional-method sparkling wine made just from Parellada, it has a soft and fruity charm.

Can Vendrell de la Codina, 08739 Sant Pau d'Ordal, Barcelona
www.albetinoya.com

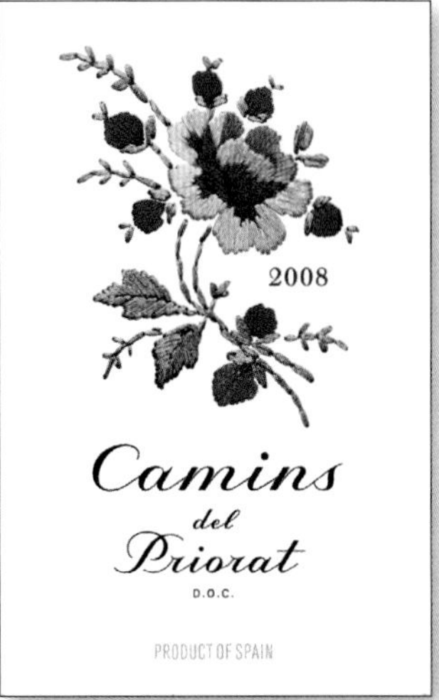

Alvaro Palacios Priorat, Catalonia

Camins del Priorat (red)

Alvaro Palacios was born in Rioja to a winemaking family, but he made his name with his pioneering work at the eponymous estate he founded in Priorat in the late 1980s. Palacios arrived in this remote, rugged corner of Catalonia after a period at the legendary Bordeaux estate, Château Pétrus. Back in Spain, working with very old vines, he was soon producing wines that attracted the world's attention. Today, his most accessible wine (in price and flavour) is the Camins del Priorat. A taste of the Alvaro Palacios style, it has baked plum fruits, supple tannins, and notes of ginger and liquorice.

Afores, 43737 Gratallops, Tarragona
977 839 195

Alvear Montilla-Moriles, Andalucia

PX Solera 1927 (fortified)

The Montilla-Moriles DO near the city of Córdoba is close to the sherry production zone, and produces similar styles of wine, all from the Pedro Ximénez grape variety. The wines are made from dried grapes, so the wines naturally reach an alcohol level of 15% ABV, and do not require (although they sometimes receive) fortification by the addition of neutral spirit (as is the case in sherry). Alvear is one of the best producers in the region, and the PX Solera 1927 one of its best wines. Young Pedro Ximénez wine is fortified to 16% ABV then left slumber in a solera dating back to 1927. The result is dark, silky, and supple, exceptionally sweet, and raisined.

María Auxiliadora 1, 14550 Montilla
www.alvear.eu

Amézola de la Mora Rioja
Viña Amézola Crianza (red)

Iñigo Amézola, great-grandson of the estate's founder, had developed Amézola de la Mora into a fine producer before he died in a car accident in 1999. His family is keeping up the good work, however, with first his widow and now his daughters working the 100ha (245 acre) of vines in the Rioja Alta, which are planted to Tempranillo, Graciano, and Mazuelo. The Viña Amézola Rioja Crianza is a lively modern Rioja that blends ripe redcurrants with a dart of citrus freshness, and the classic underlying notes of mocha from ageing in fine oak barrels.

Paraje Viña Vieja, 26359 Torremontalvo, La Rioja
www.bodegasamezola.net

Ameztoi Chacolí de Guetaria, Basque Country
Chacolí (white)

Having made wine in the Chacolí de Guetaria DO (one of two Chacolí DOs) for seven generations, the Ameztoi family know a thing or two about how to get the best out of this distinctive Basque speciality. The family's vineyards are near to San Sebastián by the Atlantic coast, where they receive abundant rain and an ocean influence. With its distinctive light green tinge and powerful zesty freshness, the family's white Chacolí is vibrant with citrus fruits and fresh-cut green herbs. It is made from the Hondarribi Zuri grape with a splash of the local red grape, Hondarribi Beltza.

20808 Getaria, Gipuzkoa
www.txakoliameztoi.com

Anta Banderas Ribera del Duero, Castilla y Léon
a4 (red)

Spain's very own Hollywood film star, Antonio Banderas, bought a stake in what was then Bodega Anta Natura in 2009, and it was not long before his name had been incorporated into the estate's new name. He picked an excellent property to make his entrance into the wine world. Founded in the late 1990s by the Ortega family, it is housed in an arresting modern winery built from glass and wood. It produces a series of wines that are somewhat enigmatically named after the period of time they spend in oak (a10, a16 etc). From its four-month sojourn in French oak barrels, the a4 has lush ripe blueberry and damson fruit. The little brother of the a16, this young wine is built for drinking now.

Carretera Palencia-Aranda de Duero Km 68, 09443 Villalba de Duero, Burgos
www.antabodegas.com

Artazu Navarra
Artazuri (red)

Artazu is a significant side-project of Rioja producer, Artadi, in the neighbouring Navarra region. It was started in 1996, and it has been living up to the very high reputation of the wines produced by the parent company ever since. It takes its name from the village of the same name in the Valdizarbe district, where the company has built a modern winery. Garnacha (or Grenache) is the focus here, and the company has invested heavily in revitalizing a number of old vineyards planted to the variety in the past decade. The value of that work can be seen in the Artazuri red, which, like all of the wines in the Artadi stable (including the El Seque project started in Alicante in 1999), manages to balance traditional virtues and grape varieties with modern winemaking techniques. Based on fruit from young Garnacha vines, Artazuri is a fine example of Artadi's excellence. It is expressive and full of fruit which is surrounded by mocha, liquorice, and spice.

Carretera Logroño, 01300 Laguardia, Alava
www.artadi.com

Baron de Ley Rioja
Finca Monasterio (red)

Though Baron de Ley is based in a 16th-century Benedictine monastery, it is in fact a fairly recent arrival on the Rioja wine scene. It started producing wine in 1985, when the owners snapped up the Ima estate beside the River Ebro. Though the property included some very old vineyards, some 90ha (225 acres) of vines were planted, mostly to Tempranillo, but also with a substantial patch of Cabernet Sauvignon. The focus here is on reserva- and gran reserva-level wines, and a mixture of French and American oak barrels is used. The Finca Monasterio is very much a Rioja in the modern style, with an emphasis on bright fruit, bolstered by creamy vanilla, and smoky oak. It is made for enjoying young.

Carretera Mendavia-Lodosa 5, 31897 Mendavia, Navarra
www.barondeley.com

Beronia Rioja
Beronia Reserva (red)

Beronia has raised its game since it was acquired by the González Byass sherry family. Indeed, the family – who also have interests in Somantano (Viñas del Vero), Cava (Vilarnau), and Toledo (Finca Constancia) – have transformed what was an underperforming estate. Where once the wines were tired, heavy, and fruit-free, today they are bright and full of charm. The investment is apparent in the lively fresh fruits, and fine oak aromas of Beronia Reserva, which has a powerful, punchy palate with notes of citrus and oak.

Carretera Ollauri-Nájera, Km 1800, 26220 Ollauri, La Rioja
www.beronia.es

Bilbaínas Rioja
Viña Pomal Reserva (red)

Viña Pomal Reserva is a classic Rioja with the elegant aromas of toasty oak, roasted redcurrants, and roses, which opens out to a midweight wine, bright with a dry finish. It is made by an estate with a long tradition in Rioja, having been established in 1901 under this name in Haro in the Rioja Alta. Today it is owned by the Cava house Codorníu, who have done much to bring about a change of fortunes at the bodega, although its style remains classic rather than modernist. Unlike many Rioja bodegas, it has significant vineyard holdings that extend to some 250ha (617 acres).

Calle de la Estación 3, 26200 Haro, La Rioja
www.bodegasbilbainas.com

Borsao Campo de Borja, Aragón
Gran Tesoro Garnacha (red)

Throughout history, Garnacha has been a mainstay of Spain's winegrowers, but it had a dip in fortunes for much of the 20th century. Revived today it fetches top prices in Priorat, but it also makes brilliant value, juicy wines in other areas, as in the well-priced Gran Tesoro Garnacha from Campo de Borja. The wine comes from Borsao, a company that dates back to 1958, when it was formed by a group of growers. It has some of the oldest vines in the region at its disposal, grown in the shadow of the Moncayo Mountain, where the cool nights lead to wines of great freshness.

50540 Borja, Zaragoza
www.bodegasborsao.com

Buil i Giné Priorat, Catalonia
Giné Giné (red)

Who could resist such a merry name? Or a Priorat at such a low price? As a true Priorat wine there are mineral notes from the slate soils, and fresh ripe fruits in Buil i Giné's Giné Giné red. The arresting name comes from the owners' grandfather, who, like his father before him, had made wine in the region. The current generation returned to Priorat in 1996, after a long period away from wine in the food retail business. They produced their first wine (Giné Giné) in 1997, and have since expanded to Montsant, Rueda, and Toro, but food remains a passion: there is a fine restaurant at the winery.

Carretera Gratallops, Vilella Baixa Km 11, 5, 43737 Gratallops, Priorat
www.builgine.com

DECANTING AND BREATHING

Merely uncorking a bottle of wine does not let it breathe. A gasp is all it will get. A large surface area of wine needs to be exposed to air so it can breathe. Many young, concentrated red wines, such as top Cabernet Sauvignon or Bordeaux that can age for several years, undergo a sort of micro-ageing process by getting lots of air into them. The same goes for a young and concentrated or especially astringent white wine, such as a Chablis. The reason is that forced exposure to air begins to oxidize a wine, causing subtle chemical changes that bring out more complex flavours and smooth out the texture. That is where decanting comes in.

SPLASH

Prompt your wine to breathe by pouring the wine into the decanter from the greatest height you can. You will only need a candle for old wines where you need to observe the sediment accumulated in the bottle.

Let the wine splash into the decanter to maximize the wine's contact with air and help release aromas.

SWIRL

Swirl the wine in the decanter so that more of it is exposed directly to the air. Sommeliers use this trick especially on young red wines that ideally need five or ten more years to mature – the difference can be remarkable.

Hold the decanter at an angle with one hand underneath for support and swirl the wine.

WHEN TO DECANT

Red wines from recent vintages with rather high levels of tannin – that pucker-inducing compound that comes from grape skins and seeds – always benefit from decanting.

The only time not to decant these wines is if the whole bottle will not be drunk in one sitting and you want to keep the remainder fresh for the next day or two. Generally speaking, bargain wines will not get better with decanting because they are made for immediate consumption. But serious wines will. Also, serious red wines that are perhaps ten years and older, may need gentle decanting to pour the wine off the sediment that collects in the bottom or along the side of the bottle.

Wines to decant include

Serious reds

Amarone
Barbaresco
Barolo
Bordeaux
Cabernet Sauvignon
Chianti Classico
Malbec
Nebbiolo
Rhône
Ribera del Duero
Rioja
Syrah/Shiraz
Tempranillo
Zinfandel

Serious whites

Alsace Riesling, Pinot Gris
Bordeaux
Burgundy
Chablis
Chardonnay
Pouilly-Fumé
Savennières

Campo Viejo Rioja
Campo Viejo Reserva (red)

Few brands are more intimately associated with one region than Campo Viejo is with Rioja. The bottle, with its orange-and-yellow-coloured label, is immediately recognizable and widely available around the world. Owned by the French Pernod Ricard drinks group (putting it in the same stable as the Australian wine brand, Jacob's Creek, and New Zealand's Brancott Estate), the brand does a good job of introducing consumers to Rioja, with consistent quality throughout the range. The Reserva is particularly good value. This grown-up version of the popular basic Rioja has three years' age to give the roasted redcurrant Tempranillo a greater depth of flavour and a vanilla lift.

Camino de Lapuebla 50, 26006 Logroño, La Rioja
www.campoviejo.com

Casa de la Ermita Jumilla, Murcia
Viognier (white)

There is a modern approach to winemaking at Casa de la Ermita that has done much to improve the reputation of Jumilla. A relative newcomer to the region, this producer has made an immediate impression, producing wines that are well-tuned to the tastes of the international market – no wonder those wines are now widely distributed throughout the world. Ermita's wines are all great value, but a real standout in terms of quality for the price is the Casa de la Ermita Viognier. The company's newest wine it is made from a grape variety (Viognier) that is itself relatively new to Spain. Finely balanced with plenty of creamy apricot and white peach fruit, it is a delicious addition to the range.

Carretera del Carche, Km. 11,5, 30520 Jumilla, Murcia
www.casadelaermita.com

Castaño Yecla, Murcia
Hecula (red)

Back in 1950, when Ramón Castaño launched his wine business, Yecla was not known for producing top-notch wines. At that time, producers in this small region, which is based around the village of the same name towards Spain's east coast, were very much focused on quantity rather than quality. Castaño was different, and has remained so ever since, maintaining a position at the forefront of developments in Yecla. Under the guidance of Ramón Castaño and his children, it took all the necessary steps for the production of good wine, such as introducing temperature-controlled fermentation tanks and sorting tables. Castaño's wines also benefit from access to the winery's prized asset: the 300ha (741 acres) of Monastrell vines owned by the family. Powerful and spicy with redcurrant fruit, Monastrell flourishes at Castaño, in wines such as Hecula. After six months ageing in American oak, this great example of modern Yecla red wine develops a rounded toasty individuality.

Carretera Fuentealamo 3, 30510 Yecla, Murcia
www.bodegascastano.com

Castell d'Encus
Costers del Segre, Catalonia
Susterris Negre (red)

The setting for Castell d'Encus has a long pedigree in the wine business. Dating back to the 11th century, you can still see the stone basins that the monks who once lived here used to make their wines. The monks have departed and today it is the setting for ex-Torres winemaker Raúl Bobet's ambitious new project, which draws on high altitude (800–1,000m/2,620–3,280ft) vineyards in the Costers del Segre DO. Bobet has certainly made a great start with Susterris Negre, a blend of Bordeaux varieties with a dash of Syrah.

Carretera Tremp a Sta. Engracia, Km 5, 25630 Talarn, Lleida
www.encus.org

Castell del Remei Costers del Segre, Catalonia

Gotim Bru (red)

The influence of Bordeaux made its presence felt at Castell del Remei in the late 1800s. A relatively large estate, there were as many as 50 families living here in its heyday, and it was widely admired for the impressive wines that the French-inspired winemaking techniques produced. Quality dropped off somewhat in the 20th century, until the Cusiné family, one of the most important names in the Costers del Segre DO, bought the estate in 1982. The family immediately set about restoring Castell del Remei to its former glories, renovating the winery and completely overhauling production. Today they make a range of excellent wines, of which the lively and highly individual Gotim Bru is a particular highlight. The blend of Tempranillo and Garnacha with Cabernet Sauvignon and Merlot makes for a dense, concentrated mix of ripe fruits, with sweet spices.

Finca Castell del Remei, 25333 Penelles, Lleida
www.castelldelremei.com

Castillo de Monjardin Navarra

Castillo de Monjardin Barrel Ferment Chardonnay (white)

Chardonnay flourishes in the Navarra region, where white burgundy has clearly been a strong influence on winemakers. That certainly seems to be the case at Castillo de Monjardin, a relatively recent arrival here having first been established in 1993. The Monjardin winery looks deceptively traditional from the outside; inside it contains all the winemaking bells and whistles required by a modern producer. Winemaking here is carefully and gently done, the winery's position on a hillside allowing the winemakers to use gravity to pass the wines through the various stages of the production process. Monjardin's successfully Burgundian-style Barrel Ferment Chardonnay has three months in oak and is creamy, with exotic undertones.

Viña Rellanada, 31242 Vilamayor de Monjardin
www.monjardin.es

Castillo Perelada Empordà, Catalonia

Castillo Perelada Brut Reserve (sparkling); 5 Fincas Empordà (red)

Holidaymakers in Catalonia in search of a day out from the beaches of the Costa Brava would do well to call in on Castillo Perelada's estate. Alongside the winery, there is a fine hotel, a spa, and a restaurant in a well-preserved castle. For some time, the hospitality options rather overshadowed the wines produced here, but, as quality improves, that is increasingly an out-of-date view. Castillo Perelada Brut Reserve is a traditional-method sparkling wine made from the three classic Cava varieties (Macabeo, Xarel-lo, and Parellada). It is pure, vibrant, and refreshing. The estate's 5 Fincas, a blend of six different grape varieties, shows the benefit of selecting from five fincas (estates): it has intense brambly fruit and is gently spicy.

Plaça del Carme 1, 17491 Perelada, Girona
www.castilloperelada.com

Castrocelta

Rías Baixas, Galicia

Albariño (white)

Formed by a group of 20 growers and producers, Castrocelta has only been going for half a decade, but it is already attracting attention. Located in the Val do Salnés zone, its name harks back to the Celts, the area's original inhabitants. The group has 37ha (91 acres) of Albariño, and their Albariño Castrocelta is a hugely impressive expression of this grape variety, revealing all of its sunny peachiness, but also the strong maritime influence of the climate – there is a freshness here that only cool nights and sea breezes can bring.

LG Quintáns,
17 Sisán 36638,
Ribadumia
www.castrocelta.com

Celler de Capçanes Montsant, Catalonia

Mas Collet (red)

Celler de Capçanes started its life in 1933, and is today one of Spain's top co-ops – indeed, many believe it is the very best. It made its name with a kosher wine, produced at the request of Barcelona's Jewish community, and it has since become associated with a host of good-value, well-made wines. A blend of Garnacha, Cariñena, Tempranillo, and Cabernet Sauvignon that has been aged in oak for eight months, Mas Collet is a bright, approachable wine for drinking young: there is a warm mouthful of spicy, juicy, brambly fruit with a lightly crunchy, grainy texture.

Carrer Llaberia 4, 43776 Capçanes, Tarragona
www.cellercapcanes.com

Chivite Navarra

Chivite Gran Feudo Reserva Especial (red)

Blending Bordeaux varietals with Tempranillo – a mix of the international and the Spanish – is a typically Navarran pursuit. It is something that Chivite does really well as can be seen in its Gran Feudo Reserva Especial, where the blend is full of pure, vibrant fruit. The Chivite name has been a feature of the Navarra wine landscape since 1647, making the Chivite family one of the oldest producers in Spain. More recently, it has expanded to include interests in Rioja, Rueda, and Ribera del Duero, but it remains associated with its original home. The family upped its presence in Navarra with the acquisition of the Señorío de Arínzano estate in 1988, which they subsquently transformed into a showpiece old-meets-new winery, where historic architecture mingles with gleaming examples of all the latest winemaking equipment.

Ribera 34, 31592 Cintruenigo
www.bodegaschivite.com

Cillar de Silos Ribera del Duero, Castilla y Léon

El Quintanal (red)

With just three months' ageing in French oak, Cillar de Silos El Quintanal is a wine intended to be enjoyed "joven" – it is young and vibrant and ready to drink. Densely flavoured, it certainly fulfils its promise. It is made by an impressive family-run business, that has some 48ha (119 acres) of Tempranillo vineyards on the slopes and amid the forests of Quintana del Pidio and Gumiel de Mercado. Yields here are kept very low by the brothers-and-sister team of Oscár, Roberto, and Amelia Aragón. The winemaker is Oscár Aragón, who studied winemaking for five years in Rioja, before moving to Jerez and travelling the winemaking world from South Africa to California.

Paraje el Soto, 09370 Quintana del Pidio, Burgos
www.cillardesilos.es

Codorníu Cava

Codorníu Pinot Noir Rosé (sparkling)

Codorníu has been instrumental in the development of Cava, since it was founded by Josep Raventós in 1872. Raventós was inspired by his studies of the traditional method of making champagne, and he decided there was a future for quality sparkling wine in his native Catalonia. He made the required investment, constructing a winery designed by a student of Gaudí that is still a popular stop on the wine tourist trail in Penedès today. Recent years have seen a renewed level of commitment to high quality production, and there has been a noticeable improvement in the wines. Among them is the Pinot Noir Rosé, which Codorníu claims is the first Cava to be made from Pinot Noir. Whether or not that is genuinely the case is immaterial, since the champagne grape variety certainly makes a successful transfer to Spain in this wine, which is light in colour but with baskets of berry fruits.

Avenida Jaume Codorníu, 08770 Sant Sadurní d'Anoia
www.codorniu.es

CVNE Rioja
CVNE Reserva (red)

An historic producer in Rioja, the Compañia Vinícola del Norte de España, or CVNE (pronounced coo-nay) for short, first began making wine in 1879. It is still owned by the descendants of the two founders, the brothers Eusebio and Raimundo Real de Asúa, and it is still based in its original home in the railway station district of the town of Haro, where many of the other great names of Rioja have their headquarters. A visit to the CVNE bodega today offers an insight into how things used to be in the region, but that does not mean the winery is stuck in the past. CVNE has always been receptive to winemaking innovations, and there have been a great number of additions to the winery over the years. The CVNE Reserva is one of the bodega's most popular wines. Medium-bodied with crunchy red fruits, it has a supple overcoat of smoky tobacco with a hint of cream. A classic and well-loved style of Rioja, it will drink well now, but it can also be kept in the cellar to develop for two or three more years.

Barrio de la Estacíon, 26200 Maro, La Rioja
www.cvne.com

Dehesa Gago Toro, Castilla y León
Dehesa Gago (red)

The engaging Telmo Rodríguez is a dynamo of Spanish wine. He refers to himself as a "driving winemaker", a nod to the "flying" consultant winemakers that became famous for making wines at different wineries all over the world in the 1980s and 1990s. Rodríguez, however, prefers to stick to his native land, where he spends much of his time driving between the various vineyards where he has an interest, making wines both under his own labels and those belonging to retailers. Rodríguez first became known for reviving his family estate, Remelluri. He then started his own business in 1994, seeking out neglected vineyards and styles to fashion into delicious wines. The Dehesa Gago is a great example of Rodríguez at work. This is him reviving Toro's powerful Tinta de Toro (Tempranillo) heritage, to create a forthright, full-flavoured, inky, earthy wine, with mocha undertones.

No visitor facilities
www.telmorodriguez.com

FOOD & WINE RIOJA TEMPRANILLO

Spanish wine is closely associated with the Tempranillo grape variety, and in Rioja it produces elegant, dry, Bordeaux-like reds. The wines are balanced, expressive, and supple.

In general Tempranillo has a firm, tannic structure, often from lavish oak ageing. The notes of the wine vary from delicate and feminine strawberry, cherry, and vanilla to bolder olive, stewed meats, tobacco, and cedar.

Both pork and lamb are widely looked upon as ideal meats for Rioja, with dishes as simple as the classic potato and chorizo stew, pork chops simmered in peppers and onions, and pork with tomato sauce with pimentos and pepper. The hearty *cocido*, a stew made with caparron beans, onions, bacon, and chorizo, pairs nicely with a lighter Rioja. A juicy roast lamb would showcase the richest, most mature Rioja.

For weeknight Rioja food pairings, think bold, rustic ingredients with gutsy flavours. Roasted red peppers, tomatoes, onions, garlic, and chilli in dishes such as ratatouille, chilli con carne, and spicy meatballs are worthy matches as is a more earthy Porcini mushroom risotto. Often served with the cheese course, Rioja has a special affinity with the fruity *Murcia al Vino* (or "Drunken Goat"), a wonderfully grapey cheese that is submerged in red wine to age, and hard cow's milk cheeses including mature Cheddar.

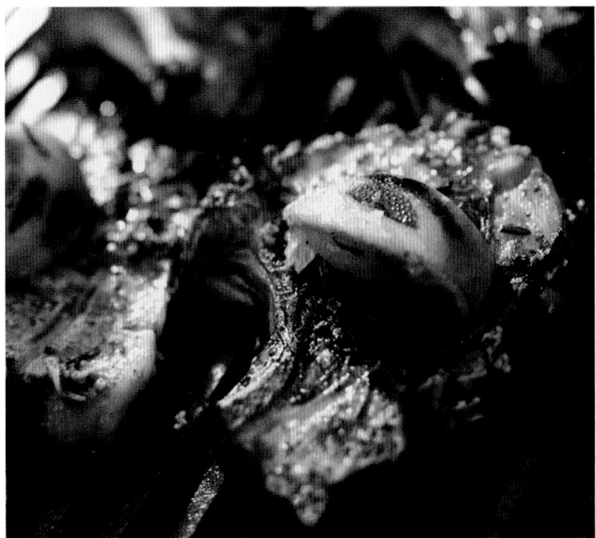

Pork chops on the grill: the perfect match for classic Rioja.

Descendientes de J Palacios Bierzo, Castilla y Léon

Pétalos (red)

An exceptional project in Corúllon in the rising-star DO of Bierzo, Descendientes de J Palacios is the work of two "descendants": Alvaro Palacios (of the legendary, eponymous Priorat estate) and his nephew, Ricardo Pérez. Started in 1999, the estate has some 30ha (74 acres) of bush vines, which are farmed biodynamically and were first planted by monks. The grape variety is the local Mencía, which Palacios and Pérez have proved can be crafted into exceptional red wines; indeed, the pair have achieved a similar transformative effect on the Bierzo region as Alvaro Palacios had previously managed in Priorat. An impressive introduction to Bierzo, the Pétalos has floral and smoky aromas, and is a delicate, dancing wine in the mouth, fresh and zesty, with a lingering elegant finish. This is supposedly the estate's entry-level wine, but it knocks the socks off the "top" wines of many estates.

Avenida Calvo Sotelo 6, 24500 Villafranca del Bierzo, León
987 540 821

Dominio de Tares Bierzo, Castilla y Léon

Baltos (red)

Located in an industrial estate, the headquarters of Dominio de Tares are not in the least bit glamorous when compared to the beautiful and historic architecture of many other Spanish bodegas. But there is a reason for being here: the vineyards of Bierzo are scattered far and wide across a number of different locations in the DO, and building a winery in one of those sites would simply make the other vineyards less accessible. No matter. The home may not be aesthetically pleasing, but the wines produced there most certainly are. In fact, Dominio de Tares is right up there among the top three or four producers in the Bierzo DO. Produced from Mencía grapes grown on 25- to 40-year-old vines, Baltos is a deeply coloured, and equally powerfully flavoured, red wine. It has a fine balance of crunchy red fruits, backed up by keynote mineral highlights and a bright toasty finish from the four to seven months the wine spends ageing in a mix of French and American oak.

Los Barredos 4, 24318 San Román de Bembibre, León
www.dominiodetares.com

Dominio de Valdepusa Vinos de Pago, Castilla-La Mancha

El Rincón Vinos de Madrid (red)

Pioneer is a word that is often attached to winemakers, but few have a bigger claim to the title in Spain than Carlos Falcó, the Marqués de Griñon. Falcó studied wine at the University of California, Davis, and planted Cabernet Sauvignon in his 3,000ha (7,413 acre) estate on the boundary of Méntrida. Because his estate was not contained in – and was therefore not constrained by the rules of – a Denominación de Origen, Falcó experimented with numerous different grape varieties and with such viticultural techniques as drip irrigation and canopy management. At his El Rincón estate in the Vinos de Madrid DO, all of the knowledge he has accrued is applied to a darkly coloured Syrah, filled out by 10% Garnacha. The fruit is ripe, while the French oak adds polish and glamour. One of Madrid's stars.

Finca Casa de Vacas, 45692 Malpica de Tajo, Toledo
www.pagosdefamilia.com

Edetària Terra Alta, Catalonia

Via Edetana (red)

Terra Alta is a neighbour of Montsant and Priorat, but it is determined not to be overshadowed by these two better-known DOs. In Via Edetana, Edetària uses the local red grape varieties to powerful effect; rich fruit, balsamic notes, and a mineral purity. Started in 2003, Edetària is a recent addition to the wine scene in Catalonia, with a spanking new (and very stylish) winery, but it draws on a stock of old vines. The company has some 24ha (59 acres) of vineyards, many of which are more than 50 years old, with the balance being between 20 and 25 years old.

Finca El Mas, Carretera Gandesa, Vilalba, 43780 Gandesa, Tarragona
www.edetaria.com

Elias Mora Toro, Castilla y León

Elias Mora (red)

The wines of Toro are never discreet, but with 12 months in French and American oak, the powerful Elias Mora red develops a fine texture with an overlay of savoury, delicate spice and liquorice. It is made by a company which produces wines in Toro and Rueda, and which is based around the "two Victorias": Victoria Pariente and Victoria Benavides. Pariente works in Rueda, Benavides in Toro, where she makes the most of the dry, continental climate and some great old-vine material.

San Román de Hornija, 47530 Valladolid
www.bodegaseliasmora.com

Emilio Moro Ribera del Duero, Castilla y Léon

Emilio Moro (red)

Since starting his winery in the late 1980s, the style at Emilio Moro has evolved considerably. Moro now draws on some 70ha (173 acres) of Tinto Fino (Tempranillo), and he no longer uses the reserva or gran reserva categories, preferring instead to give each wine its own individual name – and identity. The wine that takes Moro's own name is a refreshing blend of red fruits with notes of aniseed and spice from French and American oak barrels. Taken from vineyards aged between 25 and 50 years old, it is Moro's largest production wine, and it is big and vibrant, finishing with an elegant, savoury tobacco sign-off.

Valoria, Peñafiel Road, 47315 Pesquera de Duero, Valladolid
www.emiliomoro.com

Estancia Piedra Toro, Castilla y León

Piedra Azul (red)

Bursting with energy, Piedra Azul is an unoaked Tinta de Toro (Tempranillo) from one of the region's most exciting new producers. Full-bodied, it has a bucket of black cherries matched with balsamic notes and dark chocolate. Estancia Piedra was founded in 1998, by the Scottish-born Grant Stein, who had had enough of life as a tax lawyer. Stein has invested a great deal in the estate, and he now has some 70ha (173 acres) of Tinta de Toro vines, which include both young and old plots, and a small parcel that dates back to the 1920s.

Carretera Toro-Salamanca Km 5, 49800 Toro
www.estanciapiedra.com

Etim Montsant, Catalonia

Etim Negre (red)

Although not quite in the same league as neighbouring Priorat, the prices of the wines of Montsant are notoriously high. In this context, those produced by Etim are a positive steal. The co-op in Falset, based in a distinctive winery designed by a Gaudí-inspired architect, is the winery responsible for this great value range, of which the Etim Negre is arguably the best value of all. Here, Garnacha and Cariñena, with just a few months in oak, make for a black-fruited wine, with savoury spice and a long fresh finish.

Calle Miquel Barceló 13, 43730 Falset, Tarragona
977 830 105

Faustino Rioja

Faustino 1 Gran Reserva (red)

Faustino 1 Gran Reserva Rioja is very much in the classic style of Rioja: light- to medium-bodied with delicate cherry fruit, a crisp, almost citrus freshness, and the complexity of flavour that only comes from age. It is one of the region's most recognized brands. That recognition is down, at least in part, to the memorable packaging, which, with the aristocratic-looking character on the label, the frosted bottles, and the metallic cage, looks like it has been around since the 1600s, but is, in fact, a clever pastiche developed for the brand's launch in 1960.

Carretera de Logroño, 01320 Oyón-Oion, Alava
www.bodegasfaustino.es

Finca Sandoval

Manchuela, Castilla-La Mancha

Salia (red)

It is very rare, in any field, for a critic to cross the line into creating what they had previously only written about. But that is what Victor de la Serna, one of Spain's most respected wine journalists, has done at Finca Sandoval since 2000. And he has done it very well, too. Syrah clearly flourishes here: blended with Monastrell and a dash of Bobal, the Salia is deeply coloured, aromatic, a lively blend of blackcurrant, mocha, and citrus, with freshness from the altitude of the vineyards, which lie between 800m and 1,000m (2,625–3,281ft).

16237 Ledaña,
Cuenca, Castilla-La Mancha
616 444 805

TEMPRANILLO

Spain's most celebrated red grape variety is the main component in the wines of Rioja and Ribera del Duero, although you rarely see its name on the labels. Tempranillo can make young, fruity, affordable wines or deep, rich, and long-ageing estate-bottled reds. It is Spain's most widely planted variety.

It tends to give medium- to full-bodied wines with rather similar fruit flavours to the Bordeaux varieties of Cabernet Sauvignon and Merlot, but with more dusky, herbal, and leather aromas. Tempranillo's flavours marry beautifully with the effect of ageing in oak barrels.

EARLY BLOOMER

While Tempranillo has some similarities to Cabernet Sauvignon in terms of flavour, they don't extend to its ripening habits. Tempranillo ripens rather early, more like Merlot, so winemakers get the flavours they like before the autumn weather can turn problematic.

TEAM PLAYER

Tempranillo is great for blending with other varieties. Winemakers in Spain's Rioja region like to blend it with Garnacha, Mazuelo, and other varieties to create more complex flavours and to add a more tannic texture.

SMALL BERRIES

Winemakers ferment their reds with the skins, juice, seeds, and pulp all mixed together. Since smaller berries give relatively more skins to the mix and relatively less juice, and since skins contain most of the flavour compounds, small berries in Tempranillo equal big flavours.

SPLIT PERSONALITY

Tempranillo is known as Tinta Roriz in the Douro Valley of Portugal (the same river as the Duero in Spain) where it is one of several grape varieties used in the famous fortified, sweet port wines and in dry red table wines.

WHERE IN THE WORLD?

Fans of Spanish wine have been drinking Tempranillo for centuries without necessarily knowing what grape variety makes their favourite wine.

It is considered a native of northern Spain, where Rioja and Ribera del Duero are located. Lots of wines are also made with Tempranillo in the regions of Navarra, Penedès, and Valdepeñas, where the grape variety appears more often on the label.

Tempranillo is enjoying a small boom in popularity in Oregon and California, where a sizeable acreage has been planted with Tempranillo for decades under the local synonym, Valdepeñas. In the past, these grapes were largely used in inexpensive wines. Argentina, Chile, and Mexico are other good sources.

The following regions are among the best for Tempranillo. Try bottles from these recommended vintages for the best examples:

Rioja: 2009, 2008, 2006
Ribera del Duero: 2009, 2006
Navarra: 2010, 2009, 2008, 2007

A few wineries in Oregon, such as Abacela, produce high-quality Tempranillo.

Finca Valpiedra
Rioja
Cantos de Valpiedra (red)

Nestling in a bend of the River Ebro, Finca Valpiedra is one of Rioja's most spectacular estates. Now in the fifth generation of ownership by the Martínez Bujanda family, the estate is a technical feat as well as an aesthetic one, with every last vine and parcel of soil mapped with precision. The winemaking is similarly conscientious, and so it is perhaps not all that surprising that the wines are of a very high standard, too. Cantos, the second wine, is deeply coloured with smoky cedar and floral aromas. It is bold, fine textured, packed with blackcurrant fruit, and lifted by a crunchy freshness.

Término Montecillo, 26360 Fuenmayor, La Rioja
www.familiamartinezbujanda.com

Freixenet Cava
Freixenet Excelencia Brut (sparkling)

Freixenet (pronounced fresh-eh-nay) Excelencia Brut is a modern Cava that shows it is possible to deliver crisp citrus and apple purity using the traditional Cava grape varieties. It has a wonderful supple finish, and it is rounded and creamy. A family of wine producers, the Ferrer family began making Cava in 1914. Typically Catalan in their entrepreneurial spirit, they invested heavily in advertising and marketing, and built brands that were known the world over, bringing global renown to Cava in the process. The family now has interests around the world, with projects in California and France as well as Spain.

Joan Sala 2, 08770 Sant Sadurní d'Anoia
www.freixenet.com

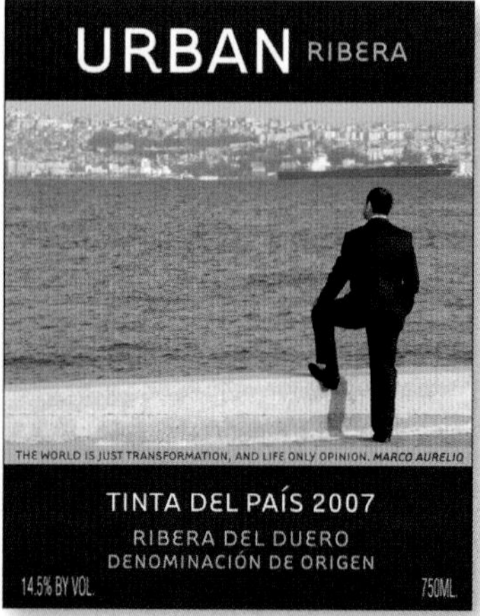

O Fournier Ribera del Duero, Castilla y Léon
Urban (red)

Bright, punchy, and vivacious, Urban Ribera del Duero is definitely a city-dweller's wine, its fresh red fruit with mocha and liquorice spice designed for drinking now. It is made by the Fournier family, and is part of their mission to produce quality wine in Spanish-speaking countries around the world – the family also have interests in Chile and Argentina. They use the same branding for all their projects, with Urban the entry-level range in the portfolio. Their Spanish home is the Ribera del Duero, where they have 60ha (148 acres) of stony vineyards that are mainly planted to Tinta del País (Tempranillo).

Finca El Pinar, 09316 Berlangas de Roa, Burgos
www.bodegasofournier.com

González Byass Jerez-Xérèz-Sherry
González Byass Tío Pepe Fino (fortified); González Byass Viña AB (fortified)

González Byass is one of the Spanish drinks industry's most familiar names. It has vinous interests throughout Spain, as well as producing a range of high-quality brandy. It is most associated with sherry, however, with its Tío Pepe Fino, its best-known brand. Widely distributed, Tío Pepe is a model of the lighter style of Fino Sherry. Look out for the "en rama" (straight from the barrel) version, which is seasonally available in some countries. Viña AB is the award-winning Amontillado style that comes from the Tío Pepe solera. It is weightier and nuttier, but it is still fresh.

Calle Manuel Maria González 12, 11403 Jerez de la Frontera
www.gonzalezbyass.com

Gramona Cava
Gramona Imperial Gran Reserva Brut (sparkling)

The local varieties Xarel-lo and Macabeo get a brisk boost from Chardonnay to give the confident Cava Gramona Imperial Gran Reserva Brut a classic biscuit aroma and a reassuringly long finish in the mouth. It is the kind of wine that challenges preconceived notions about Cava as a bland or unexciting style, but that is typical of Gramona. Harnessing their technical and artistic talents, Jaume Gramona and his cousin Javier make a range of thrilling wines, both sparkling and still, and they are forever experimenting with new ideas and techniques.

Calle Industria 36, 08770 Sant Sadurní d'Anoia
www.gramona.com

Hidalgo-La Gitana Jerez-Xérèz-Sherry
Pastrana Manzanilla Pasada (fortified)

First, a little explanation. Manzanilla is Fino matured in the Sanlúcar area; Pasada means it has longer ageing. For a fine example of this style, look no further than Hidalgo-La Gitana. From a single vineyard the wine has an impressive savoury, nutty depth. The bodega is currently run by Hector Hidalgo, the seventh generation to manage the firm. It has more than 200ha (495 acres) of vineyards, and it is based in Sanlúcar, where the maritime influence gives the flor (the layer of protective yeast that grows over the wines in barrel during ageing) a different character to other parts of the region.

Calle Clavel 29, 11402 Jerez de la Frontera
www.emiliohidalgo.es

Inurrieta Navarra
Inurrieta Norte (red)

Made from the international grape varieties Merlot and Cabernet Sauvignon with a dollop of Petit Verdot, Inurrieta Norte Navarra spends just five months in oak, ensuring the fruit remains vibrant, dark, and determinedly youthful. It is delicious proof that this relatively young winery has already found its feet in the years since it was founded in 2001. A family business, Inurrieta enjoys the considerable advantage of being able to source its fruit from some 230ha (570 acres) of its own vineyards.

Carretera de Falces-Miranda de Arga Km 30, 31370 Falces
www.bodegainurrieta.com

Jiménez-Landi
Méntrida, Castilla y Léon
Sotorrondero (red)

Jiménez-Landi Sotorrondero Méntrida is a wine produced with a philosophy of minimal intervention. Largely made from Syrah, the grapes are organically grown, and the wine is bottled unfiltered. It results in a wine that is ripe, almost roasted, with savoury, mineral notes. It will benefit from two to three years in the cellar. Another of Spain's new wave of wineries, Jiménez-Landi started out in a 17th-century family home in 2004. It has 27ha (67 acres) of vineyards in the continental climate of the Méntrida region. Elegant and expressive, the wines already have an international reputation.

Avenida de la Solana, No 45, 45930 Méntrida, Toledo
www.jimenezlandi.com

Joan d'Anguera Montsant, Catalonia
La Planella (red)

Wine has been made at the Joan d'Anguera estate for the best part of 200 years, but its fine reputation today is largely due to the work of the brothers, Joan and Josep d'Anguera. The brothers had their father to thank for introducing the grape variety with which they are most associated, Syrah. But it was very much their idea to introduce biodynamics, and the estate is in the process of full conversion to the practice. For an introduction to the d'Anguera style – and the intriguing flavours offered in the Catalan region of Montsant – the La Planella red blend is a worthy candidate. Dark and expressive, this wine's Cabernet Sauvignon, Garnacha, Syrah, and Mazuelo fruit, which is aged for six months in American oak, has a deliciously rich coating of mocha and spice.

C/Major, 43746 Darmós, Tarragona
www.cellersjoandanguera.com

José Pariente Rueda, Castilla y León
José Pariente Verdejo (white)

José Pariente is the Rueda operation of Victoria Pariente, one of the celebrated "two Victorias", a pair of talented winemakers (the other being Victoria Benavides at Elias Mora in Toro) who started a winemaking business together in the late 1990s. At José Pariente, Victoria Pariente works on hillside vineyards, where cold nights, savage winters, and pebbly soils are the ideal conditions for producing crisp, fresh wines. Those vineyards were planted with Verdejo by Victoria's late father, José, and Victoria is now one of the star producers of Verdejo, giving the variety international appeal. The José Pariente Verdejo shows why. Ringingly pure and resoundingly fresh, it is a wine to set the tastebuds dancing.

Carreterade Rueda Km 2,5, 47491 La Seca, Valladolid
www.josepariente.com

Juan Gil Jumilla, Murcia
Juan Gil Monastrell (red)

Juan Gil founded his eponymous winery in 1916, and since then the Gil Vera family have been prime movers in proving that Jumilla could be a venue for fine wine production. Despite numerous changes, the family have been consistent in their commitment to quality throughout the winery's first century of existence, and today's management, Juan Gil's great-grandchildren, are upholding the family traditions in fine style, having built a new winery, Termino de Arriba, at the highest point in Jumilla. At the core of their production is the Monastrell grape variety, which flourishes in this area of Spain. And you can discover the intriguing flavours of old-vine Monastrell (otherwise known as Mourvèdre elsewhere in the world) in the Juan Gil Monastrell Jumilla. Using fruit from low-yielding, 40-year-old vines grown on sandy soils, the wine spends just a little time in oak, and offers powerful raisin and blackberry fruit flavours that shine with undertones of mocha.

Portillo de la Glorieta 7, Bajo, 30520 Jumilla, Murcia
www.juangil.es

Juvé y Camps Cava
Cinta Purpura (sparkling)

Juvé y Camps Cinta Purpura is a blend of the three traditional Cava varieties, made using the traditional method, and sold as a vintage wine. It has floral and toast aromas, and it is well-balanced and full-bodied, with a creamy fizz. The Juvé family behind it are one of the traditional names of the town of Sant Sadurní d'Anoia, and have been making wines for more than 200 years. They began producing Cava somewhat later, in 1921, since when they have become associated with a distinctive winemaking style that produces classic wines of great weight and intensity, although always with an incisive streak of acidity, and fine bubbles.

Calle de Sant Venat 1, 08770 Sant Sadurní d'Anoia
www.juveycamps.com

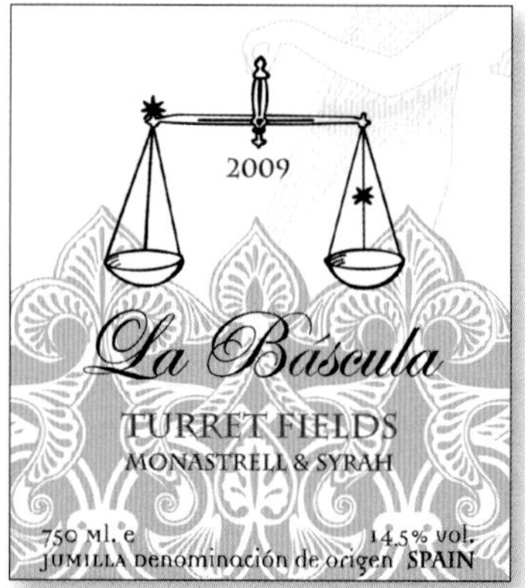

La Báscula Yecla and Jumilla, Murcia
Turret Fields Jumilla (red)

La Báscula has an interesting back story. It is the project of an English Master of Wine, Ed Adams, and a South African winemaker, Bruce Jack, who set out to make wines in a number of locations across Spain. Among the most interesting so far is Turret Fields in Jumilla. Made at the Juan Gil winery, this robust and bold red is a blend of Monastrell and Syrah. It is produced in a confident, modern style, and is released with a few youthful edges that will soften if left to cellar for a couple of years.

No visitor facilities
www.labascula.net

La Rioja Alta Rioja
Viña Alberdi (red)

With its enchanting, atmospheric headquarters filled with thousands of barrels of slowly maturing wine in the station district of Haro, La Rioja Alta is an historic presence in the region. It is also responsible for some of its finest wines. The company was founded in 1890, when five wine producers came together to form Sociedad Vinicola de la Rioja Alta. As with so many of the classic Rioja bodegas, a French influence was apparent from the beginning, with the first technical director being a M Vigier. Today the bodega owns a sizeable 360ha (890 acres) of vineyards. It makes a broad range of styles under numerous different labels, with representatives that fit into both the highly traditional and the more modern camp. Whatever the style, the wines are always worth a look, and some, such as the Viña Alberdi, are great value, too. The only one of Rioja Alta's wines to age in new oak, Alberdi is an elegant, lighter Rioja, with abundant red fruits. It is characterized by wonderful freshness, that gives it great drinkability, even in warm vintages.

Avda de Vizcaya 8, 26200 Haro, La Rioja
www.riojalta.com

Luis Cañas Rioja

Luis Cañas Seleccion de la Familia (red)

Juan Luis Cañas has made an enormous success of the established business he inherited from his father in 1989. He built a new winery (in 1994) and added a raft of high quality wines to the bodega's roster. The Luis Cañas Seleccion de la Familia is one such wine. A generous, modern, supple, rounded, red cherry- and vanilla-flavoured red, it is aged in French and American oak for a year, and is a fine example of why Rioja is so popular.

Carretera Samaniego 10, 01307 Villabuena, La Rioja
www.luiscanas.com

Lustau Jerez-Xérèz-Sherry

Palo Cortado Vides Almacenista (fortified); Emilin Moscatel (fortified)

Among the stars of Lustau's extensive portfolio is the range of Almacenista wines. These are sourced from almacenistas, stockholders who buy sherry or must and mature it in their own bodegas but who are not licenced to commercialize the wines themselves. The Palo Cortado Vides Almacenista is an example of Jerez's most celebrated style. Neither Amontillado nor Oloroso, it is a real original: intense and dry, relieved by notes of chocolate and roasted walnuts. Emilin Moscatel is a great sweet wine. Much more interesting than most Muscats, it is aromatic, silky, and floral.

Calle Arcos 53, Apartado Postal 69, 11402 Jerez de la Frontera
www.emilio-lustau.com

IS ALL THAT SPARKLES CHAMPAGNE?

The world is full of sparkling wine, but true champagne only comes from the northern French region of Champagne. But that does not mean sparkling wines made elsewhere are not enjoyable, do not have great history, or do not get great reviews from wine critics – they just cannot be officially labelled as champagne.

Put yourself in the position of the people working in the wine business near Reims, the ancient French city and the picture becomes clear. The centuries-old wine businesses here include Moët et Chandon, Taittinger, Veuve-Clicquot, and Mumm. These growers and winemakers get angry when a winery in the US, Australia, or China borrows the name of their homeland to help sell a product made elsewhere.

Still, it is not a crime to go shopping for champagne and instead buy a light, bubbly Prosecco from Italy, a smooth, sparkling Cava from Spain, or a Sekt from Germany. Many of the world's best sparkling wines are made using the same techniques and grape varieties as the Champagne winemakers use. The technique involves a secondary fermentation where yeast and sugar are added to the bottle to help develop flavour and bubbles. Champagne is always made in this way; other sparkling wines don't have to be. When you look for a champagne-like wine, find key words on the label including "bottle-fermented", "metodo classico", or "méthode classique".

Freixenet produces fine Cava using champagne techniques.

Malumbres Navarra
Malumbres Garnacha (red)

Garnacha is a grape whose reputation is rising and Malumbres is a bold, generous example of what Spain can achieve with it. Ripe, with baskets of black and red fruits, it is a well-made and delicious red wine. Malumbres has been producing wines since the inauspicious year of 1940, when founder Vicente Malumbres started the business. The company concentrated on bulk wine for the best part of half a century, until it began its modern orientation towards quality production in 1987. Vicente's son, Javier, now makes the wines in an environmentally sensitive way, with minimal winemaking interventions.

Calle Santa Bárbara 15, 31591 Corella
www.malumbres.com

Marqués de Cáceres Rioja
Marqués de Cáceres Reserva (red)

Rioja has three world-renowned marquesses; Cáceres, Murrieta, and Riscal. Founded in 1970, Cáceres is the youngest of these and it has made its name with a correspondingly modern approach to winemaking. Emile Peynaud, the celebrated winemaking consultant from Bordeaux, was originally responsible for this approach, introducing stainless steel vats, temperature controls, shorter times in new French, rather than old American, oak barrels. His legacy can be seen in the bodega's Rioja today. An appealingly aromatic red, with savoury and keynote citrus aromas, it reveals a supple, smooth character in the mouth without heavyweight oak.

Carretera Logroño, 26350 Cenicero, La Rioja
www.marquesdecaceres.com

Marqués de Riscal Rioja
Marqués de Riscal Rueda Blanco (white)

The image that immediately springs to mind when the Marqués de Riscal name is mentioned is the world-famous Frank Gehry-designed hotel that sits next to the winery at Riscal's Rioja headquarters. But Marqués de Riscal has a long history of making wine in Spain. It was one of the first to absorb the influence of Bordeaux winemaking that swept through the region in the late 19th century, and today it makes a number of wines that live up to its aristocratic name. The Marqués de Riscal Rueda Blanco comes from the company's operation in Rueda, where Riscal was one of the first producers. It is made in a young style and has a delicate tropical emphasis rather than the brisk lime and green leaf of some other producers in the region.

Calle Torrea 1, 01340 Elciego, Alava
www.marquesderiscal.com

Martín Códax Rías Baixas, Galicia
Martín Códax Albariño (white)

Albariño has become a very fashionable grape variety, a staple on many a restaurant wine list throughout the world. As an introduction to its charms, the widely available example produced by the Martín Códax winery takes some beating. The mouthwatering zestiness, the squeeze of citrus freshness, the rounded creamy finish all combine to explain Albariño's appeal. Martín Códax was founded in 1985 as a co-operative, and today it is one of the most significant producers in the Rías Biaxas region, and one of the largest producers of Albariño in the world.

Burgáns 91, 36633 Vilariño Cambados, Pontevedra
www.martincodax.com

Maurodos Toro, Castilla y León

Prima (red)

To many, Mariano García is Spain's best winemaker. Formerly at the legendary Ribera del Duero estate, Vega Sicilia, García has spent the past decade developing his own interests. Those include Aalto, the company, which he founded with Javier Zaccagnini, former director of the Ribera del Duero *consejo regulador* (regulatory body) with support from a group of investors in 1999, and a number of consultancy positions. But they also takes in his family wineries, Mauro in Tudela del Duero and, most pertinently for this guide, Maurodos in Toro. The second wine of the San Román label, Prima is made from the younger grapes of Tinta del Toro (Tempranillo). It is younger perhaps, and lighter in body, than its big brother, but it is still exuberant, with appealing aromas.

Paraje Valjeo de Carril, 47360 Quintalla de Arriba
www.aalto.es

Muga Rioja

Muga Rosado (rosé)

Muga has been a reliable fixture of the Rioja wine scene since 1932, when it was founded by the offspring of two winemaking families: Isaac Muga Martínez and his wife, Auro Caño. The couple installed themselves in the centre of Haro, although the bodega moved to new cellars, complete with tower and an in-house cooperage, after Martínez died in 1969. Today the bodega makes well-regarded reds and whites, but for everyday drinking, few wines can rival Muga Rosado Rioja. Pale in colour but surprisingly full of flavour, it has an abundance of strawberry and cherry fruit, with a refreshingly tangy edge. A wine that proves there is so much more to Rioja than oak.

Barrio de la Estación, 26200 Haro, La Rioja
www.bodegasmuga.com

Mustiguillo Vino de la Tierra de Terrerazo, Valencia

Mustiguillo Mestizaje (red)

Deeply coloured with plenty of oak aroma, Mustiguillo Mestizaje is a fine example of a red wine made from a famously "difficult to grow" variety – Bobal. Blended with Tempranillo, Syrah, and Cabernet Sauvignon, Bobal's savoury characters dominate the wine, which has a long finish. It is made by Mustiguillo, one of a handful of producers to treat Bobal with respect, believing it can be so much more than a base for cheap blends. The company's headquarters formed in eastern Valencia and the location of its vineyards would place it in the Utiel-Requena DO if it so desired. Mustiguillo prefers the flexibility of working outside the DO's restrictions, however, and bottles its wines as Vino de la Tierra de Terrerazo.

Carretera N-330, Km 195, 46300, Las Cuevas de Utiel, Valencia
962 304 483

Naia Rueda, Castilla y León

Naia (white)

Naia has become a star of Rueda in a little less than a decade. Established in 2002, its rapid rise can be attributed to two factors: the fine vineyards planted on deep gravel soils, and the talent of winemaker Eulogia Calleja. Calleja's fastidious approach ensures that the fruit is selected with great care at harvest, and the winemaking is all about preserving the fresh fruit flavours and developing aroma and texture, with the grapes left to macerate in cold temperatures in their juice before fermenting. The eponymous estate wine reveals the depth of flavour that such careful winemaking can bring out of the Verdejo grape. There is the keynote grapefruit peel on the finish, but also a creamy richness.

Camino San Martín, 47491 La Seca
www.bodegasnaia.com

Nekeas Navarra

El Chaparral de Vega Sindoa Garnacha (red); Nekeas Crianza Tempranillo-Cabernet (red)

The Nekeas winery gets its name from the Nekeas Valley area of Navarra that it calls home. It was set up in 1990 by a group of eight families who believed they could make the most of the fine terroir they found nestling in the shadow of the Sierra Perdón mountain range. In a manner that is typical for Navarra, the company uses a mix of international grape varieties, such as Cabernet Sauvignon, and more traditional and local ones, such as Tempranillo and Garnacha. The wines can be astonishingly good value for money. El Chaparral de Vega Sindoa Garnacha marries deliciously drinkable fresh, lively fruit with some characteristic Garnacha spice. The Nekeas Crianza Tempranillo-Cabernet Navarra is a thoroughly modern Navarran blend that is vibrant with dark and red fruits, and finishes with an echo of tobacco and spices from a year spent ageing in French and American oak barrels.

Calle Las Huertas, 31154 Añorbe
www.nekeas.com

Ochoa Navarra
Ochoa Tempranillo Crianza (red)

Bright and rounded, Ochoa Tempranillo Crianza is a wine for drinking young. It combines typical cherry fruit character with the vanilla and tobacco hints from barrel-ageing. With its good-natured, easy-going charm, the wine very much reflects the personality of its creator, Adriana Ochoa, who has taken up the reins of this Navarra estate from her father, Javier. One of the leaders of oenological research in the region, Javier is among the most widely respected figures in the region. But thanks to her talent, Adriana is already attracting considerable attention of her own.

Alcalde Maillata, No 2, 31390 Olite
www.bodegasochoa.com

Pago de los Capellanes Ribera del Duero, Castilla y Léon
Pago de los Capellanes Joven (red)

Tinto Fino (Tempranillo) with just a little Merlot and Cabernet Sauvignon makes Pago de los Capellanes Joven Ribera del Duero a wine with plenty of character, more than your usual "joven" youth. Like all jovens, it is perfect for drinking young, but it is worth taking your time to savour and enjoy the complexity of the flavour. The estate's intriguing name translates as "Land of the Chaplains", a nod to the fact that it was owned by the church until the 19th century. The Rodero-Villa family built a winery on the property in 1996, and they now have 110ha (272 acres) of vineyards.

Camino de la Ampudia, 09314 Pedrosa de Duero, Burgos
www.pagodeloscapellanes.com

Palacios Remondo Rioja
La Montesa (red)

One of the great names of modern Spanish wine, Alvaro Palacios, became world-renowned after developing his own estate in Priorat. But he proved his greatness once again when he returned to manage his family estate in Rioja Baja after his father died in 2000. Palacios has made several changes at the bodega, including shifting the balance of the 100ha (247 acres) from 100% Garnacha to majority Tempranillo. A blend of the Rioja varieties, sometimes with the juicy Garnacha dominant, that is aged in large vats and smaller barriques, La Montesa Rioja is a generous, appealing wine, with plenty of complex back notes.

Avenida Zaragoza 8, 26540 Alfaro, La Rioja
941 180 207

Parés Baltà Penedès, Catalonia
Mas Petit Penedès (red)

Parés Baltà Mas Petit Penedès is a blend of Cabernet Sauvignon and Garnacha that is made by the wives of the two brothers who own this family winery. Using organically grown grapes, they have created a midweight wine with plenty of lively fruit. An old estate founded in 1790, Parés Baltà was bought by Joan Cusiné Hill in 1978. Born to a winemaking family in 1917, Cusiné Hill still lends a hand in running the family's vineyards – and his son and successor is also active in the company – but it is Joan's grandsons, Joan and Josep Cusiné, who run the show today, with their wives, Maria Elena Jimenez and Marta Casas, as winemakers.

Masía Can Balta, 08796 Pacs del Penedès, Barcelona
www.paresbalta.com

Peique Bierzo, Castilla y Léon
Tinto Mencía Bodegas Peique (red)

The year 1999 was a significant one for the Bierzo DO. It was then that many of the bodegas that have gone on to make Bierzo's rising reputation were founded. Among them was Peique, established by the family of the same name in Valtuille de Abajo, near the heartland of the old gold-mining industry that the region used to be famous for. Today members of three generations of the family work for the winery, which specializes in boutique productions of the local red grape variety, Mencía. The family's straight Tinto Mencía Bodegas Peique Bierzo is pure and unoaked, allowing the variety's character to shine through. There are plenty of jammy, red berry fruits, interwoven with notes of herbs.

24530 Valtuille de Abajo, Villafranca del Bierzo, León
www.bodegaspeique.com

Pesquera Ribera del Duero, Castilla y Léon
El Vinculo La Mancha (red)

Alejandro Fernández is proving that there is more to Spanish wine than a handful of famous regions. A one-time industrialist, Fernández went into the wine business at his family's vineyard in Ribera del Duero. The vineyard was certainly well placed – the neighbours are Vega Sicilia – but Fernández made his wines in a different style, and used all the skills and tenacity he had developed in his previous career to sell them. He has since gone on to take his formula to many other, less well-known corners of Spain, including La Mancha. El Vinculo La Mancha is a deeply coloured, deeply flavoured, supple, and spicy red wine that shows that, in the right hands, La Mancha is capable of competing with any of the Spanish wine regions.

Calle Real 2, 47315 Pesquera de Duero, Valladolid
www.pesqueraafernandez.com

GRENACHE

Grenache (or Garnacha as it is known in Spain) is the red wine grape variety that people often don't realise they are drinking. It is found in some Spanish wines from Priorat, Châteauneuf-du-Pape, and Côtes-du-Rhône, but the name Grenache rarely appears on the labels.

Why Grenache has not become a star under its own name is a mystery, but it makes great wine, often at great prices. This prolific and versatile grape is known as a Rhône variety because it has traditionally been used in the Rhône Valley of France – it is the most popular grape grown in the southern part of the region.

Spanish vine growers argue that the grape is as much Spanish as it is French. Garnacha may have evolved in northern Spain and spread later to southern France. It is the third most widely grown variety in Spain and suffered from a lack of respect among wine drinkers until recent times, when the revival of old Garnacha vineyards in the Priorat region resulted in remarkably concentrated wines that gained world attention.

Grenache delivers generous, ripe fruit flavours with rather high alcoholic strength but a soft texture compared to many other full-bodied reds. By itself Grenache has a light red colour and not much tannin, so winemakers often blend in other, darker and more tannic grapes such as Syrah or Carignan. In Australia, Grenache is blended with Shiraz and Mourvèdre in wines labelled GSM.

Grenache grapes can cope with very little water.

Portal del Montsant Montsant, Catalonia

Brunus (red)

The architect Alfredo Arribas started his Portal winemaking project in Priorat at the beginning of the new millennium. A couple of years later, Arribas added a second estate, this time in Montsant. The winemaking is headed up by Ricardo Rofes, who has been assisted, since 2007, by the celebrated Australian winemaker Steve Pannell. Between them, the team have conjured up a selection of wines that are full of character, including the Brunus. The new face of Montsant, it has bold aromas of black fruit, spice, oak, and liquorice followed by polished fruits and a firm, brisk finish.

Carrer de Dalt, 43775 Marçá, Priorat
www.portaldelpriorat.com

Rafael Palacios Valdeorras, Galicia

Louro Godello (white)

The Palacios family is a talented bunch. The great Alvaro Palacios is very much a king of Spanish red wines in Priorat and Rioja, and he enjoys worldwide fame. But his brother, Rafael Palacios, is proving himself to be just as adept as a winemaker, only his preference seems to be for white wines. Certainly that is the case at his estate in Valdeorras (the "Valley of Gold"), where Rafael has adapted the skills he developed making Palacios Remondo's excellent Placet white Rioja to local grape varieties, such as Godello. His style of winemaking is quite unlike his brother's: where Alvaro is all about power, Rafael is all about elegance and intensity. The distinction is nowhere more evident than in the pure Godello of Rafael Palacios, Louro Godello Valdeorras, with its singing freshness.

Avenida Somoza 81, 32350 A Rúa, Ourense
www.rafaelpalacios.com

Raimat Costers del Segre, Catalonia

Viña 24 Albariño (white)

The influence of Raimat in the Catalan DO of Costers del Segre has been huge. Indeed, it almost singlehandedly brought the region to the attention of drinkers first in Spain, and then the world. The driving force behind the estate's rise was Manuel Raventós, the former head of the family that owns Cava house, Codorníu. Raventós bought what was then a delapidated estate in 1914 and gradually turned it into a quality wine producer. The work has not stopped since, and the company has invested greatly in planting its vineyards with the right vines and clones, and has employed a number of big-name consultant winemakers from the US and New Zealand. One of the fascinating newer arrivals, Raimat Viña 24 Albariño Costers del Segre uses a grape variety (Albariño) from Spain's east coast. It has lime and lemon curd freshness, with a little tartness at the end.

Carretera Lleida, 25111 Raimat
www.raimat.com

Ramón Bilbao Rioja

Ramón Bilbao Reserva (red)

The past decade has seen an injection of new life into the longstanding Rioja name, Ramón Bilbao. It was founded by wine merchant Ramón Bilbao Murga in Haro in 1924, although Bilbao had been a wine merchant on the same site for almost 30 years before that. The company stayed in the family until the 1960s, and was then bought by Diego Zamora, a large Spanish drinks company that also makes the Licor 43 brand, in 1999. Diego Zamora's investment has been coming through in the wines, made by managing director and winemaker, Rodolfo Bastida. The Ramón Bilbao Reserva is a lively, modern style for drinking now: the fruit is bright and jammy balancing the vanilla spice from the oak, with a dash of citrus to underpin the whole.

Avenida Santo Domingo 34, 26200 Haro, La Rioja
www.bodegasramonbilbao.es

Raventós i Blanc
Cava
L'Hereu Brut (sparkling)

L'Hereu Brut is a reliable Cava that is made in traditional fashion from the three local varieties – Macabeo, Xarel-lo, and Parellada – and aged for 15 months. It is a little nutty, with crisp apple fruit, and plenty of sparkle. It hails from a property that is surrounded by its own vineyards (the company buys in just 20% of the grapes required for its production) and that sits right across the road from the elegant headquarters of Codorníu. That is convenient, since it is owned by the same family, the Raventóses. It is considerably younger, however (founded in 1986 as opposed to 1551 for Codorníu), although quality is just as high.

Placa del Roure, 08700 Sant Sadurní d'Anoia
www.raventosiblanc.com

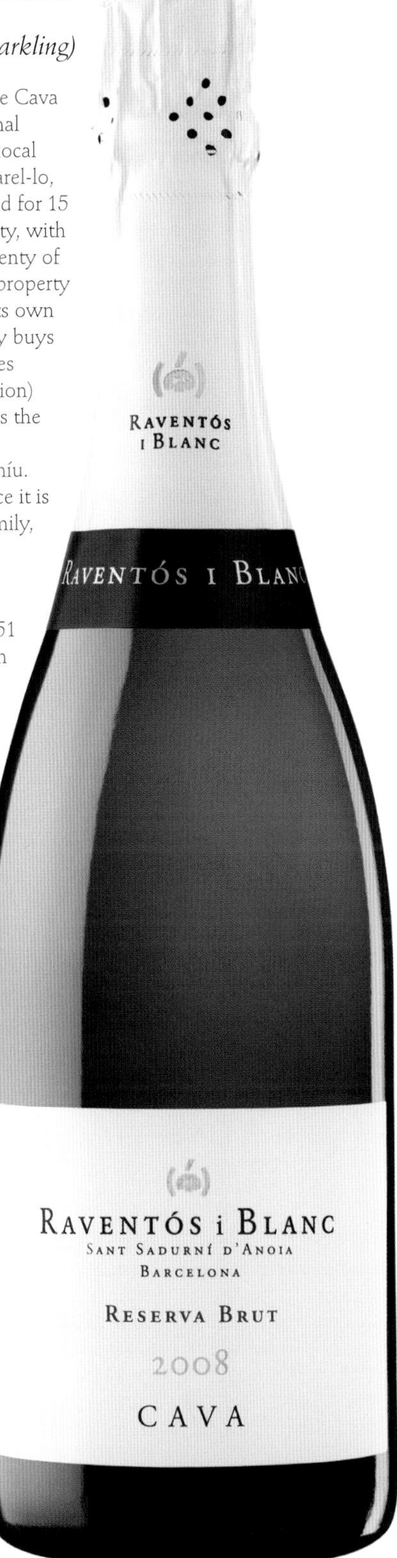

Señorío de Sarría Navarra
Señorío de Sarría Rosado (rosé)

Secreted away in a charmingly beautiful estate just off the pilgrim's road to Santiago de Compostela, Señorío de Sarría is a hidden gem. There has been a history of wine production here for many years, but it was not until recently that the quality has matched the gorgeous surroundings. Today production draws on fruit sourced from 210ha (519 acres) of vineyards, which are planted in numerous plots on the slopes of the Sierra del Perdón mountains to a mix of Spanish and international varieties including Tempranillo, Graciano, Mazuelo, Cabernet Sauvignon, and Merlot. The Señorío de Sarría Rosado Navarra is one of Navarra's brightest modern rosés. With plenty of colour and vibrant berry fruit, it is not at all cloying, and it is balanced by a good, savoury finish.

Señorío de Sarría, 31100 Puente la Reina
www.bodegadesarría.com

Tandem Navarra
Ars in Vitro (red)

As with Señorío de Sarría, this wine is produced at the heart of the pilgrim's route to Santiago de Compostela. Indeed, at Tandem you can see the pilgrims walk or cycle by. They make an intriguing contrast with the gravity-fed winery itself, which, with its concrete-and-glass facade, is the very opposite of traditional. The winemaking, too, has a distinctly modernist edge. Focusing on Tempranillo, Cabernet Sauvignon, and Merlot from 20-year-old vines, the accent is on clarity of fruit, and the wines are aged in concrete fermentors and French oak. Despite being a mere decade old, Tandem, which is run by general manager José María Fraile and winemaker Alicia Eyralar, is already established as one of Navarra's top estates, thanks to wines such as Ars in Vitro Navarra. An unoaked Tempranillo-Merlot blend, it is young and juicy and ready to drink.

Carretera Pamplona-Logroño, Km 35,9, 31292 Lácar
www.tandem.es

Tobia Rioja
Oscar Tobia (red)

Oscar Tobia's family have been making wine in Las Cuevas in San Asensio for many years. But it was not until Oscar himself returned to the family fold in 1994 that the winery took off. Tobia, who had trained first as an agricultural engineer and then as a winemaker, arrived back in San Asensio with the intention of using the family's 40- to 50-year-old vineyards to craft wines that would be the epitome of the modern style of Rioja. His first move was to renovate the cellar. From there, he introduced an entirely new approach to the winemaking, de-stemming the bunches for improved clarity of fruit character, and introducing new French oak for depth and texture. The result of all this careful winemaking was bold, modern wine, such as the Oscar Tobia Rioja, which is a powerful expression of dark fruit, married to oak.

Carretera Nacional 232, Km 438, 26340 San Asensio, La Rioja
www.bodegastobia.com

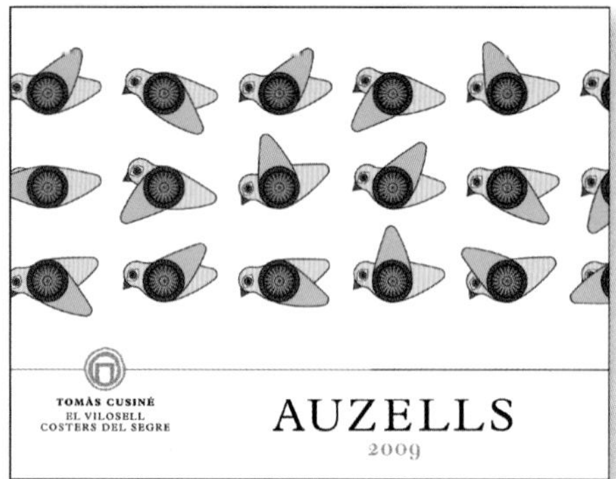

Tomàs Cusiné

Costers del Segre, Catalonia

Auzells (white)

Auzells Costers del Segre is one of Spanish wine's true originals. In composition it is a fantastically complex white blend of Macabeo, Sauvignon Blanc, Parellada, Viognier, Chardonnay, Müller-Thurgau, Muscat, Riesling, Albariño, and Roussanne. In flavour it is no less complex. In fact, it would be foolish even to try to identify the different tastes and aromas you can find leaping from the glass. It is better, perhaps, to simply savour the elegance and the freshness and marvel at the work of Tomàs Cusiné, the winemaker behind it. Remarkably, the first vintage at Tomàs Cusiné, his eponymous solo project after working at Castell del Remei and Cérvoles, was as recent as 2006.

Plaça de Sant Sebastià 13, 25457, El Vilosell, Lleida
www.tomascusine.com

Torres Catalonia

Viña Esmeralda (white); Gran Coronas (red)

Miguel A Torres is a legendary figure in Spanish wine, a genuine pioneer who has built a global empire that takes in wines from a number of Spanish regions and other countries besides. He has been at the forefront of a number of important developments in Spain. Among other things, he has championed screwcap closures and endangered grape varieties. He pioneered single-vineyard, de-alcoholized, and icon wines. He developed the idea of wine tourism in Spain with well-equipped visitor centres. And now he is widely acknowledged to be leading the way in environmentally responsible wine production, not merely in the sense of organic viticulture, but also in responding to climate change. It is quite a list, and that is before we even get around to mentioning his excellent repertoire of affordable wines. That repertoire includes wines such as Viña Esmeralda, a justly popular summery white made from headily fragrant grapes, and refreshingly light in alcohol (11.5% ABV). It also features Gran Coronas, a Torres modern classic red blend of Cabernet Sauvignon and Tempranillo aged in American and French oak, and is rich in vanilla, mocha, with delicious dark fruit.

M Torres 6, 08720 Villafranca del Penedès
www.torres.es

Txomin Etxaniz Chacolí de Guetaria, Basque Country

Chacolí (white)

There is an eye-watering tang about the wines from the chilly north coast of Spain. However, the spritziness and the low (11.5% ABV) alcohol make Chacolí, such as the crystal-clear example produced by Txomin Etxaniz, the smart choice to drink with seafood. According to the archives of Guetaria, Domingo de Etxaniz dates back as far as 1649. Rather more recently, the winery on this site was a major player in lobbying for the creation of the Chacolí Guetaria DO, which was granted in 1989. It has a fine collection of vineyards situated on a headland above the Atlantic, west of San Sebastián. Just two grape varieties are grown here: Hondarribi Zuri (white) and Hondarribi Beltza (red).

No visitor facilities
www.txominetxaniz.com

Valdelosfrailes Cigales, Castilla y León

Vendimia Seleccionada (red)

The Matarromera group is a dynamic company with vinous interests throughout northern Spain. It includes six wineries, three in the Ribera del Duero DO (Matarromera, Emina, and Renacimiento), one in Rueda (also called Emina), and, the best source for value, Valdelosfrailes in the Cubillas de Santa Marta region of the Cigales DO. Valdelosfrailes was founded by the Moro family, who went on to grow and make wine for many years, specializing in rosado. In 1998, Carlos Moro decided to make some reds in the region, and the family built a winery in 1999. Today Valdelosfrailes makes a range of wines from Tinto Fino, Verdejo, and Garnacha, which are sourced from the family's own vines in Cubillas and Quintanilla de Trigueros. The Vendimia Seleccionada Cigales is typical of the bright modern reds of Cigales. In this 100% Tinta Fino (Tempranillo), the ripe, rounded berry fruit is complemented by an equally bold expression of toasty, creamy oak.

Renedo-Pesquera Road, Km 30, 47359 Valbuena de Duero
www.matarromera.es

Valdespino Jerez-Xérèz-Sherry
Candado PX (fortified)

Decorated with a padlock ("candado"), Candado PX is one of Valdespino's many treasures. A succulent example of the lusciously sweet Pedro Ximenez style, it is drenched in treacly raisins and figs, with a zip of freshness. Among the most respected quality producers in the sherry region, Valdespino is today part of the Grupo Estevez sherry group, which comprises five top wineries across the sherry region and 700 vineyards, including the well-known La Guita Manzanilla. Valdespino is in fact a pago, or single-vineyard, that was presented by the king as a gift to a knight in 1430 and registered in the 17th century. It stayed in the knight's family until Grupo Estevez bought it in 1999. Valdespino's wines have always been well known for their focus and clarity, and quality has not dipped under the new ownership.

Carretera National IV, Km 640, 11408 Jerez de la Frontera
www.grupoestevez.es

Viñas del Vero Somontano, Aragón
La Miranda de Secastilla (red)

There is a touch of the pick-and-mix about the Somontano DO. A vast range of grape varieties is planted in the region, including Gewürztraminer, Chardonnay, Merlot, Pinot Noir, Cabernet Sauvignon, Garnacha, and Syrah. For some this diversity is illustrative of an identity crisis in the region. Others suggest it displays a lack of focus and imagination. Either way, the consensus seems to be that most would prefer it if the region's growers would concentrate on one thing. When it comes to Viñas del Vero, however, such criticisms seem a little facile. Though it is very much the classic Somontano producer, making wines from all of the above listed grapes, the quality of the wines it produces rather makes all the questions about authenticity and identity seem redundant. Take a wine like La Miranda de Secastilla, for example. This, the second wine of the estate's top Secastilla bottling, is a selection from the Garnacha vines together with new plantings of Syrah and Parraleta. It is highly expressive, with dark plums, medium weight and a terrifically long, savoury finish. Quality has been maintained since ownership of the estate was passed to the González Byass group in 2008.

Carretera de Naval Km 3, 722300 Barbastro
www.vinasdelvero.es

Viñedos de Nieva Rueda, Castilla y León
Blanco Nieva Verdejo (white)

In the Rueda region, the oldest vines can be found towards the east of the DO. This is the home of Viñedos de Nieva, a little winery whose greatest asset is a parcel of those very old vines. These are planted on stony soils at high altitude, some at 850m (2,789ft), and with many on their own rootstocks (a rarity for a European vineyard; most vines are grafted onto American rootstocks, which are more resistant to a pest that wiped out many Europen vineyards in the 19th century). Owned and run by José María and his brother, Juan Miguel Herrero Vedel, Nieva uses those vines to produce Verdejos with punchy, powerful expression. Of these, Blanco Nieva is a straightforward young Verdejo but is nevertheless bursting with characteristic grapefruit-edged flavour and citrussy fresh life.

Camino Real, 40447 Nieva, Segovia
www.vinedosdenieva.com

Vinos Valtuille Bierzo, Castilla y Léon
Pago de Valdoneje Mencía (red)

Many wineries claim to be small or boutique, believing it suggests a certain kind of artisanal charm. Some boutique producers are nothing of the sort, but the tiny Vinos Valtuille has a genuine claim to the title. Marcos García Alba is the man in charge of this family business. He does most of the work himself: tending the 20ha (49 acres) of vines, and applying his self-taught winemaking skills in the winery. He started producing wines under the Pago de Valdoneje label in 2000, bringing in his own winemaking kit after several years of private winemaking. He specializes in Mencía, Bierzo's keynote red varietal, which can be just a tad tough. But in Alba's hands it is nothing of the sort, with elegant floral aromas, and a fine texture.

La Fragua, 24530 Valtuille de Abajo, León
987 562 112

Virgen de la Sierra Calatayud, Aragón
Cruz de Piedra Garnacha (red)

Today, Calatayud is one of Spain's trendiest wine regions. Back in 1950, when Virgen de la Sierra started its life, the region barely registered. Indeed, the region was so obscure that, even though it is only 60 years old, Virgen de la Sierra is today one of the oldest producers in Calatayud. After several years making consistently good wine in relative obscurity, however, Virgen de la Sierra has enjoyed its time in the spotlight over the past decade. As with most producers in the DO, the company is a co-operative, and it draws on its members' extensive stock of 100-year-old (or more) bush vines, which thrive in dry, stony soils in extremes of temperature. Garnacha dominates the red plantings, and the old vines make for some distinctive, concentrated, powerful, and, crucially, exceptionally good value reds. The Cruz de Piedra Garnacha Calatayud is a great example of Calatayud's identity. Made to be drunk young, it is full of flavour and character.

Avenida de la Cooperativa 21-23, Villarroya de la Sierra, 50310 Zaragoza
www.bodegavirgendelasierra.com

Portugal

Though Portugal is world famous for its great fortified wines – port and Madeira – its light wines have never had quite the same level of attention. But that is changing fast. The country's wine producers are making the most of the vast array of distinctive indigenous grape varieties at their disposal, using them to fashion idiosyncratic but delicious wines. Attracting the most attention, perhaps, are the fine reds of the Douro Valley, produced from the same grape varieties (and often by the same producers) as port, and with the same mix of power and complex fruit flavours. But the intriguingly aromatic yet structured reds of the neighbouring Dão region can be equally good, while the heat of the Alentejo brings spice and richness to its wines. For enthusiasts of crisp, light, utterly refreshing whites, meanwhile, look north to the Minho region, home of Vinho Verde.

Afros Vinho Verde

Vinhão, Vinho Verde (red); Loureiro, Vinho Verde (white)

With all wines produced biodynamically, Afros is a top producer of both red and white Vinho Verde. The company's 20ha (49 acre) property, Quinta do Casal do Paço, is planted with the white Loureiro and red Vinhão (also known as Sousão) grape varieties. The Vinhão makes a remarkable wine. Almost impenetrably dark in colour, it is aromatic, and shows vivid blackberry, plum, and raspberry fruit with a meaty, savoury twist. It is certainly unusual – but utterly wonderful, too. The crisp, fresh Loureiro shows precise lemony fruit with lovely weight and freshness. Benchmark Vinho Verde, it is highly food compatible.

Quinta Casal do Paço, Padreiro (S Salvador), 4970-500 Arcos de Valdevez
www.afros-wine.com

H M Borges Madeira

5 Year Old Sweet Madeira (fortified)

Established by Henrique Menezes Borges back in 1877, H M Borges is still owned by the fourth generation of the family. They make a vast array of products, some of them rather ordinary, many of them exceptional. The 10-year-old and 15-year-old and Colheitas (single-vintage wines that are not old enough to be called vintage Madeiras) certainly qualify in the latter category. But so too – and perhaps surprisingly – does the better priced 5 Year Old Sweet Madeira. This is a rarity: an affordable Madeira that is actually quite complex. It is sweet, grapey, and raisiny with good freshness provided by the bracing acidity. Tangy, expressive, and delicious.

Rua 31 de Janeiro, No 83, 9050-011 Funchal
www.hmborges.com

CARM Douro

Reserva, Douro (red)

The full name of this estate – Casa Agrícola Roberodo Madeira – is something of a mouthful, so thankfully it is usually abbreviated as CARM. The estate is renowned for being organic. Indeed, the Madeira family's 62ha (153 acres) of vines in the Douro Superior, spread across six estates (Quinta do Bispado, Quinta de Calabria, Quinta do Côa, Quinta das Marvalhas, Quinta da Urze, and Quinta das Verdelhas) have been farmed organically since 1995, making them something of collector's item in this region. The Douro Reserva is ripe, juicy, and richly fruited with focused berry fruits and some meaty savouriness – a prime example of winemaker Rui Madeira's stylish, fruit-driven approach.

Rua da Calábria, 5150-021 Almendra
www.carm.pt

Churchill Estates Douro

Tinto, Douro (red)

Is Churchill Estate's Douro Tinto the region's best value red wine? It is most certainly a candidate for that title. A really quite serious expression of Douro terroir, it has lovely crunchy structure under the plummy, dark cherry fruit, and it finishes with a twist of spiciness. It is a wine worth cellaring for a few years, too. The producer behind it – though you would not guess it from its utterly traditional name(!) – is the most recent of the British-owned companies to make a home in the Douro. It was established 30 years ago by Johnny Graham, scion of the family that once owned the Graham port house, which is one of the best-known port houses (and which is now owned by fellow British port family, the Symingtons). Johnny Graham started his wine career at Cockburn before setting up his own port company, Churchill Graham (Churchill is his wife's name), using fruit from the vineyards of the Borges de Sousa family. The business was boosted in 1999 when Churchill acquired the 100ha (250 acre) Quinta da Gricha in the Cima Corgo, and Quinta do Rio in the Rio Torto valley.

Rua Da Fonte Nova 5, 4400 – 156 Vila Nova De Gaia
www.churchills-port.com

Conceito Douro
Contraste Tinto, Douro (red)

Contraste Tinto is a vivid, vibrant Douro red with lovely berry and cherry fruit character. Fine-grained and with bright acidity, it can be drunk now, but is also worth setting aside to see how it changes when aged. It is produced by Conceito ("concept"), which is one of the Douro Superior's newer producers. The individual behind it is the talented young winemaker, Rita Ferriera Marques. She works with fruit provided by her mother, Carla Ferriera, who owns three vineyards in the Teja valley: Quinta da Veiga, Quinta do Chão-do-Pereiro (both 20ha/50acres), Quinta do Cabido (23ha/57 acres), plus a 10ha (25 acre) vineyard further up the valley for white wines.

Largo da Madalena 10, Cedovim 5155-022
www.conceito.com.pt

Dourum Douro
Dourum Tinto, Douro (red)

The Dourum project brings together the talents of winemakers Jose Maria Soares Franco and João Portugal Ramos. Franco is best known for the 27 years he spent overseeing the production at Barca Velha, for many years the Douro's best and most expensive table wine. Ramos is widely known as the king of the Alentejo, a former wine consultant and now wine grower, whose estate is now one of the best in the region. Appropriately, the name of the estate comes from the latin for "from two", which also applies to the source of the fruit, which comes from two parts of the region, the Cima Corgo and the Douro Superior. The Dourum Tinto overdelivers in terms of quality. It is quite dense and fresh, with rich dark fruits and nice spicy structure. A new star in the making.

Estrada 222, 5150-146 Vila Nova de Foz Coa
www.duorum.pt

Fonseca Guimaraens Douro
NV: Terra Prima (fortified)

In general, the Douro has not really taken to organic viticulture, and ports made from organically grown grapes are as rare as hen's teeth. But the NV: Terra Prima is a fine exception. It may be just a humble ruby, but this is really good quality, with lovely vibrant, well defined sweet, pure blackberry and plum fruit, and a good spicy finish. It is just delicious, but then what else could be expected of Fonseca, a producer that is at the very pinnacle of port production. It was established in 1822, becoming the second-largest port producer shortly a decade or so later. It was acquired by the Taylor Fladgate Partnership (owners of the Taylor and Croft houses) just after WW II, but it was the work of the brilliant late Bruce Guimaraens as winemaker from 1960 to 1992, followed by his son, David (from 1994 to the present), that established its current pre-eminence. The company takes its fruit from three key properties: Quinta do Panascal, Quinta de São António, and Quinta do Cruzeiro.

Rua Barão de Forrester 404, Vila Nova de Gaia
www.fonseca.pt

Graham's Douro
Crusted Port (fortified)

Crusted Port is a bit like a mini-vintage port, in that it is top quality port that has spent a short time in wood, and then continues its development in bottle. It is usually a blend across vintages, and this example from Graham's is one of the best, with brooding spicy, savoury depth to the sweet dark fruits, and a hint of mint on the finish. The Graham family started in the port trade in 1820, but since 1970 the house has been part of the Symington family's empire. It has a justified reputation as one of the top port houses, with the Quinta dos Malvedos vineyard at the heart of its operations.

Rua Rei Ramiro 514, Vila Nova de Gaia
www.grahams-port.com

Herdade do Mouchão Alentejo

Dom Rafael Tinto, Alentejo (red)

One of the Alentejo's most interesting estates, Herdade do Mouchão has been in the hands of the Reynolds family for more than a century. Vines have to fight for space with cork oaks here, but there are still more than 38ha (94 acres) of vines, with the majority planted to Alicante Bouschet. A more affordable, earlier drinking red than the flagship Mouchão estate wine, Dom Rafael Tinto is really delicious, with dense cherry and plum fruit with nice freshness and a spicy finish. It's great value for money, and balances traditional and modern styles nicely.

7470-153 Casa Branca
www.mouchaowine.pt

Lavradores de Feitoria Douro

Três Bagos Sauvignon Blanc, Douro (white); Três Bagos Tinto, Douro (red)

An ambitious and unusual project, Lavradores de Feitoria was founded in 1999. It involves growers from 18 quintas from across the Douro region, who are collaborating to make some arresting wines. The wines are made by a central winemaking team. If a quinta provides grapes that are particularly good, it lends its name to the wine; otherwise, the grapes go into blends. The thinking behind the project is that the collaboration will be able to make brands that will have more impact than the quintas would have on their own. Some of the wines are highly unusual. The Três Bagos Sauvignon Blanc Douro is certainly rare, for example. But it works well. From vines in a cooler part of the region, it captures the fresh, vigorous, fruity character of Sauvignon effectively, and is quite delicious. The Três Bagos Tinto Douro is more conventional. Juicy, bright, and focused, this cherry- and berry-infused red has plenty of Douro personality. Fresh and quite delightful, it is good value for money.

Zona Industrial de Sabrosa, Lote 5, apartado 25, Paços, 5060 Sabrosa
www.lavradoresdefeitoria.pt

Niepoort Douro

Drink Me! Douro (red); Sénior Tawny Port (fortified); Junior Ruby Port (fortified)

Dirk Niepoort is a formidably talented man who has transformed his family business into one of Portugal's most successful wine producers. Everything he makes is interesting; whether it's red wines, white wines, or ports, the Niepoort style is always about extreme purity and fresh drinkability. The humorously packaged Drink Me! Douro red is at the affordable end of the fantastic Niepoort range, and it really delivers with deliciously focused dark fruits and a savoury, spicy twist. The Sénior Tawny Port, meanwhile, is a wonderfully spicy port that makes an inexpensive introduction to the tawny style. It is partnered by the equally good Júnior Ruby Port, and the two show the contrast between the styles really well.

Quinta de Nápoles, Tedo, 5110-543 Santo Adriao
www.niepoort-vinhos.com

Quinta do Ameal Vinho Verde

Quinta do Ameal Branco Loureiro, Vinho Verde (white)

From the Loureiro grape variety, Quinta do Ameal makes a superb aromatic white Vinho Verde. It is characterized by some subtle peach and pear fruit which is kept fresh by good acidity. On the finish it has gentle minerality. This wine justifies Pedro Araújo's more serious approach to the wines of a region that, historically, has had a tendency to churn out inexpensive, easy-drinking but somewhat dull, fare. Based in the Lima sub-region of Vinho Verde – an area where the Loureiro variety is at its best – Araújo prefers to put the emphasis on quality rather than quantity. His vineyards are low yielding, and he manages to extract a remarkable degree of concentration and finesse in his wines, whether working with or, as in the case of the wine featured here, without oak.

4990–707 Refóios do Lima, Ponte do Lima
www.quintadoameal.com

Quinta do Côtto Douro

Paço de Teixeiro, Vinho Verde (white)

The iconoclastic Miguel Champalimaud is not afraid to do things a little differently. Based in the Baixo Corga, he is one of a group of innovative table wine producers that have put this cooler part of the Douro on the map as a fine wine destination. Champalimaud also courted controversy – and attracted a fair degree of criticism – when he became the first Portuguese producer to bottle a wine under screw cap (Portugal is the home of the cork industry, and by far the dominant producer of cork stoppers). He makes a small quantity of excellent wines, including Paço de Teixeiro Vinho Verde. This is a fresh, bright example of Vinho Verde that blends the Avesso and Loureiro grape varieties. Unusually for a wine from this region, it is partly aged in oak, and this adds a bit of richness to the mineralic, pure citrussy fruit. Certainly, this is a wine that has a lot more depth and weight than traditional Vinho Verde.

Quinta do Côtto Cidadelhe, 5040-154 Mesão Frio
www.quintadocotto.pt

Quinta do Crasto

Douro

Branco, Douro (white)

The Douro is best known for its reds, but Quinta do Crasto's assertive, crisp white – a blend of Rabigato, Gouveio, and Roupeiro – shows that this is a region where the whites can also excel. It is hard not to like the grapefruit, passion fruit, and lemon characters, not to mention the great price. Owned by the Roquette family, Quinta do Crasto is one of the most beautiful and well regarded estates in the Douro, and it is depicted in the celebrated tiles that decorate the railway station at Pinhão. The quinta is planted with some 130ha (320 acres) of vineyards, with another 100ha (250 acres) in the Douro Superior. Dominic Morris, an Australian, makes the wines, aided by Manuel Lobo.

Gouvinhas, 5060-063 Sabrosa
www.quintadocrasto.pt

Quinta das Maias Dão

Tinto, Dão (red)

Quinta das Maias is the sister estate of fellow Dão producer, Quinta dos Roques. It was bought (well, 94% of it anyway) by the owners of dos Roques in 1997, although the das Maias wines had in fact been made at dos Roques from the 1992 vintage onwards. The das Maias estate extends to some 35ha (86 acres), with the vineyards planted at higher altitudes than dos Roques, up in the foothills of the Serra de Estrela. Today, the two estates share the same winemaking team, which is headed by Luís Lourenço, ably assisted by the consultant winemaker, Rui Reguinga. But the wines are bottled under different labels so that their individual characters are allowed to shine through. You can certainly feel the influence of the higher altitude in the Quinta das Maias Dão Tinto. An elegant red wine, and a great expression of the Dão style, it is fresh and slightly peppery, with firm dark cherry fruit and good acidity. It is a really good wine at a great price.

Rua da Paz, Abrunhosa do Mato, 3530-050 Cunha Baixa
www.quintaroques.pt

Quinta Nova de Nossa Senhora do Carmo Douro

Pomares Tinto, Douro (red)

Pomares Tinto is an example of brilliant winemaking. In style, it is a fresh, juicy, expressive Douro red with cherry and berry fruit to the fore. But it is not just a simple fruit bomb: there are hints of complexity, too. The beauty of this wine reflects the beauty of the estate where it is made: Quinta Nova de Nossa Senhora do Carmo is in a lovely spot, just a quick boat trip upstream from Quinta do Crasto in the Cima Corgo. With access to some 85ha (210 acres) of vineyards, this estate has risen towards the top of the Douro's ranks of table wine producers, with a portfolio of reds and whites.

Largo da Estação, 5085-034 Pinhão
www.quintanova.com

Quinta do Noval Douro

Unfiltered Late Bottled Vintage Port (fortified); Cedro do Noval, Douro (red)

Entirely rejuvenated after a difficult period in the 1980s by Brit Christian Seeley, the great Quinta do Noval is once again making wines that live up to its name. All the wines and ports are sourced from the 130ha (320 acres) of estate vineyards in the Pinhão Valley. The Unfiltered Late Bottled Vintage (LBV) is a high-quality port, sealed with a driven cork. It is rich and quite concentrated, with sweet dark fruits and fine definition. Almost Vintage Port level in terms of quality, it's good value for money. The Cedro do Noval, which takes its name from the beautiful cedar tree on the patio at the Quinta, is Noval's second table wine, and is just as well priced. It's an elegant, expressive red wine with cherry and berry fruits over a mineral, fresh core, and more than a hint of complexity.

Rua do Vale, 5060 Sabrosa
www.quintadonoval.com

CHOOSE THE RIGHT GLASSWARE

Elegant stemware with thin glass and gracefully shaped bowls doesn't just look good on the dinner table, it makes wine taste better. Glassmakers working with winemakers have decisively shown that certain shapes and sizes of glasses bring out the best qualities of certain wines. Buy the glasses that fit your budget and realize that you don't need all of the types shown here at once. A set of six or eight large glasses with the standard oval shape is a great start. These can be stemmed or unstemmed. Add other pieces of the collection shown here when you can to make your dinner table decorative and your wine drinking more enjoyable.

FLUTE

These tall, narrow glasses are popular for any sparkling wine. The small amount of surface area of liquid exposed to air means that the bubbles will last longer. The narrow opening is fine for bubbly because the bubbles spread the aroma, which also means the glass can be filled to near the top.

CRISP WHITE WINE GLASS

A small glass with a relatively narrow opening enhances the fresh acidity and bright flavours of crisp white wines such as Pinot Grigio, Sauvignon Blanc, or Vinho Verde. Pour to around a third full.

FULL-BODIED WHITE WINE GLASS

Rich, full-bodied whites including most New World Chardonnay, white burgundy, Viognier, ripe Riesling, and Chenin Blanc (and rosés) benefit from glasses that have a slightly larger bowl than crisp white glasses to allow air to interact with the wine, bringing out complex aromas. They have a smaller opening than red wine glasses to keep the wine cool. Pour to around a third full.

BORDEAUX GLASS

This familiar, oval shape is good for hearty red wines including red Bordeaux, Merlot, Cabernet Sauvignon, Syrah/Shiraz, Zinfandel, and most styles of Italian, southern French, and Spanish red wines because the large surface area means that more wine is exposed to air to release the wine's aromas. Pour the wine to around a third full.

BURGUNDY GLASS

Red burgundy is traditionally served in a wide glass, sometimes with an outward flaring rim to let the wine spread onto the tongue. As with all red wine glasses, it is slightly larger to allow more air to interact with the wine and develop aromas. Pour to around a third full.

DESSERT/ FORTIFIED WINE GLASS

Small servings are normal for sweet and fortified wines. These are quite aromatic and don't need a wide opening to enhance their aromas. A miniature glass with the classic tulip-shaped bowl works well.

Quinta de la Rosa Douro
douROSA Tinto (red)

Owned by the Berqvist family for more than 100 years, Quinta de la Rosa is a beautiful estate, just a short distance along the river from Pinhão. The estate is managed today by Sophia Berqvist and, since 2002, she has been helped by the highly skilled winemaker, Jorge Moreira. The change in winemaking has certainly contributed to a significant rise in quality in the range of ports and table wines created here. Another factor has been the acquisition, and subsequent partial replanting, of a new vineyard, Quinta deas Bandeiras, in the Douro Superior. The new site is right opposite the celebrated Quinta do Vale Meão, and it now supplements the 55ha (136 acre) vineyard holdings around Quinta de la Rosa. Showing vibrant, expressive cherry and berry fruit, the cunningly named douROSA is a deliciously balanced, inexpensive red with an attractive spicy bite on the finish. A lovely wine, it has all the trademark elegance of Moreira's winemaking, at a good price.

Pinhão 5085-215
www.quintadelarosa.com

Quinta de Sant'Ana Lisboa
Alvarinho, Lisboa (white)

An Anglo-German venture in the lesser-known (for wine) region of Lisboa, Quinta de Sant'Ana is a family property belonging to Englishman James Frost and his German wife, Ann. The couple took on the property from Ann's parents, Gustav and Paula von Fürstenberg, and it was James who was the prime mover in introducing vines and wine to the estate in 1999. James drew on the advice of the leading viticulturist, David Booth, and his winemaking colleague, António Maçanita, before making the decision about what and where to plant. The couple now have 11.5ha (28 acres) of vineyards interwoven with woodland, orchards, and open paddocks in the 44ha (109 acre) estate. The overperforming estate now makes a range of reds and whites that have attracted rave reviews, challenging preconceptions about the Lisboa region's potential for fine wine. A star of the range is the new Alvarinho. A lively, aromatic dry white with white peach and lime cordial flavours, it is fresh and full flavoured, and quite serious.

2665-113 Gradil, Concelho de Mafra
www.quintadesantana.com

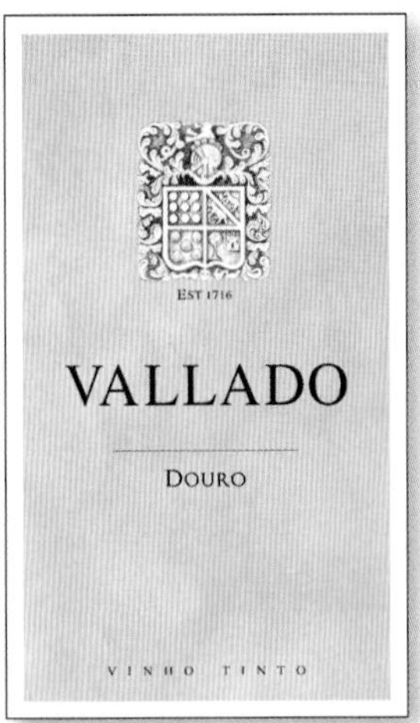

Quinta do Vallado Douro
Tinto, Douro (red)

Quinta do Vallado's Douro Tinto is all you could ask for from an inexpensive Douro red. There's the characteristic streak of minerality from the schistous soils, and there's an underlying forward dark cherry and blackberry fruit character, made all the more attractive by a savoury, meaty edge. Vallado is based in the Baixo Corgo area of the Douro, and it has been owned by the Ferreira family since the early 19th century. In the 1960s, Jorge Maria Cabral Ferreira oversaw a major renovation of the vineyards. His brother-in-law, Guilherme Álvares Ribeiro, took up the reins following Jorge Maria's death, and it was Ribeiro who started making estate-bottled port and table wine, helped by his cousin, the winemaker Xito Olazabal (of Quinta do Vale Meão), his nephew, Francisco Ferreira (general manager), and Cristiano van Zeller (who added commercial nous).

Vilarinho dos Freires, 5050-364 Peso da Régua
www.wonderfulland.com/vallado/

Ramos Pinto Douro
Duas Quintas, Douro (red)

An elegant, expressive red at a good price, Ramos Pinto's Duas Quintas Douro has attractive pure dark cherry fruit with some spice and mineral notes adding complexity. The draw here is the purity of the fruit: it doesn't try too hard to be something it is not. This is a typically fine wine from Ramos Pinto, a company that has done much to shape the identity of today's Douro wine business. The company draws on four estates for its range of excellent ports and table wines: two of these are located in the Douro Superior with the other two sites near Pinhão in the Cima Corgo. Of these sites, perhaps the most interesting – and most influential for the region – is Quinta de Ervamoira. Planted in 1974, it served as a kind of experimental vineyard, and the discoveries there informed the planting approach taken by producers throughout the region.

Quinta do Bom Retiro
www.ramospinto.pt

Sogrape Vinho Verde
Callabriga Tinto, Douro (red); Quinta de Azevedo, Vinho Verde (white)

Sogrape is a hugely important producer in Portugal. It made its name with the globally ubiquitous Mateus Rosé brand, but Portugal's largest family-owned wine company has much more to offer than that. It produces wines all over the country, many of them of excellent quality – and good value. The company's Callabriga brand shows off this multi-regional approach to very good effect, with wines from the Douro, Dão, and Alentejo. The Callabriga Douro Tinto delivers the most value for money in the range: fresh, bright, and focused, this affordable Douro red offers dark cherry and plum fruit supplemented by good acidity and a bit of grip on the finish. No less successful is the company's excellent Quinta de Azevedo Vinho Verde. A benchmark Vinho Verde, it shows laser-sharp fresh citrus fruit with a hint of spritz and keen acidity. Light and low in alcohol, it is perfect for summer sipping.

Apartado 3032, 4431-852 Avintes
www.sograpevinhos.eu

Symington Family Estates Douro
Altano Organically Farmed, Douro (red)

Altano is the name given to the table wine project of the celebrated Symington Family Estates, the celebrated British port dynasty behind such big port names as Dow's, Graham's, and Warre's. The Altano Organically Farmed Douro is a bit of a rarity: a Douro red from organically grown grapes. A real step up from the regular Altano red produced at the same estate, it has fresh, vibrant dark cherry fruit and admirable purity. Fortunately for drinkers, this extra level of quality is not reflected in the price.

5130-111 Ervedosa do Douro, S João da Pesqueira
www.chryseia.com

Taylor's Douro
Taylor's Late Bottled Vintage Port (fortified)

The British-owned and run port house, Taylor's, part of the Fladgate Partnership which also includes the Fonseca and Croft brands, is without question one of the leading port producers, and has been a genuine innovator in the development of this fortified wine. The house was the first to introduce a single quinta port, with the 1958 Quinta da Vargellas. And it was the first to market a Late Bottled Vintage (LBV) port – a style that was to prove highly popular – with the 1965 Taylor's LBV. The house's operations are centred around the Vargellas estate in the Douro Superior, which it acquired in 1893, with two properties in the Cima Corgo, Terra Feita and Junco, also making important contributions to the company's blends. Today, the flagship LBV is a well balanced port that offers plenty of sweet, spice-infused, pure dark fruits with a mellow edge.

Rua do Choupelo 250, Vila Nova de Gaia
www.taylor.pt

LOOK FOR SMALLER REGIONS AND APPELLATIONS

A good way to increase the odds of finding the highest quality wine in a given price range is to remember that smaller is often better – when it comes to wine regions, that is.

In California, for example, a wine labelled merely as coming from California is likely to be the lowest common denominator in terms of flavour. A wine labelled Central Coast, which is an area within California, is likely to be better. One labelled Santa Ynez Valley, which is within Central Coast, is likely to be better still. So if a wine labelled as "California" Chardonnay is priced similarly to one labelled as "Santa Ynez Valley" it is a good bet to buy the Santa Ynez Valley.

The same is true in French regions such as Burgundy, for example, where the hierarchy runs from the generic regional labels (Bourgogne) through more specific sub-regions (Bourgogne Hautes-Côtes de Nuit or Hautes-Côtes de Beaune) and villages (such as Mersault or Pommard), up to the smallest and best "regions", Premier Cru and Grand Cru, which is the status officially conferred on the very best vineyard sites.

Wine region names that attest to the origin of the grapes used to make the wine are called appellations. They are regulated and protected by government agencies in all major wine-producing countries to prevent fraud by wineries.

Appellation systems acknowledge that wine quality comes largely from the grapes. Grape quality in turn derives largely from the location of the vineyard in which they were grown and the local climate, soil conditions, and lay of the land. Over time, vineyard land in places that consistently produce high-quality grapes has become more expensive because people are willing to pay more for wine from these places. Wineries that buy grapes from these areas must pay more, too. For that reason, wineries seeking to make inexpensive wines normally look to less expensive places for their grapes. There are exceptions to this rule, however. And when you find these exceptions – those rare affordable wines from good, small appellations – then you should stock up.

Germany

Germany is the home of what many believe is the world's greatest white grape variety, Riesling. A hardy vine that copes well in cool climates, Riesling can deliver a range of styles beyond the reach of any other variety, and is loved by winemakers for its ability to express the region where it is grown. Throughout Germany, this versatility is given free rein, with wines that range from the delicate, floral, off-dry styles of the Mosel Valley, to the more powerful dry styles of the Pfalz, and an array of magnificent dessert wines. While Riesling hogs the limelight, there is much else of interest in Germany, however, from succulent light reds from Pinot Noir (known here as Spätburgunder), to crisp, dry aromatic whites from Scheurebe, Silvaner, and the Pinots Blanc and Gris (also known as Weissburgunder and Grauburgunder).

Aldinger Württemberg
Untertürkheimer Gips Spätburgunder Trocken QbA (red)

The Aldinger family has been tending vines in the Württemberg region since 1492, and the Aldinger enterprise remains very much a family concern today, with three generations involved in managing the business. Gerd Aldinger has the ultimate responsibility for the estate's success, but he draws on his father Gerhard's knowledge of the family's holdings, while his mother, Anne, looks after the catering, and his sons, Hans Jörg and Matthew, help with both winemaking and viticulture. Between them they make a wide range of excellent wines, of which the Untertürkheimer Gips Spätburgunder Trocken QbA is a standout. A complex, barrel-aged Pinot Noir, it is medium-bodied, dry, and has notes of cherry and cedar.

Schmerstrasse 25, 70734 Fellbach/Württemberg
www.weingut-aldinger.de

Friedrich Altenkirch Rheingau
Weissburgunder QbA (white)

Friedrich Altenkirch may not be among Germany's best-known wineries. In fact, based as it is in one of the region's lesser-known communes, Lorch is not even very well known in the Rheingau. Things are changing, however. In 2007, winemaking responsibilities were passed to the Japanese winemaker, Tomoko Kuriyama, and quality has been rising steeply ever since, with critical recognition following. Kuriyama's winemaking style is based on taking the characteristically steely, precise acidity of Lorch and fleshing it out with plenty of ripe fruit, giving the wines an attractive weight on the palate, with complex mineral and citrus elements. The resulting wines have great finesse and punch. As an introduction to this style, it would be hard to beat the estate's Weissburgunder QbA. Made with a minimalist approach and bottled with an easy-to-open screw cap, this medium-bodied dry white has lively notes of lemon, cream, and hazelnut.

Binger Weg 2, 65391 Lorch
www.weingut-altenkirch.de

Karl Friedrich Aust Sachsen
Müller-Thurgau Sächsischer Landwein (white)

Although the estate at Karl Friedrich Aust in Sachsen may be small, it has history to spare. You only need visit the beautiful house that stands at its centre to get a sense of this heritage, but the vineyards also have a long pedigree. Current director and winemaker Friedrich Aust has redeveloped a number of these historic terraced vineyards over the past decade, and he has earned a justified reputation for making some of the finest, and most innovative, whites in Sachsen. Friedrich's best wines are dry, and the humble Müller-Thurgau Sächsischer Landwein is no exception. It is racy and herbaceous with juicy notes of apple and grapefruit along with a touch of minerality for added complexity.

Weinbergstrasse 10, 01445 Radebeul, Sachsen
www.weingut-aust.de

Bassermann-Jordan
Pfalz
Riesling Trocken QbA (white)

Consistent high quality is the hallmark of this fine Pfalz estate. One of four producers in the region owned by Achim Niederberger, a local businessman, Bassermann-Jordan extends over 50ha (120 acres), which are sensibly and creatively managed by the longstanding duo of director, Gunther Hauk, and winemaker, Ulrich Mell. Although such varieties as Traminer, Muskateller, Goldmuskateller, and Sauvignon Blanc can be found here, it is Riesling that dominates. The benchmark Riesling Trocken QbA is a nervy, fruit-forward, medium-bodied white that has notes of lime, apricot, minerals, and white pepper, and is very dry.

Kirchgasse 10, 67146 Deidesheim
www.bassermann-jordan.de

Bickel-Stumpf Franken

Buntsandstein Silvaner Kabinett Trocken (white)

Matthias Stumpf is a renegade young winemaker, someone who is not afraid to innovate and challenge Franken's winemaking conventions. But there is nothing wild or unkempt about his wines, which are incredibly slick and beautifully balanced. He has a selection of vineyards at his disposal: some of his vines are grown on limestone soil in Frickenhausen, others on sandstone soil in Thüngersheim. The Buntsandstein Silvaner Kabinett Trocken, his medium-bodied dry white, is mellow and fruity with light floral, herb and spice notes.

Kirchgasse 5, 97252 Frickenhausen
www.bickel-stumpf.de

Klaus Böhme Saale-Unstrut

Bacchus Dorndorfer Rappental Trocken QbA (white)

The wines of Saale-Unstrut can be expensive, but Klaus Böhme bucks this trend, without ever compromising on quality and flavour, as his Bacchus Dorndorfer Rappental Trocken QbA shows. This light, dry white has notes of Asian pear, gooseberry, and white rose. It is less acidic than most German whites but very full-flavoured and delicious.

Lindenstrasse 43, 06636 Kirchscheidungen
www.weingut-klaus-boehme.de

Brüder Dr Becker Rheinhessen

Ludwigshoher Silvaner Trocken QbA (white)

Brüder Dr Becker's barrel-aged Ludwigshoher Silvaner Trocken QbA is one of the best Silvaners in Germany. Medium-bodied, dry, and crisp, it has some spicy notes intermingling with the soft, appley fruit. Like all of the wines here it is organic; the estate converted to this form of viticulture in the 1970s.

Mainzer Strasse 3–7, 55278 Ludwigshöhe
www.brueder-dr-becker.de

Georg Breuer

Rheingau

GB Spätburgunder Rouge QbA (red)

Georg Breuer GB Spätburgunder Rouge QbA is an elegant, dry, light red. Notes of wild strawberry, dried mushroom, and cranberry float through the palate, along with the house's signature mineral streak. It is a wine that shows just how well Theresa Breuer has done in keeping up the quality levels at this celebrated Rheingau estate since she took up the reins from her father after his death in May 2004. A breath of fresh air in this sometimes stultifyingly conservative region, she is helped considerably in her endeavours by longstanding winemaker, Hermann Schmoranz.

Grabenstrasse 8, 65385 Rüdesheim
www.georg-breuer.com

Reichsrat von Buhl Pfalz
Sauvignon Blanc Trocken QbA (white)

A famous old name of the Pfalz, Reichsrat von Buhl is currently producing wines as good as any in its long history. The 60ha (150 acre) Reichsrat von Buhl (along with three other estates) is now in the hands of local businessman, Achim Niederberger, with the day-to-day running led by director Stefan Weber, winegrower Werner Sebastian, and winemaker Michael Leibrecht. The team's zesty, dry Sauvignon Blanc Trocken QbA is not as elegant as examples from Sancerre or as brash as some from New Zealand, but lies somewhere in between. It is juicy and lively with gooseberry and herb notes and has Germany's distinctive backbone of acidity.

Weinstrasse 16, 67146 Deidesheim
www.reichsrat-von-buhl.de

Dr Bürklin-Wolf Pfalz
Riesling Trocken QbA (white)

Dr Bürklin-Wolf is the most celebrated estate in the Pfalz and, like many other top producers around the world, it is worked biodynamically. Indeed, with vineyards that extend to more than 80ha (200 acres), it is Germany's largest biodynamic producer. With yields kept low, prices can be steep for the estate's single-vineyard wines, but the estate's quality carries over into its more everyday wines, too. The dry, steely, and minerally Riesling Trocken QbA, for example, is an excellent value white wine.

Weinstrasse 65, 67157 Wachenheim
www.buerklin-wolf.de

Clemens Busch Terrassenmosel, Mosel
Trocken Mosel (white)

Clemens Busch is an estate that has always been anxious to prove that the Mosel's dry whites can be just as interesting as the off-dry and sweet styles with which the valley is traditionally associated. Managed organically by Clemens and Rita Busch with their son, Florian, the dry wines produced here are always concentrated and deeply textured. The Trocken Mosel is sourced from one of Germany's new first growth designations, and the wine has an added depth of character. It is light, fresh, minerally, and dry.

Kirchstrasse 37, 56862 Pünderich
www.clemens-busch.de

Castell Franken
Schloss Castell Silvaner Trocken (white)

The vineyards at Castell have been producing top quality Silvaner in Franken for almost 400 years. Indeed, it was an ancestor of the current owner, Earl Ferdinand Castell, who first planted the variety in Germany, in 1659. Today Silvaner occupies a significant part of the 70ha (173 acres) of vineyards owned by this, the largest privately owned estate in Franken, whose full name is Fürstlich Castell'sches Domänenamt. And these vineyards are the source of such delicious wines as the Schloss Castell Silvaner Trocken, a softly fruity style which is fresh, full, and fairly dry, with an appealingly creamy edge.

Schlossplatz 5, 97355 Castell
www.castell.de

A Christmann Pfalz
A Christmann Riesling QbA (white)

A leading figure in German wine, Steffen Christmann is known to many as the the president of the association of leading winegrowers, the VDP. But his talents extend far beyond industry politics and administration. Christmann has his own estate in the Pfalz, from where he produces wines that are a match for any in the VDP. Having recently converted the estate to biodynamic practices, the wines at A Christmann are now even more elegant, and a little lighter in alcohol, than ever before, with real depth and complexity. An inexpensive way into this fine portfolio is offered by the A Christmann Riesling QbA. With lovely fragrant notes of peaches, apricots, and sage, this light-bodied white represents the exotic Pfalz style of Riesling beautifully.

Peter-Koch-Strasse 43, 67435 Gimmeldingen
www.weingut-christmann.de

Crusius Nahe
Crusius Traiser Weissburgunder Trocken QbA (white)

From one of the better sites in the Nahe, Crusius Traiser Weissburgunder Trocken QbA is a clean, fresh, medium-bodied dry white with notes of pink grapefruit, baked apple, toasted almonds, and minerals. It is just part of the proof that all the work put in here by Dr Peter Crusius is now paying considerable dividends. After all, this was an estate that, despite the best efforts of Peter's father, Hans, had consistently underperformed before Peter took over at the beginning of the 2000s; an estate that was struggling to live up to its reputation as one of the best in the Nahe. In the past decade, however, it has once again been producing wines worthy of its history, with a house style that is all about purity and focus, where elegance and delicacy mix with fine fruit and mineral depths. First established in 1586, Crusius has parcels in such top sites as Bastei and Rotenfels, and has plantings of Müller-Thurgau, Silvaner, and, the largest proportion, Riesling, as well as a proportion of Weissburgunder and Grauburgunder.

Hauptstrasse 2, 55595 Traisen
www.weingut-crusius.de

Schlossgut Diel Nahe
Diel de Diel QbA (white)

The influential journalist Armin Diel is the first person that springs to mind when German wine lovers consider Schlossgut Diel. In fact, today it is Diel's daughter, Caroline, who is in charge of making the wines at this fine Nahe estate. Caroline has done much to raise the quality of the dry wines produced here, so much so that they are now on an equal footing with the already well-loved sweet styles. Among those dry styles is the Diel de Diel QbA. A blend of Pinot Gris, Pinot Blanc, and Riesling, it has lemony, tangy notes along with fig jam, honey, and nutmeg. Medium-bodied and dry, it shows that, under Caroline's talented stewardship, Schlossgut Diel continues to be one of Germany's finest wine producers.

Burg Layen 16-17, 55452 Burg Layen
www.schlossgut-diel.com

Dönnhoff Nahe
Dönnhoff Riesling QbA (white)

One of the contemporary German wine scene's genuinely great producers, Helmut Dönnhoff has helped put the Nahe on the international wine map, with a portfolio of Rieslings that display an unmatched finesse and subtle power. The unique qualities of Dönnhoff's wines can be felt throughout his range, from the very top to the supposedly everyday wines. Satisfyingly smooth and creamy, the medium-bodied, fairly dry Dönnhoff Riesling QbA has complex notes of peach, mint, and tangy pineapple and a refreshing sweet-and-sour aftertaste.

Bahnhofstrasse 11, 55585 Oberhausen
www.doennhoff.com

Bernhard Ellwanger Württemberg
Trollinger Trocken Gutswein (red)

Sven and Yvonne Ellwanger are part of the Junges Schwaben ("Young Swabia") group of young Württemberg winemakers that, thanks to its members' great energy and imagination, is responsible for some of Germany's most intriguing wines right now. Representing the current generation of a family of winegrowers, the Ellwangers have attracted attention for themselves, their estate, and their region with original and well-made wines such as the very drinkable Trollinger Trocken Gutswein, a forthright, plummy, and spicy dry red.

Rebenstrasse 9, 71384 Grossheppach/Württemberg
www.weingut-ellwanger.com

Karl Erbes Mittelmosel, Mosel
Ürziger Würzgarten Riesling Spätlese Mosel (white)

Karl Erbes set up his eponymous Mosel estate in 1967, and, since taking over the running of the business, his son, Stefan Erbes, has carried on the family tradition of producing what is generally referred to as the "classic" style of Mosel Riesling. These are wines that marry scintillating natural acidity with abundant fruit flavours and aromas and natural grape sweetness. Unabashedly fruity with plenty of that grapey sweetness, the Ürziger Würzgarten Riesling Spätlese Mosel is a quite lovely, approachable white, that offers notes of Golden Delicious apple, celery, and honey.

Würzgartenstrasse 25, 54539 Urzig
www.weingut-karlerbes.com

Eva Fricke Rheingau
Lorcher Riesling Trocken (white)

Eva Fricke is a busy woman. A well-travelled winemaker with experience of working at several of the world's top estates in France, Italy, Spain, and Australia, Fricke moonlights from her full-time job as operations manager at fellow Rheingau producer, Johannes Leitz, to make Lorcher Riesling Trocken at her own boutique operation. From excellent old vine fruit from Lorch, this dry, white wine is sheer, snappy, and lip-smackingly good with notes of green apple, guava, and sea salt.

Suttonstrasse 14, D 65399 Kiedrich
www.evafricke.com

Rudolf Fürst Franken
Riesling Pur Mineral Trocken QbA (white)

Paul Fürst and his son, Sebastian, are part of a line of Franken winegrowers whose roots in the region go back as far as 1638. Paul took up the reins at the family estate in Bürgstadt in 1975, when he was just 21 years old and still a student, after his father, Rudolf, died suddenly. With the help of his wife, Monika, Paul has expanded the vineyard holdings from 2.5ha (6 acres) to 20ha (50 acres), as well as building a new winery in 1979. Today, Paul and Sebastian together create some of the most innovative wines in the Franken region. Intriguingly, the majority of those wines are fermented and aged in barrel, but they are never lacking in charm, freshness, or minerality. The Riesling pur mineral Trocken QbA, for example, is deliciously focused and precise, with a series of inviting aromas and flavours including pear tart, quince, and chalk.

Hohenlindenweg 46, 63927 Bürgstadt
www.weingut-rudolf-fuerst.de

Garage Winery Rheingau
Wild Thing Riesling Spätlese (white)

The unconventional Anthony Hammond is not your average German winemaker. That he is American is unusual enough. That he is entertainingly eccentric and pony-tailed makes him stick out like a Zinfandel vine in the Rheingau. Hammond's exotic (for the German wine scene) personality has led many critics to ignore him. They are missing out. Hammond's wines are excellent. And he continues to shake up the industry with controversial releases such as Wild Thing Riesling Spätlese, a convincing, medium-sweet, earthy, and perfumed white.

Friedensplatz 12, D 65375 Oestrich
www.garagewinery.de

Geil Rheinhessen
Bechtheimer Geyersberg Grüner Silvaner Trocken Spätlese "S" (white)

Geil Bechtheimer Geyersberg Grüner Silvaner Spätlese "S" is quite a mouthful – in both senses of the phrase. Generally (and thankfully, for non-German speakers) referred to as Silvaner "S" for short (with the "S" standing for "reserve"), it is the work of the very talented and humble winemaker, Johannes Geil.
A beautifully opulent, multi-layered and luscious dry white, it is a magnificent representative of the new generation of wines from Rheinhessen, where Geil is among the group of leading producers.
It is a benchmark example of Silvaner, a grape variety that is still all too often underrated, but which can be capable of great things when the viticulture and winemaking is right.

Kuhpfortenstrasse 11, 67595 Bechtheim
www.weingut-geil.de

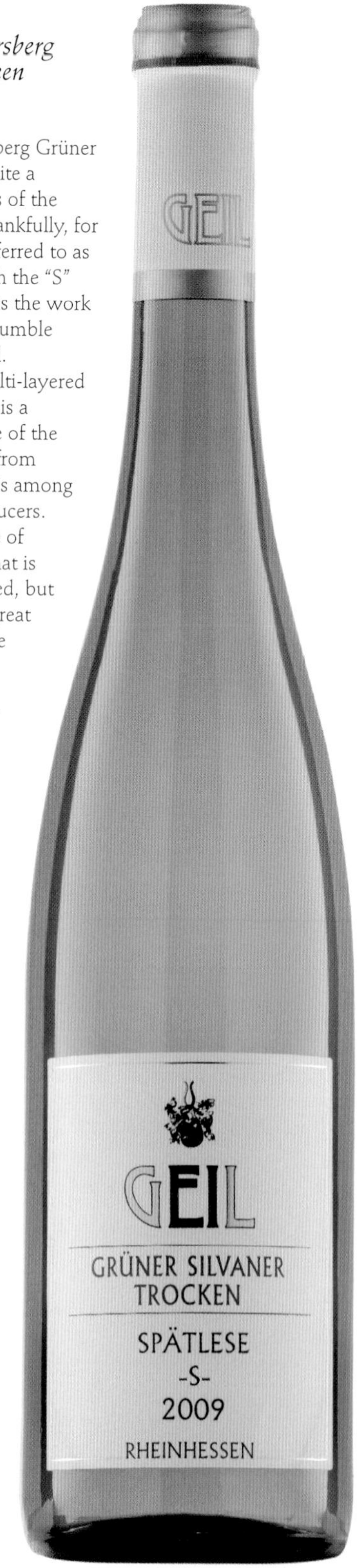

Forstmeister Gelt-Zilliken Saar, Mosel
Butterfly Riesling Mosel (white)

With notes of ginger ale, lemon sherbert, Bosc pear, and talc, Forstmeister Gelt-Zilliken's medium-dry, light-bodied Butterfly Riesling Mosel gives a great sense of the high quality being produced at this modest estate. Hanno Zilliken is the man responsible for the wine, which accounts for 50% of the total output from the 11ha (27 acre) estate, and which caused a fair amount of consternation among the more conservative members of the local wine community thanks to its unusual name. Zilliken, who is now assisted by his daughter, Dorothee, has been making top-notch Saar Rieslings at Forstmeister Gelt-Zilliken since the 1970s. However, the past decade has seen him step up another gear in quality.

Heckingstrasse 20, 54439 Saarburg
www.zilliken-vdp.de

Gies-Düppel Pfalz
Spätburgunder Illusion Weissherbst Trocken (rosé)

Top Pfalz winemaker Volker Gies has the knack of making great wines at pretty much any style he turns his attention to. He is perhaps best known for his series of dry Rieslings named after the different soils on which they are grown, but he also makes top Spätburgunder and Weissburgunder. For truly excellent value for money, however, look no further than the Spätburgunder Illusion Weissherbst Trocken. This delicate rosé is light and dry with notes of wild strawberries, pink grapefruit, and violet.

Am Rosenberg 5, 76831 Birkweiler
www.gies-dueppel.de

Gunderloch Rheinhessen
Diva Riesling Spätlese (white)

Fritz and Agnes Hasselbach understand the problems many consumers have with gothic labels. And so their Diva Riesling Spätlese is packaged in an accessible way that befits the consumer-friendly wine inside. In style Diva is medium-sweet and tart at the same time, with lovely notes of nectarine and Honeydew melon. It is yet another great wine from Fritz and Agnes, who have the nickname "Mr and Mrs 100 points" after receiving this prized rating from the American wine magazine, *Wine Spectator*, three times.

Carl-Gunderloch-Platz 1, 55299 Nackenheim
www.gunderloch.de

Fritz Haag Mittelmosel, Mosel
Riesling Trocken QbA Mosel (white)

For the best part of 50 years, the remarkable Fritz Haag estate has managed to create consistently excellent quality wines with a distinctive stylistic flair. The transition from Wilhelm Haag to his son Oliver was seamless, with Oliver sticking to Wilhelm's blueprint and creating wines that are unmatched in their pinpoint purity and clarity, and their aromatic intensity. Oliver draws on

FOOD & WINE
GERMAN RIESLING

Riesling has thrived in Germany since the 15th century, and quite possibly as far back as Roman times, most notably in the Mosel-Saar-Ruwer, Rheingau, and the Pfalz.

The great German Rieslings of the late 19th and early 20th centuries were highly sought after. Much of what is available today is commercial, and sweet, but Germany's top producers make vivid, pure, expressive wines of varying levels of sweetness, as well as a new, rich, and dry style.

All of these wines have keen acidity and are fairly low in alcohol, giving them the ability to pair with spicy dishes from Asia, the Americas, and India. They often have notes of green apple, peach, tropical fruit, and chalky minerality. Petrol, lanolin, wax, and honeysuckle emerge with age.

The lightest of these are found in the Mosel. They pair well with subtle dishes such as crab cakes, or cod with pea shoots in lemon cream sauce, as well as spicy pumpkin curry, Szechuan prawns, or egg rolls. In the Rheingau, where the wines are richer, pairings to consider include *zwiebelkuchen* (onion tart), prawn and vegetable tempura, pad Thai, sushi, or sashimi. The spicy Pfalz Rieslings offer refreshment with boudin, Cajun gumbo, bratwurst and mustard, or pork with apples and sauerkraut. The sweeter wines are ideal with desserts such as raspberry tart, papaya soufflé, or Black Forest Gâteau.

Choose clean, crisp Rieslings to match delicate sushi.

12ha (30 acres) of vineyards to create his range of Rieslings. The lively Riesling Trocken QbA Mosel is low in alcohol and dry. Like the other wines produced here, it is subtle in character with notes of white peach, apricot, pink grapefruit, and chalk.

Dusemonder Strasse 44, 54472 Brauneberg
www.weingut-fritz-haag.de

Reinhold Haart Mittelmosel, Mosel
Heart to Haart Riesling QbA Mosel (white)

The amusingly named Heart to Haart Riesling QbA Mosel is an everyday quaffer that offers an excellent demonstration of the quality on offer at this fine estate. It is fairly opulent, a word not often used in the Mosel, with peach, mint, sage, and mineral notes, and is easy to open – it has a screw cap. Theo Haart, the main man at Reinhold Haart, is known for his quiet modesty, but his eloquently opulent wines do the talking for him.

Ausoniusufer 18, 54498 Piesport
www.haart.de

Hensel Pfalz
Aufwind St Laurent Trocken QbA (red)

Hensel is a tiny producer that is well known for colourfully named and unusual blends. It is the project of the supercool Thomas Hensel, who converted his 20ha (50 acre) estate from a vine nursery to a wine producer at the beginning of the 1990s. Hensel swiftly became known for breaking away from the Riesling pack to make red wines that are unusually big, ripe, rich, and full-flavoured for Germany; indeed, some believe his wines are almost Californian in profile. Today, the most accessible red wine in Hensel's extensive portfolio (of reds and whites) is Aufwind St Laurent Trocken QbA. A delightfully fresh light red, it has notes of mushroom, berry, and rose petal with excellent balance.

In den Almen 13, 67098 Bad Dürkheim
www.henselwein.de

Heymann-Löwenstein Terrassenmosel, Mosel
Schieferterrassen Riesling Mosel (white)

Reinhard Löwenstein and his wife Cornelia Heymann were pioneers of dry whites in the Mosel. They started their estate in 1980, and they have been proving the Mosel's ability to make fine dry whites, in a powerfully textured, spice-filled style, ever since. In doing so, they have helped transform attitudes about what the Mosel Valley is capable of. Their Schieferterrassen Riesling Mosel shows the Heymann-Löwenstein approach in full effect. A light-bodied and spicy dry white, it expresses its origin with a distinct minerality. The grapes are planted in blue slate (schiefer) on some of the steepest slopes in the area.

Bahnhofstrasse 10, 56333 Winningen
www.heymann-lowenstein.de

Hofmann Franken
Spätburgunder Trocken QbA (red)

Jürgen Hofmann is a young winemaker based in a region – the Tauber Valley – that is often neglected by critics, no doubt because it sits at the confluence of three different regions, with parts of it officially located in Franken, Baden, and Württemberg. Hofmann has done much to improve recognition of the area, however, with a range of red and white wines, including the excellent value Spätburgunder Trocken QbA. Delicious, clean, and fruity but balanced Pinot Noir is hard to find at this price, but Hofmann is a master of this perfumed, sexy red varietal.

Strüther Strasse 7, 97285 Röttlingen
www.weinguthofmann.de

---

von Hövel Saar, Mosel
Oberemmeler Hütte Riesling Kabinett Mosel (white)

Eberhard von Kunow does not have quite the high profile of some of his winemaking colleagues on the Saar. But that can only be good news for drinkers, since the wines he makes at von Hövel remain almost criminally underpriced in the context of the sometimes expensive wines produced in this region. The Riesling Kabinett Mosel he makes from his monopole site (meaning he owns the whole vineyard) at Oberemmeler Hütte, for example, is amazing value. Light, zesty, and fairly dry, it has notes of star fruit, lemon sherberts, and ginger.

Agritiusstrasse 5–6, 54329 Konz-Oberemmel
www.weingut-vonhoevel.de

Achim Jähnisch Baden
Gutedel Trocken QbA (white)

The Chasselas grape is perhaps best known in Switzerland, where it produces crisp, delicate whites. The grape is also present in Baden, however, where it is known as Gutedel, and where it is made into a deliciously light and drinkable white by Achim Jähnisch, Gutedel Trocken QbA. Brisk and lemony with a touch of minerality, the wine is perfect for oysters or mussels. Achim Jähnisch established this small estate at the end of the 1990s, after graduating from the Geisenheim wine school. He has since become one of Southern Baden's best producers of dry whites. He is known for using oak barriques in his winemaking, but, because the oak is never new, the influence on the taste is minimal: it is all about adding texture and depth to the wines.

Hofmattenweg 19, 79238 Kirchhofen
www.weingut-jaehnisch.de

Schloss Johannisberg Rheingau
Riesling Gelblack Trocken QbA (white)

The sense of history is palpable at Schloss Johannisberg. It started its life as a Benedictine monastery way back in 1100 AD, and, with vines planted to the variety as early as 1720, it is widely thought of as the spiritual home of modern German Riesling. The estate struggled somewhat in the latter part of the 20th century, with wines that failed to live up to their classical billing. However, since 2006, the estate's director, Christian Witte, has turned things around, and restored this fine producer to its former glories. Even the entry-level wine, Riesling Gelblack Trocken QbA, is full of class. Medium-bodied and fruity, this is a benchmark white that gives drinkers a sense of the classic Rheingau style at a very decent price.

Schloss Johannisberg,
65366 Johannisberg
www.schloss-johannisberg.de

Toni Jost Mittelrhein
Riesling Bacharacher Kabinett Trocken (white)

The husband-and-wife team of Toni and Linde Jost have been behind some of the most consistently impressive dry and sweet Rieslings in the Mittelrhein for more than 20 years now. Their Riesling Bacharacher Kabinett Trocken is a step above their house wine in price, but this complex, ripe white offers a magnitude of flavours including peach, star fruit, and honey. It is light and crisp.

Oberstrasse 14, 55422 Bacharach
www.tonijost.de

Juliusspital Franken
Würzburger Silvaner Trocken QbA (white)

Juliusspital is a hugely impressive estate. That is certainly true in terms of scale – at 170ha (420 acres) the Juliusspital estate is arguably the largest single wine estate in Germany. But, crucially, it is also true in terms of the quality of its production – this is one of the very best producers in Franken. You can taste for yourself in the lovely Würzburger Silvaner Trocken QbA, an earthy dry white with notes of orange, spice, and minerals. Round and creamy in texture, it is as easy to open as it is to drink – the winery has made the decision to bottle its wines with screw caps.

Klinikstrasse 1, 97070 Würzburg
www.juliusspital.de

Karlsmühle Ruwer, Mosel
Kaseler Nies'chen Riesling Kabinett Mosel (white)

Showing the spice and richness of the Ruwer without the price tag, Karlsmühle Kaseler Nies'chen Riesling Kabinett offers notes of blackcurrant, lemon curd, and crushed slate. It is light and fairly dry, and reveals a tasty glimpse of the talents of Peter Geiben, one of the Ruwer's most intriguing producers. Gieber is known for his intuitive, almost improvisational way with Riesling, and his wines favour power and intense character over subtlety and delicacy.

Im Mühlengrund 1, 54318 Mertesdorf
www.weingut-karlsmuehle.de

Karthäuserhof/ Tyrell Ruwer, Mosel

Karthäuserhof Eitelsbacher Karthaüserhofberg Riesling Feinherb Mosel (white)

Karthäuserhof/Tyrell is fortunate to have the entirety of the 19ha (47 acre) Karthäuserhofberg vineyard at its disposal. Indeed, all of the production at this estate is sourced at this monopole vineyard. It is a quite beautiful spot, with the vineyards leading down to a cluster of historic buildings. Director Christoph Tyrell and long-time winemaker Ludwig Breiling specialize in ringingly aromatic, pure whites, where fruit flavours and pinpoint acidity are fleshed out by natural sweetness or a touch of alcohol. The Eitelsbacher Karthäuserhofberg Riesling Feinherb Mosel is medium-dry, with appealing notes of red apples, hay bale, lemon, and honey. It is light and refreshing with a hint of spice.

Karthäuserhof, 54292
Trier-Eitelsbach
06515 121

Kees-Kieren Mittelmosel, Mosel

Mia Riesling Lieblich QbA Mosel (white)

The Kees brothers, Ernst-Josef and Werner, are well-known for their dedication and attention to detail. And, for more than 20 years now, they have applied their skills to the consistently good, boutique-scale Kees-Kieren estate in the Mittelmosel. The brothers' Mia Riesling Lieblich QbA is a classic, gently sweet Mosel Riesling that is light and fresh with complex notes of orange, vanilla, pink grapefruit, and petrol.

Hauptstrasse 22, 54470 Graach
www.kees-kieren.de

Keller Rheinhessen

Grauer Burgunder Trocken QbA (white)

The town of Flörsheim-Dalsheim used to be very much off the beaten track when it came to wine production. Not anymore. Klaus Keller and, for the past decade, his son Klaus-Peter, have worked wonders at their small-scale family estate, and they have put this corner of the Rheinhessen firmly on the map. The enticing, dry, lemony Grauer Burgunder Trocken QbA shows why: with layers of fruit and minerality it is much more complex than most wines produced from this grape variety.

Bahnhofstrasse 1, 67592 Flörsheim-Dalsheim
www.keller-wein.de

August Kesseler Rheingau

Riesling R QbA (white)

August Kesseler Riesling R QbA gives drinkers the chance to sample fruit from old vines in the top Rheingau vineyard sites of Lorch, Lorchhausen, and Rüdesheim at a very competitive price. The estate's racy style is clearly apparent in this light, fairly dry Riesling which, thanks to the pedigree of the vineyard sources, is of a very high quality. It is the work of two men, August Kesseler and his winemaker Matthias Himstedt, who have spent the past 20 years developing the polished and focused style with which they have become associated.

Lorcher Strasse 16, 65385 Assmannshausen
www.august-kesseler.de

Reichsgraf von Kesselstatt Ruwer, Mosel

RK Riesling QbA (white)

Reichsgraf von Kesselstatt is a top estate in this corner of Germany, with some 35ha (86 acres) of vineyards divided roughly a third each between the Mittelmosel, Saar, and Ruwer. It has roots dating back to the mid-14th century, when the von Kesselstatt family arrived in the town of Trier, although the estate as it is today largely goes back to the 19th century, when the family acquired four monasteries and the vineyard land that came with them. It has been run for the past two decades by Annegret Reh-Gartner and her husband Gerhard, with Christian Steinmetz, in charge of viticulture, and, since 2005, Wolfgang Mertes, as winemaker. Mertes has now settled into his role, and is making a range of classic wines. The accessibly priced RK Riesling QbA is one such wine. Using fruit from those estate-owned vineyards on the steep slopes above the river, it is off-dry, medium-bodied, and has juicy, inviting notes of apple, anise, and slate.

Schlossgut Marienlay, 54317 Morscheid
www.kesselstatt.com

Kloster Eberbach Rheingau

Rüdesheimer Berg Roseneck Riesling Feinherb (white)

Kloster Eberbach is one of Germany's larger wineries, owned by the state and with new, decidedly modern cellar facilities dug into the ground alongside the Steinberg monopole vineyard site. Despite the new facilities, it retains its historic headquarters in the medieval monastery, Kloster Eberbach, which came to fame after being used as a location in the Sean Connery film of the Umberto Eco novel, *The Name of the Rose*. The wines here have been on a consistently upward curve since the 2008 vintage, taking on much more life, vigour, and fruit. Kloster Eberbach produces wines from a number of fine sites, including Rauenthaler Baiken, Assmannshausen, and Rüdesheim. The Rüdesheimer Berg Roseneck Riesling Feinherb is medium-bodied and medium-dry in style, and is an appealing and supple white wine with intense notes of pear tart, lemon curd, and lilies that make it perfect for a picnic.

Kloster Eberbach, 56346 Eltville
www.weingut-kloster-eberbach.de

Knebel Terrassenmosel, Mosel

Riesling Trocken Mosel (white)

Though Beate Knebel is known for her small production of rich sweet, botrytis-influenced Rieslings in the Terrassenmosel, her dry white wines can be just as good, and considerably less demanding on the wallet. Her Riesling Trocken Mosel, for example, is light, dry, pungent, and crisp with nectarine, pear, lanolin, beeswax, and mineral notes.

August-Horch-Strasse 24, 56333 Winningen
www.weingut-knebel.de

Koehler-Ruprecht Pfalz

Weissburgunder Kabinett Trocken (white)

When making wines under the Koehler-Ruprecht label, Bernd Philippi is very much a traditionalist. Indeed, he has been staying true to the winemaking blueprint of his grandfather for more than four decades. His portfolio includes dry Riesling, which Philippi was making exceptionally well for years before the grape variety became a norm in the Pfalz. But for sheer value for money it is tough to beat his acclaimed Weissburgunder Kabinett Trocken. Surprisingly opulent in style for those used to the stereotype of German wine, this creamy, round dry white has appealing notes of Golden Delicious apple, toasted almond, and hay bale.

Weinstrasse 84, 67169 Kallstadt
06322 1829

Korrell/Johanneshof Nahe

Müller Thurgau QbA (white)

With its headquarters on the edge of the town of Bad Kreuznach, Korrell/Johanneshof is now in the sixth generation of family ownership, with a winemaking pedigree dating back to 1832. That sixth generation is represented by Martin Korrell, who, since taking over the estate in 2002 after learning his trade in the Ahr and Australia, has proved himself one of the most gifted winemakers to be found working anywhere along the Rhine and its tributaries. He makes a broad range of wines that includes some fine Riesling, Weissburgunder, and Grauburgunder, but he has also worked his magic on the Müller-Thurgau grape variety. Very light in alcohol but softly sweet and mellow, this delicious and unique white has notes of pear, orange blossom, and quince.

Parkstrasse 4, 55545 Bosenheim
www.korrell.com

Kruger-Rumpf Nahe

Schiefer Riesling Feinherb (white)

Over the past 20 years, Stefan Rumpf has been one of the Nahe's best producers, drawing on top sites such as Münster, the Dautenpflänzer, and Pittersberg for a consistently high-quality portfolio. Assisted now by his son, Georg, the wines continue to reflect the Nahe personality with their combination of power and finesse, and a distinct mineral taste. The Schiefer Riesling Feinherb is a medium-dry light white which has a slate note along with some pear, lime, and moss.

Rheinstrasse 47, 55424 Münster-Sarmsheim
www.kruger-rumpf.com

Peter Jakob Kühn Rheingau

Oestrich Riesling Trocken QbA (white)

The wines of Peter Jakob Kühn are uncompromising in their sheer force of personality. It is hardly surprising, then, that they divide opinion, with some finding the extremes of character a little too much. But the sceptics are outnumbered by Kühn's many fans, who love the expression and flavour that he can extract from the Riesling grape. Kühn, and his wife Angela, assumed control of the family producer in 1979, guiding it from provider of bulk wines to a respected estate that became a member of the VDP association of Germany's top estates in 2001. From biodynamically farmed vineyards in Oestrich, the powerful, dry Oestrich Riesling Trocken QbA has notes of dried apricots, Meyer lemon, apple pie, and chalk, and is packaged with a screw cap for easy opening.

Mühlstrasse 70, 65375 Oestrich
www.weingutpjkuehn.de

Franz Künstler

Rheingau

Spätburgunder Tradition (red)

It was while tasting wines in California that Gunter Künstler, the driving force at the Franz Künstler estate, first had the inspiration to change his approach to winemaking. Returning to Germany, he began to look for more ripeness in his grapes, adding power, fruit, and minerality to the wines, such as the Spätburgunder Tradition. Künstler plants part of the Holle vineyard to Pinot Noir (Spätburgunder) to make the firm, well-structured but still light and fruity wine. It has notes of blackcurrant, black cherry, and mushroom.

Geheimrat-Hummel-Platz 1a, 65239 Hochheim am Main
www.weingut-kuenstler.de

Alexander Laible Baden
Spätburgunder Rosé Trocken QbA

The Alexander Laible estate is a relative newcomer to the Baden wine scene, although the man behind it is not. It is owned and run by Alexander Laible, who bought this former bakery and the surrounding land in his home town of Durbach, producing his first vintage as recently as 2007. The estate is already enjoying a growing reputation, however, and Laible himself is part of a new generation of winemakers who are changing the way this part of Germany is perceived. He produces a full range of wines, including Chardonnay, Weissburgunder, and Grauburgunder. And with a flair for simple marketing, the labels on wines such as his Spätburgunder Rosé Trocken QbA are as easy to read as this crisp, dry wine is easy to enjoy.

Unterwewiler 48, 77770 Durbach/Baden
www.weingut-alexanderlaible.de

Langwerth von Simmern Rheingau
Erbacher Marcobrunn Riesling Kabinett (white)

In its heyday, which ran roughly from the immediate post-war period to the 1980s, Langwerth von Simmern was a great aristocratic Rheingau estate. Quality fell off somewhat for a period of a few years after that. In the past decade or so, however, the estate has enjoyed a revival, which has been led by Georg-Reinhard Freiherr Langwerth von Simmern and his wife, Andrea. From day one, the couple have set about improving the 30ha (75 acre) estate with gusto, and the wines are now once again showing the estate's hallmark elegance and balance. The refined Erbacher Marcobrunn Riesling Kabinett, for example, is an ethereal, lacy Riesling which is closer to the Mosel Valley than the Rheingau in terms of style, and which has appealing notes of nectarine, white pepper, and a definite streak of minerality.

Kirchgasse 6, 65343 Eltville
www.langwerth-von-simmern.de

Peter Lauer Saar, Mosel
Riesling Fass 6 "Senior" (white)

The Peter Lauer estate is a great place to visit. Alongside the winery there is a fine restaurant where the family's portfolio of dry and off-dry wines can be tasted against a variety of tasty dishes. Thanks to the work of Peter Lauer, who is among the region's top winemakers, this has long been one of the most interesting estates in the Saar. But if anything, the wines have improved still further since Lauer's son, Florian, started working here in 2006. The house style is based on low alcohol, but with real depth of flavour, complexity, and texture, and a characteristic mineral edge to the acidity. The Riesling Fass 6 "Senior" is a spectacular off-dry, mid-weight Riesling with a concentration of flavours that comes from using fruit from 80-year-old vines. It is muscular and concentrated with notes of laurel, red apple, and fennel seed.

Trierstrasse 49, 54441 Ayl
www.lauer-ayl.de

Josef Leitz Rheingau
Rüdesheimer Drachenstein Dragonstone Riesling QbA (white)

Generally speaking, if a winery grows rapidly in scale, there is a trade-off in terms of quality. But that has not been the case at the Leitz estate. Despite growing from a small family firm to a 32ha (80 acre) property that also buys in grapes from other growers, the quality level of the wines has never once dipped. The expressive, medium-bodied Rüdesheimer Drachenstein Dragonstone Riesling QbA has been heralded as one of the best value German Rieslings around. It has a bracing interplay of racy acidity, succulent sweetness, and a core of yellow cherry and apple fruit.

Theodor-Heuss-Strasse 5, 65385 Rüdesheim
www.leitz-wein.de

Loch Saar, Mosel
QuaSaar (white)

QuaSaar is not your typical lean Saar wine; it is ripe and fleshy with juicy apple and tangerine notes along with lanolin and chalk. But then, Claudia and Manfred Loch are not your typical Saar producers. The couple, who built their business from scratch starting in 1992, farm organically on their tiny 3ha (7 acre) patch of vineyards, making Loch the smallest top-class estate on the Saar. Everything they do is done by hand, and they have a highly original approach, with vanishingly low yields and minimal intervention in the winery.

Hauptstrasse 80–82, 54441 Schoden
www.lochriesling.de

Carl Loewen Mittelmosel, Mosel
Quant Riesling Mosel (white)

Carl Loewen's range of organic Mosel Rieslings is highly impressive. And for value, few wines anywhere match Quant. Light, fresh, and slightly sweet with peach, apricot, and mango notes, it has a fresh, green apple tartness. The estate is owned and run by Karl Josef Loewen, who looks after some 8.5ha (21 acres) of vineyards, many of which are in top sites such as Laurentiuslay and Ritsch, with Riesling by far the most dominant grape variety.

Matthiasstrasse 30, 54340 Leiwen
www.weingut-loewen.de

RIESLING

As grown in the picturesque Rheingau and Mosel Valleys of Germany, Riesling is famous for its compelling aromas of apples and peaches, and its lively texture. The wines also age well, especially the sweet, late-harvest styles, and develop a mellow, nutty richness when five, 10, or 20 years old. It has been the premier grape variety of Germany for centuries.

Winemakers craft Riesling into an array of white wines from light and tangy to elegant and refined, to rich, honeyed, and age-worthy, depending on vineyard locations. It's one of the few classic table wines that many people prefer in a slightly sweet style.

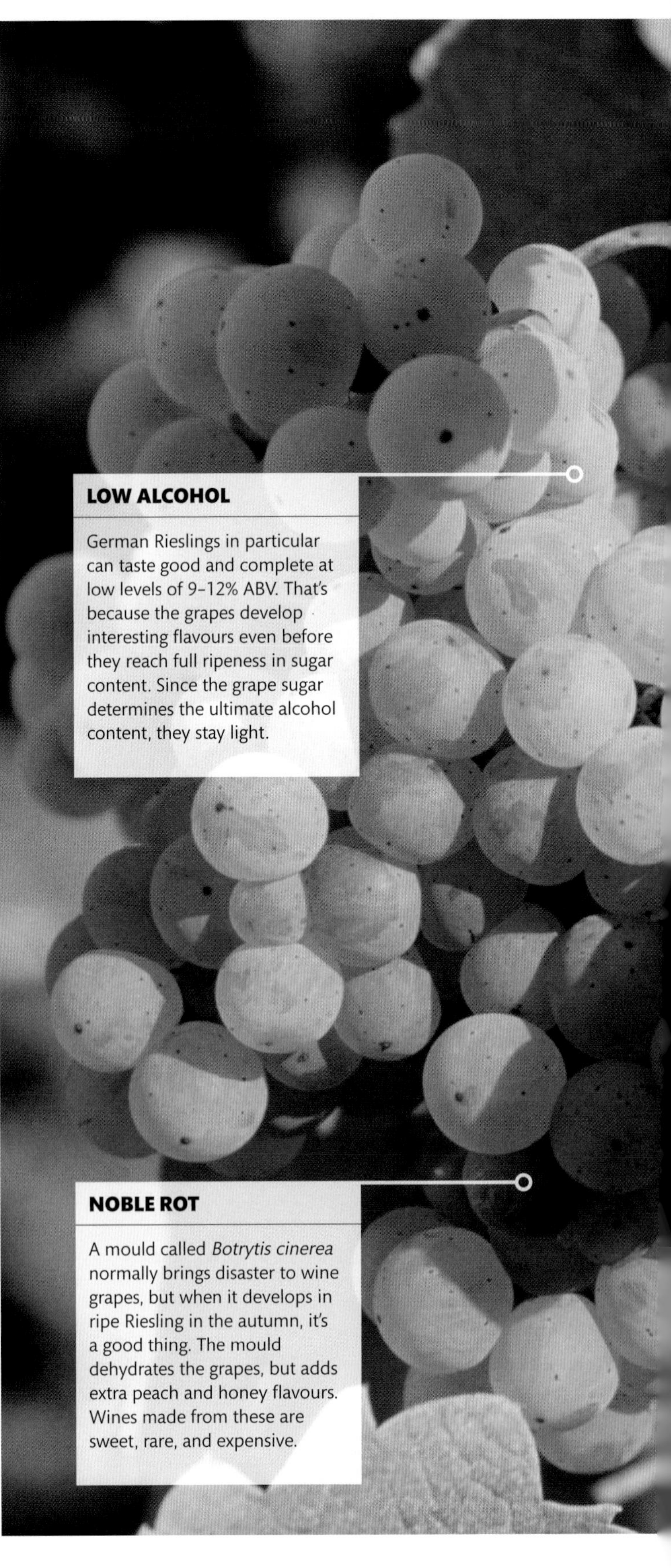

LOW ALCOHOL

German Rieslings in particular can taste good and complete at low levels of 9–12% ABV. That's because the grapes develop interesting flavours even before they reach full ripeness in sugar content. Since the grape sugar determines the ultimate alcohol content, they stay light.

NOBLE ROT

A mould called *Botrytis cinerea* normally brings disaster to wine grapes, but when it develops in ripe Riesling in the autumn, it's a good thing. The mould dehydrates the grapes, but adds extra peach and honey flavours. Wines made from these are sweet, rare, and expensive.

HILL CLIMBER

German vine growers learned centuries ago to plant Riesling on the steep slopes of their river valleys. Slopes facing south are the most prized in this country of short summers, because they face the midday sun and aid ripening in the grapes.

IN FASHION

While Riesling has long been popular among some consumers and especially connoisseurs, it is finally taking its bow in the spotlight worldwide. Sommeliers, wine merchants, and wine writers are happy that their love of Riesling is more widely shared.

WHERE IN THE WORLD?

Germany claims Riesling as its own. But just across its southern border the variety is also well known in the French region of Alsace, accounting for more than 20% of vines.

Austria, South Africa, Chile, and several eastern European countries make Riesling, too. In Ontario and British Columbia, Canada, winemakers take advantage of severe winters to make Icewine from Riesling grapes frozen on the vine just as German winemakers do when conditions permit.

In the US, the Finger Lakes area of New York State is renowned for high-quality Riesling, and on the West Coast, Washington State has massive plantings that make mostly very affordable and refreshing wines. Australian winemakers take special pride in their lime-driven Rieslings.

The following regions are among the best for Riesling. Try bottles from these recommended vintages for the best examples:

Germany: 2010, 2009, 2008, 2007
Alsace: 2010, 2009, 2008, 2007
New York State: 2010, 2008, 2007

Rieslings of the warm Pfalz region are very rich, such as this one by Basserman-Jordan.

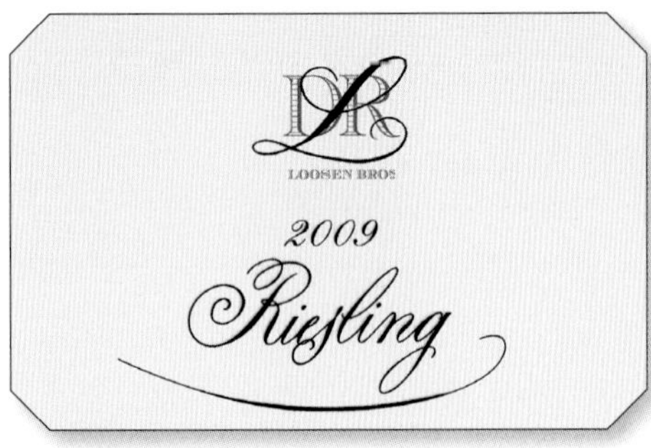

Dr Loosen Mittelmosel, Mosel
Dr L Riesling (white)

Ernst Loosen didn't set out to be a winemaker. He trained as an archaeologist, but the lure of wine called him back to take over his family's estate, and in the past couple of decades he has invested his considerable intellect and energy into changing global perceptions of German wine. At his Mosel estate – he also has a winery in the Pfalz and makes wine in Washington – he has a wealth of vineyards in top sites such as Bernkasteler Lay, Graacher Himmelreich, Wehlener Sonnenuhr, Erdener Prälat, and Erdener Treppchen, from where he makes a superb portfolio of Rieslings. His top wines rank among the best of the country, but the Dr L series offers similar styles and excellent quality at entry level prices. The Dr L Riesling is a semi-sweet, light white with notes of green apple, lime, tar, and yellow rose.

St Johannishof, 54470 Bernkastel
www.drloosen.com

Fürst Löwenstein Rheingau
CF Riesling QbA Trocken (white)

The historic Fürst Löwenstein estate in the village of Hallgarten in the Rheingau has maintained a consistent record of quality production throughout the 21st century. This despite the fact that the grapes harvested at the 20ha (50 acre) site are driven from the Rheingau to owner Prince Löwenstein's other estate in Kreuzwertheim/Franken to be both pressed and vinified. The focus is on zippy Rieslings, where the characteristically high acidity of Hallgarten (which is at relatively high altitude) is tempered by ripeness from late picking. At 12.5% ABV, the CF Riesling QbA Trocken is richer than most dry styles. With notes of apricot, peach, and white flowers, it is also very zesty and nicely tart on the finish.

Niedertwaldstrasse 8, 65375 Hallgarten
www.loewenstein.de

Maximin Grünhaus/von Schubert Ruwer, Mosel
Herrenberg Superior Riesling QbA (white)

After a difficult few years, director Dr Carl von Schubert and winemaker Stefan Kraml have ensured that the fine 31ha (77 acre) Maximin Grünhaus/von Schubert estate is now firmly back on the right course. The estate certainly should be among the best in the region, because the team here have some fantastic vineyard material to draw on. Two of the three estate vineyards here are first growths, or Erste Lage, and each one has its own unique character – Bruderberg offers blackberries, Herrenberg berries, and some herbal hints, Abtsberg gives peachy flavours. The quality of the vineyards shows throughout the estate's production, including the Herrenberg Superior Riesling QbA. This fairly dry light white has notes of minerals, herbs, and pink grapefruit. It is the kind of delightful, highly drinkable, and refreshing wine that is just made for summer and springtime afternoon picnics.

Hauptstrasse 1, 54318 Mertesdorf
www.vonschubert.com

Herbert Messmer Pfalz
Spätburgunder Trocken QbA (red)

Gregor Messmer is a remarkable winemaking talent, someone who has spent the past two decades building an enviable portfolio of first-class wines. That he has done so in one of the lesser-known corners of the southern part of the Pfalz only adds to his achievement. The wines – made from a number of different grape varieties, both red (Spätburgunder and St Laurent) and white (Riesling, Weissburgunder, Grauburgunder, and Chardonnay) – seem to get better with every passing vintage, making this experienced winemaker a perpetually rising star. For an introduction to Messmer's skill and sure touch, look for his beautiful Spätburgunder Trocken QbA. Packaged in one litre rather than 750ml bottles, this nicely priced light dry red has appealing notes of tart red cherry, lemon peel, and pomegranate.

Gaisbergstrasse 5, 76835 Burrweiler
www.weingut-messmer.de

Meyer-Näkel Ahr
Spätburgunder Illusion Trocken QbA (rosé)

The production of top quality Spätburgunder on the Ahr is a relatively recent phenomenon. Take Meyer-Näkel, for example. This excellent producer has been making fine Spätburgunder for as long as anybody in the region, but even they only began during the 1980s. Winemaking here is a family affair, with Werner Näkel, a former secondary school mathematics teacher, accompanied in the cellar for the past five years or so by his elder daughter, Meike, and since 2008, by her sister, Dörte, both of them graduates from Germany's top winemaking school, Geisenheim. The sisters' arrival has only helped add to the consistent quality here, where the influence of Burgundy is clearly apparent. The family look for very low yields in the estate's 15ha (37 acres) of vineyards, with sites in Walporzheimer Kräuterberg, Dernauer Pfarrwingert, and Bad Neuenahrer Sonnenberg. They also employ a very light touch in the winery. The Spätburgunder Illusion Trocken QbA is a slightly off-dry rosé of Pinot Noir with notes of cherry and quince and a sweet-sour sensation.

Friedenstrasse 15, 53507 Dernau
www.meyer-naekel.de

Theo Minges Pfalz

Riesling Halbtrocken QbA (white)

Theo Minges is one of the most exciting producers in the Pfalz right now. In style, his wines owe as much to the Mosel as they do to Minges' home region, with a pronounced minerality and elegance as well as plenty of richness and concentration. Minges works some 15ha (37 acres) of vineyards in sites including Gleisweiller Hölle and Flemlinger Vogelsprung, with a spread of varieties including Gewürztraminer, Spätburgunder, Weissburgunder, and Grauburgunder. But it is for his Rieslings that he is best known. The Riesling Halbtrocken QbA is the perfect, unpretentious introduction to his style. This is an everyman's Riesling – snappy, punchy, fruity, and just slightly sweet, it is the perfect wine for a warm afternoon or evening, and in the one-litre bottle there is more to go around.

Bachstrasse 11, 76835 Flemlingen
www.weingut-minges.com

Markus Molitor Mittelmosel, Mosel

Haus Klosterberg Riesling QbA (white)

Markus Molitor took up the reins at his family estate at the tender age of 20 years old in 1984, since when he has forged a reputation for pushing his wines to the stylistic limit. Now working on an estate of some 38ha (94 acres – he had a mere 3ha/7.5 acres when he started) in a number of fine sites (his largest holdings are in Zeltinger Sonnenuhr and Wehlener Klosterberg), his wines are highly concentrated, fruity, and spicy. With the grapes picked late, his winemaking favours long fermentations with an extended period on the lees. The Haus Klosterberg Riesling QbA is an almost dry white that is moderate in alcohol and characteristically creamy on the palate, with notes of elderflower, dried pineapple, green grapes, and slate.

Haus Klosterberg, 54470 Bernkastel-Wehlen
www.markusmolitor.com

Mosbacher Pfalz

Forster Riesling Kabinett (white)

Generally speaking, Rieslings from the Pfalz are known for their full-flavoured fruit and a general air of ripeness and succulence. The best examples marry these qualities with finesse and elegance, as well as the ability to mature gracefully for years in bottle. Certainly, that is the case at Mosbacher. The wines are made today by Sabine Mosbacher-Düringer and her husband Jürgen Düringer, the third generation of the family to manage the estate. The couple succeeded Sabine's father, Richard Mosbacher, who put this estate on the map from the 1960s onwards, and who still provides advice today. Grapes are sourced from the family's 18ha (38 acres) of vineyards in a number of top sites in Forst. The Forster Riesling Kabinett is full of the trademark elegance and minerality this producer is now so well known for. A light dry white, it also has engaging notes of white peach, mandarin orange, and celery seed.

Weinstrasse 27, 67147 Forst
www.georg-mosbacher.de

Müller-Catoir Pfalz

Muskateller Kabinett Trocken (white)

During the 1970s and 1980s, owner Heinrich Catoir and estate manager Hans-Günther Schwarz helped Müller-Catoir rise to a position of prominence in the Pfalz with a string of magnificent wines, both dry and sweet. Today, Philipp Catoir and estate manager Martin Franzen have formed a similarly dynamic duo, and the wines they are now making from this historic estate – nicknamed "MC²" – are once again ranked among the most scintillating in Germany. The Muskateller Kabinett Trocken is a benchmark Muskateller, perhaps the best produced anywhere in the world. In style it is full-bodied, dry, and spicy, but it has a backbone of racy acidity to balance out the invitingly rich tropical fruit.

Mandelring 25, 67433 Haardt
www.mueller-catoir.de

Egon Müller-Scharzhof/Le Gallais
Saar, Mosel
Scharzhof Riesling QbA Mosel (white)

A wonderful sense of tradition and history pervades the twinned estates of Egon Müller-Scharzhof/Le Gallais. The wines here are all about finesse, delicacy, and refinement, no matter what style is being made. They are the work of the highly respected Egon Müller IV, who is generally regarded as one of the greatest winemakers in the Saar district, and who can command seriously high prices for his top wines. There is plenty in the portfolio to satisfy palates on a more everyday budget, however, not least the startlingly good Scharzhof Riesling QbA Mosel. Ethereal is the word that first springs to mind with this wine, with its graceful texture. It reveals peachy, honey, and floral tones that blend seamlessly with a vein of minerality. It is not technically dry – Müller makes no dry styles – but with its perfect balance, you never notice the sweetness.

Scharzhof, 54459 Wiltingen
www.scharzhof.de

Pfeffingen/Fuhrmann-Eymael Pfalz
Pfeffo Estate Riesling Kabinett Halbtrocken (white)

At first punchy and firm, the medium-bodied, medium-sweet Pfeffo Estate Riesling Kabinett Halbtrocken soon softens and becomes fruity and inviting with notes of citrus, mineral, and melon. The wine takes its name from Pfeffo, the Roman who first settled in this part of the Pfalz, and whose residence was located where the Pfeffingen/Fuhrmann-Eymael has its headquarters today. The estate, something of an institution in the Pfalz, first rose to prominence in the 1950s and 1960s, when it was run by Karl Fuhrmann. Now managed by Fuhrmann's grandson, Jan Eymael, it has been thoroughly updated and it produces some of the region's most intriguing wines in a plethora of styles.

Pfeffingen 2, 67098 Bad Dürkheim
www.pfeffingen.de

Joh Jos Prüm Mittelmosel, Mosel
Riesling Kabinett Mosel (white)

When wine lovers around the world think of great Mosel Riesling, Joh Jos (or "JJ") Prüm is often the first name that springs to mind. This estate's reputation has been developed over several generations by the Prüm family, starting with Joh Jos himself, who inherited half of an existing family estate in 1911. Joh Jos's son, Sebastian, his grandson, Manfred, and today's custodian, Joh Jos's great granddaughter, Katharina, have each added in turn their own touch to the estate, refining the model but always retaining the elegant but concentrated house style of Mosel Riesling in all its guises. The always affordable and reliable Riesling Kabinett Mosel makes a great primer for students of German wine styles. A quintessentially elegant expression of Mosel Riesling, it is light and lacy, with notes of green apple, white pepper, lily, and quince. It is fruity but dry.

Uferallee 19, 54470 Wehlen
www.jjpruem.com

S A Prüm
Mittelmosel, Mosel
Essence Pinot Blanc Trocken QbA Mosel (white)

Not to be confused with Joh Jos Prüm (see previous entry), S A Prüm is another classic Mosel estate that has grown considerably in the past few years, acquiring parcels of vineyard in the Urziger Würzgarten and Erdener Treppchen, to add to its existing holdings in the celebrated Wehlener Sonnenuhr and Graacher Himmelreich. The father-and-daughter team behind it are unique in the area for working with Weissburgunder (Pinot Blanc). The medium-bodied dry white Essence Pinot Blanc Trocken is lemony and round with vanilla hints.

Uferallee 25–26,
54470 Wehlen
www.sapruem.com

Schloss Saarstein Saar, Mosel
Pinot Blanc Trocken QbA (white)

This estate's fine postwar reputation begins with its acquisition by Dieter Ebert in 1956. Ebert saw the potential of the 10ha (25 acre) Schloss Saarstein, which had been a founder member of the Grosser Ring group of quality producers, but which had been somewhat ravaged during the war. Ebert soon set about the task of making the estate, with its steeply terraced vineyards above the Saar River, into one of the most consistently excellent producers in the region. Dieter's son, Christian, a graduate of the Geisenheim wine school, took over the operation in 1986, and assisted by his wife, Andrea (a member of the Wirsching wine family from Franken), he makes a small range (around 5,000 cases each year) of exceedingly good, ripe, but fresh white wines. A real bargain from this estate is Christian's fresh, appley and nutty Pinot Blanc (Weissburgunder) Trocken. It is a delicious wine at a very appealing price that is just about the perfect match for pork dishes.

Schloss Saarstein, 54455 Serrig
www.saarstein.de

St Urbans-Hof Mittelmosel, Mosel
Urban Riesling Mosel (white)

Some winemakers excel at making small amounts of the highest quality wine. Others are better at producing large amounts of very good wine. Very few are capable of doing both, but Mosel star Nik Weis is certainly one. At St Urbans-Hof, the 32ha (80 acre) family estate based in the Mittelmosel, Weis makes an almost bewildering array of top vineyard-designated wines from sites such as Okfener Bockstein on the Saar and Piesporter Goldtröpfchen and Leiwener Laurentiuslay on the Mosel. But each year he also makes hundreds of thousands of bottles of very affordable and very high quality estate Riesling, and it is this, as much as his top wines, that have helped earn him his fine international reputation. The Urban Riesling Mosel is an entry level Riesling made with fruit from vineyards near Weis's estate. It is light, low in alcohol, and refreshingly off-dry with notes of lilac, talc, Bosc pear, and slate. It is hard to imagine finding a better aperitif wine at this kind of price.

Urbanusstrasse 16, 54340 Leiwen
www.urbans-hof.de

KEEPING OPENED WINE FRESH

The simplest, most reliable way to keep an open bottle of wine fresh – whether sparkling, white, red, or even fortified – is to store it in the refrigerator. The cold temperature slows down various chemical reactions in the wine that begin when the wine is exposed to air and that could otherwise spoil it in as little as one day's time in some cases.

It is the process of oxidation that will eventually make an opened wine undrinkable. This occurs when chemicals called phenols in the wine are exposed to oxygen, and results in a loss of aroma, colour, and flavour. At lower temperatures, this reaction occurs much more slowly than it otherwise would.

Retailers sell various devices to preserve wine that has been opened but not finished. You could, for example, buy a can that will shoot nitrogen into the bottle, or a small hand-pump that will draw the air out. Both of these aim to protect the wine from oxygen, which is its main enemy in terms of freshness. But these devices can be difficult to use, and are not appreciably more effective than putting the cork back in the bottle and placing it in the trusty refrigerator. Don't bother with putting a spoon in an opened bottle of sparkling wine, however – it is a myth that it stops the wine from losing its fizz. But special stoppers for sparkling wines do work well.

Half-empty bottles of white, rosé, and bubbly should go straight back into the refrigerator after pouring. Many reds, particularly lighter styles such as Beaujolais and inexpensive Pinot Noir, will benefit from chilling after opening until they are needed. If a red wine is too cold when you bring it out, let it warm up on the kitchen counter or in the glass for 20 minutes before drinking. As unsavoury as it may sound, you can even use the microwave (cautiously) for about 10 seconds to warm a glassful of red wine (if no guests are looking).

A few types of age-worthy red wines and even fewer age-worthy rare whites can handle being exposed to air for a day or two, and even taste better for it. A half-empty, young, tannic bordeaux will soften overnight at room temperature in a rough approximation of its ageing arc over several years.

Horst Sauer Franken

Escherndorfer Lump Silvaner Kabinett Trocken (white)

Over the years, the winemakers of Franken have often felt like second-class citizens in the world of German wine. While regions such as the Rheingau, the Mosel, and the Pfalz attracted national and global renown, the wines of Franken were largely ignored outside the region itself. That this situation has changed somewhat in the past decade or so is down to innovative producers such as Horst Sauer. Sauer shot to fame in the late 1990s with his gloriously fruity yet elegant and distinctively mineral wines, putting Franken very much in the spotlight in the process. Sauer's daughter, Sandra, is now responsible for much of the winemaking, but the house style remains intact; with Sandra reluctant to tamper with what has been a highly successful formula. The Sauer signature is certainly evident in the Escherndorfer Lump Silvaner Kabinett Trocken. From one of Germany's historic grand cru vineyards, this fleshy, fruity dry white has notes of peach, pear, and chalk and finishes with a burst of racy tartness.

Bocksbeutelstrasse 14, 97332 Escherndorf
www.weingut-horst-sauer.de

Willi Schaefer Mittelmosel, Mosel

Graacher Domprobst Riesling Kabinett (white)

Willi Schaefer and his son, Christoph, have a somewhat cautious approach to expanding their business. They have acquired several parcels of vineyards over the years, but even after all this activity their holdings still only amount to 4ha (10 acres) in the great sites of Graacher Himmelreich and Domprobst. For wine lovers around the world this can pose problems: there are many more potential customers for the Schaefer's portfolio of wines than there are bottles produced each year. Those customers are attracted by a house style where natural grape sweetness is underpinned by pinpoint-focused acidity; wines that are full of life, energy, and personality. Like that icon of American candy, salt water taffy, the lovely fruity white Graacher Domprobst Riesling Kabinett offers a salty minerality as a counterpart to the sweet flavours – in this case of Asian pear and tart grapefruit.

Hauptstrasse 130, 54470 Bernkastel-Graach
06531 8041

Selbach-Oster Mittelmosel, Mosel

Riesling Kabinett Fish Label (white)

Johannes Selbach is so dedicated to the cause of spreading the word about Riesling from Germany and the Mosel, that you are as likely to come across him at an event in Tokyo or New York as you are to find him at home. Selbach's wines are no less eloquent ambassadors for the cause than the man himself, however. His sweet Kabinett and Spätlese wines, which are considerably less sweet than is the case at other estates in the region, are consistently excellent, full of minerality and verve. Sourced mainly from Zeltingen, the lively, fresh dry white, Riesling Kabinett Fish Label, has notes of strawberry, mango, and tart green apple.

Uferallee 23, 54492 Zeltingen
www.selbach-oster.de

Rudolf Sinss Nahe

Spätburgunder Trocken QbA (red)

Rudolf Sinss is a small estate on a distinctly upwards trajectory since Johannes Sinss started helping his father, Rudolf, make the wines from the 1997 vintage. Now a leading light in the Nahe it has a fine reputation for its dry white Rieslings, Weissburgunders, and Grauburgunders. But it is also one of the top producers of red wines in the region, particularly Pinot Noir (Spätburgunder). For sheer value it is hard to beat the Spätburgunder Trocken QbA. Barely coppery-pink in colour, this medium-bodied dry red wine offers delicious strawberry, cherry, and spice notes and is round and supple in texture. It is a fine introduction to this evolving part of the German wine scene.

Hauptstrasse 18, 55452 Windesheim
www.weingut-sinss.de

Spreitzer Rheingau

Riesling 101 QbA (white)

Two of the Rheingau's brightest winemaking talents, the Spreitzer brothers, Bernd and Andreas, deserve applause for sticking to their own path rather than following received wisdom. At a time when many of their contemporaries in the Rheingau were copying the richer, riper dry styles of regions to the south, the Spreitzers went back to the lighter, fresher, lower alcohol style of dry and off-dry whites. The snappily named Riesling 101 QbA showcases this style perfectly. With moderate alcohol and just a touch of sweetness, it is brimming with lemon drop, ripe pear, and gingerbread notes.

Rheingaustrasse 86, 65375 Oestrich
www.weingut-spreitzer.de

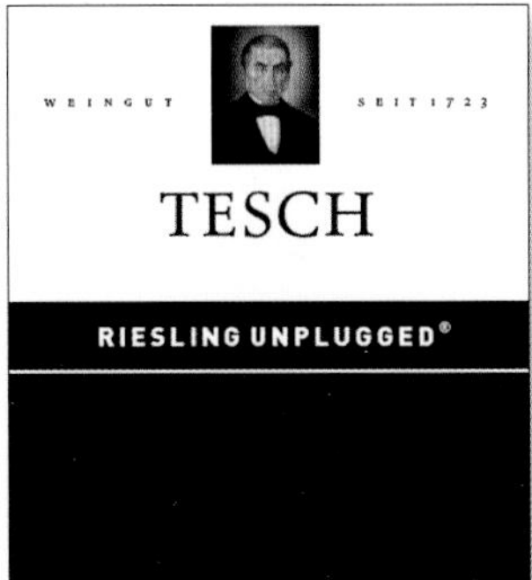

Tesch Nahe

Unplugged Riesling Kabinett Trocken (white)

Martin Tesch is a controversial figure in the German wine scene, someone who has borrowed the imagery, marketing techniques, and spirit of rock music, to produce and sell his wines – shaking up this occasionally staid and conservative world in the process. Tesch trained as a microbiologist before taking over his family estate in 1996. And from the moment he took charge he has consistently innovated, bucking convention at every turn. His portfolio includes a series of colour-coded wines from single vineyards, all of them distinctive in both flavour and packaging, but the best introduction to his unusual approach is the Unplugged Riesling Kabinett Trocken. As its name suggests, this is made with as little winemaking influence (or amplification) as possible. A pure, unfiltered Riesling, it positively sings with notes of apple, tar, and fruit cake, and is very dry.

Naheweinstrasse 99, 55450 Langenlonsheim
www.weingut-tesch.de

Dr H Thanisch - Erben Thanisch

Mittelmosel, Mosel

Bernkasteler Badstrube Riesling Kabinett (white)

The wines produced at the Thanisch estate have always been marked by elegance and finesse. But in the past ten years they have added a notch of concentration to those qualities. This is a famous estate, known particularly for its wines from the Bernkasteler Doctor, but its prices, especially for the wines from Bernkasteler Badstrube, are in no way prohibitive. The Bernkasteler Badstrube Riesling Kabinett is a dry light white that offers lots of minerality, tartness, and ripe pear notes. It is enticingly plump on the palate and is ever so slightly sweet.

Saarallee 31, 54470 Bernkastel-Kues
www.thanisch.com

Daniel Vollenweider

Mittelmosel, Mosel

Wolfer Goldgrübe Riesling Spätlese (white)

The switched-on young Swiss, Daniel Vollenweider, was a complete outsider – and entirely unknown in the wine world – when he first arrived in the Mosel. Determined to make wine, in 2000 he took out a loan to buy a tiny 1.6ha (4 acre) patch of vineyards in the dizzyingly steep, long-neglected, but historically significant, Wolfer Goldgrübe site. This was the beginning of a remarkable rise for his eponymous estate, and Vollenweider was soon outstripping his more established peers with his fine selection of Rieslings. The Wolfer Goldgrübe Riesling Spätlese is a lovely lithe, semi-sweet white wine. It is light and lively with peach skin, pear, and stony notes.

Wolfer Weg 53, 56841
Traben-Trarbach
www.weingut-vollenweider.de

CREATE A WINE "CELLAR"

Keeping a stock of your favourite types of wine at home is easily within reach even if you don't have a cellar. When it comes to finding a storage place, the cooler the better, short of freezing. The ideal temperature is that of a deep cave, about 13°C (55°F), but just find the coolest spot you can, away from direct sun, on or close to the floor, in a wardrobe, or under a bed. A spare refrigerator adjusted to a warm-ish setting will suffice. A high shelf in the kitchen will not. Racks are useful and don't have to be fancy but wine boxes are satisfactory. If the bottle is sealed with a cork, remember to store it on its side so that the cork does not dry out, split, and then cause the wine to spoil. To help get you started, here is a suggestion of what wines to stock in a cellar of 100 bottles.

RICH REDS

In a cellar of 100 bottles, around 35 could be full-bodied reds, which can be enjoyed both now and later when they have taken on an added dimension of complexity. Most Bordeaux, even inexpensive ones, will age well for a few years, as will international Cabernet Sauvignons, higher-priced burgundies, and Italian and Spanish reds.

LIGHT REDS

Most supermarket varietal reds go in this category, along with rosé, Beaujolais, simple Chianti, and generic red burgundies. Many of these are great for simple pizza or pasta, but few of them will improve with age, so aim for 20 bottles of these styles, and drink them soon after purchase, while they are still lively and full of fruit.

RICH WHITES

Full-bodied white wines to be drunk both with and before a meal could account for 15 bottles in your cellar. Drink most now, but try to age a few bottles of good white burgundy or other high-quality Chardonnay, German Riesling, or Loire Valley Chenin Blanc to see how they change over a year. Some rich whites can keep for years.

SPARKLING

Sparkling wine including champagne is not just for special occasions. It works as an aperitif or with appetizers and fish courses, too. Sparkling wines are released when they are ready to drink, so there is no need to age them. However, some top champagnes will develop nicely if they are left to age, so it's worth having up to 10 bottles of fizz in your cellar.

LIGHT WHITES

At any time of the year, but especially in warm weather, light and refreshing white wines are essential. Sauvignon Blanc, Albariño, Pinot Grigio, and others are perfect for lunches and appetizers. These are best drunk young and could provide 10 bottles in your cellar.

DESSERT AND FORTIFIED

Include a small stock of dessert or after-dinner wines – up to 10 bottles in your cellar – to add another dimension to dinner parties. The sweetness of Sauternes, late-harvest Riesling, and Vin Santo, and the raised alcohol of sherry, port, and Madeira make them suited to ageing.

Giné Giné from the Priorat region of Catalonia in Spain.

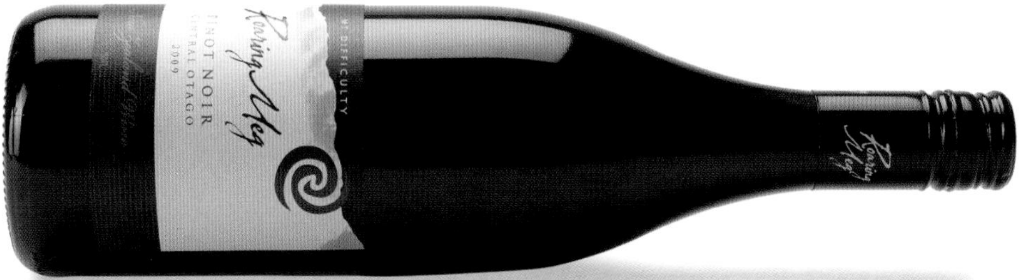

Roaring Meg Pinot Noir from Central Otago in New Zealand.

Hess Select Chardonnay from Monterey, California.

Louis Roederer Brut Premier Champagne NV.

Martin Códax Albariño from Rías Baixas in Galicia, Spain.

Taylor's Late Bottled Vintage Port from Portugal.

Schloss Vollrads
Rheingau

Riesling Kabinett Feinherb (white)

Consistently ranked among the best deals in German Riesling, and easy to find in shops and on restaurant lists around the world, Schloss Vollrads Riesling Kabinett Feinherb is a delicious, racy, and lemony off-dry white. It is an ideal aperitif and perfect for warmer weather. This historic estate, based around a beautifully maintained castle, has been operating since 1211, and it claims to be the oldest winery in the world. In recent years, it has improved rapidly under the stewardship of Rowald Hepp, and, although it produces some 500,000 bottles of wine each year, it always has its eye on quality – which is not something that many of its rivals of a similar scale can say. Dealing exclusively in Riesling, the estate has some 60ha (148 acres) of vineyards.

Vollradser Allee, 65375 Winkel
www.schlossvollrads.de

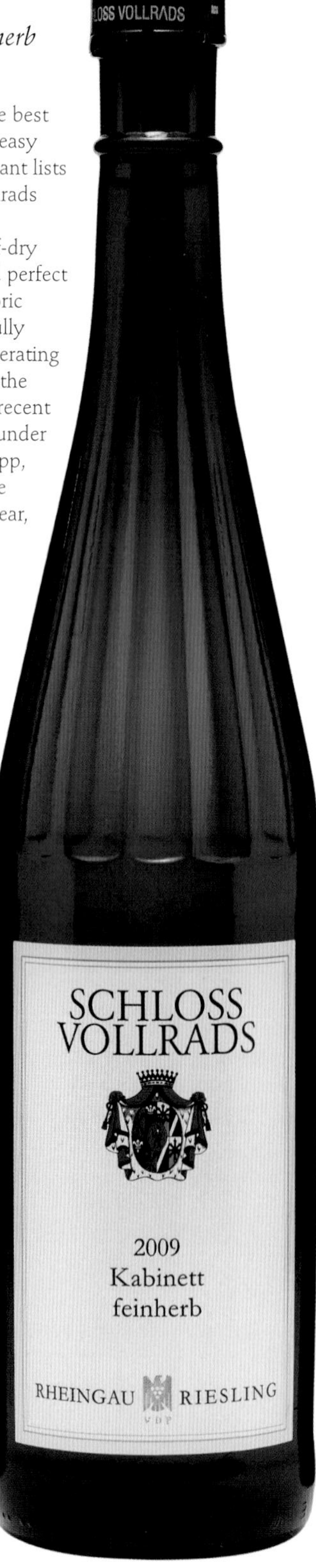

Wagner-Stempel Rheinhessen

Silvaner Trocken QbA (white)

Complex and impressive, Wagner-Stempel's bold dry white Silvaner Trocken QbA showcases the new Rheinhessen style. It is medium-bodied and has lovely apple, pear, and moss notes. It was made by Daniel Wagner who for many years now has developed a focused, precise, aromatic, and concentrated winemaking signature that stands as a riposte to anyone who might claim that Rheinhessen can only produce the broad and the round. That style is a faithful rendition of the vineyards at Wagner's disposal, which are planted at a relatively high altitude in the far west of Rheinhessen, and include sites such as Heerkretz and Höllberg. One of Germany's very best winemakers, recent vintages have shown that Wagner is currently operating at the height of his powers.

Wöllsteiner Strasse 10, 55599 Siefersheim
www.wagner-stempel.de

Wegeler Rheingau and Mosel

Gutssekt Riesling Brut (sparkling)

The driven Dr Tom Dreisberg has overseen a remarkable transformation at Wegeler in recent years. Formerly known as Wegeler-Deinhard, the wines have become significantly better since Dreisberg took over, with an extra dimension of fragrance and lift. The estate is well known in Germany for supplying many of the country's best restaurants with its celebrated dry Riesling. But the Gutssekt Riesling Brut is equally good. Produced from grapes sourced in the company's Bernkastel (in the Mosel) and Oestrich (Rheingau) vineyards, this fine and exceedingly well-priced Sekt spends more than 15 months on its lees. It is gracefully soft, fragrant, yet vivacious.

Friedensplatz 9-11, 65375 Oestrich
www.wegeler.com

Dr Wehrheim Pfalz

Chardonnay Spätlese Trocken (white)

There are many winemakers operating around the world who do not have the renown they deserve. But few are as criminally undervalued as Karl-Heinz Wehrheim, who has proved himself time and time again to be a quite exceptional winemaker without ever receiving the international recognition doled out to many of his lesser contemporaries. Then again, you get the distinct impression Wehrheim himself is not all that concerned; he would certainly much prefer to spend a day hunting than put in the long hours away from home required by a PR mission. For the lucky ones who have tasted his wines, however, there is no doubt they are among the best being made in Germany today. Any renown Wehrheim does have is centred on his multi-faceted Weissburgunder Grosses Gewächs, but his talents extend to many other wines and varieties. His Chardonnay Spätlese Trocken, for example, is a delicious, medium-bodied dry white that has notes of tropical fruit, butter, and vanilla.

Weinstrasse 8, 76831 Birkweiler
www.weingut-wehrheim.de

Robert Weil Rheingau
Riesling Trocken QbA (white)

Owned by Wilhelm Weil and the Japanese drinks group, Suntory, Robert Weil is the paradigmatic modern Rheingau producer. It has 73ha (180 acres) of vineyards – taking in acclaimed sites in Kiedrich, Gräfenberg, Turmberg, and Klosterberg – from which it makes a full range of wines, from dry to headily sweet and sumptuous dessert styles. The core of the estate's activities, in that it accounts for a significant amount of its annual production, is the Riesling Trocken QbA. Several hundred thousand bottles of this splendidly luscious dry Riesling are made each year, but it is always full of intensity and drive. In terms of flavour profile, it has inviting notes of star fruit, guava, and honey, with a precise, fresh, focused, and racy palate that finishes clean.

Mühlberg 5, 65399 Kiedrich
www.weingut-robert-weil.com

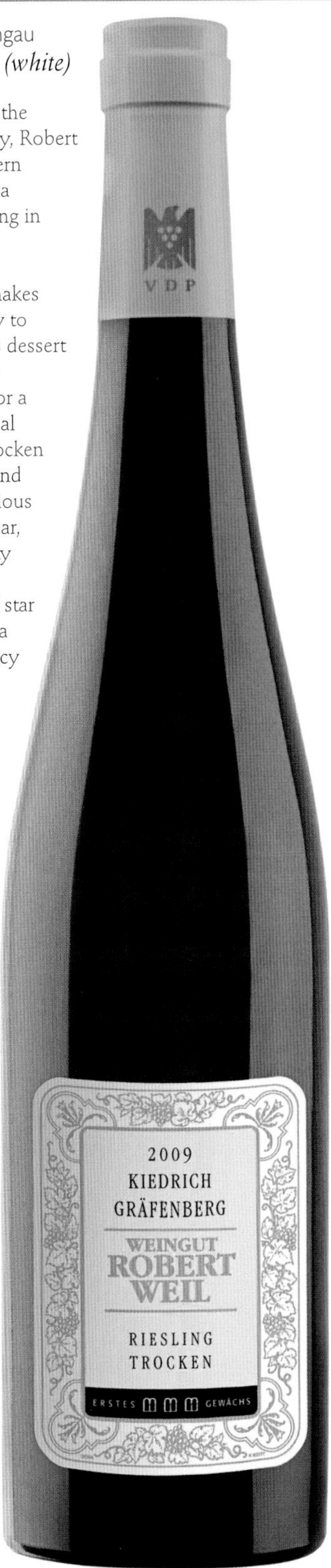

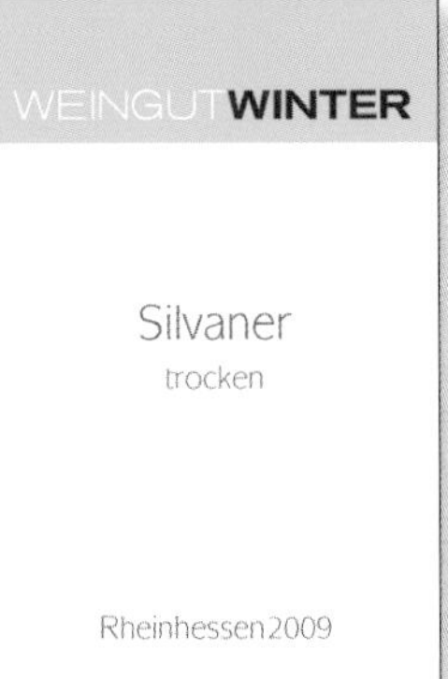

Winter Rheinhessen
Silvaner Trocken QbA (white)

Stefan Winter is a name to watch. Until this young winemaker arrived on the scene in 2003 with his Leckerberg (which translates as "delicious hill") Riesling, very few people had even heard of Dittelsheim-Hessloch. They do now, and Winter has gone on to prove that his first release was no flash in the pan, with great-value wines such as the Silvaner Trocken QbA. Medium- to full-bodied and bone-dry, it has notes of Asian pear, chalk, and spice.

Hauptstrasse 17, 67596 Dittelsheim-Hessloch
www.weingut-winter.de

J L Wolf Pfalz
Villa Wolf Gewürztraminer QbA (white)

Ernst Loosen came to fame with his rejuvenation of the Dr Loosen estate in Bernkastel in the Mosel. But this restless star winemaker was soon casting his net wider, with the J L Wolf estate in the Pfalz the first in a series of ventures around the world. From its headquarters in a beautiful set of mid-19th century buildings, the company produces a range of consistent quality, including this classic off-dry Gewürztraminer, which comes at a fraction of the price of those from neighbouring Alsace. Exotic and spicy, it has rose petal perfume and a musky note.

Weinstrasse 1, 67157 Wachenheim
www.jlwolf.de

Zipf Württemberg
Blauer Trollinger Steillage Trocken QbA (red)

Blauer Trollinger Steillage Trocken QbA is a light, soft, fruity, and dry red made with grapes grown on steep slopes (steillage). It is seriously delicious when served slightly chilled as an aperitif. It is the work of Jürgen Zipf and his wife, Tanya, who have developed their small family estate, with its high altitude vines and forest-influenced climate, into one of the best in the Pfalz.

Vorhofer Strasse 4, 74245 Löwenstein/Württemberg
www.zipf.com

Austria

In the past 20 years, Austria has re-emerged onto the international wine scene with some of the world's most thrilling white wines. At the heart of this revival has been the country's calling-card white grape, Grüner Veltliner. Grown only in tiny quantities elsewhere in the world, Grüner Veltliner makes highly distinctive white wines that are now a fixture on restaurant wine lists around the world. As successful – and delicious – as Grüner is, however, don't miss out on Austria's other top whites. From dry to lusciously sweet, the Rieslings, particularly those from the Wachau region of Lower Austria, are a match for the best examples from Alsace and Germany. Fine dry whites are also being made from Chardonnay, Weissburgunder (Pinot Blanc), and Sauvignon Blanc. Meanwhile, the reds, produced in the eastern region of Burgenland from a mix of international and local varieties (such as Blaufränkisch), get better and better.

Alzinger Wachau

Federspiel Frauenweingarten Grüner Veltliner (white)

The dedication and approach of the father-son team of Leo and Leo Alzinger mean that many of the Alzinger wines are more expensive than the other wines in this book, but the Grüner Veltliner Federspiel Frauenweingarten is a real bargain. It is worth parting with the money for a classic Grüner Veltliner that has a creamy mouthfeel and flavours of spice, pepper, and strawberry, plus more unusual elements such as lentils and rhubarb. This is a wine that can be drunk considerably sooner than much of the Alzinger portfolio, but it is a fine insight into this producer's highly individual style.

Unterloiben 11, 3601 Dürnstein
www.alzinger.at

Bründlmayer Kamptal

Zobinger Heiligenstein Riesling (white)

Willi Bründlmayer has a well-deserved reputation for his outstanding top wines. But his abilities are just as visible no matter what wine you pick up from his portfolio. Indeed, it is remarkable that he manages to sustain the quality he does across the 350,000 bottles he makes each year, and that he has done so for more than 20 years. The Zobinger Heiligenstein Riesling is a fine case in point. A Riesling that is well worth tucking away for a few years, it combines racy acidity with some simple floral and citrus fruit flavours that will develop and broaden in flavour with time in bottle. Older vintages show delicious complexity with apricot, tangerine, and floral elements to the fore. The winery itself is situated in Langenlois, in the Kamptal region of Lower Austria, and the 75ha (185 acres) of vineyards are tended with environmentally sensitive practices, with no chemical fertilizers.

Zwettlerstrasse 23, 3550 Langenlois
www.bruendlmayer.at

Christian Fischer Thermenregion

Premium Chardonnay (white)

A wonderfully bright rendition of Chardonnay, the Christian Fischer Premium Chardonnay offers a nicely full-bodied and rich glass of wine. There is plenty of citrus and vanilla flavour, all wrapped up in a blanket of subtle oak. It shows that the warm, dry Thermenregion can produce excellent whites along with the reds that have become a speciality in this part of Austria in recent years. Christian Fischer first assumed control of his family's winery in 1982, and he has won numerous awards for his winemaking since then. His winemaking style is avowedly Burgundian, marked by a judicious employment of oak.

Hauptstrasse 33, 2500 Sooss
www.weingut-fischer.at

Domäne Wachau Wachau

Terraces (white); Grüner Veltliner Achleiten Smaragd (white)

Domäne Wachau Terraces is an excellent introduction to the style of Grüner Veltliner emanating from this small but quality-focused region. The "basic" Terraces offers a crisp, clean wine with a touch of minerality adding to the clean-cut pear flavours. A step up in quality from this excellent co-operative is the Grüner Veltliner Achleiten Smaragd. This uses fruit from the famed Achleiten vineyard, whose steep terraces provide superior quality grapes resulting in a more weighty, powerful, fuller wine but still with those characteristic Grüner flavours.

Domäne Wachau, 3601 Dürnstein
www.domaene-wachau.at

Ernst Triebaumer Burgenland

Triebaumer Sauvignon Blanc (white); Triebaumer Blaufränkisch Rosé

Making vibrant, striking wines is where Ernst Triebaumer excels. The Triebaumer Sauvignon Blanc is bright and vibrant with plenty of elderflower and cut grass flavours with a grapefruit-like acidity. There is a tightness to the palate which is typical of the Triebaumer style, and is also evident in their rosé: the Triebaumer Bläufrankisch Rosé. This has a rounded, easy drinking style, a touch of spritz to keep it lively, and a strawberry-based fruit flavour.

Raiffeisenstrasse 9, 7071 Rust
www.triebaumer.com

Feiler-Artinger
Burgenland
Blaufränkisch (red)

If you take the juice from a handful of blackberries, add more juice from redcurrants, and a few cherries, then add a little oak you have the delicious red wine of Feiler-Artinger Blaufränkisch. Made from grapes grown with care on family-owned vineyards, it is an affordable step towards the estate's celebrated (and somewhat pricier) red wines, Solitaire and 1000. The man behind these wines, Kurt Feiler, has done as much as anyone to develop the modern-day reputation of the Rust area of Burgenland, with both reds and superb dessert wines.

Hauptstrasse 3, 7071 Rust
www.feiler-artinger.at

Gerhard Markowitsch Carnuntum
Pinot Noir (red); Carnuntum Cuvée (red)

Here are two great little wines from the fine Markowitsch stable. The pale-coloured Markowitsch Pinot Noir is light but firm with a lovely complex flavour combining spice and savoury elements with a refreshing lick of red berries, such as raspberry – a superb match for roast chicken. The Markowitsch Carnuntum Cuvée is a more serious mix of Pinot Noir with the local Zweigelt grape which has been formed into a soft and elegant wine with wild cherries and spice flavours. Carnuntum is named after the nearby Roman settlement.

Pfarrgasse 6, 2464 Göttlesbrunn
www.markowitsch.at

Heidi Schröck Burgenland
Weinbau Weissburgunder (white); Furmint (white)

Austrian Pinot Blanc is often overlooked, but Heidi Schröck's rendition is a beautiful example of the variety. The Weinbau Weissburgunder is yeasty on the palate with touches of spice and minerals among the fruit. Crisp and quite full, it is an affordable example of Schröck's distinctive textural style. Equally stunning is the Furmint, a variety not often seen outside Hungary's Tokaj region. A complex, spicy, and exotic dry white, it is packed with the robust flavours of ginger and spice, and again has that distinctive textural quality.

Rathausplatz 8, 7071 Rust
www.heidi-schroeck.com

Hiedler Kamptal
Löss Grüner Veltliner (white)

Broadly speaking, Ludwig Hiedler makes wines in two styles at his organically run family estate: rich, bold, and serious; and light, graceful, and characterful. The Hiedler Löss Grüner Veltliner is a terrific member of the latter group. It is made in a light and refreshing style and is a near perfect mid-week drink – and a great example of the Austrian tradition of affordable, easy-drinking summer wines. There is a touch of sweetness to this medium-bodied wine but this just adds to the rounded, easy-drinking style.

Am Rosenhügel 13, 3550 Langenlois
www.hiedler.at

Johanneshof Reinisch Thermenregion

Pinot Noir Reserve Grillenhuegel (red); Rotgipfler (dessert)

Johanneshof Reinisch makes wines that challenge preconceptions about Austrian reds. Whether working with international or local grape varieties, his wines always maintain a distinctively Austrian identity. The Pinot Noir Reserve Grillenhuegel, for example, is a big and intense wine, concentrated and individual – a fine modern Austrian red. Reinish, who is the fourth generation to manage the family estate near the village of Tattendorf, some 30km (19 miles) from Vienna, is not only about red wines, however. The estate's Rotgipfler, made from the indigenous white grape variety, is no less remarkable for its concentration of aromas and flavours, and would make an excellent aperitif. The estate began its life in 1932 with a mere half hectare (1.2 acres) of vines in the Ried Mitterfeld vineyard. Today it has grown to some 40ha (99 acres), with the largest concentration in the area surrounding Tattendorf, but with significant parcels in Gumpoldskirchen and Guntramsdorf.

Im Weingarten 1, 2523 Tattendorf
www.j-r.at

Jurtschitsch Sonhof Kamptal

Stein Grüner Veltliner (white)

2006 marked the beginning of a new era at Jurtschitsch in the Kamptal. That was the year when this family-owned estate, which has a long and celebrated history of winemaking, decided to convert its entire 72ha (180 acre) vineyard holdings to organic practices. At the same time, the work in the cellar was switched to a non-interventionist, "natural" approach, moving to wild, rather than cultivated, yeasts for fermentations. The young winemaker Alwin Jurtschitsch was the prime mover behind the switch, and one wine that fully displays the intensely mineral edge that he and the rest of the new generation in charge here is now squeezing from their fruit is the Jurtschitsch Stein Grüner Veltliner. Tightly focused with plenty of pepper-backed fruit, this Grüner is lighter bodied than many with a touch of spritz to add to the freshness.

Rudolfstrasse 39, 3550 Langenlois
www.jurtschitsch.com

Laurenz V Kamptal

Grüner Veltliner Friendly (white); Silver Bullet Grüner (white)

Many of the less expensive bottlings from Laurenz V are well worth seeking out. The Grüner Veltliner Friendly is not only friendly on the wallet but friendly to a host of food too. The array of flavours is excellent with a dash of pepper added to peach, pear, and apple. The Silver Bullet Grüner is a notch higher price-wise, but is only sold in 50cl bottles, which makes this excellent wine affordable. In the glass, the wine is all white pepper and white flower aromas. It is a thoroughly lovely creamy mouthful, and is an absolute star that is well worth hunting down. A global brand for Grüner? Let us hope so.

Mariahilfer Strasse 32, 1070 Wien
www.laurenzfive.com

Loimer Kamptal
Riesling Terrassen (white); Grüner Veltliner (white)

Over the past few years, Fred Loimer has made a perceptible change to his winemaking, adding extra layers of intensity, minerality, and spice to wines that were already very good. In 2005, he built a striking winery, a kind of hi-tech black box, to house his production facilities. The Loimer Riesling Terrassen is a wonderful, individualistic style of Riesling blended from prime vineyards. It verges on the tart and acidic when young but is nicely balanced, and there is a lovely floral edge to the aromatics. Just as good is the estate Grüner Veltliner, which combines spice, peach fruit, and white pepper into a crisp, fresh, perfectly poised whole with tense, racy acidity. Deliciously sleek.

Haindorfer Vögerlweg 23, 3550 Langenlois
www.loimer.at

GRÜNER VELTLINER

Now internationally recognized as a white grape variety that makes distinctive wines, Grüner Veltliner has long been a local favourite in Austria, where it is the country's most widely planted variety. Its wines range from lean and light, to reasonably rich and spicy depending on the vineyard site and winemaking techniques used.

Grüner Veltliner remains unknown to a lot of wine drinkers, but it has caught on widely among sommeliers and the wine trade. The relative trendiness of "Gru Vee", as it is sometimes called, is all the more remarkable because the name is dramatically foreign in non-German speaking countries.

Grüner is usually light- to medium-bodied, rather crisp and bracing to taste, and similar in weight to a Sauvignon Blanc. But its flavours have much less of the herbal and citrus components of Sauvignon and more spicy, white-pepper accents and minerality. Sommeliers love Grüner because its fresh acidity makes it a good match for a wide variety of foods, particularly spicy Thai and Vietnamese dishes, various seafoods, and even sushi.

Neighbouring Slovakia and the Czech Republic also grow significant quantities of Grüner, and there is a small amount grown in the US and other New World countries.

The flavours of Grüner Veltliner depend on where it is grown.

Meinklang/Michlits Burgenland
Pinot Noir Frizzante Rosé (sparkling)

Firmly committed to biodynamic production, Werner Michlits is responsible for some of the most original and downright delicious wines being made in Austria today. There is eccentricity here – he makes a wine in egg-shaped concrete vats from St-Laurent, for example – but it is always in the service of flavour. If you are looking for something a little unusual, then the individual, indeed perhaps totally unique, Pinot Noir Frizzante Rosé is well worthy of attention. The funky bottle featuring a label dominated by a cow and butterflies contains a wine that will be unlike anything you have sampled before. Liquid strawberry sponge cake is one way of describing it. It is great chilled for long lazy sunny days.

Hauptstrasse 86, 7152 Pamhagen
www.meinklang.at

Moric Burgenland
Blaufränkisch (red)

The Moric estate is the place to go if you want to see just how good the red Blaufränkisch grape variety can be. The estate is run by the engaging Roland Velich, a former casino croupier who is a deep-thinker when it comes to wine. Velich first established Moric in 2001, but his way with Blaufränkisch has already attracted a great deal of attention. He makes a number of cuvées from the grape, with vines grown both in the heavy soils surrounding Lutzmannsburg and the slate-dominated Neckenmarkt, but his style always emphasizes primary fruit, floral, and spice characters over oak. The Moric Blaufränkisch is packaged in a rather off-putting bottle, with a somewhat harsh, brutal label – but the wine inside is far from being either of those things. Instead it offers a winning combination of ripe red fruits, a smidgen of oak to add interest, and a smooth, delicious texture.

Kirchengasse 3, 7051 Grosshöflein
www.moric.at

Nikolaihof Wachau
Vom Stein Federspiel Riesling (white)

Austria is something of a hotbed for biodynamic viticulture, which is perhaps not surprising when you consider that the founding father of the movement, Rudolf Steiner, was himself Austrian. Nikolaihof was among the very first to make the move to the practice, however, using biodynamic methods way before the movement had become fashionable. This is a genuinely historic estate: the winery has evidence suggesting wine was made here as far back as 470 AD. Run today by the Saahs family, with winemaking in the hands of Nikolaus Saahs, the wines remain among the best in the Wachau. The Nikolaihof Vom Stein Federspiel Riesling is full of minerality. Steely dry, with an almost piercing acidity tempered by some fine fruit, it is distinctive and age-worthy, developing hugely in the bottle and taking on some fine grass and lime characters.

Nikolaigasse 3, 3512 Wachau
www.nikolaihof.at

Prieler Burgenland
Familie Prieler Blaufränkisch Ried Johanneshöhe (red)

Blaufränkisch is a speciality at Prieler estate, where oenologist and microbiologist Dr Silvia Prieler makes some of the best reds in Burgenland, including the Familie Prieler Blaufränkisch Ried Johanneshöhe. In the past, this wine has sometimes been described as a touch rustic. However, these days it is much more polished, and with the fuller, riper black fruits and the tannins tamed a little, the wine is a joy to drink.

Hauptstrasse 181, 7081 Schützen am Gebirge
www.prieler.at

Rainer Wess Wachau
Grüner Veltliner (white)

The Wachau region had not had a new producer for an astonishing 476 years until Rainer Wess founded his tiny (with just 3ha/7acres of vineyards) estate in 2003. Wess supplements his own grapes with those bought in from local growers, and he has proved himself a worthy addition to the Wachau scene with wines that are ripe, fruity, and spicy but always balanced. As an introduction to this wonderful producer's excellent range hunt out the "basic" Grüner Veltliner, which offers apricot and green apple flavours with a twist of white pepper and a smoky finish. Delicous now, it can also be set aside for a couple of years to take on more complexity.

Kellergasse, 3601 Unterloiben
www.weingut-wess.at

Sepp Moser Kremstal
Breiter Rain Grüner Veltliner (white); Sauvignon Blanc (white)

For a Grüner Veltliner with weight, style, and a full, flavoursome mouthfeel the Breiter Rain Grüner Veltliner from the Sepp Moser estate in Kremstal is perfect. Showing the pear and mineral naunces typical of this grape, it offers more than a dash of personality and complex flavours that justify the rising-star status of this producer. The Sauvignon Blanc is a medium-sweet wine that is perfect for sipping on its own. It is full of the Sauvignon Blanc traits of greengage, grapefruit, and gooseberry that the slight sweetness seems to enhance.

Untere Wienerstrasse 1, 3495 Rohrendorf bei Krems
www.sepp-moser.at

Umathum Burgenland

Zweigelt (red); Traminer (white)

Josef Umathum has a fine reputation in Austria for his bold, powerful Burgenland reds. One of Umathum's regular varietal bottlings, the Umathum Zweigelt is certainly impressive. It's a big wine with lashings of personality and robust, deep forest fruits; rich and flavoursome with a slice of minerality to add even more interest. The Umathum Traminer, by contrast, is an exotic rendition of this white grape, with a lovely full-bodied mouthfeel. While the aroma suggests sweet roses, the palate is certainly dry.

St-Andräer Strasse 7, 7132 Frauenkirchen
www.umathum.at

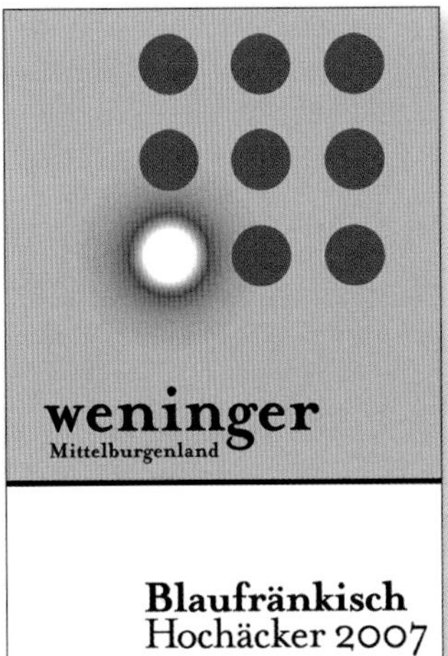

Weninger Burgenland

Blaufränkisch Hochäcker (red)

The Weninger family is lucky to have two very talented winemakers in its ranks. Just over the border from Burgenland in Sópron, Hungary, Franz Weninger Jr makes impressive reds and dry whites. In Burgenland itself, in Horitschon, his father, Franz Weninger Snr, is responsible for an equally impressive series of characterful, fleshy, and spicy red wines. A lovely example of what the Burgenland region does so well, the Weninger Blaufränkisch Hochäcker is an elegant wine with a delightful softness and warming character that makes the plum and black-fruit flavours so moreish. A dangerously drinkable wine, that will have you coming back for a second glass.

Florianigasse 11, 7312 Horitschon
www.weninger.com

Zull Weinviertel

Lust & Laune Grüner Veltliner (white); Lust & Laune Blauer Portugieser (red)

Run by Werner Zull and his son Phillip, this estate makes a collection of superbly elegant, fresh wines that marry ripe fruit with fine aromatics – wines that show just how good Weinviertel, a region that is often overlooked, can be. The wines are the result of very carefully considered work in the vineyard, where the search for quality is always the guiding principle. The two wines recommended here are easy to spot, thanks to the arresting packaging with its funky multi-coloured stripy labels. For value, it is hard to beat the wonderfully light and zippy Lust & Laune Grüner Veltliner, for example. The soft, fruity, gently spicy Blauer Portugieser is a perfect red for easy weekday drinking.

Schrattenthal 9, 2073 Schrattenthal
www.zull.at

North America

North American wine is dominated by California, which is now firmly established as one of the world's most important quality wine regions. With a collection of vine-growing regions that is more diverse than many countries, California offers a range of signature styles, such as Napa Valley Cabernet Sauvignon, Sonoma Chardonnay, and ripe juicy Zinfandel reds and rosés from across the state. Elsewhere in the US, the Pacific Northwest states of Washington and Oregon are making great reds inspired by, respectively, Bordeaux and Burgundy, while Rieslings from the Finger Lakes area of New York State can be exceptional. North of the border, Canada makes a range of fine dry whites and reds and some fantastic sweet Icewine.

California

The long sunny days of California's growing season are what give the wines from the US' most important wine region their full-flavoured style. Napa Valley Cabernet Sauvignon and Sonoma County Chardonnay are the most famous names here, but vines thrive throughout the state, and exciting wines are being made from a diversity of grape varieties from Temecula in the south to Mendocino in the north.

Acacia Carneros

Chardonnay, Carneros (white)

Restrained use of new oak contributes creamy aromas to precisely focused ripe pineapple and tropical fruit in Acacia's fine yet affordable example of Carneros Chardonnay. It is a wine that positively shimmers on its way to a refreshingly crisp finish. The estate began its life in 1979, and was one of the key figures in establishing Carneros' reputation as a producer of top-quality Chardonnay and Pinot Noir. Under the guidance of winemaker Matthew Glynn, the estate today is still well regarded for producing consistent quality at fair prices.

2750 Las Amigas Rd, Napa, CA 94559
www.acaciavineyard.com

Acorn Winery/Alegria Vineyards

Russian River Valley, Sonoma

Rosato, Russian River Valley (rosé)

The practice of making a "field blend" used to be common all over the world. It involves a vineyard planted to a number of different varieties which are harvested and vinified together. In its Alegria Vineyards, Acorn Winery is one of the few producers in the US to do field blends. Owned by Bill and Betsy Nachbaur, the vineyard is an eclectic mix of Zinfandel and Italian and French grape varieties. The excellent Rosato shows that it is a worthwhile approach: it is simply bursting with rose and strawberry aromas and creamy berry, watermelon, and zippy citrus flavours.

12040 Old Redwood Highway, Healdsburg, CA 95448
www.acornwinery.com

Anaba Sonoma Valley, Sonoma

Corial Red Rhône Blend, Sonoma Valley; Corial White, Sonoma Valley

New Sonoma estate Anaba specializes in Rhône-style wines, including an excellent pair bottled under the Corial name. The red is a fuller-bodied, New World-style blend of juicy Rhône varieties that shows plenty of black pepper spice from Syrah throughout, as well as darker fruit and cedar flavours. The white version leads with peachy Viognier and citrus zest that precede creamy flavours of ripe citrus and minerals in a weighty blend that has been called a "red-wine-drinker's white".

60 Bonneau Rd, Sonoma, CA 95476
www.anabawines.com

Artesa Carneros

Pinot Noir, Carneros (red)

The Spanish Codorníu Group, best-known for its widely available range of Cavas, first came to Napa to apply its sparkling wine know-how to the valley's wine scene. By 1997, however, the company had decided that still wines in this part of the world held more allure, and they switched the name of the winery from Codoníu Napa to Artesa. In its current guise, the winery produces a wide range of wines from across the region, of which the Pinot Noir from Carneros is a particular highlight. Though the production is high, this has no bearing on the quality. Rather, it simply means that this silky, balanced Pinot Noir with red cherry flavours and subtle layers of dark chocolate and clove is readily available to drinkers on a budget.

1345 Henry Rd, Napa, CA 94559
www.artesawinery.com

Au Bon Climat Santa Barbara County, Central Coast

Pinot Noir, Santa Barbara County (red)

Winemaker Jim Clendenen is one of California's more outsize personalities, someone who is not afraid to call things as he sees them in sometimes colourful fashion. As if to disprove the notion that wines are a straight reflection of the winemaker's personality, however, the wines he makes at Au Bon Climat are very much on the elegant and restrained end of the spectrum. Clendenen founded Au

Bon Climat in 1982 with partner Adam Tolmach (now of Ojai Vineyard). The winery specializes in Pinot Noir and Chardonnay, and the entry-level Pinot Noir is elegant and slightly earthy, with supple cherry and raspberry flavours; a good reflection of the winery's style.

No visitor facilities
www.aubonclimat.com

Baker Lane Sonoma Coast, Sonoma
Cuvée Syrah, Sonoma Coast (red)

Balanced and ageworthy, Baker Lane's juicy Syrah, Sonoma Coast has floral and red fruit scents and some darker, almost chewy black fruits on the palate that persist through the finish. It is a fine example of the Old-World inspiration that fires this estate, which was founded by restaurateur Stephen Singer. Using a mix of bought-in grapes and those sourced from the estate's sustainably farmed vineyards outside of Sebastopol in the Sonoma Coast AVA, there is a cool-climate edge to production here. A boutique concern, total production stands at just 18,000 bottles.

No visitor facilities
www.bakerlanevineyards.com

Beckmen Vineyards Santa Barbara County, Central Coast
Cuvée le Bec, Santa Ynez Valley (red)

Santa Barbara meets the Côtes du Rhône in Beckmen Vineyards' structured red blend from the Santa Ynez Valley, Cuvée le Bec. Made in a ripe but still food-friendly style, it has lively flavours of cherry, blackberry, lavender, and spice. Beckmen Vineyards is the project of father-and-son duo, Tom and Steve Beckmen. The pair started out with a 16ha (40 acre) vineyard outside Los Olivos. The operation multiplied several times in size with the acquisition of a 148ha (365 acre) hillside parcel in Ballard Canyon, Purisima Mountain Vineyard. With its high elevations (256m/750ft to 380m/1,250ft) Purisima has shown itself to be a happy home for red Rhône grapes such as Syrah and Grenache.

2670 Ontiveros Road, Los Olivos, CA 93441
www.beckmenvineyards.com

Benessere Vineyards St Helena, Napa Valley
Pinot Grigio, Carneros (white)

Owned since 1994 by John and Ellen Benish, the 17ha (42 acre) Benessere Vineyard provides the ingredients for the couple's Italianate wines. The vineyard is planted to, among others, the red varieties Sangiovese and Aglianico, but it is the Pinot Grigio that offers the best value here. More like an Alsace Pinot Gris (a synonym for Pinot Grigio) in style, it opens with floral and mineral aromas, before ripe citrus, nectarine, and mango flavours build a lush mouthfeel and a crisp, fruity finish.

1010 Big Tree Rd, St Helena, CA 94574
www.benesserevineyards.com

Benziger Family Winery Sonoma Valley, Sonoma
Finegold Merlot, Sonoma Mountain (red); Stone farm Syrah, Sonoma Valley (red)

Formerly a producer of mass-market wines under the Glen Ellen label which it sold in 1993, Benziger Family Winery has reinvented itself in recent years. The focus now is on sustainable production in wines such as the medium-bodied Finegold Merlot, with its red fruit and sweet toasty aromas and plum-pudding flavours; and the Rhône-like Stone farm Syrah, which has ripe fruit, roasted meat, and baking spice aromas, and distinct with smoky, black pepper flavours.

1883 London Ranch Rd, Glen Ellen, CA 95442
www.benziger.com

Bernardus Winery Monterey County, Central Coast
Sauvignon Blanc, Monterey County (white)

The Dutch native, ex-racing driver, Bernardus "Ben" Pon, is the man behind Bernardus Winery. It is one of the leading producers in the Carmel Valley AVA, where the local climate offers hot days and cool nights, leading to wines that mix ripeness with definition. Made from the aromatic Musqué clone, Pon's Sauvignon Blanc is fresh and bright, with melon, passion fruit, and hints of grass and smoke.

5 West Carmel Valley Rd, Carmel Valley, CA 93924
www.bernardus.com

Boeger Winery El Dorado County, Inland California
Hangtown Red, El Dorado

Much more than a novelty, Boeger Winery's Hangtown Red recognizes California's Gold Rush history with a blend of grapes as eclectic and adventurous as the prospectors themselves, yielding a robust yet easily quaffable wine that unfolds with engaging complexity. The estate it comes from can be found right in the middle of Gold Rush territory, in El Dorado, and dates back to that era. It is owned by Greg and Sue Boeger, who bought the property in the early 1970s, before planting some vines. Though they always have one eye on the region's traditions, the Boegers strive to make it relevant to new generations. They were the first to make wine in the region after Prohibition. The Boegers' son, Justin, is now the winemaker.

1709 Carson Rd, Placerville, CA 95667
www.boegerwinery.com

Bogle Vineyards Yolo County, Inland California
Pinot Noir, California (red)

While Bogle winery is itself located in California's Central Valley, it pulls grapes for its Pinot Noir from such cool coastal enclaves as Russian River Valley and Santa Barbara. Those sources lead to an interpretation that is light and frisky, charmingly delicate on the surface, surprisingly multi-faceted in its depth. The Bogle family have been farming the fertile land of the Sacramento and San Joaquin River Delta, south of Sacramento, for six generations, but it was not until 1968 that they entered the wine business, as growers. They now produce nearly 14.5 million bottles each year.

37783 County Rd 144, Clarksburg, CA 95612
www.boglewinery.com

Bonny Doon Vineyard Santa Cruz Mountains, Central Coast
Syrah Le Pousseur, Central Coast (red); Contra (red)

You might mistake Bonny Doon's Le Pousseur Syrah for something from the Northern Rhône: it is dark, dense, and peppery, with blackberry and baking spice, and fine, ripe tannins. But then, this estate, founded by Randall Grahm in 1981 with the intention of making great Pinot Noir, has long had an association with the Rhône Ranger movement in California. It also has a reputation for witty marketing and for being experimental, both in winemaking techniques and its use of grape varieties, such as the six found in Central Coast Contra. Led by 55% old-vine Carignane, Contra is both fruity and savoury, with ample boysenberry and spice flavours.

328 Ingalls St, Santa Cruz, CA 95060
www.bonnydoonvineyard.com

Bonterra Vineyards Mendocino
Chardonnay, Mendocino County (white)

Bonterra Vineyards' Mendocino County Chardonnay is a smooth, fruit-forward Chardonnay made from organically grown grapes. With abundant fresh pear and apple flavours and just touches of butter and almond from oak barrels, it makes a great supporting actor at lunch or dinner. Bonterra is known for being the first mainstream US wine brand to work exclusively with organically grown grapes. The winery is a sister project to Fetzer Vineyards, and operates from its own winery in Mendocino County, with production overseen by winemaker, Robert Blue.

12901 Old River Road, Hopland, CA 95449
www.bonterra.com

The Brander Vineyard Santa Barbara County, Central Coast
Sauvignon Blanc, Santa Ynez Valley (white)

Though Fred Brander also makes reds such as Cabernet Sauvignon and Merlot, it is for his mastery of Sauvignon Blanc that he has been justly celebrated in California. Whatever the style of the (several) Sauvignon Blancs he makes, the flavour profile is always a world away from the flavours that drinkers reared on New Zealand's pungently herbaceous, gooseberry-bush Sauvignon Blancs have come to expect. The entry-point Santa Ynez Valley Sauvignon Blanc takes a middle road: crisp and a little grassy, with a splash of barrel fermentation adding texture.

2401 Refugio Rd, Los Olivos, CA 93441
www.brander.com

Buena Vista Carneros
Pinot Noir, Carneros (red); Chardonnay, Carneros (white)

Buena Vista is an important estate in the early history of California wine. It was established by the Hungarian Count Agoston Haraszthy in 1857, which means it is one of the oldest wineries in the state. The latest of its many owners since then is the Ascentia Wine Group, and under the steadying influence of winemaker Jeff Stewart, the estate has re-established itself. Scents of strawberry, cherry, and earth lead to strawberry jam-on-toast and plum with vanilla and sweet cinnamon in the Buena Vista Pinot Noir. The Buena Vista Chardonnay, meanwhile, offers sweet vanilla, mango, and pineapple with creamy, toasty aromas and yellow apple and pear on a toasted coconut finish.

18000 Old Winery Rd, Sonoma, CA 95476
www.buenavistacarneros.com

Calera Winery San Benito County, Central Coast

Chardonnay, Mt. Harlan (white); Viognier, Central Coast (white)

Having learned his trade in Burgundy, Calera founder, Josh Jensen, believes limestone soils are vital for producing world-class Pinot Noir and Chardonnay. And it was a hunt for this kind of soil that informed Jensen's search for land on which to plant his first vines. The site he found, Mt. Harlan vineyard, is full of limestone, and it shows in this Chardonnay, which has a lot of minerality to go with its bright lemon and pear fruit. There is also plenty of minerality in Calera's fleshy Central Coast Viognier, a very drinkable white from a grape variety originating in France's Rhône Valley, that also offers plenty of ripe peach flavours, with a firm core of acidity.

11300 Cienega Rd, Hollister, CA 95023
www.calerawine.com

Cambria Winery Santa Barbara County, Central Coast

Pinot Noir, Julia's Vineyard, Santa Maria Valley (red)

Another component of ex-lawyer Jess Jackson's California wine empire, Cambria Winery's story begins with the planting of the Tepusquet Vineyard in the Santa Maria Valley in the 1970s. Jackson bought the vineyard in 1986 with his wife, Barbara Banke, and it became the estate vineyard for Cambria Winery. The vineyard has been significantly replanted since then, mostly to Chardonnay and Pinot Noir, and it is the source for the consistently good, relatively high-production (some 500,000 bottles) Julia's Vineyard Pinot Noir. A good example of Santa Maria Valley Pinot Noir, it offers pretty raspberry and cherry fruit, some spicy notes, and a silky texture.

5475 Chardonnay Lane, Santa Maria, CA 93454
www.cambriawines.com

Carol Shelton Wines Russian River Valley, Sonoma

Monga Zin Old Vine Zinfandel, Cucamonga Valley (red); Wild Thing Zinfandel, Mendocino County (red)

After 19 years as a winemaker, Carol Shelton started her eponymous label in 2000 as a Zinfandel specialist. She now makes a number of intriguingly named wines from the grape. Monga Zin Old Vine Zinfandel has ephemeral fruit and aromas of graphite with contrasting flavours of cool, lean minerality and concentrated spicy, blue fruit. The complex, earthy aromas of Wild Thing Zinfandel, meanwhile, become racy blue and black fruit seasoned with dried herbs and cedar in a pure, mineral-laden finish.

3354-B Coffey Lane, Santa Rosa, CA 95403
www.carolshelton.com

Ceja Carneros

Vino de Casa White Blend, Napa Valley (white)

Mexican émigré, Pablo Ceja worked for several years at a number of different Napa wineries before joining forces with the rest of his family to start the 6ha (15 acre) family estate in Carneros. The Ceja Vino de Casa white blend proves that all that hard work was worthwhile. Chardonnay, Pinot Gris, and a smattering of Rhône varieties give this blend its lively green apple and citrus aromas, crisp mineral-driven flavours, and an oh-so-lush finish.

1248 First Street, Napa, CA 94559
www.cejavineyards.com

Chappellet Vineyards Napa Valley

Chenin Blanc, Napa Valley (white); Zinfandel, Napa Valley (red)

Donn and Molly Chappellet's vineyards have an elevated position some 366m (1,200ft) up on Pritchard Hill. Here they produce some refined wines with a European influence. Their Chenin Blanc has floral aromas with crisp lemon and apricot flavours, and is the closest Napa comes to the Loire. The Zinfandel, by contrast, is full-bodied and lengthy. Sweet, cigar-box spice perfumes a generous, mouth-filling bite of ripe blackberry pie seasoned with a twist of black pepper.

1581 Sage Canyon Rd, St Helena, CA 94574
www.chappellet.com

Chateau St Jean Sonoma Valley, Sonoma

Fumé Blanc, Sonoma County (white); Chardonnay, Sonoma County (white)

Having been founded in 1973, Chateau St Jean is part of the advanced guard in Sonoma. Now owned by Australian brewer, Foster's, it has also grown to become one of the area's bigger wineries, producing a range of wines that, while not always the most exciting, nonetheless includes a couple of genuine diamonds in the rough. With its crisp, delicate pear and citrus aromas, and lean, focused citrus flavours, Chateau St Jean's Fumé Blanc is comfortably one of the best-value wines in Sonoma. The Chardonnay is equally good value for money. It opens out with richly toasted citrus and tropical fruit aromas before delivering medium-bodied flavours of ripe, buttery citrus, sweet vanilla, and a round finish. Winemaker Margo Van Staavere has been making the Chateau St Jean wines for more than two decades.

8555 Sonoma Highway, Kenwood, CA 95452
www.chateaustjean.com

Cline Cellars Carneros

Cool Climate Syrah, Sonoma County (red); Oakley Five Reds Blend, California

Fred Cline started his wine-growing career in Contra Costa County, where he made his name as a producer of top-quality, old-vine Zinfandel and Mourvèdre. He has since broadened his horizons to take in a number of other varieties, and in 1991 he expanded his land holdings considerably with the acquisition of a 142ha (350 acre) estate in Carneros. The estate, on the site of an old Spanish mission, now produces a number of excellent, good-value wines. Labels to look out for include the Cline Cellars Cool Climate Syrah, which is a classic example of Syrah from the Sonoma coast where the blueberry, black pepper, and subtle aromas of cedar shavings are amplified by a full body and velvety texture. The Cline Cellars Oakley Five Reds Blend, meanwhile, is a happy (if unlikely) blend of Merlot, Zinfandel, Barbera, Alicante Bouschet, and Petite Sirah with spicy blackberry flavours that stands up to spicy Tex-Mex and tomato-based dishes.

24737 Arnold Drive, Highway 121, Sonoma, CA 95476
www.clinecellars.com

Clos LaChance Santa Cruz Mountains, Central Coast

Hummingbird Series Zinfandel, Central Coast (red)

Bill and Brenda Murphy, the owners of Clos LaChance, were just enjoying a hobby when they planted some Chardonnay vines in their back garden. But things turned progressively more serious, and they started to source additional Chardonnay as well as Pinot Noir from the Santa Cruz Mountains. By the late 1990s the couple had begun work on building a winery and planting a commercial vineyard in the Santa Clara Valley. In this warmer spot they planted Syrah and Zinfandel and other warm-climate grapes. The Hummingbird Series Zinfandel is a medium-weight version of the grape and is loaded with ripe, spicy berry flavours.

1 Hummingbird Lane, San Martin, CA 95046
www.closlachance.com

Clos du Val

Stags Leap District, Napa Valley

Merlot, Napa Valley (red)

French by name, and French by nature, Clos du Val has been attracting plaudits for its elegant take on the traditional Napa Valley virtues of ripe fruit since it started its life in 1972. It is owned by businessman John Goelet, and he has employed the same winemaker, Frenchman Bernard Portet, since the very beginning. Signature toasty oak layered with complex aromas of black fruit, black olive, and dried herbs are supported by plenty of structure in Clos du Val's Napa Valley Merlot, which is made in quite a ripe New World-style for this producer.

5330 Silverado Trail, Napa, CA 94558
www.closduval.com

Dashe Cellars San Francisco Bay, Central Coast

Zinfandel, Dry Creek Valley (red)

The globetrotting Michael and Anne Dashe have made wine all over the world. In fact, their collective experience includes winemaking stints on three continents, as well as at a number of top California wineries, and between them they have worked with several of the world's best winemakers. In 1996, they decided to use all of that experience and make their own wine. They specialize in Zinfandel, from which they make a number of wines including the affordable Dry Creek Valley Zinfandel, a wine that offers bright, brambly blackberry fruit with a tobacco note.

55 4th St, Oakland, CA 94607
www.dashecellars.com

Deerfield Ranch Sonoma Valley, Sonoma

Red Rex, Sonoma County Blend (red); Sauvignon Blanc, Windsor Oaks Vineyard, Chalk Hill (white)

Seven varieties make up the Red Rex Sonoma County Blend from the unassuming, but highly competent Sonoma winery, Deerfield Ranch. Cabernet Sauvignon leads the way in a wine that delivers a whopping mouthful of complex flavours that are balanced and bright. No less interesting is Deerfield Ranch Sauvignon Blanc, from the Windsor Oaks Vineyard. A perfectly balanced expression that defines pure, concentrated varietal aromas and flavours transmitted from the chalky site where it grows. Delicious.

10200 Sonoma Highway, Kenwood, CA 95452
www.deerfieldranch.com

DeLoach Vineyards Russian River Valley, Sonoma

Vinthropic Chardonnay, Sonoma (white); Pinot Noir, Russian River Valley (red)

Retired fireman Cecil DeLoach founded DeLoach Vineyards in 1973, since when it has become one of Sonoma's most famous brands. The French wine businessman, Jean-Charles Boisset, bought the vineyards in 2003. There are some great bargains to be found. The Vinthropic Chardonnay has aromas of green apple, pineapple, and guava with crisp, transparent flavours of apple skin and vanilla in a light-weight body. The Russian River Valley Pinot Noir has bright red fruit and sweet spice that intensify in medium-bodied, candied cherry, and caramelized vanilla with balanced acidity.

1791 Olivet Rd, Santa Rosa, CA 95401
www.deloachvineyards.com

CG Di Arie Winery El Dorado County, Inland California

Verdelho, Shenandoah Valley (white)

The Madeira grape Verdelho is finding a receptive new home in California's Sierra foothills. At its best, as it most certainly is in CG Di Arie Winery's version from the Shenandoah Valley, it yields a medium-bodied white wine as fragrant as a farmers' market when the tangerines, grapefruit, quince, and pear are at prime ripeness. The man behind all these wonderful flavours, Chaim Gur-Arieh, used to take a different route to people's tastebuds: he was for some time a food scientist. Ten years ago he swapped lab for vineyard, and with the help of his wife, the artist Elisheva Gur-Arieh, he has turned CG Di Arie into one of El Dorado County's most exciting new wineries. The couple use a wide range of grape varieties, and their wines are a blend of Old and New World sensibilities.

19919 Shenandoah School Rd, Plymouth, CA 95669
www.cgdiarie.com

Domaine Carneros Carneros

Sparkling Brut, Carneros

Eileen Crane is following in a long and distinguished tradition of strong women at the head of sparkling wine houses. And, like Barbe-Nicole Ponsardin (La Veuve Clicquot) and Lily Bollinger before her, she has made a strong impression. After helping to set up Gloria Ferrer, she was tapped by Champagne's Claude Taittinger to run Domaine Carneros in the late 1980s, and she has been at the estate, with its imposing château-style Napa winery, ever since. She makes wines in the Champagne style, with the second fermentation taking place in bottle. Aged for three years prior to release, Domaine Carneros Sparkling Brut is a blend of Pinot Noir and Chardonnay that has it all: bright citrus and red fruit aromas with complex, mineral-driven flavours.

1240 Duhig Rd, Napa, CA 94559
www.domainecarneros.com

Dry Creek Vineyards

Dry Creek Valley, Sonoma

Sauvignon Blanc, Dry Creek Valley (white); Heritage Zinfandel (red)

Started by David Stare in 1972, the family owned and run Dry Creek Vineyards is intimately associated with the valley of the same name. Most certainly one of the original producers in the valley, it also has a claim to being one of the best. In its pungent Sauvignon Blanc, pink grapefruit aromas gain complexity and clean, concentrated tropical fruit flavours from a dose of Sauvignon Musqué. In the Heritage Zinfandel, spicy blue fruits are the dominant aromas which deepen to brambly, peppery fruit on the palate that shows plenty of concentration and grip.

3770 Lambert Bridge Rd, Healdsburg, CA 95448
www.drycreekvineyard.com

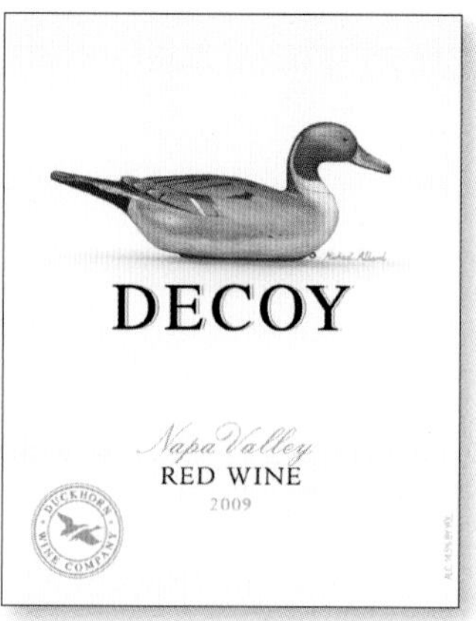

Duckhorn Vineyards St Helena, Napa Valley

Decoy, Napa Valley Blend (red)

Duckhorn Vineyards has grown considerably since Dan Duckhorn and his wife Margaret founded the label in 1976. As well as the thriving main label, it has diversified into names such as Paraduxx, and Goldeneye in Anderson Valley. Duckhorn owes at least some of its success to the fashion for Merlot that gripped the world, particularly the US, in the 1990s, when the high-quality wines it was making from the grape were perfectly placed to take advantage of the trend. New Zealander Bill Nancarrow is now in charge of making a consistently strong range of wines that includes the accessible – in both price and style – Decoy Napa Valley blend. Though it is made to be ready to drink immediately on release, the Decoy does not skimp on complexity. There are mulberry, baking spice, and cedar aromas aplenty, moving to generous, lingering flavours of cassis, liquorice, and mocha.

1000 Lodi Lane, St Helena, CA 94574
www.duckhorn.com

Eberle Winery San Luis Obispo County, Central Coast

Syrah, Steinbeck Vineyard, Paso Robles (red)

In 1973, when Gary Eberle first arrived in Paso Robles, the winemaking scene (if you could call it that) was still very much in its infancy. There were, in fact, just three wineries operating in the area. Eberle, who had been studying for a doctorate before getting the wine bug, could see the potential in this part of California, however, and he started the now-defunct Estrella Rivery Winery to grow grapes and make wines. In 1978, he became the first California wine producer to make and release a wine from 100% Syrah, and for a long time he was the go-to guy for other producers looking for Syrah vines. By 1983, he had opened Eberle Winery, where he consolidated his reputation for Syrah and Cabernet Sauvignon. He continues to make fine Syrah, including the Steinbeck Vineyard expression. Quite a structured wine, the Steinbeck has lively blackberry, plum, and clove notes: the perfect introduction to the work of a California Syrah producer.

3810 Highway 46 East, Paso Robles, CA 93447
www.eberlewinery.com

Edmunds St John San Francisco Bay, Central Coast

Gamay Noir Bone-Jolly, El Dorado County (red)

The Edmunds St John estate takes its name from the two proprietors: Steve Edmunds and his wife Cornelia St John. The couple have been making excellent wines inspired by the Rhône in Berkeley, and a number of other parts of the East Bay, since 1985, when the fashion for all things Rhône in California was just beginning. Edmunds is something of a traditionalist when it comes to winemaking, and he believes in minimal intervention in the winery, resulting in wines that are designed to exhibit a sense of where they come from. There is a quirky edge to the Edmunds St John portfolio that is fully on display in the Gamay Noir Bone-Jolly from El Dorado County. An easy-to-drink, lively wine, it has aromas and flavours of raspberry, spice, and violets that jump from the glass. Firm acidity makes it very refreshing, too.

No visitor facilities
www.edmundsstjohn.com

Elke Vineyards Mendocino

Pinot Noir, Anderson Valley (red)

Few affordable Pinot Noirs deliver as much smoothness and flavour interest as Elke Vineyards Pinot Noir from the Anderson Valley. Its colour is on the light side, but the aromas of toasted bread and sandalwood, and flavours of baked cherries, cinnamon, and nutmeg make it exceedingly tasty. The wine is so good it makes you wonder if all winemakers shouldn't start their career in the same way as Elke Vineyards' Mary Elke, who began her drink-making life crafting apple juice. Mary Elke Organic Apple Juice is still made in small quantities, but wine is now the main business and the Elke family have owned vineyards for 20 years in Napa and Mendocino. They sell a lot of their production to other producers, but since 1997 have built a loyal following for their own bottlings.

12351 Highway 128, Boonville, CA 95415
www.elkevineyards.com

Enkidu Winery Sonoma Valley, Sonoma

Humbaba Rhône Red Blend, Sonoma; E Cabernet Sauvignon, Sonoma Valley (red)

After spending almost a decade making wines at Carmenet Vineyards in the late 1980s and 1990s, Phillip Staehle left to start the Enkidu project. Taking its name from a character in the Indian epic saga, Gilgamesh, Enkidu makes a variety of wines from fruit that Staehle buys from growers in and around Sonoma and Napa. Staehle makes small quantities of wines with great attention to detail, preferring to let the fruit itself do the talking, rather than applying a heavy winemaking hand, and minimizing any oak influence. The Humbaba Rhône Red Blend is black as night with complex tarry, blue fruit aromas that gain depth and spice from Petite Sirah. The E Cabernet Sauvignon is an easy-drinking style that shows bright, savoury fruit-forward aromas and a mouthful of soft, ripe blackberries that persist through the finish.

No visitor facilities
www.enkiduwines.com

OAK FLAVOURS

Words such as "oak", "oaky", and "toasted oak" are popular wine descriptors. If you've ever been in a cabinet-maker's shop where freshly sawn oak is stacked you will know what oak smells like. But even people who have not experienced oak flavours in that direct way, almost definitely have tasted the effect of oak in wine.

Oak flavours resemble vanilla, coconut, cedar, toasted bread, maple syrup, and even cured bacon. They are often the main flavour components in wine other than grapes. Winemakers around the world use oak containers to hold their wine while it ages, and have done so for centuries. Originally, oak barrels were intended only for storage, not to increase quality, but winemakers learned that oak containers added flavour and texture. Eventually barrels became integral to the wine's personality.

Since the 1970s, winemakers have learned to get an approximation of oak flavour without using barrels, which are expensive. They add oak chips, powder, and other permutations to the wine while it is fermenting and ageing.

Some winemakers advocate "unoaked", "non-oaked", and "naked" wines that are fermented and aged in containers made of stainless steel, plastic, or old oak casks that no longer give flavour to the wine. This is an approach that strives to allow the natural personalities of the grapes to come through.

Ageing in oak barrels gives both flavour and texture to wine.

HOST A WINE TASTING IN YOUR HOME

Hosting a wine tasting party in your home exposes you and your guests to new wines and provides an excellent excuse for a modest Bacchanalia that should be fun for everyone including you. Why not try to make this wine tasting the first in a series? Ask a friend to host at his or her house in a month or two. Soon you'll have a semi-official wine tasting group and a great ongoing source of wine recommendations from the ultimate expert sources – yourself and your friends.

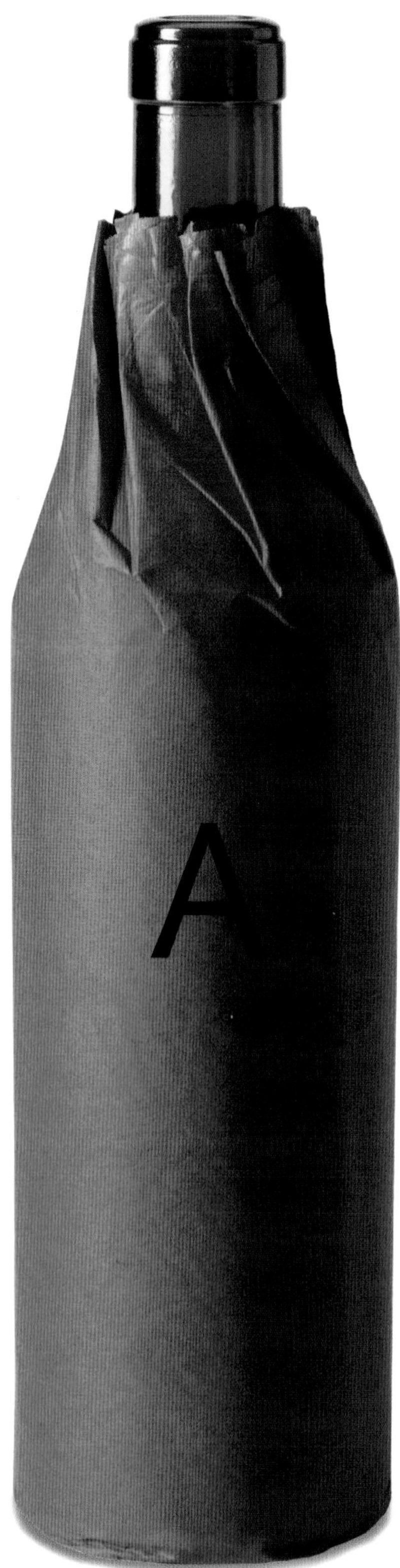

Concealing the identity of the wines exposes your guests' true opinions.

1 Choose a theme Everyone will benefit if you narrow the field of wines before you invite the guests. Think about the time of year and try to choose appropriate wines: if hosting just before Christmas, choose champagne so people know what to buy for gifts, or in the summer, choose rosés so people have an idea what to serve at their next outdoor party. Select a type of wine and make it as specific as possible. The easiest themes are horizontal tastings, where all the wines are the same vintage, but come from different vineyards and wineries. You could also try a vertical tasting where the wines are all from the same winery and vineyards but the vintage is different.

2 Invite your guests Invite six to eight people or couples and ask each to bring along one bottle that fits in with your theme. Ask them also to bring their own wine glasses, so you are not left with 36 glasses to wash up at the end of the evening (assuming you even have that many glasses in the first place). That leaves you to provide the inspiration, location, and good portions of finger food (see panel) to mop up the wine.

3 Blind the bottles Hide the identity of the wines. When the guests arrive with their bottles, slip them into paper bags or wrap a couple of sheets of paper around each and tape tight. Mark the bottles A, B, C, and so on, and, if you want to feel really professional, lay out place mats for each guest marked with the same series of letters, making it easy for them to compare the wine. Remove other clues to the brand identities. Cut off the foil capsules, and pull the corks or twist the tops off and hide them.

4 Explain the rules Take a minute to explain the rules before anyone takes a sip. "We're sampling red Southwest French wines, all from the same village, and from vintage 20XX." Supply pens and note-pads (or pre-printed score cards with spaces for wines A, B, C, and so on) and encourage your friends jot down their impressions and rankings. Then, taste, drink, eat, discuss the wines, and have fun, but save "the reveal" until all guests have tried as many wines as they want to.

5 The result Get your guests to commit to their favourite wines by handing their note-cards to you, or raising hands for their top picks as you unwrap the bottles one by one. It can be hilarious to watch your friends try to take back their votes when they see a famous brand name to which they gave low scores.

Wait until everyone has chosen their favourite wine before the big reveal.

FINGER FOOD

You don't want the wine to hit empty stomachs but nor do you want to supply food that is so spicy or flavoursome that it may interfere with the aromas and tastes of the wine.

Go for mild savoury crackers and vegetable crudités (but avoid dips) instead of fancy canapés.

A good way to add dimension to a wine tasting party is to incorporate a particular food-pairing element. When hosting a tasting of a particular wine type, you can plan two or three small bites that test the recommended food pairings with that type, and guests can be polled as to their favourites.

Examples could include a couple of steaks cut up into bite-sized pieces for a tasting of Argentine Malbecs, or some simply cooked seafood, such as prawns in olive oil, for a run of global Sauvignon Blancs.

If you're feeling particularly generous, you could even prepare a small main course of a food-matching element for your guests to enjoy with their favourite wine of the tasting once the main event is over.

Choose simple, plain food such as crackers.

Etude Carneros

Pinot Gris, Carneros (white)

An unusual winery in that it has a great reputation for making top Pinot Noir *and* Cabernet Sauvignon, Etude also has a number of other aces up its sleeve. It was founded by, and made its reputation under, Tony Soter, who later sold on the project to the Foster's Australian beer and liquor group. Winemaker Jon Priest has kept up the good work since the acquisition, however, in wines such as the delicious Pinot Gris. From fruit that is Alsatian in origin (the original vines came from the French region) and style, opulent floral and white stone fruit aromas elevate focused flavours of white peach and crisp citrus.

1250 Cuttings Wharf Road, Napa, CA 94558
www.etudewines.com

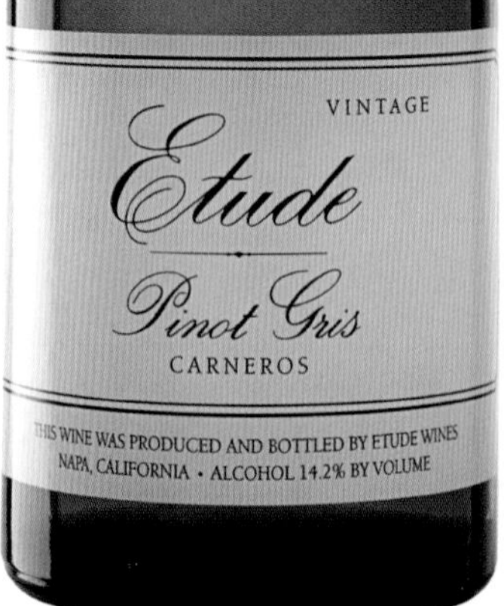

Ferrari-Carano Vineyards

Dry Creek Valley, Sonoma

Siena Sangiovese-Malbec Blend, Sonoma (red); Fumé Blanc (white)

Famed for its delightful gardens, Ferrari-Carano is a regular part of the itinerary for tour parties visiting the area. Founded by Don Carano in 1985, the estate today has more than 567ha (1,400 acres) of vineyards and two distinct wineries. It makes a number of intriguing and tasty wines, but two stand out for their quality and value. The Siena is a seamless red blend of Sangiovese and Malbec with amplified aromas of red fruit and a tasty balance of juicy flavours. The white Fumé Blanc, meanwhile, has delicate aromas of lime and freshly mown hay unfolding to concentrated flavours of ripe lemon and mango with a weighty finish.

8761 Dry Creek Rd, Healdsburg, CA 95448
www.ferrari-carano.com

Flora Springs St Helena, Napa Valley

Sangiovese, Napa Valley (red)

Originally started by Jerry and Flora Komes a quarter of a century ago, Flora Springs is a family operation that is now in the third generation of family ownership. The Komes-Garvey family has a number of vineyard holdings in the valley, adding up to a little under 263ha (650 acres), making them significant growers. Having worked as assistant winemaker for some time, Paul Steinauer was made head winemaker in 2008, and he is ensuring that Flora Springs remains at the forefront of the winemaking scene in this part of California. Flora Springs has attracted a great deal of attention for Trilogy, its top-of-the-range blend of Cabernet Sauvignon, Cabernet Franc, and Merlot, but it is the very fine Sangiovese that leads the way here for drinkers on an everyday budget. Neutral oak ageing lets the fruit and acidity take centre stage in this balanced bottling with aromas and intense flavours of cherry, cranberry, and spice.

1978 West Zinfandel Lane, St Helena, CA 94574
www.florasprings.com

Folie à Deux Winery St Helena, Napa Valley

Cabernet Sauvignon, Napa Valley (red); Chardonnay, Napa Valley (white)

One of the best-known names in California wine, Sutter Home began its life in 1874 and was bought some 74 years later by the Trinchero family. The company's name became associated with off-dry rosé wines in the 1980s thanks to its top-selling White Zinfandel, but it has a strong range of other brands, including the consistently good-value Folie à Deux. The medium-bodied Cabernet Sauvignon has lifted aromas of black cherry, a round texture and generous black fruit flavours complemented by sweet, dark spice. The Chardonnay has tropical fruit salad and toasted coconut aromas with round, creamy flavours of vanilla bean and ripe stone fruit custard with a crisp, nutmeg-dusted finish.

7481 St Helena Highway, St Helena, CA 94562
www.trincherowinery.com

Foursight Wines Anderson Valley, Mendocino

Sauvignon Blanc, Charles Vineyard, Anderson Valley (white)

The young boutique operation Foursight Wines is a family concern: four members of the Charles family tend the vines and make the wines at their site in the Anderson Valley. Having first planted a vineyard (to Pinot Noir, Sauvignon Blanc, and Semillon), and then constructed a winery, the family have gone about things their own way, with wines that are bright and elegant. The Sauvignon Blanc is particularly electric. Fresh apple, ripe melon, and a citrus-like tang light up this crisp, refreshing wine. It is best served well chilled with lunch or a fish course at dinner.

14475 Highway 128, Boonville, CA 95466
www.foursightwines.com

Francis Ford Coppola Winery

Alexander Valley, Sonoma

Diamond Collection Claret, California (red); Director's Cut Cabernet Sauvignon, Alexander Valley (red)

Legendary Hollywood director, Francis Ford Coppola, is perhaps just as famous these days for his successful wine business as he is for films such as *The Godfather*. The Sonoma end of his empire offers the best bet for bargain hunters. The Diamond Collection Claret is a classic Bordeaux blend that over delivers in optimal vintages with rich berry and plum fruit and firm, balanced structure. The Director's Cut Cabernet Sauvignon features signature Alexander Valley aromas of savoury red fruit, and is full-bodied with forward darker berry flavours and a refined texture.

300 Via Archimedes, Geyserville, CA 95441
www.franciscoppolawinery.com

Freemark Abbey St Helena, Napa Valley

Chardonnay, Napa Valley (white)

Concentrated and rich with intense tropical and ripe stone fruit aromas, Freemark Abbey Chardonnay offers a mélange of Key lime, mandarin, grapefruit, and mineral flavours with a crisp, fruit-laden finish. It hails from an estate that was bought by Josephine and John Tychson in 1886. When John died from tuberculosis, Josephine continued the business for a while, and it then passed through a number of different hands before being snapped up by Jackson Family Estates in 2006. The Jackson family has since invested a large amount of capital here, and the wines, already good, are improving all the time.

3022 St Helena Highway North, St Helena, CA 94574
www.freemarkabbey.com

Gloria Ferrer Winery Carneros

Brut, Sonoma (sparkling); Blanc de Noirs, Carneros (sparkling)

Owned by the Ferrer family of Freixenet Cava, Gloria Ferrer is one of California's best sparkling wine estates.The Brut features a creamy, almost dense mousse atop Ferrer's signature aromas of pear and citrus with flavours of baked apple. It is crisp with lively minerality building to a toasty finale. The Blanc de Noirs (Pinot Noir with just a splash of Chardonnay) is a fuller-bodied sparkler that blushes with vanilla-scented strawberry and creamy black cherry fruit.

23555 Carneros Highway, Sonoma, CA 95476
www.gloriaferrer.com

Greenwood Ridge Vineyards Mendocino

White Riesling, Mendocino Ridge, Estate Bottled (white)

A good wine does not need to be complicated, as Greenwood Ridge Vineyards' Mendocino Ridge White Riesling Estate Bottled proves time and again. A charming, light, and aromatic sipper, it is easy to enjoy and smooth to swallow. It has alluring honey and apple aromas, is fresh, slightly sweet, and offers delicate fruit flavours. One of the oldest wineries in Anderson Valley (it was founded in 1980), Greenwood Ridge is a hive of ingenious activity. Visitors can find innovations such as the widespread use of solar power and biodiesel-fuelled vehicles. They can also enjoy the artwork of owner Allan Green, who used to be a graphic artist, and who designed the arresting silk-screened wine labels. A creative soul, he also thought up an annual wine tasting competition for his wine club members, and is responsible for the bright pennants that fly over the tasting room.

5501 Highway 128, Philo, CA 95466
www.greenwoodridge.com

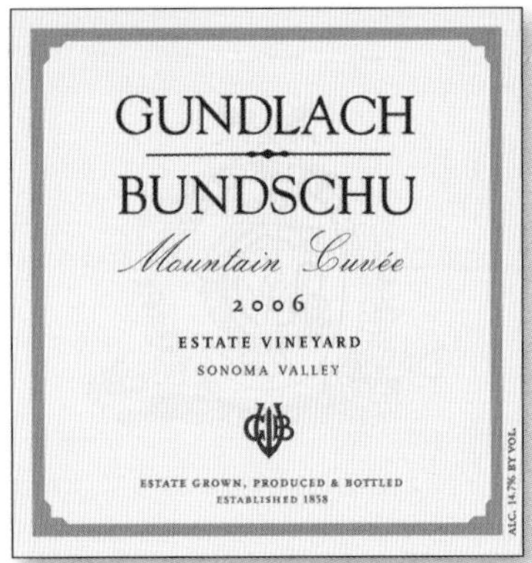

Gundlach Bundschu Winery Sonoma Valley, Sonoma

Gewürztraminer, Sonoma Coast (white); Mountain Cuvée Bordeaux Blend, Sonoma Valley (red)

Gundlach Bundschu Winery was founded in 1858 by Bavarian immigrant Jacob Gundlach. Originally known as the Rhinefarm vineyard, it had earned a good reputation for its wines in the region, until Prohibition put a stop to things. The family went back into growing grapes in 1938, but did not start to make wine again until 1970. Quality has been on the rise since the turn of the millennium, when the winery decided to make wines using only its own fruit. Wines worth looking out for here include the gorgeous Gewürztraminer, which is a crisp, mineral-driven white, with aromas of lychee and stone fruit evolving into broad, green citrus flavours in this savoury, bone-dry-style. The lean, lighter-bodied red known as Mountain Cuvée Bordeaux Blend, by contrast, has some upfront aromas of pure red fruit – plum and pomegranate – turning to savoury flavours spiced with anise.

2000 Denmark St, Sonoma, CA 95476
www.gunbun.com

Hahn Estates Monterey County, Central Coast

Hahn Winery, Pinot Noir, Monterey (red)

When Nicky Hahn first made his mark on the Monterey County wine scene it was with the Smith & Hook Cabernet Sauvignon from the Santa Lucia Highlands. The appellation was not, in fact, the best site for growing Cabernet Sauvignon – it is really too cool to ripen the grape reliably every vintage – and so Hahn went on to develop the Hahn Estates label by adding vineyards in other regions (as well as more in the Santa Lucia Highlands). The business expanded, too, with the development of a popular brand, Cycles Gladiator. Hahn now grows his Cabernet Sauvignon in Paso Robles, and attention in the Monterey County vineyards has instead shifted to cooler climate varieties, such as Pinot Noir. Hahn produces several tiers of wines made from Pinot Noir, many of them very high quality, but the one labelled Hahn Winery is the best value. It is bright and fruity with a slight leafy, savoury note.

37700 Foothill Rd, Soledad, CA 93960
www.hahnfamilywines.com

Handley Cellars
Mendocino

Chardonnay, Estate Vineyard, Anderson Valley (white); Pinot Noir, Anderson Valley (red)

Handley Cellars Anderson Valley Chardonnay has great complexity of pear, vanilla, fig, and butter flavours that define a very concentrated, ripe, almost sweet wine that is modest in alcohol content. The Pinot Noir, by contrast, is nicely balanced, appetizingly dry, and begs for a roast pheasant or grilled salmon. It holds back a bit on the ripeness, yet shows pretty cinnamon and cherry flavours and firm tannins in the texture. Both wines are great examples of Milla Handley's unpretentious style.

3151 Highway 128, Philo, CA 95466
www.handleycellars.com

Hanna Winery Russian River Valley, Sonoma

Sauvignon Blanc, Russian River Valley (white); Chardonnay, Russian River Valley (white)

Syrian-born heart surgeon, Dr Elias Hanna, was an amateur winemaker before being drawn more seriously into the wine business with the acquistion of 5ha (12 acres) in the Russian River Valley in 1970. He now farms 100ha (250 acres) of estate vineyards in the Russian River Valley, Alexander Valley, and Sonoma Valley AVAs. His Sauvignon Blanc is zippy with grapefruit and herbaceous floral aromas, vibrant ripe citrus, and juicy stone fruit flavours. The Chardonnay has powerful varietal aromas of ripe, creamy citrus, and apple that build towards richer, nutty flavours and a bright mineral finish.

9280 Highway 128, Healdsburg, CA 95448
www.hannawinery.com

Hess Collection Mount Veeder, Napa Valley

Select Chardonnay, Monterey (white); Cabernet Sauvignon, Allomi Vineyard, Napa Valley (red)

The Hess Collection winery is one of a number owned by the Hess family, and it generally produces good quality wines. The crisp, Monterey-grown Select Chardonnay has citrus and sweet vanilla flavours that strike a balance between fruit and oak with aromas of ripe pineapple and tropical fruit. The Allomi Vineyard Cabernet Sauvignon has black cherry and caramel aromas expanding to concentrated, ripe flavours of black plum, baking spice, and dark, toasty oak with a lingering finish.

4411 Redwood Rd, Napa, CA 94558
www.hesscollection.com

Honig Vineyard and Winery Rutherford, Napa Valley

Sauvignon Blanc, Napa Valley (white)

Honig Napa Valley Sauvignon Blanc is a veritable fruit basket of a white wine, with orange, melon, and peach aromas all amplified by balanced, juicy flavours that are underscored by racy minerality. Produced by the talented Kristen Belair, it is the kind of flavour-packed wine that the Honig winery has become famous for. Belair is supported by the proprietor Michael Honig, a man who has been at the forefront of promoting sustainable viticulture in the valley.

850 Rutherford Rd, Rutherford, CA 94573
www.honigwine.com

Hook & Ladder Winery

Russian River Valley, Sonoma

Tillerman Cabernet Blend, Russian River Valley (red); Pinot Noir, Russian River Valley (red)

The Hook & Ladder brand takes its name from one of founder Cecil DeLoach's past lives as a fireman. It was started after the DeLoach family made a fortune from selling off their eponymous wine brand, which had become one of the most successful in the

ORGANIC WINE

The word "organic" implies health and environmental benefits, and promises the absence of chemical pesticides and fertilizers.

By refusing synthetic inputs to boost soil nutrition and omitting synthetic sprays on the leaves and grape bunches, growers can eliminate many foreign substances from the vineyard. Instead, organic growers use organic sprays to prevent mildew, compost to fertilize, and plant low-growing crops between vine rows to encourage a living soil full of worms, insects, and micro-organisms.

In terms of taste and quality, organic wines have come a long way and many can compete in price with conventionally made wine. Still, organic means different things when applied to different wines, and labelling is different from country to country. For example, wine labelled as "made from organically grown grapes" is not necessarily the same as wine labelled as "organic". The former – which is the only officially sanctioned organic labelling permitted in the European Union – means the wine can be made from grapes sprayed with copper-sulphur compounds and dosed with sulphur dioxide as a traditional preservative in the winery. In the US, however, the use of added sulphur dioxide is not permitted on wines labelled "organic". So, "wines made from organically grown grapes" are now much more common than "organic wines".

Ultimately, organic wines vary about as much in quality as non-organic wines, but they carry a moral benefit for those concerned about the environment.

Cover crops encourage beneficial micro-organisms.

history of California. The family's new brand specializes in good-value wines sourced from the family's 152ha (375 acres) of vineyards. Among them is the fine Tillerman Cabernet Blend, in which the Cabernet Franc has a savoury, herbal character that lends complexity to the black fruit and cedar aromas and bright, chocolate cherry flavours. The Pinot Noir, meanwhile, is in a ripe, New World-style with spicy cherry aromas, chocolate-covered cherry and cola flavours building to medium-weight with a toasty, brown-spice finish.

2027 Olivet Rd, Santa Rosa, CA 95401
www.hookandladderwinery.com

Hop Kiln Winery Russian River Valley, Sonoma

Chardonnay, Sonoma (white); Pinot Noir, Russian River Valley (red)

Hop Kiln Winery derives its name from the massive building it calls home: one of the country's best-preserved examples of a hop kiln. Produced solely from estate-grown fruit with showy floral and stone fruit aromas, the Chardonnay here is well balanced and round with flavours of ripe, grilled pear. The Pinot Noir is a full-bodied yet finely textured, signature expression of the variety, with aromas of violet, red cherry, and blackberry and a spicy finish.

6050 Westside Rd, Healdsburg, CA 95448
www.hopkilnwinery.com

Imagery Estate Sonoma Valley, Sonoma

Grenache, Sonoma Mountain (red); Muscato di Canelli, Lake County (white)

Imagery Estate began its life as the project of Joe Benziger, who used the family estate to work with lesser-spotted grape varieties. An example of the output of what has since become a more serious proposition is the medium-bodied Grenache with its candied red fruit aromas and its spicy, stewed cherry and plum flavours dusted with baking spice on the finish. The Muscato di Canelli has attractive citrus blossom and floral aromas giving way to medium-bodied and striking flavours of sweet, ripe apple and Crenshaw melon.

14335 Highway 12, Glen Ellen, CA 95442
www.imagerywinery.com

J Vineyards Russian River Valley, Sonoma

J Cuvée 20 Brut NV, Russian River Valley (sparkling); Cooper Vineyard Pinot Gris, California (white)

The J Cuvée 20 Brut NV is a great introduction to Jane Jordan's J Vineyard's style of fizz. Lemon zest and honeysuckle aromas unfold to toasted brioche, lemon, and spicy pear flavours that are vibrant and complex. The estate also produces an excellent range of still wines, such as the Cooper Vineyard Pinot Gris, with its inviting floral and citrus aromas, mineral-driven flavours of baked stone fruit and candied orange peel, and its crisp, dry finish.

11447 Old Redwood Highway, Healdsburg, CA 95448
www.jwine.com

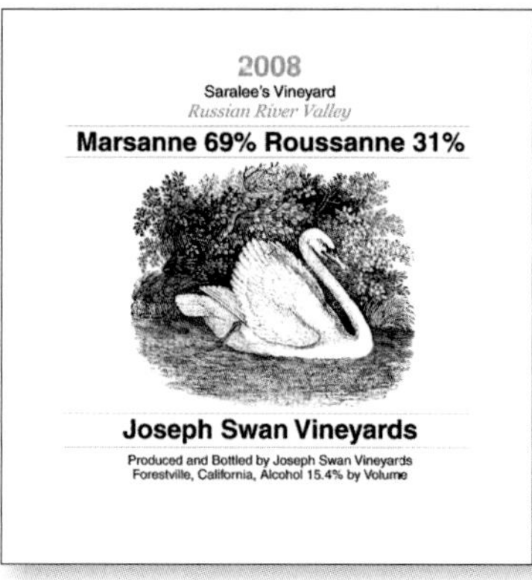

Joseph Swan Vineyards

Russian River Valley, Sonoma

Cuvée du Trois Pinot Noir, Russian River Valley (red); Marsanne-Roussanne, Russian River Valley (white)

Joseph Swan had a long and distinguished career as an airline pilot before switching to the wine business as a retirement project at the end of the 1960s. The project started with a small vineyard near Forestville, where he planted some Chardonnay and Pinot Noir. But Swan first made his name with the acclaimed Zinfandels he made from bought-in fruit while he waited for his vines to mature. Today the winery is known for a slightly rustic style of both Zinfandel and Pinot Noir, but one of the best bets is the Cuvée du Trois Pinot Noir, easily one of the best-value Pinot Noirs in Sonoma. Dark-natured with savoury aromas of red cherry, earth, and tea; darker berry flavours are seasoned with toasted spices and caramel. No less good value is the estate's blend of Marsanne and Roussanne. Perfumed aromas of baked apple are the signature of this rich, mineral-infused Rhône-inspired blend, with its crisp pear and hazelnut flavours.

2916 Laguna Rd, Forestville, CA 95436
www.swanwinery.com

Karly Wines Amador County, Inland California

Sauvignon Blanc, Amador County (white)

When he founded Karly Wines in 1978, Buck Cobb sensed that Sauvignon Blanc would be the green grape most at home in the hot Sierra foothills. Each vintage he backs up that early theoretical viewpoint (or hunch) with the best kind of empirical proof – the kind that his customers can taste in the glass. A full-bodied and slightly sweet take on the grape variety, the Amador County Sauvignon Blanc has enough tropical fruit to make it as welcome with Thai dishes as it is when it is served as an aperitif. Intriguingly Cobb was a fighter pilot before he landed in the wine business with his wife, Karly, who lent her name to their estate. Located in Amador County's Shenandoah Valley, they also work with the red varieties Mourvèdre and Zinfandel in wines that are never less than full of character, and that always display a deep imprint of the region's terroir.

11076 Bell Rd, Plymouth, CA 95669
www.karlywines.com

Kendall Jackson Wine Estates

Russian River Valley, Sonoma

Grand Reserve Cabernet Sauvignon, Sonoma (red); Vintners' Reserve Pinot Noir, California (red)

Kendall Jackson Wine Estates is one of the most successful wine producers in the US, and also one of the largest in the world – it is currently number 10 in the list of the US's largest wine producers. Founded by the lawyer Jess Jackson in 1982, it has since grown to include a bewildering array of different names and projects, not just in California, but all over the world. Not everything produced under the Kendall Jackson name is worth seeking out, but at least a couple of its wines stand out for producing genuinely great quality at affordable prices. The Grand Reserve Cabernet Sauvignon has bright, black fruit and cassis aromas revealing a full body with plenty of dark fruit and toasty oak flavours. The Kendall Jackson Vintners' Reserve Pinot Noir, meanwhile, has delicate aromas of strawberry and cherry, with lighter-bodied flavours of dark fruit and earth that get a boost from a subtle toastiness.

5007 Fulton Rd, Santa Rosa, CA 95403
www.kj.com

Kenwood Vineyards Sonoma Valley, Sonoma

Cabernet Sauvignon, Jack London Vineyard (red); Pinot Gris, Sonoma County (white)

It would be easy to discount Kenwood Vineyards as a quality producer. After all, in its four decades of winemaking, it has upped production levels to some 3.6 million bottles, and a number of its entry-level wines are far from exciting. But just because it is one of California's larger producers (part of the Korbel company) does not mean Kenwood is not capable of greatness. The top-of-the-line Artist Series Cabernet Sauvignon is well worth a look if you are feeling flush. But so, too, are the wines of the Jack London Vineyard, such as the Cabernet Sauvignon, which has refined aromas of currant and plum that deepen with complex, full-bodied black fruit judiciously seasoned with dried herbs and cedar. The Kenwood Sonoma County Pinot Gris, meanwhile, is full of bright tropical fruit and citrus aromas, and the mineral-driven stone fruit and ripe citrus flavours linger in a crisp, silky finish.

9592 Sonoma Highway, Kenwood, CA 95452
www.kenwoodvineyards.com

Laetitia Vineyard San Luis Obispo County, Central Coast

Brut Cuvée Estate, Arroyo Grande Valley (sparkling); Syrah Estate, Arroyo Grande Valley (red)

Laetitia Vineyard in the cool-climate Arroyo Grande Valley, started its life as a sparkling wine project called Maison Deutz. It still produces bubbly, and the non-vintage Brut Cuvée Estate Arroyo Grande Valley is crisp and citrussy, with a hint of strawberry and a fine texture. However the new owner, Selim Zilkha, is much more focused on still wines, such as the Syrah Estate Arroyo Grande Valley. As befits a cool-climate Syrah, it is bright and smoky, with blackberry fruit, a dash of white pepper, and fine tannins.

453 Laetitia Vineyard Drive, Arroyo Grande, CA 93420
www.laetitiawine.com

LangeTwins Winery Lodi, Inland California

Moscato, Lodi and Clarksburg (white)

Twin brothers Bradford and Randall established their eponymous winery in 2003. They employ nine members of their family, but then, grapegrowing expertise is in the family blood: the Langes have had a presence in Lodi since the 1870s, first as watermelon farmers and then, since 1916, as grape growers. The refreshing Moscato Clarksburg white – a successor to the winery's Muscat Frizzante – is spritzy, floral, and barely off-dry, with lively aromas and flavours of orange blossom and tangerine.

1525 East Jahant Rd, Acampo, CA 95220
www.langetwins.com

Langtry Estate Lake County

Guenoc, Sauvignon Blanc, Lake County (white)

Langtry Estate has the whole of the Guenoc Valley area in Lake County to itself. The estate owns some 8,500ha (21,000 acres) of land and it makes good use of the relatively small (182ha/449 acre) parcel planted to vines. It takes its name from the founder, one Lillie Langtry, a renowned Victorian beauty and performer. One of the tastier parts of her legacy is the tropical fruit flavour of Guenoc Langtry Estate Sauvignon Blanc. Guenoc is a second wine of Langtry.

21000 Butts Canyon Road, Middletown, CA 95461
www.langtryestate.com

J Lohr Vineyards San Luis Obispo County, Central Coast

Syrah, South Ridge, Paso Robles (red)

A grape-growing presence in Monterey County since the 1970s, Jerry Lohr expanded his empire to Paso Robles in 1988 and now has a combined 1,215ha (3,000 acres) in Monterey, Paso Robles, and Napa Valley. Powerful reds are the focus in the Paso Robles operation, and Lohr makes a number of different tiers and varietals. From the winery's Estates tier, the South Ridge Paso Robles Syrah is plump and easy to drink, with ripe blackberry, roasted coffee, and spice notes and fine tannins.

6169 Airport Rd, Paso Robles, CA 93446
www.jlohr.com

Lolonis Mendocino

Chardonnay, Redwood Valley (white)

Lolonis Redwood Valley Chardonnay is an unabashedly "big" California Chardonnay. It shows aromas such as toasted and buttered French bread, luscious ripe pear and fig flavours, a drippingly rich texture, and a lingering finish. Ah, for some fresh Maine lobster. It is produced, by winemaker Lori Knapp, from grapes that have been grown organically by one of the oldest family-owned vineyards in Mendocino County – and one that has improved a great deal in the past decade.

1905 Road D, Redwood Valley, CA 95470
www.lolonis.com

Long Meadow Ranch Napa Valley

Ranch House Red Blend, Napa Valley

The Ranch House Red blend from Long Meadow Ranch is an easy-drinking blend of Cabernet Sauvignon, Merlot, Sangiovese, and Petite Sirah. It has generous amounts of dark, spicy fruit and a substantial but finely textured finish. It comes from an estate, run by Ted and Laddie Hall and their son Christopher, that produces olive oil, grass-fed Highland beef, eggs, and other produce, on their main 263ha (650 acre) ranch and from a couple of smaller properties.

738 Main St, St Helena, CA 94574
www.longmeadowranch.com

MacRostie Winery Carneros

Pinot Noir, Carneros (red)

Before starting out on his own operation at MacRostie Winery in 1987, Steve MacRostie spent 12 years making wine at Sonoma's Hacienda Winery. He brings all his almost 40 years of winemaking experience to bear on the series of top wines he makes both from grapes he has grown himself, and those he buys in from growers. Among the latter is the excellent value Carneros Pinot Noir. Dark and ripe, this full-bodied Pinot Noir explodes with smoky black cherry, cinnamon, and cola aromas. A superbly balanced structure makes it both accessible and age-worthy.

21481 8th St East 25, Sonoma, CA 95476
www.macrostiewinery.com

Madroña Vineyards El Dorado County, Inland California

New-World Port, El Dorado (fortified)

Start with seven traditional Portuguese grape varieties, grow them 914m (3,000ft) up the Sierra foothills, and then pack their ripe fruit flavours and ticklish spice into a distinguished emulation of classic port, as warmly welcome as an embracing hug on a cold winter night. That is the recipe for Madroña Vineyards' El Dorado New-World Port, and it is just one of the envelope-pushing adventures embarked on here by the Dick Bush family since they planted Madroña's first vines in 1973. The family have one of the more varied portfolios of grape varieties to draw on, from which they produce consistently good wines.

2560 High Hill Rd, Camino, CA 95709
www.madronavineyards.com

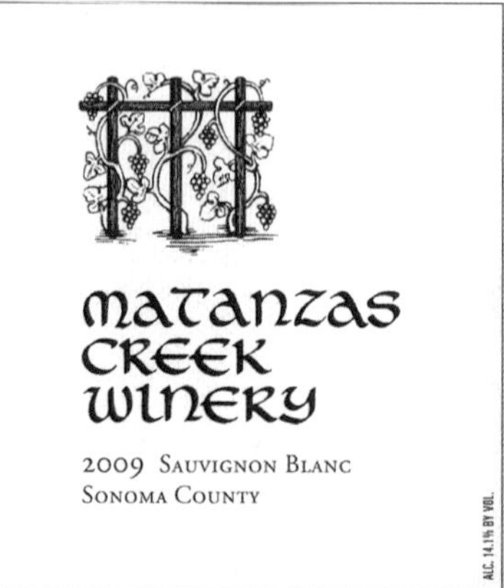

Matanzas Creek Winery Bennett Valley, Sonoma

Sauvignon Blanc, Sonoma County (white)

A pedigreed Sauvignon Musqué blend with vibrant floral and citrus aromas, Matanzas Creek Winery's Sonoma County Sauvignon Blanc offers a minerally array of medium-weight tropical and stone fruit, along with some citrus and fig flavours. It was made in typically understated style by Frenchman François Cordesse, who learned his trade in Bordeaux, Australia, and his native Languedoc in France, before moving to California. Matanzas is a beautiful property, complete with lovingly tended lavender gardens, in Bennett Valley. It was founded – in what was then still largely unmapped territory for the California wine business – in 1977. And it has since made a name for itself as both a trailblazing and, more importantly, a consistently high-quality producer, with a recognizable style that favours lower alcohol and elegance over raw power and steamroller alcohol.

6097 Bennett Valley Rd, Santa Rosa, CA 95404
www.matanzascreek.com

McManis Family Vineyards
San Joaquin County, Inland California
Viognier, California (white)

Winemakers at McManis Family Vineyards are not adverse to oak, but with their Viognier they know the grapes deliver enough richness, weight, and depth all on their own, so they let it be, releasing an interpretation that is all honeysuckle, tangerine, apple, and peach. The decision seems to have pleased the experts: the wine was voted best Viognier in California at the 2010 State Fair. The McManis family have been growing grapes in this corner of the northern San Joaquin County for more than 70 years, after starting out in 1938. But it took until 1997 for members of the fourth generation of the family to finally take the plunge and start making their own wines from those grapes, building a winery at Ripon to do so. The style of winemaking here – with both red varieties and the Viognier and other whites – is to make wines that show off bright, abundant fruit flavours, but always at everyday prices.

18700 East River Rd, Ripon, CA 95366
www.mcmanisfamilyvineyards.com

Morgan Winery Monterey County, Central Coast
Un-oaked Chardonnay Metallico, Monterey (white); Syrah, Monterey (red)

Chardonnay is part of the DNA at Morgan Winery. The first wine produced here by owner Dan Lee after he started the business in 1982 was a Chardonnay – and one that quickly earned him acclaim. Lee still produces a number of different Chardonnay bottlings at a range of prices. But the standout in terms of value is the Un-oaked Chardonnay Metallico Monterey. Unlike some of the more wimpy examples of unoaked Chardonnay available on the market today, Metallico has a real punch to it. It is packed with racy lemon and Granny Smith apple flavours, with a hint of creaminess. Chardonnay is by no means the only string to Morgan Winery's bow these days, however; both Pinot Noir and Syrah are important here today. The Monterey Syrah combines grapes from several Monterey appellations to make a wine that is smoky and smooth, with bright berry and a hint of lavender.

204 Crossroads Blvd, Carmel, CA 93923
www.morganwinery.com

FOOD & WINE NAPA VALLEY CABERNET SAUVIGNON

For Californians, Napa Valley Cabernet Sauvignon is the quintessential expression of this strapping grape variety. Its flavour profile is different from the green pepper and vegetal notes sometimes found in the Cabernets of Bordeaux – here, it is all about ripe fruit and sweet toasty oak.

With delicious notes of blackberry, blackcurrant, and plum accented with hints of olive, sage, moss, and, with age, cigar and leather, these rich, concentrated, fruity, and voluptuous wines pair easily with a variety of foods.

In Napa Cabernets, there is plenty of lush, ripe fruit as well as higher alcohol (and lower acidity) than in Bordeaux, both of which serve to cover up the sometimes aggressive tannins. The remaining tannins are easily dealt with by pairing the wine with fatty dishes. Beef is a natural – try prime rib *au jus* or a Kobe burger topped with local blue or Cheddar cheese. For vegetarians, an oven-roasted aubergine matches some of the bitterness in the wine, while seitan skewers with chimichurri is a meat-free take on the Argentine Asado (barbecue).

Lamb is ideal for the earthier French Cabs, but for riper Napa versions a rosemary and mustard crust would bring the pairing into beautiful balance. Adding a blackberry or blackcurrant component (or the wine itself) to the sauce also helps, as does the addition of black olives.

Roast lamb with rosemary is ideal for lush, ripe Napa Cabernets.

Mount Eden Vineyards Santa Cruz Mountains, Central Coast

Chardonnay, Wolff Vineyard, Edna Valley (white)

You have to go back to World War II to trace the beginnings of the winery known today as Mount Eden. It was established in 1942 by Martin Ray, one of the key figures in the history of Santa Cruz Mountains viticulture and the one-time owner of the Paul Masson winery. Ray did not get along with his investors, however, and after a series of quarrels he was banished from the estate, and its name was changed to Mount Eden in the 1970s. Since 1981, the wines have benefited from the consistent presence of winemaker Jeffrey Patterson. The centrepiece is a very individualistic Chardonnay from the low-yielding estate vineyard, which rises from 490m to 680m (1,600ft to 2,000ft). Much cheaper is the Wolff Vineyard Chardonnay he makes from purchased grapes from the Edna Valley. This Chardonnay is fleshier and more tropical than Mount Eden's estate Chardonnay, but it is still elegant and well-balanced.

22020 Mt Eden Rd, Saratoga, CA 95070
www.mounteden.com

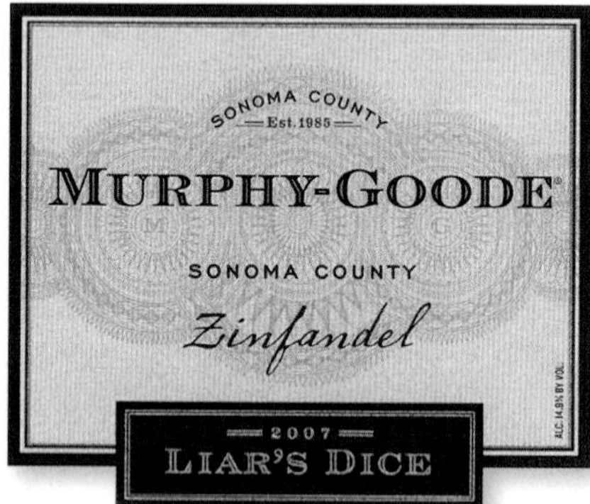

Murphy-Goode Winery

Alexander Valley, Sonoma

Liar's Dice, Zinfandel, Sonoma (red); Fumé, Sauvignon, Alexander Valley (white)

Murphy-Goode is every inch the modern winery. Indeed, it is perhaps better known for its associations with that most 21st century of pursuits, blogging, than it is for its wines. Back in 2009, the winery ran a competition to hire a resident wine blogger, a successful viral marketing campaign that garnered it plenty of publicity in both old and new media. The estate is now a member of the Jackson Family Wines portfolio, but its wines are made by the son of one of the founders and, like many Jackson-owned operations, it is run with a certain degree of independence from the mother ship. The Liar's Dice Zinfandel is gushing with black raspberry and cassis aromas and sweet, juicy black fruit and jammy spice flavours that are softly medium-bodied. The Sauvignon Fumé, by contrast, is full of delicate, grassy, and citric aromas that open up to lots of creamy, tropical fruit and crisp minerality that extends all the way through the finish.

20 Matheson St, Healdsburg, CA 95448
www.murphygoodewinery.com

Navarro Vineyards Anderson Valley, Mendocino

Dry Gewürztraminer, Anderson Valley (white)

Navarro Vineyards' appetizing and affordable Dry Gewürztraminer Anderson Valley has been fermented in large oak casks as in Alsace, and delivers quite similar sensations: fragrant floral aromas, crisp apple flavours, and a spicy aftertaste. It is refreshingly tasty and light. Producers Ted Bennett and Deborah Cahn were among the earliest of the wave of city-dwellers that switched to making wine in Mendocino County in the 1970s, and they still embody the green-thinking that flourished there in the 1970s. The wines are made with complete respect for the environment, and there are a number of initiatives at the estate aimed at keeping the vineyards healthy.

5601 Highway 128, Philo, CA 95466
www.navarrowine.com

Newton Vineyard Spring Mountain District, Napa Valley

Red Label Claret, Napa Valley

Newton Vineyard's Red Label Claret is a Merlot-dominated, Bordeaux-style blend. It is winningly full of black fruit and dark spice aromas that carry through to mountain-fruit flavours with chocolate, white pepper, and soft, black plums. It is a terrific value introduction to a fine estate that is now in the hands of the luxury goods behemoth, LVMH. The estate is based around the steep, terraced Spring Mountain vineyards, where varied exposures and soils, produce strong, firm, mineral-rich Cabernet Sauvignon, Cabernet Franc, and Merlot, and some well-made Chardonnay. LVMH has invested substantially in improving the property, with serious attention paid to the vineyards, and it seems likely these will see the wines improve still futher in the near future. The winemaker is the well-regarded Chris Millard, formerly of Sterling Vineyards.

2555 Madrona Ave, St Helena, CA 94574
www.newtonvineyard.com

Obsidian Ridge Lake County

Cabernet Sauvignon, Lake County, Red Hills (red)

The Molnar family, owners of Obsidian Ridge, have gone to unusual lengths to make a success of the wine business. Having invested in planting vineyards in the Carneros district in 1973 when few considered it winemaking country, they also bought a barrel cooperage in Hungary (the Molnars are of Hungarian extraction), and then, in the 1990s, sought out high altitude sites in Lake County (an area now known as Red Hills). The Cabernet Sauvignon they have made from that site is comparable in quality to more expensive Napa Valley Cabernets. This full-bodied, barrel-aged red wine combines cherry-like flavours with spicy oak nuances and a layered and velvety mouthfeel.

Winery and vineyards open by appointment only
www.tricyclewineco.com

Owl Ridge/Willowbrook Cellars

Russian River Valley, Sonoma

Sauvignon Blanc, Sonoma County (white)

When you first put your nose in the glass, assertive New Zealand-style aromas of gooseberry and juicy melon mark out Owl Ridge's Sauvignon Blanc. Those aromas soon give way to quieter flavours of lemon and pear on the palate that are lighter-bodied and refreshingly crisp to the finish. The Owl Ridge brand is the work of the computer business entrepreneur John Tracy, who followed a well-trodden path in swapping Silicon Valley for Russian River Valley in the 1990s. Aided by winemaker Joe Otos, he founded Willowbrook Cellars, making the wine in rented space – and he soon saw an opportunity to build his own winery with space and facilities enough to rent out to other smaller wineries. Owl Ridge was developed as a second label in similarly entrepreneurial spirit.

No visitor facilities
www.owlridge.com

Pacific Star Winery Mendocino

Dad's Daily Red

Pacific Star Winery is aptly named: it is in the enviable position of being one of the world's rare wineries with a view that looks out directly onto an ocean. Owner and winemaker, Sally Ottoson, reckons that the proximity to the sea has a more profound effect on proceedings here than merely cheering up the staff, however. Ottoson believes the salty sea air, and the waves of the ocean itself as it crashes into a cave beneath her cellar, are what give her wines that little extra something in taste and texture. She produces her wines on a small scale, and gives them eccentric names, such as It's My Fault (named after a seismic fault that runs under the estate) and Dad's Daily Red. The latter is the wine Ottoson's father, who died aged 87, liked best and it is easy to see why. The smooth blend of pioneer grape varieties – Carignane, Petite Sirah, Zinfandel, and Charbono – comes off like a very drinkable California version of classic Côte du Rhône.

401 North Main Street, Fort Bragg, CA 95437
www.pacificstarwinery.com

Parducci Wine Cellars Mendocino

True Grit, Petite Sirah, Mendocino (red)

During much of its existence during the 20th century, Parducci Wine Cellars represented Mendocino County wine pretty much all by itself. For most of that time, it was the only producer to sell its wines directly to the public rather than shipping it off in bulk for other producers to use anonymously in their blends. The estate's owner, John Parducci, was also the public face of the area's winemaking. Parducci made many different wines from a number of different grape varieties, with the Petite Sirah widely regarded as the best. Today, current owners the Thornhill family are keeping up the good work, with Paul Dolan – a former president of Fetzer Vineyards and a vocal advocate of biodynamic principles – leading the winemaking. The Mendocino Petite Sirah True Grit has deep colour, rich blackberry flavours, and full body – there is, in fact, nothing "petite" about the wine at all. The jammy flavours and firm texture will taste best with rich meat and cheese dishes. It can age well for five or more years.

501 Parducci Road, Ukiah, CA 95482
www.parducci.com

CHARDONNAY

Chardonnay is one of the world's most versatile grape varieties. It has adapted to such varied climates and winemaking styles as those of Burgundy (the French region where it originated), Australia, California, Chile, Greece, India, and at least 30 other countries.

If Chardonnay has been fermented in oak barrels, it has flavours of butter, hazelnuts, and vanilla. It develops a luscious richness and full body when grown in warm places such as California and Australia, but stays more lean, crisp, and refreshing in cooler spots like France's Chablis region and New Zealand.

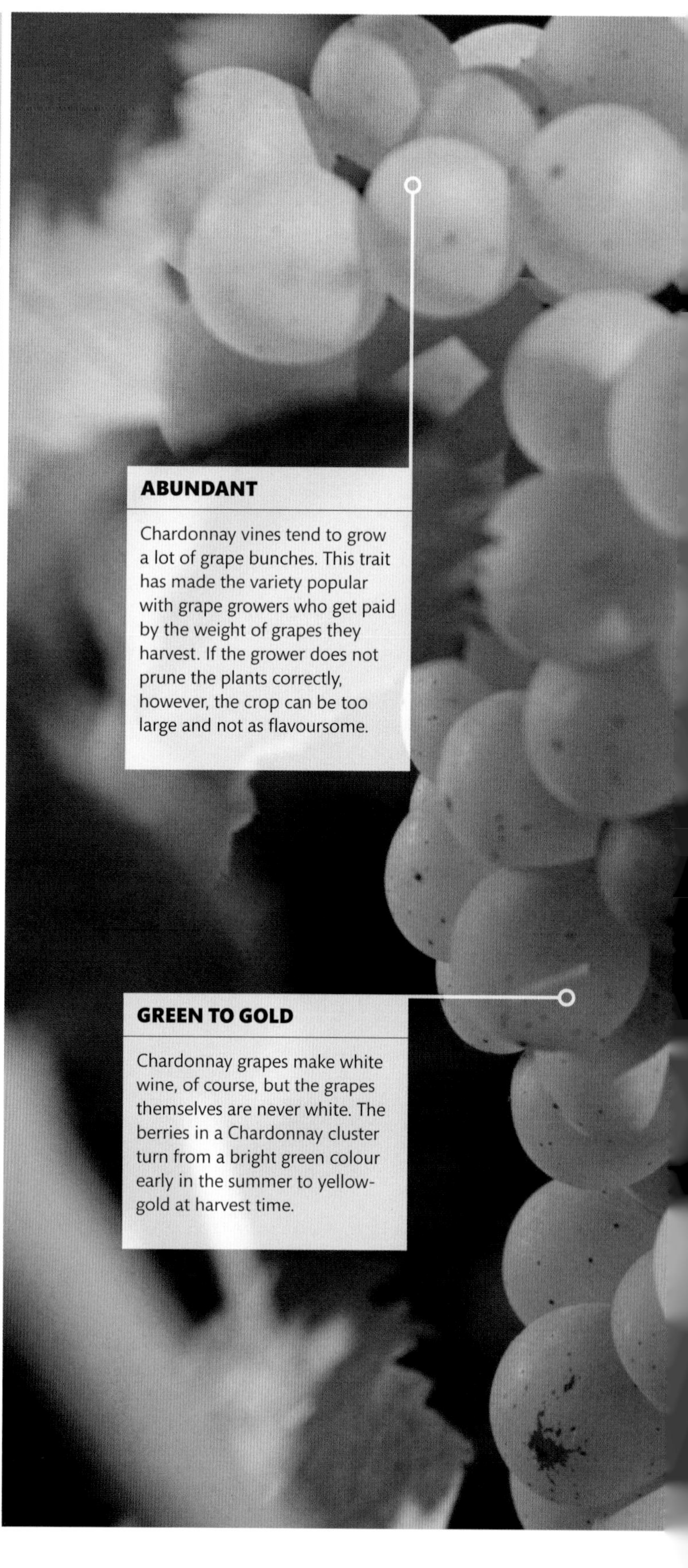

ABUNDANT

Chardonnay vines tend to grow a lot of grape bunches. This trait has made the variety popular with grape growers who get paid by the weight of grapes they harvest. If the grower does not prune the plants correctly, however, the crop can be too large and not as flavoursome.

GREEN TO GOLD

Chardonnay grapes make white wine, of course, but the grapes themselves are never white. The berries in a Chardonnay cluster turn from a bright green colour early in the summer to yellow-gold at harvest time.

THIN-SKINNED

The skins on Chardonnay grapes are thin, so they are easily damaged by mould, mildew, and other pests and diseases that can penetrate through the skins and negatively affect the juice inside. Chardonnay growers have to be extra careful to protect their crops.

TRANSPARENT

Chardonnay is no easier to see through than other white wines, but the grapevines themselves are good at transparency, meaning the wines made from them vary significantly according to where they were grown. This taste of place is known in the winemaking world as "terroir".

WHERE IN THE WORLD?

Great-value Chardonnay comes from almost all parts of the globe. One reason is that Chardonnay grew so fast in popularity in recent decades that many farmers planted it to get in on the action.

Now, there is a huge supply in France, Australia, California, Chile, and other places. Since Chardonnay comes in many styles, one can match one's taste to an appropriate Chardonnay-producing region.

White burgundy from the Mâcon and Chalonnaise districts and Chablis is rather lean, buttery, and lemony. Many Italian and Chilean versions fall on the leaner side of the spectrum, too. Australian and California Chardonnays, however, are often fatter, riper, and not as tangy, especially those with broad place names on the label such as California or Southeast Australia. Also, some champagnes, referred to as Blanc de Blancs, use only Chardonnay grapes.

The following regions are among the best for Chardonnay. Try bottles from these recommended vintages for the best examples:

Côte de Beaune: 2009, 2008, 2007
Côte Chalonnaise: 2009, 2007
Mâconnais: 2009, 2007, 2006
Sonoma County: 2009, 2007, 2006

Saint Véran in the Mâconnais is a reliable source of delicious Chardonnay.

Patianna Organic Vineyards Mendocino

Sauvignon Blanc, Mendocino, Estate Vineyards (white)

As much savoury as fruity in character, Patianna Organic Vineyards' Mendocino Estate Vineyards Sauvignon Blanc is a distinctive wine. It has white pepper, grapefruit, and melon notes, crisp balance, and a lingering finish. In its flavours and texture it tastes more like the Austrian white grape variety, Grüner Veltliner, than it does a more conventional Sauvignon Blanc. It is made, like everything else at this Fetzer family operation, with organic grapes. Indeed, the Fetzer family is committed to organic grape production, and many people believe that explains why the wines made here are so distinctively pure. Do these wines have a certain depth of flavour and sense of life that is directly attributable to the lack of chemicals used to grow the grapes? The best way to find out, of course, is to taste for yourself!

13340 Spring Street, Hopland, CA 95449
www.patianna.com

Pey-Marin Marin County

Punchdown, Syrah, Spicerack Vineyards (red)

One of Marin's best producers, Pey-Marin has been carving out a path for others to follow in the area for a decade now. It was founded by Jonathan Pey, who for several years plied his trade in wineries in Burgundy, Australia, and Napa. Pey's wife Susan, meanwhile, is a top restaurant wine buyer, and together they make a successful team. The couple work their vineyards organically, and their location – on steep, foggy hillsides inland from the Pacific – makes for a cool climate that gives the wines freshness. In the Spicerack Vineyards Punchdown Syrah, peppery dark fruit and dried herb aromas intensify in the mouth with meaty, smoky plum, and blue fruit flavours that are full-bodied and finely structured.

10000 Sir Francis Drake Blvd, Olema, CA 94950
www.marinwines.com

Pine Ridge Winery Stags Leap District, Napa Valley

Chenin Blanc-Viognier, Clarksburg (white)

After the excitement of being an Olympic skier, Gary Andrus came down to earth a little when he switched to winemaking. He established Pine Ridge, a 101ha (250 acre) estate, in 1978, and later went on to found Archery Summit in Oregon. Both wineries have since been bought by the Crimson Wine Group, and the wines are now made by Michael Beaulac, who used to work at California's St Supéry. Though the focus at Pine Ridge has traditionally been Cabernet Sauvignon produced from a number of different appellations in California, it has a good reputation, too, for its white wines, including Chardonnay. In terms of value, however, the best offering is an unusual Rhône-meets-Loire white blend, the Pine Ridge Chenin Blanc-Viognier. This is a unique marriage of Viognier's heady, perfumed aromas – jasmine, lychee, and citrus – with the ripe melon and peach flavours of Chenin Blanc that is just off-dry but fresh.

5901 Silverado Trail, Napa, CA 94558
www.pineridgewinery.com

Porter Creek Vineyards

Russian River Valley, Sonoma

Old Vine Carignan, Mendocino (red)

Porter Creek Vineyards' Old Vine Carignan is charming in a way that only old-vine Carignan can be. Sourced from some of the oldest vines in the Alexander Valley, it has a transparency that reveals complex aromas of elderflower and raspberry with precisely balanced flavours of juicy, brambly fruit. This family-run operation takes its name from the creek that runs right next door to the winery. Founded in 1982, it is run today by Alex Davis, who succeeded his father with the 1997 vintage, and, having been frequently overlooked in the past, it is becoming increasingly well-known as one of the best producers in the Russian River Valley. The house style here is highly distinctive, and the presentation is laid-back and unstuffy, with an old shack serving as the tasting room for visitors. The portfolio of wines is small but perfectly formed, and the vineyards are run according to strict biodynamic principles.

8735 Westside Rd, Healdsburg, CA 95448
www.portercreekvineyards.com

Pride Mountain Vineyards St Helena, Napa Valley, Sonoma

Viognier, Sonoma (white)

If you were collecting evidence of the sometimes absurd demands made by winemaking bureaucracy, then Pride Mountain Vineyards would be the first port of call. Its premises skirt the boundary between Sonoma and Napa counties which means it is obliged to have two wineries, one on the Sonoma side, and the other in Napa. Its labelling is equally schizophrenic (sometimes Napa, sometimes Sonoma), but the wines have a consistent (and consistently good) identity. Wines have been made here since the 1890s, and Pride Mountain's reputation was elevated first by winemaker Bob Foley and more recently by Sally Johnson. The Sonoma County Viognier is robust in all ways with rich quince and stone fruit aromas, weighty texture, and honeyed white peach flavours that show best at a cooler serving temperature.

4026 Spring Mountain Rd, St Helena, CA 94574
www.pridewines.com

Quivira Vineyards
Dry Creek Valley, Sonoma
Grenache, Wine Creek Ranch (red)

An early pioneer of sustainable viticulture and green thinking in the California wine scene, Quivira Vineyards started its life in 1987. Now under new ownership and with a new winemaker, Steven Canter, at the helm, it is finally becoming as famed for its wines as its use of biodynamic farming and solar power. It is one of the few producers in Dry Creek to make a Grenache, and it is a standout wine. Savoury, spicy plum, and strawberry aromas that show as deep, pure flavours; round and well balanced with a brightness that makes for easy drinking.

4900 West Dry Creek Rd, Healdsburg, CA 95448
www.quivirawine.com

Qupé Wine Cellars Santa Barbara County, Central Coast
Syrah, Central Coast (red)

Winemaker and owner at Qupé, Bob Lindquist, is a specialist in making California wines with a Rhône influence. With his experience from working at Zaca Mesa Winery, Lindquist founded Qupé as a means to experiment with his own wines, but the project soon took off. Lindquist is renowned for making wines that are somewhat more subtle than the big, beefy examples made by many other winemakers in this area. Today he makes several Syrah wines, but the affordable Central Coast Syrah bottling has plenty of the signature cool-climate character: bright berry, spice, tobacco, and tea.

2963 Grand Ave, Los Olivos, CA 93441
www.qupe.com

Rancho Zabaco Winery
Dry Creek Valley, Sonoma
Zinfandel, Heritage Vines, Sonoma (red)

One of the many brands in the Gallo Family Vineyards stable, Rancho Zabaco has become closely associated with best value Zinfandel. Made by winemaker Eric Cinnamon, the Heritage Vines Zinfandel is particularly good value for money. It has intense vanilla-scented aromas of raspberry jam, mouth-coating flavours of spicy blackberry and dark cherries, with a soft, robust structure and complex, spicy finish.

3387 Dry Creek Rd, Healdsburg, CA 95448
www.ranchozabaco.com

Ravenswood Sonoma Valley, Sonoma
Old Vine Zinfandel, Lodi (red)

Ravenswood is one of the most recognized of California brands, exported all over the world. It is known for making big, full-flavoured wines, particularly from Zinfandel. In the words of founder Joel Peterson, who has turned Ravenswood from a small producer to a major player since the 1980s, there are "no wimpy wines" here. The Old Vine Zinfandel has aromas of raspberry and vanilla which become darker flavours of plums and blueberries spiced with black pepper and anise while the addition of a little bit of Petite Sirah boosts the overall structure.

18701 Gehricke Rd, Sonoma, CA 95476
www.ravenswood-wine.com

Robert Hall Winery San Luis Obispo County, Central Coast
Rhône de Robles, Central Coast (red)

The eponymous founder of Robert Hall Winery made his money developing shopping malls. On retirement, he moved to Paso Robles, bought a vineyard, and built a winery soon after. His winemaker, Don Brady, now crafts wines that are unusual for the area – well balanced and elegant rather than big and ripe.

Dominated by Grenache and Syrah, the aptly named Rhône de Robles Central Coast is ripe yet lively, with flavours of raspberry and spice supported by firm tannins.

3443 Mill Rd, Paso Robles, CA 93446
www.roberthallwinery.com

Robert Mondavi Winery Oakville, Napa Valley
Cabernet Sauvignon, Napa Valley (red)

A driving force in the development of California wine, the late Robert Mondavi and his family sold their operation to the drinks multinational, Constellation Brands, in 2004. The family is no longer involved but, under the guidance of Genevieve Janssens, a winemaker here since the 1970s, it continues to live up to the name with some high quality wines. The Napa Cabernet Sauvignon has dense and complex aromas of blackberry, currants, and a sprinkle of dried thyme that give way to concentrated flavours of black fruit and savoury black olive.

7801 St Helena Highway, Oakville, CA 94562
www.robertmondaviwinery.com

Robert Sinskey Vineyards
Stags Leap District, Napa Valley
Vin Gris Los Carneros (rosé)

Salmon-coloured with spicy floral and lime aromas, Robert Sinskey Vineyards Vin Gris Los Carneros is a rich rosé produced from Pinot Noir. It has savoury strawberry and melon flavours that stand up well to heavier dishes. It is made at a winery that sits right on the Silverado Trail in Stags Leap, although most of the fruit comes from Carneros, where the family first established their vineyards. All of the fruit is sourced from vineyards that are farmed either organically or biodynamically.

6320 Silverado Trail, Napa, CA 94558
www.robertsinskey.com

Rocca Family Vineyards Yountville, Napa Valley
Bad Boy Red Blend, Yountville

A relatively new operation, Rocca Family Vineyards was founded in Yountville in 1999, when Mary Rocca and her husband, Dr Eric Grigsby, snapped up a 8.5ha (21 acre) vineyard. They enlisted the services of consultant winemaker, Celia Welch Masyczek, and they began making a handful of well-received reds. Bad Boy Red Blend is a fine-tuned mix of a trio of Bordeaux varieties, Cabernet Sauvignon, Cabernet Franc, and Petit Verdot. Vanilla warms up cherry and blueberry aromas and robust, concentrated flavours dissolve in a pretty finish.

129 Devlin Rd, Napa, CA 94558
www.roccawines.com

Rued Winery Dry Creek Valley, Sonoma
Sauvignon Blanc, Dry Creek (white); Zinfandel, Dry Creek (white)

Rued Winery is run by Steve Rued and his wife, Sonia, long-time grape growers who decided to make their own bottlings after decades of growing grapes in Sonoma County to sell to other wineries. Their Dry Creek Sauvignon Blanc has pungent Meyer lemon and gooseberry aromas revealing medium-bodied, crisp flavours of vanilla-infused melon and stone fruit, with a crisp finish. The Dry Creek Zinfandel has blackberry pie and complex baking spice aromas that lead into meaty flavours of blackberry, chocolate, and anise.

3850 Dry Creek Rd, Healdsburg, CA 95448
www.ruedvineyards.com

St Supéry Rutherford, Napa Valley
Merlot, Napa Valley (red); Oak-Free Chardonnay, Napa Valley (white)

A Franco-US operation on Highway 29 in Rutherford, St Supéry is the work of the major southern French wine producer Robert Skalli and his family. It produces a broad range of wines across a number of different prices, including a handful that are excellent value. The Napa Valley Merlot has fruit, leather, and spice aromas followed by big, sweet flavours of black plum, a round texture, and savoury anise on the finish. The Oak-Free Chardonnay is Chablis-like in style with tropical fruit and green apple aromas; medium-bodied with citrus flavours, white pepper-driven minerality, and a clean, bright finish.

8440 St Helena Highway, Rutherford, CA 94573
www.stsupery.com

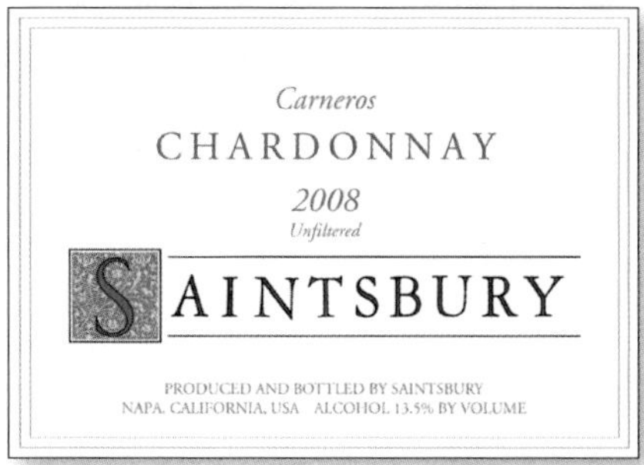

Saintsbury Carneros
Chardonnay, Carneros (white)

A Burgundian influence rules at Saintsbury, which was founded in 1981 by two US lovers of the French region's wines, David Graves and Richard Ward. They focused on Burgundy's two great grape varieties, Pinot Noit and Chardonnay, and the winemaker is the French-born Jerome Chery. In 2011, Saintsbury sold the Garnet Pinot Noir label to the people behind Silverado Winegrowers, but the company's Chardonnay remains the best in California. The toasty Carneros Chardonnay, for example, is a study in pear and citrus. Creamy and round in the mouth it has smoky lemon and orange flavours and a crisp finish.

1500 Los Carneros Ave, Napa, CA 94559
www.saintsbury.com

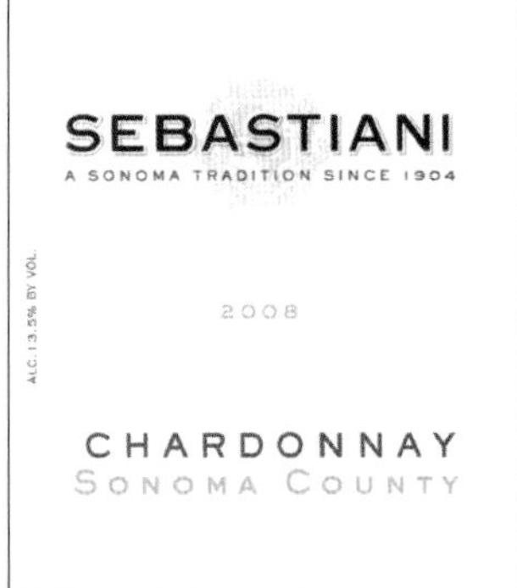

Sebastiani Winery Sonoma Valley, Sonoma
Chardonnay, Sonoma (white)

Effusive green apple, high-toned banana, and limestone characterize the nose of Sebastiani's Sonoma Chardonnay. On the palate it has pure stone fruit and ripe apple concentrated by pervasive minerality and a structured finish. It is a great value Sonoma Chardonnay from a producer that has been forging the region's reputation since 1904, when it was founded by Samuele Sebastiani. Today, production exceeds 96 million bottles, and Sebastiani wines are a fixture on retailers' shelves throughout the US.

389 Fourth St East, Sonoma, CA 95476
www.sebastiani.com

HOW MUCH ALCOHOL IS TOO MUCH?

Grapes naturally ferment, turning the sugar into alcohol. When a winemaker adds yeast to freshly picked grapes, fermentation begins. This inevitable process converts the sugar content in the grapes to alcohol. Table wines usually range from about 10% to 14%, while fortified wines such as port and sherry go up to about 18% because winemakers "strengthen" them by adding spirits (usually neutral-tasting vodka).

The traditional 20th-century table wine from France, Italy, and Spain rarely developed more than 13% alcohol, and even in sunny Napa Valley, wines with 12% alcohol or less were common in the 1970s. Yet today, Australian Shiraz, French Châteauneuf-du-Pape, California Cabernet Sauvignon, and other wines often reach 15% alcohol or higher. It is largely because grape growing practices have advanced to help grapes create more sugar in the vineyard. Many vineyard owners in colder regions such as Germany are convinced that climate change has had an effect, too.

Alcohol, of course, is the element in wine that makes us relax and enjoy ourselves. But there is some controversy about how much alcohol is too much. A modern wine at 15% alcohol carries 25% more punch than its predecessor a generation ago at 12%. It tastes riper and fuller, which many drinkers like. But it also brings a hangover 25% more quickly, and some argue that it overpowers the meals it is supposed to enhance.

The wine drinker gets to choose higher or lower alcohol, just by looking closely at the label. At 13% or under, the average-sized woman can drink about a third of a bottle (250ml/9fl oz) and the average sized man slightly less than half a bottle over two hours and not get too intoxicated. At 15%, it's different. Everyone can find his or her own comfort zone, and the wine that keeps him or her in it.

Seghesio Family Vineyards
Alexander Valley, Sonoma
Zinfandel, Sonoma (red)

Ted and Peter Seghesio made a brave decision in 1993. Believing that the family business had become too big for its own good, they decided to cut back production from a peak of 1.5 million bottles and make wine exclusively with fruit they grew on their own vineyards, which were first planted 100 years ago. It is a move that has won many friends for this archetypal Sonoma winery, founded in 1895 by Edoardo Seghesio and run by his descendants (including Ted and Peter) ever since. And it has had a positive effect on the quality of wines such as the big, ripe Sonoma Zinfandel, with its scents of berry patch and toast, its complex, layered palate of sweet cinnamon and cocoa dust, and its deep, creamy finish.

14730 Grove St, Healdsburg, CA 95448
www.seghesio.com

Silverado Vineyards
Stags Leap District, Napa Valley
Merlot, Napa Valley (red)

There is a touch of Hollywood glamour at Silverado Vineyards. It was founded towards the end of the 1980s by Walt Disney's daughter, Diane, and her husband Ron Miller, a former professional American football player and one-time CEO of Walt Disney Productions. But unlike many other examples of the rich and famous moving into the wine business, this most certainly is not a vanity project. The Millers clearly take wine very seriously indeed, and they now own six vineyards in various sites across the Napa Valley. The wines are consistently good and often well priced, too. The Napa Valley Merlot, for example, is aromatic and complex. It is a balanced expression of Merlot that has plenty of grip with generous amounts of ripe red and black fruit seasoned with dried herbs and toasty vanilla.

6121 Silverado Trail, Napa, CA 94558
www.silveradovineyards.com

Sobon Estate
Amador County, Inland California
Old Vines Zinfandel, Amador County (red)

Though "Amador County" and "Old Vines" usually translate into Zinfandels that are ruthless in their bulk and power, Sobon Estate is very much an exception. Each vintage, this fine estate turns out a member of the Zinfandel genre that is unusually fresh and lithesome, its fruit restrained and balanced, more raspberry jelly than blackberry jam. The man behind this delicious aberration is Silicon Valley rocket scientist Leon Sobon, who moved his family to Amador County's Shenandoah Valley in 1977 to follow his passion for making port-style fortified wines (which Sobon still makes). The family established Shenandoah Vineyards in 1989, before acquiring the D'Agostini Winery nearby (which dates from 1856) and then renaming it Sobon Estate.

14430 Shenandoah Rd, Plymouth, CA 95669
www.sobonwine.com

Sonoma-Cutrer Vineyards
Russian River Valley, Sonoma
Chardonnay, Sonoma Coast (white)

Sonoma-Cutrer is a Chardonnay specialist that is well-known to customers at the US's better restaurants. Started in 1972 by former US Air Force pilot Brice Cutrer Jones, its reputation for Chardonnay really got going after 1981, when Cutrer Jones decided to focus exclusively on the variety. Owned since 1999 by the Brown Forman Corporation, the specialization continues with wines such as the focused, balanced Sonoma Coast Chardonnay with its citrus-scented ripe, yellow apple and pear aromas and emphatic citrus flavours of Key lime, baked apple, and juicy stone fruit.

No visitor facilities
www.sonomacutrer.com

Spring Mountain Vineyards

Spring Mountain, Napa Valley

Cabernet Sauvignon, Chateau Chevalier, Spring Mountain (red)

Spring Mountain Vineyards' Chateau Chevalier Cabernet Sauvignon is lean and savoury with a bouquet of bright berry, anise, and cedar and a more concentrated palate of black cherry and black tea. Tart tannins and medium-weight structure complete the picture of a wine that is far more serious that you might expect from a winery that provided the setting for the opening credits of the US soap opera, Falcon Crest.

2805 Spring Mountain Rd, St Helena, CA 94574
www.springmountainvineyard.com

Stephen Ross Wine Cellars

San Luis Obispo County, Central Coast

Pinot Noir, Central Coast (red)

Steve Dooley's wines have come a long way from his first efforts, which were produced from rhubarb and dandelions when he was still a schoolboy in Minnesota. Today his eponymous (Ross is his middle name) estate deals in high quality Pinot Noir rather than the stuff Dooley once found in his back garden. The Central Coast Pinot Noir is the lightest-bodied of the Pinots in the winery's line up. It is a pretty wine with strawberry and cherry flavours, some vanilla and spice, and a smooth finish.

178 Suburban Rd, San Luis Obispo, CA 93401
www.stephenrosswine.com

Summers Estate Wines Calistoga, Napa Valley

La Nude Chardonnay (white)

Bright, unsullied aromas of pineapple and tropical fruit can be found on the nose of Summers Estate Wines' La Nude Chardonnay. There are more complex, medium-weight flavours of melon and citrus zest in the mouth, and a lively finish of crisp pear. The wine is typical of the ripe, fruit-forward styles favoured by Jim and Beth Summers and their vineyard manager and winemaker, Ignacio Blancas. The couple have replanted the property with 30ha (50 acres) of vines since acquiring it in 1996.

1171 Tubbs Lane, Calistoga, CA 94515
www.summerswinery.com

Tablas Creek Vineyard

Paso Robles, Central Coast

Côtes de Tablas, Paso Robles (red)

The Perrin family, owners of Château Beaucastel, one of the greatest estates in Châteauneuf-du-Pape in France's Rhône Valley, lend some serious class to Tablas Creek in Paso Robles. A joint-venture between the Perrins and ex-wine importer, Robert Haas, it began its life in 1989, and uses vinestock imported from France in the organically worked vineyard. Paso Robles Côtes de Tablas is a traditional Rhône-style blend, with an obvious influence from the Grenache component showing through in the bright strawberry flavours accented by a tobacco note and firm tannins.

9339 Adelaida Rd, Paso Robles, CA 93446
www.tablascreek.com

Talbott Vineyards Monterey County, Central Coast

Kali Hart, Pinot Noir, Monterey (red)

Kali Hart is the only Pinot Noir produced at Talbott Vineyards containing non-estate fruit. But the character of this high-quality winery nonetheless shines through when you taste the finished wine. This is a wine that is plump and supple, with a range of sprightly berry flavours, accented by vanilla and spice. Like all of the Pinots produced at Talbott, which is owned and managed by Robb Talbott, Kali Hart has improved immeasurably since the arrival of the talented Dan Karlsen as winemaker. Karlsen was previously at Chalone Vineyard, and is renowned as a specialist in Pinot Noir and Chardonnay. He has been working hard on moving the style towards greater purity and ripeness. Talbott is famed for its two great vineyards, Sleepy Hollow in the Santa Lucia Highlands, and Diamond T, which is a short drive from Carmel Valley. As well as wine, the Talbott family also owns and runs a longstanding upmarket clothing business.

53 West Carmel Valley Rd, Carmel Valley, CA 93924
www.talbottvineyards.com

Tangent Winery San Luis Obispo County, Central Coast

Albariño, Edna Valley (white)

Tangent Winery is owned by the Niven family, who, as owners of Paragon Vineyards, have been grape growers in the Edna Valley for many years. They are also partners with Diageo in Edna Valley Vineyard. Around 20 years ago, Catharine Niven decided she would like to make wines on a smaller scale than the family had been used to, and she founded Baileyana. That operation soon grew, however, to include a new vineyard, Firepeak, a new winery (that doubles up as a custom crush facility), and a sister brand by the name of Tangent Winery, the size of which has now outgrown Baileyana. Among the most exciting of the wines produced by the Nivens under the Tangent label is the fine Edna Valley Albariño. It demonstrates the Spanish grape variety Albariño's potential when grown in the right location, and it is fresh, crisp, and a little floral, with white peach flavours.

5828 Orcutt Rd, San Luis Obispo, CA 93401
www.baileyana.com

Tantara Winery Santa Barbara County, Central Coast

T. Solomon Wellborn Pinot Noir, Santa Barbara County (red)

In a relatively short space of time, Bill Cates and Jeff Fink have turned Tantara into a fine producer of Pinot Noir. Founded in 1997, the winery is based in the Santa Maria Valley, and sources fruit from top Central Coast vineyards, such as Garys' and Pisoni Vineyards in the Santa Lucia Highlands, and Bien Nacido, Dierberg, and Solomon Hills in the Santa Maria Valley. The bargain-priced T. Solomon Wellborn Pinot Noir is juicy and aromatic, with lively raspberry, cherry, and notes of vanilla and spice.

2900 Rancho Tepusquet Rd, Santa Maria, CA 93454
www.tantarawinery.com

Terra Valentine Spring Mountain, Napa Valley
Amore Super Tuscan, Napa Valley (red)

Decanting will unleash the ripe cherry fruit, mocha, and raspberry flavours of Terra Valentine's full-bodied Sangiovese-dominated blend, the Amore Super Tuscan. A bit of air will also reveal complex and spicy tannins. Terra Valentine is a winery that has come back from the brink. The estate, in all its Greco-Roman glory, was hand-built by the inventor and engineer Fred Aves in the 1960s, and has been entirely restored, with the vineyards replanted, by new owners, Angus and Margaret Wurtele.

3787 Spring Mountain Rd, St Helena, CA 94574
www.terravalentine.com

Unti Vineyards Dry Creek Valley, Sonoma
Petit Frère, Dry Creek Valley (red); Zinfandel, Dry Creek Valley (red)

Unti Vineyards specializes in Mediterranean-style wines. The Petit Frère is a Rhône-style blend that emphasizes Grenache, and features floral aromas giving way to earthy, baked fruit and a bright, mineral finish. The estate's Zinfandel is also made in a blockbuster style with unctuous aromas of brambly, jammy black fruit. It is full-bodied with complex black spices that dress up the rich, massive flavours and dry finish.

4202 Dry Creek Rd, Healdsburg, CA 95448
www.untivineyards.com

Valley of the Moon Winery Sonoma Valley, Sonoma
Syrah, Sonoma (red); Pinot Blanc, Sonoma (white)

Valley of the Moon has been a working winery since 1863, but has changed name (once) and owners (twice) since then. Today, the winery makes an array of reasonably priced, good-quality wines, including a Syrah, which is true to form with blackberry, white pepper, and cedar aromas; firm and round with juicy blueberry and baking spice flavours. The Pinot Blanc has Alsace-style aromas of stone fruit and honeysuckle complementing creamy flavours of apples, pears, and citrus and a bright, balanced finish.

777 Madrone Rd, Glen Ellen, CA 95442
www.valleyofthemoonwinery.com

Viader Vineyards
Howell Mountain, Napa Valley
DARE Rosé, Napa Valley

The formidable Delia Viader is a force to be reckoned with: she raised four children (all of them now in the family business) while managing her estate's rise to prominence in the 1990s. Planted to Bordeaux varieties (plus a bit of Syrah) on steep slopes in Howell Mountain, the wines are made with the assistance of consultant winemaker, Michel Rolland. The estate is responsible for some very smart wines, but one of the less expensive highlights here is the DARE Rosé. A vibrant, concentrated wine from Cabernet Sauvignon, it has floral, Bing cherry, and cassis aromas amplified by bursting flavours of rose and blue flowers on a clean, fresh finish.

1120 Deer Park Rd, Deer Park, CA 94576
www.viader.com

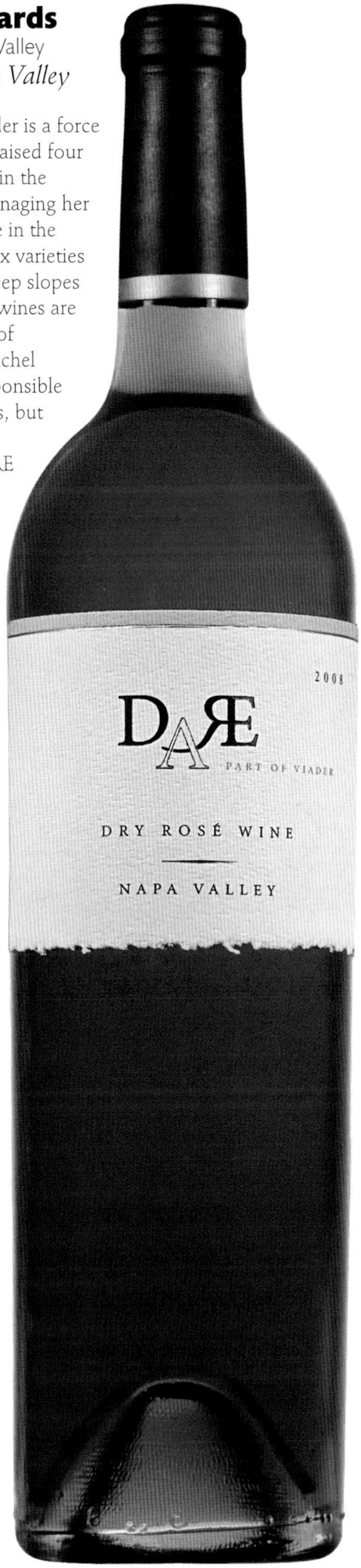

Vina Robles

San Luis Obispo County, Central Coast

White4 Huerhuero, Paso Robles (white)

Vina Robles arrived in Paso Robles in the late 1990s and has been making consistent wines ever since. A Swiss-flavoured operation, it is owned by Hans Nef, an engineer, with fellow Swiss, Matthias Gubler, making the wines. Nef owns some 486ha (1,200 acres) of vines, but most of the fruit is sold to other producers. The White4 Huerhuero is a refreshing blend of four grapes – usually dominated by Vermentino or Verdelho – with aromas of jasmine and flavours of white peach and citrus.

3700 Mill Rd, Paso Robles, CA 93446
www.vinarobles.com

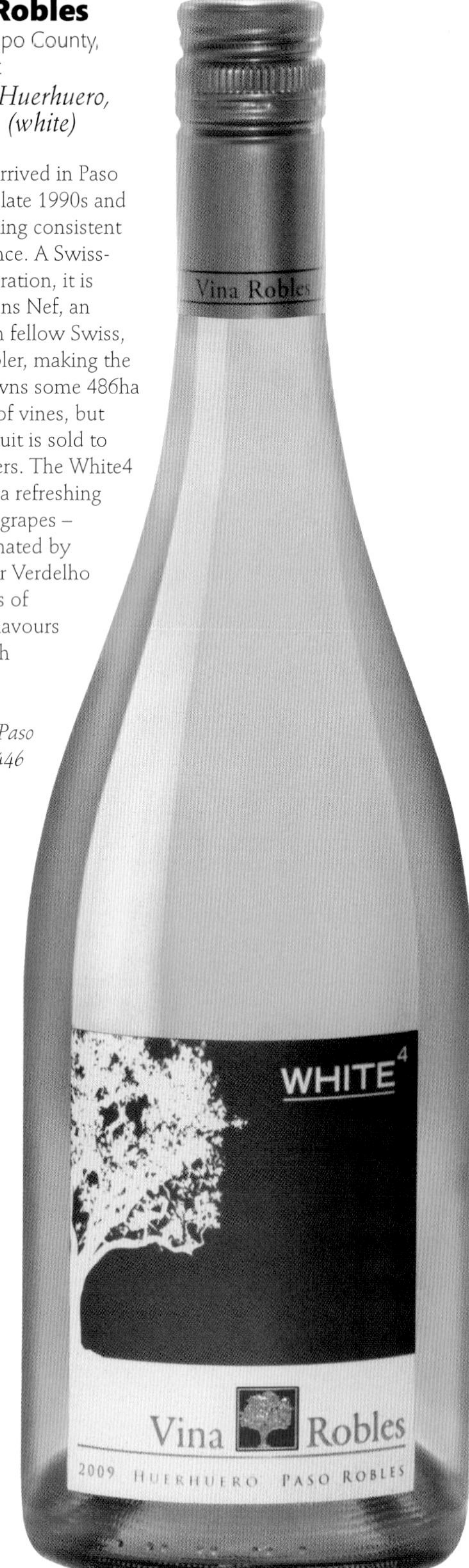

Vino Noceto Amador County, Inland California

Moscato Bianco Frivolo, California (white)

Spring arrives in Northern California when the first bottle of Vino Noceto California Moscato Bianco Frivolo is opened, brightening the day with its sunny fruit and amiable nature. It is a tangy mix of Moscato Bianco and Orange Muscat, crackling with a touch of spritz, decidedly sweet, full-figured, and low in alcohol. It is the work of Jim and Suzy Gullett, who arrived in the Sierra Foothills in the 1980s in search of new winemaking frontiers. The couple are much admired – loved even – for the charming way they have gone about their business, which has focused on making original wines with an Italianate inspiration, using the Italian grape varieties that they believe suit the warm climate in Amador County. Having made a modest 110 cases in their first vintage in 1990, they now produce around 9,000 cases a year. As well as the Moscato, they are known for their fine Sangiovese, which they make in a number of different styles, including grappa. Winemaking is now in the hands of Rusty Folena, who used to work for the Renwood/Santino Winery, with Stacey Gregersen employed as a consultant.

11011 Shenandoah Rd, Plymouth, CA 95669
www.noceto.com

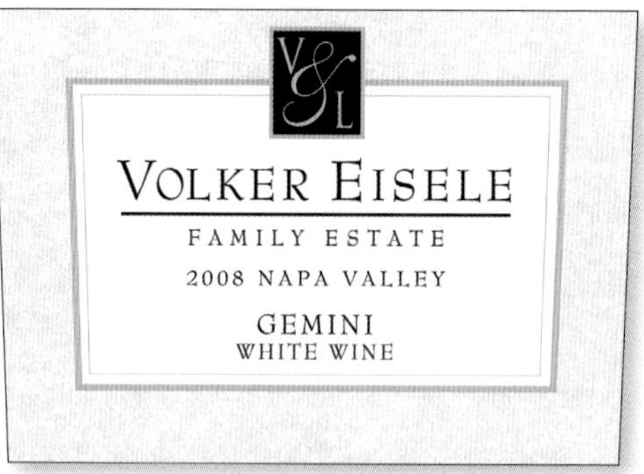

Volker Eisele Family Estate Chiles Valley, Napa Valley

Gemini White Blend, Chiles Valley

Founded more than 35 years ago by Volker and Liesel Eisele, Volker Eisele is one of the finest producers in the Chiles Valley, a rugged, cool-climate outpost of the Napa Valley. Organic production is very much at the heart of operations at the 160ha (400 acre) family estate, and it has proved – almost by itself – that the Chiles Valley, which is located to the east of the other Napa Valley AVAs, is capable of producing fine wine. Today the wines are made by Volker and Liesel's son, Alexander Eisele, who impresses with his careful, skilful, and fastidious approach in a range of complex, intense wines. All that skill is immediately apparent in the Volker Eisele Family Estate Gemini White Blend. A weighty Semillon-dominated blend, it features showy fig and melon flavours contributed by Sauvignon Blanc coupled with savoury green tea, ginger, and vanilla on the appetizingly spicy finish.

3080 Lower Chiles Valley Rd, St Helena, CA 94574
www.volkereiselefamilyestate.com

Wente Vineyards San Francisco Bay, Central Coast
Charles Wetmore, Cabernet Sauvignon, Livermore Valley (red)

Karl Wente, the founder of Wente Vineyards, was one of the pioneers of the Livermore Valley. He started the family business way back in 1883, and today this flagship of the region is still owned and run by the fourth and fifth generations of the Wente family, making it the oldest continuously operating family-run winery in the US. Wente is well-known throughout the world, thanks to an enlightened and energetic export policy that puts many California wineries to shame. The business has also been partly responsible for rescuing Livermore's vineyards from housing developers. The range here is broad, covering a vast array of wines, both still and sparkling, but it is of a consistently good quality, too. Named after another Livermore winemaking pioneer, the Charles Wetmore Cabernet Sauvignon is a medium-weight red that offers ripe black cherry and roasted coffee flavours with an attractive hint of cedar.

5565 Tesla Rd, Livermore, CA 94550
www.wentevineyards.com

Whitehall Lane Winery Rutherford, Napa Valley
Merlot, Napa Valley (red); Sauvignon Blanc, Napa Valley (white)

Based in Rutherford, the Whitehall Lane Winery is a small- to medium-sized producer with a reputation for producing consistently good quality and well-priced wines. The business has been owned since 1993 by the Leonardini family, and the family's house style is very much of the classical old school, eschewing excessive weight and alcohol for a touch of elegance. This is certainly true of the bargain Napa Valley Merlot, where a touch of aromatic Syrah perfumes the dark cherry aromas of velvety Merlot while sandalwood and vanilla enrich darker mocha, raspberry, and cherry flavours. The lighter-bodied Napa Valley Sauvignon Blanc is equally well made, and has a profile that takes in intense tropical fruit and green citrus scents with riper citrus notes on the palate. Refreshing acidity keeps the wine squeaky clean right through to the finish.

1563 St Helena Highway, St Helena, CA 94574
www.whitehalllane.com

ZINFANDEL

Is it Zinfandel, Primitivo, or the tongue twister Crljenak Kastelanski? That depends on where this affordable, fresh, ripe, and fruity red is made. In California, Zinfandel has been a mainstay of wine-grape vineyards for more than 150 years.

The most popular style of wine made from the variety in California is a light, slightly sweet rosé called white Zinfandel. But a California red Zinfandel is usually full-bodied, with more than 15% alcohol in some cases, deep in colour and dripping with ripe boysenberry and blackberry flavours.

Primitivo is this grape's name in Italy, where winemakers have used it for centuries. Specialists in ampelography, the study of plant subspecies, puzzled over Zinfandel's origin for decades. Californians claimed it as practically indigenous. Italians said Zinfandel was similar to Primitivo but the variety belonged to them. In the 1990s Carole Meredith of the University of California at Davis confirmed that Zinfandel and Primitivo are basically identical genetically, and that both are descendants of the ancient Croatian grape variety, Crljenak Kastelanski, which still grows along the Dalmatian Coast.

White Zinfandel is an easy-to-drink, hot-summer-day kind of refreshment. Red Zinfandel is big in alcohol, but not austere in texture and has a sweet-seeming ripeness that goes well with cheese, pasta, slow-cooked pork, grilled chicken, or can even be enjoyed after the meal, like a port.

Zinfandel grapes become raisins quickly if harvested too late.

Washington

Divided perpendicularly by the Cascade Mountains, it is no surprise that Washington's biggest and best appellations lie in the rain-shadow of this volcanically formed barrier, to the east of the state. Here irrigation is essential, but the combination of an arid climate and long daylight hours during the growing season creates close to perfect conditions for producing quality wines, noted for their complex fruit flavours and bright acidity.

Amavi Cellars Walla Walla
Syrah, Walla Walla Valley (red)

Amavi Cellars is one of several Walla Walla Valley wineries that are owned and run by Norm McKibben and his sons and daughter, Travis, Ray, and Diana Goff, and winemaker Jean-François Pellet. Their finely tuned teamwork produces lovely, approachable wines that age well. These include a rich, barrel-fermented Semillon-Sauvignon Blanc, a highly popular rosé, and a scattering of dessert wines. The main focus, however, is on their estate-grown Cabernet Sauvignon and their powerful Syrah. Bursting with fresh New-World juiciness, as well as Old-World character and complexity, the Syrah is a good introduction to the high quality that Amavi consistently offers. It presents a sophisticated balance between a firm core of juicy, ripe dark berry fruits – blueberries, cranberries, and raspberries – and subtle accents of smoked meats and spices.

3796 Pepper Bridge Rd, Walla Walla, WA 99362
www.amavicellars.com

Cadaretta Walla Walla
SBS Sauvignon Blanc-Semillon, Columbia Valley (white)

Established in 2005, Cadaretta is a newish winery in the Walla Walla Valley. It is run by an old farming family, the Middletons, who only planted their own vineyards in 2008, and currently rely on grapes purchased from across the state. A good-value example of their fine craftsmanship is the highly popular, crisp, unoaked Sauvignon Blanc-Semillon SBS blend. An artful balance between the lean, zesty profile of Sauvignon and the broader, richer character of Semillon, with notes of white melon and citrus, it is a consistent winner at the table.

1102 Dell Ave, Walla Walla, WA 99362
www.cadaretta.com

CADARETTA
sbs
sauvignon blanc / semillon | columbia valley | 2009

Chateau Ste Michelle Woodinville

Dry Riesling, Columbia Valley (white); Cabernet Sauvignon, Cold Creek Vineyard Columbia Valley (red)

The largest winery in Washington, with the oldest vineyards in the Columbia Valley, Chateau Ste Michelle can trace its history back to the Repeal of Prohibition. However, the company as it stands today did not take off until 1954, with the merger of the Pommerelle Wine Company and National Wine Company to form American Wine Growers. In 1967, American Wine Growers introduced a new range of wines, "Ste Michelle Vintners", produced under the direction of the renowned California winemaker André Tchelistcheff. The company then changed its name to Chateau Ste Michelle in 1976 and is best known for its fine Rieslings, of which the crisp, delicate, and clean yet remarkably intricate Columbia Valley Dry Riesling is a wonderful introduction. However, Ste Michelle is also noted for its selection of high-quality Merlot and Cabernet Sauvignon. The full-bodied Cold Creek Vineyard Cabernet boasts typically ripe fruit for Washington and wonderfully firm tannins. Both wines offer outstanding quality at an amazing price.

14111 NE 145th St, Woodinville, WA 98072
www.ste-michelle.com

Chinook Wines Prosser

Cabernet Franc, Yakima Valley (red)

In 1983, husband-and-wife team Clay Mackey and Kay Simon, both former employees of Chateau Ste Michelle, combined their broad experience to set up Chinook Wines. The couple grows Chardonnay, Sauvignon Blanc, Semillon, Merlot, Cabernet Franc, and Cabernet Sauvignon grapes, but possibly one of their most interesting wines is the delicious, true-to-form Yakima Valley Cabernet Franc. A very rare New World example of this varietal, it shows enough softness and delicacy to echo Chinon, but also enough juicy fruit to reflect its Washington roots.

220 W Wittkopf Loop, Prosser, WA 99350
www.chinookwines.com

Columbia Crest Winery Prosser

H3 Merlot, Horse Heaven Hills (red); H3 Cabernet Sauvignon, Horse Heaven Hills (red)

Owned and operated by Chateau Ste Michelle, Columbia Crest planted its own vineyards in 1978, from which it released its first wine in 1985. From the outset, the focus of this winery has been to balance high-quality with affordability. The excellent Horse Heaven Hills Merlot H3 and Cabernet Sauvignon H3 certainly run true to form, with the smooth Merlot featuring soft notes of plums and cherries, while the Cabernet displays a more structured profile, based on gutsy tannins and intense, dark fruit.

Hwy 221 Columbia Crest Drive, Paterson, WA 99345
www.columbia-crest.com

Columbia Winery Woodinville
Cellarmaster's Riesling, Columbia Valley (white)

Columbia was led for many years by David Lake MW, the first winemaker to produce Syrah, Cabernet Franc, and Pinot Gris wines in the region. It is now part of Icon Estates, a division of the American multinational, Constellation Wines. Columbia's offerings are generally well made and have a broad appeal. The good-value Columbia Valley "Cellarmaster's Riesling" is no exception. Finely balanced, its opulent sweetness is perfectly countered by a sharp citrus edge that lifts the finish. Notes of apricot and tangerine fruit add character and interest.

14030 NE 145th St, Woodinville, WA 98072
www.columbiawinery.com

Fielding Hills Winery Wenatchee
Cabernet Franc Riverbend Vineyard, Wahluke Slope (red)

Fielding is a young winery, which released its first wine in 2002, using grapes from vineyards that were planted in 1998. The Wahluke Slope Riverbend Vineyard Cabernet Franc presents a gentler introduction to its good-value wines than its delicious but powerful, spicy Syrah, and Cabernet Sauvignon-Syrah blend. Ripe with a sweet, soft finish, the Cabernet Franc features lush, dark overtones of cherries and cassis, which mingle beautifully with subtle but distinct leafy, herbal aromas.

1401 Fielding Hills Drive, East Wenatchee, WA 98802
www.fieldinghills.com

Hedges Family Estate Benton City
Red Mountain Red Wine

Washington native Tom Hedges began his adventures in the wine industry in 1986, soon setting up what was then Hedges Cellars. However, the beginnings of Hedges as a serious estate winery really date to 1991, when Tom and his wife Anne-Marie purchased land on the then largely unknown Red Mountain, the state's warmest growing region, now with a reputation for producing many of its best wines. Since then, they have concentrated their efforts on high-quality but affordable reds, centred on Cabernet Sauvignon and Merlot. The excellent Red Mountain Red Wine is a balanced blend, combining these classic Bordeaux varieties with Syrah. The result is a spicy and complex red, packed with rich flavour, but with a soft underlying structure that makes for easy drinking.

53511 N Sunset Rd, Benton City, WA 99320
www.hedgesfamilyestate.com

J M Cellars Woodinville
Syrah Boushey Vineyard, Rattlesnake Hills (red)

John Bigelow became a professional winemaker in 2006, when he founded J M Cellars in Woodinville with his wife Peggy. Together, they craft wines from grapes grown in top vineyard sites across the entire Columbia Valley, including their signature Tre Fanciulli blend, as well as the modestly priced Rattlesnake Hills Boushey Vineyard Syrah. The latter offers great value, without cutting corners on complexity. Lingering notes of smoked meats and sweet tannins give definition to the highly expressive aromas of raspberries and dark blackberries that form the solid core of this rich, character-filled wine.

14404 137th Place NE, Woodinville, WA 98072
www.jmcellars.com

L'Ecole No. 41 Lowden
Semillon, Columbia Valley (white)

Based in a former schoolhouse from which it takes its name, L'Ecole No. 41 is owned and run by Marty Clubb, who fashions grapes from top vineyards in the Walla Walla and Columbia Valleys into stylish wines. As well as a range of prized Cabernet Sauvignon-based blends, Clubb makes a trio of fine Semillons, of which the Columbia Valley bottling, although the cheapest, is possibly the most outstanding. Great value for such high quality, this remarkably consistent offering features light floral aromas, backed by broad sweeps of satisfying fruit, reminiscent of melons and fresh figs.

41 Lowden School Rd, Lowden, WA 99360
www.lecole.com

Michelle Loosen Woodinville

Riesling Eroica, Columbia Valley (white)

Produced at Chateau Ste Michelle as part of a joint project with Germany's Dr Loosen Estate of the Mosel Valley, the Columbia Valley Riesling Eroica, gets heaped with praise by the critics. A perfect mix of Old- and New-World styles, it delivers an intricate combination of soft floral aromas and fresh citrus notes, sealed by a precisely balanced finish. Its crisp acidity and touch of sweetness make it a good match for a variety of foods. Even alongside many of the world's top, and far more costly, Rieslings, it still shines.

14111 NE 145th St, Woodinville, WA 98072
www.eroicawine.com

Pacific Rim West Richland

Riesling Wallula Vineyard, Columbia Valley (white)

Celebrated California winemaker Randall Grahm's project to promote the versatility of Riesling – Pacific Rim – is now an independent winery, with offices in Portland and a winery in the Columbia Valley. It remains obsessed with Riesling, and even produces a useful pamphlet on the subject (available from its website). Among the wide range of Rieslings produced by Pacific Rim are four single-vineyard wines, including the vibrant, well-priced Columbia Valley Wallula Vineyard offering. Fresh and lively, with notes of apricot and mandarin and a pleasant hint of citrus-rind bitterness, the faint sweetness of this wine is beautifully balanced by energetic acidity.

8111 Keene Rd, West Richland, WA 99353
www.rieslingrules.com

Poet's Leap Winery Walla Walla

Riesling, Columbia Valley (white)

Poet's Leap is part of Long Shadows Vintners, a group of premium wineries brought together by Washington wine pioneer Allen Shoup. It is operated by a partnership of some of the world's most highly acclaimed winemakers, each of them producing a single Columbia Valley wine that represents the best of its kind, and reflects their signature style. The Poet's Leap Riesling is a great value introduction to this expressive collection of fine vintages. Crafted by Armin Diel, one of Germany's top Riesling producers, it is at once generous but also light and delicate. Lovely rich aromas, recalling fresh citrus and kumquat, are followed by vivid notes of ripe melon, apricot, and peach, and a final flourish of crisp acidity.

1604 Frenchtown Road, Walla Walla, WA 99362
www.longshadows.com

Reininger Winery Walla Walla

Cabernet Sauvignon, Walla Walla Valley (red)

Chuck and Tracy Reininger started making wine from bought-in grapes in the Walla Walla Valley in 1997. In 2000, their project went up a gear when they planted their first vineyard. Another vineyard and new winery followed in 2003. They specialize in producing well-structured red wines, largely from Walla Walla Valley fruit. Concentrated, but restrained in terms of ripeness, the Walla Walla Valley Cabernet Sauvignon represents a great budget introduction to their wines. With a little Petit Verdot and Cabernet Franc blended in, this classy, complex wine has sweet notes of dark chocolate, red berries, and cinnamon, finely balanced by a light touch of acidity.

5858 W Highway 12, Walla Walla, WA 99362
www.reiningerwinery.com

Seven Hills Winery Walla Walla

Merlot, Columbia Valley (red)

Casey and Vicky McClellan set up the Seven Hills Winery in 1988, and since then have made two pioneering moves: bottling Walla Walla's first varietally labelled Malbec, and planting its first Tempranillo. Their focus, however, is on Cabernet Sauvignons and Bordeaux-varietal reds, which are widely recognized as some of the finest wines that Washington has to offer. The soft, lush Columbia Valley Merlot is an absolute charmer, thanks to deep flavours of black plums and cherries, mixed with subtle accents of toffee and liquorice, plus finely-grained tannins, and a long, lingering finish.

212 North 3rd Ave, Walla Walla, WA 99362
www.sevenhillswinery.com

Syncline Wine Cellars Lyle

"Cuvée Elena", Columbia Valley (red)

James and Poppie Mantone opened Syncline Wine Cellars in 1999, and immediately started working with vineyards planted with classic French varieties, such as Cinsault, Counoise, Grenache, Mourvèdre, Roussanne, Syrah, and Viognier. Their passion is evident in wines such as the Columbia Valley "Cuvée Elena", a Southern Rhône-inspired blend of Grenache, Mourvèdre, Carignan, Cinsault, and Syrah. This makes for a stunningly elegant, full-bodied wine, which delivers vibrant flavours of wonderfully concentrated, juicy red fruit and hints of fig, topped by sweet spicy aromas and silky finishing tannins.

111 Balch Rd, Lyle, WA 98635
www.synclinewine.com

Oregon

Though Oregon is a relative newcomer to the world of quality wine, it has already developed a strong identity. The Willamette Valley is the home of some of America's finest Pinot Noirs, wines that are a match for many a burgundy. On the white side, Pinot Gris has become a speciality, and varieties such as Tempranillo and Chardonnay are also proving successful both in Willamette and elsewhere in the state.

A to Z Wineworks Dundee

Pinot Noir, Oregon (red)

A to Z Wineworks Oregon Pinot Noir is consistently a top performer among relatively affordable expressions of Oregon Pinot. It shows focused dark cherry flavours with supple tannins and just the faintest whiff of oak. It is the fruit of a successful partnership between the winemakers Sam Tannahill (who used to be at Archery Summit) and his wife Cheryl Francis (formerly at Chehalem) with Deb and Bill Hatcher (the former managing director of Domaine Drouhin Oregon). The two couples initially ran the business as a négociant, starting in 1998, before becoming the state's largest winery after snapping up Rex Hill Vineyards in 2007.

Dundee, OR 97115
www.atozwineworks.com

Abacela Roseburg

Tempranillo, Southern Oregon (red)

Few wineries outside Spain have made a success of Tempranillo, but Abacela is certainly an exception. Earl and Hilda Jones, helped by their son, Greg Jones (himself a world authority on the effects of climate change on wine), conducted a country-wide search for the right spot to plant Tempranillo, before settling on southern Oregon in 1992. In their Southern Oregon Tempranillo, grippy, gutsy flavours of dark cherry and black plum show plenty of fruit with balanced structure and minimal oak. It is a genuinely convincing – not to mention delicious – rendition of a great grape.

12500 Lookingglass Rd, Roseburg, OR 97471
www.abacela.com

Adelsheim Vineyard Newberg

Pinot Noir, Willamette Valley (red)

David Adelsheim is one of the Oregon wine scene's most important and influential individuals, someone who has played a key role in drafting Oregon's wine laws, as well as founding one of its best producers. The latter project began with 6ha (15 acres) planted near Adelsheim's home, and it now has 77ha (190 acres) of vineyards, and an annual production of 40,000 cases a year. Always a model of purity and restraint, the Willamette Valley Pinot Noir shows fresh notes of red and black cherries that are framed by soft, fine-grained tannins. It is made by Dave Paige, the winemaker since 2001.

16800 NE Calkins Lane, Newberg, OR 97132
www.adelsheim.com

Bergström Wines Newberg

Pinot Noir Old Stones, Willamette Valley (red); Chardonnay Old Stones, Willamette Valley (white)

Both the Chardonnay and Pinot Noir in Bergström Wines' Old Stones label show a ripe, generous style offering deep flavours and a rounded texture. Restrained use of oak results in them seeming balanced and natural rather than manipulated, with great versatility for the table. This kind of finesse is just what wine drinkers have come to expect from the Bergström family, ever since John and Karen Bergström first planted a 6ha (15 acre) estate after moving to Dundee from Portland. Today the couple's son Josh is the winemaker (he trained in Burgundy) while Josh's four siblings all work in a business which has now grown to 16ha (40 acres) of vineyards, producing 10,000 cases of top-notch wines a year.

18215 NE Calkins Lane, Newberg, OR 97132
www.bergstromwines.com

Chehalem Wines Newberg

Dry Riesling Reserve, Willamette Valley (white); Chardonnay Inox, Willamette Valley (white)

Chehalem's Willamette Valley Dry Riesling Reserve is very generous in flavour despite its restrained sweetness, with juicy notes of quince and mandarin orange edged with energetic acidity. In quality, it is matched by the unwooded Willamette Valley Chardonnay Inox, which shows subtle aromas but open, expressive flavours of peaches and baked apples. The company behind this duo began its life in 1980 when the founder, Harry Peterson-Nedry, planted his first Pinot Noir vineyard in Ribbon Ridge. It soon went from hobbyist's plaything to full-blown commercial winery, and by 1990, Chehalem had been born. Peterson-Nedry has recently been joined in the winery by his daughter, Wynn.

31190 NE Veritas Lane, Newberg, OR 97132
www.chehalemwines.com

The Eyrie Vineyards McMinville
Pinot Gris, Dundee Hills (white)

The Eyrie Vineyards was founded by the late David Lett, who was a pioneer of Pinot Noir Oregon, having planted the first Pinot Noir vines in the state in the mid-1960s. Today, Lett's son, Jason, is carrying on the family tradition with a range of top wines produced in the Dundee Hills, at the northern end of the Willamette Valley. The Dundee Hills Pinot Gris shows a ripe, almost honeyed richness akin to renditions of the grape variety from Alsace, yet an edge of balancing acidity keeps it refreshing sip after sip.

935 NE 10th Ave, McMinnville, OR 97128
www.eyrievineyards.com

King Estate Eugene
Pinot Gris Signature Series, Oregon (white)

With its 400ha (1,000 acres) of beautiful prime vineyard land near Eugene to the south of the Willamette Valley, King Estate is a fine place to spend a few hours. There is a restaurant and visitor centre, and the company also makes a range of jams. Aside from its contribution to wine tourism, King Estate is also a very reliable source of affordable wines. The Oregon Pinot Gris Signature Series, which is sourced from vineyard sites across the state, is a consistently strong value option. Alluring aromas lead into flavours suggesting ripe peaches and poached pears in this well-made white, with medium body and a fresh, lifted finish.

80854 Territorial Rd, Eugene, OR 97405
www.kingestate.com

Soter Vineyards Yamhill
Pinot Noir North Valley, Willamette Valley (red)

Tony Soter first made his name as a winemaking consultant to a number of top properties in the Napa Valley. But these days Soter is much more involved in the pair of winemaking projects he has established with his wife, Michelle: Etude in the Napa Valley, and Soter Vineyards in Oregon. Both are dedicated to Soter's speciality, Pinot Noir, and his world-class winemaking skills are evident even in the entry-level bottling, Willamette Valley Pinot Noir North Valley. A very high-quality wine for the money, this is more delicate and subtle than many bottles at twice the price.

Carlton, OR 97111
www.sotervineyards.com

FOOD & WINE WILLAMETTE VALLEY PINOT NOIR

Pinot Noir makes an intensely flavoured, complex, high-acid wine with incredible longevity. No other grape delivers a wine with such heady perfume, silky texture, and primal, earthy flavour and the fruity, juicy versions from Oregon's Willamette Valley are a blend of Old World restraint and New World richness.

Generally the wines are light- to medium-bodied and light in colour, and they do not overpower delicate dishes. They have gorgeous raspberry, spice, mushroom, earth, and floral notes – often pink rose petal, and varying levels of vanilla from oak.

Local specialities include the freshly caught salmon prepared *a la plancha* (on a cedar plank over fire), which pairs beautifully with the delicate, berry-imbued wine. Even with the char, the fish itself is rather delicate and sweet, so a Willamette Valley Pinot Noir is perfect. Wild mushrooms and Oregon truffles are also incorporated into many dishes here, providing a flavour bridge to the wine. Roasted quail with morels – a dish often served in Burgundy – or, for vegetarians, linguine with black truffles, pair nicely. Pinot Noir's natural acidity gives it the ability to pair well with cheeses, too. A baked truffled Brie en croute illustrates both flavour and structural compatibility. Adding Parmesan cheese to a dish provides a flavour and textural contrast.

Roasted quail echoes some of the flavours of Pinot Noir.

The rest of the US

Winemaking is a rapidly growing business in the US, and there are wineries in nearly every state. New York, in fact, has one of the country's oldest winemaking traditions, with the Finger Lakes area and Long Island being noted for their exceptional vintages. Vineyards and wineries are proliferating in Ohio, Michigan, and Missouri, and an increasing number of world-class wines are now coming out of Texas and New Mexico.

Château LaFayette Reneau New York

Dry Riesling, Finger Lakes (white); Riesling Late Harvest, Finger Lakes (white)

When Château LaFayette Reneau's Dick Reno purchased a dilapidated farm in 1985, making wine was never part of his retirement plan. But finding himself in the pocket of wineries on Seneca Lake's southeastern shores, he was soon planting plots of *vinifera* vines, mostly Chardonnay and Riesling, which yield top-class wines. The Finger Lakes Dry Riesling is a lively mouthful, with generous aromas of citrus, stone fruits, and summer flowers, lifted by a touch of spritziness. By contrast, the Finger Lakes Riesling Late Harvest coats the palate with rich flavours of peach, apricot, and baked apple, a wave of juicy acidity, punctuated with spice, carrying them through to a long, balanced finish.

5081 Route 414, Hector, New York 14841
www.clrwine.com

Dr Konstantin Frank Vinifera Wine Cellars New York

Semi-Dry Riesling, Finger Lakes (white); Salmon Run Riesling (white)

In 1962, the Dr Konstantin Frank winery on Keuka Lake ignited the *vinifera* revolution in the Finger Lakes area and throughout the northeast. Current owner Fred Frank employs a diverse team of top international winemakers, and the excellent Dr Konstantin Frank Finger Lakes Rieslings have become a benchmark for quality in the region. The semi-dry version is ripe with apple and tropical fruit flavours, offset by a deft balance of sugar and crisp acidity that ends with a distinct mineral edge. The more widely available Salmon Run Riesling, from Frank's more affordable Salmon Run label, is a terrific bargain. It is eminently enjoyable, with a lean and steely palate, fine flowery aromas, and a delicate dash of ripe pear.

9749 Middle Rd, Hammondsport, New York 14840
www.drfrankwines.com

Gruet Winery New Mexico

Blanc de Noir (sparkling); NV: Blanc de Blancs Sauvage (sparkling)

The high desert plateaux of New Mexico may seem an unlikely source of high-class sparkling wine, but after a quarter of a century of excellence, the quality of Gruet Winery's offerings is no longer a surprise. The Gruet family blends Chardonnay and Pinot Noir to create their elegant, top-value Blanc de Noir. With lovely clean bubbles and a creamy texture, it shows a rich complexity of summer-berry aromas. The bone-dry NV: Blanc de Blancs Sauvage also delivers an amazing amount for your money. Bright and minerally, with a delicate mousse and bead of fine bubbles, notes of green apple and lemon lead to a light but lingering finish.

8400 Pan American Frwy NE, Albuquerque, New Mexico 87113
www.gruetwinery.com

Kinkead Ridge Winery Ohio

Cabernet Franc, Ohio River Valley (red); Viognier-Roussanne, Ohio River Valley (white)

Among the more than 100 wineries in Ohio, Kinkead Ridge is one of the state's most compelling. Unlike the offerings of so many of its peers, Kinkead wines are never thin or insignificant, but have rich, varietal character, and great balance. Owner Ron Barrett's gentle touch with Cabernet Franc has produced a full-bodied, richly complex wine with fragrant aromas of violet and black cherry, and enticing notes of spice, plum, and red berries. It is an outstanding offering at a very modest price. The floral, honeyed Viognier-Roussanne is delicious, too. Its elegant mix of orange blossom and tropical fruit flavours is set off by sharper notes of kiwi and guava. A crisp acidic finish makes for a truly satisfying experience.

904 Hamburg St, Ripley, Ohio 45167
www.kinkeadridge.com

Left Foot Charley Michigan

Pinot Blanc (white); Riesling MD (Medium Dry) (white)

Bryan Ulbrich has crafted superb vintages for others over the years, so it is no surprise that his own Left Foot Charley label now sets the standard for Michigan wine. When writers use words like "grace" and "purity" to describe his products, they are not exaggerating. His ability with aromatic white grapes has been on display since the winery was founded in 2004, crafting vintages of great delicacy and balance that highlight perfectly the distinctive nature and vibrancy of each individual grape variety. The Pinot Blanc is flush with dense flavours of ripe apple and pear that lead to a long, drawn-out finish. Floral and citrus notes float over the peachy sweetness and crisp acidity of the hugely popular Riesling MD.

806 Red Drive, Traverse City, Michigan 49684
www.leftfootcharley.com

Macari Vineyards & Winery New York

Sauvignon Blanc, Long Island (white); Sette, Long Island (red)

The Macari family have farmed their waterfront estate for over 50 years, but grapes only arrived on the scene in 1995. True to his heritage, Joseph Macari Jr has applied sustainable practices and biodiversity to his 70ha (180 acres) of vines. Macari's wines are very affordable for Long Island examples. The Sauvignon Blanc shows good grassy varietal character that will appeal greatly to fans of New Zealand-style Sauvignon. Its characteristic grapefruit and grassy aromas mingle with tangy lime and citrus to reach a crisp finish. The non-vintage Sette, a soft blend of Merlot and Cabernet Franc, shows astonishing complexity for its price, wrapping flavours of black plum and blackcurrants in a warm blanket of chocolate and spice.

150 Bergen Ave, Mattituck, New York 11952
www.macariwines.com

McPherson Cellars Texas

Tre Colore (red)

A passion for wine runs in the McPherson family. They have been pioneering grape growing and winemaking in Texas for over 40 years. The father of McPherson Cellars' owner and winemaker Kim McPherson was a university professor and a founder of one of the first post-Prohibition wineries in Texas, and his younger brother has been making fine wines for decades in southern California. McPherson's laid-back, folksy demeanour belies the dedicated and passionate winemaker behind some of the state's most interesting wines, all showing true varietal character as well as elegance – a word that is often hard to apply to Texas wines. The utterly charming Tre Colore is a wonderfully smooth, Rhône-style blend of Carignan, Syrah, and Viognier, with a soft lingering finish. It is one of McPherson's most complex wines. Packed with dense earthy aromas, flavours of lush ripe raspberries and blackcurrants burst out across the palate with every mouthful.

1615 Texas Ave, Lubbock, Texas 79401
www.mcphersoncellars.com

Stone Hill Winery Missouri

Norton Port (fortified); Dry Vignoles (white)

Stone Hill is one of the oldest wineries in the US, dating back to 1847, and for many Americans it represents the pinnacle of Midwestern wine. Closed during Prohibition, the Held family re-opened the winery in 1965, and under the tutelage of chief winemaker David Johnson, it has led the way for the rest of the country with its use of relatively unknown grapes, such as Norton and Vignoles. Johnson continues to oversee production of the great fortified wines, such as the rich dark Norton Port. Produced in limited quantities, using traditional methods, it delivers a powerful punch of blackberry and cassis. The full-bodied Dry Vignoles displays lively, zingy aromas of pineapple, strawberries, and lime, with a hint of sweetness that is perfectly balanced by a vibrant acidity.

1110 Stone Hill Hwy, Hermann, Missouri 65041
www.stonehillwinery.com

Wölffer Estate New York

Rosé, Long Island

Christian Wölffer founded his wine estate in 1988 on former potato fields. The victim of a tragic accident in 2008, he would be proud of the ongoing achievements of technical director and chief winemaker Roman Roth, whose dry rosé, a blend of red grapes and Chardonnay, has become a benchmark of summer drinking on Long Island. As the price of Provençal rosé continues to climb, this stylish drink deserves a place in every picnic basket. Refreshing, and complex, its fresh lively aromas of pear and peach, plus a hint of rose petals, mingle with lovely melon, peach, and strawberry flavours, leading to a clean, dry finish.

139 Sagg Rd, Sagaponack, New York 11962
www.wolffer.com

Canada

Though vines for the production of wine were first planted in Canada in the 1630s, it is only very recently that the country's winemakers have begun to make a quality impression. There has been a wave of investment in the industry in the past two decades, mostly focused on British Columbia (particularly the Okanagan Valley) in the west and Ontario in the east, and many distinctive, good-value wines of all styles are now being made.

Averill Creek Vineyards Vancouver Island, West Canada

Pinot Noir (red)

Dark fruit flavours match the ruby hue in Averill Creek's Pinot Noir. A hint of smokiness from ageing in French oak give it a soft, seductive feel – this is a premium everyday wine you will not regret buying. It is an impressive achievement for a winery that only planted its first grapes in 2001. It is owned by Andy Johnston, a doctor by profession who had dreamed of having his own winery. The first wines from those vineyards arrived with the 2004 vintage, and they have since gone on to win several awards.

6552 North Rd, Duncan, British Columbia V9L 6K9
www.averillcreek.ca

Blasted Church Vineyards Okanagan Valley, West Canada

Hatfield's Fuse (white)

One of the most popular wines currently coming out of Okanagan's burgeoning wine scene, Blasted Church Vineyard's Hatfield's Fuse is an aromatic blend of eight grapes led by Gewurztraminer, Optima, and Pinot Blanc. The blend yields notes of honeydew melon and pear, brightened by hints of Granny Smith apple. As well as its quality, the popularity of this wine is helped by the highly distinctive labels used by Chris and Evelyn Campbell since the couple took over the estate in 2002. The estate used to be known as Prpich Hills, after the Croatian-born ex-proprietor, Dan Prpich.

378 Parsons Rd, Okanagan Falls, British Columbia V0H 1R0
www.blastedchurch.com

Cave Spring Cellars Niagara Peninsula, East Canada

Riesling, Estate Bottled, Beamsville Bench (white)

Cave Spring Cellars' Estate Bottled Riesling is a dry Riesling made from fruit sourced from the Beamsville Bench, a narrow strip of land where the Niagara escarpment meets Lake Ontario, that produces excellent quality grapes. It offers a warm spiciness on the nose, and baked apple on the palate. The winery behind it started life as a producer in 1986, after several years as a grower, specializing in various *Vitis vinifera* varieties on the Beamsville Bench. Diversity still rules here, but it is the rich Rieslings that are best known.

3836 Main St, Jordan, Ontario L0R 1S0
www.cavespring.ca

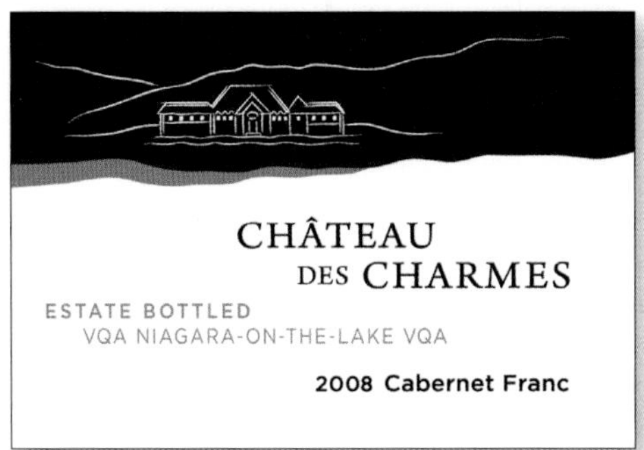

Château des Charmes Niagara Peninsula, East Canada

Cabernet Franc, Estate Bottled, Niagara-on-the-Lake (red)

Wines that are deep in flavour and rich in minerality have placed the family-run Château des Charmes among the Niagara Peninsula's best producers. The wines have a distinctly Gallic character, in fact, something which must be attributable, at least in part, to the French pedigree of the ownership. There is a desire to experiment, too, and the winery has pioneered Gamay Droit and Chardonnay Musqué. The Estate Bottled Cabernet Franc is a serious, deeply coloured wine that bears Cabernet Franc's characteristic blackberry and cherry flavours. The hint of pepper and spice comes from the Niagara terroir and the period the wine spends ageing in oak.

1025 York Rd, Niagara-on-the-Lake, Ontario L0S 1J0
www.chateaudescharmes.com

Gray Monk Estate Okanagan Valley, West Canada

Gewürztraminer (white)

George and Trudy Heiss, the couple behind Gray Monk, are big fans of aromatic white grape varieties. So much so they named both their first vineyard and their winery after one: Gray Monk is a reference to the Pinot Gris variety. While Pinot Gris may therefore be Gray Monk's signature grape, the couple's popular off-dry version of another aromatic white, Gewürztraminer, is no less worthwhile – and is excellent value, too. It wins with notes of bergamot on the nose, and papaya and mango on the palate, responding well to the cool climate of North Okanagan.

1055 Camp Rd, Okanagan Centre, British Columbia V4V 2H4
www.graymonk.com

Hillebrand Winery Niagara Peninsula, East Canada

Trius Riesling (white)

Hillebrand Winery is a hugely impressive operation. It attracts a number of visitors to its destination winery complex, which includes a restaurant and guided tours. The success of this venture is a tribute to the quality of the wines the company has produced since it became one of the first wineries to make premium wines in Niagara some 30 years ago. Winemaking here is now entrusted to the Australian, Craig McDonald, who looks after a broad portfolio that is led by the single-vineyard Showcase Riesling. The Trius Riesling is a great everyday alternative to that superb wine, however. A lighter expression of the grape and the local terroir, it is just as crisp with hints of starfruit and luscious mango.

1249 Niagara Stone Rd, Niagara-on-the-Lake, Ontario L0S 1J0
www.hillebrand.com

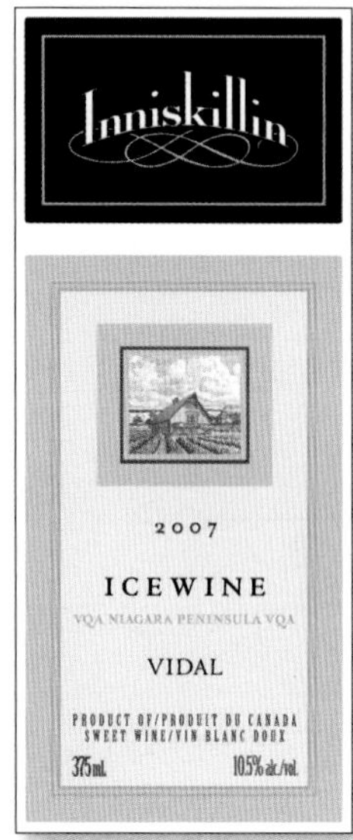

Inniskillin Niagara Niagara Peninsula, East Canada

Vidal Icewine (dessert)

Stonefruit characters usually tend to dominate the Icewines of British Columbia. But rich notes of smooth honey characterize this Icewine, made from the Vidal grape by Inniskillin, Ontario's pioneering Icewine producer. Though it may be a tad expensive for everyday drinking, it is included here because it is so much more affordable than the majority of its counterparts; it is certainly the best-value way into a great North American wine. Inniskillin has arguably done more to popularize Icewine – a wine made from grapes that are harvested when frozen on the vine – than any other winery in Canada. Founded by Donald Ziraldo and Karl Kaiser in 1975 (Ontario's first winery since the end of Prohibition in 1927), Inniskillin Niagara did not make the first Ontario Icewine (that was Hillebrand Estates in 1983). But it did make the first to capture international attention and prizes.

1499 Line 3, Niagara-on-the-Lake, Ontario L0S 1J0
www.inniskillin.com

Jost Vineyards Malagash Peninsula, East Canada

Oak-Aged L'Acadie Blanc, Nava Scotia (white)

L'Acadie Blanc is Nova Scotia's signature grape, a white that is suited to the crisp maritime climate, and which characteristically yields bright apple flavours. In Jost Vineyards' oak-aged example, those apple flavours are augmented by hints of pear and lemon, helping it to match – what else? – seafood. Jost Vineyards can be found on the north shore of Nova Scotia, right by the warm waters of the Northumberland Strait. Originally licensed in 1983, the winery opened to the public in 1986, and the wines (and other local products) are made today by Hans Christian Jost.

48 Vintage Lane, Malagash, Nova Scotia B0K 1E0
www.jostwine.com

Lailey Vineyard Niagara Peninsula, East Canada
Chardonnay (white)

The success of Lailey Vineyard rests on the shoulders of two talented individuals: Derek Barnett and Donna Lailey. As a top viticulturist, it is Lailey – who was officially dubbed Ontario's "Grape Queen" in 1991 – who manages the vineyards planted by her father-in-law, William Lailey, in the 1950s. Barnett fashions that fruit (some of it sourced from the oldest Chardonnay vines in the region) into a portfolio of intense, yet elegant wines. These include the estate Chardonnay, which is replete with flavours of McIntosh apple and decent acidity, and even has cellar potential.

15940 Niagara Parkway, Niagara-on-the-Lake, Ontario L0S 1J0
www.laileyvineyard.com

Le Clos Jordanne Niagara Peninsula, East Canada
Village Reserve Pinot Noir (red)

Le Clos Jordanne is a joint venture between the Canadian drinks firm, Vincor, and the Burgundian wine producer, Boisset. It is housed in what used to be a warehouse operated by a plant nursery business which looks right out over Lake Ontario. Winemaking is today led by Sébastien Jacquey, who took over from his ex-boss, Thomas Bachelder, once the project was established in the mid-2000s. The Village Reserve Pinot Noir is a fine but affordable expression of the Niagara Escarpment's terroir. It is a delicate wine that offers the earthiness of the terrain alongside the plum and tart cherry characters of the grape. Chardonnay is also produced here, and the winery has picked up a number of international awards, beating off competition from more established corners of the wine world such as Burgundy and California.

2540 South Service Rd, Jordan Station, Ontario L0R 1S0
www.leclosjordanne.com

Mission Hill Family Estate Okanagan Valley, West Canada
Cabernet Sauvignon-Merlot, Five Vineyards (red)

Mission Hill has arguably done more to put the Okanagan Valley on the map than any other wine producer. It is the work of Anthony von Mandl, who was inspired by the pioneering California wine producer, Robert Mondavi. Von Mandl constructed a hugely impressive winery overlooking Lake Ontario, and he oversaw the production of a no-less impressive range of wines, which have won numerous top international prizes all over the world. Among Mission Hill's most remarkable bottlings is the top wine, Oculus, a rich Bordeaux blend. But an affordable glimpse into the flavours and style of what is one of Canada's most expensive reds, can be found in the Five Vineyards Cabernet Sauvignon-Merlot. Produced from the same South Okanagan vineyards as Oculus, it has subtle pepper and spice to point up flavours of red berries and dark cherries.

1730 Mission Hill Rd, West Kelowna, British Columbia V4T 2E4
www.missionhillwinery.com

Quails' Gate Estate Winery Okanagan Valley, West Canada
Chasselas-Pinot Blanc-Pinot Gris (white)

A blend of Chasselas, Pinot Blanc, and Pinot Gris is not one that you come across very often. Chasselas is a grape variety more commonly associated with Switzerland, while Pinots Blanc and Gris are usually vinified on their own in Alsace and elsewhere. But Quails' Gate has proved these grapes can come together to make something refreshing, and at an affordable price, too. It starts with hints of citrus, moves through starfruit, and ends with apples and matches well with seafood. It is produced by a medium-sized but extremely professional winery, that has been working in this region since it was founded by the Stewart family in 1960, and has been doing a fine job with non-hybrid grapes since the 1990s.

3303 Boucherie Rd, Kelowna, British Columbia V1Z 2H3
www.quailsgate.com

Road 13 Winery Okanagan Valley, West Canada
Honest John's Red

In Honest John's Red, Cabernet Sauvignon and Merlot, enriched by Cabernet Franc and Syrah, meld to offer characteristic South Okanagan fruit that does not overpower. Its earthy cherry flavours end in sun-tanned spice. Made by Jean-Martin Bouchard, it is a worthy entry point to Mick and Pam Luckhurst's Road 13 Winery, which the couple bought in 2003, when it was still known as Golden Mile Cellars. Production here is now increasingly devoted to blends, which the team believes offer more complexity and interest than single-varietal wines. Road 13 also believes in working carefully with oak, and the team have been looking carefully at different sources, toasting levels, and periods of ageing.

13140 Road 13, Oliver, British Columbia V0H 1T0
www.road13vineyards.com

Sandhill Estate Winery Okanagan Valley, West Canada

Pinot Gris (white)

Andrew Peller's Sandhill Estate Winery has been a trailblazer when it comes to producing single-vineyard wines made from grapes including Cabernet Sauvignon and Sangiovese. Peller's winemaker, Howard Soon, produces wines taken from four vineyards – Sandhill Estate, King Family, Phantom Creek, and Osprey Ridge – each of which has its own unique characteristics. While Sandhill's portfolio of "Small Lot" wines deserve a following, there is no doubt that its single-vineyard Pinot Gris is a very fine wine in its own right. A crisp, refreshing white, it uses fruit sourced from the King Family vineyard (operated by the eponymous family) in Naramata in Okanagan, where Lake Okanagan has a cooling influence on the climate. In taste it is redolent of apples and Bartlett pear with citrus highlights.

1125 Richter St, Kelowna, British Columbia V1Y 2K6
www.sandhillwines.ca

Sumac Ridge Estate Winery Okanagan Valley, West Canada

Steller's Jay Brut (sparkling)

Steller's Jay Brut is British Columbia's signature sparkling wine. Made using the traditional method (the same as is used in Champagne, where the fizz-providing second fermentation happens in the bottle), it is a blend of Chardonnay, Pinot Blanc, and Pinot Noir that spends three years ageing on its lees before release. Its flavour spectrum is light on yeastiness and rich with apple and hazelnut, and, like a good champagne, it has the structure and acidity to age for several years in bottle. The wine was one of the many reasons that Canadian drinks group, Vincor, became interested in the estate, which is one of the oldest in British Columbia (founded in 1981), around the turn of the millennium. Vincor eventually bought it from the founder, Harry McWatters, for Can$10 million in 2000. The head winemaker today is Jason James, who assumed control in 2010 after five years working under previous head winemaker, Mark Wendenburg.

17403 Highway 97N, Summerland, British Columbia V0H1Z0
www.sumacridge.com

Tawse Winery

Niagara Peninsula, East Canada

Sketches of Niagara Riesling (white)

There is a real Old World influence at Riesling specialist, Tawse Winery. In part that is down to the current winemaker, Frenchman Pascal Marchand. But Marchand is following a tradition started by Deborah Paskus, and thoroughly endorsed by owner, Moray Tawse. Sketches of Niagara Riesling is a blend of Niagara Peninsula grapes with an attractive, aromatic character. Stone fruit and clover on the nose give way to pineapple and cream on the palate.

3955 Cherry Ave, Vineland, Ontario L0R 2C0
www.tawsewinery.ca

South America

The two giants of South American wine, Argentina and Chile, help make this continent the largest producer of wine outside Europe. In the past, producers in both countries tended to focus on their domestic markets. Since the 1980s, however, exports have become the priority, and quality has risen exponentially. Argentina, particularly in the Mendoza region in the foothills of the Andes, has made a name for itself with its lush take on Malbec, while Chile has turned Carmenère, another red grape of southwestern French origin, into a speciality. Both countries produce reliably good and affordable reds from classic red grapes such as Cabernet Sauvignon, Merlot, Syrah, and Pinot Noir. For whites, look to Sauvignon Blanc from Chile's cooler climate regions and aromatic Torrontés from Salta in northern Argentina. And don't ignore the sparkling wines and Merlot-based reds coming out of the third country in this section, Brazil, where quality is rising fast.

Chile

Few countries are better at providing good quality everyday wines than Chile. Thanks to the excellent growing conditions across the country, with long, dry summers and plentiful sun, value for money goes with the territory here. For reds, look for brightly fruited wines from Cabernet Sauvignon, Merlot, Syrah, Pinot Noir, and the local speciality, Carmenère. For whites, great value Sauvignon Blanc and Chardonnay are reliable choices.

Amayna (Viña Garcés Silva) San Antonio

Sauvignon Blanc, Leyda Valley (white)

One of Chile's richest families, the Garcés Silva clan, first bought some 700ha (1,730 acres) of land in Leyda in San Antonio for their livestock business. They soon saw the potential for wine in this coastal area, however, planting vines in 1999 and releasing their first wine in 2003. That wine – a Sauvignon Blanc – received a rapturous response, showing Leyda's thrilling potential for the grape variety. With its powerful flavours of grapefruit and herbs, and its bright natural acidity, it was a wine that reflected its terroir. Though other successful wines have since been added to the portfolio, the Sauvignon Blanc remains the original and best at this estate.

Fundo San Andres de Huinca, Camino Rinconada de San Juan, Leyda, San Antonio
www.vgs.cl

Antiyal Maipo

Kuyen, Maipo Valley (red)

A marvellous blend of Syrah, Cabernet Sauvignon, and Carmenère, Maipo Valley Kuyen starts with a blast of ultra-expressive New World fruit but then finishes with a host of intriguing subtleties. It is one of two wines made by the family project of the renowned winemaker Alvaro Espinoza, who has been the most significant figure in the development of organic and biodynamic winemaking in Chile. Started as a homespun garage operation on his parents' farm, the estate now has its own vineyards and a proper winery.

Padre Hurtado 68, Paine, Santiago
www.antiyal.com

Casa Marin San Antonio

Sauvignon Blanc Cypress Vineyard, San Antonio Valley (white)

Sourced from steep slopes just inland from the Pacific, Casa Marin Cypress Vineyard Sauvignon Blanc shows cool-climate crispness and cut, but also generous breadth and depth of flavour. It is typical of the uncompromising approach at Casa Marin, an approach that derives directly from its energetic, driven owner, Mariluz Marín, for whom this project is very much a labour of love. An experienced winemaker, she conceived the project as a vehicle for making terroir wines, wines that express the individuality of the different vineyard plots she planted in the hills some 4km (2½ miles) from the cool waters of the Pacific Ocean. It is among Chile's best boutique wineries, in a country still dominated by large producers.

Lo Abarca, Valle de San Antonio
www.casamarin.cl

Casas del Bosque Casablanca

Sauvignon Blanc Reserva, Casablanca Valley (white)

In Casas del Bosque's Sauvignon Blanc Reserva, the expressive aromas of dried herbs and freshly sliced grapefruit are very appealing. They are backed by citrus and white melon fruit leading to a bright, lifted finish. It proves once again that the Cuneo family have managed to transfer the talents that have made them a success in the realm of department stores to the wine business. That transition began in the 1990s, with plantings in the cool-climate Casablanca Valley, and the company now has some 245ha (605 acres) of high quality vineyard land to draw on in the west of the valley. Winemaking is now in the hands of the talented New Zealander, Grant Phelps (formerly of Viu Manent), who has carried on the consistent progress made here in the past decade.

Hijuela 2 Ex Fundo, Santa Rosa, Casablanca
www.casasdelbosque.cl

Concha y Toro Maipo

Casillero del Diablo Cabernet Sauvignon Reserva, Central Valley (red); Marqués de Casa Concha Carmenère, Peumo Valley (red)

Concha y Toro is a hugely important presence in the Chilean wine scene. It is the country's largest producer, but it is also behind some of the country's best bottles, both at the high-end and, just as importantly for Chile's international image, in its broad and consistently excellent range of affordable wines. The company has three of Chile's best winemakers in Marcelo Papa, Enrique Tirado, and Ignacio Recabarren, who head up a fine team. The entire Casillero del Diablo line offers exceptional value, but the Cabernet Sauvignon shines brightest, with dark berry fruit and just a whiff of oak. The Carmenère in the Marqués de Casa Concha line features remarkable aromatic complexity and an uncanny combination of concentration and softness.

Avenida Virginia Subercaseaux 210, Pirque, Santiago
www.conchaytoro.com

Cono Sur Colchagua
Bicycle Cabernet Sauvignon, Central Valley (red)

Cono Sur certainly benefits from the financial muscle of its parent company, Concha y Toro, but this young company is run as an independent concern and has blazed its own trail since it was established in 1993. It has a range of fine vineyards across the country (including its headquarters at Chimbarongo in the Rapel Valley and extensive holdings in the cool-climate Bío-Bío), where it has been a pioneer of ecologically sensitive viticulture. It has also been at the forefront of a number of other developments in Chile, such as using screwcap closures for premium wines and being among the first wineries in the country to take Pinot Noir seriously. The company is led by the extravagantly talented winemaker, Adolfo Hurtado, who makes good wine across his wide portfolio. Among the highlights is the Bicycles label Central Valley Cabernet Sauvignon. Offering remarkable quality for very little money, this Cabernet is medium-bodied but full of flavours recalling dark berries and cherries, with subtle dried herb aromas.

Chimbarongo, Rapel Valley
www.conosur.com

Cousiño Macul Maipo
Antiguas Reservas Cabernet Sauvignon, Maipo Valley (red)

There is a long and distinguished history of wine production at Maipo Valley stalwart, Cousiño Macul. The company was founded in 1856 by the industrialist Matías Cousiño, basing his headquarters in a part of the Maipo Valley which had first been planted to vines by the Conquistadors. For many years Cousiño Macul was at the forefront of quality Chilean wine, and, after a period in the doldrums, it has spent the past decade regaining its status, with a new winery and vineyards in Buin, further south from Santiago. The Antiguas Reservas is something of a Chilean classic – arguably the stylistically definitive Cabernet in a great Cabernet country – that showcases the brighter, more fruit-driven style sought out by Macul in recent years, without losing the winery's hallmark sophistication and complexity. It shows black cherry fruit with aromas of dried herbs, cedar, and seaweed.

Quilin 7100, Penalolen, Santiago
www.cousinomacul.cl

De Martino Maipo
Organically Grown Cabernet-Malbec, Maipo Valley (red)

De Martino's Organically Grown Cabernet-Malbec blend is tough to beat for generosity of flavour and attractiveness of price, with a very deep colour and well flavoured fruit recalling dark berries, cassis, and blackberries. It is one of many wines produced here that are worthy of the company motto: "Reinventing Chile". This project piggy-backs on the company's bulk wine and juice business, providing the funds for skilled winemaker Marcelo Retamal to experiment and allowing him to travel across the country to find the best regions for the range of different grape varieties he grows.

Manuel Rodríguez 229, Isla de Maipo
www.demartino.cl

Emiliana Colchagua
Natura Chardonnay, Casablanca Valley (white); Natura Merlot, Rapel Valley (red)

Emiliana is a branch of the Concha y Toro family, run as an independent company. Thanks to its work at its Emiliana Orgánico offshoot, it has become one of the world's largest organic and biodynamic wine producers: it currently has some 1,000ha (2,470 acres) of vineyards managed under organic and biodynamic methods. The unoaked, organically grown Chardonnay Natura Casablanca Valley is a delicious tropical fruit salad in a glass, with zesty acidity lifting the finish and inviting repeated sipping. The Merlot Natura Rapel Valley is every bit as good, showing perfectly ripened, exceptionally pure fruit recalling plums and cherries.

Nueva Tajamar 481 Torre Sur 701, Las Condes, Santiago
www.emiliana.cl

Errázuriz Estate Aconcagua
Sauvignon Blanc, Casablanca Valley (white)

Owned by the Chadwick family, Errázuriz Estate has been an important and pioneering producer in Chile for decades. It has been among the first to experiment with such innovations as organic and biodynamic viticulture and hillside plantings, using wild yeast for fermentations, and establishing profile-raising joint ventures with companies from other countries (with Mondavi from California, for example). The range is consistently good, with the Sauvignon Blanc Casablanca Valley among the standouts. This attention-grabbing white is highly aromatic and full of zesty flavours, with just a touch of sweetness to take the edge off the driving acidity.

Avenida Antofagasta, Panquehue, V Region
www.errazuriz.com

Falernia Elqui
Carmenère-Syrah Reserva, Elqui Valley (red)

The Elqui Valley used to be better known for producing grapes for pisco, Chile's national spirit (a form of brandy), than wine, but the Italian-run Falernia has changed all that. Taking advantage of the endless clear blue skies (the valley is also known for its stargazers – both astronomers and astrologers), Falernia makes a range of fine, bright, pure wines. The Carmenère-Syrah Reserva is an unusual blend that proves instantly convincing, marrying Carmenère's intense black fruit with Syrah's more open, juicy, red berry character into a seamless whole.

Ruta 41, Km 46, Casilla 8 Vicuña, IV Region
www.falernia.com

Haras de Pirque Maipo
Carmenère, Maipo Valley (red)

Haras de Pirque's Carmenère, Maipo Valley is a dark and assertively flavoursome red that is packed with black fruit and accents of anise and espresso coffee beans. The finish is firm and geared toward robust foods. It is produced at a visually arresting horseshoe-shaped winery that has been constructed in a hilly amphitheatre, surrounded by vines and paddocks full of thoroughbred horses. With the vineyards established in the Pirque sub-region of Maipo in 1992, Eduardo Suave and his son, also Eduardo, run this ambitious operation that includes a wine made in partnership with Piero Antinori, the celebrated Tuscan producer.

Camino San Vicente, Sector Macul, Pirque, Casilla 247 Correo Pirque
www.harasdepirque.com

Kingston Family Vineyards Casablanca
Tobiano Pinot Noir, Casablanca Valley (red)

Sourced from the Casablanca Valley, Kingston Family Vineyards Pinot Noir Tobiano is a contender for Chile's best Pinot Noir. It is perfectly ripened and very tastefully wrought, with delicate notes of strawberry and cherry and commensurately restrained oak. Kingston began its life back in the 1900s, when Carl John Kingston arrived in Chile from Michigan on the look out for gold. He soon purchased a 3,000ha (7,410 acre) farm in coastal Casablanca, on which his descendants planted a vineyard in the late 1990s. Today, the family use about 10% of the fruit from the vineyard in their own excellent range of distinctive wines, with the rest sold on to other producers.

No visitor facilities
www.kingstonvineyards.com

La Reserva de Caliboro Maule
Erasmo, Maule Valley (red)

The debonair Italian Francesco Marone Cinzano is the heir to both a counthood and an iconic drinks business (his family owns the Cinzano brand among others). But he is also a vital presence in the recent renaissance of Chile's Maule Valley wine scene, thanks to his involvement in La Reserva de Caliboro. Cinzano teamed up with the Chilean Manzano family for the project, which is located in the rolling hills of the highlands that lie to the east of the central valley, with the vineyards themselves part of a large 19th-century estate. The project is focused on just one wine: the red blend Erasmo. The fruit – Cabernet Sauvignon, Merlot, and Cabernet Franc – is sourced from low-yielding, dry-farmed vineyards by the Perquilauquén River. The wine has a firm edge of spicy, smoky oak that makes it a candidate for cellaring, yet the pure, fresh berry fruit notes enable it to excel immediately with robust foods.

Carretera San Antonio, Caliboro Km 5.8, San Javier
www.caliboro.com

Lapostolle
Colchagua

Casa Carmenère, Rapel Valley (red); Cuvée Alexandre Chardonnay Atalayas Vineyard, Casablanca Valley (white)

The Marnier Lapostolle family – the people behind the Grand Marnier liqueur brand – have brought the know-how to this project, headquartered in Apalta in the Colchagua Valley where Michel Rolland is the consultant winemaker. The entry-level Carmenère Casa Rapel Valley shows admirably deep colour and flavour with blackberry fruit and lots of gutsy tannin. The Cuvée Alexandre Chardonnay is exceptional for its combination of ripe, rich fruit with a zesty, spicy finish that is driven by outstanding acidity.

Camino San Fernando a Pichilemu, Km 36, Cunaquito, Comuna Sta Cruz
www.casalapostolle.com

Leyda San Antonio

Pinot Noir Las Brisas Vineyard, Leyda Valley (red)

As the name suggests, this fine producer, one of the very best to have emerged in Chile in the past decade, was the first to arrive in San Antonio's Leyda Valley. Thanks largely to Leyda Valley, San Antonio, which benefits from cooling ocean breezes due to its proximity to the Pacific Ocean, has become a vinous hotspot, with a number of producers planting vineyards. The region depends for its life on an 8km (5-mile) pipeline (constructed in 1997) that brings water from the Maipo River. Leyda (both the region and the producer) captured attention from its first releases, for wines that were unusually elegant, fresh, and refined. If you need convincing that Chile can make top Pinot Noir, then the Las Brisas Vineyard expression is a great place to start. It does the trick nicely with bright cherry and strawberry fruit with freshness, lift, and an endearingly spicy edge.

Avenida Del Valle 601 of.22, Ciudad Empresarial, Santiago
www.leyda.cl

Loma Larga Vineyards Casablanca

Chardonnay, Casablanca Valley (white)

Loma Larga Vineyards Chardonnay is a beautifully balanced expression of Casablanca Chardonnay. It shows tasteful oak notes recalling toasted nuts and woodsmoke that are nicely interwoven with juicy hints of ripe peaches. Like all the wines produced at this coastal Casablanca estate, it is marked by finesse and a lively freshness. Owned by the Diaz family – who have been involved in wine since the late 19th century – the company began planting in Casablanca in 1999. Today, they have some 148ha (365 acres) of vineyards planted in hillside and foothills, although it uses only the best blocks for its own wines (amounting to some 40ha/97 acres in total), with the rest sold off to other wineries. From low yields, the French winemaker Emeric Genevière-Montignac makes seriously characterful and incisive wines that are not afraid to challenge ideas about what Chilean wine can do.

Avenida Gertrudis Echeñique 348, Depto. A, Las Condes, Santiago
www.lomalarga.com

Los Vascos Colchagua

Cabernet Sauvignon, Colchagua Valley (red)

Ripe and generously fruity without being obvious, Los Vascos Cabernet Sauvignon from the Colchagua Valley is all about blackberry fruit, with very subtle oak but plenty of fine-grained tannins that lend a gutsy, structured feel to the finish. It comes from a traditionally minded winery that, since 1988, has benefited from the investment and know-how of the Rothschild family behind legendary Bordeaux first growth, Château Lafite. In recent years, the company has taken a number of steps to improve quality, such as new plantings on the hillsides and sourcing its white wines from the cooler climate of the Casablanca Valley.

Camino Pumanque Km 5, Peralillo, VI Region
www.vinalosvascos.com

NAVIGATE A WINE LIST

When friends or family have gathered at a restaurant for a relaxing meal, few things can interrupt the flow of conversation like a big wine list. The host, or appointed wine "expert", can spend too much time studying the options and making decisions – unless that person remembers a few wine list shortcuts. Trust the waiter or sommelier to give generally good advice, just as you trust the chef to make good food, but use these tips to make the process of ordering wine less stressful and time-consuming.

1 **Look for half-bottles** Save money and make the meal more interesting by ordering two or more 375-ml half-bottles; this works particularly well if there are two of you. Try matching wines to different courses. If one of you is having fish as a starter and the other is having duck, you can each choose a completely different wine appropriate for your dish.

2 **Look for champagne alternatives** When ordering bubbly, remember that you pay a premium for sparkling wine produced in the Champagne region of France. Many alternatives from Spain, California, and elsewhere are made from the same grape varieties and use the same methods as those that are used in Champagne. Try a Spanish Freixenet Excelencia Brut, for example, or a Californian Laetitia Vineyard Brut Cuvée.

3 **Point to prices** A good way to subtly indicate your desired price range to the waiter or sommelier – without blurting out, "We'll have the cheapest plonk on the list!" – is to have the waiter watch while you point to one or two of the prices on the wine list and say, "We would like something in this range". The waiter or sommelier should then help you to find something in that price bracket to suit your palate and to complement your meal.

4 **Least but not last** The least expensive wine on the list may actually be a very nice bottle, but few people buy it for fear of appearing stingy. It's better to be wary of the second lowest-priced wine. Restaurants know that many people will edge up one step from the lowest, and so they may offer a truly cheap wine and put a much higher mark-up on it. Ask the waiter or sommelier if they would recommend the wine and, if in doubt, choose the next bottle up.

5 Location, location, location

Understand that wine prices tend to increase as the region in which a wine was made shrinks. A red burgundy labelled Bourgogne (Burgundy), meaning that its grapes could have come from virtually anywhere in the greater Burgundy wine region, would be the least expensive burgundy on the list; a burgundy from a smaller area, such as the Hautes-Côtes, would be more expensive; one from a highly rated village, such as Gevrey-Chambertin, would be costlier still, and a Gevrey-Chambertin with an individual vineyard name on the label would be the most expensive burgundy on the list.

6 Don't let star power sway you

Sometimes a modest-sounding wine at a low price will be a better choice than a more expensive bottle from a famous estate. For example, Château Greysac's "Grand Vin" in most vintages will be smoother and less pricey than the second wine from the highly rated Château Calon Ségur.

7 Beware of vaguely famous names

Do not let a famous-sounding name persuade you to buy unless you really know what it is. The famous Château Lafite-Rothschild, for example, is often confused with similar sounding châteaux. These may be great estates, but they are not Lafite-Rothschild.

8 Ensure fortified wine is ready to drink

Restaurants may offer expensive vintage port that is too young to be enjoyable. Ideally it needs more than a decade after the vintage to come round. If in doubt, choose crusted and late-bottled vintage styles that are designed for immediate drinking.

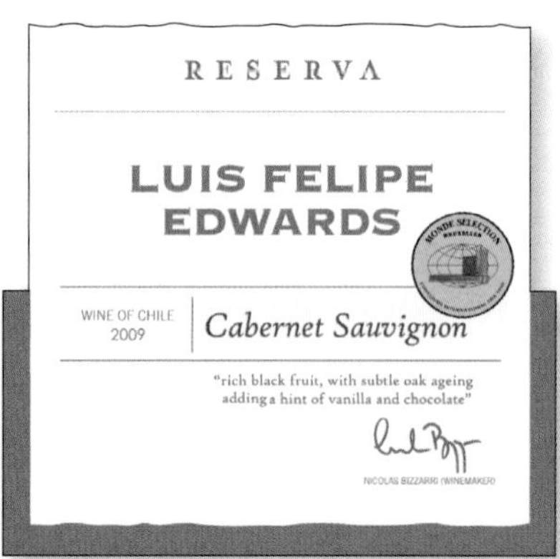

Luis Felipe Edwards Colchagua

Cabernet Sauvignon Reserva, Colchagua Valley (red)

A transformation has occurred at LFE in the past decade. Formerly a producer of formulaic bulk wine, the company started bottling its own brands in the 1990s, the first step on a road that has seen it become one of Chile's most improved producers. Rapid expansion followed, with LFE adding new plantings in Leyda on the hillsides in the Colchagua Valley where the winery is based. The Cabernet Sauvignon Reserva, Colchagua Valley, offers a delicious taste of the company's improvement. Softly ripe but still packed with character and utter sophistication, this shows lovely dark berry fruit edged with soft tannins.

Fundo San Jose de Puquillay, Nancagua, VI Region
www.lfewines.com

Miguel Torres Curicó

Santa Digna Carmenère Reserva, Central Valley (red)

Already world-renowned for his pioneering work in his native Catalonia, Miguel Torres arrived in Chile in the 1970s and promptly repeated the trick. Torres invested heavily in the country, planting vineyards and importing all the latest winemaking equipment, helping to inspire a generation of Chilean producers to take the steps they needed to make high quality premium wine. He also pioneered wine tourism and organic viticulture. The Santa Digna Carmenère Reserva is among the most graceful and restrained of Chile's more affordable Carmenères, and features ripe, deeply flavoured fruit recalling black plums and juicy Bing cherries.

Panamericana Sur Km 195, Curicó
www.migueltorres.cl

Montes Colchagua

Limited Selection Apalta Vineyard Cabernet Carmenère, Colchagua Valley (red); Limited Selection Pinot Noir, Casablanca Valley (red)

The world clamours for good, affordable Pinot Noir but almost never gets it. But they do with Montes Limited Selection Pinot Noir, Casablanca Valley, which is pure, delicate, true to the variety, and downright delicious. In the Limited Selection Apalta Vineyard Cabernet Carmenère, the blend uses Carmenère's intensity to kick Chile's reserved Cabernet into a higher gear, with indisputable success. The company behind this pair of excellent value reds is an old-favourite of Chilean wine drinkers. Over the past quarter of a century, winemaker Aurelio Montes has brought about a number of improvements, but has never forgotten the company's primary raison d'être: crowd-pleasing premium wines.

Avenida del Valle, Huechuraba, Santiago
www.monteswines.com

Odfjell Vineyards Maipo

Armador Merlot, Maipo Valley (red)

Softly ripe but still packed with character and surprising class for the asking price, Odfjell Vineyards Armador Merlot shows lovely dark berry fruit edged with soft tannins. It is part of a fine portfolio of characterful wines produced by a firm that was set up by the Norwegian shipping magnate Dan Odfjell, who fell in love with Chile during a business trip. Odfjell bought some land in the hills to the west of Santiago, planting his first vines in 1992.

Camino Viejo a Valparaiso 7000, Padre Hurtado, Santiago
www.odfjellvineyards.cl

Pérez Cruz Maipo

Cabernet Sauvignon Reserva, Maipo Valley (red)

There is something winningly humble about Pérez Cruz's winery in Huelquén. Formerly a store house for alfalfa, almonds, and cattle, today it plays host to the Pérez family winemaking operation that has quietly established itself as a fine producer of authentic Alto Maipo red wines since the family first planted vines here in 1994. The Pérez Cruz Cabernet Sauvignon Reserva is a fine introduction to the philosophy here: a traditionally styled Maipo Cabernet, it features dried herb and cedar aromas, dark cherry fruit, and a gutsy finish that calls out for a grilled steak.

Fundo Liguai de Huelquén, Paine, Maipo Alto
www.perezcruz.com

Quintay Casablanca

Clava Sauvignon Blanc, Casablanca Valley (white)

Zesty and refreshing, Quintay Sauvignon Blanc from the Casablanca Valley shows lively aromas of citrus and freshly cut grass, leading into persistent flavours of Honeydew melon and grapefruit. It is one of the products of an intriguing (relative) newcomer on the Chilean scene, which started in 2005 with the intention of making top-quality Sauvignon Blanc. Eight partners, most of them grape-growers, came together to form the project, which has gone on to develop a range of wines that always show an impressive attention to detail and no lack of ambition.

San Sebastián 2871, Office 201, Las Condes, Santiago
www.quintay.com

San Pedro Curicó

Castillo de Molina Sauvignon Blanc Reserva, Elqui Valley (white)

San Pedro is one of Chile's biggest wine producers, with a huge range of wines sold both domestically and in export markets around the world. When it comes to quality, it has been through some peaks and troughs, however, and the beginning of the 2000s was certainly an example of the latter, when management changes and a policy of pursuing quantity over quality had a deleterious effect on the wines. In the latter part of the past decade, however, San Pedro has been soaring again, thanks in no small part to the work of the talented head winemaker, Marco Puyo, who has put the emphasis on terroir and elegance in a series of excellent releases. An intense but still civilized expression of the grape variety from the Elqui Valley, the Castillo de Molina Sauvignon Blanc Reserva shows cut grass, gunflint, and grapefruit aromas backed by citrus and white melon fruit.

Avenida Vitacura 4380, Piso 6, Vitacura, Santiago
www.sanpedro.cl

Santa Rita Maipo

Sauvignon Blanc 120, Central Valley (white); Cabernet Sauvignon Medalla Real, Maipo Valley (red)

Santa Rita may have a long history of wine production, but it has not sat still. Recent years have seen the winery, owned by the Claro group, spread its wings with new plantings in quality regions such as Colchagua and Limarí, and the company has employed the celebrated Australian winemaker and thinker, Brian Croser, as a consultant. The "120" Sauvignon Blanc is a great value wine with aromas that are expressive but not pungent and citrus fruit that is zesty but never sour. The Medalla Real Cabernet Sauvignon combines world-class complexity with a firmly Chilean distinctiveness and wonderful cedar and spice accents.

Camino Padre Hurtado 0695, Alto Jahuel/Buin, Maipo
www.santarita.com

Tabalí Limarí

Chardonnay Reserva Especial, Limarí Valley (white)

Tabalí is a project of Guillermo Luksic, head of the powerful family behind the San Pedro Tarapacá empire, one of Chile's richest families. In essence it is a joint-venture between Luksic and San Pedro, the same ownership in fact as Viña Leyda. Like Leyda, Tabalí has been a pioneer in one of Chile's exciting new cool-climate regions, in this case the remote dry southern Limarí plateau, around 400km (250 miles) north of Santiago. The first vines were planted in 1993, and they have led to robust wines with a distinctive edge of fresh, bright, fruit. Boldly oaked but still balanced, the Chardonnay Reserva Especial starts with aromas of woodsmoke and toasted nuts, giving way to peach and pineapple fruit with a spicy finish.

Hacienda Santa Rosa de Tabalí Ovalle, Rute Valle del Encanto, Limarí Valley
www.tabali.cl

Undurraga Maipo

Undurraga TH Series Sauvignon Blanc, Leyda Valley (white)

Undurraga TH (for "Terroir Hunter") Series Sauvignon Blanc is a striking expression of this variety of grape with zingy, lively aromas yet a broad, textured feel. The fruit tastes of citrus and white melon and finishes on the palate with a zesty lemon note. It is evidence of the transformation of a producer that had been in some trouble at the end of the 1990s, thanks to a lack of leadership caused by divisions in the ownership. Now solely in the hands of the Colombian Picciotto family, with a new winemaking team, it is back on track.

Camino Melipilla, Km 34, Santa Ana, Maipo
www.undurraga.cl

Valdivieso Curicó

Cabernet Sauvignon Reserva, Maipo Valley (red)

In Chile, Valdivieso was once all but synonymous with sparkling wine. That is no surprise: it was founded in Santiago in 1879 by Alberto Valdivieso, who was inspired by the sparkling wines he loved from France and set about recreating them in his native land. Valdivieso continued as a fizz specialist until the 1990s, when the company began to experiment with still wines, and today it is the latter that attract the most critical attention, although sparkling wines are still made in high volumes. The New Zealander Brett Jackson is now in charge of winemaking, and he turns out a broad selection of good quality bottles in a range that includes both reds and whites. The Cabernet Sauvignon Reserva from the Maipo Valley is rich and deeply flavoured, a satisfying Cabernet that is driven by dark berry fruit and structured by supple tannins and toasty oak.

Luz Pereira 1849, Lontué
www.valdiviesovineyard.com

Ventisquero Maipo

Sauvignon Blanc Root 1, Casablanca Valley (white); Cabernet Sauvignon Root 1, Colchagua Valley (red)

As the name of the brand, Root 1, might suggest, this pair of wines is made from un-grafted vines (vines that are planted with their own rootstocks; most vines in the world have the fruiting variety grafted onto a different rooting variety). Though opinion is split in the wine world about whether this makes any difference to the finished wine, these wines are most certainly delicious. The Sauvignon Blanc is crisp and refreshing, with white melon fruit accented with a lemon-lime edge. The Cabernet Sauvignon is deeply flavoured and quite soft in texture, with herbal aromas. First established in 1998, Ventisquero is a relatively recent addition to the Chilean wine scene and has been backed with massive investment (US$60m by 2006) from parent company, Agrosuper. It has a talented winemaking team headed by Felipe Toso, with ex-Penfolds Grange winemaker, John Duval, a consultant.

La Estrella Avenida, 401, Office 5P, Punta de Cortés Sector, Rancagua
www.ventisquero.com

Veramonte Casablanca

Chardonnay Reserve, Casablanca Valley (white)

Veramonte's Chardonnay Reserve from the Casablanca Valley seems impossibly complex and complete for the money, with toasty aromas, broad peach and tropical fruit, and a citrus-tinged finish. A fine wine that exemplifies the quality on offer at this Casablanca Valley pioneer, which first sprang to world attention with crisp whites from Sauvignon Blanc in the 1990s. Managed by the Huneeus family, it remains identified with the Casablanca Valley – and its headquarters remain in the elevated eastern part of the valley. But it has begun to expand its horizons for its red wines, and has built a new winery for that purpose in Marchihue (Colchagua).

Ruta 68, Km 66 Casablanca
www.veramonte.com

Viña Casablanca
Casablanca

Cefiro Merlot Reserva, Maipo Valley (red); Cefiro Cabernet Sauvignon Reserva, Maipo Valley (red)

Viña Casablanca was among the first to put the eponymous, cool-climate valley on the map in the 1980s and 1990s. But for some time now it has been associated with other regions, too, as in this pair of Maipo reds from the Cefira range. The Cefira Merlot shows a core of plum fruit with appealing aromas of cedar, autumn leaves, and subtle oak, whereas the Cefira Cabernet Sauvignon has scents of dried herbs and flavours of dark berries. Both wines show restrained ripeness in a European style.

Rodrido de Araya 1431, Macul, Santiago
www.casablancawinery.com

Viu Manent Colchagua

Estate Collection Chardonnay, Colchagua Valley (white); Cabernet Sauvignon Reserva, Colchagua Valley (red)

Viu Manent started its life as a provider of basic jug wines, headquartered in Santiago, in the 1930s. It began to get more serious about its output after acquiring some vineyards of its own in its current base in Cunaco in the Colchagua Valley in 1966, and today it has become an exciting quality producer. Viu Manent makes exquisite reds, but the Estate Collection Chardonnay should not be eclipsed, as it is generously fruity but very deftly oaked. The Cabernet Sauvignon Reserva, meanwhile, is phenomenally complex for the money, with intriguing notes of cedar, dried herbs, black fruits, and subtly spicy oak. Recently the company has expanded its vineyards with new plantings in western Colchagua, Casablanca, and Leyda.

Santa Cruz, Colchagua
www.viumanent.cl

Von Siebenthal Aconcagua

Parcella #7, Aconcagua Valley (red)

Von Siebenthal's Parcella #7 is a sophisticated Bordeaux-style blend (Cabernet Sauvignon, Merlot, and Cabernet Franc) that is so complex, convincing, and classy it should cause sleepless nights for wine producers in Bordeaux. Intricate, yet remarkably harmonious, it is a fine example of the stylish wines being produced at Von Siebenthal, which has had a remarkably swift ascent towards the top of the list of Chile's best wineries. Owned by the charming and ambitious Swiss lawyer Mauro von Siebenthal, along with four business partners, it arrived on the scene with an impressive debut vintage in 2002, but quality has only improved since then. Today it produces a range of fine red wines, all of them designed to showcase the potential of the Aconcagua Valley, with its three main vineyards located in the Panquehue area of the valley.

Calle O'Higgins, Panquehue, Aconcagua
www.vinavonsiebenthal.com

Argentina

Cosmopolitan Argentina has always been one of the world's largest consumers of wine; now it is also one of its best producers. Lush, powerful Malbec from Mendoza is the country's flagship red variety; aromatic, floral Torrontés from northern Salta its most distinctive white. But waves of Spanish and Italian immigrants in the 19th and early 20th century brought a a huge selection of grape varieties with them, and diversity still rules here.

Alta Vista Luján de Cuyo, Mendoza

Malbec Classic, Mendoza (red)

With a background in champagne – they were formerly owners of the Piper-Heidsieck brand – it is no surprise that the French d'Aulan family arrived in Argentina in the 1980s with the intention of making sparkling wines. By 1996, however, they had switched their attentions to Malbec, starting up Alta Vista in a restored 19th-century winery. The wines have developed significantly since then, with better balance and more judicious use of oak, as in the Malbec Classic, Mendoza. Juicy and soft, it has deep flavours of dark cherry that show lovely purity and just a hint of spice around the edges.

Alzaga 3972, Luján de Cuyo, Mendoza
www.altavistawines.com

Altos Las Hormigas Luján de Cuyo, Mendoza

Malbec, Mendoza (red)

Always among the most intense expressions of Argentine Malbec, Altos Las Hormigas Malbec, Mendoza is nearly black in appearance, with blackberry fruit accented with liquorice and espresso. The name of the project translates as "ants heights", relating both to the colonies of ants that were found here when the vineyard was planted and the Argentine expression for hard, careful work, "a job for ants". An Italian-Argentine joint-venture, it has become increasingly successful since its foundation in the mid-1990s, with vineyard manager Carlos Vazquez and Italian winemaker Attilio Pagli helped by the consultant winemaker, Alberto Antonini.

9 de Julio, 309-5500 Mendoza
www.altoslashormigas.com

Benegas Luján de Cuyo, Mendoza

Don Tiburcio, Mendoza (red)

The Benegas family have been involved in wine for many years, having owned the Trapiche winery until the 1970s, and with Tiburcio Benegas widely considered one of the founding fathers of Mendoza's wine industry. After a hiatus from the forefront of the industry, the family returned in 1998 with the launch of Benegas. Drawing on fruit from a family vineyard in Maipú, Benegas specializes in reds such as Don Tiburcio, a delicious blend of all five Bordeaux varieties with ripe, open fruit and serious structure from fine-grained tannin and spicy French oak.

Cruz de Piedra, Maipú, Mendoza
www.bodegabenegas.com

Catena Zapata Luján de Cuyo, Mendoza

Chardonnay, Mendoza (white); Malbec, Mendoza (red)

After decades of hard work and intelligent experimentation, Catena Zapata is justly regarded in the very highest echelon of Argentine wine. Led by Nicolás Catena and his daughter, Laura, Catena has broken new ground in the understanding of high-altitude viticulture and Malbec clones, and it now produces excellent wines across its broad portfolio. Catena's Chardonnay from Mendoza is a marvel of integrated complexity that outperforms many wines costing twice as much. Their Malbec is pure and poised at every turn, with a very precise balance of components that leaves a sense of seamlessness and supreme quality.

J Cobos, Agrelo, Luján de Cuyo, Mendoza
www.catenawines.com

Chacra Río Negra, Patagonia

Pinot Noir Barda, Patagonia (red)

One of Argentina's most exciting wineries proves that this country is about much more than the two "Ms" for which it is internationally known: Malbec and Mendoza. Based in Patagonia, Chacra specializes in Pinot Noir, produced from extremely old vines, including some planted as far back as the 1930s. The project has a serious fine wine pedigree: it was founded in 2004 by Piero

Incisa della Rocchetta, of the famous Super Tuscan wine, Sassicaia, who purchased a plot of abandoned Pinot Noir vines. He recruited the Danish winemaker Hans Vinding-Diers (of nearby Noemía), who makes impressively silky, elegant Pinot Noirs such as Barda.

Avenida Roca 1945, General Roca, Rio Negro 8332
www.bodegachacra.com

Clos de los Siete Uco Valley, Mendoza

Mendoza Red Wine

Michel Rolland, the internationally renowned, Bordeaux-based winemaking consultant, is the driving force behind this unique, ambitious project. Rolland recruited a group of investors to plant some 850ha (2,100 acres) of vineyards in the high-altitude Vista Flores in the Uco Valley, and then divided the property into seven parts, with each partner making their own wines plus providing a proportion of a single, shared wine. That wine, Clos de los Siete, is a five-grape blend based predominantly on Malbec. It is strikingly polished but certainly not lacking in power, with concentrated fruit and amazingly fine-grained tannins.

Tunuyán, Mendoza
www.dourthe.com

Cobos Luján de Cuyo, Mendoza

Felino Chardonnay, Mendoza (white); Felino Malbec, Mendoza (red)

The history of Cobos dates back to 1997, when the husband-and-wife winemaking duo of Luis Barraud and Andrea Marchiori went on a tour of California wine country. Inspired by what they saw, they returned to Argentina to found Cobos in partnership with the Californian winemaker, Paul Hobbs. In time, they added a high-tech winery and they are now making some top quality modern wines, with some of the fruit drawn from Andrea's father's vineyard in Perdriel. Felino Chardonnay is opulent but still fresh and beautifully balanced, with ripe peach and pineapple fruit edged with spicy oak. The Malbec is ripe and rich without seeming heavy, showing plum and dark berry notes and highly polished tannins.

Costa Flores y Ruta 7, Perdriel, Luján de Cuyo, Mendoza
www.vinacobos.com

Colomé Calchaquí Valley, Salta

Torrontés, Calchaquí Valley (white); Estate Malbec, Calchaquí Valley (red)

Owned since 2001 by Swiss businessman Donald Hess, Colomé is one of Argentina's oldest wineries, dating back to 1831. But what really marks this producer out is its altitude: the winery itself is at 2,200m (7,200ft) above sea level; its highest vineyards are at more than 3,100m (10,200ft), among the highest in the world. The wines are as arresting as their home. Torrontés is flamboyantly floral and opulently flavoursome, but balanced by bright acidity. The Estate Malbec is full of weighty, dark-toned fruit braced by fine-grained tannins and restrained oak.

Ruta Provincial 53 Km 20, Molinos 4419, Provincia de Salta
www.bodegacolome.com

Decero Luján de Cuyo, Mendoza

Malbec Remolinos Vineyard, Agrelo District (red)

One of Argentina's most exciting new producers, Decero started from scratch ("decero" in Spanish) in the early 2000s, with its first vintage in 2006. Its home is Agrelo, at 1,050m (3,400ft) altitude, where it concentrates exclusively on reds grown in its Remolinos estate vineyard. Few wines from anywhere can match the appeal of the delicious, plum-flavoured Remolinos Vineyard Malbec's texture, which is uncanny in its balance of inviting softness and focused structure.

Bajo las Cumbres 9003, Agrelo, Mendoza
www.decero.com

Dominio del Plata Winery Luján de Cuyo, Mendoza

Crios de Susana Balbo Torrontés, Salta (white); Crios de Susana Balbo Cabernet Sauvignon, Mendoza (red)

Trained as a nuclear physicist, Susana Balbo chose instead to apply her intellect to making wine. She made her name working at Catena Zapata, founding Dominio del Plata with her husband and colleague, the viticulturist Pedro Marchevsky, in 1999. With fruit from Salta in the north of Argentina, the Crios Torrontés is among Argentina's most perfumed and luscious, with sweet richness balanced by refreshing acidity. The Cabernet Sauvignon achieves a laudable combination of grace and muscle, with fruit recalling dark cherries and blackberries with tastefully restrained oak.

Cochabamba 7801, Agrelo (5507), Mendoza
www.dominiodelplata.com

Doña Paula Luján de Cuyo, Mendoza

Estate Torrontés, Cafayate Valley (white)

Doña Paula make a remarkably balanced and complete rendition of the exciting Torrontés grape variety with gorgeous floral aromatics followed by rich flavours and a focused finish. It is one of the flagship wines of this consistently good but forward-looking producer, which is owned by the Claro Group, a major player in wine across the Andes in Chile. Energetic winemaker Edgardo del Popolo makes a wide range of wines, both red and white, and is well respected in Argentina for his fastidious and skilful approach.

Av Colón 531, CP 5500, Ciudad, Mendoza
www.donapaula.com.ar

Fabre Montmayou Luján de Cuyo, Mendoza
Malbec Reserva, Mendoza (red)

In 1992, the Frenchman Hervé Joyaux Fabre set up his Argentine wine business with his partner Montmayou. Somewhat confusingly, the Mendoza part of the operation was named Domaine Vistalba, while the Patagonian subsidiary was called Infinitus, although today both wineries make wines under both the Fabre Montmayou and Phebus labels. No matter, the wines, such as the Malbec Reserva from Mendoza, are consistently good. Dark cherry fruit is what this is all about, with very deep flavours and just a hint of sweetness that peeks out from under the soft tannins.

Roque Saenz Peña, Vistalba, Luján de Cuyo, Mendoza
www.domainevistalba.com

Familia Zuccardi Maipú, Mendoza
Santa Julia Malbec Reserva, Mendoza (red); Tempranillo Q, Mendoza (red)

José Alberto Zuccardi is an irresistible force of nature, who has charmed and willed his family company to the forefront of Argentine wine. He's a man who understands that a successful wine business is not solely about wine: clever marketing and a convivial approach to wine tourism (Zuccardi's eastern Mendoza HQ features a restaurant, art gallery, and hot air balloon tours alongside the production facilities) can also raise the profile. It helps that the quality of wines produced in his burgeoning empire are as good as they are. The Santa Julia Malbec Reserva is consistently satisfying, with delicious dark plum and berry fruit enveloped in soft, ripe tannins. The Tempranillo Q is wonderfully flavoursome and very well made with spicy oak framing gorgeous dark cherry fruit.

Ruta Provincial 33 Km 7.5, Maipú, Mendoza
www.familiazuccardi.com

Finca Sophenia Uco Valley, Mendoza
Cabernet Sauvignon Reserve, Tupungato (red)

Dark colour and deep flavours recalling black fruits suggest that Finca Sophenia Cabernet Sauvignon Reserve might be a rough wine. But looks can deceive: the texture is soft and the finish is delicate and detailed. The estate has shot to fame in Argentina thanks to two key factors: carefully designed and tended, high-altitude (1,200m/3,900ft) vineyards and smart winemaking.

Ruta 89 Km 12.5, Camino a los Arboles, Tupungato, Mendoza
www.sophenia.com.ar

O Fournier San Carlos, Mendoza
B Crux, Uco Valley (red)

Banker-turned-wine producer José Manuel Ortega Gil-Fournier has developed a mini-empire of wineries around the Spanish-speaking world, with operations in Chile, Spain, and Argentina. The standards are high at all three operations, including Argentina, where Ortega blends fruit from both his own vineyards (around 30% of production) and local producers (70%) in the high-altitude (1,200m/3,900ft) vineyards around San Carlos. His portfolio divides into three ranges: Urban, B Crux, and A Crux, but for quality-value ratio it is hard to beat the B Crux red. A blend based on Tempranillo with Cabernet, Syrah, and Malbec, this is lavishly oaked but still wondrously fruity, with soft texture and a very persistent finish.

Calle Los Indios 5567, La Consulta, Mendoza
www.ofournier.com

Kaiken Luján de Cuyo, Mendoza
Malbec, Mendoza (red); Cabernet Sauvignon, Mendoza (red)

Auerlio Montes is a star in his native Chile, but in recent years he has engaged in winemaking projects in California and Argentina, too. His Argentine business takes its name from the geese that fly across the Andes, and the wines follow on from the style Montes developed back home. Very expressive aromas and invitingly juicy flavours get Kaiken Malbec off to a great start, and a pure, persistent finish is equally impressive. The Cabernet Sauvignon shows darker fruit tones and more grip in the finish, with intense blackberry fruit.

Roque Saenz Pena 5516, Vistalba, Luján de Cuyo, Mendoza
www.kaikenwines.com

Luigi Bosca Luján de Cuyo, Mendoza
Malbec Reserva, Luján de Cuyo (red)

There is a great sense of history at Luigi Bosca: wines have been made here by successive generations of the Arizu family since the 1900s. But this splendid winery is in no way stuck in the past, and the current (fourth) generation of ownership, brothers Alberto and Gustavo, are making modern wines that draw on all the latest winemaking thinking, from their six family-owned vineyards across Luján de Cuyo and Maipú. The Malbec Reserva is an object lesson in the symmetry of Argentine Malbec, with deep, tender fruit that is supported by perceptible – but never overt-tannin and oak.

San Martin 2044, Mayor Drummond, Luján de Cuyo, Mendoza
www.luigibosca.com.ar

Masi Tupungato

Uco Valley, Mendoza

Malbec-Corvina Passo Doble, Uco Valley (red)

With roots in Northeastern Italian wine dating back some six generations, the Boscaini family came to Argentina to make wines with "Argentine soul" and "Venetian style". Using fruit from their high-altitude vineyard in Tupungato, they have certainly fulfilled their brief in the distinctive and delicious Passo Doble. Inspired by the Northeastern Italian technique of making wines from dried grapes, this starts with 70% Malbec that undergoes a second fermentation with 30% semi-dried Corvina. It has notes of ripe black cherries and prunes.

No visitor facilities
www.masi.it

FOOD & WINE
MENDOZA MALBEC

Argentine Malbec, considered the world's best, combines rugged New World characteristics with a gentle Italian sensibility. In the wine, there is plenty of accessible, pure, clean fruit, but the acid backbone gives incredible food-matching ability.

Malbec is the principal grape variety in Mendoza, where it produces wines that are firm, supple, and ripe with notes of plum, cassis, blueberry, black tea, orange rind, violet, and vanilla. The best are arguably from Mendoza's central subzone of Luján de Cuyo, commonly known as the "Bordeaux of Argentina". Here, in addition to the characteristic plummy notes, the wines exhibit anise and floral notes and are paired with discreetly flavoured dishes such as Beef Wellington or Involtini (thin meat slices rolled up around a mixture of Parmesan cheese, eggs, and flavourings).

Mendoza Malbecs pair beautifully with rich, juicy meat dishes like Asado (barbecued meats), fillet of beef with rosemary and tomato confit, and a fragrant spiced rack of lamb. Malbec pairs well with Asian-inspired dishes too, such as wok charred beef tenderloin with lily bulbs, lotus root, and a warm citrus broth. The local empanadas mendocinas, with olives, onions and eggs added to the meat pie, are often served with Malbec rosé.

Malbec's acidic backbone goes well with soy beef and lime.

Mauricio Lorca
Luján de Cuyo, Mendoza
Opalo Malbec Vistaflores Vineyards, Mendoza (red)

With his impressive work at the Eral Bravo, Enrique Foster, and Viña Alicia wineries, Mauricio Lorca had already established himself as a rising star in Argentine wine; someone who has a remarkably deft, light touch for such a big man. Now he is applying his many skills to his own project, which draws on fruit from high-altitude (1,050m/3,400ft) vineyards in the Vista Flores area of the Uco Valley to make some vibrantly characterful and finely balanced wines that are among the best in Argentina. Very dark in colour but supremely soft and succulent, the Vistaflores Vineyards Opalo Malbec shows interesting aromas of wild mushrooms followed by deep, soft fruit flavours that recall black plums.

Brandsen 1039, Perdriel, Luján de Cuyo, Mendoza
www.mauriciolorca.com

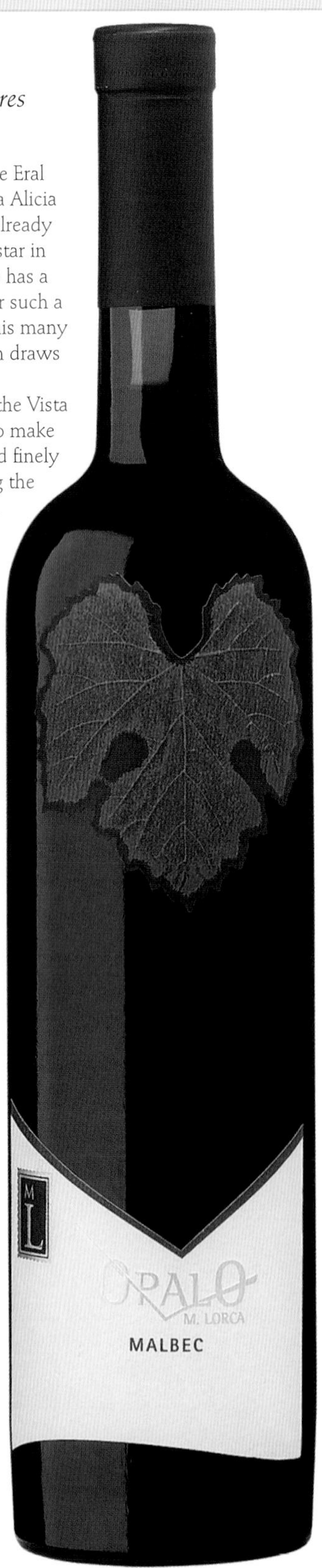

Mendel Wines Luján de Cuyo, Mendoza
Lunta Malbec, Mendoza (red); Mendel Malbec, Mendoza (red)

Few winemakers come with a bigger reputation in Argentina than Roberto de la Mota. Widely respected for his work at Terrazas de los Andes (including making the company's joint-venture with Bordeaux's Château Cheval Blanc, Cheval de los Andes), his own venture with the Sielecki family is now the showcase for his talents. The Lunta bottling is intended for earlier drinking than the flagship wine, but is nevertheless remarkably concentrated and flavoursome. The top wine, Mendel, is one of the best in all of Argentina, with great density but also real refinement.

Terrada 1863, Mayor Drummond (5507), Luján de Cuyo, Mendoza
www.mendel.com.ar

Pascual Toso Maipú, Mendoza
Cabernet Sauvignon, Mendoza (red)

Malbec from Pascual Toso can be very good, but Cabernet Sauvignon really excels. The straight Mendoza bottling features precise balance and meaty, pleasantly earthy flavours in a traditional style that proves irresistible. The wine has benefited from the assistance of the Californian winemaker, Paul Hobbs, who is the consultant at this traditional winery, that was established in the late 19th century, and which is most commonly associated with sparkling wine. Fizz still dominates production – to the tune of 90% – but in the past ten years the company has invested heavily (some US $25 million) in establishing itself in still wines.

Alberdi 808, San Jose 5519, Mendoza
www.bodegastoso.com.ar

Pulenta Estate Luján de Cuyo, Mendoza
Cabernet Sauvignon, Luján de Cuyo (red)

As part of the family that, until the late 1990s, owned the enormous Peñaflor group, the brothers Hugo and Eduardo Pulenta were born into one of Argentina's most powerful wine families. Today they run a business based on a 135ha (335 acre) estate planted by their father, Antonio, in 1991, that specializes in good, polished premium wines. No expense has been spared at Pulenta, which the brothers founded in 2002, and the winemaking kit is second to none. Pick of the wines at everyday prices is the Cabernet Sauvignon, Luján de Cuyo. Soft, suave and sumptuous in all respects, this recalls very ripe plums with a lightly spicy edge but a strikingly smooth, rounded texture.

Gutiérrez 323 (5500), Ciudad, Mendoza
www.pulentaestate.com

Ruca Malén Luján de Cuyo, Mendoza
Cabernet Sauvignon Reserva, Mendoza (red)

Two Frenchmen head up Ruca Malén, bringing a decidedly Gallic flair to proceedings. Jean Pierre Thibaud, former chairman of Bodega Chandon in Argentina, and the Burgundian Jacques Louis de Montalembert source their fruit from Luján de Cuyo and Uco, and the wines have great purity, verve, and aromatic lift. A marvel of softness and subtlety with plenty of restrained power based on perfectly ripened fruit, their Cabernet Sauvignon Reserva could lure a Malbec lover into infidelity.

Ruta Nacional No 7 Km 1059, Agrelo, Luján de Cuyo, Mendoza
www.bodegarucamalen.com

Salentein Uco Valley, Mendoza
Chardonnay Reserve, Uco Valley (white)

With investment from Holland combined with Argentine winemaking experience, Salentein helped pioneer the Uco Valley in the late 1990s from their stunning location high up on the Uco plateau. They have now planted some 700ha (1,730 acres) of vines in the 2,000ha (4,940 acre) estate, with some touching 1,700m (5,600ft) in altitude. Carefully ripened and judiciously oaked, the Chardonnay Reserve, Uco Valley is richly satisfying but also focused and refreshing, with soft peach fruit and a finishing spritz of lemon.

Ruta 89, Los Arboles, Tunuya, Mendoza
www.bodegasalentein.com

Terrazas de los Andes Luján de Cuyo, Mendoza
Malbec, Mendoza (red); Malbec Reserva, Mendoza (red)

Part of the LVMH luxury goods stable that owns top champagne brands Moët & Chandon and Veuve Clicquot among others, Terrazas emerged from the sparkling wine producer, Chandon Argentina. Supple and sweet but nevertheless structured and serious, the entry-level Malbec from Terrazas is exceptionally versatile, with lovely fruit recalling black plums and cherries. The Reserva is more firmly oaked, but is so generously fruited that the finish remains luxuriously soft.

Thames y Cochabamba, Perdriel, Luján de Cuyo, Mendoza
www.terrazasdelosandes.com

Trapiche Maipú, Mendoza
Malbec Broquel, Mendoza (red)

Part of the Peñaflor group – an enormous concern that also includes Finca las Moras, Santa Ana, and Michel Torino – Trapiche is one of Argentina's biggest wine producers. Production exceeds 35 million bottles each year, and the company owns more than 1,250ha (3,090 acres) of vineyards, as well as buying fruit from 300 producers across Mendoza. The operation has been greatly enhanced by the arrival of Daniel Pi as head winemaker, and the range is now much more reliable than has been the case in the past. Boldly oaked but always up to the challenge of counterbalancing the wood with ripe fruit, the Malbec Broquel is a consistent winner thanks to its ripe but energetic core.

Nueva Mayorga, Coquimbito, Maipú, Mendoza
www.trapiche.com.ar

MALBEC

This traditional red grape variety of Bordeaux had to move to the other side of the world to get respect. Now it is the most popular varietal wine of Argentina. Wine drinkers internationally have also fallen for the deep-coloured, full-bodied, velvet-textured, tongue-tingling-spicy red wine.

Malbec is one of the five classic red-wine varieties of Bordeaux, along with Merlot, Cabernet Sauvignon, Cabernet Franc, and Petit Verdot. Another region of Southwest France, Cahors, grows Malbec traditionally, too, and blends it with Tannat and sometimes Merlot. Historically Cahors was known as "the black wine", thanks to its inky-dark colour, and it was often used to give structure to the less powerful wines of Bordeaux. Though this practice no longer occurs today, Malbec in France (sometimes known by the synonyms Côt and Auxerrois) can still tend towards the severe, with abundant palate-drying tannins and a rather tough texture.

Malbec has grown in Argentina for 150 years, and there, too, the wines were traditionally astringent. It is only really in the past decade, however, that Argentine winemakers have learned how to manage the grape so that it produces the more succulent and sensuous style that is the country's signature. Vineyard owners cut back on irrigation to reduce their crop sizes and this helped pump up the flavours. Winemakers handled the grapes more gently to extract those flavours from the grape skins into the wine.

Malbec performs well in Argentina's high-altitude vineyards.

Brazil

Brazil – the land of carnival, football, and beautiful beaches – is starting to make a name for itself as a wine producer with real potential. The country's winemaking heartland is in the relatively cool-climate province of Rio Grande do Sul in the south of the country near to the borders with Argentina and Uruguay. Here you can find good value, high quality sparkling wines, and some excellent Merlot, Brazil's flagship grape variety.

Angheben Encruzilhada do Sul (vineyards)

Touriga Nacional (red)

The founder of Angheben, Idalencio Francisco Angheben, is a highly respected winemaker and professor of oenology. A Brazilian by birth, his family's roots go back to the Austrian-Italian border, where the Angheben name derives from an 11th-century tribe of Celts. Angheben worked for some 30 years teaching viticulture and consulting to Brazilian wineries – and made a number of trips to vineyards around the world – before establishing the winery in 1999. Angheben now manages the estate with his son, Eduardo, and between them they make a broad range of high quality wines that are among the best being produced in Brazil today. Their vineyards are in the Encruzilhada do Sul area of Rio Grande do Sul – Brazil's most important winemaking area – and one of the highlights of their range is the Touriga Nacional. This is a fine Brazilian take on the great Portuguese grape variety, dark and rich with notes of violets and coffee, it has excellent varietal definition.

RS 444, Km 4, Vinhedos Valley, Bento Gonçalves, 95700-000
www.angheben.com.br

Cave Geisse Vinhos da Montanha

Cave Geisse Espumante Brut (sparkling)

Across South America, Brazil is known for making sparkling wines, and few producers have contributed more to its burgeoning reputation for fizz than Cave Geisse. The estate was founded by Mariou Geisse, who originally left his native Chile behind to take up a job at Chandon Brazil, part of the same stable as champagne brand, Moët & Chandon. Having seen just how good the potential was in Brazil for sparkling wine, however, Geisse decided to start out on his own. His project was based in the stunningly picturesque scenery of Serra Gaúcha in the Pinto Bandeira district of Bento Gonçalves. He planted the vineyards to the same grape varieties used in Champagne (Pinot Noir and Chardonnay) and constructed a winery capable of making wines in the same way as the best champagne houses. Quality is very high here in wines such as the deliciously fresh and elegant Espumante Brut.

Linha Jansen, Distrito de Pinto Bandeira-Bento Gonçalves
www.cavegeisse.com.br

Dal Pizzol Faria Lemos

Dal Pizzol Touriga Nacional (red)

There is much to attract the visitor to Dal Pizzol's Faria Lemos headquarters, where the extensive grounds include a restaurant, lakes, a collection of exotic plants, and an enoteca (wine library). The winery itself is a small-scale operation, making 28,000 cases each year. It has a wide range of grape varieties planted, but the standout is the deliciously drinkable, rich, full-fruited red Touriga Nacional.

RST Km 4,8 Faria Lemos, Bento Gonçalves, 95700-000
www.dalpizzol.com.br

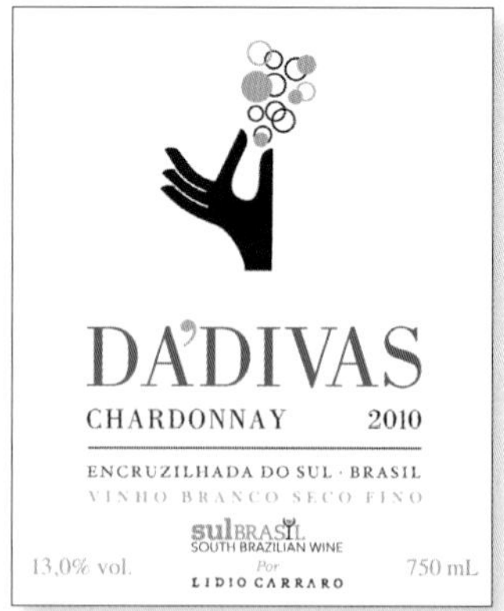

Lidio Carraro Vinhedos Valley and Encruzilhada do Sul

Da'divas Chardonnay (white)

The Carraro family had been growing vines for five generations before they made the decision to start up their own label. This they did in 1998, after a long period of research led them to develop two new vineyards in two areas of southern Brazil: the Vinhedos Valley and Encruzilhada do Sul. By 2002, the first wines were released, and Lidio Carraro began to attract attention for its hand-crafted, artisanal wines. Today the family exports to 15 countries, and they follow a winemaking philosophy that emphasizes terroir and purity of fruit – a purity that is enhanced by eschewing the use of oak. In the Brazilian context, the prices for these wines are high. Internationally speaking, however, wines like the beautifully pure and concentrated Da'divas Chardonnay are an absolute bargain.

RS 444 Km 21, Vinhedos Valley, Bento Gonçalves, 95700-000
www.lidiocarraro.com

Miolo Vinhedos Valley

Miolo Merlot Terroir (red)

An Italian influence is very much in evidence at Miolo. Its roots go back to the turn of the 20th century, when Giuseppe Miolo, one of the many Italian immigrants to arrive in Brazil at that time, invested his savings in a small plot of vineyard. Today, Miolo is a major player in Brazilian wine, encompassing six subsidiaries, and owning a total 1,150ha (2,840 acres) of vineyards. If volumes are high, quality has not suffered, and French consultant winemaker Michel Rolland has made his presence felt in quality wines such as the luscious, juicy, refined, and serious Miolo Merlot Terroir.

RS 444 Km 21, Vinhedos Valley, Bento Gonçalves, 95700-000
www.miolo.com.br

Perini Farroupilha

NV: Casa Perini Prosecco Spumante (sparkling)

Though the Perini family has been making wine in Brazil for generations, it was not until Benildo Perini took the helm at the family firm in 1970 that it began to take on its modern form. Before then, the family had specialized in making simple wines for the undemanding local market, but Benildo had other, more ambitious ideas. He set about the task of making wines that would appeal to wine drinkers across the country and internationally, and the winery grew in scope and size. Today, the family have some 92ha (227 acres) of vineyards and they produce around 16.5 million litres (4.3 million gallons) of wine a year at their base in Garibaldi in the Trentino Valley where an Italian influence remains strong. By common consent, the sparkling wines are the highlight of the large range, specifically the deliciously light, effervescent, crisp, and refreshing NV: Casa Perini Prosecco Spumante, which would not be out of place in Prosecco's Italian homeland, the Veneto.

Santos Anjos, Farroupilha-RS Caixa Postal 83 CEP 95180-000
www.vinicolaperini.com.br

Pizzato Vinhedos Valley

Pizzato Fausto Merlot (red)

Another leading Brazilian winemaking family with Italian roots, the Pizzato family came to Brazil from Venice in the latter part of the 19th century. They first started in the wine business as suppliers of wines to the local hospital, which used them for strictly medicinal purposes. Their entrance into the arena of serious quality wine production didn't happen until 1999, however, when the family established a modern winery. The family now have some 42ha (104 acres) of vineyards from which they make a limited production of artisanal wines – just 7,000 cases in total. The winningly energetic team have a fastidious approach to winemaking, which results in superb quality reds based on Merlot. The Pizzato Fausto Merlot is a deep, rich, spicy red with great balance.

Via dos Parreirais, Vinhedos Valley, Bento Gonçalves, 95700-972
www.pizzato.net

Vinhos Don Laurindo Vinhedos Valley

Don Laurindo Merlot Reserva (red)

Like many Italian families in Brazil, the Brandellis have been making wine for themselves and their friends through successive generations ever since they arrived in the country from Verona in 1887. Today, the latest generation of the Brandelli line, Don Laurindo Brandelli and his sons, have taken things a step further, having set up their quality-driven family wine estate, Vinhos Don Laurindo, in 1991. The wines have shown a steady upwards curve since then, using such grapes as Merlot, Cabernet Sauvignon, and Malbec, as well as the indigenous Italian grape, Ancellota. For an insight into this estate's ability with Merlot, try the satisfyingly smooth, dark-fruited, and long-lasting Merlot Reserva.

Estrada do Vinho 8, da Graciema, Vinhedos Valley, 95700-000
www.donlaurindo.com.br

South Africa

South Africa has a surprisingly long history of wine production: the first vines arrived here with Dutch settlers in the middle of the 17th century. Today, having emerged from an extended period of political exile during which winemaking fell behind the rest of the world, South African wines are better than they have ever been. On the white side, South Africa specializes in two varieties from France's Loire Valley: rich, complex Chenin Blanc, and Sauvignon Blanc pitched in style between the freshness of the Loire and the pungency of New Zealand. For reds, fine Syrah/Shiraz is made in both spicy Rhône-like and richer Australian-inspired styles, while Bordeaux-blends can be extremely impressive. And don't forget the local speciality, Pinotage, a love-it-or-hate-it grape variety where abundant fruit is matched with a distinctive smoky edge.

Avondale Paarl, Western Cape
Syrah (red); Chenin Blanc (white)

Avondale is committed to organic, biodynamic practices when it comes to cultivating vines, and this is certainly reflected in the wines that are produced there, under the watchful eye of general manager and winemaker Jonathan Grieve. The estate's leathery but refined reds and refreshing whites exhibit purity of fruit, finesse, and style. The well-rounded Syrah offers satisfying aromas of liquorice, dark plum, and spice, with ripe fruit flavours that unfold in waves on the tongue. Delicate notes of lime, honey, peach, and tropical fruits add interest and depth to the clean and bright quality of the mouthwatering Chenin Blanc.

Klein Drakenstein, Suider Paarl 7624
www.avondalewine.co.za

Backsberg Estate Cellars Paarl, Western Cape
Chenin Blanc (white); Pinotage (red)

The Backsberg Estate was founded in 1916. Dedicated to working in harmony with the environment, it was the first of South Africa's wineries to be declared carbon neutral. It offers a good-value range of stylish wines that are both well-structured and food friendly. Owner Michael Back and winemaker Guillame Nell are staying true to Backsberg's noted creativity, which is particularly marked in their classy Chenin Blanc, with its mix of pear and tart apple flavours, and crisp acidity. The Pinotage is also easy to love, as soft tannins, a touch of spice, and juicy red-berry flavours curl around the tongue.

Suider Paarl 7624
www.backsberg.co.za

Boekenhoutskloof Winery Franschhoek, Western Cape
Wolftrap Red Blend; Porcupine Ridge Syrah (red)

Lauded winemaker Marc Kent, one of Boekenhoutskloof's partners, is a key player on the Franschhoek wine scene, having helped to make the region one of South Africa's top winemaking sites. His distinctive, plucky Wolftrap Red Blend is a crowd-pulling favourite. Hints of black fruit, spice, and raspberries mingle in this smooth blend of Syrah, Mourvèdre, and Viognier. When it comes to Syrah, Boekenhoutskloof is a true leader. Its bottlings exhibit a dense, dark character, and the Porcupine Ridge Syrah runs true to form. Violets, ripe red berries, plus a dash of pepper, dominate the aromas and flavours, all topped off with a minerally spin that helps to keep this classic wine clean on the tongue.

Excelsior Road, Franschhoek 7690
www.boekenhoutskloof.co.za

Bouchard-Finlayson Walker Bay, Western Cape
Blanc de Mer (white); Sauvignon Blanc (white)

Old World-style Pinot Noir is the main focus at this winery, set amid the cool maritime breezes of Walker Bay. But Peter Finlayson, the widely acclaimed winemaker, also produces some deliciously interesting red blends and very classy, well-priced whites, such as the pretty Blanc de Mer and subdued Sauvignon Blanc. Dominated by Riesling and Viognier, the former has notes of orange blossom, gooseberry, and lemon, while the Sauvignon Blanc displays tropical fruit flavours, some smoke, and the linear, mineral character that is distinctive of the region.

Klein Hemel en Aarde Farm, Hemel en Aarde Vall, Hermanus 7200
www.bouchardfinlayson.co.za

Bradgate Wines Stellenbosch, Western Cape
Chenin Blanc-Sauvignon Blanc (white); Syrah (red)

Bradgate Wines are part of the Jordan stable, established in 1982 by Gary and Kathy Jordan, an ambitious winemaking team. The winery produces almost equal parts reds and whites, all food-friendly and packing in plenty of complexity for their price. The Chenin Blanc-Sauvignon Blanc blend is a lively offering, with notes of pepper and green fig, mixed in with a clean citrus spin. Violet, and ripe plum flavours give the Syrah a sultry character, while notes of pepper and crushed herbs add a savoury touch that keeps the wine anchored and poised.

Stellenbosch 7600
www.jordanwines.com

Cape Chamonix Wine Farm Franschhoek, Western Cape
Sauvignon Blanc (white); Rouge Red Blend

When innovative young winemaker Gottfried Mocke arrived at Cape Chamonix, he believed that Franschhoek had the potential to be a world-class contender in the fine-wine market. His dedication to refined wines with unique character has resulted in award-winning bottlings that consistently strike a perfect balance between fruit and wood. The alluring Sauvignon Blanc offers a wave of fragrant herbs, accompanied by aromas and flavours of lemon, fig, and tropical fruit, while the soft, plush Rouge Red Blend would sit quite comfortably with some of the best Bordeaux. Its beautiful mix of ripe black fruit, spice, and minerality give it weight and real finesse.

Franschhoek 7690
www.chamonix.co.za

Cederberg

Cederberg, Western Cape

Sauvignon Blanc (white); Chenin Blanc (white)

At 1,000m (3,280ft) above sea level, Cederberg is South Africa's highest-lying vineyard, with snow in the winter and intense sun in the summer. Here, fifth-generation winemaker David Nieuwoudt grows vines in a range of soil types, from shale-slate to clay, producing a celebrated portfolio of terroir-driven wines. Aromas of lemon, lime, and pineapple lift off the luscious Sauvignon Blanc, while fig and slate flavours make it fresh yet mouth-filling. The Chenin Blanc is powerful, its melon and grapefruit notes combining with tropical fruit flavours and a crisp minerality.

Clanwilliam 8135
www.cederberg-wine.com

De Grendel Durbanville, Western Cape

Merlot (red); Sauvignon Blanc (white)

Established in 1720 and in the same family for five generations, De Grendel is an expanding operation, focusing on wines that are layered and lush, with expressive exotic fruit, balanced by the minerality of Durbanville's cool climate. Winemaker Elzette du Preez and cellarmaster Charles Hopkins claim an obsession with value and quality. Their polished Merlot is perfect proof of this. Elegant and poised, its aromas of anise, tobacco, and dark plum make for a wine that is reminiscent of French offerings, while dried herb, mushroom, and peppery flavours add appealing complexity and character. The passion fruit, green fig, and herbal notes of the estate's acclaimed Sauvignon Blanc give it a classic South African style. Crisp but generous, it makes a lovely partner for rich fish and poultry dishes, and oriental-style cuisine.

Panorama 7506
www.degrendel.co.za

Durbanville Hills Durbanville, Western Cape

Sauvignon Blanc (white); Pinotage (red)

Cellarmaster Martin Moore's finely balanced, food-friendly wines are a direct result of the cool maritime breezes found in Tygerberg, home of the Durbanville Hills winery. Here the relatively low temperatures for South Africa ensure slow-ripening of the grapes, helping to develop the deep flavours that make for wines of the very best quality. The region has a diverse spread of soils and microclimates that are reflected in the winery's bottlings. Typically South African in style, the crisp but giving Sauvignon Blanc sports dense aromas of lime and gooseberry, which mingle beautifully with lively flavours of tropical fruit, lemon, fig, and slate. The full-bodied Pinotage is laden with character. Rich and fruity, it is bursting with ripe red berries, pepper, and exotic spices.

Durbanville 7551
www.durbanvillehills.co.za

Fairview/Spice Route Paarl, Western Cape

Beacon Shiraz (red); Goats Do Roam White

A tower inhabited by goats greets the many visitors to Fairview's Paarl winery – an indication of the management's playful edge. Fairview, however, is a serious producer, with an ongoing quest to create the next great South African wine. Owner Charles Back and winemaker Anthony de Jager use grapes from across the Cape, and their wines speak of that diversity. Rhône-style Shiraz is king here, with the Beacon Shiraz fitting firmly into that mould. Aromas and flavours of tobacco, spiced meat, dark plums, and pepper give it a decidedly masculine edge. Whites are a beautiful balance of warm-climate richness and crisp acidity. The fruit-focused Goats Do Roam White blend is like a tropical island in a glass, presenting a whirl of exotic fruit, spice, and straw aromas, with ripe apple, apricot, and a host of tropical fruit flavours.

Suid Agter Paarl Road, Suider-Paarl 7646
www.fairview.co.za

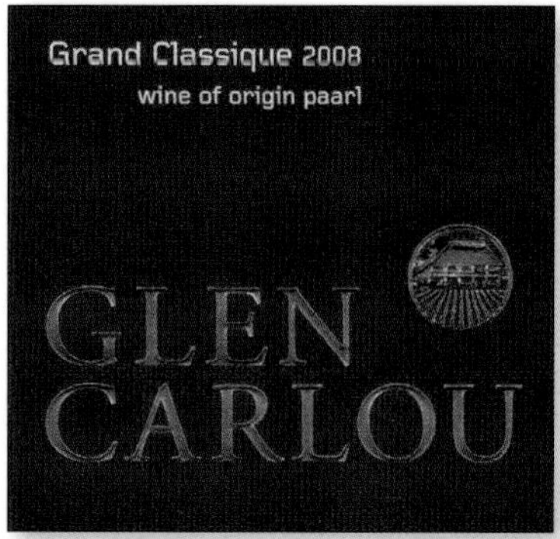

Glen Carlou Paarl, Western Cape

Cabernet Sauvignon (red); Grand Classique (red)

Glen Carlou's South African operation is owned by Hess Family Estates, a Swiss company that also has vineyards and wineries in Australia, California, and Argentina. Everything about this wine estate evokes drama and power. This includes its spectacular setting in the foothills of the scenic Paarl Valley, as well as the rich, well-structured bottlings that are so skilfully crafted by winemaker Arco Laarman and his team. The earthy Cabernet Sauvignon, with its brooding aromas and flavours of ripe black plums and roasted herbs leading to a finish that is dry and spicy, demands close attention. The Grand Classique is a finely balanced Bordeaux-style blend of Cabernet Sauvignon, Merlot, Cabernet Franc, Malbec, and Petit Verdot. Silky smooth, fruity, and easy on the palate, it displays lingering notes of dark chocolate, sandalwood, smoke, and warming spice, which add both interest and depth. Both of these top-value reds exhibit great ageing potential.

Simondium Road, Klapmuts 7625
www.glencarlou.co.za

Graham Beck Wines Robertson, Western Cape

The Game Reserve (red); Chardonnay-Viognier (white)

Founded in 1983 by pioneering winemaker Graham Beck, the Robertson estate is entering its third generation as a family-run enterprise. Beck's goal to establish a world-class winery in the Robertson region has been fully realized and has also been extended to estates in both Stellenbosch and Franschhoek. The Beck business model is noted for its efforts in conservation, biodiversity, and staff empowerment, as well the high quality and keen pricing of its wines. The Game Reserve is an elegant but hefty Cabernet Sauvignon that will make a perfect match when served with grilled meats or robust stews. Intense blackberry fruit, cassis, and tobacco aromas and flavours dominate, supported by a spicy minerality and firm, well-structured tannins. The Chardonnay-Viognier offers a brilliant balance of zippy citrus notes from the Chardonnay and apricot- and peach-laden notes from the Viognier. Mixed with a solid core of lush tropical fruit flavours, the result is both bright and sultry, with a clean, sharp, and lingering finish.

Robertson 6705
www.grahambeckwines.com

Groot Constantia

Constantia, Western Cape

Sauvignon Blanc (white); Blanc de Noir (rosé)

Founded in 1685, Groot Constantia is South Africa's oldest operating winery, and draws in visitors as much for its beautiful Cape Dutch architecture and lush grounds as for its attractive wines. Winemakers Boela Gerber and Michelle Rhodes produce a diverse range of solid reds and elegant classic whites. Aromas of fig and citrus, plus intense gooseberry, fig, and citrus flavours give the Sauvignon Blanc an unmistakably South African character. The Blanc de Noir rosé is both refreshing and fun, with notes of grapefruit, strawberry, and citrus dancing on the palate. A finishing flourish of red cherry adds style.

Constantia 7848
www.grootconstantia.co.za

Groote Post Darling, Western Cape

The Old Man's Blend White; Unwooded Chardonnay (white)

Venturing into the rural backwaters of the Darling Hills is well worth the effort, when the charming 18th-century Groote Post winery lies at the end of the trail. The classy food-friendly wines being produced by owners Peter and Nicholas Pentz have done a brilliant job of promoting this emerging wine region, where deep soils with good water retention and a cool climate yields crop after crop of superlative fruit. Zippy and fresh, The Old Man's Blend White – a mix of Sauvignon Blanc, Chenin Blanc, and Semillon – is a delicate balance of fruit, acid, and minerals. It has nuances of honeyed apricot and flowers that help to round out the citrus, making for everyday enjoyment. The perfect accompaniment to a spicy Asian meal, the Unwooded Chardonnay has sharp cutting aromas of lime and lemon that float over an alluring mix of ripe orange, ginger, and spice flavours, to culminate in a lingering and zesty finish.

Darling 7345
www.grootepost.com

Hartenberg Stellenbosch, Western Cape

Cabernet Sauvignon (red); Sauvignon Blanc (white)

The approachable, stylish, and good-value wines that the Hartenberg winery produces with such great consistency have made it a hugely popular brand in the international market. Especially worthy of attention is the highly characterful, medal-winning Cabernet Sauvignon. Easy drinking enough to have broad appeal, its deep aromas of black fruit, anise, and violet, coupled with lovely jammy flavours of red fruit, make it a versatile match for a wide range of hearty meat dishes. Another of the estate's growing list of critically acclaimed bottlings is the Sauvignon Blanc. Also easy to love, without missing out on both interest and depth, it features inviting tropical fruit and fresh herbal aromas that lead on to a broad sweep across the palate of pineapple and citrus. Coupled with a crisp lingering finish, all of this makes for a refreshing wine with some considerable substance that is lovely on its own, but also goes brilliantly with Asian-style dishes and grilled fish.

Bottelary Road, Stellenbosch 7605
www.hartenbergestate.com

Iona Vineyards Elgin, Western Cape

Sauvignon Blanc (white); The Gunnar (red)

Andrew Gunn, the organically minded owner of Iona Vineyards, is on a mission to harness the elegant exuberance of Elgin Valley grapes, and his critically acclaimed range of stylish wines prove that he is getting it right. The flinty Sauvignon Blanc is a much-praised trademark example, reflecting the core characteristics of Elgin's crops. Its herbaceous quality is rounded out with a delicious mix of citrus, floral, and grapefruit flavours. Crisp plucky green apple and lime notes add an extra dimension. The Gunnar, a refined deep red blend of Cabernet, Merlot, and Petit Verdot is pretty but earthy, with rich flavours of black cherry, anise, and mushroom, set over a firm spicy base.

Grabouw 7160
www.iona.co.za

WHEN TO SEND WINE BACK

When a waiter brings a plate of ravioli to the table, he doesn't stick a fork in one and present it to you for approval. So when a waiter or sommelier presents the bottle of wine to you, then pulls and presents the cork, then pours you a taste, this procedure is done for a reason, at least an historical one. Restaurants have long acknowledged that wine is variable, and an individual bottle can in fact be so distasteful that you might reject it. The ritual lets the customer decide if something is technically wrong with the wine. It might be "corked", or damaged by heat, or simply too hot or too cold for your taste. It is unlikely that you will have to send a wine back, as faulty bottles are much less common than they used to be.

1 Is it the wine you ordered? Look closely at the bottle and label. Check the label for the winery and type of wine, confirm the vineyard or region it came from, and the vintage date. You may send it back if these don't agree with what you saw on the wine list. Also, be suspicious if the wine has been uncorked somewhere out of sight and brought to you already opened. It could be a different wine in the bottle.

2 Look at the cork. A cork tells you a lot about a wine's quality and authenticity. If it is dated, is the year the same as the label states? If it is wet on top or has a definite wine streak that runs from the wet end to the other, this probably indicates leakage, which means it could have been spoiled by heat and/or premature oxidation.

If the top of the cork is wet, the wine may have leaked.

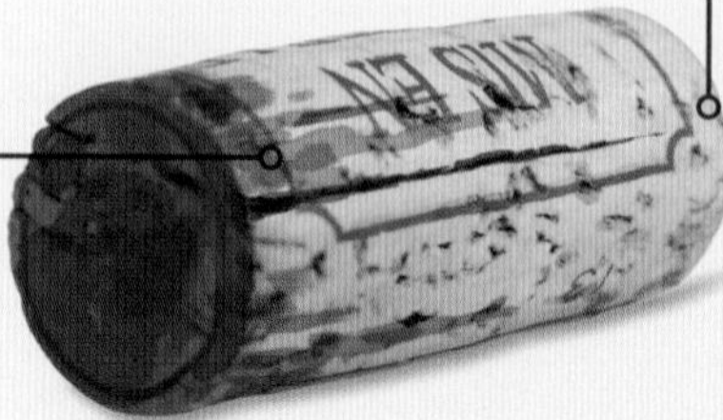

Streaks down the side suggest leakage.

3 Examine the poured wine. If the "rim" or edge of a red wine against the glass looks brown rather than red or purple, then a leaking cork might have prematurely oxidized it. If a white is brassy or amber rather than golden or yellow-green it might be oxidized. If it is unusually cloudy looking, you should also send it back because it might have bacterial spoilage. Don't worry about small crystals; these are often found in unfiltered wines and are harmless.

Take a sniff A white table wine that smells like sherry, or a red that smells like gar or a horse stable is probably spoiled. orked" wine smells mouldy, as it has been cted with the harmless but unpleasant-lling compound, TCA, usually found in the . Taste the wine. Is it cool enough? If not, for an ice bucket. If the taste corroborates a blem that your nose or eyes have detected, should certainly send the wine back.

Mulderbosch Stellenbosch, Western Cape

Cabernet Sauvignon Rosé; Chenin Blanc Steen Op Hout (white)

The vision and efforts of the much-lauded Mike Dubrovic helped to bring both the Mulderbosch winery, and South African wines generally, to the forefront. His successors at Mulderbosch, Richard Kershaw and his team, continue the company's tradition by producing a good range of consistently high quality, terroir-driven vintages. All are wildly popular internationally, both with the general public and the critics. A warm-weather winner, the Cabernet Sauvignon Rosé draws you in with its mouthwatering punch of wild strawberries and perfectly ripe red berries, overlaid by a distinct aroma of rose petals, all of this mingling on the palate with a soft brush of nutty spice. Finely balanced but with plenty of weight, the curvy Chenin Blanc Steen Op Hout is also a clear winner. A lightly oaked white with elegance and style, it has a showy streak. Its warm tropical fruit, clove, and citrus flavours are topped by forceful aromas of lemon, pineapple, and warming spice.

R304, Stellenbosch 7599
www.mulderbosch.co.za

Neil Ellis Stellenbosch, Western Cape

Sauvignon Blanc (white); Shiraz (red)

Trailblazing négociant Neil Ellis and innovative businessman Hans-Peter Schroder have teamed up to produce a range of finely crafted wines that offer a comprehensive expression of South Africa's varietal character and diversity. Ellis has been seeking out the best grapes in South Africa's winelands since 1986. Whether it is Stellenbosch for its dense power, the Darling Hills for their maritime crispness, or the Elgin Valley for its delicate reserve, all the wines his and Schroder's partnership have produced so far are firmly terroir-driven. Their fresh and lively Sauvignon Blanc is a perfect warm-weather sipper that goes magnificently with barbecued fish and seafood. Redolent of juicy lime, a touch of fragrant herbs and a chalky minerality give it an extra dimension. Full-bodied and well-balanced, the Shiraz is brimming with flavours and aromas of blackberry fruit, anise, and violets, with an earthy spin of pepper and cedar giving it weight.

Oude Nektar Farm, Stellenbosch 7600
www.neilellis.com

Paul Cluver Estate Wines Elgin, Western Cape

Sauvignon Blanc (white); Gewürztraminer (white)

The Paul Cluver Estate's crisp sophisticated whites, dessert wines, and reds have played a key role in putting the emerging, cool-climate region of Elgin Valley firmly on the map for value and quality. Under the direction of the Cluver family, winemaker Andries Burger focuses on the elegant expression of Elgin's coastal terroir – which he achieves in abundance in both the award-winning Sauvignon Blanc and the Gewürztraminer. Fleshed out with a touch of oak-aged Semillon, the Sauvignon offers green pepper and gooseberry aromas, followed by a blast of minerality and rich tropical fruit flavours. The exotic and refreshing Gewürztraminer has opulent notes of rose, citrus, and spice, with delicate but lingering sweet and spicy flavours.

Grabouw 7160
www.cluver.com

Rudera Wines Stellenbosch, Western Cape

Chenin Blanc (white); Noble Late Harvest Chenin Blanc (white)

Rudera Wines, established in 1999, has a track record for excellence, especially with its terroir-focused line of stunning Chenin Blancs, produced under the direction of winemaker Eleonor Visser. A favourite among Chenin lovers, the winery's basic Chenin Blanc offering is a golden sip, with tropical citrussy aromas and flavours, plus a rounded note of baked apple and spice. Beautifully balanced, it has a richly satisfying and lingering finish. The lovely indulgent Noble Late Harvest Chenin Blanc is a unique and memorable find. Each richly honeyed mouthful delivers a stunning mix of tangerine, apricot, and pineapple, plus a dash of spicy smoked oak.

No visitor facilities
www.rudera.co.za

Rustenberg Stellenbosch, Western Cape

Brampton Sauvignon Blanc (white); Brampton Chardonnay (white)

Vines grown on the rich red slopes of the Simonsberg and Helderburg mountains tend to produce wines with power and grace – a trademark of Rustenberg bottlings. This includes those of its great-value, second label Brampton range, which have substance and depth that is especially evident in the Sauvignon Blanc and the unoaked Chardonnay. The crisp, vegetal Sauvignon flaunts grassy notes of asparagus and green pepper, rounded out by tropical lychee and passion fruit flavours. The Chardonnay is quite a surprise. Refreshing and bold, it has the expected aroma of lemon and fresh white fruits, but there is also a spin of orange and pine in the glass.

Schoongezicht Street, Stellenbosch 7600
www.rustenberg.co.za

Simonsig Stellenbosch, Western Cape

Chenin Blanc (white); Labyrinth Cabernet (red)

A highly respected voice in the South African wine industry, Johann Malan, cellarmaster and winemaker of the famed Simonsig estate, produces wines of power and grace. His Chenin Blanc does real justice to this varietal. Opulent but firmly structured, it is lively and fresh with a carefully balanced layering of tropical fruit and honey. The Labyrinth Cabernet could easily slip into being an overly studied and serious red, but its friendly blackberry fruitiness, with notes of chocolate and spice and a dry finish, assure its easy appeal.

De Hoop Krommerhee Road, Stellenbosch 7605
www.simonsig.co.za

Steenberg Constantia, Western Cape

Nebbiolo (red); Sauvignon Blanc (white)

Under the analytical eye of manager John Loubser, Steenberg is a force to be reckoned with in Constantia wine. Wines to watch are the lauded reds such as the Nebbiolo – an unusual varietal for South Africa – with its spice and strawberry aromas, followed by flavours of plum and red berries, and refreshing whites such as the Sauvignon Blanc, which marries grassy crispness with tropical fruit.

Steenberg 7947
www.steenberg-vineyards.co.za

Stormhoek Wellington, Western Cape

Sauvignon Blanc (white); Pinotage (red)

Stormhoek focuses firmly on food-friendly, affordable wines, and its approachable bottlings are fast gaining a loyal following. This is partly due to sharp online marketing, but it is the wines' sheer quality and exuberant fruit that brings customers back for more. The Sauvignon Blanc, with lively gooseberry and citrus aromas and peppery lemon flavours, makes a fun yet interesting introduction to Stormhoek's offerings. The Pinotage also entices, with a slightly eccentric mix of berry, spice, smoked-meat, and chocolatey notes.

No visitor facilities
www.stormhoek.co.za

Warwick Estate Simonsberg-Stellenbosch, Western Cape

The First Lady (red); Pinotage (red)

Michael Ratcliffe is the third generation of his family to run the Warwick Estate. A Pinotage pioneer and promoter of South African wines worldwide, his ambitious expansion has not diminished the company's reputation for consistency and excellence in any way. Ambitious yet accessible wines remain the goal here, with intense yet friendly reds, such as The First Lady and the Pinotage leading the way. A dark, full-bodied Cabernet Sauvignon, The First Lady is gregarious and easy-drinking. Its red-berry, cassis, and currant aromas, and smooth, dark-fruit flavours are punctuated by bursts of black pepper. The hearty Pinotage is a wine you will want to take a big "bite" out of. Here, notes of cocoa powder, coffee, tobacco, pepper, cloves, and cherry mingle in a delicious, mouth-filling mix.

Elsenburg 7607
www.warwickwine.com

Australia

Australia is strongly associated with two distinctive types of wine: full-on, rich, smooth Shiraz, and big, buttery, tropical fruit-flavoured Chardonnay, both of which became top sellers in the 1980s and 90s. Things have moved on in the past decade, however, and the country has added a great many other strings to its bow, with the grapes often sourced from cooler-climate sites than in the past. Today, you're as likely to find subtle, complex whites from Riesling, Viognier, and Semillon as you are intense Chardonnay, while the Chardonnays themselves have become much more subtle and restrained. For reds, Shiraz remains the king, but Australia is also a fine producer of vibrant Cabernet Sauvignon and Cabernet-based blends, and elegant Pinot Noirs (particularly from the state of Victoria), as well as a host of other wines from intriguing grape varieties.

Battle of Bosworth McLaren Vale, South Australia
Shiraz Viognier, McLaren Vale (red)

In 1995, Joch Bosworth took over the Edgehill Vineyard, founded by his parents 25 years earlier, and decided to switch to organic cultivation. The result is his broad Battle of Bosworth range of attractively packaged wines, of which the reds all share the McLaren Vale trademarks of dark, ripe fruit flavours and high acidity. In the medium-bodied Shiraz Viognier, however, the splash of white-grape Viognier gives a decidedly aromatic, floral lift to the blend, with vibrant notes of ripe peach and raspberry fruit sweeping over the tongue to a bright, refreshing finish.

McLaren Vale, SA 5171
www.edgehill-vineyards.com.au

Bremerton Langhorne Creek, South Australia
Verdelho, Langhorne Creek (white)

Langhorne Creek is the site of some of the most prized winelands in Australia, and Bremerton is considered by many to be the area's best producer. The Willson family are the owners, with daughters Rebecca and Lucy in charge of winemaking and marketing respectively. They have successfully steered Bremerton towards highly individualistic, top quality wines at a keen price. The broad sweep of their house style is for lush, intense wines with prominent but well-integrated oak. However, they use Verdelho beautifully to craft a really fresh, unwooded white with instant "drink-me-now" appeal. Made only from free-run juice, its lovely light tropical fruit aromas and subtle pear and citrus flavours move gently towards a soft but lingering finish.

Strathalbyn Rd, Langhorne Creek, SA 5255
www.bremerton.com.au

Brokenwood Hunter Valley, New South Wales
Semillon, Hunter Valley (white)

Brokenwood has evolved from a weekend hobby into being one of Australia's most reputable wine labels. Set up in 1970 by a consortium of three wine-lovers, which included the famed wine writer James Halliday, its distinctive winery was built in 1975, and in 1978 its famous Graveyard Vineyard, the source of the company's legendary and elegant Graveyard Shiraz, was purchased. Iain Riggs, the current custodian, joined as winemaker in 1982, opening a new state-of-the-art winery, which he dedicated to the production of premium-quality whites. The brilliant Semillon is one of its most dazzling offerings. A classic Hunter Valley example of this varietal, it presents a perfect balance of fruit, alcohol and acidity. Brimming with sharp lemon fruit and mineral flavours, it is deliciously fresh and bright when young, but also has the potential to age well, developing rich and complex toasty notes. This is a superb bottling that delivers in abundance – far more than its price would ever lead you to expect.

401-427 McDonalds Rd, Pokolbin, NSW 2320
www.brokenwood.com.au

Brown Brothers King Valley, Victoria
Tarrango, Victoria (red)

The Brown Brothers estate's 750ha (1,853 acres) of vineyards are spread right across the state of Victoria, supplying most of the needs of their massive million-case winery. The company is very well known, both in Australia and internationally, for its broad range of affordable varietal wines, all of consistently high quality. These include a number of interesting oddities too, such as stylish fizz made from Prosecco, and the extremely popular, Beaujolais-style, cherry-fresh Tarrango. Here the unusual, slow-ripening Tarrango grape has been crafted into a quite unique wine. An alluring, jewel-like, bright magenta in colour, it is full of fresh, rather tart cherry and raspberry fruit, topped by a hint of spice, and winding down gently to a delicate dry finish. All this makes for a perfect drink to serve slightly chilled on a sultry summer's evening.

239 Milawa Bobinawarrah Rd, Milawa, VIC 3678
www.brownbrothers.com.au

By Farr Geelong, Victoria
Farr Rising Pinot Noir, Geelong (red)

Legendary Australian winemaker Gary Farr has joined his son Nick to form the By Farr venture, which produces an adventurous range of highly individual, terroir-led wines. There are two labels: the premium By Farr wines, produced solely from estate-grown grapes, and Nick's more price-conscious Farr Rising range. In 2009, By Farr released three single-vineyard designated Pinot Noirs for the first time – all of them world-class, but for complexity, interest, and high quality at a great price, the second-label Farr Rising Geelong Pinot Noir takes some beating. The nose of this light-bodied, softly perfumed Pinot gem builds subtly and gradually. Flush with flavours of ripe, sweet cherry fruit, it has an attractive grassy and herb complexity and finely rounded texture that builds to a long and savoury finish. Good for immediate drinking, it also has several years' ageing potential.

Bannockburn, VIC 3331
www.byfarr.com.au

Campbells Rutherglen, Victoria

Muscat, Rutherglen (fortified)

Campbells is run by brothers Colin and Malcolm, who bring over 30 years' experience to their enterprise. The company makes a range of solid table wines, but it is its fortified bottlings that really demand attention – hardly a surprise, considering Campbells' Rutherglen location. This hot area is now famous as the home of one of Australia's unique contributions to fine wine – the sweet and powerful Muscat and Tokay wines that are commonly referred to as "stickies". Campbells is one of the best producers, and its Rutherglen Muscat makes a perfect introduction to their sensual qualities. Typically super-concentrated and viscous, with a hint of tar in the aroma, it has rich raisin, fudge, and herb flavours that linger on the tongue.

Murray Valley Hwy, Rutherglen, VIC 3685
www.campbellswines.com.au

Cape Mentelle Margaret River, Western Australia

Sauvignon Blanc-Semillon, Margaret River (white)

Cape Mentelle's first vineyard was planted in 1970, making it a Margaret River pioneer. Today, the company has four vineyards and also sources fruit from a dozen growers. Bold, structured Cabernet is the star here, but the Cape Mentelle Sauvignon Blanc-Semillon, considered one of the best of this classic Margaret River blend, is also worth seeking out. Fragrant with aromas of passion fruit, lime, and wild blackberry, its delicate citrus flavours are coupled with a hint of green pepper and spice, finishing with a firm, crisp acidity.

331 Wallcliffe Rd, Margaret River, WA 6285
www.capementelle.com.au

Chain of Ponds Adelaide Hills, South Australia

Pilot Block Sangiovese-Barbera-Grenache, South Australia (red)

An ambitious Adelaide Hills producer, Chain of Ponds sources grapes from all around the Adelaide Hills, making a range of wines, with Italian varieties the speciality. Silky smooth and highly accessible, the Pilot Block, a blend of Sangiovese, Barbera, and Grenache offers alluring, deep notes of cherry fruit with a dash of spice. It makes an easy-drinking tipple that also has some depth and genuine character.

Adelaide Rd, Gumeracha, SA 5233
www.chainofponds.com.au

Chalkers Crossing Hilltops, New South Wales

Cabernet Sauvignon, Hilltops (red)

Chalkers Crossing focuses on premium quality, cool-climate wines, with fine Riesling, Semillon, Shiraz, and Cabernet Sauvignon produced under the direction of Bordeaux-trained Celine Rousseau. The first wines were made here in 2000, and in a relatively short time have acquired a devoted following. The silky Cabernet Sauvignon is an award winner. A full-bodied offering, its dark wild-berry flavours and classic cool-climate aromas of olive, mint, cedar, and cassis sit in perfect balance with fine-grained tannins.

285 Henry Lawson Way, Young, NSW 2594
www.chalkerscrossing.com.au

Chapel Hill McLaren Vale, South Australia

Foundation Verdelho, McLaren Vale (white)

Chapel Hill works sustainably using biodynamic principles to reduce chemical input in its vineyards. When winemaker Michael Fragos joined in 2004, Chapel Hill was already a McLaren Vale star, but his input has clearly made even further improvement, producing outstanding wines that express perfectly the qualities of McLaren Vale grapes. The super-fresh, nervy Verdelho, from the keenly priced Foundation range, makes a versatile food wine. Crisp and unoaked, its honeyed tropical fruit flavours are countered by crisp appley notes and finely tuned acidity.

Corner Chapel Hill and Chaffey's Rd, McLaren Vale, SA 5171
www.chapelhillwine.com.au

Crawford River Henty, Victoria

Riesling Young Vines, Henty (white)

John Thompson took quite a leap of faith when he set up his vineyard in Henty, southwest Victoria, where the cool maritime breezes create a climate that is quite marginal for grape growing. But his gamble paid off, and over 30 years later Crawford River is firmly established as one of Australia's leading Riesling producers. Limey and minerally in their youth, Crawford River bottlings show that Riesling can age well too. The well-priced Riesling Young Vines, although not as complex and deep as some of the vintages made with grapes from older plantings, is still beautifully expressive and stylish. Terroir-driven, it shows lovely balance as its lively lemon and lime fruit and chalky minerality sweep crisply over the palate.

741 Upper Hotspur Rd, Condah, VIC 3303
www.crawfordriverwines.com

D'Arenberg McLaren Vale, South Australia

The Custodian Grenache, McLaren Vale (red)

D'Arenberg has been a leading light on the McLaren wine scene since 1912, but has been transformed in recent years by the dynamism of Chester Osborn and his winemaking team into one of Australia's most interesting and visible producers. The range of imaginatively labelled wines has widened, with the top wines largely deserving of the considerable hype they receive. Quality across the entire range is both consistent and impressive, especially considering the high rate of production. Most of the wines are made from old, low-yielding vines, using traditional techniques that catch amazing levels of fruit and intensity. The Custodian Grenache is no exception to this. Likeable and highly approachable, like most D'Arenberg reds, it presents intriguing aromas of lavender, violet, spice, and bright red fruit, plus a rich mouthful of cherry and plum fruit, all of which is countered by a balancing smokey, spicy underlayer. A firm backbone of tannins lends structure and potential for some interesting ageing.

Osborn Rd, McLaren Vale, SA 5171
www.darenberg.com.au

De Bortoli Riverina, New South Wales

Noble One, Riverina (dessert); Show Liqueur Muscat, Riverina (dessert)

Set up by a family of immigrants from northern Italy in 1928, De Bortoli is one of the key players in Australian wine. The company's huge winery at Riverina produces around 4.5 million cases a year, covering a range of styles that also offer outstanding value. These include Noble One, which since its first vintage in 1982, has gone on to become one of Australia's most revered dessert wines. A rich, botrytized Semillon, its lush mix of citrus and apricot flavours mingles with undertones of honey and spice. The Show Liqueur Muscat, another sweet offering, is as an affordable introduction to Australian Muscat, showing concentrated flavours of toffee, raisin, and spice.

De Bortoli Rd, Bilbul, NSW 2680
www.debortoli.com.au

Delatite Goulburn, Victoria
Pinot Gris, Victoria (white)

Established in 1982, the family-run Delatite winery is located in the Upper Goulburn, a fairly cool region in northeastern Victoria. It specializes in aromatic whites, which include a rare serious Australian interpretation of Pinot Gris. With a distinctive minerally, smoky edge to its grapey fruit, and some dry straw complexity, it is generous and lush in the mouth. Soft sultry flavours of pear, musk, and spice are balanced by a fine crisp acidity.

Stoney's Road, Mansfield, VIC 3722
www.delatitewinery.com.au

Domaine A Tasmania
Sauvignon Blanc Stoney Vineyard, Tasmania (white)

Domaine A is possibly Tasmania's best producer. Winemaker Peter Althaus personally selects the fruits that he crafts into highly seductive Pinot Noir and Cabernet Sauvignon, as well as the superb, good-value Stoney Vineyard Sauvignon Blanc. Beautifully aromatic, its mouthfilling, ripe pear fruit and grassy gooseberry notes wind down gently to a lovely, sweet, lingering finish.

Tea Tree Rd, Campania, TAS 7026
www.domaine-a.com.au

Dutschke Wines Barossa, South Australia
Shiraz GHR (God's Hill Road), Barossa (red)

Dutschke Wines is a collaboration between winemaker Wayne Dutschke and his uncle, grower Ken Semmler. In 1990, instead of selling all their grapes, they decided to keep some for themselves to produce wine under the Willowbend label. Volumes increased significantly in the late 1990s, when these wines became a hit in the US, and the name Dutschke Wines was adopted. Noted for their Shiraz, the GHR bottling is a classy offering at a great price, with lots of ripe, lush blackberry fruit and a distinctive spicy edge.

God's Hill Rd, Lyndoch, SA 5351
www.dutschkewines.com

"CONTAINS SULPHITES": SHOULD YOU WORRY?

Virtually all wines contain tiny quantities of sulphites, or sulphur dioxide, which act as a fruit preservative. But only a small number of countries, such as the US and Australia, require wineries to declare this on the labels. In the US, the wording is "contains sulfites" and in Australia it is "contains sulphites".

But should you worry? Most of us should not. Many people believe erroneously that sulphites can bring on headaches, but extensive medical research has shown that there is absolutely no connection between the two. A connection has been identified, however, between rare cases in which high percentages of sulphites have been applied to foods, and negative health effects for people with a tendency to suffer from asthma attacks.

Winemakers around the world add an average of about 80 parts per million of sulphites to their wines to help keep them fresh, and have done so for at least 100 years. This concentration is far below the amount that has been connected to asthma attacks. A wine on sale in Europe need not mention any sulphites it contains. However, the same wine from the same barrel, when put on sale in the US or Australia, must declare the presence of sulphites.

Most wines produce a small quantity of sulphites on their own, so even a wine that contains no added sulphites can have a few parts per million. In the US and Australia the label need not mention sulphites unless the level is at least 10 parts per million. Organic wines in the US may not contain added sulphites, but organic wines in many other countries may contain added sulphites.

In recent years, a number of winemakers have sought to reduce the amount of sulphur dioxide they use in the winemaking process, or eliminate it entirely. These winemakers, who also prefer to use wild yeasts naturally present on the grape skins for fermentation rather than adding cultivated yeasts that have been developed commercially, and who farm organically or biodynamically, have become known as "natural winemakers". At present, however, there is no official list of rules for natural winemakers, so if you are interested in finding out more, talk to your local independent wine merchant.

Evans & Tate Margaret River, Western Australia

Classic White, Margaret River

One of Australia's most innovative and consistent producers, Evans & Tate have never failed to turn out fantastic wines, even when they were experiencing a period of financial turmoil in the early years of the 21st century. Now part of the long-established and reputable McWilliam's Wines Group, their top wines are some of the finest available in Western Australia. However, even those on a budget can enjoy this winery's amazing quality and originality of style by selecting from their less expensive Classic label. The Classic White, a beautiful blend of Semillon and Sauvignon Blanc, is extremely pure and refreshing on the palate. It is bright and well focused, with pithy grapefruit and citrus flavours that wind down gracefully to a zingy, acidic finish.

Corner of Metricup Rd/Caves Rd, Wilyabrup, WA 6280
www.mcwilliamswines.com.au

First Drop Barossa, South Australia

Two Percent Shiraz, Barossa (red)

Award-winning winemaker Matt Gant of St Hallett winery – The Wine Society's (in Australia) Young Winemaker of the Year in 2004 – and manager John Retsas of Schild Estate make up the young and ambitious team behind First Drop. They source their grapes from all corners of the Barossa Valley, Adelaide Hills, and McLaren Vale, producing a wide range of premium wines, including several very interesting oddities, such as Barbera, Arneis, Nebbiolo, and Montepulciano, and a number of different and highly idiosyncratic Barossa Shirazes. However, their Two Percent Barossa Shiraz demonstrates that First Drop can also do the classics with great panache. Complex, dense, and deliciously seductive, this is a particularly exuberant example of Barossa Shiraz, showing a lovely focus and freshness to the sweet, lush fruit. Earthy flavours of ripe black berries mingle with enticing notes of dark chocolate, spice, and tobacco, all set off with an attractive savoury, meaty edge and given a gentle lift by the subtle use of oak.

No visitor facilities
www.firstdropwine.com

Gemtree Vineyards McLaren Vale, South Australia

Bloodstone Shiraz, McLaren Vale (red)

The Buttery family first started growing wine grapes in McLaren Vale in 1980, and have been using some of their crop to make their own wines since 1998. Today, Gemtree owns 130ha (330 acres) of prime vineyards, which are managed by the founders' daughter, Melissa Buttery, with the winemaking in the hands of her husband, Mike Brown. Sustainable viticulture is practiced here, and the entire farm has been run along biodynamic lines since 2007. Minimal intervention is the policy when it comes to crafting the varied range, and it is largely choices made in the vineyard that determine the ultimate character of Gemtree's wines. They are beautifully focused, with rich, lush fruit but also great definition. With a dash of Viognier in the blend, the appealing Bloodstone Shiraz makes for a bold, highly concentrated glassful. Meaty notes mingle with aromas and flavours of lush, dark fruit, leading to a fresh hint of mint in the long, drawn-out finish.

184 Main Road, McLaren Vale, SA 5171
www.gemtreevineyards.com.au

Giant Steps/Innocent Bystander Yarra Valley, Victoria

Chardonnay Sexton Vineyard, Yarra Valley (white)

Wine buff and entrepreneur Phil Sexton had already developed and sold a wine company (Devil's Lair) and a beer brand (Little Creatures) before setting his sights on a set-up in the Yarra Valley. The innovative Giant Steps winery and cellar door, in downtown Healesville, opened for business in 2006. Giant Steps' bottlings, including those in its more affordable second label, Innocent Bystander, are absolutely in the first rank. Terroir-driven qualities, reflecting the cool, crisp climate and flinty soils of the heart of the Yarra Valley, are particularly evident in the company's superlative Chardonnays. The complex Sexton Vineyard Chardonnay, typical of Sexton's beautifully crafted and charismatic wines, delivers a huge amount for its price. Minerally and flinty notes complement the delicate white peach, nectarine, and melon fruit, all topped by notes of refreshing citrus and warm toast. This is a focused and elegant wine with real interest and depth.

336 Maroondah Hwy, Healesville, VIC 3777
www.innocentbystander.com.au

Grosset Clare Valley, South Australia
Springvale, Watervale Riesling, Clare Valley (white)

Jeffrey Grosset has been making exceptional Riesling in the Clare Valley since 1981. The powerful wines produced from grapes grown in his Polish Hill vineyard are justifiably highly acclaimed, but the more restrained, better-value bottlings made from Grosset's Springvale-Vineyard vines can be just as satisfying. Fresh and citrussy, with a deliciously prolonged delivery of lime and grapefruit flavours, these are lovely Rieslings with some complexity and a light but seemingly endless, bone-dry finish. They also age well, developing richly honeyed notes.

King St, Auburn, Clare Valley, SA 5451
www.grosset.com.au

Heartland Langhorne Creek, South Australia
Dolcetto & Lagrein, Langhorne Creek (red)

A sizeable, collaborative venture that includes vineyards in Limestone Coast and Langhorne Creek, Heartland grows grapes for sale to other wineries as well as for their own bottlings. But what is impressive about Heartland is not the size and scope of their venture, but the quality and sheer value of their wines, especially considering the quantities in which they are made. They outclass many wines twice the price. The richly flavoured Dolcetto & Lagrein, a blend of two Italian grape varieties, is a particularly noteworthy offering. Bright and focused, with lovely dark cherry fruit, and coffee-bean and chocolate aromas, it rounds off with mouth-tingling, fresh, clean acidity.

34 Barossa Valley Way, Tanunda, SA 5352
www.heartlandwines.com.au

Hewitson Barossa, South Australia
Gun Metal Riesling, Eden Valley (white)

The Hewitson winery, set up in 1998, makes expressive and interesting wines, using grapes from vineyards across a range of South Australia's best vine-growing regions, including Barossa, Eden Valley, McLaren Vale, and the Adelaide Hills. The Gun Metal Riesling is made from grapes cultivated in the Eden Valley, an area noted for its world-class Rieslings. There is nice citrussy intensity and complexity to this elegant bottling. Not as dry and austere as many Eden Valley examples, it is bursting with lime and lemon flavours, rounding off to a lovely minerally finish.

No visitor facilities
www.hewitson.com.au

Hope Estate Hunter Valley, New South Wales
The Cracker Cabernet Merlot, Western Australia (red)

In 1994, Michael Hope decided to abandon his successful pharmacy business to follow his dream and make wine in the Hunter Valley. As well as 100ha (247 acres) in the Hunter Valley, he owns vineyards in Victoria and Western Australia. The Cracker Cabernet Merlot is crafted with grapes trucked from Western Australia. Rich and bold, it bursts with mouth-filling blackberry flavours and hints of liquorice and chocolate, balanced by notes of mint and eucalyptus. Ripe tannins and sweet vanilla oak provide a firm framework.

2213 Broke Rd, Pokolbin, NSW 2320
www.hopeestate.com.au

Houghton Swan Valley, Western Australia
The Bandit Shiraz-Tempranillo, Western Australia (red)

Houghton, part of the important Accolade Wines Group, is Western Australia's largest wine producer. However, this does not detract in any way from the quality of its offerings. They are excellent, and have attracted critical acclaim, as well as numerous awards. Most of the fruit that Houghton uses in its wines is sourced from Western Australia's premium grape-growing regions. Vibrant and affordable, The Bandit Shiraz-Tempranillo is an unusual blend of these two grape varieties, but works extremely well. The result is a bright, vivid, juicy red with lots of pure dark cherry, raspberry, and blackberry fruit, complemented by lingering notes of chocolate and bolstered by a lovely, fresh acidity.

Dale Rd, Middle Swan, WA 6065
www.houghton-wines.com.au

SYRAH / SHIRAZ

Shiraz brought Australian wine onto the international stage in the late 20th century, and it continues to inspire some of the greatest winemaking efforts in that country. Australian Shiraz is usually made in a different style than French Syrah (which is the identical grape variety under a different name), with riper fruit flavours, a thicker texture, and a greater impression of sweetness.

At lower price levels Shiraz can be plump, pleasantly viscous, jammy, and sweet. High-level Shiraz is more complex, with blueberry and violet aromas, a touch of anise, and mouth-filling richness. Big and bold, then, but not rough.

VARIETY OF FLAVOUR

In Australia, Shiraz grapes develop a different spectrum of flavour when they get extra "hang-time" on the vine, and their sugar content and flavour development increases beyond what French Syrah can. Less ripe Shiraz or Syrah often tastes smoky and peppery, while riper versions are jammy.

OVER-DOING IT

Syrah/Shiraz vines tend to grow aggressively, a tendency that is bad for wine quality if not managed by the vine-grower. When too many grape bunches form per plant this reduces the flavour concentration in each. The grower needs to prune the vines thoroughly.

SENSITIVE TO CLIMATE

Wine drinkers like their Syrah/ Shiraz wines in varying styles. It's a good thing, because this grape variety tastes quite different depending largely on the climate in which it is grown. In the variety's home region, France's Rhône Valley, Syrah wines taste leaner and spicier than most of those from Australia.

WRINKLED

Grape growers know their Syrah/ Shiraz is getting really ripe when the berries begin softening and the skin wrinkles or puckers. For a full-bodied style of Syrah/ Shiraz, this is the time to harvest.

WHERE IN THE WORLD?

While Australian winemakers have made Shiraz since the 19th century, the variety is much more established in the Rhône Valley of France, where its history stretches back at least 1,000 years.

It is the signature red grape variety of the Northern Rhône Valley in France, responsible for the distinguished and long-lived wines of Côte-Rôtie and Hermitage, among others. It grows in less abundance in the Southern Rhône and can be part of the famous Châteauneuf-du-Pape blend or in affordable red wines labelled Côtes du Rhône. Syrah is planted widely in other parts of France, California, Australia, South Africa, Italy, and elsewhere.

Australia may have the best examples at everyday prices, but California Syrah has come down in price, and South African examples, sometimes blended with other grapes, are well worth a look.

The following regions are among the best for Syrah/Shiraz. Try bottles from these recommended vintages for the best examples:

Australia: 2010, 2009, 2006, 2005
Northern Rhône: 2009, 2006, 2005
California Central Coast: 2008, 2007

Boekenhoutskloof in South Africa is a Syrah leader, producing dense, dark examples.

Howard Park
Margaret River, Western Australia
Sauvignon Blanc, Western Australia (white)

Howard Park started out in the Great Southern region in 1986, and set up vineyards in Margaret River in 1996, followed by a winery in 2000. It is one of the star attractions of the region. Wines are made under the direction of Tony Davis, who upholds the company's reputation for excellence with a pure and focused house style. Ageworthy Cabernet Sauvignons, steely Rieslings, and taut Sauvignons are all first-rate. Fresh and intense, the Margaret River Sauvignon Blanc is dominated by a fresh herb and green pepper character, with notes of tropical fruit and citrus, a chalky edge, and a crisp acidic finish. This is a true gastronomic wine that packs quite a punch.

Miamup Rd, Cowaramup, WA 6284
www.howardparkwines.com.au

Jacob's Creek Barossa, South Australia
Steingarten Riesling, Barossa (white); Reserve Cabernet Sauvignon, Coonawarra (red)

Parent-company Pernod Ricard has brought high-end Orlando Wines under the banner of Jacob's Creek. This means that the acclaimed Steingarten Riesling, from Barossa, is now a Jacob's Creek wine. Concentrated, fresh, and limey, this minerally classic has a track record for ageing brilliantly. Also great for both quality and value is the fruit-driven Cabernet Sauvignon from Jacob's Creek Reserve range, made with Coonawarra grapes. It shows luscious, ripe blackcurrant and plum fruit, bolstered by creamy, spicy oak.

Barossa Valley Way, Rowland Flat, SA 5351
www.jacobscreek.com

Jim Barry Wines Clare Valley, South Australia
The Lodge Hill Dry Riesling, Clare Valley (white); The Lodge Hill Shiraz, Clare Valley (red)

The legendary Jim Barry was the first college-trained winemaker to operate in the Clare Valley, purchasing one property in 1959 and another in 1964. He began by selling grapes to other winemakers, setting up his own operation in 1974. His son Peter took over the reins as managing director in 1985, expanding to 10 vineyards across the Clare Valley, plus one in Coonawarra. Two of the company's Clare Valley offerings stand out for value and style. An award winner, The Lodge Hill Dry Riesling is zingy and minerally. Dry, verging on the austere, it displays notes of kumquat, lime, and pink grapefruit, with a firm acid backbone, immense length, and great ageing potential. Inky and highly drinkable, The Lodge Hill Shiraz packs vibrant dark berry and plum fruit, mixed with hints of chocolate and mint. All of this makes for an immense mouthful, beautifully supported by delicate and sensual tannins.

Craigs Hill Rd, Clare, SA 5453
www.jimbarry.com

Kalleske Barossa, South Australia
Pirathon Shiraz, Barossa Valley (red)

A true Barossa star, Kalleske is considered by many to have some of the best vineyards in the region, all certified organic. They are located in Greenock, east of the Barossa heartlands, at an altitude of 350m (1,148ft), which helps to moderate temperatures during the growing season. Shiraz and Grenache are the main plantings, with a bit of Cabernet Sauvignon and a smidgen of Chenin Blanc. The winery was set up by brothers Troy and Tony Kalleske, who are the seventh generation of their family to live and work in Barossa since 1853. Their first wines were released in 2004 and are simply brilliant, and that includes the highly affordable Pirathon Shiraz. Really expressive, it has sweet, ripe berry and plum fruit in abundance, with some meatiness, along with bright floral, chocolate, and peppery notes. It is beautifully structured with subtle oak and fine tannins, and has a persistent yet fresh finish.

Vinegrove Rd, Greenock, SA 5360
www.kalleske.com

Katnook Estate Coonawarra, South Australia

Founder's Block Cabernet Sauvignon, Coonawarra (red)

Winemaking at Katnook dates back to 1896, but the first of the estate's current 200ha (494 acres) of vines was not planted until 1971, and the first wines made under the Katnook label only appeared in 1980. Winemaker Wayne Stehbens was responsible for those debut bottlings, and remains firmly at the helm despite several changes of ownership along the way – Katnook was sold to Freixenet in 2008. Cabernet Sauvignon dominates here, as you might expect for Coonawarra, and the wines are consistently good, as well as offering great value. They are made in a rich, very ripe, and sometimes rather oaky style, but tend to settle down with age. The medium-bodied Founder's Block Cabernet Sauvignon shows generous quantities of sweet, well-defined blackcurrant and blackberry fruit, with alluring aromas of ripe berries and violets, plus a hint of mint. A lovely lingering finish crowns the experience of this elegant and well balanced wine.

Riddoch Hwy, Coonawarra, SA 5263
www.katnookestate.com.au

K T and the Falcon Clare Valley, South Australia

Watervale Riesling, Clare Valley (white)

Kerri Thompson – "KT" – a talented winemaker with a particular passion for Riesling, and viticulturalist Stephen Farrugia – "the Falcon" – have teamed up to produce a premium-quality, terroir-driven range of wines from vines cultivated on their 8ha (20-acre) farm, using sustainable, organic practices. They make some noteworthy Shiraz, but Riesling is their main focus. The luscious, exotic Watervale Riesling is crafted from hand-picked grapes, grown at a single vineyard, the Churinga Vineyard in the township of Watervale. Inspired by richer, sweeter styles of Riesling, it is extravagantly aromatic, with beautiful floral, lime, and mineral notes on the nose. In the mouth, there is an abundance of concentrated limey citrus fruit, enhanced by a touch of fragrant spicy and a subtle herby character. All of this finishes with a refreshing burst of bright, crisp acidity. With enough complexity to delight on its own, this wine is a perfect match for spicy, Asian dishes.

Watervale, SA 5452
www.ktandthefalcon.com.au

The Lane

Adelaide Hills, South Australia

Viognier, Adelaide Hills (white)

The Lane wines come from John Edwards' own 52ha (128.5 acres) of vines, which are located high up, above 450m (1,476ft), near Hahndorf. Nine grape varieties are grown here, and wines are made under two labels: Ravenswood Lane and The Lane. The Viognier, from The Lane's Black Label range is a sensuous and powerful but ultra-sophisticated offering. Redolent with aromas of orange blossom, nectar, and almond, with floral, pear, and peach notes, it presents deep, rich flavours of sweet apple, honey, and warm spice on the palate.

Ravenswood Lane, Hahndorf, SA 5245
www.thelane.com.au

THE LANE
VINEYARD
ADELAIDE HILLS

Larry Cherubino Wines Frankland River, Western Australia

The Yard Whispering Hill Vineyard Riesling, Mt Barker, Western Australia (white)

In 2005, Larry Cherubino, one of Australia's most acclaimed young winemakers, launched his own winery business, producing wines from grapes grown in some of Western Australia's finest growing regions. Cherubino is his top label, followed by The Yard, and Ad Hoc. The Whispering Hill Vineyard Riesling is one of The Yard's highly sought-after, single-vineyard bottlings. Pretty, delicate, and very approachable, it is an intensely savoury, dry Riesling, with tight, lime and mineral aromas, and lovely, taut citrus fruit. It shows real presence and potential for further development.

15 York St, Subiaco, Perth WA 6008
www.larrycherubino.com.au

Leasingham Clare Valley, South Australia

Magnus Riesling, Clare Valley (white)

Owners Constellation have sold off the famous, old Leasingham Winery in the Clare Valley, although The Leasingham brand remains part of its stable, offering some extremely interesting and good value wines, including the Magnus Riesling. A very tasty expression of Clare Riesling, especially for its modest price, it is bone-dry and zingy, with intense citrussy fruit. There are distinct signs that it will age well in the medium term, too.

No visitor facilities
www.cbrands.com

Mac Forbes Yarra Valley, Victoria

Riesling rs37, Strathbogie Ranges (white)

The talented Mac Forbes is best known for its Yarra Valley Pinots, but his small, 2,000-case enterprise also produces interesting Riesling from grapes grown in the cool climate of the Strathbogie Ranges, to the northeast of Melbourne. So far, Forbes has produced two of these stunningly precise wines – the rs9 and the rs37 – the names indicating the residual sugar level in each. The rs37, especially, offers astonishing value for such exceptional quality and individuality. It is lively, off-dry, and has real vibrancy. Bright, pure, and minerally, it displays citrus aromas and flavours with soft floral notes, winding down to a satisfying, lengthy finish.

770 Healesville Koo Wee Rup Rd, Healesville, VIC 3777
www.macforbes.com

Majella Coonawarra, South Australia

The Musician, Coonawarra (red)

The Lynn family, Majella's owners, planted their first vines in the late 1960s, and began supplying Wynns in 1980. Their first wine, a Shiraz, appeared in 1991, followed by a Cabernet Sauvignon in 1994 and by their top wine, The Malleea, in 1996. Increasingly, grapes from Majella's 60ha (148 acres) of vineyards are finding their way into the company's own wines, which have attracted numerous awards. Majella is now considered to be one of the best and most consistent Australian wine producers. Among its many highly impressive offerings is a great-value Cabernet-Shiraz blend called The Musician. Lively, aromatic, and moreish, it combines vibrant blackcurrant fruit and herbal flavours with a dash of vanilla and some finely-grained, silky tannins. This is a smooth, complex, yet approachable wine that has a lovely, fresh and pleasantly acidic finish.

Lynn Rd, Coonawarra, SA 5263
www.majellawines.com.au

McGuigan Hunter Valley, New South Wales

The Shortlist Chardonnay, Adelaide Hills (white)

Four generations of the McGuigan family have been involved in the Australian wine industry. Their Hunter Valley operation focuses on producing small batches of super-premium wines, under the skilled eye of winemaker Peter Hall. These include multi-award-winning wines from The Shortlist range, among which sits McGuigan's brilliant crack at high-end Chardonnay. Surprisingly affordable for such a refined bottling, there is a delicious toasty, minerally undercurrent to its ripe pear, peach, and grapefruit flavours. Wonderfully rounded, it has a lingering, refreshing finish.

Rosebery, NSW 1445
www.mcguiganwines.com.au

McHenry Hohnen Margaret River, Western Australia

3 Amigos, Margaret River (red and white)

In 2003, David Hohnen, founder of Cape Mentelle and Cloudy Bay, linked up with brother-in-law Murray McHenry and began crafting wines with grapes from four family-owned Margaret River vineyards. Their excellent 3 Amigos range offers two good-value and unusual blends – a Shiraz-Grenache-Mataro red and a Marsanne-Chardonnay-Roussanne white. Fresh and assertive, the red combination works well, its deep black cherry and plum fruit being perfectly complemented by a firm, spicy core. The intriguing white is intensely aromatic and offers dense, slightly toasty, citrus-laden fruit, plus appealing spicy complexity.

Margaret River, WA 6285
www.mchv.com.au

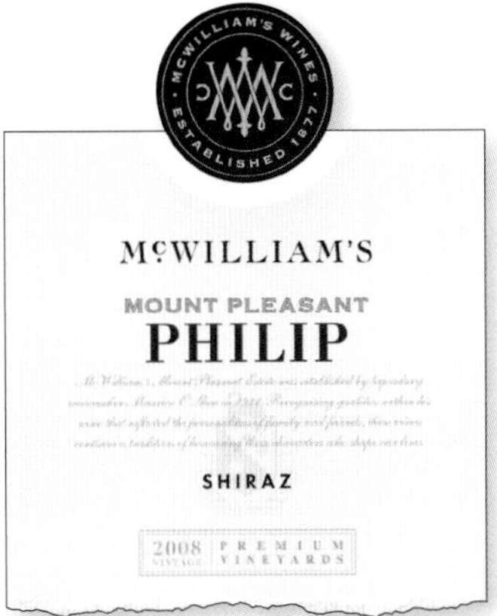

McWilliam's Mount Pleasant Hunter Valley, New South Wales

Mount Pleasant Elizabeth Semillon (white); Mount Pleasant Philip Shiraz (red)

The McWilliam family acquired the Mount Pleasant winery in 1941, retaining the legendary Maurice O'Shea, whose famous wines remain an inspiration to the new generation of Australian winemakers. Now crafted by Phil Ryan, Mount Pleasant's wines are classic Hunter Valley in style. Both the Elizabeth Semillon and Philip Shiraz are absolute bargains. The lively, unoaked Semillon is intensely lemony, with great purity and some decent ageing potential. The moreish Philip Shiraz offers lush, ripe blackberry and blackcurrant fruit, nicely balanced by firm yet fresh acidity.

401 Marrowbone Rd, Pokolbin, NSW 2320
www.mcwilliams.com.au

Mitchell Wines Clare Valley, South Australia

Watervale Riesling, Clare Valley (white); Sevenhill Cabernet Sauvignon, Clare Valley (red)

Andrew and Jane Mitchell set up their small, independent Clare Valley winery in 1975. Today it produces around 30,000 cases a year, entirely from its own 75ha (185 acres) of vineyards. Their Rieslings are among the region's best. Fresh and limey, the Watervale Riesling offers rounded, elegant fruit. Great for drinking now, it also ages well. The Sevenhill Cabernet Sauvignon also stands out. With appealing, ripe blackcurrant fruit, there are lovely spice, gravel, and herby notes that add complexity. The chewy tannins suggest great ageing potential.

Hughes Park Rd, Sevenhill, SA 5453
www.mitchellwines.com

CORK OR SCREWCAP?

Will the pop of a wine cork become a sound heard only in our memories, like the ring of a dial telephone? This friendly little explosion is music to the ears of most wine drinkers, but corks no longer have the wine-stoppering stage to themselves.

Cork-free packaging options now abound, as one wine brand after another appears on the market in a screwcapped bottle, box, carton, and even a pouch. The sound of any of these being opened may never be as inviting as hearing a cork pop, but that doesn't mean they don't contain high quality wine.

Screwcaps and synthetic "corks" became popular largely because they are not subject to the mould that sometimes taints natural corks. Wineries and wine drinkers in New Zealand and Australia were among the first to switch to screwcap wines for this reason. They found that not only were the wines free of cork taint, but they were also easy to open, without the need for a special tool (the corkscrew), and were easy to reseal. Plus, the taste of the wine was unaffected.

Pressured by growing competition from screwcaps, the producers of natural corks have improved their quality control to the point where there are far fewer bad corks in existence today.

Screwcaps are well-suited to perhaps 95 per cent of the world's wines – those that are meant to be opened and enjoyed immediately. Scepticism about the effect of screwcaps on wine quality remains only in the small but expensive category of wines that are meant to sit and age in the bottle for years. Many producers and other experts believe that screwcaps are unable to replicate the way cork lets a small amount of oxygen into the bottle over time, softening the wine and allowing the development of complex aromas and tastes. So, for the foreseeable future, corks are most certainly here to stay, but they are no longer alone, and in the near future, you can expect increasing amounts of everyday wines to be bottled with screwcaps.

Mitchelton

Nagambie Lakes, Victoria

Airstrip Roussanne Marsanne Viognier, Central Victoria (white)

Mitchelton was launched in 1967, when Colin Preece was commissioned by Ross Shelmerdine, a Melbourne businessman, to prospect for a great place to make wine. Preece identified a grazing estate in Nagambie Lakes, because of its combination of soil, climate, and access to water. Since 2007, talented winemaker Ben Haines has been in charge of winemaking here, and makes a solid range of well-priced wines. The rich, distinctive Airstrip white is a popular example. A Rhône-style blend of Roussanne, Marsanne, and Viognier, it offers dense herby melon fruit, followed by some fine subtle nutty notes.

Mitchellstown Rd, Nagambie, VIC 3608
www.mitchelton.com.au

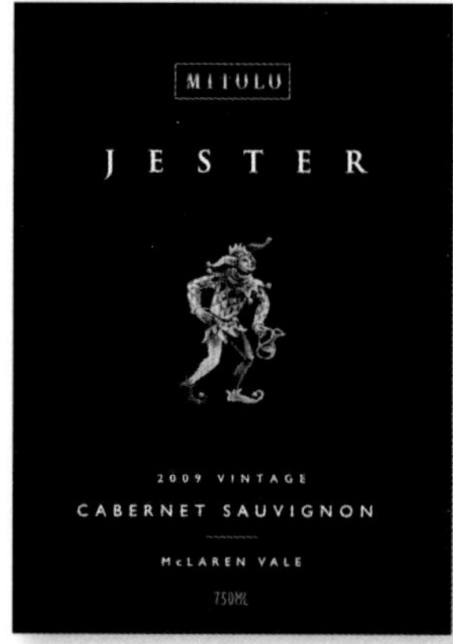

Mitolo McLaren Vale, South Australia

Jester Vermentino, McLaren Vale (white); Jester Cabernet Sauvignon, McLaren Vale (red)

Businessman Frank Mitolo and Barossa winemaker Ben Glaetzer created Mitolo in 1999. Most of the grapes come from Woolunga, at the southern end of the McLaren Vale. Jester are Mitolo's good-value, entry-level wines. They all offer lovely fruit purity. The refreshing Vermentino is a fresh, edgy, lemony white, with sharp acidity. A proportion of the grapes for the Cabernet Sauvignon are dried on racks before fermentation, resulting in a rich red wine with clean blackberry and blackcurrant fruit and a firm, spicy finish.

Angel Vale Rd, Angel Vale, Virginia, SA 5120
www.mitolowines.com.au

Moss Wood Margaret River, Western Australia

The Amy's Blend, Margaret River (red)

Keith Mugford and his wife Clare run one of Margaret River's most highly acclaimed wineries at Moss Wood, producing 15,000 cases of premium-quality wines a year from their 20ha (49.5 acres) of vines. The top-value The Amy's Blend is a deliciously focused Bordeaux-style Cabernet Sauvignon. Approachable and easy-drinking, this velvety red shows delightful red-berry aromas, with deep flavours of dark blackberry fruit, a hint of soft spicy oak, and an attractive minerally edge. Fine yet firm tannin hold it all together.

Metricup Rd, Wilyabrup, WA 6284
www.mosswood.com.au

Mount Langi Ghiran Grampians, Victoria

Billi Billi Shiraz, Victoria (red)

In a spectacularly dramatic setting, at the southern end of the Great Dividing Range in the Grampians region of Western Victoria, the cool climate and soils enjoyed by the vineyards here create a unique environment for cultivating wine grapes. One of the most celebrated results is some of Australia's finest Shiraz. This includes Mount Langi Ghiran's remarkably inexpensive and deliciously forward Billi Billi Shiraz. Based on fruit from 80 to 100-year-old vines, this approachable, fruit-driven red displays a high concentration of ripe, dark berry fruits and distinct notes of uplifting mint and spice. Such complexity and ageing potential are rare at this price level.

80 Vine Rd, Bayindeen, VIC 3375
www.langi.com.au

Nepenthe Adelaide Hills, South Australia
Sauvignon Blanc, Altitude Range, Adelaide Hills (white)

Founded by the Tweddell family in 1994, and owned since 2007 by Australian Vintage, Nepenthe is now a key player in the Adelaide Hills. The wines are commercially astute, and sometimes very good indeed, with Sauvignon Blanc being the pick of the whites. The price-conscious Altitude Range offers a racy, lively expression of Sauvignon, with powerful aromas and flavours of guava, pineapple, and passion fruit, supported by grassy, citrussy notes. Fresh, bright, and pure on the palate, it has a lovely crisp and lasting finish.

Jones Rd, Balhannah, SA 5242
www.nepenthe.com.au

Penfolds Barossa, South Australia
Koonunga Hill Seventy Six Shiraz-Cabernet, South Australia (red)

Dating back to 1844, Penfolds is probably the most famous name in Australian wine. The company's extensive portfolio contains a large range of fine reds, including the celebrated Grange. The good-value Koonunga Hill Seventy Six Shiraz-Cabernet blend is a new wine that sets out to capture the alluringly popular qualities of the original Koonunga Hill offering, first released in 1976. It packs a densely packed punch of spicy, dark berry and plum fruits, with notes of liquorice and dark chocolatey oak adding complexity. While utterly delicious now, it has great ageing potential.

Tanunda Rd, Nuriootpa, SA 5355
www.penfolds.com.au

Petaluma Adelaide Hills, South Australia
Hanlin Hill Riesling, Clare Valley (white)

Petaluma was founded by visionary winemaker Brian Croser in 1976, with the aim of producing top-of-the-class vintages, based on grapes grown on sites that were particularly well-matched for specific varietals. Although now owned by drinks giant Lion Nathan, the company have continued to follow the pure, lean, unadorned, terroir-led wine style set by Croser. Their focused and interesting Hanlin Hill Riesling comes from grapes grown at one of Petaluma's oldest vineyards in the Clare Valley, first planted in 1968. Limey, fresh, and extremely inviting, it displays a charming hint of floral sweetness that adds a rounded texture to the bright passion fruit and lemon flavours. Backed by a lovely, firm acidity, it shows clear potential to age gracefully for decades.

Spring Gully Rd, Piccadilly, SA 5151
www.petaluma.com.au

Peter Lehmann
Barossa, South Australia
Back to Back Grenache, Barossa (red); Wigan Eden Valley Riesling (white)

Peter Lehmann took quite a risk by setting up his own winery in 1979, at a time when many Barossa businesses were struggling, due to serious overproduction. His first vintages were processed in 1980, using grapes from across the entire region. Part of the Hess Family beverage group since 2003, the company now makes around 750,000 cases a year, using fruit from 180 Barossa growers. Many of these wines really excel, particularly for their price. The beautifully balanced Back to Back Grenache is exquisitely light and fruity, offering fine cherry and plum fruit, matched by a subtle herbiness and a hint of pepper. The Wigan Riesling is a superb example of what the Eden Valley does best. Deliciously fresh, with typical limey fruit for this area, it also has the depth and concentration to suggest that it will age well.

Para Rd, Tanunda, SA 5352
www.peterlehmannwines.com.au

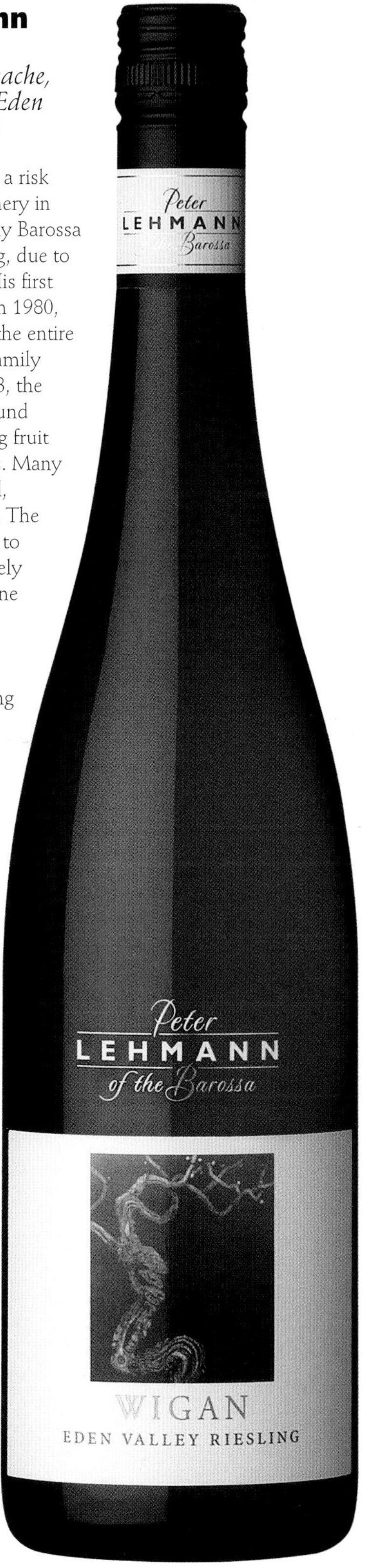

Pirie Tasmania Tasmania

South Pinot Noir, Tasmania (red)

Pirie Tasmania was set up in 2002 by Dr Andrew Pirie, and has a justified reputation for having put Tasmania firmly on the viticultural map. The wines here are produced in four distinct ranges, with the fruit-focused South collection being both deliciously fresh and highly affordable. The South Pinot Noir is certainly worth seeking out. It may not be overly complex, but the delightful cherry fruit is pure and appealing, and is kept lovely and fresh by good firm acidity.

1A Waldhord Drive, Rosevears, TAS 7277
www.pirietasmania.com.au

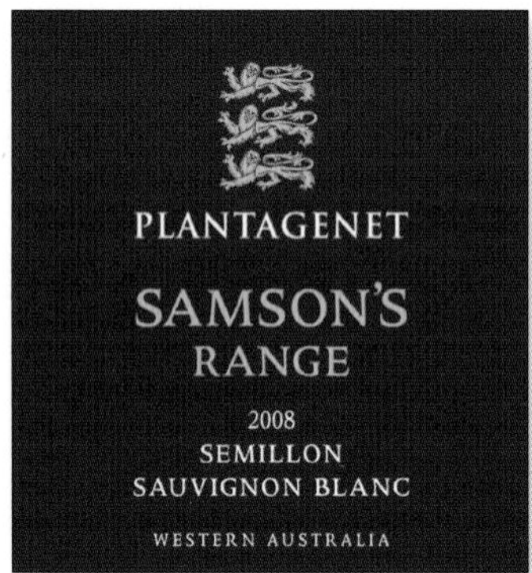

Plantagenet Mount Barker, Western Australia

Samson's Range Semillon Sauvignon Blanc, Western Australia (white)

The first winery in the Mount Barker region, Plantagenet released its debut bottlings in 1974. Founder Tony Smith put quality and style high on his agenda, and after selling to Lionel Samson & Son in 2000, remained as chairman. He and his acclaimed winemaker John Durham, hired in 2007, have kept the winery's top reputation firmly on track. Their approachable Samson's Range Semillon Sauvignon Blanc is an elegant, clean, and grassy blend, with delightfully crisp, citrus notes. Beautifully fragrant and fresh, it is packed with sufficient fruit to give ample weight to drink alone or be matched with a wide range of food.

Lot 45, Albany Hwy, Mount Barker, WA 6324
www.plantagenetwines.com

Rolf Binder Wines Barossa, South Australia

Bulls Blood Shiraz Mataro Pressings, Barossa (red)

With access to fruit from a spread of fine Barossa vineyards, Rolf Binder crafts a distinguished array of good-value, consistently high quality wines at the family-owned Veritas winery that his parents set up in 1955. The company has received a number of awards for both its red and white wines over the years. Its famous Bulls Blood Shiraz Mataro Pressings, renamed the Hubris for some export markets, has been produced at Veritas for more than 40 years. It is a beautifully dense, vibrant, and affordable red. A really robust, gutsy wine, it contains fruit from century-old vines. With firm tannins and a rich, multi-layered texture, it is a red for those who relish plenty of impact and complexity.

Cnr Seppeltsfield Rd and Stelzer Rd, Tanunda, SA 5352
www.veritaswinery.com

Rusden Barossa, South Australia

Christian Chenin Blanc, Barossa Valley (white)

Overproduction leading to low prices made life tough for Barossa grape growers in the late 1970s and early 1980s. Coupled to that, Dennis and Christine Canute were continually being told that the grapes they were struggling to grow on the 16ha (40 acres) they had purchased in 1979 were of inferior quality. Eventually, in 1992, Dennis and a friend, Russell, decided to make a barrel of Cabernet Sauvignon for their own consumption, and so the Rusden label (from their names: Russell and Dennis) was born. From these humble beginnings, a range of sought-after, well-structured wines, with the focus on traditional Barossa grapes and blends, has developed. The Christian Chenin Blanc is named after its creator and current Rusden winemaker, the Canutes' son Christian. A rare Australian example of this varietal, it is an interesting wine. Subtly toasty, it displays forceful aromas of tropical fruit that mingle with a gorgeous palate of ripe pear fruit, grassy herbal notes, and a pithy, citrus freshness. Crisp acidity balances and gives a firm framework to this intriguing complexity.

Magnolia Rd, Tanunda, SA 5352
www.rusdenwines.com.au

St Hallett Barossa, South Australia

Gamekeeper's Reserve, Barossa (red)

At the forefront of the revival of the Barossa Valley wine industry in the 1980s, St Hallett became famous for its Old Block Shiraz, a dense and structured, yet lushly fruited classic, with a record for ageing magnificently. Now part of the Lion Nathan group, St Hallett has made a slight shift in a more commercial direction, but it still manages to produce some very classy wines. From its more budget-conscious range, the Gamekeeper's Reserve offers a lovely depth of flavour at a great price. A delightful, finely tuned blend of Shiraz, Grenache, and Touriga Nacional, its mouthwatering mix of ripe, dark fruit is lifted by a spicy twist, and supported by meaty tannins.

St Hallett Rd, Tanunda, SA 5352
www.sthallett.com.au

Scotchmans Hill Geelong, Victoria

Swan Bay Pinot Noir, Geelong (red)

Quality and value for money are what the Scotchmans Hill vineyard and winery are known for. A major player in the Geelong region, the heart of this family-owned enterprise, founded in 1982, is located close to its main vineyard on the Bellarine Peninsula. Grapes from here and from other Geelong vineyards go into five separate premium-wine ranges. Impressive and complex, especially for its price, the medium-bodied Swan Bay Pinot Noir offers rich aromas of plum and strawberry with attractive notes of violet and spice that lead into a juicy palate of ripe cherry fruit. A dash of toasty oak, silky tannins, and firm acidity give the wine its fine structure and balance.

190 Scotchmans Rd, Drysdale, VIC 3222
www.scotchmans.com.au

Shaw + Smith Adelaide Hills, South Australia
Sauvignon Blanc, Adelaide Hills (white)

One of the Adelaide Hills' most consistent, high performers, Shaw + Smith was launched by cousins Martin Shaw and Michael Hill Smith over a long lunch in 1989. Their exciting reds and vibrant, interesting whites are all greatly revered, but it is their Sauvignon Blanc that first captured the attention of the international wine community. Now a benchmark for Australian Sauvignons, it remains an important wine for the company and makes a great-value entry point into the excellent Shaw + Smith range. A truly superb offering, it combines fresh, zippy, grassy notes with a rich, mouth-filling blast of ripe peach, pear, and pink grapefruit flavours. Racy acidity makes this a really refreshing wine that is at its best when young.

Jones Rd, Balhannah, SA 5242
www.shawandsmith.com

Skillogalee Clare Valley, South Australia
Riesling, Clare Valley (white)

The Palmers, David and Diana, make all their wines at Skillogalee from grapes grown on the estate's 50ha (124 acres) of vineyards, which were originally planted with vines in the early 1970s. The first wines appeared in 1976, and included a dry Riesling that helped put the estate on the map. Current Skillogalee bottlings of this varietal continue to draw praise from the critics and public alike. With lively lime and floral aromas lending interest to a palate of intense citrussy fruit, a crisp acidity leads to a long, bright finish.

Trevarrick Rd, Sevenhill via Clare, SA 5453
www.skillogalee.com.au

Spinifex
Barossa, South Australia
Lola, Barossa Valley (white)

Pete Schell and Magali Gely have been strongly influenced by the south of France in deciding the direction their Spinifex winery, one of the Barossa's most exciting ventures. Pete began making Spinifex wines back in 2001, while he was still working elsewhere, but he now devotes all his energies to the estate's brilliant wines. Lola is a remarkable blend that brings together six different grapes varieties – Semillon, Marsanne, Viognier, Ugni Blanc, Grenache Blanc, and Vermentino. The result is a superb and highly unusual, dry wine that shows distinctly savoury aromas with some minerally notes, leading to dense, creamy lemon and nutty flavours.

Biscay Road, Bethany, SA 5352
www.spinifexwines.com.au

SHOPPING FOR GREAT VALUE

How do you increase the odds of finding excellent quality wines at affordable prices? A good place to start, of course, is to look for wines listed in this book. Beyond that, the most important thing is learning what makes a great value wine. Many shops and restaurants try to entice you to buy the wines on which they make the most profit. These might be poorly made wines with a very low wholesale price, or high-quality wines with enough brand appeal that the merchant marks them up excessively and still finds buyers. To see through the marketing, search for wines that meet one or more of the following simple criteria.

UNDER-APPRECIATED GRAPE VARIETALS

Some grape varietals and types are underrated in particular regions. In the US, for example, low-quality California Chenin Blanc has given the grape a bad name, so even high-quality examples from better regions such as the Loire Valley and South Africa, tend to be underpriced. Sémillon, Gewürztraminer, and even Grenache can fit this mould.

UNDER-VALUED REGIONS

Regions that are known for being the best in the world at making a specific style are not the places to look for good value in that style. Sancerre, in the Loire Valley, for example, makes great Sauvignon Blanc, but it tends to be expensive. Try wines from the nearby Touraine appellation or from countries such as Chile instead.

SECOND WINES

Top Bordeaux châteaux make "second" and "third" wines to ensure that their top "*grand vins*" are as good as they can be. They do it by "selection" – the cellarmaster tastes from every barrel or tank and selects the best ones for the first wine. Selection improves the first wine by excluding the lower-quality batches of wine. In most years these "leftovers" make for excellent drinking in the second wine.

HOUSE BLENDS

Wineries typically have leftover quantities of wine. This may be due to the selection process (see "Second Wines"), an especially large harvest, or light orders from their usual customers. A winery may blend this to make an unusual but good-tasting non-varietal wine and sell it at a price just high enough to make a slim profit and empty the cellar. These are sometimes called cuvées, house blends, or simply red and white.

WINERIES THAT VALUE VALUE

Some wineries simply choose to make good wines for low prices, and it's worth remembering their names when you encounter them. They may have bought their vineyards decades ago and have no mortgages to pay, or the owners may be content with simple lifestyles. In some cases a business plan dictates making large quantities of good-quality wine and selling it at the slimmest margins.

Stonier Mornington Peninsula, Victoria

Pinot Noir, Mornington Peninsula (red); Chardonnay, Mornington Peninsula (white)

One of the Mornington Peninsula's first wineries, Stonier remains one of the best. Beautifully textured and elegant Pinot Noirs and Chardonnays have sealed its reputation, with even the regular and less costly bottlings standing out for their excellence. The basic Pinot Noir is a deliciously affordable example of a Mornington Peninsula wine. Elegant, with a soft, supple texture, it is packed with delicious ripe, sweet red cherry and berry fruit. A light brush of oak adds character to the Chardonnay, also crafted from Mornington Peninsula grapes. This fruity offering, with aromas and flavours of fresh citrus, plus pear notes and a hint of toast, has a stylish, fresh, clean finish.

2 Thompsons Lane, Merricks, VIC 3916
www.stoniers.com.au

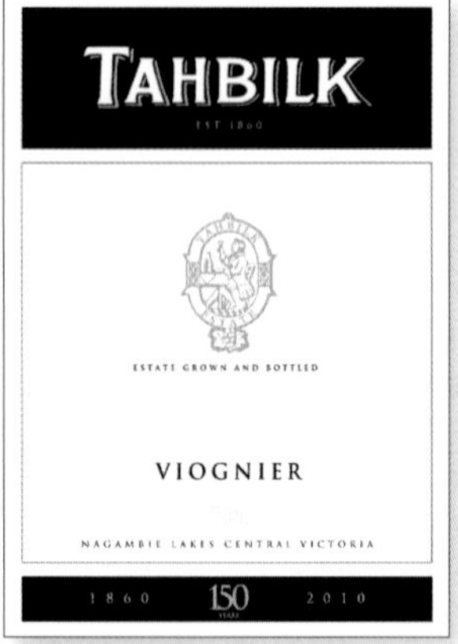

Tahbilk Nagambie Lakes, Victoria

Marsanne, Nagambie Lakes (white); Viognier, Nagambie Lakes (white)

With around 200ha (495 acres) of vines, the Tahbilk operation is sizeable. Winemaking here dates back to 1860, and is steeped in tradition – the ageworthy and affordable Marsanne being a bit of a legend. A characterful wine, with a reputation for ageing beautifully, it is dominated by concentrated, bright lemon and lime fruit in its youth, developing with a decade's bottle age to reveal notes of toast, beeswax, and honey. Also worth looking out for is the powerful, aromatic Viognier. There is intensity of flavour here, with a zip of pithy grapefruit freshness, touched by notes of peach and pear.

Goulburn Valley Hwy, Nagambie, VIC 3608
www.tahbilk.com.au

Tamar Ridge Tasmania

Devil's Corner Pinot Noir, Tasmania (red)

Now owned by Brown Brothers, Tamar Ridge is a large venture, with around 300ha (741 acres) of vines located in three different sites, all overseen by leading viticultural consultant Richard Smart. Another top name here is that of the CEO and chief winemaker, Dr Andrew Pirie. Under their stewardship, Tamar Ridge is fast emerging as a Tasmanian star, with its impressive cool-climate wines. Especially noteworthy are the Sauvignon Blanc and Pinot Noir, of which there is a lovely, well-judged example in the price-conscious Devil's Corner range. This is a light, fresh style of Pinot, with pure, juicy cranberry and cherry fruit and just a hint of balancing tannins to provide some structure.

653 Auburn Rd, Kayena, TAS 7270
www.tamarridge.com.au

Taylors/Wakefield Clare Valley, South Australia

Cabernet Sauvignon, Clare Valley (red)

Labelled as Wakefield for the export market, the wines produced at the 500,000-case Taylors winery, under the direction of chief winemaker Adam Eggins, are truly excellent. Cabernet Sauvignon is generally the Clare Valley's most popular wine, and the basic example made here is one of the best from a very good range. It offers lots of lively, sweet blackcurrant and berry fruit, with a subtle, spicy, and minerally core, finishing off with some nice, lingering crisp acidity. If cellared well, this well-balanced red shows potential for some interesting development.

Taylors Rd, Auburn, SA 5451
www.taylorswines.com.au

Teusner Wines Barossa, South Australia

The Riebke Shiraz, Barossa Valley (red)

A newcomer to the wine business, Kym Teusner is a young winemaker who is establishing quite a reputation in the Barossa Valley. The Teusner label was launched by Kym and his brother-in-law, viticulturalist Michael Page, in 2002. Their range has grown considerably over the years, and as well as some superb high-end vintages, there are several very affordable ones too. Most affordable is The Riebke Shiraz, a deliciously pure and sophisticated Barossa example of this grape variety. Sweetly scented with aromas of plum, blackberry, and cherry, it displays lush, velvety, ripe blackberry and blackcurrant fruit with floral notes, all finely balanced by an uplifting edge of spice and meaty tannins.

Cnr Research Rd & Railway Terrace, Nuriootpa, SA 5355
www.teusner.com.au

Tim Adams Clare Valley, South Australia

Semillon, Clare Valley (white); Riesling, Clare Valley (white)

Tim Adam launched the business that bears his name in 1987, after a brief partnership with a local cooper, Bill Wray, ended on Bill's death. Since then, the company's Clare Valley wines have established an international reputation for quality and value. Just over 1,000 tonnes (984 tons) of grapes annually, sourced from 11 vineyards across the valley (of which Tim owns four), go into making the winery's expanding range. The best wines here are the powerful, ageworthy Semillon and the limey, intense Riesling. With its crisp, taut fruit, vanilla notes, some melony richness and high acidity, the Semillon is a really fine, good-value food wine. The Riesling is a bone-dry, Clare Valley classic – limey and minerally, with good acidity and a lemony zip.

Clare, SA 5453
www.timadamswines.com.au

FOOD & WINE BAROSSA VALLEY SHIRAZ

Australian Shiraz, especially from the excellent growing regions of McLaren Vale and the Barossa Valley, is inky in colour, with very forward raspberry, cherry, boysenberry, lilac, lavender, menthol, and sweet vanilla notes (from oak-ageing). There is nothing shy or understated about these wines. They are outgoing, warm, friendly, and instantly likeable.

Despite relatively high alcohol, generous oak usage, and sweet, ripe fruit, the top Australian versions are well balanced. There are also plenty of options at everyday prices. These jazzy reds are smooth, clean, round, warm, and spicy enough to satisfy the palate on their own, and are enjoyed by drinkers around the world as you might enjoy a cocktail or aperitif. However, they pair beautifully with a wide range of dishes.

Lighter versions of Barossa Valley Shiraz are easygoing enough to serve with pizza, burgers, kebabs, and ribs, or a lightly spiced dish of sausagemeat sauce with pasta. Medium-bodied Shiraz is ideal for braised beef, grilled steak, roasted pork loin, or roast leg of lamb. The richest Shiraz is perfect for rich meat dishes as well as game. Creating a flavour bridge from the mint notes in the wine to the mint jelly served with roast lamb is another great pairing. Venison, or local kangaroo in Australia, would pair nicely too, with the ripe fruit acting as a contrast to the dark, gamey meat.

Pizza topped with sausagemeat contrasts with fruity Shiraz.

Torbreck Barossa, South Australia
Cuvée Juveniles, Barossa Valley (red)

Ever since founder and chief winemaker David Powell released Torbreck's first vintages in 1997, they have attracted a substantial following, particularly in the US. The house-style here is for big, rich, aromatic reds, but they are never over-ripe and always retain some definition and a clear structure, despite their size. Everything from Torbreck is good and enticing, and that includes one of its most affordable bottlings – the Cuvée Juveniles, named after a cult wine bar in Paris that Torbreck made an exclusive wine for in 1999. It is a wonderfully expressive, meaty, unoaked red, reflecting David Powell's and the Juveniles owner's passion for the Rhône Valley varietals – Grenache, Mataro (Mourvèdre), and Shiraz – that go into the blend. Soft and sensual, bold and seductive, its ripe, juicy blackberry and dark cherry fruit just sing out at you. All this is held in check by crisp acidity and fine, silky tannins. Although alluring when young, a few years of cellaring should be rewarding.

Roennfeldt Rd, Marananga, SA 5355
www.torbreck.com

Two Hands Barossa, South Australia
Gnarly Dudes, Barossa Valley (red)

Former wine exporter Michael Twelftree and his ex-accountant, business partner Richard Mintz are the "two hands" here. They have stormed the American market with their boldly flavoured, ripe, and sometimes quite alcoholic, reds. The wines are well made and brilliantly packaged, although some may find their styling a little overblown, flaunting ripeness at the cost of definition. However, if you like full-flavoured wines that pack a real punch then Two Hands' offerings will certainly appeal. The extensive range draws on grapes from a wide spread of premium regions, including McLaren Vale, Padthaway, and Heathcote, in addition to Barossa. The affordable Gnarly Dudes, made from Barossa Shiraz, is a good choice to start with. Very full, rich, and intense, there is a delicious vibrancy and freshness to the super-ripe, dark berry and cherry fruit that holds all its exuberance in check.

Neldner Rd, Marananga, SA 5355
www.twohandswines.com

Tyrrell's Hunter Valley, New South Wales
Heathcote Shiraz, Victoria (red)

Murray Tyrrell and his son Bruce, the current managing director, are the driving force behind the continuing success of the family-owned Tyrrell's winery in the Hunter Valley. Dating back to 1858, it is one of the pioneering forces in the region. Tyrrell's grew rapidly during the 1980s and 1990s, but recently sold its non-Hunter, Long Flat brand in order to focus more on premium wines. Its range contains some of Australia's best wines, including the famous, award-winning Semillons. But some lovely reds also come out of Tyrrell's winery. The Shiraz from Victoria's Heathcote region is an attractive, deep-coloured wine that shows sweet, well-focused blackberry and dark cherry fruit, accompanied by some spice and vanilla from the oak it was aged in.

1838 Broke Rd, Pokolbin, NSW 2320
www.tyrrells.com.au

Wirra Wirra McLaren Vale, South Australia
The 12th Man Chardonnay, Adelaide Hills (white)

In 1969, the late Greg Trott and his first cousin Roger re-opened this historic McLaren Vale winery, which had fallen into total ruin, and began making wine here again. Around 100,000 cases a year now make their way from Wirra Wirra's doors to customers across the globe. The portfolio includes a broad range of well-made wines, mostly crafted from McLaren Vale grapes. The 12th Man Chardonnay is an exception, being made from vines grown in the nearby Adelaide Hills. A stylish, oak-matured offering, it displays alluring toasty peach and citrus notes that lead to a complex mix of zesty lime and grapefruit flavours, with rounded spicy and nutty overtones. A tight, crisp acidity brings texture and balance to this delicious, great-value wine.

McMurtrie Rd, McLaren Vale, SA 5171
www.wirrawirra.com

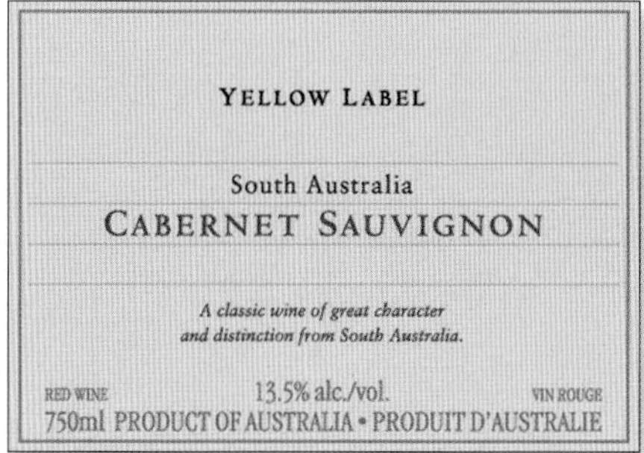

Wolf Blass Barossa, South Australia
Yellow Label Cabernet Sauvignon, South Australia (red)

Wolf Blass is one of the top brands in the Foster's Group drinks stable. It offers admirable quality at a wide range of prices – quite a remarkable feat for an operation that turns out around 4 million cases of wine a year. The ranges are tiered by label colour, and start to get interesting with the Yellow Label, while remaining good value. The Cabernet Sauvignon from this grouping is cheap, widely available, and still utterly delicious, with its lovely, finely poised combination of ripe blackcurrant fruit and some spicy, slightly tarry oak. There should be a lot more good, inexpensive wines like this on the market.

97 Sturt Hwy, Nuriootpa, SA 5355
www.wolfblass.com.au

Wyndham Estate Hunter Valley, New South Wales
George Wyndham Shiraz Cabernet (red)

An old Hunter Valley producer, the Wyndham Estate is now just a cellar door, with the wines made elsewhere. Many of the entry-level bottlings are over-produced and suffer as a consequence, but the new George Wyndham range marks a significant step up in quality for only a small increase in price. The dense, fruity Shiraz Cabernet has immediate appeal. Deliciously rounded, its sweet berry, spice, and minty aromas, enhanced by notes of nutty oak, mingle beautifully with the blackcurrant and cassis flavours. With a clean finish and fine tannins, it has everything in the right place.

700 Dalwood Rd, Dalwood, NSW 2335
www.wyndhamestate.com

Yabby Lake Mornington Peninsula, Victoria
Red Claw Chardonnay, Mornington Peninsula (white); Red Claw Pinot Noir, Mornington Peninsula (red)

Yabby Lake wines are made with grapes harvested from four separate properties owned by the Kirby family. Their celebrated winemaker and general manager, Tom Carson, has crafted a selection of wines here that all offer a brilliant balance of class, complexity, and elegance. The Chardonnay and Pinot Noir from the Red Claw range are perfect examples of this, and also deliver astonishing interest for their price. The superb Chardonnay is bold and fruity, with nutty, toasty notes, and a natural, crisp acidity that leads to a long, drawn-out finish. The Pinot is silky and smooth, its fragrant cherry fruit highlighted by hints of spice, mint, and oak.

112 Tuerong Rd, Tuerong, VIC 3933
www.yabbylake.com

Yalumba Barossa, South Australia
Y Series Viognier, South Australia (white); Riesling Pewsey Vale, Eden Valley (white)

Founded in 1849, Yalumba is the oldest family-owned winery in Australia. It is big – producing almost a million cases a year – but it is also very good. Its Y Series varietals offer fantastic value for money, especially the expressive Viognier. It shows bright peach and pear fruit, with a pithy, satisfying finish. Yalumba also now runs Eden Valley's first vineyard, Pewsey Vale, noted for its fine, well-priced Riesling. It shows refreshing citrus and lime fruit, with some floral, honeysuckle notes. Drink it now, or enjoy the rewards of careful cellaring, any time over the next 20 years.

Eden Valley Rd, Angaston, SA 5353
www.yalumba.com

Yering Station Yarra Valley, Victoria
Willow Lake Old Vine Chardonnay, Yarra Valley (white)

Yering Station, Victoria's first vineyard, was originally planted in 1837. Purchased by the Rathbone Wine Group in 1966, it developed a reputation for distinctive, world-class wines under the direction of star winemaker Tom Carson. Willy Lunn, who succeeded Carson in 2008, continues to craft winners, although the much-lauded Willow Lake Old Vine Chardonnay is actually a Carson-era wine. Lean and lemony, this is a beautifully taut, unoaked styling. Lifted by notes of green apple and wet slate, it makes a striking mouthful, displaying great minerality and a long smoky finish.

38 Melba Hwy, Yarra Glen, VIC 3775
www.yering.com

New Zealand

New Zealand exploded onto the global wine stage in the 1980s with the wine style that remains its signature and still dominates production: Marlborough Sauvignon Blanc. The appeal was easy to understand: with their pungent, ripe gooseberry and passion fruit aromas and flavours, and their crisp acidity, these white wines were highly drinkable and instantly recognizable. In recent times, New Zealand has followed up its success with Sauvignon with its bright-fruited, accessible take on Pinot Noir in supple reds that are much more consistent (and considerably cheaper) than those produced in the grape variety's home in the Burgundy region of France. It does not stop there, however. Many would argue that New Zealand's complex Chardonnays, voluptuous Pinot Gris, and refreshing Rieslings are better than its Sauvignons, while the Syrahs from the Hawkes Bay area are spicy rivals for France's Northern Rhône.

Ara Marlborough

Composite Pinot Noir, Marlborough (red); Composite Sauvignon Blanc, Marlborough (white)

Top winemakers have been drawn to this fine operation in Marlborough. Until early 2011, the wines were made by Dr Damian Martin, a Bordeaux-trained winemaker whose wines were a little more European in style than many of his peers. Martin's influence can be felt in the angular Composite Pinot Noir, which has bright cherry and berry fruits kept in check by a savoury, spicy, slightly earthy dimension, with good acidity that make it worth sticking a few bottles in the cellar. The Composite Sauvignon Blanc also has some European styling: dominated by crisp, grassy, grapefruit notes, as well as some attractive minerality, it is not showy, but quite serious. The future looks bright at Ara, which has recruited Jeff Clarke – the man who oversaw the rise of Montana/ Brancott Estate for 17 years – as Martin's successor.

Renwick, Marlborough
www.winegrowersofara.co.nz

Ata Rangi Martinborough

Crimson Pinot Noir, Martinborough (red)

While Ata Rangi's estate Pinot Noir is one of New Zealand's most highly sought after wines, the second wine, labelled Crimson, is much more affordable and easier to get hold of. On the palate it delivers plenty of bright, forward red cherry fruit, and there's some sappy, herbal complexity too, making this a delicious wine. Founded with very little investment or fanfare in 1980 by Clive Paton, and then run along similar lines for much of its early life, Ata Rangi has gone on to be a major player in Martinborough, and undoubtedly one of the best producers anywhere in the country. Today the vineyards extend to some 30ha (74 acres) and winemaking is in the hands of the highly talented Helen Masters, producing a fine range of wines from Sauvignon Blanc, Riesling, the Bordeaux varieties, Syrah, Pinot Gris, as well as Pinot Noir.

Puruatanga Rd, Martinborough, South Wairarapa
www.atarangi.co.nz

Bilancia Hawkes Bay

Bilancia Pinot Gris, Hawkes Bay (white)

Bilancia, founded in 1997, takes its name from the Italian name for Libra, a star sign shared by owners Warren Gibson (of fellow New Zealand producer, Trinity Hill) and his wife Lorraine Leheny. Just as pertinently, Bilancia also means "balance" or "harmony", two adjectives that certainly fit the wines and the winemaking ethos at this high-end Hawkes Bay producer. The couple are perhaps best known for their Syrah, but the Italian influence discernible in the estate's name is possibly more apparent in the excellent Bilancia Pinot Gris. This is a long way from the average, neutral Pinot Gris style: instead, it is full flavoured and complex with notes of pear and spice, and a smooth, full texture.

Stortford Lodge, Hawkes Bay
www.bilancia.co.nz

Blind River

Awatere, Marlborough

Sauvignon Blanc, Marlborough (white)

From the Awatere Valley, Blind River's Sauvignon Blanc is one of the best from New Zealand, offering vivid, bright passion fruit and grapefruit notes as well as an attractive grassiness. An extra dimension of flavour and texture comes from fermenting 10% of the juice in old oak barrels. Blind River is a small operation that started its life as a retirement project for Barry and Diane Feicker. It soon became more serious, however, and it is now run by their three daughters: Debbie (a winemaker with experience in Australia and California), Suzie, and Wendy.

Redwood Pass, Awatere Valley, RD4, Blenheim, Marlborough
www.blindriver.co.nz

BLIND RIVER
MARLBOROUGH
2010
SAUVIGNON BLANC

Brancott Estate Marlborough
Sauvignon Blanc, Marlborough (white)

With the 2010 vintage, the name of New Zealand's largest wine company was changed from Montana to Brancott Estate, a name it was already using in the US. Established in the 1970s, and now owned by Pernod Ricard, it crushes 20,320 tonnes (20,000 tons) of Sauvignon Blanc each year, and produces high volumes of its benchmark Marlborough Sauvignon Blanc. Crisp, fresh, and vibrant with a lovely passion fruit edge to the focused grapefruit and citrus fruit, this entry-point wine is best drunk young.

State Hwy 1, Riverlands, Blenheim, Marlborough
www.brancottestate.com

Cloudy Bay Marlborough
Pelorus Brut NV, Marlborough (sparkling)

There can be few more famous names in New Zealand than Cloudy Bay, which played a huge role in establishing the country's wine industry on the global stage with its legendary Marlborough Sauvignon Blanc. That wine is perhaps not quite what it once was – it is certainly produced in much higher volumes than it used to be – but this producer is still an important and quality-conscious player in New Zealand. Indeed, the sparkling wine, Pelorus Brut NV Cloudy Bay is still unequivocally superb. It's fresh, citrussy, and quite toasty with good acidity and lovely purity of fruit. There's also a delicate grapefruit pith character here.

Jacksons Rd, Blenheim, Marlborough
www.cloudybay.co.nz

Craggy Range Winery Hawkes Bay
Te Kahu, Hawkes Bay (red); Sauvignon Blanc Old Renwick Vineyard, Marlborough (white)

A blend of Merlot and Cabernet Sauvignon by a top producer from the famed Gimblett Gravels in Hawkes Bay, Craggy Range Te Kahu is a deliciously poised red with savoury, gravelly dark cherry, and blackcurrant fruit. Quite dense, with some chocolate and tar complexity, it is a lovely mix of Old and New World style, a description that also applies to the Old Renwick Vineyard Sauvignon Blanc. This isn't your usual in-yer-face Marlborough-style Sauvignon, but instead offers precisely focused citrussy fruit with a restrained herbal, mineral character, making it both classy and food friendly.

253 Waimarama Rd, Havelock North, Hawkes Bay
www.craggyrange.com

Delta Vineyard Marlborough
Hatter's Hill Pinot Noir, Marlborough (red)

London-based wine merchant David Gleave and roving New Zealand winemaker Matt Thomson set up Delta Vineyard with the help of two other investors in the Waihopai Valley in Marlborough in 2000. The pair had previously worked together on a series of winemaking projects in Italy, and in the many hours they spent travelling together, they hatched a plan to make wine together. They planted the first vineyards – in sites found by Thomson where the soil was low in vigour and rich in clay – in 2001 and 2002, and soon began making some high quality Pinot Noir. The Delta Vineyards, Hatter's Hill, from vines planted on the hillsides, is a great value Pinot Noir, offering focused cherry and berry fruit with a hint of earthy depth and good acidity. Expressive and quite pure.

2A Opawa St, Blenheim, Marlborough
www.deltawines.co.nz

Dog Point Vineyard Marlborough
Chardonnay, Marlborough (white)

The influence of Cloudy Bay looms large at Dog Point Vineyard: James Healy and Ivan Sutherland were respectively winemaker and viticulturalist at the famed Marlborough producer before setting up Dog Point Vineyard. Using fruit sourced from top vineyards around the Wairau Valley, they make a range of high quality wines from Pinot Noir, Chardonnay, and Sauvignon Blanc. The Chardonnay is one of the most exciting examples of this grape variety currently being produced anywhere in the New World. It spends 18 months in French oak, some of it new, and it has a lovely toasty, flinty edge to the bold peach and pear fruit, finishing with lively acidity. It is utterly superb stuff.

Dog Point Rd, Renwick, Marlborough
www.dogpoint.co.nz

Esk Valley Estate
Hawkes Bay
Esk Valley Verdelho, Hawkes Bay (white)

Fortified wines used to be the speciality at this Hawkes Bay producer, which started its life way back (in the New Zealand context) in the 1930s as Glenvale. The Esk Valley brand was acquired by George Fistonich, the man behind Villa Maria, in the 1980s, after Glenvale had gone into receivership, but it has remained a separate concern, and the wine team has been led by the same man, Gordon Russell, since 1993. Russell is a *terroiriste* who takes a minimal approach to making wines such as the Esk Valley Verdelho. The only wine made from this grape variety in New Zealand, it is of more than just novelty value, offering fresh, herby fruit with a rich texture and some fruit sweetness, finishing with good acidity.

Main Rd, Bay View, Napier, Hawkes Bay
www.eskvalley.co.nz

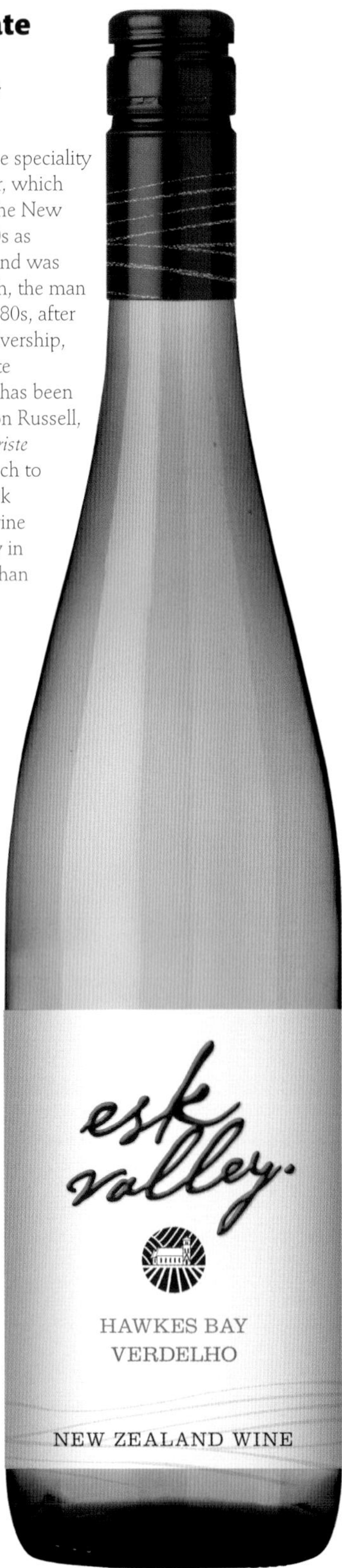

Foxes Island Wines Marlborough
Riesling, Marlborough (white); Fox by John Belsham Pinot Noir, Marlborough (red)

From a stony-soiled vineyard in the Awatere, Foxes Island Riesling is a pure, mineralic dry expression of the grape variety with focused limey fruit. Quite delicious, it has the potential for development in bottle. The Fox by John Belsham Pinot Noir is perhaps even more impressive. Silky smooth and light, it is a perfectly poised Pinot offering red cherry and cranberry fruit with a spicy twist. It is expressive and elegant, and very good value. The "John Belsham" in the wine's name started out in wine at Château de Saturnin in Bordeaux in 1977. His vinous career continued back in New Zealand at Matua Valley and Hunter's, before he set up first Vintec, a contract winemaking facility, and then Foxes Island, after planting his own vineyard in 1988.

8 Cloudy Bay Drive, Cloudy Bay Business Park, RD4, Blenheim, Marlborough
www.foxes-island.co.nz

Framingham Marlborough
Classic Riesling, Marlborough (white)

Framingham are New Zealand's specialists in Riesling, and they make quite a few of them. The Classic Riesling may be the cheapest of these, but it's wonderful, showing lovely rounded citrus fruit character, with great balance. Given the very high quality, it's brilliantly affordable, too. The estate's history dates back to the beginning of the 1980s, when Rex Brooke-Taylor first started planting vines in Marlborough. The first wines from the estate arrived in 1994, and a new winery was constructed in 1997. Framingham's Riesling reputation is largely down to winemaker Andrew Headley, who has shown a real affinity for the grape.

no visitor facilities
www.framingham.co.nz

Gladstone Vineyard Wairarapa
Pinot Gris, Wairarapa (white)

Christine and David Kernohan left their native Scotland in the 1970s, when David became a professor at the faculty of architecture at Wellington University. The couple went into wine when they bought Gladstone Vineyard, a slice of the Gladstone sub-region of Wairarapa that had been developed in the mid-1980s. In the past 15 years the operation has grown to include a restaurant and a winery, and the vineyards have expanded. The work here is all done in a sustainable manner, with cover-crops planted between the vines to provide an environment for beneficial insects, and a generally light touch in both the vineyard and the winery. As well as making a serious Pinot Noir, Gladstone are also doing good things with Pinot Gris. The Gladstone Vineyard Pinot Gris is textured, broad, and full flavoured with lovely rich melony fruit, kept fresh with a citrus pith edge.

Gladstone Rd, RD2, Carterton, Wairarapa
www.gladstonevineyard.co.nz

Jackson Estate Marlborough
Shelter Belt Chardonnay, Marlborough (white)

New Zealand Chardonnay is underrated, as Jackson Estate's Shelter Belt Chardonnay, one of the country's best examples of the grape variety, proves. It's rich but fresh with complex spice and toast notes complementing the pear and peach fruit, and is boldly flavoured yet really harmonious. Founded by John Stichbury in 1987, with the first wines released in 1991, Jackson Estate is right up there as one of New Zealand's top producers. The talented chief winemaker, Mike Paterson, is behind a consistently good portfolio, which uses fruit sourced in five vineyards.

22 Liverpool Street, Renwick, Marlborough
www.jacksonestate.co.nz

Kumeu River Wines Auckland
Kumeu River Village Chardonnay, Auckland (white)

Kumeu River Wines is a Chardonnay specialist, an estate that proves that New Zealand versions of this grape variety deserve to be much better known around the world. It is a family business, run by the three Brajkovich brothers, Michael, Milan, and Paul, whose grandparents had emigrated to New Zealand from Croatia. Though the family had been involved in grape growing since the 1940s, it was the three brothers that made the estate what it is today, and between them they do everything from winemaking to viticulture and marketing. The operation is located in Kumeu, northwest of the city of Auckland, and it produces a little Pinot Noir as well as a variety of Chardonnays. The entry-level Kumeu River Village Chardonnay represents simply brilliant stuff for the money: fresh, fruity, and a bit toasty with appealing citrus notes and hints of ripe apple. It's like a really good Chablis, but a bit richer.

550 State Hwy 16, Kumeu
www.kumeuriver.co.nz

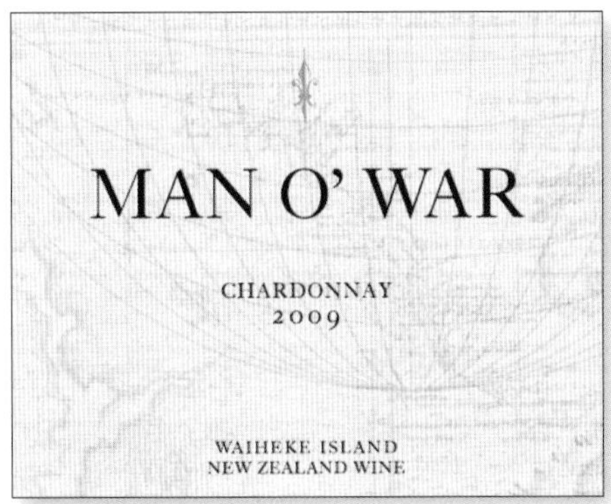

Man O' War Waiheke Island
Man O' War Chardonnay, Waiheke Island (white)

Mostly tank fermented, with a portion in wood, Man O' War Chardonnay is fruit-dominated, with incredible aromatics and a bit of toasty richness, as well as notes of melon, pineapple, pear, and

FOOD & WINE NEW ZEALAND SAUVIGNON BLANC

Although Sauvignon Blanc originates in Bordeaux, the most varietally expressive version is found in New Zealand, where the climate and intense sunlight allow for full flavour expression at the ripest extreme.

New Zealand Sauvignon Blanc is internationally renowned for its exuberant fruit and ripeness with tropical fruit notes of guava, mango, star fruit, passion fruit, and pineapple. As the grapes ripen with age on the vine the herbaciousness becomes less intense, but without some grassiness the wines may be unbalanced, so many winemakers confess to mixing in some less ripe fruit for that gooseberry/grassy kick.

While these very full flavoured, fresh, zingy wines are easily enjoyed on their own as an aperitif, they are delicious with a range of dishes, especially those that are easy going and uncomplicated. With local dishes, such as fish and chips and coconut fish with cucumber salad, their acidity cleanses and refreshes the palate.

For more internationally known dishes, these wines are light enough for ceviche, and perfect with weeknight dishes such as prawns with melon salsa, grilled stuffed chillies, lemon chicken, or a light fennel, tangerine, and goat's cheese salad.

Fish and chips: perfect with zingy Sauvignon Blanc.

peach. It is a quite brilliant effort from this excellent Waiheke Island producer. Man O' War was founded in 1993, when the Spencer family planted a vineyard on their large (1,821ha/4,500 acre) and spectacularly beautiful estate at the far northeastern end of the island. Their first releases were marketed as Stoney Batter, the name of fortifications found on the estate, but they soon switched to Man O' War. The family now have 61ha (150 acres) of vineyards which are divided into 90 small plots, with all work carried out by hand, led by the man who first planted the vines, vineyard manager, Matt Allen. Winemaking is in the hands of Duncan McTavish.

Man O' War Bay Rd, Man O' War Bay, Waiheke Island
www.manowarvineyards.co.nz

Martinborough Vineyard Martinborough
Te Tera Pinot Noir, Martinborough (red)

Te Tera Pinot Noir, Martinborough Vineyard's second-label Pinot, is a really fantastic wine in its own right, offering bright cherry fruit with some herbal, sappy undertones. Elegant, fresh, and well balanced, it is the latest piece in a long line of evidence supporting the claims made by soil scientist Dr Derek Milne, in a report he published in 1978, that Martinborough was the best place in New Zealand for Pinot Noir. Milne put his money where his mouth was, becoming one of the investors in the Martinborough Vineyard, which was first planted in 1980. The vineyard yielded its first commercial wines in 1984, and by 1986 the investors had hired Larry McKenna as winemaker. McKenna was succeeded first by Claire Mullholland and then by Paul Mason, and between them the three have consistently, and deliciously, helped prove Dr Milne's prescience.

Princess St, Martinborough, South Wairarapa
www.martinborough-vineyard.com

Matakana Estate Matakana
Sauvignon Blanc, Marlborough (white)

Matakana Estate makes a concentrated, lively expression of Sauvignon Blanc with melon, passion fruit, grapefruit, and herb notes. It's no shrinking violet, with exuberant flavours and a fresh finish. The estate takes its name from the small wine region to the north of Auckland where it, and a handful of others, has made its home. The Matakana region is spread across two peninsulas, and, in climate, it is similar to Waiheke Island. A boutique operation, Matakana Estate sources the fruit for its impressive range from both Matakana region and other regions in New Zealand.

568 Matakana Rd, Matakana
www.matakanaestate.co.nz

The Millton Vineyard Gisborne
Millton Chenin Blanc Te Arai Vineyard, Gisborne (white)

Is Millton Chenin Blanc Te Arai Vineyard New Zealand's best Chenin Blanc? It is hard to think of a wine that does a better job with this grape variety. Wonderfully aromatic with notes of herbs, citrus, apricot, and spice, together with honey and wax, in the mouth it is waxy, spicy, and apricotty with some minerals; a really distinctive wine. It is made by James Millton, who is a pioneer in biodynamic production in New Zealand. This despite being located in Gisborne, one of New Zealand's warmer, damper areas, and a difficult spot to work without the assistance of chemicals.

119 Papatu Rd, CMB 66, Manutuke, Gisborne
www.millton.co.nz

Mt Difficulty Central Otago
Roaring Meg Pinot Noir, Central Otago (red)

Consistent, affordable, and produced in relatively large quantities, Mt Difficulty's Roaring Meg Pinot Noir is a good introduction to the joys of Central Otago Pinot Noir. It offers bright, juicy cherry fruits with a savoury, herbal twist, finishing fresh. Mt Difficulty is among the largest wine producers in Central Otago. It was founded by five partners, each of whom owned a vineyard, with the first releases coming in 1998. It is now owned by a single company and has a new winery on the Felton Road. Pinot Noir is very much the focus here, bottled under both Roaring Meg and Mt Difficulty labels, including some very serious single-vineyard bottlings. Since 1999, the winemaking has been in the hands of Matt Dicey, who spent four years making wines overseas before returning to Bannockburn.

Cromwell, Bannockburn, Central Otago
www.mtdifficulty.co.nz

Neudorf Vineyards Nelson
Brightwater Riesling, Nelson (white)

Neudorf Vineyards Brightwater Riesling is a precise, quite complex wine with pure lemon and grapefruit freshness, good acidity, and some of that ethereal quality known as minerality. The high acid is nicely offset with just a hint of sweetness. It is one of several fine wines made at this boutique operation, which has been around since 1978, a very long time for a winery in this part of the world. It is still run by the original founders, Tim and Judy Finn, who have vineyards in two sites: the home block at Moutere, and also at Brightwater, south of Nelson.

138 Neudorf Rd, RD2 Upper Moutere, Nelson
www.neudorf.co.nz

Palliser Estate
Martinborough

Sauvignon Blanc, Martinborough (white)

It's not just the Marlborough region that makes lively, aromatic Sauvignon Blanc in New Zealand. In Martinborough, Palliser Estate make a really superb example with lovely contrast between the passion fruit aromatics and the grapefruit and citrus freshness in the mouth. Palliser has been a trailblazer in the region, having planted its first vines back in 1984. Run by founding shareholder Richard Riddiford, one of the region's most engaging characters, it now has more than 80ha (198 acres) of vineyards, making it one of Martinborough's biggest producers.

Kitchener St, Martinborough, South Wairarapa
www.palliser.co.nz

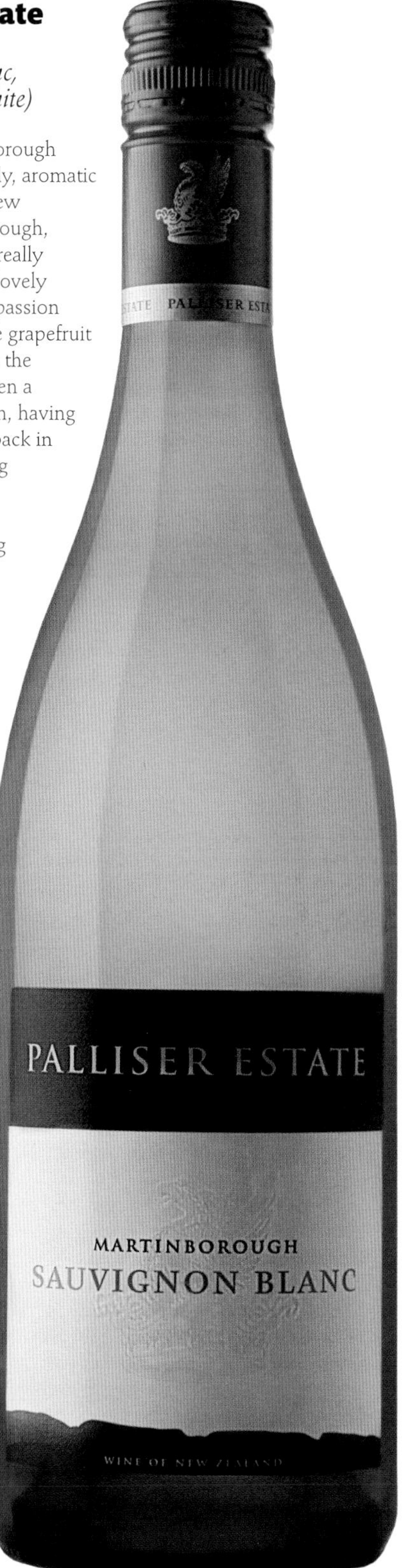

C J Pask Winery Hawkes Bay

Gimblett Road Syrah, Hawkes Bay (red)

The Gimblett Gravels district of Hawkes Bay is today responsible for some of New Zealand's best wines, something that is all the more amazing when you consider there were no vines there until 1981. The man responsible for the first vines was Chris Pask, and the company he founded, C J Pask Winery, now has more than 60ha (148 acres) planted on the Gravels, with a further 30ha (74 acres) in other areas of Hawkes Bay. Today, the operation is helmed by managing director and chief winemaker, Kate Radburnd, who joined in 1991. Radburnd makes a consistently strong range of wines that includes the Gimblett Road Syrah. Some whole-bunch fermentation adds complexity to this lovely expression of Gimblett Gravels Syrah. It's bright and aromatic with violetty floral notes and a hint of pepper, showing precision and freshness.

1133 Omahu Rd, Hastings, Hawkes Bay
www.cjpaskwinery.co.nz

Pegasus Bay Waipara

Main Divide Riesling, Waipara (white)

Main Divide Riesling is a stylish off-dry white with complex, textured limey fruit and a sweet finish. It is a pleasantly poised and well balanced Riesling from Pegasus Bay, a Waipara producer with a real talent for this variety. Owned by the Donaldson family, who have been involved in the New Zealand wine business since the 1970s, the wines are made by the eldest son, Matthew Donaldson, a graduate of the Australian winemaking school, Roseworthy, and his wife, Lynette Hudson, who studied winemaking at Lincoln University. Donaldson's father, Ivan Donaldson, a professor and consultant neurologist by profession, who is also a wine writer and wine show judge, still has a hand in overseeing the viticulture and winemaking, and Donaldson's younger brother, Edward, looks after the marketing. Between them the Donaldsons have some 40ha (99 acres) of estate vineyards to draw on, with the Main Divide label also using fruit from South Island contract growers.

Stockgrove Rd, Waipara, RD2, Amberley, North Canterbury
www.pegasusbay.com

Sacred Hill Hawkes Bay

Syrah, Hawkes Bay (red)

The Mason family hired top winemaker Tony Bish when they started Sacred Hill in Hawkes Bay in 1985. Bish left to make wine in Australia, Martinborough, and Central Otago, but the family lured him back to the burgeoning business in 1994. Today Bish oversees a production of some 300,000 cases a year, and the wines have been a success in international markets. One of the best wines at this estate for both taste and value is the Hawkes Bay Syrah. This style of wine is hot stuff among wine lovers at the moment, and there are few better or more affordable examples. It's fresh and bright with a black pepper/clove twist to the forward berry fruits.

1033 Dartmoor Rd, Puketapu, Napier
www.sacredhill.com

SAUVIGNON BLANC

This versatile, assertively flavoured, and often affordable white grape variety originated in France, but it took New Zealanders applying the latest vine-growing techniques to bring it global popularity.

Sauvignon Blanc is an aromatic grape variety, with sometimes-aggressive flavours and vibrant acidity. It offers diverse fruit and herbal notes, depending on where and how it is grown. From the coolest parts of New Zealand it gives grassy aromas and tangy grapefruit flavours. From slightly warmer areas in California and Chile it can be herbal, or more complex and ripe with melon nuances.

CABERNET'S PARENT

Genetic studies have proved that Sauvignon Blanc, a white variety, is a parent of Cabernet Sauvignon, a red one. Both are traditional in Bordeaux, where white wines are often made with blends of Sauvignon Blanc and Sémillon.

STEEL VERSUS OAK

The international style of crisp Sauvignon Blanc is made in stainless steel tanks, cooled to preserve the grapes' freshness. Some is fermented and/or aged in oak barrels, however, to round the texture and add vanilla and spice accents.

OVER GROWTH

Sauvignon Blanc vines tend to grow fast and spread their branches and leaves. Vine growers learned to prevent this over-growth, because too many leaves and branches shade the grape bunches and encourage green, coarse flavours.

MOOD SWINGS

The flavours of Sauvignon Blanc swing dramatically depending on the climate and sun exposure of the vines. In cooler regions, the herb and citrus flavours dominate. In warmer areas softer, melon-like flavours develop.

WHERE IN THE WORLD?

While the New World regions of New Zealand and California make lots of Sauvignon Blanc, the variety also remains important in its traditional home of France.

In the Loire region the variety makes crisp white Sancerre, smoky Pouilly Fumé, and other wines. In Bordeaux, it makes dry table wines for great and minor châteaux, and contributes to the famous dessert wines of Sauternes and Barsac.

Since the vines are vigorous, produce large crops, and ripen their grapes early in the season, Sauvignon Blanc is a good variety with which to make large quantities of relatively inexpensive wine, as many growers in southern France, Chile, and California have done. But quality and styles vary enormously, so it pays to try several examples to find the wines that fit your taste and your spending habits.

The following regions are among the best for Sauvignon Blanc. Try bottles from these recommended vintages for the best examples:

Bordeaux: 2009, 2008, 2007
Loire Valley: 2009, 2008
Napa Valley: 2010, 2009, 2008
New Zealand: 2010, 2007

Blind River makes a vibrant Sauvignon Blanc in classic New Zealand style.

Seresin Estate
Marlborough

Leah Pinot Noir, Marlborough (red)

One of six top quality, single-vineyard Pinot Noirs made by Seresin Estate, the Leah Pinot Noir is a really exciting wine, showing dark cherry and plum fruit flavours with lovely definition and minerality. It is further proof that this estate, owned by the film maker Michael Seresin, is now one of the best in the Marlborough region. It has extensive vineyard holdings which are run on biodynamic lines (and certified organic), and the wines are made with great care and skill by Clive Dougall who started here in 2006.

85 Bedford RD, Renwick, Marlborough
www.seresin.co.nz

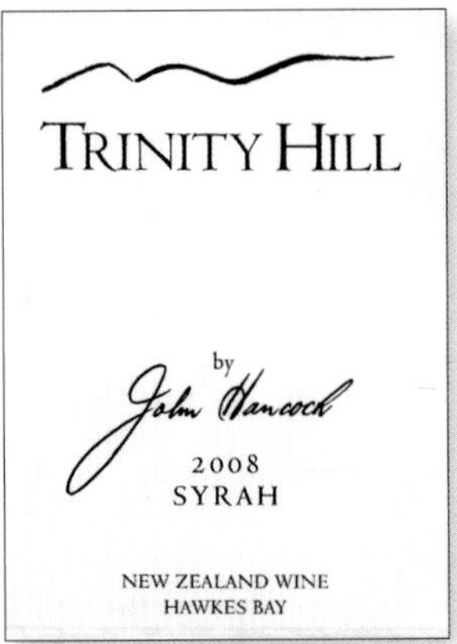

Trinity Hill Hawkes Bay
Trinity Hill Syrah, Hawkes Bay (red)

John Hancock makes some impressive Syrahs from his Hawkes Bay vineyards. The Trinity Hill Syrah, Hawkes Bay, is the entry-level wine, but it's actually quite serious, with elegant, bright, peppery red berry and cherry fruit. Fruity and expressive, it is dangerously easy to drink. Hancock entered into a partnership with Robert and Robyn Wilson, and Trevor and Hanne James, to bring about Trinity Hill. They bought a 20ha (49.5 acre) vineyard in Gimblett Gravels in 1993, and their debut commercial vintage was 1996. Since then they have added another 20ha (49.5 acres) of vineyard in the Gravels, and they constructed an arresting winery in 1997.

2396 State Hwy 50, RD5, Hastings, Hawkes Bay
www.trinityhill.co.nz

Urlar Wairarapa
Urlar Pinot Noir, Gladstone, Wairarapa (red)

Urlar Pinot Noir, from Gladstone in Wairarapa, is a delicious young, full-bodied Pinot Noir with reach, featuring meaty, spicy dark cherry and plum fruit. It has lots of presence and admirable freshness with cherries and spice on the palate. It is the work of a Scotsman, Angus Thomson, who swapped his family farm back home for a new life in New Zealand making wine. He settled in the Wairarapa, and began his biodynamic estate Urlar (from the Gaelic for "earth") in 2004. His first commercial vintage was 2008, and he now has 31ha (77 acres) of vines.

No visitor facilities
www.urlar.co.nz

Vidal Wines Hawkes Bay
Vidal Pinot Noir, Hawkes Bay (red); Vidal Syrah, Gimblett Gravels, Hawkes Bay (red)

Vidal Pinot Noir, Hawkes Bay is an oddity, in that it is a deliciously expressive Pinot Noir from the Hawkes Bay region. The key to its quality is that it's from a cool spot, and it offers bold flavours of dark cherry, blackberry, and spice. Gimblett Gravels Vidal Syrah

Hawkes Bay, is a more conventional variety for the area, and it shows the Gimblett Gravels trademark fresh white pepper character, along with lovely, juicy red berry and cherry fruit – light and delicious. Vidal has a long history in Hawkes Bay that goes back to 1905. It now makes a full range of wines that draw on a number of premium wine regions, with Hawkes Bay still the focus.

913 St Aubyn St East, Hastings, Hawkes Bay
www.vidal.co.nz

Villa Maria Estate Marlborough

Private Bin Pinot Noir, Marlborough (red); Private Bin Sauvignon Blanc, Marlborough (white)

It's hard to find good, cheap Pinot Noir, but the deliciously drinkable Villa Maria Private Bin Pinot Noir is a prime example. From one of New Zealand's biggest and best wine companies, it shows bright, sappy cherry fruit with a bit of spice and some gravelly grip, combining fruitiness with a pleasant savoury dimension. The zesty Private Bin Sauvignon Blanc is lively and aromatic with notes of fresh passion fruit, grapefruit, and herbs.

Cnr Paynters Rd and New Renwick Rd, Fairhall, Blenheim, Marlborough
www.villamaria.co.nz

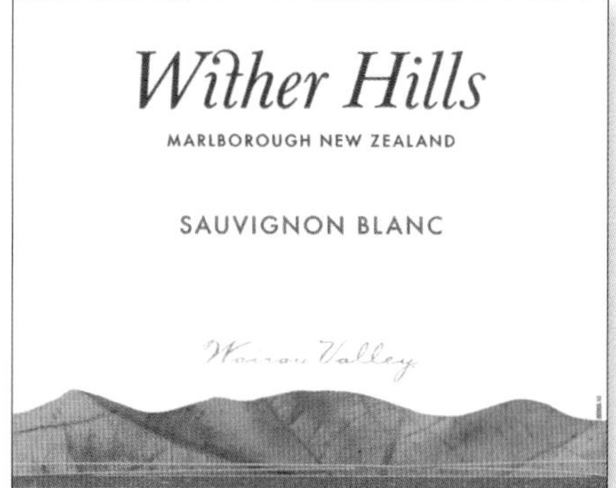

Wither Hills Marlborough

Pinot Noir, Marlborough (red); Sauvignon Blanc, Marlborough (white)

Satisfyingly broad, and with a silky texture, Wither Hills' sweetly fruited Pinot Noir is a good example of the Marlborough style of this grape variety. It's quite rich, but avoids being jammy or heavy, and delivers lots of red fruit character. The Sauvignon Blanc, meanwhile, is consistently good, and is a delicious introduction to Wairau Sauvignon, offering both passion fruit and peach richness as well as citrus and grassy freshness in nice combination. Wither Hills is owned today by the Lion Nathan wine group, but it was Brent Marris who made it one of the region's best wineries, both before he sold it in 2002, and as winemaker until 2007. Marris's former deputy, Ben Glover, is now in control and doing a fine job.

211 New Renwick Rd, RD2, Blenheim, Marlborough
www.witherhills.co.nz

Yealands Estate

Marlborough

Sauvignon Blanc, Awatere Valley, Marlborough (white)

With a first vintage in 2008, Yealands Estate is one of Marlborough's youngest and most promising wineries. It was founded by Peter Yealands, an entrepreneur who has previously made a success farming both green mussels and deer. The Sauvignon Blanc Awatere Valley is highly aromatic, and has elements of grass, tomato leaf, geen pepper, and passion fruit. In the mouth, it's concentrated and well balanced, with smooth tropical fruit notes countered by green pepper and citrus characters. Really lively.

Cnr Seaview Rd and Reserve Rd, Seddon, Blenheim, Marlborough
www.yealands.com

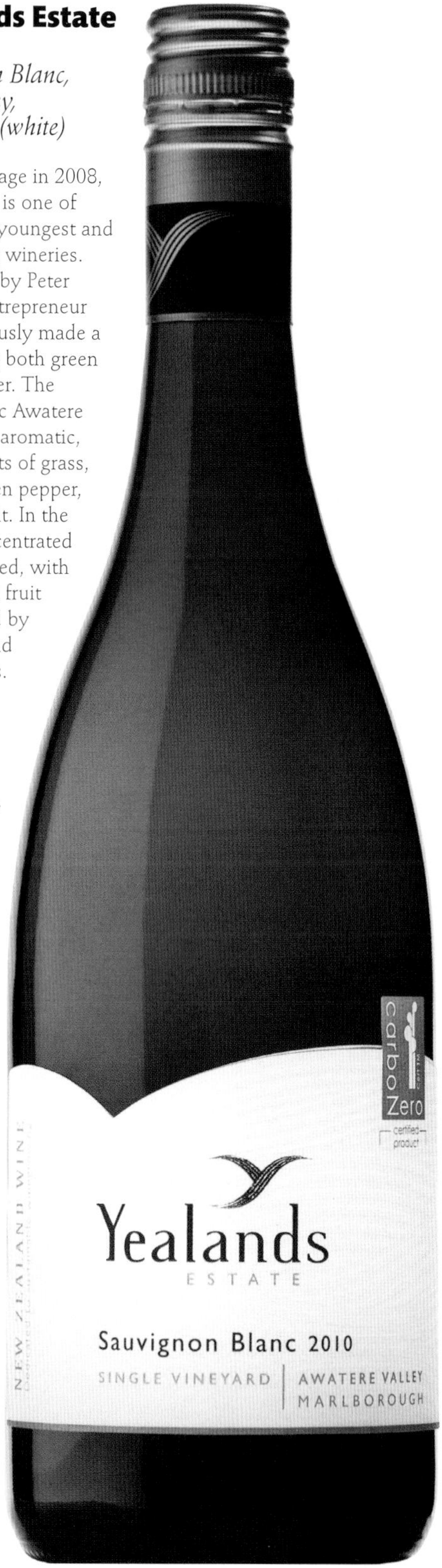

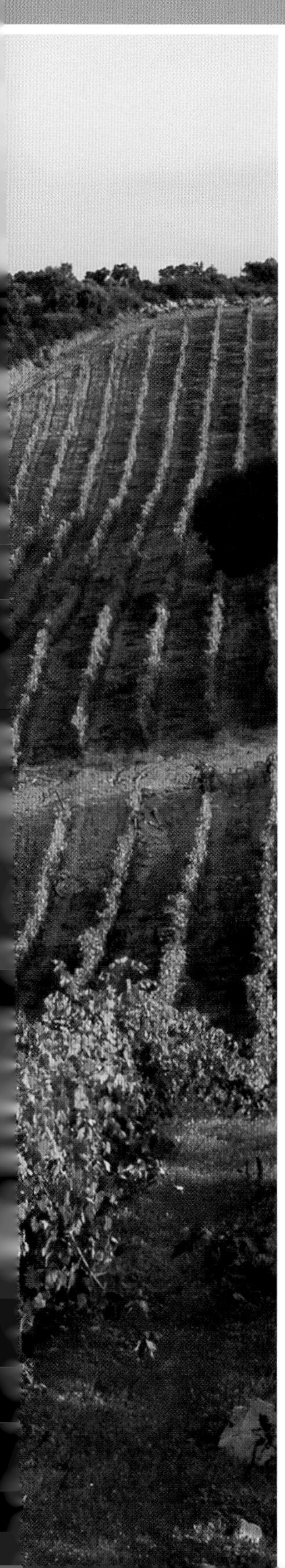

Emerging Regions

Exciting affordable wines are made in every continent of the world (with the obvious exception of Antarctica). In Asia, the emerging middle-classes of China and India have encouraged thriving wine scenes with some well-priced examples of international varieties. In northern Europe, Luxembourg makes whites to rival Germany, and the UK produces some excellent champagne-style sparkling whites. Moving south, Switzerland is a fine source of crisp whites, while Greece, Cyprus, Turkey, and the ex-Yugoslavian countries (such as Croatia, shown here) have a range of exciting indigenous varieties. In eastern Europe, Bulgarian Cabernet Sauvignon, Romanian Pinot Noir, and Georgia's Saperavi are all well-priced red gems, while Morocco's bold reds and the Lebanon's sophisticated whites and reds fly the flag for quality in North Africa and the Middle East. Finally, in the Americas, Uruguay specializes in reds from Tannat, and Mexico is a warm red wine region to watch.

Acorex Wine Holding

Southern (Chişinău), Moldova

Amaro de la Valea Perjei Private Reserve (red)

It has all happened very quickly for Acorex Wine Holding. In 20 years it has transformed itself from being a wine exporter and merchant to become one of the most individual and important wine producers in Moldova. It produces its wines in Chaul, in the south of the country, and has 3,000ha (7,410 acres) of organically farmed and certified vineyards. Among its best wines is the highly original Amaro de la Valea Perjei, in the Private Reserve range. Made with partially dried grapes, it is a Moldovan take on the Italian style, Amarone.

45 G.Banulescu-Bodoni St, MD-2012 Chişinău
www.acorex.net

Arman Istria, Croatia

Chardonnay, Teran (white)

The Arman family have been established as producers of wine in Istria, the Croatian peninsula near Italy, for more than 100 years, having started out back in the 1800s. The tradition is strong, then, but they have also been innovators, and they were one of the first producers to move their production towards more modern techniques after the unrest of the early 1990s. Their vineyards are planted on south- and southwest-facing slopes, which means the grapes ripen in a consistent way, and the cool of the nearby Mirna River lends a moderating influence to take the edge off any climatic extremes. Marijan Arman makes the wines in a way that emphasizes their texture as well as their bouquet. The Chardonnay, which sees some oak, is a good example of what Croatian whites can be, with great richness and varietal expression.

Narduci 3, 52447 Vizinada
www.arman.hr

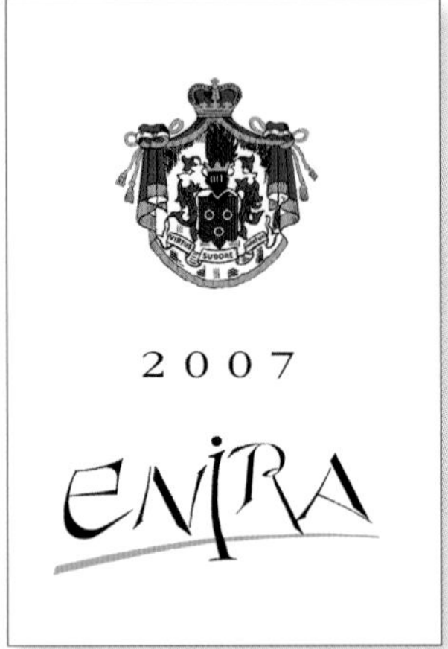

Bessa Valley Thracian Lowlands, Bulgaria

Enira (red)

Bessa Valley is a real Bulgarian original. It was established by Count Stephan von Niepperg, the man behind the famous Bordeaux estate, Château La Mondotte, and Dr Karl Hauptmann, a Czech-based venture capitalist, in 2001. They decided to follow the estate concept, planting an impressive 140ha (346 acres) of its own vineyards on an abandoned former vineyard on the lower slopes of the Rhodope Mountains in the Thracian Lowlands area of Bulgaria. The winery focuses exclusively on red grapes, under the guidance of highly skilled French winemaker Marc Dworkin. In Enira, Dworkin produces a delicious red wine, with a slightly different blend of grapes each year, although it is always led by Merlot. Varying amounts of one or all of Syrah, Cabernet Sauvignon, and Petit Verdot are also used in the blend. Aged in oak barrels, Enira is a bright, fruity, and well-made modern red wine.

Zad Baira, Pazardjik, 4417 Ognianovo
www.bessavalley.com

Breaky Bottom Vineyard East Sussex, England
Cuvée John Inglis Hall (sparkling)

Tucked away in the beautiful heart of the South Downs in East Sussex, the Breaky Bottom estate is a quintessentially English pastoral scene. It also happens to be home to one of England's best winemakers. Peter Hall is the far-sighted farmer behind the project, and he has been producing trailblazing wines from the Seyval Blanc variety since he made his first foray into the wine business by planting vines in 1974. Seyval Blanc is Hall's great love, and the Cuvée John Inglis Hall, a distinctively English version of traditional method sparkling, proves just how good the variety can be.

Rodmell, Lewes, East Sussex BN7 3EX
www.breakybottom.co.uk

Camel Valley Cornwall, England
Bacchus Dry (white); White Pinot (sparkling)

Retired RAF fighter pilot, Bob Lindo, has turned his beautiful estate in the Camel Valley in Cornwall into one of England's most recognized wine producers. Now run by Lindo's son, Sam, Camel Valley has been such a success that it has to buy in some grapes from other growers to meet demand. Its location, on the sunny banks of the Camel River, certainly helps: many tourists visit the site in summer and pick up a bottle. But the quality here is excellent – the wines have picked up a raft of awards from wine competitions over the years – and the Lindos have been tireless ambassadors both for their own estate and for English wine more generally. The estate is well known for its sparkling wines, and the White Pinot (a Blanc de Noirs) is a top UK fizz. For still styles, meanwhile, try the lovely, Sauvignon Blanc-like Bacchus.

Nanstallon, Bodmin, Cornwall PL30 5LG
www.camelvalley.com

Carmel Shomron, Israel
Appellation Carignan Old Vines (red)

The Carmel estate has been blazing a trail on the Israeli wine scene for more than a century, and it remains the country's biggest and, to many, its best producer. It began life in 1882, with the backing of Baron Edmond de Rothschild, and for a time it was responsible for a remarkable 90% of all wine produced in the country. Since the turn of the millennium, however, the emphasis has shifted considerably towards quality, rather than quantity, of production, with CEO Israel Izvan leading a move to reduce output, improving the wines significantly – both here and at the company's Yatir project in the Negev – in the process. For fine value, there are few better bottles in Israel than those in Carmel's Appellation series, of which the Carignan Old Vines is a standout with its textured, cherry-scented character.

Winery St, Zichron Ya'acov 30900
www.carmelwines.co.il

Casa de Piedra Valle de Guadalupe, Mexico
Chardonnay (white)

Hugo D'Acosta learned his winemaking trade in France, Italy, and California. But by 1997 he was ready to return to Mexico to start up Casa de Piedra with his brother, the architect Alejandro D'Acosta, in the Valle de Guadalupe. In the following decade, the D'Acostas became the leading lights in the valley's winemaking scene, working on their own range of projects, and as consultants. For an insight into what they are capable of, look for their rich and crisp Casa de Piedra Chardonnay.

Km 93.5 Mexico Highway 3, San Antonio de las Minas
www.vinoscasadepiedra.com

Castra Rubra Danube Plain and Thracian Lowlands, Bulgaria
Castra Rubra (red)

Telish in the Pleven area of Bulgaria has a reputation for affordable, drinkable reds. But, in 2005, Jair Agopian wanted to prove it could offer something more serious, and he employed top French consultant, Michel Rolland, to help with his new Castra Rubra project. Rolland lent advice on planting the (organic) vineyards and on the construction of the stone winery. Today the wine is already a fine, rich, ripe, and, yes, serious addition to the Bulgarian scene.

Kolarovo, 6460 Haskovo
www.telish.bg

Château Ksara Bekaa Valley, Lebanon
Reserve du Couvent (red)

Founded more than 150 years ago, Château Ksara is Lebanon's largest wine producer. Each year it puts out some 2.7 million bottles of wine, which is more than a third of the country's total output. Thankfully, quality is kept high across the company's portfolio, and the Château Ksara has been a significant influence in the great strides Lebanon has taken as a quality producer. It used wire training for the plantings of Cabernet Sauvignon and Syrah at the beginning of the 1990s, for example, and it employs French winemaker, James Palgé, one of the best working in Lebanon today. One of the top wine of the range is the Château Ksara label, and the Reserve du Couvent is balanced and has red fruits and earthy flavours.

Zahle, Bekaa Valley
www.ksara.com.lb

Château Musar Bekaa Valley, Lebanon
Hochar Père et Fils (red)

Château Musar is one of the world's most famous wine estates, a producer that has done more than any other to put Lebanese wine on the map. It exports some 80% of its 700,000-bottle annual production, and it has developed a winemaking style that divides opinion. Certainly, that style is not for everyone. Some say it is too oxidized and too high in volatile acidity; others love it for its originality and complexity. Either way, you certainly know a Château Musar wine when you taste it. For an introduction to this great estate's style, the Hochar Père et Fils red is the best place to start. Made with the same approach as the Château wines, it is juicy and approachable.

Dlebta Rd, Ghazir, Mount Lebanon
www.chateaumusar.com.lb

Château de Val Danube Plain, Bulgaria
Claret Reserve (red)

There is a rags-to-riches tale behind Château de Val. The company's founder, Val Markov, fled the communist regime of Bulgaria, making it all the way to the US, where he built a career in high-tech engineering. Some years later, he returned home to his family's vineyards, and entirely rejuvenated them, converting to organic viticulture, and implementing a minimal intervention approach in the winery. The Claret Reserve, produced from Saperavi, Storgozia, and Buket, is full of life and flavour.

201 Parva St, Gradetz, Vidin
www.chateaudeval.com

Corvus Vineyards Island of Bozcaada, Turkey
Rarum (red)

On the Turkish island of Bozcaada, Corvus Vineyards is one of the first Turkish wineries to attract international attention. Established by a Turkish-born architect, it has made its name by using both local and international varieties to produce a broad range of high quality and distinctive wines. Rarum is among the standouts in a consistently good range. A serious red, it is made with the indigenous grape varieties, Kuntra and Karalahna.

Bozcaada
www.corvus.com.tr

Domaine Skouras
Nemea, Greece

Nemea Grande Cuvée (red)

The influential George Skouras travelled to Dijon in France to learn winemaking, before returning home to set up his eponymous winery in the mid-1980s. Since then, Skouras has been at the forefront of the Greek wine revival, producing a consistent range from both international (Cabernet Sauvignon, Merlot, and Chardonnay) and indigenous grapes. It is the latter that really excites Skouras, however, specifically the red Aghiorghitiko variety. If you want to know just how good Aghiorghitiko can be, then Skouras's Nemea Grande Cuvée, a 100% Aghiorghitiko, provides an excellent indication. With its cherry-laden flavours, it is spicy and bold but with plenty of finesse.

10th km Argos-Sternas, Malandreni, Argos, Peloponnese 21200
www.skouras.gr

Golan Heights Winery Golan Heights, Israel

Gamla Cabernet Sauvignon (red)

Before Golan Heights Winery arrived on the scene, cool-climate winemaking had not really been on the radar for Israel's winemakers. The success of Golan Heights Winery changed all that for good. The winery had first planted vines in Katzrin, way up in the Golan Heights, in 1976, but it did not make its first wine until 1984. Almost as soon as those wines were released, however, it was clear that they had something different to offer: definition, deliciously crisp and fresh acidity, and bright fruit flavours. It was not long before other wineries began to look for similar sites for their own ventures. Today, Golan Heights is managed by winemaker Victor Schoenfeld, who oversees an annual production of around 380,000 cases of wine a year, spread out across three distinct labels. Of these the Gamla label provides incredible quality for the price. Look for the Gamla Cabernet Sauvignon with its mix of power, pure black cassis fruit, and freshness.

Katzrin 12900
www.golanwines.co.il

Great Wall Hebei Province, China

Cabernet Sauvignon (red)

Unless you live in China, it is not always easy to come across examples of Chinese wine. But Great Wall is an exception, with its brand of the same name distributed in Asian supermarkets all over the world. The winery itself is a vast enterprise. Indeed, the cellar – complete with a barrel room that seems to have been copied exactly from the one at Château Lafite Rothschild in Bordeaux – is the largest winery building in Asia. Great Wall is also unusual in China for being 100% Chinese-owned, whereas many of its peers are joint-ventures with foreign partners.The popular Great Wall Cabernet Sauvignon is this estate's most accessible wine. With its blackcurrant pastille flavours, it calls to mind a Chilean red.

Tianjin, Hebei Province
www.huaxia-greatwall.com.cn

Grover Vineyards Karnataka, India

Cabernet-Shiraz (red)

Kanwar Grover became interested in wine during the many business trips he made to France during his career in high-tech engineering. He believed he could recreate these fine bottles in his native India, and he spent the best part of two decades contemplating and researching the best sites, and the most suitable grape varieties. By 1988, years before anyone else had thought about making fine wine in India, he had found his ideal site in the Nandi Hill region of Karnataka. With longstanding assistance from top consultant, Michel Rolland, he has consistently shown that this cool-climate site is the most promising area for wine in India. Try the Cabernet-Shiraz for a ripe, smooth, and fruity red.

Raghunathapura, Devanahalli, Doddaballapur Road, Doddaballapur, Bangalore 561203
www.groverwines.com

Halewood Dealu Mare, Murfatlar-Cernavodă, Sebeş-Apold, Romania

Single-Vineyard Pinot Noir (red); Cantus Primus (red)

The entrepreneurial Englishman, Sir John Halewood, has been the most significant exporter of Romanian wines for more than a decade now. He bought what was then known as the Prahova Company from the Romanian government in 1998, and he now oversees a project with four winemakers managing a total of 400ha (988 acres) of vineyards. Wines to look out for here include the serious Cantus Primus, a 100% Cabernet Sauvignon joint-venture with Italian firm Antinori, and the juicy, bright Single-Vineyard Pinot Noir from the Dealu Mare.

Tohani Village, Gura Vadului, Prahova District
www.halewood.com.ro

Hatzidakis Santorini, Greece

Santorini Assyrtiko (white)

There is a rough-and-ready charm to the Hatzidakis Winery – it is really just a roof over a hole in the ground. That "hole" is a hive of activity, however, full of barrels and tanks, and it produces some fine wines. At the centre of it all is Haridimos Hatzidakis, ex-head oenologist at Boutari's Santorini winery, who started out on his own in 1997. From organic vineyards planted by his family in the 1950s, he makes some gorgeously textured whites such as the lemon-fresh Santorini Assyrtiko.

Pyrgos Kallistis, Santorini, 84701
www.hatzidakiswines.gr

Kavaklidere Winery Central Anatolia, Turkey

Vin-Art Emir-Sultaniye (white)

Not everything produced by the Kavaklidere Winery is worth more than cursory attention. One of the largest producers in Turkey, much of its output is mass-produced table wine for early and easy-drinking. The Vin-Art Series, however, is a rather more serious proposition that is made with indigenous and international grapes. Using two Turkish grapes, the Emir-Sultaniye is a crisp, fresh dry white.

Çankırı yolu 6.km, 06750, Akyurt/Ankara
www.kavaklidere.com

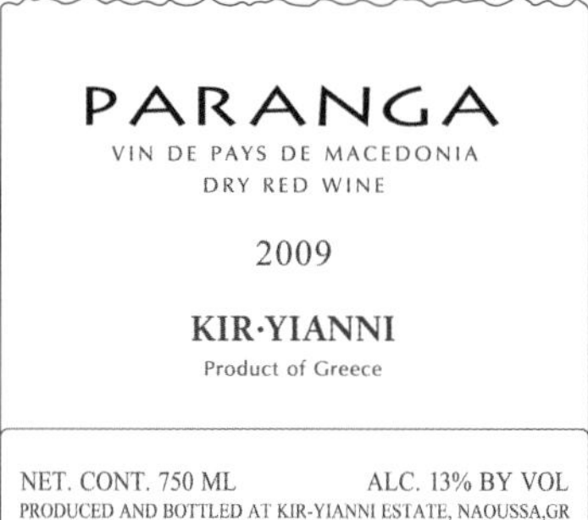

Kir-Yianni Naoussa, Greece

Paranga, Vin de Pays de Macedonia (red)

The "Kir-Yianni" (Mr John) in question here is Yiannis Boutari, a seminal figure in Greek wine, a fount of vinous wisdom and kindness, and a tireless worker for the international cause of Greek wine. Until the mid-1990s, Boutari looked after the Boutari winery with his brother Constantinos, before leaving to establish a vineyard in Yianakohori, Naoussa's highest point. From bought-in fruit, he makes the Paranga Vin de Pays de Macedonia, a blend of Xinomavro, Merlot, and Syrah; it is a gorgeously rich red, which is given life and charm by its streak of vivid acidity.

Yianakohori, Naoussa, 59200
www.kiryianni.gr

Kogl Podravje, Slovenia

Mea Culpa Sämling (white)

Founded in the 17th century, this eastern Slovenian estate has a long history, but its story as a quality winemaker really starts in the 1980s, when it was acquired by the Cvetko family. Today it makes a fine range of never-less-than-intriguing wines from a mix of grape varieties. Look for the white Mea Culpa Sämling, which shows off the bright, crisp, and utterly charming flavours of the Sämling variety in an unoaked style.

Velika Nedelija 23, 2274 Velika Nedelija
www.kogl.net

Korak Dalmatia, Croatia

Riesling (white)

Velimir Korak's engaging operation is typical of Croatia's burgeoning boutique scene. With a winery based just 30km (19 miles) to the west of Croatia's capital, Zagreb, Korak has some 5ha (12 acres) of his own vineyards, and he buys in a comparable amount from other growers. His clean, fresh wines consistently show good varietal character, as can be seen in his excellent Riesling. This is made with a hint of sugar in an off-dry style, and it has plenty of mineral complexity and good depth of flavour.

Plešivica 34, 10450 Jastrebarsko
www.vino-korak.hr

Les Celliers de Meknès Morocco, North Africa

Château Roslane Premier Cru (red and white)

It sometimes comes as a surprise to learn that Muslim countries produce wine, but North Africa has a long tradition of viticulture, and Morocco is no exception. Les Celliers de Meknès is the largest producer in the country, and has been enjoying something of a renaissance in recent years. Today the company makes a range of wines under the guiding hand of Rene Zniber, who draws on some 50 years of winemaking experience, and is widely considered to be the godfather of modern Moroccan wine. Among his most impressive projects is the company's Château Roslane estate in Morocco's sole AC region, Coteaux d'Atlas. Both the red (a Merlot-Syrah-Cabernet Sauvignon blend), and the white (Chardonnay) Premier Cru wines produced here offer great sophistication, personality, and depth of flavour.

11 Rue Ibn Khaldoune, 50,000 Meknès
www.lescelliersdemeknes.net

Malatinszky Villány, Hungary

Pinot Bleu (red)

The Malatinszky estate in the Villány area of Hungary is very much on the rise. It has been run since 1997 by Csaba Malatinszky, who revived his family estate after returning from a vinous career that had seen him work as an assistant winemaker at some of Bordeaux's best estates, as a sommelier, and as the owner of a wine shop. Malatinszky has a 30ha (74 acre) estate to work with, which is planted to the Cabernet Franc and Cabernet Sauvignon grape varieties. He is a big believer in preserving the local identity of his wines, and so he only uses barrels that have been made exclusively from Hungarian wood. Among his most interesting wines is his Pinot Bleu, which is a blend of Pinot Noir and the local Kékfrankos variety. Made in a distinctly Burgundian way, it offers distinctive pure and profound red and black berry fruit, and an attractive spiciness. Powerful, yet exceptionally elegant, it is a great introduction to this fine producer.

H-7773 Villány 12th, Batthyany L. u.27
www.malatinszky.hu

Marc Gales Luxembourg

Marc Gales Riesling (white); Marc Gales Pinot Gris (white)

The Marc Gales business is behind a number of Luxembourg's most popular bottles. Having recently added the historic Krier Frères business – including its highly regarded Remich Primerberg vineyards – to the portfolio, quality here is higher than ever before, with the minerally Marc Gales Riesling and Pinot Gris both great value. The estate, on the northern fringes of Remich, is well worth a visit, too. The cellars have been carved deep into chalky fels (cliffs) right beside the River Mosel, and there is a restaurant from where you can take in the view, accompanied by local food and the estate's wines.

6, rue de la Gare, L-5690 Ellange
www.gales.lu

Massaya Bekaa Valley, Lebanon

Classic Red

The cream of French wine is involved at Massaya in Lebanon's Bekaa Valley. Both Dominique Hébard (once of Château Cheval Blanc in Bordeaux) and the Brunier family (of Châteauneuf-du-Pape's Domaine du Vieux Télégraphe) have been enlisted as partners by the Lebanese Ghosn brothers. The project began in 1998, and, with its creative marketing and well-made wines, it has quickly established itself as one of Lebanon's rising stars. It now makes some 250,000 bottles of wine each year, with 90% going overseas. Made without oak, the Classic Red is an elegant blend of Bordelais and Mediterranean varieties.

Tanail Property, Bekaa Valley
www.massaya.com

Mathis Bastian Moselle Luxembourgeoise, Luxembourg

Rivaner (white)

The Mathis Bastian family estate is situated in a picturesque spot above the vineyards and town of Remich in Luxembourg. Here Mathis Bastian, his daughter, Anouk, and his vineyard manager, Hermann Tapp, make some lovely elegant, floral white wines, from around 12ha (30 acres) of vineyards, including a delightful, tropical fruit-inflected off-dry white. Because the wines are produced in small quantites and at fair prices, they often sell out fast.

29, route de Luxembourg, L-5551 Remich
23 69 82 95

Mercouri Estate Ilias, Greece

Foloi White; Estate Red

In terms of setting, Mercouri is one of Greece's – indeed, the world's – most jawdropping estates. It can be found towards the west of the Peloponnese, where it spreads across overgrown gardens with views to the sea. Founded in the 1870s, it has been a serious wine producer since Hristo and Vassilis Kanellakopoulos assumed control in the mid-1980s. The fresh, aromatic Foloi white blends Roditis and Viognier; the fine, balanced, ageworthy Estate Red is a deft mix of Refosco and Mavrodaphne.

Korakohori, Ilias, Peloponnese 27100
www.mercouri.gr

Nyetimber Sussex, England

Classic Cuvée (sparkling)

Nyetimber has seen considerable expansion of both its vineyards and its winery since it was bought by the Dutchman, Eric Hereema, in 2006. The fruit of this expansion has not yet reached the market, but the current releases show that this producer is a standard-bearer for quality English sparkling wine. Cherie Spriggs, installed as winemaker when Hereema took over the business, oversees a portfolio that includes the excellent Classic Cuvée, which is full of complex yeasty, toasty flavours.

No visitor facilities
www.nyetimber.com

Pisano Progresso, Uruguay

Río de los Pájaros Torrontés (white); Río de los Pájaros Tannat (red)

Few Uruguayan producers have done more to promote the country's image overseas than Pisano. With its expansive estate based on calcerous soil in the middle of the Río del Plata region, Pisano produces some 380,000 bottles of consistently good wine each year. Because the estate is relatively close to the ocean, the grapes are grown in a climate where big differences between day and night temperatures create freshness and intensity. This can be seen across the portfolio, but particularly in its excellent Río de los Pájaros range, which includes a lovely aromatic Torrontés and a punchy, bright-fruited example of Uruguay's flagship grape, Tannat.

No visitor facilities
www.pisanowines.com

Provins Valais, Switzerland
Mâitre de Chais, Vieilles Vignes (white)

Provins dominates production in Switzerland's Valais region. Indeed, with its 1,100ha (2,700 acres) of vineyards, it accounts for more than a quarter of the region's total production. Fortunately, it does a very good job, particularly since the estimable Madeleine Gay took charge. Gay has overseen enormous improvements here, with the winemaking now of a very high standard, and the vineyards treated with great care. What is particularly striking here, given the volumes, is the personality and natural flair of the wines: they do not feel in any way forced or clumsy. One of the highlights of the range is the curious Vieilles Vignes Maître de Chais. Based on an intriguing, almost certainly unique blend of Marsanne, Pinot Blanc, and the indigenous Swiss varieties, Amigne and Heida, it is wonderfully rich and aromatic, yet delicate and refreshing.

Rue de l'Industrie 22, 1951 Sion
www.provins.ch

Ridgeview Wine Estate Sussex, England
Ridgeview Cuvée Merret Bloomsbury (sparkling)

Mike Roberts never seems to stop promoting English wine. The paterfamilias at the top English family estate, Ridgeview, he has long been a believer in England's potential for making great sparkling wines. It is a potential that is being fully realized at Ridgeview, where Mike's son, Simon, now looks after the winemaking operation. The family focuses exclusively on sparkling wines, and has access to all the best and most up-to-date equipment, such as a Coquard champagne press. A number of wines are produced in a variety of styles, but the standout – both at the estate and in England – is the great Ridgeview Cuvée Merret Bloomsbury. Based on a classic mix of the three champagne varieties – Chardonnay, Pinot Noir, and Pinot Meunier – it is a wonderfully rich, deep, and complex fizz, with sparkling acidity and a delicate mousse.

Fragbarrow Lane, Ditchling Common, East Sussex, BN6 8TP
www.ridgeview.co.uk

Santomas Primorje, Slovenia
Malvazija (white)

Santomas is a fine Slovenian estate with a long, long history. Indeed, the Glavina family has roots dating back to the Middle Ages, although the Santomas estate as it is today really began in the middle of the 19th century, when this branch of the family began growing and making wine in the Primorje region. Ludvik Nazarij Glavina is now in charge of the 19ha (47 acres) of vineyards, and he is ably assisted by his daughter, Tamara, who looks after the winemaking. One of the estate's specialities is the local Malvazija grape variety. Santomas makes one of the best examples currently on offer in Slovenia – an elegant interpretation of Malvazija Istriana with bright, clear acidity, and floral aromatics.

Ludvik Nazarij Glavina, Smarje 10, 6274 Smarje
www.santomas.si

ALTERNATIVES TO GLASS BOTTLES

Good-value wines in alternative packaging, such as boxes, cans, pouches, and plastic bottles, are increasingly popular. They make sense on several levels. The main reason is that using them costs less for the winery and, therefore, the consumer.

The costs are lower for at least three reasons. First, the materials for alternative packaging are cheaper than glass bottles. Second, they eliminate the need for separate labels, since graphics and text can be printed directly onto the packaging. Third, all forms of alternative packaging weigh less than glass bottles and so save on transportation costs. Furthermore, some boxes and pouches enable a larger quantity of wine to be transported by squeezing the equivalent of two or four bottles of wine into a single 1.5-litre or 3-litre unit.

From the wine drinker's point of view, boxes and pouches are also more convenient. They take up less space on a shelf or in a refrigerator; and they do not break – so parks, outdoor concerts, and sporting events sometimes allow them while banning glass.

Why then, have boxes, plastic, cans, and pouches not overtaken glass? Primarily it is because people are generally conservative about wine. Since glass is the traditional wine packaging, people find it difficult to accept that good and even great wine can come in a box or a can.

Glass bottles are still best for wines that age. Boxes keep wine fresh for up to a year, and during that time the wine tastes as it would in a glass bottle. After that, however, the wine quality fades. Glass protects collectible wines for decades. But since these account for perhaps 1% of the wine sold, it is not a concern for most people.

Schuchmann Wines Kakheti, Georgia

Saperavi (red)

The practice of ageing wines in *kvevri* (clay jars) goes back to antiquity, but the method had rather fallen from favour in Georgia until it was revived by Schuchmann Wines. The company was the first to make wines using a modern adaptation of the practice in 2002, a revival prompted by the third-generation winemaker, Gogi Dakishvili and the top consultant winemaker, David Maisuradze. The pair also developed new microbiological controls for wines fermented with their skins and pips, and Schuchmann has become known for its commitment to the great Georgian grape variety, Saperavi. This full-flavoured, powerful example is a great introduction to the grape's charms.

37 Rustaveli St, Telavi 2200
www.schuchmann-wines.com

Sula Vineyards Maharashtra, India

Sauvignon Blanc (white); Chenin Blanc (white)

Outside its rapidly growing middle-class, in India wine is still far from being a mass-market proposition. But no company has done more to try to change that than Sula Vineyards, which continues to go from strength to strength. The company has steadily added to its range over the years, and it now has a portfolio that takes in a number of styles and grape varieties. Although it has started making some highly promising red wines from Cabernet Sauvignon and Shiraz, it is the white wines that first captured attention, and they continue to offer the highest points in the range today. The original Chenin Blanc is a true expression of the variety with an Indian accent; the Sauvignon Blanc is a tropical fruit salad of flavours.

Survey 36/2, Govardhan, Off Gangapur-Savargaon Road, Nashik 422222, Maharashtra
www.sulawines.com

Szeremley Badacsony, Hungary

Riesling Selection (white); Badacsonyi Kéknyelű (white)

The Szeremley family estate sits in a beautiful spot in the Balaton Uplands National Park, between Mount Badacsony and the shores of Lake Balaton. It has been the subject of considerable renewal since 1992, when Huba Szeremley began to realize his vision for the 115ha (284 acres) of vineyards, based on volcanic soils. Szeremley works with a number of different grape varieties, many of them native to the region, such as Kéknyelű, Budai Zöld, Zeus, and Riesling Italico, and the single-varietal Kéknyelűis well worth seeking out for its finesse and grace. No less interesting is the Riesling Selection blend, a laser-guided white with great concentration and verve.

H-8258 Badacsonytomaj, Főút 51–53
www.szeremley.com

Telavi Wine Cellar Kakheti, Georgia

Marani Separavi (red)

Telavi Wine Cellar is comfortably Georgia's largest wine producer, but its wines are consistently good. It has more than 450ha (1,112 acres) of vineyards to its name, spread throughout three districts of Kakheti, and it also purchases a number of grapes from growers in Kakheti and the outlying western wine regions. Winemaking here is in the hands of the talented young Georgian, Beka Sozashvili, who is ably assisted by the Frenchman, Raphael Jenot. The pair make a number of excellent wines from Georgia's Saperavi grape variety, although they often use a little Malbec to soften and fill out Saperavi's naturally astringent tannins. Most of the company's output is focused on the Marani brand name, and the basic Separavi produced in this line shows just how good the variety can be. A full-bodied wine, with plenty of grip and structure, it has plenty of crunchy, fresh red fruit.

Kurdgelauri, Telavi 2200
www.tewincel.com

Tsiakkas Winery Pitsilia, Cyprus

Dry White; Rosé Dry; Vamvakada (red)

Costas Tsiakkas took to the wine world as an escape from the banking industry in the 1980s. Since then, he has ploughed all of his considerable energy into building his eponymous estate into one of the best in Cyprus. Its home is a tile-roofed winery that can be found more than 1,000m (3,281ft) up on the south side of the Troodos Mountains, looking down on the town of Pelendri. Tsiakkas makes a range of wines, of which the best are the citrussy fresh Dry White made from Xynisteri; a rosé made from Grenache that is just about the perfect al fresco summer sipper; and the vanilla-infused, fruity Maratheftiko, which is sold under the local name of Vamvakada. With several recently planted vineyards soon to be ready, and with Tsiakkas's son, Orestes, learning winemaking in Adelaide, this is an estate to watch.

4878 Pelendri
www.swaypage.com/tsiakkas

Vinakoper Koper, Slovenia
Malvazija (white); Refosk (red)

Situated in the Adriatic town of Koper on the Istrian peninsula to the south of Trieste, Vinakoper is one of Slovenia's most productive and successful co-operatives. It was founded in 1947, and, particularly in recent years, it has become identified with fine examples of two local specialities: the Refosk red and the Malvazija white. The former, known as Refosco elsewhere, produces vibrantly fruity reds with marked acidity and an attractive savoury edge that make it perfect for winter dishes. The Malvazija, by contrast, is all about the summer, both in its flavours – Mediterranean herbs, lemons, and a bracing blast of salty fresh acidity – and the drinking occasions – try this with seafood on a warm evening.

Smarska cesta 1, 6000, Koper
www.vinakoper.si

Vinos LA Cetto Valle de Guadalupe, Mexico
Petite Sirah (red)

With considerable hard work and dedication, and no little adventure, Camillo Magnoni has helped make Vinos LA Cetto into a consistently strong performer. Mexico's largest winery, Vinos LA Cetto has an annual production in excess of 900,000 cases, making it the market leader in terms of size by some distance. But Magnoni, the winemaker here since the company was formed in 1974, has made the most of the raw ingredients he has been given in the challenging growing conditions of the Valle de Guadalupe in Baja California Norte. Not surprisingly given the warm climate here, the reds are the winery's strong point. The rich and warming Petite Sirah is a very drinkable red for winter evenings.

Km 73.5 Carretera Tecate El Sauzal, Valle de Guadalupe, BC
www.lacetto.com

Zambartas Winery Limassol Wine Villages, Cyprus
Shiraz-Lefkada (red); Xynisteri (white)

For many years, the Cypriot winemaking community seemed bent on ignoring its rich array of indigenous varieties, allowing many to fall to the brink of extinction as growers rushed to plant international varieties instead. But Akis Zambartas took a different view. In the long period he spent as the head of the island's biggest producer, KEO, he worked tirelessly to save those varieties for future generations, and he was able to draw on this experience when he set up his own winery in 2006 with his son, Marcos. The slogan at Zambartas is "New World Wines on Old Soil", and they put this idea into practice. The idea is to take local grape varieties, blending them with international varieties using the most up-to-date techniques. The result is wines with a polished feel such as the Shiraz-Lefkada, a powerful, plush, sophisticated red, and the fresh Xynisteri, which is augmented by a splash of Sémillon. Total production at the moment is only 2,300 cases for the entire estate, but the plan is to double it in the next few years.

Gr. Afxentiou 39, 4710 Agios Amyrosios
www.zambartaswineries.com

Zlatan Otok Dalmatia, Croatia
Ostatak Bure (white)

Originally formed in 1986 under the name Vitis, before taking on its current name in 1993, Zlatan Otok is a small but extremely well managed producer. Operating from a headquarters in the southern part of the island of Hvar, the company also has vineyards in Makarsko Vinogorje, and it is currently working towards organic certification. Among other things, Zlatan Otok is widely respected for its work with native Croatian varieties, such as the white Pošip, Žilavka, and Malvazija. These varieties are very much to the fore in the excellent white wine, Bure (the name refers to a strong northern wind). A crisp, nutty white, with peachy fruit, it is a summer wine par excellence.

Sveta Nedjelja, 21465 Jelsa
www.zlatanotok.hr

Glossary

Use this glossary to get to grips with the wine words you'll need to make the most of affordable wines, many of which appear throughout this book. Grape varieties (with the exception of those treated in depth elsewhere), wine tasting terms, and grape growing and winemaking techniques, are all covered here.

Acid, acidity Good acidity brings crispness or tanginess to a wine. The acidity comes mostly from the grape as tartaric and malic acids, but can include lactic acid, too.

Aftertaste The taste that lingers in the mouth after swallowing wine. *See* Finish.

Ageing A wine ages in barrels or tanks at the winery, and in bottles after it is ready for release. Many wines improve with time in the bottle, becoming softer and more complex.

Albariño, Alvarinho White grape variety from Galicia in Spain. Called Alvarinho in Portugal.

Alcohol The intoxicating component of wine. Ethyl alcohol or ethanol is a natural by-product of fermentation as yeast converts the sugar in grape juice into alcohol and carbon dioxide.

Aligoté White grape variety associated with Burgundy. Also planted in eastern Europe.

Amarone Red wine from Valpolicella, Northeast Italy made from partially dried grapes.

Amontillado Well-aged, amber-coloured sherry with a rich nutty flavour.

AOC Abbreviation for the French legal term that designates geographical origins for wine and other agricultural products – Appellation d'Origine Contrôlée. Often shortened to AC.

Apéritif A pre-dinner drink.

Appellation The name of the place where the grapes were grown. Appellations in most wine-growing countries are regulated by law.

Appellation d'Origine Contrôlée *See* AOC.

Aroma The fragrance of a wine.

Assemblage The assembly of a wine from component batches from different vineyards, grape varieties, barrels, and tanks.

Asti Spumante Sweet, sparkling, low-alcohol wine from Asti in northern Italy.

Astringency Mouth-drying sensation mainly caused by tannins, particularly in red wine.

Auslese German term for a wine made from fully ripened grapes.

Autolysis What happens when a wine is left to age on the lees, or dead yeast cells, remaining in a barrel, tank, or bottle after fermentation.

Auxerrois In Cahors Auxerrois means Malbec or Côt. In Alsace it refers to a white variety.

AVA American Viticultural Area. Vine-growing area recognized by the US government.

Balance, balanced A wine where the flavour, acidity, tannins, and body enhance each other.

Banyuls French dessert wine from around the village of Banyuls near the Mediterranean coast.

Barbera Italian red grape variety.

Barrel Traditional, portable wooden container for holding wine, almost always made of oak. The typical size holds about 225 litres (50 gals).

Barrel ageing Period a wine spends in oak barrels after fermentation.

Barrel fermented The process of fermenting wine in the barrel to deepen the texture.

Barrique French term for an oak barrel of about 225 litres (50 gals).

Bâtonnage *See* Lees stirring.

Bianco Italian for white, or white wine.

Big Term that refers to a wine with high alcohol, a rough or tannic texture, and robust flavours.

Biodynamic A method of farming related to organics that limits chemical fertilizers and pesticides, and requires attention to natural cycles including the phases of the moon.

Blanc de Blancs A white wine, often a sparkling wine, made from white grape varieties.

Blanc de Noirs White wine made from black grapes, most often applied to sparkling wines.

Blaufränkisch *See* Lemberger.

Blending Winemaking practice that combines separate lots of wine into a final blend for sale.

Blush wine American term for a form of rosé.

Bodega Spanish term for winery or wine cellar.

Body Perceived weight of a wine, detemined largely by its alcohol content. Light-bodied wines are usually under 12% alcohol, medium-bodied, roughly 12–13.5%, and full-bodied above that.

Bonarda Name for at least three different red grape varieties in Italy and one in Argentina.

Bordeaux varieties Five classic red grape varieties used in red wine in the Bordeaux region and by winemakers around the world emulating Bordeaux: Cabernet Franc, Cabernet Sauvignon, Malbec, Merlot, and Petit Verdot.

Botrytis In its malignant form this fungus, also known as grey rot, can spoil a grape crop. But when it affects ripe bunches of certain grapes destined for dessert wines, it earns the name noble rot. Full name *Botrytis cinerea*.

Bouquet A flowery term for a wine's aroma.

Breathing What a wine does when a bottle is opened, and the wine is poured into glasses or a decanter, bringing it into contact with oxygen.

Brut Dry-tasting style of sparkling wine, standard in most Western countries. A brut wine must have less than 1.5% sugar.

Brut Nature Very dry style of champagne without any sugar added at the dosage stage.

Bush vines Vines grown without trellising, usually in older vineyards in warmer regions.

Butt A wooden cask or barrel (650 litres/142 gals) used mainly in the Sherry region of Spain.

Cabernet Franc Red grape variety popular in the Loire Valley, Bordeaux, and globally wherever Bordeaux blends are made.

Canaiolo Italian red wine grape popular in Tuscany, the Marches, and Sardinia.

Cap The layer of grape skins that rises to the top of a container of grape must during fermentation.

Carignan Red grape variety common in Spain and southern France. *Cariñena* in Spain, *Carignano* in Italy, and *Carignane* in California.

Carmenère A late-ripening black grape variety of French origin popular in Chile.

Cask Container, usually wooden, larger than the common 225 litre (50 gal) barrel. In Australia the term can also refer to a box of wine.

Cava Traditional-method Spanish sparkling wine, mostly made in the Penedès region.

Cave French term for wine cellar and/or winery.

Cellar A place suitable for storing wine.

Cement tank Vessel for storing wine.

Cépage French term for grape variety.

Chai A storage place for wine on the premises where it is fermented or bottled.

Charmat Economical (in time and money) method of sparkling wine production where the secondary fermentation takes place in a sealed tank, rather than in a bottle as in champagne.

Chasselas White grape variety closely identified with Switzerland, but also planted in parts of France, Germany, Italy, and other regions.

Château "Castle" or "grand house" in French. The term is most often used for Bordeaux wines that are grown on one property.

Chef de cave French for the person directly in charge of winemaking at a given facility.

Cinsault A red wine grape variety widely planted in southern France.

Claret The English term for dry red wine from Bordeaux.

Clarify *See* Fining.

Classico An Italian wine of a classic origin, from a wine region or small district known for producing the best wines of a type.

Classified growth *See* Cru Classé.

Clean A fresh, well-made wine with no defects.

Climat Burgundian term for specific vineyard sites and for sub-sections of vineyards.

Clonal selection The practice of carrying forward favourable genetic material from an existing grapevine to new vines or a whole new vineyard grown from cuttings of that vine.

Clone Wine grapes are differentiated by species, then by varieties, then by clones. Multiple clones are created by mutations of individual vines.

Clos French term for a walled or fenced vineyard.

Cloudy Murky appearance in a wine.

Cloying Term to describe overly sweet wine.

Colheita "Vintage" or "crop" in Portuguese. Also describes a port or Madeira made from one vintage and aged for several years in casks before bottling. Not the same as vintage port.

Colombard White grape variety common in France, California, South Africa, and Australia.

Commune Describes a village and the surrounding area in French wine regions.

Cooperage Company making wooden barrels.

Co-operative An association of wine-grape growers with winemaking facilities.

Cork Bottle stopper made from cork oak bark.

Corked, corky Term for a wine spoiled by the mouldy odour of trichloroanisole, also known as TCA, carried by corks, in wood barrels, or in cardboard within a winery.

Cortese White grape variety of Gavi in Italy.

Corvina Italian black grape variety common in Valpolicella and Bardolino.

Côte "Hillside" or "slope" in French.

Cream sherry A sweet-tasting blend of dry and very sweet sherries.

Crémant French term for a sparkling wine that is not from the Champagne region.

Crianza Spanish term used to indicate a wine aged for a minimum period. In Rioja, it is two years, including six months in barrel.

Crisp Attractively acidic and appetizing wine.

Cru French for "growth", but it more accurately indicates an individual vineyard property or plot, rather than the growth of the vines.

Cru Bourgeois Quality level for Bordeaux châteaux below Cru Classé.

Cru Classé A classed or classified vineyard in France that has been officially singled out for the quality of its wine over time. In Bordeaux, Cru Classé properties range from first growth (Premier Cru) at the top end, to fifth growth.

Crush To crush grapes is to squeeze or break open the berries just after harvesting to release the juice from the skins before fermentation. "Crush" also refers to the harvest season.

Crusted port A full-bodied port blended from multiple vintages.

Cuvée In French a tank or vat is a cuve. The wine in that tank is a cuvée.

Decant To draw the clear wine off its lees or sediment. This is done in the winery by siphon or pump for clarification of a young wine, and called "racking". At home, decanting refers to pouring a wine from a bottle to another vessel, such as a decanter or pitcher.

Decanter Container into which a wine is decanted before serving.

Declassify To set aside a portion of wine in the winery as lesser quality.

Demi-muid A barrel of about 600 litres (132 gals).

Demi-Sec "Half-dry" in French; tastes rather sweet.

Dessert wine Generic term for sweet wines.

Destemming Removing the grape berries from the stems to prepare for fermentation.

Disgorging A step in making bottle-fermented sparkling wine for the market. The process removes the dead yeast cells (lees) from the bottle, where a second fermentation has occured, so that the remaining wine is clean and clear of sediment.

DO Spanish appellation system, Denominación de Origen, which seeks to guarantee that a wine's origin is accurately portrayed on its label.

DOC/DOCG Italian categories for wines that come from a specific growing region. The rules for DOCG (Denominazione di Origine Controllata e Garantita), are stricter and the wines should be of a higher quality than DOC (Denominazione di Origine Controllata).

Dolcetto Northwest Italian red grape variety.

Domaine Term for a vineyard holding owned by one family or company.

Dornfelder Red German grape variety.

Dosage Process of adding a shot of sweetness and flavouring to a bottle-fermented sparkling wine just after disgorging and before corking.

Double Magnum Bottle containing 3 litres or the equivalent of 4 standard bottles.

Doux Sweet; used for still and sparkling wines.

Dry Lacking sweetness. Dry wines have fermented fully, to the point where virtually all the grape sugar has been converted to alcohol.

Dry-farmed, dry-grown Vineyards grown without the use of irrigation.

Earthy A tasting term signifying an aroma of damp soil – a positive attribute in some complex red wines.

Eiswein Also known as Icewine, a sweet wine made from grapes that have been left to partially freeze on the vine.

Elbling Traditional white grape variety grown in Germany and Luxembourg.

Elegant A tasting term for well-balanced, lighter, high-quality wines.

Enology *See* Oenology.

Enoteca Often translated as "wine library", this Italian term means a repository of wine. In Italy an enoteca is often a wine shop.

Erben Seen in the names of many German wineries, it means "heirs".

Erstes Gewächs Term used for the highest level of quality wines from specific sites in the Rheingau region of Germany.

Erzeugerabfüllung Term that means "bottled by the producer" in German.

Estate-bottled Wines that are bottled by the owner of the vineyard where the grapes grew.

Extra Brut A very dry sparkling wine, made with just a drop of sweetness in the dosage.

Extra Dry Term used for sparkling wines that are sweeter than brut, but drier than demi-sec.

Extract The flavour, colour, and texture components of a wine, derived from the grape skins, extracted during the winemaking process.

Fat Describes a wine where the sweetness and/or body overwhelms the acidity and tannins.

Fattoria Italian word often used for winery.

Fermentation Natural process conducted by yeast cells which consume the sugar in grape juice and produce alcohol and carbon dioxide gas as by-products.

Filtering Most wines are filtered before bottling to remove spoilage micro-organisms and to clarify. Some winemakers avoid filtration to make what they believe are more natural wines.

Finesse Describes an elegant, memorable wine.

Fining Process for clarifying wine, in which a fining agent such as gelatin, bentonite clay, milk or cream derivatives, or sometimes egg whites, is added to a wine in tanks or barrels.

Finish Aftertaste. In general terms, the longer the finish, the better the wine.

Fino A dry full-flavoured style of sherry that ages under a layer of flor yeast.

First growth English for "Premier Cru", a vineyard or winery of the first rank.

Fleshy Ample texture and body in a wine.

Flinty The smell of steel struck against flint, it is an attractive quality in some white wines.

Flor A layer of yeast that forms on the surface of sherry when the barrels are left slightly under-filled to allow air space.

Flute A tall, narrow glass for sparkling wine.

Flying winemaker Term for a winemaker who consults in different countries or continents.

Fortified wine A class of wine to which distilled spirits have been added to raise the alcohol percentage. This is often done during the fermentation to stop the yeast from completing its job, and thus retaining natural grape sugar in the wine. Examples include port and sherry.

Foudre French term for a large oak barrel.

Free run The juice that flows freely out of the grapes when they are destemmed and/or crushed, but before they are pressed.

Frizzante A lightly sparkling wine from Italy.

Frühburgunder German red wine grape variety; a mutation of Pinot Noir.

Fruity A positive description of most wines where fruit characters are evident.

Fuder Large oak wine cask in Germany.

Full-bodied A wine that tastes full and strong, usually of 13.5% alcohol or higher.

Fût French word for barrel used in Burgundy.

Garagiste/garage wines Quality wines made in recent years, primarily in Bordeaux, without a château name or official classification. Some are literally fermented in garages.

Garganega Main white grape variety used in the Soave wines of the Veneto region of Italy.

Glycerol Viscous liquid that forms in small quantities in wine during fermentation, and adds a sensation of sweetness and richness in high enough concentrations. Same as glycerine.

Grafting Grapevines, like fruit trees and roses, adapt readily to the grafting of a fruiting variety onto a rootstock of a different species or variety. This is a necessity for vineyards using the *Vitis vinifera* in areas where the phylloxera louse is present in the soil because ungrafted vinifera vines are vulnerable to phylloxera.

Gran Reserva Spanish term for a red wine that has been aged for at least five years before it is sold (with a minimum of 18 months in oak), and a white or rosé aged for at least four years.

Grand Cru Literally "great growth" in French, meaning great vineyard. The term denotes the top-rated vineyards in Burgundy (where there are 33 such) and in Alsace. The term is used in a different manner in St-Emilion (Bordeaux) and Champagne. The Grand Cru designation indicates the potentially outstanding quality of the wines made from these vineyards. Burgundy and Alsace hold the term Grand Cru above Premier Cru. In St-Emilion, 53 properties are classified as Grands Crus, while 13 more are Premiers Grands Crus (or "first great growths"). *See* Premier Cru.

Grand Vin "Great wine" in French, used to indicate the top-quality wine of an estate.

Grape A small, naturally manufactured package of winemaking ingredients that contains sugary juice, seeds, pulp, skin, and yeast.

Gravity flow Moving wine in the winery without using a pump.

Green Characterization of a wine that usually indicates unripe aromas or flavours. Considered a virtue in some fresh white wines.

Green harvest The quality-focused practice of removing a portion of a grape crop early in the growing season, usually when the grapes are still green, to reduce the yield and concentrate the vines' energy on the remaining grapes.

Grip Refers to the texture of a wine in one's mouth, and signifies a desired level of tannins, acid, and alcohol, particularly in red wines.

Grosses Gewächs First growth wine of at least Spätlese quality from a single vineyard or estate in Germany.

Grosslage "Large vineyard" in German. Usually refers to a collection of small neighbouring vineyards.

Halbtrocken "Half-dry" in German, indicating a wine with relatively low sugar content and enough balancing acidity so the wine tastes dry.

Harmonious Similar to "balanced", it refers to a wine in which all the parts blend well.

Haut "High" in French, referring either to the physical position of vineyards or to quality level.

Heavy High in alcohol or sweetness, and without sufficient balance from acidity.

Hectare Abbreviated to ha. Unit for land measurement in the metric system equal to 100m by 100m, or 10,000m^2. One hectare equals 2.47 acres.

Hectolitre Abbreviated to hl, and equal to 100 litres, or 26 US gallons, and 22 Imperial gallons.

Herbaceous Refers to a herbal taste in wine.

High-density planting Fashionable but not scientifically proven practice of planting vines extremely close together to increase quality by limiting yields in the individual vines.

Hybrid A vine type resulting from the crossing of grapevines from two different species. A true cross is a vine type created from two parent vines of the same species.

Icewine *See* Eiswein.

IGP Indication Geographique Protegée. The French interpretation of new EU labelling laws that will see the Vins de Pays and VDQS quality designations phased out in the coming years.

Johannisberg Riesling Term sometimes seen in California to distinguish the Riesling grape of Germany from the once-popular Grey Riesling.

Kabinett German term indicating a level of ripeness just below Spätlese. Kabinett wines are light and can be slightly sweet, half-dry, or dry.

Keller "Cellar" in German, often indicating a winery.

Kosher wine Wine made in a way that satisfies the Jewish dietary guidelines.

Labrusca *Vitis labrusca* grapevines are native to the northern and eastern sections of North America and produce grapey, musky wines.

Lactic acid The soft, buttery acid found also in dairy products, that is converted from malic acid in wine during the malolactic fermentation.

Lagar A large trough or low-sided vat in Portugal in which wine ferments, traditionally after the grapes have been foot-trodden.

Lambrusco Red varietal sparkling wine from Italy that can be dry or sweet.

Landwein Austrian and German classification for common table wines that are dry or nearly dry with more body than most table wines.

Late Bottled Vintage A port wine made from grapes all harvested in the same vintage, aged in casks and sold between four and six years after the vintage. Abbreviated as LBV.

Late harvest When wine grapes are picked later in the season than is required for normal dry table wine, leading to wines that are either higher in alcohol or sweeter than normal.

Lees The dregs that fall to the bottom of a barrel or tank in a winery. Composed of bits of grape skin and dead yeast cells.

Lees stirring "Bâtonnage" in French. This practice keeps the dead yeast cells (lees) in a barrel or tank in contact with the wine as it ages, to prevent oxidation and add flavour and texture.

Legs Rivulets formed by alcohol that run down the inside of a glass wetted with wine.

Lemberger Red grape variety in Württemberg, Germany. Called *Blaufränkisch* in Austria and *Kékfrankos* in Hungary.

Liebfraumilch Term meaning "mother's milk", used for sweet, low-priced wines exported from Germany, often made from Müller-Thurgau.

Lieu-dit "Place name" used in Burgundy, Alsace, and other French areas for traditional, named vineyard without official appellation status. *Climat* is a Burgundian synonym.

Liquoreux French for sweet-style wines.

Liquoroso Italian term for a fortified wine.

Litre Metric unit of measure, consisting of 1,000mls. One litre equals 33.8 fl oz.

Lodge English term for a winery in the Oporto region of Portugal where port wines are blended, aged, and bottled.

Macabeo White vine variety planted in Spain, especially in Rioja, and the Penedès region (where it is blended with Xarel-lo and Parellada to make the base wine for Cava). Also found in southern France. *Viura* and *Macabeu* are synonyms.

Maceration The practice of soaking grape skins in the juice or wine before, during, or after fermentation, to allow more colour and flavour compounds to move from the skins into the juice, and ultimately the wine.

Magnum Bottle size containing 1.5 litres or the equivalent of two standard bottles.

Malic acid A crisp, tangy fruit acid strong in apples and also in wine grapes.

Malolactic fermentation The conversion of malic acid to lactic acid to lower overall acidity and create a smoother texture and longer finish.

Malvasia Mediterranean family of white grape varieties characterized by distinctive perfume.

Manzanilla Typically light, dry style of sherry made in the town of Sanlúcar de Barrameda that is similar to fino sherry in that it ages in barrels with a layer of flor yeast on its surface.

Marsala Italian wine, best known as a dessert wine, sometimes made dry as Marsala Vergine.

Marsanne Rhône white wine grape variety.

Master of Wine/MW Title awarded to people who have passed the rigorous series of exams from the UK-based Institute of Masters of Wine.

Mataró *See* Mourvèdre.

Melon de Bourgogne White grape variety used mostly in the Loire for making Muscadet.

Méthode Champenoise Method developed in the Champagne region of France for producing high-quality sparkling wines by conducting in the individual bottles the second fermentation that produces the characteristic carbonation. Champagne wines must age on the lees from this process for at least 15 months, before disgorging and bottling. Terms used for the same process elsewhere in the world include Traditional Method, Méthode Traditionnelle, and Méthode Classique (France), Metodo Classico and Metodo Tradizionale (Italy), and Méthode Cap Classique (South Africa).

Microclimate Describes the individual climatic conditions of a vineyard or part of a vineyard.

Millésime "Vintage" year in French.

Minerality, mineral taste Term for wines that go beyond simply fruity in flavour.

Mise en bouteille au château "Bottled at the château" in French. Usually indicates that the grower and the bottler were the same entity.

Moelleux A French term to describe wine that is mellow, rather sweet, and with a soft texture.

Monastrell *See* Mourvèdre.

Mondeuse Red grape variety in Savoie, France.

Monopole A French wine district where all the vineyard property is owned by one proprietor.

Moscato Italian for "Muscat" (see below).

Moscato d'Asti Low-pressure, low-in-alcohol sparkling wine made from Moscato (Muscat) grapes in the northern Italian town of Asti in Piedmont, where Asti Spumante is made, too.

Mourvèdre Red grape variety best-known in the Rhône Valley of France, but also used in California, Australia, and elsewhere. *Mataró* and *Monastrell* are synonyms.

Mousse The foam in a glass of sparkling wine.

Müller-Thurgau Widely planted white German grape variety.

Muscadelle French white grape variety common in Bordeaux and Bergerac.

Muscat French name for a family of *Vitis vinifera* grapevines that produce aromatic, floral, and usually sweet wines of all colours.

Must Term for the liquid grape mixture before fermentation.

Négociant A firm that buys finished wine from a third party and bottles it under its own brand.

New oak Any form of oak cooperage being used for the first time, when the oak staves provide the most potent flavour.

Noble rot *See* Botrytis.

Nose Term for the smell of a wine.

Nouveau "New" in French. Nouveau wines, such as Beaujolais Nouveau, are bottled, shipped, and usually consumed within a few weeks of harvest.

Oak The type of wood preferred by winemakers around the world in which to age wine to improve its flavours and textures. Can be applied as a barrel or by adding oak chips, powder, stave inserts, nuggets, or blocks to stainless steel or concrete vats.

Oaky Descriptor for a wine that shows strong aroma and/or flavour influences from the oak used to store or age it in.

Oenologist Wine scientist, or qualified winemaker. *Enologist* in the US.

Oenology The science of wine. *Enology* in the US.

Old vines Known as "vieilles vignes" in French, the term on a label indicates that a wine was made from grapes grown on fully mature vines.

Oloroso Rich, nutty, full-bodied style of sherry, made in a different way to the lighter fino.

Organic Indicates agricultural produce grown without the use of synthetic herbicides, pesticides, and fertilizers.

Organically grown On a wine label this term means the grapes have been grown using strict organic practices. It does not indicate that the wine has been processed organically.

Overcropped A vineyard that produces too many grapes per vine so that the sugar content and flavour constituents are not concentrated sufficiently to make the desired quality of wine.

Own-rooted *See* Ungrafted vines.

Oxidation Process by which oxygen interacts with wine and changes its composition.

Oxidized Term for a stale or spoiled wine suffering from too much exposure to oxygen.

Palo cortado Rare type of sherry between an amontillado and an oloroso in style.

Palomino A white grape variety used particularly for sherry, but also table wines.

Passetoutgrains Bourgogne A basic wine in Burgundy made from Pinot Noir and Gamay.

Passito Italian term for wine from dried grapes.

Pays "Country" or "countryside" in French.

PDO Protected Designation of Origin. A new EU-wide labelling system to guarantee the origin of wines and other products.

Pedro Ximénez, PX Grape grown mostly in Spain for dry white and rich dessert wines, and also the name of a sherry made from this grape.

Perfume A wine's aroma or smell.

Pétillant French term for slightly sparkling wine.

Petit Verdot One of the five classic red grape varieties of Bordeaux.

Petite Sirah Red grape variety most closely linked to California.

PGI Protected Geographical Indication. A new EU-wide labelling system to guarantee the origin of wines and other products.

Phylloxera A tiny louse that eats grapevine roots and destroyed European and Californian vineyards in the late 19th century and forced changes in grape growing that persist today.

Picpoul Grape variety from France's Languedoc region most common as a crisp white wine.

Pigeage *See* Punching down.

Pinot Blanc The whitest variation in the grape family that also includes Pinot Noir and Pinot Gris. Grown in Burgundy, Alsace, Germany (Weissburgunder), Italy (Pinot Bianco), central and eastern Europe, and the New World.

Pinot Meunier A red grape variety, one of the three grape varieties used in champagne (the others being Pinot Noir and Chardonnay).

Pinotage Red grape variety from South Africa, a crossing of Pinot Noir and Cinsault.

Port Fortified wine made in Portugal. The grapes are grown in the Douro Valley, the wines are aged in and around the city of Oporto.

Portugieser Red grape variety, also known as Blauer Portugieser, popular in Austria, Germany, and other parts of central and eastern Europe.

Prädikat "Distinction". Used in Germany to identify wines of various quality levels based on ripeness of the grapes.

Prädikatswein The top classification level of German wine.

Premier Cru *See* First Growth.

Press Machine used to squeeze the juice or wine out of the grape skins.

Press wine Wine that flows from the wine press only after pressure is applied, and which is kept separate from the free run juice.

Primitivo Red grape variety grown in Italy, similar to the Zinfandel of California.

Prohibition Period from 1918 to 1933 when the commercial sale of most alcoholic beverages was banned in the US and Canada.

Prosecco White grape variety from the Veneto region of Italy, best known for sparkling wine.

Protected Designation of Origin *See* PDO.

Protected Geographical Indication *See* PGI.

Pumping over The act of pumping the clear juice from the bottom of a fermenting tank of red wine and spraying it over the cap of grape skins at the top. *Remontage* in French.

Punching down English term for the task of mixing the cap of grape skins back into the wine as it ferments. *Pigeage* in French.

Punt The indentation in the bottom of a wine bottle that adds structural strength to the glass.

QbA "Qualitätswein bestimmter Anbaugebiete". The broadest category for quality wine in Germany indicating that the grapes come from one of the 13 designated quality regions.

QmP "Qualitätswein mit Prädikat". German for "quality wine with distinction" based on sugar ripeness in the must with six levels: Kabinett (the lightest), Spätlese, Auslese, Beerenauslese, Trockenbeerenauslese, and Eiswein.

Qualitätswein German term for quality wine on a very broad level.

Quinta Portuguese for a farm or wine estate.

Racking Ancient technique of transferring wine from one vessel to another to leave behind the lees and thus clarify it, and to keep barrels and tanks full to preclude oxygen from spoiling the wine. Can be done via gravity or a pump.

Racy Positive tasting term for vivid acidity.

Recioto Type of wine, red or white, made from dried grapes in the Veneto area of Italy.

Récoltant French for one who harvests. Abbreviated on champagne labels to RM (récoltant-manipulant) – a grower who makes his own wine rather than selling the grapes.

Red wine Wine made from red grapes. Red wine usually indicates a dry table wine from medium to full-bodied, with a wide variety of aromas and flavours.

Reduction, reductive The opposite of oxidation or the chemical status of a wine that is cut off from oxygen during production.

Refosco A family of red grape varieties in Slovenia, Northeast Italy, and Croatia.

Reichsgraf Term for a nobleman in Germany that is used in several winery estate names.

Reserve Can mean a wine with longer ageing, but the term has no legally binding meaning.

Reserva Spanish term for wine that has been aged for at least three years (with one in oak) before selling.

Ribolla, Ribolla Gialla White grape variety grown in Northeast Italy, Slovenia, and Greece.

Ripasso Technique where partially dried grape skins are saved from fermentation tanks and "re-passed" into other vats of newly fermenting wine to add more flavour and colour.

Riserva Italian term, indicating a wine that has been aged longer than normal.

Rootstock The base vine onto which the preferred wine-grape variety is grafted.

Rosato Rosé or pink wine, in Italian.

Rosé Wine typically made from red grapes using white wine methods to create a light red, pink, or amber hue, and flavours that fall between those of white and red wines.

Rosso Italian for "red".

Rouge French for "red".

Round Term for a smooth-textured wine.

Roussanne Rhône Valley white grape variety.

Ruby port The basic level of port wine.

Saint Laurent Red grape variety, related to Pinot Noir, and grown in Alsace, Austria, the Czech Republic, Germany, and other regions.

Sauvignon Gris White wine variety related to Sauvignon Blanc, with a semi-dark or pink colour on the grape skins.

Savagnin White grape variety of Jura, France.

Scheurebe Grape variety developed in Germany by crossing Sylvaner and Riesling.

Schloss German for "castle", used in wine names in the same manner as the French use "château".

Screwcap Increasingly popular metal alternative to the cork for a wine bottle stopper.

Sec, Seco, Secco Means "dry" in French, Spanish, and Italian; the opposite of sweet.

Sediment Minute particles in wine that slowly settle out of the solution over time, and form a murky layer in the bottom of the bottle.

Sekt Sparkling wine in Germany.

Sélection de Grains Nobles Abbreviated to SGN. Used mostly in Alsace, France, for wines made from grapes affected by *Botrytis cinerea*.

Sémillon A white grape variety from Bordeaux making dry and dessert wines around the world.

Seyval Blanc French-American hybrid white grape variety common in the UK and the US.

Sherry Spanish fortified wine from the Jerez region made in a variety of styles.

Skin contact When the grape juice stays mixed with the grape skins after crushing.

Solera System of blending and ageing used especially for sherry and other fortified wines.

Sommelier French for "wine waiter".

Spätburgunder German word for Pinot Noir.

Spätlese "Late harvest" in German, it refers to wines of medium body, either dry or sweet.

Spritz A slight carbonation that is normal and pleasant in certain wines, especially very fresh, recently released white wines. In dry red wines, it can be a sign of poor quality.

Spumante Italian for fully sparkling wines with greater pressure than merely frizzante wines.

Still A wine without effervescence or fizz.

Sulphites Word used on some wine labels to indicate the presence of sulphites, bisulphites, and free and total sulphur dioxide in wine. Sulphites are used by most winemakers in small quantities as a preservative.

Super Tuscan Popular term for top wines made from non-traditional grape varieties in Tuscany.

Superiore Used to indicate Italian wines that have attained a higher level of potential quality due to riper grapes and higher alcohol content.

Supple Tasting term for soft but strong texture.

Sur Lie French for "on the lees". Refers to a wine that stayed in contact with dead yeast cells and other particles that remain after fermentation.

Sylvaner White grape variety grown mainly in Germany and Alsace.

Table wine Can mean simply a still dry wine. In areas including the European Union, it is the official term for the basic level of wine quality.

Tannin Class of compounds found in wine, black tea, and other drinks that creates a drying, astringent, puckering effect in one's mouth.

Tawny port Style of port aged for long periods in wooden casks before bottling.

TCA Acronym for 2,4,6-trichloroanisole, the mouldy-smelling compound in "corked" wines.

Tenuta "Estate" in Italian, meaning a property devoted to wine-growing.

Terra rossa "Red soil", generally with a high iron content, that is prized in regions such as Italy, Spain, Australia, and California.

Terroir Vine-growing conditions that give a taste of place to a wine.

Texture The feel of a wine in one's mouth.

Tinta, Tinto Spanish for "red".

Toasted, toasty A smell or taste similar to that of toasted bread that can derive from ageing in barrels or from ageing on lees.

Tokaji, Tokay The Hungarian and anglicized terms for the Hungarian sweet wine.

Torrontés A family of grape varieties common in Argentina, producing aromatic white wines.

Touriga Franca Widely planted red grape variety from Portugal's Douro Valley.

Touriga Nacional Highly reputed red Portuguese grape variety.

Traminer White grape variety, parent of Gewürztraminer, making floral wines.

Traditional method *See* Méthode Champenoise.

Transfer method A method of making sparkling wine where the wine undergoes its second fermentation in individual bottles which are emptied into a tank under pressure and become mixed prior to bottling.

Treading The practice of crushing grapes by foot, still widely used in port production.

Trebbiano The most widely planted white grape variety in Italy. Also common in Southwest France, where it is called Ugni Blanc.

Trocken German for "dry".

Ugni Blanc *See* Trebbiano.

Unfiltered, unfined A wine that has not been filtered or fined. *See* Filtering and Fining.

Ungrafted vines A vine grown on its own rootstocks. *See* Grafting.

Unoaked A wine made without the use of oak.

Varietal A varietal wine is a wine made from just one, or predominantly one, grape variety.

Variety A specific sub-species of grapevine.

Vat Large wine container of various sizes made of stainless steel, oak, concrete, or plastic.

VDP The association of top German wine producers.

Vendange Tardive French for late harvest.

Verdelho, Verdello Two names for what are probably identical white grape varieties grown in Portugal, Madeira, and Australia as Verdelho, and in Spain as Verdello or Godello.

Verdicchio Central Italian white grape variety.

Vermentino Italian white variety popular in Liguria, Sardinia, Corsica, and southern France.

Vidal Blanc Hybrid grape variety found in Northeast US and Canada.

Vieilles vignes French term for old vines.

Vigneron French for "vine-grower".

Vin French for "wine".

Vin de Garde French for a wine to keep or age.

Vin de Pays Official French designation for "country wine", it falls above Vin de Table and below AOC, and is being replaced by IGP.

Vin de Table The official, basic level of inexpensive, low-quality wine in France.

Vin Doux Naturel French for a naturally sweet wine.

Vin Gris French expression for a rosé wine.

Viniculture Cultivation of grapevines and growing of grapes.

Vinifera *Vitis vinifera* is the traditional Middle-Eastern and later European species of grapevine that is used for most quality wines.

Vinification Winemaking, especially the steps taken in the winery to ferment, mature, and ready a wine for the market.

Vino da Tavola Italian for "table wine".

Vino de Mesa Spanish for "table wine".

Vintage Both the year in which a particular wine's grapes were harvested, and the time of year when the grape harvest takes place.

Vintage port A high-quality, ageworthy port from a specific vintage that is bottled young.

Viognier White grape variety from the Rhône Valley in France and now widespread.

Viticulture The science and labour of vine-growing.

Vitis Scientific term for the genus of grapevines.

Viura *See* Macabeo.

Volatile acidity Abbreviated to VA and refers to acids naturally occuring in wine due to the interaction of alcohol and oxygen, primarily acetic acid (vinegar). When VA grows to a level detectable as the smell of vinegar or nail polish, then it has gone too far and the wine is flawed.

Wein German for "wine".

Weingut German for wine estate, where wine is made from grapes grown on the same property.

Weinkellerei German for a wine cellar that usually buys rather than grows grapes.

Weissburgunder German name for the Pinot Blanc white grape variety.

White Zinfandel A style of light, slightly sweet rosé made from Zinfandel grapes in California.

Wild yeast Also native yeast or indigenous yeast. A yeast type that pre-exists in a vineyard or winery environment and will go to work on grape must without the winemaker's help.

Winemaker Person whose job is to help grapes and grape juice become wine.

Winery The physical premises where wine is made, or sometimes the legal entity that is responsible for producing wine and documenting it for legal and tax purposes.

Yeasts Microscopic single-celled organisms that convert the sugar in grape juice into ethyl alcohol and release carbon dioxide in the process.

Yeasty Aroma or flavour that resembles rising bread dough, sometimes detected in wine.

Yield Proportional measure of the productivity. of grapevines in a particular vineyard.

Index

The code after the name of each wine signifies the following: (r) red (w) white (rs) rosé (s) sparkling (f) fortified (d) dessert.

A

A Christmann 184
  A Christmann Riesling (w) QbA 184
A to Z Wineworks 252
  Oregon Pinot Noir (r) 252
Abacela 252
  Tempranillo (r) 157, 252
Abadía Retuerta 144
  Rívola Sardon de Duero (r) 144
Abbazia di Novacella 106
  Müller-Thurgau (w) 106
Abel Mendoza 144
  Abel Mendoza Joven (r) 144
Acacia 216
  Chardonnay, Carneros (w) 216
Accademia dei Racemi 106
  Puglia Rosso IGT Anarkos (r) 106
Achim Jähnisch 188
  Gutedel Trocken QbA (w) 188
Acorex Wine Holding 328
  Amaro de la Valea Perjei (r) 328
Acorn Winery/Alegria Vineyards 216
  Rosato, Russian River Valley (rs) 216
Acústic 144
  Acústic Blanc (w) 144
Adelsheim Vineyard 252
  Willamette Valley Pinot Noir (r) 252
Adriano Adami 106
  Prosecco di Valdobbiadene Bosco di Gica (s) 106
Afros 172
  Loureiro Vinho Verde (w) 172
  Vinhão Vinho Verde (r) 172
Agrapart & Fils 68
  Brut Blanc de Blancs Les 7 Crus (s) 68
Agrícola Castellana 144
  Cuarto Rayas Sauvignon Blanc (w) 144
  Cuarto Rayas Verdejo (w) 144
Agustí Torelló 145
  Brut Reserva (s) 145
Aímézola de la Mora 146
  Viña Amézola Crianza 146
Albet I Noya 145
  Petit Albet (s) 145
Alcohol
  How Much Alcohol is too Much? 241
Aldinger 182
  Untertürkheimer Gips Spätburgunder Trocken QbA (r) 182
Alexander Laible 193
  Spätburgunder Rosé Trocken (rs) 193
Alois Lageder 106
  Pinot Bianco Dolomiti (w) 106
Alsace Pinot Gris, Food & Wine 101
Alta Vista 272
  Malbec Classic, Mendoza (r) 272
Alternatives to Glass Bottles 335
Altos Las Hormigas 272
  Malbec, Mendoza (r) 272
Alvaro Palacios 145
  Camins del Priorat (r) 145
Alvear 145
  PX Solera 1927 (f) 145
Alzinger 208
  Federspiel Frauenweingarten Grüner Veltliner (w) 208
Amavi Cellars 248
  Walla Walla, Valley Syrah (r) 248
Amayna (Viña Garcés Silva) 262
  Sauvignon Blanc, Leyda Valley (w) 262
Amézola de la Mora 146
  Viña Amézola Crianza (r) 146
Ameztoi 146
  Chacolí (w) 146
Ampeleia 106
  Kepos IGT Maremma (r) 106
Anaba 216
  Corial Red Rhône Blend, Sonoma Valley (r) 216
  Corial White, Sonoma Valley (w) 216
Angheben 278
  Touriga Nacional (r) 278
Anna Maria Abbona 106
  Dolcetto di Dogliani Sori dij But (r) 106
Anta Banderas 146
  a4 (r) 146
Antech 74
  Blanquette de Limoux Cuvée Françoise (s) 74
Antiyal 262
  Maipo Valley Kuyen (r) 262
Antonelli San Marco 107
  Grechetto dei Colli Martani (w) 107
  Montefalco Rosso (r) 107
Antonin Rodet 65
  Château de Chamirey Mercurey Blanc Premier Cru La Mission Monopole (w) 65
Apollonio 107
  Rocca dei Mori Salice Salentino (r) 107
Ara 316
  Composite Pinot Noir, Marlborough (r) 316
  Composite Sauvignon Blanc Marborough (w) 316
Argiolas 107
  Cannonau di Sardegna Costera (r) 107
Arman 328
  Chardonnay, Teran (w) 328
Artazu 146
  Artazuri (r) 146
Artesa 216
  Pinot Noir, Carneros 216
Ata Rangi 316
  Crimson Pinot Noir, Martinborough (r) 316
Au Bon Climat 133, 216
  Pinot Noir, Santa Barbara County (r) 216
August Kesseler 190
  Riesling R QbA (w) 190
Averill Creek Vineyards 256
  Pinot Noir (r) 256
Avide 108
  Cerasuolo di Vittoria (r) 108
Avondale 282
  Chenin Blanc (w) 282
  Syrah (r) 282

B

Backsberg Estate Cellars 282
  Chenin Blanc (w) 282, 308
  Pinotage (r) 282
Badia a Coltibuono 108
  Coltibuono Cetamura Chianti (r) 108
Baker Lane 217
  Cuvée Syrah, Sonoma Coast (r) 217
Baron de Ley 146
  Finca Monasterio (r) 146
Barossa Valley Shiraz, Food & Wine 311
Bassermann-Jordan 182
  Riesling Trocken QbA (w) 182, 195
Battle of Bosworth 292
  Shiraz Viognier, McLaren Vale (r) 292
Beckmen Vineyards 217
  Cuvée le Bec, Santa Ynez Valley (r) 217
Bellavista 108
  NV: Franciacorta Brut (s) 108
Benanti 108
  Rosso di Verzella (r) 108
Benegas 272
  Don Tiburcio, Mendoza (r) 272
Benessere Vineyards 217
  Pinot Grigio, Carneros (w) 217
Benjamin Leroux 60
  Auxey-Duresses Blanc (w) 60
  Savigny-les-Beaune Rouge (r) 60
Benziger Family Winery 217
  Finegold Merlot, Sonoma Mountain (r) 217
  Stone farm Syrah, Sonoma Valley (r) 217
Bérèche et Fils 68
  Brut Réserve (s) 68
Bergström Wines 252
  Willamette Valley Chardonnay Old Stones (w) 252
  Pinot Noir Old Stones (r) 252
Bernardus Winery 217
  Sauvignon Blanc, Monterey County (w) 217
Bernhard Ellwanger 185
  Trollinger Trocken Gutswein (r) 185
Beronia 147
  Beronia Reserva (r) 147
Bessa Valley 328
  Enira (r) 328
Bickel-Stumpf 183
  Buntsandstein Silvaner Kabinett Trocken (w) 183
Bilancia 316
  Bilancia Pinot Gris, Hawkes Bay (w) 316
Bilbaínas 147
  Viña Pomal Reserva (r) 147
Biodynamic Wine 43
Bisson 109
  Vermentino Vignaerta (w) 109
Blasted Church Vineyards 256
  Hatfield's Fuse (w) 256
Blind River 316
  Sauvignon Blanc, Marlborough (w) 316, 323
Boeger Winery 217
  Hangtown Red, El Dorado (r) 217
Boekenhoustkloof Winery 282
  Porcupine Ridge Syrah (r) 282, 299
  Wolftrap Red Blend (r) 282
Bogle Vineyards 218
  Pinot Noir, California (r) 218
Bonny Doon Vineyard 218
  Syrah Le Pousseur, Central Coast (r) 218
  Contra (r) 218
Bonterra Vineyards 218
  Chardonnay, Mendocino County (w) 218
Boroli 109
  Dolcetto d'Alba Madonna di Como (r) 109
Borsao 147
  Gran Tesoro Garnacha (r) 147
Bouchard Père et Fils 47
  Meursault (w) 47
Bouchard-Finlayson 282
  Blanc de Mer (w) 282
  Sauvignon Blanc (w) 282
Bradgate Wines 282
  Chenin Blanc-Sauvignon Blanc (w) 282
  Syrah (r) 282
Brancott Estate 317
  Sauvignon Blanc, Marlborough (w) 317
Breaky Bottom Vineyard 329
  Cuvée John Inglis Hall (s) 329
Bremerton 292
  Vedelho, Langhorne Creek (w) 292
Broglia 109
  Gavi di Gavi La Meirana (w) 109
Brokenwood 292
  Semillon, Hunter Valley (w) 292
Brown Brothers
  Terrango, Victoria (r) 292
Brüder Dr Becker 183
  Ludwigshoher Silvaner Trocken (w) 183
Brundlmayer 208
  Zobinger Heiligenstein Riesling (w) 208
Buena Vista 218
  Chardonnay, Cameros (w) 218
  Pinot Noir, Carneros (r) 218
Buil I Giné 147
  Giné Giné (r) 147, 203
By Farr 292
  Farr Rising Pinot Noir, Geelong (r) 292

C

C J Pask Winery 321
  Gimblett Road Syrah, Hawkes Bay (r) 321
Cadaretta 248
  Columbia Valley Sauvignon Blanc-Semillon (w) 248
Calera Winery 219
  Viognier, Central Coast (w) 219
  Chardonnay, Mt. Harlan (w) 219
Cambria Winery 219
  Pinot Noir, Julia's Vineyard, Santa Maria Valley (r) 219
Camel Valley 329
  Bacchus Dry (w) 329
  White Pinot Sparkling (s) 329
Campbells 293
  Muscat, Rutherglen (f) 293
Campo Viejo 150
  Campo Viejo Reserva (r) 150
Candido 109
  Salice Salentino Riserva (r) 109
Cantina del Locorotondo 109
  Primitivo di Manduria Terre di Don Peppe (r) 109
Cantina del Pino 110
  Barbera d'Alba (r) 110
Cantina Gallura 109
  Vermentino di Gallura (w) 109
Cantina Terlan 110
  Pinot Bianco Classico (w) 110
Cantina Tramin 110
  Gewürztraminer Classic (w) 110
Cantine de Falco 111
  Salice Salentino Salore (r) 111
Cantine Giorgio Lungarotti 111
  Rosso di Torgiano Rubesco (r) 111
Cantine Gran Furor Divina Costiera di Marisa Cuomo 111
  Ravello Bianco (w) 111
Cape Chamonix Wine Farm 282
  Rouge Red Blend (r) 282
  Sauvignon Blanc (w) 282
Cape Mentelle 293
  Sauvignon Blanc-Semillon, Margaret River (w) 293
Carl Loewen 193
  Quant Riesling Mosel (w) 193
CARM 172
  Reserva, Duoro (r) 172
Carmel 329
  Appellation Carignan Old Vines (r) 329
Carol Shelton Wines 219
  Monga Zin Old Vine Zinfandel, Cucamonga Valley (r) 219
  Wild Thing Zinfandel, Mendocino County (r) 219
Casa de la Ermita 150
  Viognier (w) 150
Casa de Piedra 330
  Chardonnay (w) 330
Casa Emma 111
  Chianti Classico (r) 111
Casa Marin 262
  Cypress Vineyard Sauvignon Blanc (w) 262
Casale Del Giglio 111
  Lazio Bianco Satrico (w) 111
Casas del Bosque 262
  Sauvignon Blanc Reserva (w) 262
Cascina Morassino 112
  Dolcetto d'Alba (r) 112
Castaño 150
  Hercula (r) 150
Castel de Paolis 112
  Frascati Superiore (w) 112
Castell 184
  Schloss Castell Silvaner Trocken (w) 184
Castell d'Encus 150
  Susterris Negre (r) 150
Castell del Remei 151
  Gotim Bru (r) 151
Castello Banfi 112
  Rosso di Montalcino (r) 112

Castello di Ama 112
Chianti Classico (r) 112
Castello di Brolio 112
Ricasoli Brolio Chianti Classico (r) 112
Castello di Montepò 113
Sassoalloro Toscana IGT (r) 113
Castello di Verduno 113
Verduno Pelaverga (r) 113
Castello di Volpaia 113
Chianti Classico (r) 113
Castillo de Monjardin 151
Castillo de Monjardin Barrel Ferment Chardonnay (w) 151
Castillo Perelada 151
5 Fincas Empordà (r) 151
Castillo Perelada Brut Reserve (s) 151
Castra Rubra (r) 330
Castrocelta 151
Albariño (w) 151
Cataldi Madonna 116
Montepulciano d'Abruzzo (r) 116
Catena Zapata 272
Chardonnay (w) 272
Malbec (r) 272
Cave de Mont Tauch 74
Muscat de Rivesaltes Tradition (d) 74
Cave Geisse 278
Espumante Brut (s) 278
Cave Spring Cellars 256
Estate Bottled Riesling (w) 256
Caves des Vignerons de Saumur 74
La Réserve des Vignerons Saumur Champigny (r) 74
Les Poyeux Saumur Champigny (r) 74
Cederberg 283
Chenin Blanc (w) 283
Sauvignon Blanc (w) 283
Ceja 219
Vino de Casa White Blend, Napa Valley (w) 219
Celler de Capçanes 152
Mas Collet (r) 152
Ceretto 116
Arneis Blangé (w) 116
CG Di Arie Winery 221
Verdelho, Shenandoah Valley (w) 221
Chacra 272
Pinot Noir Barda (r) 272
Chain of Ponds 293
Pilot Block Sangiovese-Barbera-Grenache, South Australia (r) 293
Chalkers Crossing
Cabernet Sauvignon, Hilltops (r) 293
Champy Père et Fils 48
Bourgogne Blanc (w) 48
Chapel Hill 294
Foundation Verdelho, McLaren Vale (w) 294
Chappellet Vineyards 219
Chenin Blanc, Napa Valley (w) 219
Zinfandel, Napa Valley (r) 219
Charles Heidsieck 68
Brut Réserve (s) 68
Chartogne-Taillet 68
Brut Cuvée Ste-Anne (s) 68
Château Beau-Séjour Bécot 14
Tournelle de Beau-Séjour Bécot (r) 14
Château Beauregard 14
Benjamin de Beauregard (r) 14
Château Beauséjour 14
Croix de Beauséjour (r) 14
Château Belgrave (r) 8, 15
Château Belle-Vue (r) 15
Château Bellevue de Tayac (r) 15
Château Bertinerie (r) 15
Château Beychevelle 16
Les Brulières de Beychevelle (r) 16
Château Brane-Cantenac
Baron de Brane (r) 16, 309
Château Calon-Ségur 16
Marquis de Calon (r) 16
Château Cambon la Pelouse (r) 16
Château Camensac 16
La Closerie de Camensac (r) 16
Château Canon 17
Clos Canon (r) 17
Château Cantelys (r/w) 18
Château Cantenac Brown 18
Brio de Cantenac Brown (r) 18
Château Cap de Faugères (r) 18
Château Caronne-St-Gemme (r) 18, 133
Château Cazal Viel 76
St-Chinian Vieilles Vignes (r) 76
Château Chasse-Spleen 18
L'Ermitage de Chasse Spleen (r) 18
Château Citran 19
Moulin de Citran (r) 19
Château Clarke 19
Rosé de Clarke (rs) 19
Château Clément-Pichon (r) 19
Château Clément Termes 77
Cuvée Tradition Rouge (r) 77
Château Climens 19
Cyprès de Climens (d) 19
Château Clos Chaumont (r) 22
Château Coucheroy (r/w) 22
Château Couhins (r) 23
Château d'Agassac 14
L'Agassant d'Agassac, (r) 14
Château d'Aussières 75
A d'Aussières Corbieres (r) 75
Château d'Esclans 77
Whispering Angel (rs) 77
Château d'Issan 28
Blason d'Issan (r) 28
Château de Beauregard 46
Pouilly Fuissé (w) 46
Château de Caraguilhes 75
Solus Corbières Blanc (w) 75
Château de Cary-Potet 48
Bourgogne Aligoté (w) 48
Château de Cazeneuve 76
Pic St-Loup Les Calcaires (r) 76
Château de Chambert 76
Chambert Gourmand, Cahors (r) 76
Château de Chantegrive (r) 18
Château de Fieuzel 24
L'Abeille de Fieuzel (w) 24
Château de Haute Serre (r) 77, 225
Château de Jau 78
Le Jaja de Jau Syrah (r) 78
Château de la Dauphine 23
Delphis de la Dauphine (r) 23
Château de la Negly 78
La Falaise Coteaux du Languedoc (r) 78
Château de la Rivière (r) 40
Château de Lussac 30
Le Libertin de Lussac (r) 30
Château de Pibarnon 79
Rosé de Pibarnon (r) 79
Château de St-Cosme 80
St-Cosme Côte du Rhône (r) 80
Château de Val 330
Claret Reserve (r) 330
Château de Valandraud 43
3 de Valandraud (r) 43
Château des Charmes 257
Estate Bottled Cabernet Franc (r) 257
Château des Erles 77
Cuvée des Ardoises, Fitou (r) 77
Château des Eyssards 77
Bergerac Blanc (w) 77
Château du Tertre 42
Haut du Tertre (r) 42
Château Duhart-Milon 23
Baron de Milon (r) 23
Château Figeac 24
Le Grande Nueve de Figeac (r) 24
Château Fonbadet (r) 25
Château Fonplégade 25
Fleur de Fonplégade (r) 25
Château Fonréaud (r) 26
Château Fourcas Dupré (r) 26
Château Fourcas Hosten (r) 26
Château Franc Mayne 26
Les Cèdres de Franc Mayne (r) 26
Château Giscours 26
La Sirène de Giscours (r) 26
Château Grand Corbin-Despagne 27
Petit Corbin-Despagne (r) 27
Château Greysac 27 (r)
Château Haut Peyrous (r) 28
Château Haut-Bailly 27
La Parde de Haut-Bailly (r) 27
Château Haut-Bergey (r/w) 28
Château Joanin Bécot (r) 28
Château Kirwan 28
Les Charmes de Kirwan (r) 28
Rosé de Kirwan (rs) 28
Château Ksara 330
Reserve du Couvent (r) 330
Château La Bécasse (r)15
Château La Canorgue (r) 75
Château La Conseillante 22
Duo La Consillante (r) 22
Château La Croix Mouton (r) 23, 39
Château La Fleur Morange 24
Mathilde (r) 24
Château La Garde (r) 26
Château La Lagune 29
Mademoiselle L (r) 29
Moulin de La Lagune (r) 29
Château La Liquière 78
Sous l'Amandier Faugères Rouge (r) 78
Château La Pointe (r) 36
Château La Roque 80
Coteaux du Languedoc Blanc (w) 80
Château La Tour de Bessan (r) 43
Château La Tour de Mons 43
Terre du Mons (r) 43
Château LaFayette Reneau 254
Finger Lakes Dry Riesling (w) 254
Late Harvest Riesling (w) 254
Château Lafon-Rochet 28
Les Pelerins de Lafon-Rochet (r) 28
Château Lagrézette 78
La Rosé de Grézette (rs) 78
Château Le Fleur de Boüard 24
Fleur de Boüard 24
Château Le Moulin 31
Le Petit Moulin (r) 31
Château Léoville Las Cases 29
Le Petit Lion (r) 29
Château Léoville-Poyferré 29
Pavillon de Poyferré (r) 29
Château Lucas (r) 30
Château Lynch-Bages 30
Echo de Lynch Bages (r) 30
Château Malartic Lagravière 30
La Reserve de Malartic (w) 30
Rosé de Malartic (rs) 30
Château Manoir du Gravoux (r) 30
Château Marjosse (r) 31
Château Mondésir-Gazin (r) 31
Château Moulin St Georges (r) 31
Château Mourgues du Grès 78
Les Galets Dorés (w) 78
Les Galets Rosé (rs) 78
Château Musar 330
Hochar Père et Fils (r) 330
Château Nenin 31
Fugue de Nenin (r) 31
Château Ormes de Pez (r) 34
Château Penin (r) 34
Château Pesquié 79
Les Terrasses (rs/r) 79
Château Petit-Village 34
Le Jardin de Petit Village (r) 34
Château Peyrabon (r) 34
Château Phélan Ségur 35
Frank Phélan (r) 35
Château Pibran 36
La Tour Pibran (r) 36
Château Pierre-Bise 79
Clos Le Grand Beaupreau Savennières (w) 79
Gamay Sur Spilite Anjou (r) 79
Château Plaisance 80
Le Grain de Folie (r) 80
Château Plince 36
Pavilion Pince (r) 36
Château Poujeaux (r) 36
Château Preuillac (r) 37
Château Rahoul 37
L'Orangerie de Rahoul (r) 37
Château Rauzan-Ségla 37
Ségla (r) 37
Château Raymond-Lafon 37
Les Jeunes Pousses de Raymond-Lafon (d) 37
Château Réal (r) 37
Château Reine Blanche (r) 37
Château Reynon (w) 40
Château Roc de Cambes (r) 40
Château Rollan de By (r) 40
Château Rouget 41
Carillon de Rouge (r)t 41
Château Seguin 41
Château Seguin Cuvée Prestige (r) 41
Château Sérilhan (r) 41
Château Siaurac 41
Le Plaisir de Siaurac (r)
Château Smith Haut Lafitte 41
Les Hauts de Smith (r) 41
Château Sociando-Mallet 41
La Demoiselle de Sociando Mallet (r) 41
Chateau St Jean 220
Chardonnay, Sonoma County (w) 220
Fumé Blanc, Sonoma County (w) 220
Château St-Jacques d'Albas 80
Domaine St-Jacques d'Albas (r) 80
Château St-Martin de la Garrigue 81
Picpoul de Pinet (w) 81
Château Ste Michelle 249
Columbia Valley Cold Creek Vineyard Cabernet Sauvignon (r) 249
Columbia Valley Dry Riesling (w) 249
Château Talbot 42
Caillou Blanc du Château Talbot (w) 42
Château Teyssier (r) 42
Château Thieuley (w) 42
Château Vieux Pourret (r) 44
Chehalem Wines 252
Willamette Valley Chardonnay Inox (r) 252
Dry Riesling Reserve (w) 252
Chéreau Carré 81
Château l'Oiselinière de la Ramée Muscadet Sèvre-et-Maine sur Lie (w) 81
Château l'Oiselinière Le Clos du Château Muscadet Sèvre-et-Maine sur Lie (w) 81
Chinook Wines 249
Yakima Valley Cabernet Franc (r) 249
Chivite 152
Gran Feudo Reserva Especial (r) 152
Choose the Right Glassware 176–7
Christian Fischer 208
Premium Chardonnay (w) 208
Churchill Estates 172
Tinto, Duoro (r) 172
Cillar de Silos 152
El Quintanal (r) 152
Cima 116
Massaretta Toscana IGT (r) 116
Clemens Busch 184
Trocken Mosel (w) 184
Cline Cellars 220
Cool Climate Syrah, Sonoma County (r) 220
Oakley Five Reds Blend, California (r) 220
Clos de l'Anhel 81
Le Lolo de l'Anhel Corbières Rouge (r) 81
Clos de la Roilettte 65
Fleurie, Cuvée Tardive (r) 65
Clos de los Siete 273
Mendoza Red Wine (r) 273
Clos du Tue-Bouef 82
Rouillon Cheverny (r) 82, 286
Clos du Val 220
Merlot, Napa Valley 220
Clos Floridène (w) 44

Clos Fourtet 44
La Closerie de Fourtet (r) 44
Clos LaChance 220
Hummingbird Series Zinfandel, Central Coast (r) 220
Clos Mireille 81
Rosé Coeur de Grain (rs) 81
Clos Nicrosi 81
Clos Nicrosi Blanc Coteaux du Cap Corse (w) 81
Clos Puy Arnaud (r) 45
Clos Ste-Magdeleine 82
Rosé Cassis (rs) 82
Cloudy Bay 317
Pelorus Brut NV, Marlborough (s) 317
Cobos 273
Felino Chardonnay (w) 273
Felino Malbec (r) 273
Collemattoni 116
Rosso di Montalcino (r) 116
Colomé 273
Estate Malbec (r) 273
Torrontés (w) 273
Colonnara 116
Verdicchio Lyricus (w) 116
Columbia Crest Winery 249
Horse Heaven Hills Cabernet Sauvignon (r) 21, 249
Horse Heaven Hills Merlot (r) 249
Columbia Winery 250
Cellarmaster's Riesling Columbia Valley (w) 250
Conceito 173
Contraste Tinto, Douro (r) 173
Concha y Toro 262
Casillero del Diablo Cabernet Sauvignon Reserva (r) 262
Marqués de Casa Concha Carmenère (r) 262
Cono Sur 263
Cabernet Sauvignon Bicycle (r) 263
Conti Costanti 116
Rosso di Montalcino (r) 116, 125
Contucci 117
Rosso di Montepulciano (r) 117
Cordoníu 152
Cordoníu Pinot Noir Rosé (s) 152
Cork or Screwcap? 303
Corvus Vineyards 330
Rarum (r) 330
COS 117
Cerasuolo di Vittoria (r) 117
Cousiño Macul 10, 263
Cabernet Sauvignon Antiguas Reservas (r) 10, 263
Craggy Range Winery 317
Sauvignon Blanc Old Renwick Vineyard, Marlborough (w) 317
Te Kahu, Hawkes Bay (r) 317
Crawford River 294
Riesling Young Vines, Henty (w) 294
Create a Wine "Cellar" 202–203
Crusius 184
Weissburgunder Trocken QbA (w) 184
Cusumano 117
Nero d'Avola (r) 117
CVNE 153
CVNE Reserva (r) 153

D

D'Arenberg 294
The Custodian Grenache, McLaren Vale (r) 11, 294
Dal Pizzol 278
Dal Pizzol Touriga Nacional (r) 278
Daniel Vollenweider 9, 201
Wolfer Goldgrübe Riesling Spätlese (w) 9, 201
Danjean Berthoux 47
Givry (r) 47
Dashe Cellars 221
Zinfandel, Dry Creek Valley (r) 221
De Bortoli 294
Noble One, Riverina (d) 294
Show Liqueur Muscat, Riverina (d) 294
De Grendel 283
Merlot (r) 283
Sauvignon Blanc (w) 283
De Martino 263
Organically Grown Cabernet-Malbec (r) 263
Decanting and Breathing 148–9
Decero 273
Remolinos Vineyard Malbec (r) 273
Deerfield Ranch 221
Red Rex, Sonoma County Blend (r) 221
Sauvignon Blanc, Windsor Oaks Vineyard, Chalk Hill (w) 221
DeForville di Anfosso 118
Langhe Nebbiolo (r) 118
Dehesa Gago 153
Delas Frères 82
Crozes-Hermitage Domaine des Grands Chemins (r) 82
Delatite 295
Pinot Gris (w) 295
DeLoach Vineyards 221
Pinot Noir, Russian Valley (r) 221
Vinthropic Chardonnay, Sonoma (w) 221
Delta Vineyard 317
Hatter's Hill Pinot Noir, Marlborough (r) 317
Denis et Didier Berthollier 82
Savoie Chignin Bergeron (w) 82
Savoie Chignin Vieilles Vignes (w) 82
Descendientes de J Palacios 154
Pétalos (r) 154
Di Majo Norante 118
Terre degli Osci Sangiovese (r) 118
Diebolt-Vallois 69
Brut Blanc de Blancs (s) 69
Dog Point Vineyard 317
Chardonnay, Marlborough (w)
Domaine A 295
Stoney Vineyard Sauvignon Blanc, Tasmania (w) 295
Domaine A et P de Villaine 67
Bougogne Aligoté (w) 67
Domaine Alain Graillot 83
Crozes-Hermitage (r) 83
Domaine Alain Jeanniard 57
Côtes de Nuits Villages (r) 57
Domaine Alain Michaud 62
Brouilly (r) 62
Domaine Alary 83
La Chèvre d'Or Côtes de Rhône Blanc (w) 83
Tradition Cairanne (r) 83
Domaine André and Mireille Tissot 84
Arbois Poulsard Vieilles Vignes (r) 84
Crémant du Jura (s) 84
Domaine André et Michel Quenard 83
Savoie Abymes (r) 83
Savoie Chignin Mondeuse (r) 83
Domaine Anne Gros 53
Haut-Côtes de Nuits, Cuvée Marine (w) 53
Domaine Arretxea 84
Rouge Tradition (r) 84
Domaine Belle 84
Blanc Les Terres Blanche (w) 84
Les Pirrelles (r) 84
Domaine Bernard Baudry 85
Les Grand Chinon (r) 85
Domaine Bernard Defaix 50
Chablis (w) 50
Domaine Bott-Geyl 85
Les Pinots d'Alsace Métiss (w) 85
Domaine Brana (r/w) 85
Domaine Carneros 221
Sparkling Brut, Carneros (s) 221
Domaine Chaume-Arnaud 86
Vinsobres (r) 86
Domaine Combier 86
Crozes-Hermitage (r) 86
Domaine Cordier Père et Fils 50
St-Véran (w) 50, 237
Domaine Cosse Maisonneuve 86
Cuvée La Fage (r) 86
Domaine Daniel Barraud 46
Mâcon-Vergisson (w) 46
Domaine Daniel Dampt 50
Chablis Premier Cru Lys (w) 50
Domaine David Clark 49
Côtes de Nuits-Villages (r) 49
Domaine de Bellivière 84
Prémices Jasnières(w)84
Domaine de Cazes 86
Muscat de Rivesaltes (d) 86
Domaine de Chevalier 45
L'Esprit de Chevalier (r) 45
Domaine de Joÿ 91
L'Etoile, Côtes de Gascogne (w) 91
Domaine de la Cotellaraie 86
Les Mauguerets St-Nicolas-de-Bourgueil (r) 86
Domaine de la Ferme Blanche 87
Cuvée Cassis Blanc (w) 87
Domaine de la Janasse 90
Côtes du Rhone (r) 90
Domaine de la Pigeade 94
Muscat de Beaumes-de-Venise (d) 94
Domaine de la Rectorie 94
L'Argile Vin de Pays de la Côte Vermeille Blanc (w) 94
Domaine de Montvac 93
Vacqueyras (r) 93
Domaine de Roally 65
Mâcon-Villages (w) 65
Domaine Denis Mortet 62
Marsannay Langeroies (r) 62
Domaine des Deux Roches 51
Macon-Villages (w) 51
Domaine des Malandes 61
Chablis Premier Cru Côte de Lechet (w) 61
Domaine des Remizières 95
Crozes-Hermitage (r) 95
Domaine des Savarines 96
Cahors Rouge (r) 96
Domaine du Cros 86
Cuvée Lo Sang del Païs (r) 86
Domaine du Grapillon d'Or 89
Cuvée Classique, Gigondas (r) 89
Domaine du Mas Blanc 92
Collioure Rouge Cosprons Levants (r) 92
Domaine du Tunnel 97
St-Joseph (r) 97
St-Péray Roussanne (w) 97
Domaine Dupasquier 87
Roussette de Savoie (w) 87
Savoie Mondeuse (r) 87
Domaine Duseigneur 87
Antarès, Lirac (r) 87
Domaine Emile Juillot 57
Mercurey Blanc (w) 57
Domaine et Maison Chanson 8, 48
Pernand-Vergelesses Premier Cru Les Caradeaux Blanc (w) 8, 48
Domaine Faiveley 51
Bourgogne Rouge Hautes-Côtes de Nuits Dames-Huguettes (r) 51
Domaine François Lamarche 57
Bourgogne Rouge (r) 57
Domaine François Parent 62
Bourgogne Pinot Noir (r) 62
Domaine Frantz Saumon 88
Minérale+ Sec Montlouis-sur-Loire (w) 88
Un Saumon dans la Loire Romorantin Vin de France (w) 88
Domaine Frédéric Mabileau 88
Les Rouillères St-Nicolas-de Bourgueil (r) 88
Racines Bourgueil (r) 88
Domaine Gauby 88
Côtes du Roussillon Villages Les Calcinaires Blanc (w) 88
Domaine Gayda 88
Gayda Cépages Syrah (r) 88
Domaine Georges Mugneret-Gibourg 62
Bourgogne Rouge (r) 62
Domaine Georges Vernay 89
Vin de Pays des Collines Rhodaniennes Viognier (w) 89
Domaine Germain, Château de Chorey 52
Chorey-Les-Beaune (r) 52
Pernand-Vergelesses Blanc (w) 52
Domaine Guffens Heynen 56
Mâcon-Pierreclos Le Chavigne (w) 56
Domaine Henri Naudin-Ferrand 62
Bourgogne Hautes-Côtes de Nuits Rouge (r) 62
Domaine Henri Perrusset 63
Macon-Villages (w) 63
Domaine Hudelot-Noellat 56
Vosne-Romanée (r) 56
Domaine J A Ferret 51
Pouilly-Fuissé (w) 51
Domaine Jack Confuron-Cotétidot 50
Bourgogne Rouge (r) 50
Domaine Jacques Puffeney 89
Arbois Chardonnay (w) 89
Arbois Poulsard M (r) 89
Domaine Jean Grivot 53
Bourgogne Rouge (r) 53
Domaine Jean Luc Matha 90
Cuvée Pèirafi, Marcillac (r) 90
Domaine Jean Marechal 61
Mercurey Les Nauges (w) 61
Domaine Jean-Luc Colombo 90
Les Fées Brunes (r) 90
Domaine Jean-Marc et Hughes Pavelot 63
Savigny-lès-Beaune Blanc (w) 63
Savigny-lès-Beaune Rouge (r) 63
Domaine Jean-Marc et Thomas Bouley 47
Bourgogne Hautes-Côtes de Beaune Rouge (r) 47
Bourgogne Rouge (r) 47
Domaine Jean-Marc Pillot 64
Chassagne-Monrachet Rouge (r) 64
Santenay Rouge (r) 64
Domaine Jean-Philippe Fichet 52
Bourgogne Aligoté (w) 52
Domaine La Grange aux Belles 89
Fragile Anjou (w) 89
Princé Anjou(w) 89
Domaine La Réméjeanne 94
Les Arbousiers (w/r) 94
Domaine La Soumade 97
Cuvée Tradition Rasteau (r) 97
Vin Doux Naturel Rasteau Rouge (d) 97
Domaine La Tour Vieille 97
Banyuls Vendanges (f) 97
Domaine Laffont 91
Cuvée Erigone (r) 91
Domaine Laurent Cognard 49
Montagny Premier Cru Les Bassets (w) 49
Domaine Le Briseau 85
Patapon Coteaux du Loir (r) 85
Domaine le Roc 96
Le Classique, Fronton (r) 96
Domaine Le Roc des Anges 96
Vieilles Vignes Cotes du Roussillon Rouge (r) 96
Domaine Leflaive 60
Bourgogne Blanc (w) 60
Domaine Leon Barral 92
Faugères Rouge (r) 92
Domaine Long-Depaquit 61
Chablis Premier Cru Les Vaucopins (w) 61
Domaine Louis Boillot et Fils 47
Gevrey-Chambertin (r) 47
Domaine/Maison Simmonet-Febvre 66
Chablis Premier Cru Les Vaillons (w) 66
Domaine Marcel Deiss 92
Vendanges Tardives Pinot Blanc (w) 92
Domaine Michel & Stéphane Ogier 92
La Roisine Syrah, Vin de Pays Collines Rhodaniennes (r) 92
Viognier de Roisine, Vin de Pays des Collines Rhodaniennes (r) 92
Domaine Michel Bouzereau et Fils 48
Bourgogne Aligoté (w) 48
Bourgogne Blanc (w) 48
Domaine Michel Gros 56
Haute Côte de Nuits (r) 56

Domaine Michel Lafarge 57
Bourgogne Aligoté (w) 57
Passetoutgrains L'Exception (r) 57
Domaine Michel Sarrazin et Fils 65
Givry Champs Lalot (r) 65
Domaine Michele et Patrice Rion 64
Bourgogne Rouge Bon Batons (r) 64
Domaine Nicolas Rossignol-Jeanniard 65
Bourgogne Pinot Noir (r) 65
Volnay (r) 65
Domaine Oratoire St-Martin 93
Réserve des Seigneurs, Cairanne (r) 93
Domaine Patrick Javillier 56
Bourgogne Blanc Cuvée Oligocène (w) 56
Domaine Paul Blanck 93
Gerwurztraminer (w) 93
Pinot Noir (r) 93
Domaine Philippe Delesvaux 93
Coteaux du Layon (d) 93
Domaine Philippe Faury 93
St-Joseph (r) 93
Domaine Philippe Gilbert 94
Menetou-Salon (r/w) 94
Domaine Pieretti 94
Coteaux du Cap Corse Vieilles Vignes (r) 94
Domaine Ricard 95
Le Petiot Sauvignon Blanc (w) 95
Domaine Roger Belland 46
Maranges Rouge (r) 46
Santenay Rouge (r) 46
Domaine Rotier 96
Renaissance Rouge, Gaillac (r) 96
Domaine Servin 66
Chablis Premier Cru (w) 66
Domaine Skouras 331
Nemea Grande Cuvée (r) 331
Domaine Sylvain Loichet 60
Ladoix Blanc (w) 60
Domaine Tariquet 97
Tariquet Classic(w) 97
Domaine Trapet Père et Fils 67
Marsannay Rouge (r) 67
Domaine William Fèvre 52
Chablis (w) 52
Domaine Yann Chave 97
Crozes-Hermitage (r) 97
Domaines Paul Mas 98
Arrogant Frog (w) 98
La Forge Varietal Wines (w) 98
Domaines Schlumberger 98
Riesling Grand Cru Saering (w) 98
Domäne Wachau 208
Grüner Veltliner Achleiten Smaragd (w) 208
Terraces (w) 208
Dominio de Tares 154
Baltos (r) 154
Dominio de Valdepusa 154
El Rincón Vinos de Madrid (r) 154
Dominio del Plata Winery 273
Crios de Susana Balbo Cabernet Sauvignon (r) 273
Crios de Susana Torrontés (w) 273
Doña Paula 273
Estate Torrontés (w) 273
Dönhoff 185
Dönhoff Riesling QbA (w) 185
Donnafugata 118
Passito di Pantelleria Ben Ryé (d) 118
Doyard 69
Brut Cuvée Vendémiaire (s) 69
Dr Bürklin-Wolf 184
Riesling Trocken QbA (w) 184
Dr H Thanisch - Erben Thanisch 201
Bernkasteler Badstrube Riesling Kabinett (w) 201
Dr Konstantin Frank Vinifera Wine Cellars 254
Finger Lakes Semi-Dry Riesling (w) 254
Salmon Run Riesling (w) 254
Dr Loosen 196
Dr L Riesling (w) 196, 309
Dr Wehrheim 204
Chardonnay Spätlese Trocken (w) 204
Drappier 69
Brut Nature Zéro Dosage (s) 69
Dry Creek Vineyards 222
Heritage Zinfandel (r) 222
Sauvignon Blanc, Dry Creek Valley (r) 222
Duckhorn Vineyards 222
Decoy, Napa Valley Blend (r) 222
Duorum 173
Duorum Tinto, Douro (r) 173
Durbanville Hills 283
Pinotage (r) 283
Sauvignon Blanc (w) 283
Dutchske Wines 295
Shiraz GHR (God's Hill Road), Barossa (r) 295

E

E Guigal 99
E Guigal Crozes-Hermitage (r) 99
Eberle Winery 222
Syrah, Steinbeck Vineyard, Paso Robles (r) 222
Edetària 154
Via Edetana (r) 154
Edmunds St John 223
Gamay Noir Bone-Jolly, El Dorado County 222
Egon Müller-Scharzhof/Le Gallais 198
Scharzhof Riesling QbA Mosel (w) 198
Elias Mora 154
Elio Grasso 119
Nebbiolo d'Alba Gavarini (r) 119
Elke Vineyards 223
Pinot Noir, Anderson Valley (r) 223
Emiliana 264
Chardonnay Natura (w) 264
Merlot Natura (r) 264
Emilio Moro 154
Enkidu Winery 223
E Cabernet Sauvignon, Sonoma Valley (r) 223
Humbaba Rhône Red Blend, Sonoma (r) 223
Ernst Triebaumer 208
Triebaumer Blaufränkisch Rosé (rs) 208
Triebaumer Sauvignon Blanc (w) 208
Errázuriz Estate 264
Sauvignon Blanc (w) 264, 308
Esk Valley Estate 318
Esk Valley Verdelho, Hawkes Bay (w) 318
Estancia Piedra 155
Piedra Azul (r) 155
Etim 155
Etim Negre (r) 155
Etude 226
Pinot Gris, Carneros (w) 226
Eva Fricke 186
Lorcher Riesling Trocken (w) 186
Evans & Tate 296
Classic White, Margaret River (w) 296

F

Fabre Montmayou 274
Malbec Reserva, Mendoza (r) 274
Fairview/Spice Route 283
Beacon Shiraz (r) 283
Goats Do Roam White (w) 283
Falernia 264
Carmenère-Syrah Reserva (r) 264
Falesco 119
Vitiano Rosso (r) 119
Familia Zuccardi 274
Santa Julia Malbec Reserva (r) 274
Tempranillo Q (r) 274
Fantinel 119
Vigneti Sant'Helena Ribolla Gialla (w) 119
Fattoria di Selvapiana 120
Chinari Rùfina (r) 120
Fattoria Fèlsina 120
Chianti Classico Berardenga (r) 120
Fattoria Le Pupille 120
Morellino di Scansano (r) 120
Fattoria Nicodemi 120
Montepulciano d'Abruzzo (r) 120
Faustino 155
Faustino 1 Gran Reserva (r) 155
Feiler-Artinger 209
Blaufränkisch (r) 209
Ferrari-Carano Vineyards 226
Fumé Blanc (w) 226
Sienna Sangiovese-Malbec Blend, Sonoma (r) 226
Ferraton Père & Fils 98
Crozes-Hermitage La Malinière (r) 98
Feudi di San Gregorio 121
Falanghina Campania Sannio (w) 121
Fielding Hills Winery 250
Wahluke Slope Riverbend Vineyard Cabernet Franc (r) 250
Finca Sandoval 155
Salia (r) 155
Finca Sophenia 274
Cabernet Sauvignon Reserve (r) 274
Finca Valpiedra 158
Cantos de Valpiedra (r) 158
First Drop 296
Two Percent Shiraz, Barossa (r) 296
Flora Springs 226
Sangiovese, Napa Valley (r) 226
Folie à Deux Winery 226
Cabernet Sauvignon, Napa Valley (r) 226
Chardonnay, Napa Valley (w) 226
Fonseca Guimaraens 173
NV: Terra Prima (f) 173
Food and Wine 17, 35, 49, 67, 79, 101, 107, 114–15, 129, 153, 187, 233, 253, 275, 311, 319
Forstmeister Gelt-Ziliken 187
Butterfly Riesling Mosel (w) 187
Foursight Wines 227
Sauvignon Blanc, Charles Vineyard, Anderson Valley (w) 227
Foxes Island Wines 318
Riesling, Marlborough (w) 318
Fox by John Belsham Pinot Noir, Marlborough (r) 318
Framingham 318
Classic Riesling, Marlborough (w) 318
Francesco Rinaldi e Figli 121
Grignolino d'Asti (r) 121
Francis Ford Coppola Winery 227
Diamond Collection Claret, California (r) 227
Director's Cut Cabernet Sauvignon, Alexander Valley (r) 227
François Crochet 98
Sancere (w) 98
François Lurton 99
Fumées Blanches Sauvignon (w) 99
Terra Sana Syrah (r) 99
Franz Künstler 192
Spätburgunder Tradition (r) 192
Fratelli Alessandria 121
Verduno Pelaverga (r) 121
Freemark Abbey 227
Chardonnay, Napa Valley (w)
Freixenet 158, 161
Freixenet Excelencia Brut (s) 158
Friedrich Altenkirch 182
Weissburgunder QbA (w) 182
Fritz Haag 187
Riesling Trocken QbA Mosel (w) 187
Fuligni 121
Rosso di Montalcino Ginestreto (r) 121
Fürst Löwenstein 196
CF Riesling QbA Trocken (w) 196

G

Garage Winery 186
Wild Thing Riesling Spätlese (w) 186
Geil 186
Bechtheimer Geyersberg Grüner Silvaner Trocken Spätlese "S" (w) 186
Gemtree Vineyards 296
Bloodstone Shiraz, McLaren Vale (r) 296
Georg Breuer 183
GB Spätburgunder Rouge QbA (r) 183
Gérard Bertrand 99
Gris-Blanc, Vin de Pays d'Oc (rs) 99
Gerhard Markowitsch 209
Carnuntum Cuvée (r) 209
Pinot Noir (r) 209
German Riesling, Food & Wine 187
Giant Steps/Innocent Bystander 296
Sexton Vineyard Chardonnay, Yarra Valley (w) 296
Gies-Düppel 187
Spätburgunder Illusion Weissherbst Trocken (rs) 187
Gladstone Vineyard 318
Pinot Gris, Wairarapa (w) 318
Glen Carlou 284
Cabernet Sauvignon (r) 284
Grand Classique (r) 284
Gloria Ferrer Winery 227
Blanc de Noirs, Carneros (s)
Brut, Sonoma (s) 227
Golan Heights Winery 331
Gamla Cabernet Sauvignon (r) 331
González Byass 158
González Byass Tío Pepe Fino (f) 158
González Byass Viña AB (f) 158
Gosset 72
Brut Excellence (s) 72
Graham Beck Wines 284
Chardonnay-Viognier (w) 284
The Game Reserve (r) 284
Graham's 173
Crusted Port (f) 173
Gramona 159
Imperial Gran Reserva Brut (s) 159
Grapes
Cabernet Sauvignon 20–1
Chardonnay 236–7
Chenin Blanc 95
Gamay 63
Gewürztraminer 87
Grenache 165
Grüner Veltliner 211
Malbec 277
Merlot 38–9
Nebbiolo 119
Pinot Gris / Grigio 136–7
Pinot Noir 58–9
Riesling 194–5
Sangiovese 124–5
Sauvignon Blanc 322–3
Syrah / Shiraz 298–9
Tempranillo 156–7
Zinfandel 247
Gray Monk Estate 257
Gewürztraminer (w) 257
Great Wall 331
Cabernet Sauvignon (r) 331
Greenwood Ridge Vineyards 227
White Riesling, Mendocino Ridge, (w) 227
Groot Constantia 284
NV: Blanc de Noir (rs) 284
Sauvignon Blanc (w) 284
Groote Post 285
The Old Man's Blend White (w) 285
Unwooded Chardonnay (w) 285
Grosset 297
Springvale, Watervale Riesling, Clare Valley (w) 297
Grover Vineyards 331
Cabernet-Shiraz (r) 331
Gruet Winery 254
Blanc de Noir (s) 254
NV: Blanc de Blancs Sauvage (s) 254
Gulfi 122
Nero d'Avola Rossojbleo (r) 122
Gunderloch 187
Diva Riesling Spätlese (w) 187
Gundlach Bundschu Winery 228
Gewürztraminer, Sonoma Coast (w) 228
Mountain Cuvée Bordeaux Blend, Sonoma Valley (r) 228
Gunk in the Bottle 91

H
H M Borges 172
 5 Year Old Sweet Madeira (f) 172
Hahn Estates 228
 Hahn Winery, Pinot Noir, Monterey (r) 228
Halewood 332
 Cantus Primus (r) 332
 Single-vineyard Pinot Noir (r) 332
Handley Cellars 228
 Anderson Valley Pinot Noir (r) 228
 Anderson Valley Chardonnay (w) 228
Hanna Winery 229
 Chardonnay, Russian River Valley (w) 229
 Sauvignon Blanc, Russian River Valley (w) 229
Haras de Pirque 264
 Carmenère, Maipo Valley (r) 264
Hartenberg 285
 Cabernet Sauvignon (r) 285
 Sauvignon Blanc (w) 285
Hatzidakis 332
 Santorini Assyrtiko (w) 332
Heartland 297
 Dolcetto & Lagrein, Langhorne Creek (r) 297
Hedges Family Estate 250
 Red Mountain Red Wine (r) 250
Heidi Schröck 209
 Furmint (w) 209
 Weinbau Weissburgunder (w) 209
Henriot 72
 Brut Souverain (s) 72
Hensel 188
 Aufwind St Laurent Trocken (r) 188
Herbert Messmer 196
 Spätburgunder Trocken QbA (r) 196
Herdade de Mouchão 174
 Dom Rafael Tinto Alentejo (r) 174
Hess Collection 229
 Cabernet Sauvignon, Allomi Vineyard, Napa Valley (r) 203, 229
 Select Chardonnay, Monterey (w) 203, 229
Hewitson 297
 Gun Metal Riesling, Eden Valley (w) 297
Heymann-Löwenstein 188
 Schieferterrassen Riesling Mosel (w) 188
Hidalgo-La Gitana 159
 Pastrana Manzanilla Pasada (f) 159
Hiedler 209
 Löss Grüner Veltliner (w) 209
Hilberg-Pasquero 122
 Barbera d'Alba (r) 122
Hillebrand Winery 257
 Trius Riesling (w) 257
Hofmann 188
 Spätburgunder Trocken QbA (r) 188
Honig Vineyard and Winery 229
 Sauvignon Blanc, Napa Valley (w) 229
Hook & Ladder Winery 229
 Pinot Noir, Russian River Valley (r) 229
 Tillerman Cabernet Blend, Russian River Valley (r) 229
Hop Kiln Winery 230
 Chardonnay, Sonoma (w) 230
 Pinot Noir, Russian River Valley (r) 230
Hope Estate 297
 The Cracker Cabernet Merlot, Western Australia (r) 297
Horst Sauer 200
 Escherndorfer Lump Silvaner Kabinett Trocken (w) 200
Houghton 297
 The Bandit Shiraz-Tempranillo, Western Australia (r) 297
Howard Park 300
 Sauvignon Blanc, Western Australia (w) 300
Hugel et Fils 100
 Hugel Muscat Tradition (w) 100
 Riesling Tradition (w) 100

I
I Clivi di Ferdinando Zanusso 122
 Galea Bianco (w) 122
I Poderi di San Gallo 123
 Rosso di Montepulciano (r) 123
Il Molino di Grace 123
 Chianti Classico (r) 123
Il Poggione 123
 Rosso di Montalcino (r) 123
Imagery Estate 230
 Grenache, Sonoma Mountain (r) 230
 Muscato di Canelli, Lake County (w) 230
Inama 123
 Soave Classico (w) 123
Inniskillin Niagara 257
 Vidal Icewine (d) 257
Inurrieta 159
 Inurrieta Norte (r) 159
Iona Vineyards 10, 285
 Sauvignon Blanc (w) 10, 285
 The Gunnar (r) 285
Is all that sparkles champagne? 161
Isole e Olena 126
 Chianti Classico (r) 126

J
J Hofstätter 122
 Lagrein (r) 122
J Lohr Vineyards 232
 Syrah, South Ridge, Paso Robles (r) 232
J Vineyards 230
 Cooper Vineyard Pinot Gris, California (w) 230
 J Cuvée 20 Brut NV, Russian River Valley (s) 230
Jackson Estate 319
 Shelter Belt Chardonnay, Marlborough (w) 319
Jacob's Creek 300
 Reserve Cabernet Sauvignon, Coonawarra (r) 300
 Steingarten Riesling, Barossa (w) 300
Jean-Louis Chave Selection 100
 Crozes-Hermitage Silène (r) 100
Jean-Marc Burgaud 48
 Cuvée Les Charmes (r) 48
Jean-Paul Brun 48
 Brouilly Terres Dorés (r) 48
Jean-Yves Devevey 51
 Bourgogne Hautes-Côtes de Beaune Blanc (w) 51
Jim Barry Wines 300
 The Lodge Hill Dry Riesling, Clare Valley (w) 300
 The Lodge Hill Shiraz, Clare Valley (r) 300
Jiménez-Landi 159
 Sotorrondero (r) 159
JL Wolf 205
 Villa Wolf Gewürztraminer QbA (w) 205
JM Cellars 250
 Rattlesnake Hills Boushey Vineyard Syrah (r) 250
Joan d'Anguera 160
 La Planella (r) 160
Joh. Jos. Prüm 198
 Riesling Kabinett Mosel (w) 198
Johanneshof Reinisch 210
 Pinot Noir Reserve Grillenhuegel (r) 210
 Rotgipfler (d) 210
José Pariente 160
 José Pariente Verdejo (w) 160
Joseph Drouhin 51
 Chorey-Les-Beaune rouge (r) 51
 Domaine de Vaudon (w) 51
 Laforêt Pinot Noir Bourgogne (r) 51
Joseph Leitz 193
 Rüdesheimer Drachenstein Dragonstone Riesling QbA (w) 193
Joseph Swan Vineyards 230
 Cuvée du Trois Pinot Noir, Russian River Valley (r) 230
 Marsanne-Rousanne, Russian River Valley (w) 230
Josmeyer 100
 Pinot Gris Le Fromenteau (w) 100, 137
Jost Vineyards 257
 Oak-Aged L'Acadie Blanc (w) 257
Juan Gil 160
 Juan Gil Monastrell (r) 160
Juliusspital 189
 Würzburger Silvaner Trocken (w) 189
Jurtschitsch 210
 Stein Grüner Veltliner (w) 210
Juvé y Camps 160
 Cinta Purpura (s) 160

K
Kaiken 274
 Cabernet Sauvignon (r) 274
 Malbec (r) 274
Kalleske 300
 Pirathon Shiraz, Barossa Valley (r) 300
Karl Erbes 185
 Ürziger Würzgarten Riesling Spätlese Mosel (w) 185
Karl Friedrich Aust 182
 Müller-Thurgau Sächsischer Landwein (w) 182
Karlsmühle 189
 Kaseler Nies'chen Riesling Kabinett Mosel (w) 189
Karly Wines 230
 Sauvignon Blanc, Amador County (w) 230
Karthäuserhof/Tyrell 190
 Karthäuserhof Eitelbacher Karthäuserhofberg Riesling Feinherb Mosel (w) 190
Katnook Estate 301
 Founder's Block Cabernet Sauvignon, Coonawarra (r) 301
Kavaklidere Winery 332
 Vin-Art Emir-Saltaniye (w) 332
Keeping Opened Wine Fresh 199
Kees-Kieren 190
 Mia Riesling Lieblich QbA Mosel (w) 190
Keller 190
 Grauer Burgunder Trocken QbA (w) 190
Kendall Jackson Wine Estates 231
 Grand Reserve Cabernet Sauvignon, Sonoma (r) 231
 Vintners' Reserve Pinot Noir, California (r) 231
Kenwood Vineyards 231
 Cabernet Sauvignon, Jack London Vineyard (r) 231
 Pinot Gris, Sonoma County (w) 231
King Estate 253
 Oregon Pinot Gris Signature Series (w) 253
Kingston Family Vineyards 264
 Pinot Noir Tobiano (r) 264
Kinkead Ridge Winery 254
 Ohio River Valley Cabernet Franc (r) 254
 Viognier-Roussanne (w) 254
Kir-Yianni 332
 Paranga, Vin de Pays (r) 332
Klaus Böhme 183
 Bacchus Dorndorfer Rappental Trocken QbA (w) 183
Kloster Eberbach 191
 Rüdesheimer Berg Roseneck Riesling Feinherb (w) 191
Knebel 191
 Riesling Trocken Mosel (w) 191
Koehler-Ruprecht 191
 Weissburgunder Kabinett Trocken (w) 191
Kogl 332
 Mea Culpa Sämling (w) 332
Korak 332
 Riesling (w) 332
Korrell/Johanneshof 191
 Müller Thurgau QbA (w) 191
Kruger-Rumpf 192
 Schiefer Riesling Feinherb (w) 192
KT and the Falcon 301
 Watervale Riesling, Clare Valley (w) 301
Kuentz-Bas 101
 Pinot Gris Tradition (w) 101
Kumeu River Wines 319
 Village Chardonnay, Auckland (w) 132, 319

L
L Aubry Fils 68
 Brut NV (s) 68
L'Ecole No. 41 250
 Semillon Columbia Valley (w) 250
La Báscula 160
 Turret Fields Jumilla (r) 160
La Goulée (r) 45
La Mozza 126
 Morellino di Scansano I Perazzi (r) 126
La Reserva de Caliboro 264
 Erasmo, Maule Valley (r) 264
La Rioja Alta 160
 Viña Alberdi (r) 160
Laetitia Vineyard 231
 Brut Cuvée Estate (s) 231
 Syrah Estate Arroyo Grande Valley (r) 231
Lailey Vineyard 258
 Chardonnay (w) 258
LangeTwins Winery 231
 Moscato, Lodi & Clarksburg (w) 231
Langtry Estate 231
 Guenoc, Sauvignon Blanc, Lake County (w) 231
Langwerth von Simmern 193
 Erbacher Marcobrunn Riesling Kabinett (w)193
Lapostolle 265
 Carmenère Casa Rapel Valley (r) 265
 Cuvée Alexandre Chardonnay Atalayas Vineyard (w) 265
Larry Cherubino Wines 302
 The Yard Whispering Hill Vineyard Riesling, Mt Barker, Western Australia (w) 302
Laurenz V 210
 Grüner Veltliner Friendly (w) 210
 Silver Bullet Grüner (w) 210
Lavradores de Feitoria 174
 Três Bagos Sauvignon Blanc (w) 174
 Três Bagos Sauvignon Tinto (r) 174
Le Clos de Caveau 101
 Fruits Sauvages Vacqueyras (r) 101
Le Clos Jordanne 258
 Village Reserve Pinot Noir (r) 258
Le Presi 126
 Rosso di Montalcino (r) 126
Leasingham 302
 Magnus Riesling, Clare Valley (w) 302
Left Foot Charley 255
 Pinot Blanc (w) 255
 Riesling Medium Dry (w) 255
Leon Beyer 101
 Gerwurztraminer (w) 101
 Pinot Gris (w) 101
Leone de Castris 126
 Salice Salentino Riserva Donna Lisa (r) 126
Les Celliers de Meknès 333
 Château Roslane Premier Cru (r/w) 333
Les Vins de Vienne 101
 Heluicum, Vins de Pays (r) 101
Leyda 265
 Pinot Noir Las Brisas Vineyard (r) 265
Librandi 126
 Cirò Riserva (r) 126
Lidio Carraro 278
 Da'divas Chardonnay (w) 278
Livio Felluga 127
 Pinot Grigio (w) 127
Loch 193
 QuaSaar (w) 193
Loimer 211
 Grüner Veltliner (w) 211
 Riesling Terrassen (w) 211
Lolonis 232
 Chardonnay, Redwood Valley (w) 232
Loma Larga Vineyards 265
 Chardonnay (w) 265

Long Meadow Ranch 232
Ranch House Red Blend, Napa Valley (r) 232
Look for Smaller Regions and Appellations 179
Los Vascos 265
Cabernet Sauvignon (r) 265
Louis Roederer 72
Brut Premier (s) 72, 203
Luigi Bosca 274
Malbec Reserva (r) 274
Luis Cañas 161
Luis Cañas Seleccion de la Familia (r) 161
Luis Felipe Edwards 268
Cabernet Sauvignon Reserva (r) 268
Lustau 161
Emilin Moscatel (f) 161
Palo Cortado Vides Almacenista (f) 161

M

M Chapoutier 74
Deschants St-Joseph (r) 74
Mac Forbes 302
Riesling rs37, Strathbogie Ranges (w) 302
Macari Vineyards & Winery 255
Long Island Sauvignon Blanc (w) 255
Sette (r) 255
MacRostie Winery 232
Pinot Noir, Carneros (r) 232
Madroña Vineyards 232
New-World Port, El Dorado (f) 232
Mailly Grand Cru 72
Grand Cru Brut Réserve (s) 72
Maison Camille Giroud 52
Maranges Premier cru Croix aux Moines Rouge (r) 52
Santenay Rouge (r) 52
Maison Frédéric Magnien 61
Marsannay Coeur d'Argile (r) 61
Maison Jean-Claude Boisset 47
Bourgogne Pinot Noir Les Ursulines (r) 47
Maison Louis Jadot 56
Bourgogne Pinot Noir (r) 56
Maison Olivier Leflaive 60
Auxey-Duresses La Macabree Blanc (w) 60
Bourgogne Blanc Les Setilles (w) 60
Maison Roche de Bellene 65
Côtes de Nuits-Villages Vieilles Vignes (w) 65
Majella 302
The Musician, Coonawarra (r) 302
Majolini 127
NV: Franciacorta Brut (s) 127
Malatinszky 333
Pinot Bleu (r) 333
Malumbres 162
Malumbres Garnacha (r) 162
Man O'War 319
Man O'War Chardonnay, Waiheke Island (w) 319
Marc Gales 333
Pinot Gris (w) 333
Riesling (w) 333
Marchesi di Gresy 127
Nebbiolo d'Alba Martinenga (r) 127
Marco Porello 128
Roero Arneis Camestri (w) 128
Markus Molitor 197
Haus Klosterberg Riesling QbA (w) 197
Marqués de Cáceres 162
Marqués de Cáceres Reserva (r) 162
Marqués de Riscal 162
Marqués de Riscal Rueda Blanco (w) 162
Martín Códax 162
Martín Códax Albariño (w) 162, 203
Martinborough Vineyard 320
Te Tera Pinot Noir, Martinborough (r) 320
Mas Amiel 102
Maury (d) 102
Mas Champart 102
St-Chinian Rosé (rs) 102
Mas de Libian 102
Khayyam (r) 102
Masciarelli 128
Montepulciano d'Abruzzo (r) 128
Masi Tupungato 275
Malbec-Corvina Passo Doble (r) 275
Massaya 333
Classic Red (r) 333
Matakana Estate 320
Sauvignon Blanc, Marlborough (w) 320
Matanzas Creek Winery 232
Sauvignon Blanc Sonoma County (w) 232
Mathis Bastian 334
Rivaner (w) 334
Mauricio Lorca 276
Vistaflores Vineyards Opalo Malbec (r) 276
Maurodos 163
Prima (r) 163
Maximin Grünhaus/von Schubert 196
Herrenberg Superior Riesling QbA (w) 196
McGuigan 302
The Shortlist Chardonnay, Adelaide Hills (w) 302
McHenry Hohnen 302
3 Amigos, Margaret River (r/w) 302
McManis Family Vineyards 233
Viognier, California (w) 233
McPherson Cellars 255
tre Colore (r) 255
McWilliam's Mount Pleasant 303
Elizabeth Semillon (w) 303
Philip Shiraz (r) 303
Meinklang/Michlits 212
Pinot Noir Frizzante Rosé (s) 212
Melini 128
Chinati Classico Granaio (r) 128
Mendel Wines 276
Lunta Malbec (r) 276
Mendel Malbec (r) 276
Mendoza Malbec, Food & Wine 275
Mercouri Estate 334
Estate Red (r) 334
Foloi White (w) 334
Meyer-Näkel 196
Spätburgunder Illusion Trocken QbA (rs) 196
Michel Loriot 72
Brut Réserve Blanc de Noirs (s) 72
Michel Tête (Domaine du Clos du Fief) 66
Domaine du Clos du Fief Juliénas (r) 66
Michele Chiarlo 129
Barbera d'Asti Le Orme (r) 129
Michelle Loosen 251
Columbia Valley Riesling Eroica (w) 251
Miguel Torres 268
Santa Digna Carmenère Reserva (r) 268
Miolo 279
Miolo Merlot Terroir (r) 279
Mission Hill Family Estate 258
Five Vineyards Cabernet Sauvignon-Merlot (r) 258
Mitchell Wines 303
Sevenhill Cabernet Sauvignon, Clare Valley (r) 303
Watervale Riesling, Clare Valley (w) 303
Mitchelton 304
Airstrip Rousanne Marsanne Viognier, Central Victoria (w) 304
Mitolo 304
Jester Cabernet Sauvignon, McLaren Vale (r) 304
Jester Vermentino, McLaren Vale (w) 304
Montes 268
Limited Selection Apalta Vineyard Cabernet Carmenère (r) 268
Limited Selection Pinot Noir (r) 268
Montesecondo 129
Toscana Rosso IGT (r) 129
Montevertine 129
Pian del Ciampolo IGT (r) 129
Morgan Winery 233
Syrah, Monterey (r) 233
Un-oaked Chardonnay Metallico, Monterey (w) 233
Morgante 130
Nero d'Avola (r) 130
Moric 212
Blaufränkisch (r) 212
Moris Farms 130
Morellino di Scansano (r) 130
Mosbacher 197
Forster Riesling Kabinett (w) 197
Moss Wood 304
The Amy's Blend, Margaret River (r) 304
Mt Difficulty 320
Roaring Meg Pinot Noir, Central Otago (r) 203, 320
Mount Eden Vineyards 234
Chardonnay, Wolff Vineyard, Edna Valley (w) 234
Mount Langhi Ghiran 304
Billi Billi Shiraz, Victoria (r) 304
Muga 163
Muga Rosado (rs) 163
Mulderbosch 288
Cabernet Sauvingon Rosé (rs) 288
Chenin Blanc Steen Op Hout (w) 288
Müller-Catoir 197
Muskateller Kabinett Trocken (w) 197
Muri-Gries 130
Lagrein (r) 130
Murphy-Goode Winery 11, 234
Fumé Sauvignon, Alexander Valley (w) 234
Liar's Dice, Zinfandel, Sonoma (r) 11, 234
Mustiguillo 163
Mustiguillo Mestizaje (r) 163

N

Naia 163
Naia (w) 163
Napa Valley Cabernet Sauvignon, Food & Wine 233
Navarro Vineyards 234
Dry Gewürztraminer, Anderson Valley (w) 234
Navigate a wine list 266–7
Neil Ellis 288
Sauvignon Blanc (w) 288
Shiraz (r) 288
Nekeas 163
El Chaparral de Vega Sindoa Garnacha (r) 163
Nekeas Crianza Tempranillo-Cabernet (r) 163
Nepenthe 305
Sauvignon Blanc, Altitude Range, Adelaide Hills (w) 305
Neudorf Vineyards 320
Brightwater Riesling, Nelson (w) 320
New Zealand Sauvignon Blanc, Food & Wine 319
Newton Vineyard 235
Red Label Claret, Napa Valley (r) 235
Niepoort 174
Drink Me! Douro (r) 174
Junior Ruby Port (f) 174
Sénior Tawny Port (f) 174
Nikolaihof 212
Vom Stein Federspiel Riesling (w) 212
Nino Franco 131
Prosecco Rustico (s) 131
Nyetimber 334
Classic Cuvée (s) 334

O

O Fournier (Spain) 158
Urban (r) 158
O Fournier (South America) 274
B Crux, Uco Valley (r) 274
Oak Flavours 223
Obsidian Ridge 235
Cabernet Sauvignon, Lake County, Red Hills (r) 235
Ochoa 164
Ochoa Tempranillo Crianza (r) 164
Odfjell Vineyards 268
Armador Merlot (r) 268
Organic Wine 229
Orsolani 131
Erbaluce di Caluso La Rustica (w) 131
Owl Ridge/Willowbrook Cellars 235
Sauvignon Blanc, Sonoma County (w) 235

P

Pacific Rim 251
Columbia Valley Wallula Vineyard Riesling (w) 251
Pacific Star Winery 235
Dad's Daily Red (r) 235
Pago de los Capellanes 164
Pago de los Capellanes Joven (r) 164
Palacios Remondo 164
La Montesa (r) 164
Palliser Estate 320
Sauvignon Blanc, Martinborough (w) 321
Parducci Wine Cellars 235
True Grit, Petite Sirah, Mendocino (r) 235
Parés Baltà 164
Mas Petit Penedè (r) 164
Pascal Granger 53
Juliénas (r) 53
Pascual Toso 276
Cabernet Sauvignon (r) 276
Patianna Organic Vineyards 238
Sauvignon Blanc, Mendocino, Estate Vineyards (w) 238
Paul Cluver Estate Wines 288
Gewürztraminer (w) 288
Sauvignon Blanc (w) 288
Paul Jaboulet-Aîné 103
Crozes-Hermitage Domaine de Thalabert (r) 103
Pegasus Bay 321
Main Divide Riesling, Waipara (w) 321
Peique 165
Tinto Mencía Bodegas Peique (r) 165
Penfolds 305
Koonunga Hill Seventy Six Shiraz-Cabernet, South Australia (r) 305
Pérez Cruz 268
Cabernet Sauvignon Reserva (r) 268
Perini 279
NV: Casa Perini Prosecco Spumante (s) 279
Pesquera 165
El Vinculo La Mancha (r) 165
Petaluma 305
Hanlin Hill Riesling, Clare Valley (w) 305
Peter Jakob Kühn 192
Oestrich Riesling Trocken ObA (w) 192
Peter Lauer 193
Riesling Fass 6 "Senior" (w) 193
Peter Lehmann 305
Back to Back Grenache, Barossa (r) 305
Wigan Eden Valley Riesling (w) 305
Pey-Marin 238
Punchdown, Syrah, Spicerack Vineyards (r) 238
Pffefingen/Fuhrmann-Eymael 198
Pfeffo Estate Riesling Kabinett Halbtrocken (w) 198
Piedmont Reds, Food & Wine 129
Pieropan 131
Soave Classico (w) 131
Pierre Gimonnet & Fils 9, 73
Brut Blanc de Blancs (s) 9, 73
Pierre-Jacques Druet 103
Bourgueil Rosé (rs) 103
Pietracupa 131
Fiano di Avellino (w) 131
Pietratorcia 134
Ischia Bianco (w) 134
Pine Ridge Winery 238
Chenin Blanc-Viognier, Clarksburg (w) 238
Pirie Tasmania 306
South Pinot Noir, Tasmania (r) 306
Pisano 334
Río de los Pájaros Tannat (r) 334
Río de los Pájaros Torrontés (w) 334
Pizzato 279
Pizzato Fausto Merlot (r) 279

Planeta 134
 Cerasuolo di Vittoria (r) 134
Plantaganet 306
 Samson's Range Semillon Sauvignon Blanc, Western Australia (w) 306
Poderi e Cantine Oddero 134
 Barolo (r) 134
Poet's Leap Winery 251
 Columbia Valley Riesling (w) 251
Pomerol, Food & Wine 17
Portal del Montsant 166
 Brunus (r) 166
Porter Creek Vineyards 238
 Old Vine Carignan, Mendocino (r) 238
Potel-Aviron 64
 Morgon Côte du Py (r) 64
Pride Mountain Vineyards 238
 Viognier, Sonoma (w) 238
Prieler 212
 Familie Prieler Blaufränkisch Ried Johanneshöhe (r) 212
Producteurs Plaimont 103
 L'Empreinte de Saint Mont Rouge (r) 103
Produttori del Barbaresco 9, 134
 Barabesco (r) 9, 134
Provins 335
 Vieilles Vignes Maître de Chais (w) 335
Pulenta Estate 276
 Cabernet Sauvignon (r) 276

Q

Quails' Gate Estate Winery 258
 Chasselas/Pinot Blanc/Pinot Gris (w) 258
Querciabella 134
 Chianti Classico (r) 134
Quinta das Maias 175
 Dão Tinto (r) 175
Quinta de la Rosa 178
 duoROSA Tinto (r) 178
Quinta de Sant'Ana 178
 Alvarinho, Lisboa (w) 178
Quinta do Ameal 174
 Branco Loureiro, Vinho Verde (w) 174
Quinta do Côtto 174
 Paço de Teixeiro, Vinho Verde (w) 174
Quinta do Crasto 175
 Branco Douro (w) 175
Quinta do Noval 175
 Cedro do Noval Douro (r) 175
 Vintage Port (f) 175
Quinta do Vallado 178
 Douro Tinto (r) 178
Quinta Nova de Nosso Senhora do Carmo 175
 Pomares Tinto Douro (r) 175
Quintay 269
 Clava Sauvignon Blanc (w) 269
Quivira Vineyards 239
 Grenache, Wine Creek Ranch (r) 239
Qupé Wine Cellars 239
 Syrah, Central Coast (r) 239

R

Rafael Palacios 166
 Louro Godello (w) 166
Raimat 166
 Viña 24 Albariño (w) 166
Rainer Wess 212
 Grüner Veltliner (w) 212
Ramón Bilbao 166
 Ramón Bilbao Reserva (r) 166
Ramos Pinto 178
 Duas Quintas Douro (r) 178
Rancho Zabaco Winery 239
 Zinfandel, Heritage Vines, Sonoma (r) 239
Ratings on the 100-Point Scale 25
Ravenswood 239
 Old Vine Zinfandel, Lodi (r) 239
Raventós i Blanc 167
 L'Hereu Brut (s) 167
Raymond Boulard/Francis Boulard & Fille 73
 Brut Nature Les Murgiers (s) 73
Reading Wine Labels
 Old World 8–9
 New World 10–11
Red Burgundy, Food & Wine 49
Reichsgraf von Kesselstatt 191
 RK Riesling QbA (w) 191
Reichstrat von Buhl 184
 Sauvignon Blanc Trocken (w) 184
Reinhold Haart 188
 Heart to Haart Riesling Mosel (w) 188
Reininger Winery 251
 Walla Walla Valley Cabernet Sauvignon (r) 251
René Geoffroy 73
 Brut Expression (s) 73
Rhône Valley Reds, Food & Wine 79
Ridgeview Wine Estate 335
 Ridgeview Cuvée Merret Bloomsbury (s) 335
Rimauresq 103
 R de Rimauresq Rosé (rs) 103
Rioja Tempranillo, Food & Wine 153
Road 13 Winery 258
 Honest John's Red (r) 258
Robert Hall Winery 239
 Rhône de Robles, Central Coast (r) 239
Robert Mondavi Winery 240
 Cabernet Sauvignon, Napa Valley (r) 240
Robert Sinskey Vineyards 240
 Vin Gris Los Carneros (rs) 240
Robert Weil 205
 Riesling Trocken QbA (w) 205
Rocca di Montegrossi 135
 Chianti Classico (r) 135
Rocca Family Vineyards 240
 Bad Boy Red Blend, Yountville (r) 240
Rolf Binder Wines 306
 Bulls Blood Shiraz Mataro Pressings, Barossa (r) 306
Ruca Malén 276
 Cabernet Sauvignon Reserva (r) 276
Rudera Wines 289
 Chenin Blanc (w) 289
 Noble Late Harvest Chenin Blanc (w) 289
Rudolf Fürst 186
 Riesling pur mineral Trocken (w) 186
Rudolf Sinss 200
 Spätburgunder Trocken QbA (r) 200
Rued Winery 240
 Sauvignon Blanc, Dry Creek (w) 240
 Zinfandel, Dry Creek (r) 240
Rusden 306
 Christian Chenin Blanc, Barossa Valley (w) 306
Rustenberg 289
 Brampton Chardonnay (w) 289
 Brampton Sauvignon Blanc (w) 289

S

S.A. Prüm 198
 Essence Pinot Blanc Trocken QbA Mosel (w) 198
Sacred Hill 321
 Syrah, Hawkes Bay (r) 321
St Hallett 306
 Gamekeeper's Reserve, Barossa (r) 306
St Supéry 240
 Merlot, Napa Valley (r) 240
 Oak-free Chardonnay, Napa Valley (w) 240
St Urbans-Hof 199
 Urban Riesling Mosel (w) 199
Saintsbury 241
 Chardonnay, Carneros (w) 241
Salcheto 135
 Rosso di Montepulciano (r) 135
Salentein 277
 Chardonnay Reserve (w) 277
San Pedro 269
 Castillo de Molina Sauvignon Blanc Reserva (w) 269
Sandhill Estate Winery 259
 Pinot Gris (w) 259
Santa Rita 269
 Cabernet Sauvignon (r) 269
 Sauvignon Blanc 120 (w) 269
Santomas 335
 Malvazija (w) 335
Sartarelli 135
 Verdicchio dei Castelli di Jesi (w) 135
Sassotondo 135
 Ciliegiolo Toscana Rosso IGT (r) 135
Sauternes, Food & Wine 35
Scarbolo 138
 Friulano (w) 138
Schloss Johannisberg 189
 Riesling Gelblack Trocken QbA (w) 189
Schloss Saarstein 199
 Pinot Blanc Trocken (w) 199
Schloss Vollrads 204
 Riesling Kabinett Feinherb (w) 204
Schlossgut Diel 185
 Diel de Diel QbA (w) 185
Schuchmann Wines 336
 Saperavi (r) 336
Scotchmans Hill 306
 Swan Bay Pinot Noir, Geelong (r) 306
Sebastiani Winery 241
 Chardonnay, Sonoma (w) 241
Seghesio Family Vineyards 242
 Zinfandel, Sonoma (r) 242
Selbach-Oster 200
 Riesling Kabinett Fish Label (w) 200
Send Wine Back 286–7
Señorio de Sarría 167
 Señorio de Sarría Rosado (rs) 167
Sepp Moser 212
 Breiter Rain Grüner Veltliner (w) 212
 Sauvignon Blanc (w) 212
Seresin Estate 324
 Leah Pinot Noir, Marlborough (r) 59, 324
Sergio Mottura 138
 Orvieto Classico (w) 138
Serving Champagne 70–1
Seven Hills Winery 251
 Columbia Valley Merlot (r) 251
Shaw + Smith 307
 Sauvignon Blanc, Adelaide Hills (w) 307
Shopping for Great Values 308–309
Silverado Vineyards 242
 Merlot, Napa Valley (r) 242
Simonsig 289
 Chenin Blanc (w) 289
 Labrynth Cabernet (r) 289
Skalli 103
 Chardonnay Vins de Pays (w) 103
Skillogalee 307
 Riesling, Clare Valley (w) 307
Sobon Estate 242
 Old Vines Zinfandel, Amador County (r) 242
Sogrape 179
 Callabriga Douro Tinto (r) 178
 Quinta de Azevedo Vinho Verde (w) 179
Sonoma-Cutrer Vineyards 242
 Chardonnay, Sonoma Coast (w) 242
Sorelle Bronca 138
 Prosecco di Valdobbiadene Extra Dry (s) 138
Soter Vineyards 253
 Willamette Valley Pinot Noir (r) 253
Spinifex 307
 Lola, Barossa Valley (w) 307
Sprietzer 200
 Riesling 101 QbA (w) 200
Spring Mountain Vineyards 243
 Cabernet Sauvignon, Chateau Chevalier, Spring Mountain 243
Steenberg 289
 Nebbiolo (r) 289
 Sauvignon Blanc (w) 289
Stephen Ross Wine Cellars 243
 Pinot Noir, Central Coast (r) 243
Stone Hill Winery 255
 Dry Vignoles (w) 255
 Norton Port (f) 255
Stonier 310
 Chardonnay, Mornington Peninsula (w) 310
 Pinot Noir, Mornington Peninsula (r) 310
Stormhoek 289
 Pinotage (r) 289
 Sauvignon Blanc (w) 289
Sula Vineyards 336
 Chenin Blanc (w) 336
 Sauvignon Blanc (w) 336
Sulphites 295
Sumac Ridge Estate Winery 259
 Steller's Jay Brut (s) 259
Summers Estate Wines 243
 La Nude Chardonnay (w) 243
Symington Family Estates 179
 Altano Organically Farmed Douro (r) 179
Syncline Wine Cellars 251
 Columbia Valley "Cuvée Elena" (r) 251
Szeremley 336
 Badacsonyi Kéknyelű (w) 336
 Riesling Selection (w) 336

T

Tabalí 269
 Chardonnay Reserva Especial (w) 269
Tablas Creek Vineyard 243
 Côtes de Tablas, Paso Robles (r) 243
Tahbilk 310
 Marsanne, Nagambie Lakes (w) 310
 Viognier, Nagambie Lakes (w) 310
Talbott Vineyards 244
 Kali Hart, Pinot Noir, Monterey (r) 244
Talenti 138
 Rosso di Montalcino (r) 138
Tamar Ridge 310
 Devil's Corner Pinot Noir, Tasmania (r) 310
Tandem 167
 Ars in Vitro (r) 167
Tangent Winery 244
 Albariño, Edna Valley (w) 244
Tantara Winery 244
 T. Solomon Wellborn Pinot Noir, Santa Barbara County (r) 244
Tasca d'Almerita 138
 Regaleali Rosso (r) 139
Tasting wine 32–3
Tawse Winery 259
 Sketches of Niagara Riesling (w) 259
Taylor's 179
 Taylor's Vintage Port (f) 179, 203
Taylors/Wakefield 310
 Cabernet Sauvignon, Clare Valley (r) 310
Telavi Wine Cellar 336
 Marani Separavi (r) 336
Temperature Matters 132–3
Tenimenti Fontanafredda 139
 Serralunga Barolo (r) 139
Tenuta Belguardo 139
 Serrata Maremma Toscana IGT (r) 139
Tenuta Pèppoli 140
 Chianti Classico (r) 140
Terra Valentine 245
 Amore Super Tuscan, Napa Valley (r) 245
Terradora 140
 Campania IGT Aglianico (r) 140
Terrazas de los Andes 277
 Malbec (r) 277
 Malbec Reserva (r) 277
Tesch 201
 Unplugged Riesling Kabinett Trocken (w) 201
Teusner Wines 310
 The Riebke Shiraz, Barossa Valley (r) 310
The Brander Vineyard 218
 Sauvignon Blanc, Santa Ynez Valley (w) 218
The Eyrie Vineyards 253
 Dundee Hills Pinot Gris (w) 253
The Lane 301
 Viognier, Adelaide Hills (w) 301

The Millton Vineyard 320
Chenin Blanc Te Arai Vineyard, Gisborne (w) 320
Theo Minges 197
Riesling Halbtroken QbA (w) 197
Thurnhof 140
Lagrein Riserva (r) 140
Tim Adams 311
Riesling, Clare Valley (w) 311
Semillon, Clare Valley (w) 311
Tobia 167
Oscar Tobia (r) 167
Tomas Cusiné 168
Auzells (w) 168
Toni Jost 189
Riesling Bacharacher Kabinett Trocken (w) 189
Torbreck 312
Cuvée Juveniles, Barossa Valley (r) 312
Torres 168
Gran Coronas (r) 168
Viña Esmeralda (w) 168
Trapiche 277
Malbec Broquel (r) 277
Trappolini 140
Orvieto Classico (w) 140
Triacca 140
Valtellina Sassella (r) 140
Trinity Hill 324
Trinity Hill Syrah, Hawkes Bay (r) 324
Tsiakkas Winery 336
Dry White (w) 336
Rosé Dry (rs) 336
Vamvakada (r) 336
Tuscan Reds, Food & Wine 107
Two Hands 312
Gnarly Dudes, Barossa Valley (r) 312
Txomin Etxaniz 168
Chacolí (w) 168
Tyrell's 312
Heathcote Shiraz, Victoria (r) 312

U
Umani Ronchi 140
Verdicchio dei Castelli di Jesi (w) 140
Umathum 213
Traminer (w) 213
Zweigelt (r) 213
Undurraga 270
TH Series Sauvignon Blanc (w) 270
Unti Vineyards 245
Petit Frère, Dry Creek Valley (r) 245
Zinfandel, Dry Creek Valley (r) 245
Urlar 324
Pinot Noir, Gladstone, Wairarapa (r) 324

V
Valdelosfrailes 168
Vendimia Seleccionada (r) 168
Valdespino 169
Candado PX (f) 169
Valdeviso 270
Cabernet Sauvignon Reserva (r) 270
Valle dell'Acate 141
Sicilia ICT Il Frappato (r) 141
Valley of the Moon Winery 245
Pinot Blanc & Syrah, Sonoma (r/w) 245
Velenosi 141
Rosso Piceno Superiore Il Brecciarolo (r) 141
Ventisquero 270
Cabernet Sauvignon Root 1 (r) 270
Sauvignon Blanc Root 1 (w) 270
Veramonte 270
Chardonnay Reserve (w) 270
Viader Vineyards 245
DARE Rosé, Napa Valley (rs) 245
Vidal Wines 324
Vidal Pinot Noir, Hawkes Bay (r) 324
Vidal Syrah, Gimblett Gravels, Hawkes Bay (r) 324
Vietti 141
Nebbiolo d'Alba Perbacco (r) 141
Vieux Château Certan 45
La Gravette de Certan (r) 45
Vieux Château Gaubert (r/w) 45
Villa Bucci 141
Verdicchio dei Castelli di Jesi (w) 141
Villa Maria Estate 325
Private Bin Pinot Noir, Marlborough (r) 325
Private Bin Sauvignon Blanc, Marlborough (w) 325
Villa Ponciago 64
Fleurie (r) 64
Viña Casablanca 271
Cefiro Cabernet Sauvignon Reserva (r) 271
Cefiro Merlot Reserva (r) 271
Vina Robles 246
White4 Huerhuero, Paso Robles (w) 246
Vinakoper 337
Malvazija (w) 337
Refosk (r) 337
Viñas del Vero 169
Miranda de Secastilla (r) 169
Vincent Girardin 52
Santenay Blanc (w) 52
Viñedos de Nieva 169
Blanco Nieva Verdejo (w) 169
Vinhos Don Laurindo 279
Don Laurindo Merlot Reserva (r) 279
Vino Noceto 246
Moscato Bianco Frivolo, California (w) 246
Vinos LA Cetto 337
Petite Sirah (r) 337
Vinos Valtuille 169
Pago de Valdoneje Mencía (r) 169
Virgen de la Sierra 169
Cruz de Piedra Garnacha (r) 169
Vittorio Bera e Figli 141
Moscato d'Asti (s) 141
Viu Manent 271
Cabernet Sauvignon Reserva (r) 271
Estate Collection Chardonnay (w) 271
Volker Eisele Family Estate 246
Gemini White Blend, Chiles Valley (w) 246
von Hövel 188
Oberemmeler Hütte Riesling Kabinett Mosel (w) 188
Von Siebenthal 271
Parcella #7 (r) 271

W
Wagner-Stempel 204
Silvaner Trocken QbA (w) 204
Warwick Estate 289
Pinotage (r) 289
The First Lady (r) 289
Wegeler 204
Gutssekt Riesling Brut (s) 204
Weninger 212
Blaufränkisch Hochäcker (r) 213
Wente Vineyards 247
Charles Wetmore, Cabernet Sauvignon, Livermore Valley 247
White Bur undy, Food & Wine 67
Whitehall Lane Winery 247
Merlot, Napa Valley (r) 247
Sauvignon Blanc, Napa Valley (w) 247
Willamette Valley Pinot Noir, Food & Wine 253
Willi Schaefer 200
Graacher Domprobst Riesling Kabinett (w) 200
Wine List Shortcuts 266–7
Winemaking 54–5
Winter 205
Silvaner Trocken QbA (w) 205
Wirra Wirra 313
The 12th Man Chardonnay, Adelaide Hills (w) 313
Wither Hills 325
Pinot Noir, Marlborough (r) 325
Sauvignon Blanc, Marlborough (w) 325
Wolf Blass 313
Yellow Label Cabernet Sauvignon, South Australia (r) 309, 313
Wölffer Estate 255
Long Island Rosé (rs) 255
Wyndham Estate 313
George Wyndham Shiraz Carbernet (r) 313

Y
Yabby Lake 313
Red Claw Chardonnay, Mornington Peninsula (w) 313
Red Claw Pinot Noir, Mornington Peninsula (r) 313
Yalumba 313
Riesling Pewsey Vale, Eden Valley (w) 313
Y Series Viognier, South Australia (w) 313
Yannick Pelletier 103
St-Chinian (r) 103
Yealands Estate 325
Sauvignon Blanc, Awatere Valley, Marlborough (w) 325
Yering Station 313
Willow Lake Chardonnay, Yarra Valley (w) 313

Z
Zambartas Winery 337
Shiraz-Lefkada (r) 337
Xynisteri (w) 337
Zipf 205
Blauer Trollinger Steillage Trocken (r) 205
Zlatan Oto 337
Ostatak Bure (w) 337
Zull 213
Lust & Laune Blauer Portugieser (r) 213
Lust & Laune Grüner Veltliner (w) 213

Acknowledgments

Jim Gordon's acknowledgments
Thanks first to my family for letting me leave them to disappear into winedom – sometimes physically and often intellectually – during many evenings and weekends. Great appreciation also to Hugh Tietjen and Chet Klingensmith of *Wines & Vines* magazine for understanding my creative tangents. And to James Laube for connecting me with a wonderful publisher, Mary-Clare Jerram, and the DK team.

Dorling Kindersley's acknowledgments
Peter Anderson for the photography; Chris Skyme and Bethan Wallace at Sopexa for supplying wines from Austria; Cécile Landau, Laura Nickoll, Danielle Di Michiel, and Alastair Laing for their editorial help; Sonia Charbonnier for her language skills; Sue Morony for proofreading; and Jane Parker for creating the index.

Picture Credits
The publisher would like to thank the following for their kind permission to reproduce their photographs: (Key: a-above; b-below/bottom; c-centre; f-far; l-left; r-right; t-top). 20-21 **Corbis:** Charles O'Rear. 55 **Corbis:** Charles O'Rear (tr). 63 **Corbis:** Morton Beebe (br). 124-125 **Getty Images:** David Epperson. 136-137 **Corbis:** Jack K. Clark / AgStock Images. 156-157 **Corbis:** Charles O'Rear. 165 **Corbis:** James Hardy / PhotoAlto (br). 211 **Getty Images:** Armin Faber (br). 326–327, 170–171 **Dorling Kindersley:** Rough Guides.

About the authors

Jim Gordon, Editor-in-Chief, oversaw this dynamic team of writers. He also wrote the features on grapes and wine enjoyment, the wine panels, and the Mendocino and Lake entries in the California section. Jim's 25-year career in the wine industry includes working as managing editor of *Wine Spectator* for 12 years and helping to set up Wine Country Living TV for NBC. Currently, he is the editor of *Wines & Vines* magazine, based in California.

Sarah Abbott MW wrote the Côte de Beaune entries in the Burgundy chapter. She is the founder of the wine events company, Swirl, is a consultant for wine importers, and judges at international wine competitions. *www.swirl-me.co.uk Twitter: SarahAbbottMW*

Jane Anson wrote the Bordeaux chapter, the Southwest France, Provence, Corsica, and Vin de Pays entries in the Rest of France chapter, and the Chablis and Beaujolais entries in the Burgundy chapter. Jane is the Bordeaux correspondent for *Decanter* magazine, and contributes to the *South China Morning Post* in Hong Kong. *www.newbordeaux.com*

Andrew Barrow was responsible for the Alsace entries in the Rest of France chapter and the Austria chapter. At the forefront of wine and food on the internet for 15 years, most recently with his top-rated blog Spittoon.biz, Andrew has also written for *Via Michelin* and *The Guardian*. *www.spittoon.biz Twitter: @wine_scribbler*

Laurie Daniel has been a journalist for over 30 years, and wrote the Central Coast entries in the California section. Based in the Santa Cruz Mountains, she began writing about wine regularly in 1993, and has contributed to newspapers, magazines, and websites. *Twitter: com/ldwine*

Mary Dowey wrote the Southern Rhône entries in the Rest of France section. She has been a wine, food, and travel writer for a range of publications for over 20 years. Specializing in the Southern Rhône from her base in western Provence, she runs a website dedicated to Provencal food and wine. *www.marydowey.com www.provencefoodandwine.com*

Mike Dunne wrote the Inland California entries. After nearly 40 years writing about the wine industry as a columnist, restaurant critic, and food editor of *The Sacramento Bee*, he now divides his time between homes in Northern California and Baja California in Mexico, exploring the wine regions of both countries. *www.ayearinwine.com*

Sarah Jane Evans MW is a writer and broadcaster, and wrote the Spain chapter. A long-term lover of Spanish wine, she has been associate editor of the BBC's *Good Food Magazine* and president of the Guild of Food Writers. A Master of Wine, Sarah is also a member of the Gran Orden de Caballeros de Vino. *www.sarahjaneevans.co.uk*

Catherine Fallis MS wrote the Côte Chalonnaise and Maconnais entries in the Burgundy chapter, the Germany chapter, and the Food & Wine panels. Catherine is the founder and president of wine consulting firm, Planet Grape LLC. *www.planetgrape.com*

Michael Franz wrote the Northern Rhône entries in the Rest of France chapter and the Washington, Oregon, Chile, and Argentina sections. He contributes to wine magazines, instructs culinary academies, and is a consultant for 13 restaurants. He is also editor and managing partner of Wine Review Online. *www.winereviewonline.com*

Doug Frost MS, MW is the author of the US Heartland and Southern states entries in the Rest of US section. He is a Master Sommelier and Master of Wine. He has written several books and also hosts Check Please!, a weekly US TV show, and is the wine and spirits consultant for United Airlines worldwide. *www.dougfrost.com Twitter: winedogboy*

Jamie Goode wrote the chapters on Australia, New Zealand, and Portugal. Formerly a science editor, Jamie was one of the first wine bloggers, writing as the Wine Anorak. He has a weekly column for *The Sunday Express* and writes for a number of magazines. His books include *The Science of Wine* and *Authentic Wine*. *www.wineanorak.com*

Susan Kostrzewa is the author of the South Africa chapter. Before relocating to Manhattan in 2005, Susan lived for 10 years in the San Francisco Bay Area, specializing in food, wine, and travel writing. Today, she is the executive editor of *Wine Enthusiast Magazine*, for whom she tasted and rated South African wines for several years.

Peter Liem wrote the chapter on Champagne. The only professional English-language wine writer currently living in the Champagne region, Peter writes for *Wine & Spirits* and *The World of Fine Wine*, as well as writing and publishing ChampagneGuide.net, an online guide to the wines and wine producers of the region. *www.champagneguide.net*

Jeffrey Lindenmuth wrote entries for New England, New York, and the Mid-Atlantic states (in the Rest of US section) He writes about wine, spirits, and beer and has travelled the world in search of a good drink. His work has appeared in *Cooking Light*, *Men's Health*, and other forums.

Wink Lorch has been a wine writer, educator, and editor for the past 20 years, having previously worked in the UK wine trade. Wink, who has a home in the French Alps, wrote the Jura and Savoie entries in the Rest of France section. She is the creator of Wine Travel Guides website, focusing on wine regions in Europe. *www.winetravelguides.com*

Greg Love wrote the Côte de Nuits entries in the Burgundy section. Greg likes to approach his wine reviews from the ground up, meaning he invests time and effort in understanding the vineyards and the personality of the winemakers and owners and their winemaking style. *www.burgundylover.co.uk*

Peter Mitham wrote the Canada chapter, drawing on more than a dozen years of tasting experience across North America. He currently writes about viticulture and the wine business in the Pacific Northwest and Canada for *Wines & Vines* magazine and other publications.

Wolfgang Weber wrote the Italy chapter. He has worked almost exclusively in the wine trade, including two vintages as a cellar rat in the mountains above the Napa Valley, and he is the former senior editor and Italian wine critic at *Wine & Spirits*. *http://spume.wordpress.com*

Deborah Parker Wong wrote the Napa Valley, Carneros, Sonoma, and Marin entries in the California section. She is Northern California editor for *The Tasting Panel* magazine, and works with winegrowers, reporting first-hand on current vintages and industry trends. She is a member of both the London-based Circle of Wine Writers and the Wine Media Guild of New York. *www.examiner.com* (consumer drinks column).